501
ENGLISH VERBS

fully conjugated in all the tenses
in a new easy-to-learn format,
alphabetically arranged

by

Thomas R. Beyer, Jr.

Professor
Middlebury College
Middlebury, Vermont

BARRON'S EDUCATIONAL SERIES, INC.

All inquries should be addressed to:
Barron's Educational Series, Inc.
250 Wireless Boulevard
Hauppauge, NY 11788

Library of Congress Catalog Card No. 97-40811

International Standard Book No. 0-7641-0304-0

Library of Congress Cataloging-in-Publication Data

Beyer, Thomas R.
    501 English verbs : fully conjugated in all the tenses in a new
easy to learn format / alphabetically arranged by Thomas R. Beyer,
Jr.
       p.   cm.
   Includes index.
   ISBN 0-7641-0304-0
   1. English language—Verb—Tables.   I. Title.
PE1273.B49   1998
428.2—dc21   97-40811
                                   CIP

PRINTED IN THE UNITED STATES OF AMERICA
9 8 7 6 5

Dedicated to the hundreds of millions
who have learned English
to communicate with the other
hundreds of millions of native speakers.

For my understanding wife, Dorothea,
my most faithful supporters,
Carina, Stefanie, and Alexandra,
and Rich who loves action words.

Contents

The English Verb

Introduction

For everything you do, or want to be or how you feel, you need a verb. A verb can indicate an action (I write, she buys, they talk) or a state of being (we feel, you care). The verb is an essential element of English—only the nouns occur more frequently in the spoken and written language. Structurally the verb is one of the easiest parts of speech, since there really are only four or five different forms. Native speakers of English rarely think about verbs. In actual practice, however, verbs are misused and abused by native speakers and learners of English alike. The English verb has confounded generations worrying whether to use "lie" or "lay," "gone" or "went," "shall" or "will." For those learning English the verb can be one of the most complex word forms, with over 300 irregular verbs and 200 possible combinations for all the possible verbal usages. It is the disparity between this paucity of verbal endings and the numerous and flexible uses of English verbs that has given birth to this book.

The English verb in comparison to many other Indo-European languages has lost most of the endings that indicate the categories of voice, mood, tense, aspect, person, and number. Most English verbs are **full verbs**, which may be either **regular** or **irregular**. **Regular verbs** form the past tense by adding "**d**" or "**ed**" to the simple form: accept**ed**, pull**ed**, mov**ed**. **Irregular verbs** (some languages call them "strong" verbs) have different ways of forming that past tense: bring–**brought**, drive–**drove**, sing–**sang**, spend–**spent**. There are about 300 hundred irregular verbs in English and all but those rarely used are found in *501 English Verbs*.

501 English Verbs gives the conjugations or conjugated forms of the irregular and regular verbs most frequently used in speech and writing. Conjugation means to "join with": we attach endings to the basic form of the verb to distinguish voice, mood, tense, aspect, person, and number. These categories may be more familiar to the learner of English than to the native speaker. Discussions and analyses of grammatical categories in English have disappeared from many American schools. The traditional categories are better suited to a highly inflected language—one with many changes such as Classical Greek and Latin, or modern Russian and German. At one time English was more heavily inflected—it had many more endings than at present.

How To Use This Book

What follows is an example of the verb **accept** accompanied by an overview and explanation of the categories of verbs and the formation of those forms as they are presented in our book.

Conjugation of the Full Verb "accept"

accept
(active voice)

PRINCIPAL PARTS: **accepts, accepting, accepted, accepted**

be accepted
(passive voice)

Infinitive: **to accept**
Perfect Infinitive: **to have accepted**
Present Participle: **accepting**
Past Participle: **accepted**

Infinitive: **to be accepted**
Perfect Infinitive: **to have been accepted**
Present Participle: **being accepted**
Past Participle: **been accepted**

INDICATIVE MOOD

Pres. I, we, you, they **accept**

he, she, it **accepts**

I **am accepted**
we, you, they **are accepted**
he, she, it **is accepted**

Pres.
Prog. I **am accepting**
we, you, they **are accepting**
he, she, it **is accepting**

I **am being accepted**
we, you, they **are being accepted**
he, she, it **is being accepted**

Pres.
Int. I, we, you, they **do accept**
he, she, it **does accept**

I, we, you, they **do get accepted**
he, she, it **does get accepted**

Fut. I, he, she, it,
we, you, they **will accept**

I, he, she, it,
we, you, they **will be accepted**

Past I, he, she, it,
we, you, they **accepted**

I, he, she, it **was accepted**
we, you, they **were accepted**

Past
Prog. I, he, she, it **was accepting**
we, you, they **were accepting**

I, he, she, it **was being accepted**
we, you, they **were being accepted**

Past
Int. I, he, she, it,
we, you, they **did accept**

I, he, she, it,
we, you, they **did get accepted**

Pres.
Perf. I, we, you, they **have accepted**
he, she, it **has accepted**

I, we, you, they **have been accepted**
he, she, it **has been accepted**

Past
Perf. I, he, she, it,
we, you, they **had accepted**

I, he, she, it,
we, you, they **had been accepted**

Fut.
Perf. I, he, she, it, we, you, they
will have accepted

I, he, she, it, we, you, they
will have been accepted

IMPERATIVE MOOD

accept

be accepted

SUBJUNCTIVE MOOD

Pres. if I, he, she, it,
we, you, they **accept**

if I, he, she, it,
we, you, they **be accepted**

Past if I, he, she, it,
we, you, they **accepted**

if I, he, she, it,
we, you, they **were accepted**

Fut. if I, he, she, it,
we, you, they **should accept**

if I, he, she, it,
we, you, they **should be accepted**

Transitive and intransitive.

Basic Form

Verbs are normally listed in English language dictionaries according to the basic or simple form. In this book, the basic form of each verb appears on the top line in **bold face**, followed by the notation "active voice" in parentheses for verbs that can be transitive. This form is used for the present tense and infinitive.

Principal Parts

In addition to their basic forms, English verbs have four other forms. These other principal parts may be listed in English language dictionaries according to their "irregularity." In the middle of the top line, we provide the other four principal parts for all verbs in this order:

- **accepts**   the third person singular present tense or "-s" form
- **accepting**   the present participle or "-ing" form
- **accepted**   the past tense or "-ed" form
- **accepted**   the past participle

The third person singular present (the "he," "she," or "it") form is made by adding "s" or "es" to the simple form: **she accepts.** Since this change is not difficult for the native speaker the form is included in dictionaries only when the correct spelling is not obvious.

The present participle or "-ing" form also poses little problem for the native speaker and it too rarely occurs in dictionaries.

The simple past is usually formed by adding to the basic form "ed" after a consonant and "d" after a vowel. Verbs that form their past tense in this way are considered **regular verbs.**

The past participle for regular verbs is the same as the past tense. Some English verbs have alternate forms for the past tense and/or the past participle. These are normally listed in the order in which they appear in the *American Heritage Dictionary of the English Language* (Third Edition).

After the principal parts the top line contains the passive voice form if the verb is transitive, followed by the notation "passive voice."

The convention of listing the active voice on the left side of the page and the passive voice on the right side is maintained throughout *501 English Verbs.*

Voice

A verb is in the **active voice** when some subject (the doer) performs some action or activity on someone or something:

Mary accepts the invitation.

When there is a complement—a direct or indirect object—for these verbs, they are transitive verbs and permit a passive construction. When a verb is in the **passive voice**, the object of the action becomes the grammatical subject of the verb:

The invitation was accepted by Mary.

In both cases "Mary" was the doer and the "invitation" was the object of "accepted."

Beneath the line following the principal parts of the verb, there are normally eight forms, four active and four passive: **infinitive, perfect infinitive, present participle,** and **past participle.**

Infinitives (non-finite verb form).

Infinitives are forms of the verb not limited by time. They have no tense or mood. Often (but not always) the infinitive is preceded by **to**:

I like **to take** showers.

The **Present Infinitive** refers to the present or future.
The Present Active Infinitive is identical to the basic form of the verb.
The Present Passive Infinitive is a compound form composed of **be** and the past participle.

The **Perfect Infinitive** relates to an activity or state existing prior to the main verb.
The Past Active Infinitive is a compound form composed of **have** and the past participle.
The Past Passive Infinitive is a compound form composed of **have been** and the past participle.

Participles

Participles also have no tense or mood, but they are used together with auxiliaries to form the progressive and perfect tenses and the passive voice.

The **Present Participle** refers to an action in the present or future.
The Present Active Participle is formed by adding "ing" to the basic form: accept**ing**. When a verb ends in a silent "e," that letter is dropped before adding the "ing": **come–coming**.
The Present Passive Participle is a compound form composed of **being** and the past participle.

The **Past Participle** refers to an action in the past. Since it is used in combination with auxiliary verbs to form the passive voice, the past participle is sometimes called the "passive participle."
The Past Active Participle is normally the same as the past tense form of the verb. For regular verbs this is the "-ed" form: accept**ed**.
The Past Passive Participle is a compound form combining **been** and the past participle.

Mood

English has three **moods** or modes of speech: **indicative**, **imperative**, and **subjunctive**.

The **Indicative Mood** is used to make a statement or an exclamation, or to ask a question:

I **like** strawberries.
Mary **was accepted** to Harvard!
Are you **going** to the movies?

Tense

Tense is used to express the time when an action takes place. Traditionally there are three primary categories of tense: **present**, **past**, and **future**. (Recent English grammars consider only the present and the past true tenses, because only they have distinct grammatical forms.)

The **Present** (*Pres.*) is used for an action or state that exists at the present moment (or the moment of speech or writing). This may also include something that began in the past and continues now in the present, and might include something that continues into the future.
The Present Active for most full verbs has two forms to distinguish between **person** and **number.**

Person and Number

In English we have three persons (**first, second, third**) and two numbers (**singular** and **plural**).

First person singular, the **I** form, refers to the speaker.
First person plural, the **we** form, refers to the speaker and one or more other persons.
Second person singular and plural, the **you** form, refers to the person or persons spoken to.
Third person singular, the **he, she, it** form, refers to someone or something other than the speaker or the person spoken to.
Third person plural, the **they** form, refers to more than one person or thing other than the speaker or the person spoken to.

The Present Active for the first person singular and plural, the second person singular and plural, and the third person plural is the **basic form**:

I **accept** your invitation.
We **accept**.
Do you **accept**?*
They **accept**!

The Present Active for the third person singular (**he, she, it**) is normally formed by adding "s" after most consonants and all silent vowels:

She runs, he plays, it snows, she moves, he hides, it drives.

After the combinations of "ss," "zz," "ch," "sh," "x," or after a vowel that is pronounced, we add "es."

She passes, it buzzes, he catches, she pushes, he boxes, he goes, she does.

When a verb ends in "y" after a consonant, the "y" changes to an "i" and is followed by "es."

He cries, she tries, it fries.

In a few instances when the basic form ends in a single "s," you add "ses":

The district busses, she focusses.

The Present Passive is a compound form combining the conjugated form of **be** with the past participle.

I **am accepted**.
We, you, they **are registered**.
He, she, it **is required**.

Aspect

In addition to the simple present, past, and future, English has a **progressive** and a **perfect** aspect relaying how an action or mood is experienced or viewed by the speaker.

The **Progressive Aspect**, sometimes called the continuous aspect, describes something in progress at the time of the verb's action.

---

* Note that English today uses **you** to refer to one or more than one person. Sometimes you may find the archaic second person singular form **thou** instead of **you**. The **thou** form is then followed by the old form of the verb.

The **Present Progressive** (*Pres. Prog.*) is an action still going on in the present.

The Present Progressive Active is formed by combining the present tense form of the verb **be** with the present participle.

> I **am reading**.
> We, you, they **are thinking**.
> He **is riding**, she **is driving**, it **is snowing**.

The Present Progressive Passive combines **am being, are being,** or **is being** with the passive participle.

> I **am being driven**.
> We, you, they **are being sent**.
> She **is being tested**.

The Intensive

This form is used for emphasis and is also a key to negation in English and for asking questions.*

The **Present Intensive** (*Pres. Int.*) emphasizes that an action can or does take place.

The Present Intensive Active is formed by combining the auxiliary form **do** or **does** with the basic form.

> I, we, you, they **do accep**t your conditions.
> He **does want** to come, but she **does not want** to come.

The Present Intensive Passive combines **do get** or **does get** with the past participle.

> I, we, you, they **do get appreciated**.
> He or she **does get presented** a variety of views.

The **Future** (*Fut.*) of a verb indicates an action or state that does not yet exist. Strictly speaking, it is not a separate tense in modern English.

The Future Active is a compound formed with the help of the auxiliary verb **will** (or **shall**)** and sometimes contracted as **'ll** followed by the basic form of the verb. (In the spoken language future time is often indicated by **am, are, is going to** and the basic form of the verb).

> I, she, he, it, we, you, they **will survive**.

The Future Passive is formed by combining **will be** and the past participle.

> I, he, she, it, we, you, they **will be discovered**.

---

* In the latest English grammar texts there is no mention of the intensive or emphatic as a separate category. The auxiliary verb **do** is called a "dummy operator" when used to form negations and questions. Because these **do** forms are so essential I have followed the convention of Hopper, *English Verb Conjugations,* and provided the present and the past intensive for each verb.

** I have consistently used **will** as the auxiliary verb for the future. Traditionally school children were taught to use **shall** for the first person singular and plurals to indicate simple future: "I shall come, we shall overcome." "I will" and "we will" were to be used for special emphasis. Similarly we were taught to write "he, she, it, you, they will" unless we wished to emphasize the statement with "she, he, it, you, they shall." The distinction was then and probably for the entire twentieth century very artificial. Recent research has indicated that this rule was rarely ever observed in actual practice and in modern standard American English **shall** is rarely used except in some specific phrases: "We shall overcome." "Shall we dance?" One should, however, be aware of the historical distinction and recognize **shall** for the first person singular and plural and in questions and some formulaic statements.

The **Past** (*Past*) tense describes some action or mood that occurred or existed prior to or before the moment of speech or writing.

The Past Active form of **regular verbs** is formed for all three persons, singular and plural, by adding "d" after a vowel:

He close**d**, continue**d**, decide**d**.

After a consonant, the letters "ed" are added:

She work**ed**, open**ed**, pass**ed**, pack**ed**.

When a "y" comes after a consonant, it changes to "i" before the ending "ed":

He cr**ied**, tr**ied**, carr**ied**, marr**ied**.

Verbs that end with a "c" sometimes have an added "k" before the "ed" ending:

She panic**ked**, because he traffic**ked** in drugs.

Sometimes a word's final consonant is doubled—when it is spelled with a single letter and the vowel before it is stressed—before adding "ed." (In words of a single syllable this is always the case.)

He beg**ged**, gun**ned**, stop**ped**.

American English differs from British English in verbs ending in a single "l" or "p." American English permits a single final consonant.

She travel**ed** (travel**led**), he worship**ed** (worship**ped**).

American English also accepts a single "m" for the past tense of verbs ending in "m":

She program**ed** (program**med**).

The Past Passive form combines **was** or **were** and the past participle.

I, he, she, it **was added** at the last moment.
We, you, they **were** all **added** later.

The **Past Progressive** (*Past Prog.*) indicates an action that was proceeding in the past.
The Past Progressive Active combines **was** or **were** with the present participle.

I, he, she, it **was riding** in a car.
We, you, they **were keeping** tabs.

The Past Progressive Passive combines **was being** or **were being** with the past participle.

I, she, he, it **was being improved**.
We, you, they **were being preserved**.

The **Past Intensive** (*Past Int.*) emphasizes that an action did take place in the past. It is also used for negation and questions in the past.
The Past Intensive Active combines **did** (the past tense of **do**) with the basic form of the verb.

I **did complete** the assignment.
She **did** not **stop** to smell the roses.
Did we **hear** you correctly?
You and they **did do** the exercises.

The Past Intensive Passive combines **did get** and the past participle.

I **did get recognized**.
It **did** not **get removed**.
Did we **get called** last evening?
You and they did not **get summoned**.

The Perfect Aspect

The three perfect tenses refer to an action or state that precedes some other action or state.

The **Present Perfect** (*Pres. Perf.*) describes an action or state begun in the past and leading up to the present.

The Present Perfect Active combines the auxiliary present tense form of **have** or **has** with the past participle.

I, we, you, they **have arrived**.
He **has worried**, she **has heard**, it **has rained**.

The Present Perfect Passive uses **have been** or **has been** plus the past participle. (This is the same as adding **have/had** to the past passive participle.)

I, we, you, they **have been wondering**.
Neither she nor he **has been supported** by their friends.

The **Past Perfect** (*Past Perf.*) (sometimes called the Pluperfect) describes an action or state begun sometime prior to another past reference point.

The Past Perfect Active form uses **had** (the past tense of **have**) with the past participle.

I, he, she, it, we, you, they **had** all **taken** the ferry.

The Past Perfect Passive uses **had been** with the past participle (which is the same as adding **had** to the past passive participle).

I, she, he, it, we, you, they **had been convinced**.

The **Future Perfect** (*Fut. Perf.*) refers to a future action or state that will have begun prior to some other future time event.

The Future Perfect Active combines **will have** (**shall have**) with the past participle.

I, he, she, it, we, you, they **will have written** the letter before tomorrow.

The Future Perfect Passive combines **will have been** with the past participle (or **will have** with the past passive participle).

I, he, she, we, you, they **will have been married** twenty-five years next fall.

The Progressive Perfect*

One can combine the perfect and progressive aspects for the compound forms Present Perfect Progressive and Past Perfect Progressive.

---

* Since these forms represent a combination of two forms already presented, they are not listed for each individual verb.

The **Present Perfect Progressive** describes an action begun in the past and continuing into the present.

The Present Perfect Progressive Active combines **have** or **has** plus **been** and the present participle form of the verb.

> I, we, you, they **have been training** since January.
> He **has been swimming** since he was three years old.

The Present Perfect Progressive Passive combines **have** or **has** plus **been being** and the past participle form of the verb.

> I, he, she, it, we, you, they **have been being observed** since our plane arrived.

The **Past Perfect Progressive** describes an action ongoing in the past that no longer exists.

The Past Perfect Progressive Active combines **had** and **been** with the present participle form of the verb.

> I, he, she, it, we, you, they **had been training** regularly before the accident.

The Past Perfect Progressive Passive combines **had** plus **been being** with the past participle form of the verb.

> I, he, she, it, we, you, they **had been being examined** when the storm began.

The **Future Perfect Progressive** describes an ongoing action in the future prior to another future action.

The Future Perfect Progressive Active combines **will have** and **been** with the present participle form of the verb.

> I, he, she, it, we, you, they **will have been playing**
> chess for ten hours before the match ends.

The Future Perfect Progressive Passive combines **will have** plus **been being** with the past participle form of the verb.

> I, he, she, it, we, you, they will **have been being examined**
> for over three months before the report will be issued.

The **Imperative Mood** is used to give an order, command, demand, or request. Sometimes it is used in giving directions.

The Active Imperative form is the same as the basic form of the verb.

> **Go. Stop. Write. Listen. Sing. Eat** and **drink.**
> **Bring** me your homework.
> Please **pass** the butter.
> **Drive** straight ahead and **turn** right at the light.

The Passive Imperative* combines **be** with the past participle.

> **Be frightened.**
> Don't **be found.**

---

* Another way to form a passive imperative is with the word **get** and past participle: "**Get hired.**" "**Get dressed.**"

The **Subjunctive Mood** is used for expressing a wish, reporting something that was said, or describing something hypothetical.

The **Present Subjunctive** is used with a "that" clause after verbs, adjectives or nouns; for a condition; in some set expressions of desire.

The Present Subjunctive Active uses the verb's basic form (except for the verb **be**). Note the third person singular form has no "s."

> We suggested that she **travel** to London this summer.
> I demanded that he **refund** my money.

The Present Subjunctive Passive is made by combining **be** and the past participle.

> I insist that you **be heard**.
> He requested that she **be invited**.

The **Past Subjunctive** describes something hypothetical or unreal. It often occurs after words like "if," "as if," "though," "wish," "suppose."

The Past Subjunctive Active* (sometimes called the **were** form) is identical to the forms of the past except for the verb **be**, in which case the form **were** is used for all persons.

> If she **tried**, she could do it.
> If we **slept**, we could have done better.
> If he **were** rich, he would buy me a diamond ring.
> I wish that I **were** in Oklahoma.

The Past Subjunctive Passive combines **were** with the past participle.

> I wish that we **were warned**.
> We would be delighted, if our invitation **were accepted**.

The **Future Subjunctive**** (should) refers to an action or state that may come into being.

The Future Subjunctive Active is formed by combining the auxiliary verb **should** with the basic form of the verb form.

> If ever you **should leave** me, I would die.
> If I **should be** in town next week, I will call you.

The Future Subjunctive Passive combines **should be** and the past participle.

> If he **should be harmed**, you will all be punished.
> **Should** she **be awoken**, please inform me immediately.

---

* In modern American English the indicative past tense is often substituted: "I wish I **was** there." A Past Perfect Subjunctive is also possible using **had** or **had been** plus the past particple: "If we **had written**, they would have come." "If we **had been driven**, we would not have arrived too late for the show."

** As with other recent references to future time, the future subjunctive is not listed in the two most recent English grammar texts. The use of **should** is considered a special use as "putative" in conditional sentences. Nonetheless, **should** is regularly used to describe a future condition: "How **should I know**?" "If I **should see** him, I'll tell him." I have followed the example of Hopper in including the future form here for the sake of consistency.

Transitive and Intransitive Verbs

Most regular verbs are either transitive or intransitive. When a single verb can be both transitive and intransitive, it has been noted at the bottom of the page.

A **Transitive verb** is one that has a complement, either a direct or indirect object.

Mary **gave** me the book.

An **Intransitive verb** is one that has no complement.

He **tires** easily.
My head **aches**.

Auxiliary Verbs

English has a dozen **auxiliary verbs**, normally divided into three categories: **primary**, **modal**, and **marginal**. Auxiliary verbs are often referred to as "helpers" or "operators." They help in the construction of English sentences.

They can come before the negative particle **not.**

> I **am** not coming.
> She **did** not buy the dress.
> He **has** not set the time.

They can be inverted in questions.

> **Are** you coming?
> **Must** I go?
> **Will** they be there?

They can form contractions.

> **I'll** be ready.
> We **can't** decide.
> They **couldn't** accept our offer.
> John **won't** use a computer.

They can be used as emphatics.

> You **should** do it.
> He **must** come.

The Primary Auxiliaries: be, have, do.

The three verbs **be, have,** and **do,** can stand alone, but they also serve as auxiliaries to form other tenses.

The verb **be** combines with the present participle to form the progressive tenses and with the past participle to form the passive.

> I **am working**.
> He **was notified**.

The verb **have** combines with the past participle to form the perfect tenses.

> You **have made** great progress.
> He **had listened**.
> She **will have arrived** by evening.

The verb **do** forms the intensive and is used in negations and questions.

> We **do like** to read often.
> They **did not come** any more.
> **Do** you **prefer** an aisle or window seat?

The Modal Auxiliaries: can/could, may/might, must, shall/should, will/would

They have no distinctive "s" form for the third person singular in the present.

> I **will go**, and she **will come**.

They combine with the basic or infinitive form without the word "to."

He **can leave**.
I **might stay**.
We **must stop** for lunch.

The Marginal Auxiliaries: dare, need, ought to, used to.
These verbs may all be used as main verbs in addition to their auxiliary function. When used as auxiliaries, the third person singular form has no "**s**."

She **dare not go**.
He **need not try**.

Phrasal Verbs

Phrasal verbs are combinations of a verb and an adverb or preposition in which the meaning cannot always be understood as the sum of its parts. One can "run up a hill," but this is not the same as the phrasal verb **run up** as in "**run up** a bill."

Some phrasal verbs are intransitive, that is, they take no complement: **act up, burn out**. Others are transitive and take an object: **call off, cut down**.

We have included a special section of the most common phrasal verbs for the 501 English verbs in this book.

Catenatives

Catenatives are verbs that are not auxiliary verbs but can be followed by another verb. They can occur with the simple form:

He **helped clean** the car.

Some have the basic form with **to**.

I always **wanted to write**.

Others are followed by the "**-ing**" form.

I **like buying** jewelry.
I **hate watching** television.
She **kept calling**.

Questions

English has two main types of questions: **yes-no**, and **wh-** (who, what, where, when, why, etc.). A question (the interrogative sentence) can be formed in English by using an auxiliary verb before the subject. Many questions in English rely on inversion—changing the position of the order of the subject and the auxiliary.

Are you coming?
Had she listened?
What can I do for you?
Where can I find that telephone number?

When the subject of the question is **who**, there is no inversion.

Who is coming to the party?

Even when the declarative sentence has no auxiliary, one is used for questions.

The baby drinks milk.   Does she drink juice?
We work every morning.   Do they work?

Negations

Negation in English is also dependent upon auxiliaries placed after the subject and before **not** plus the required form of the verb.

I am not going.
She has not been seen.
We do not feel like leaving.
You were not watching.
They will not want dinner.

Negative sentences can also be formed using another negation word, such as **never, nothing, nobody**, and so forth.

I never went to class unprepared.
Nothing can stop us now.
Nobody likes to pay taxes.

Which 501 English Verbs?

Where did these 501 English verbs come from? One cannot write a book like this without expressing a debt to those who have come before. A pioneer in attempting to list all the forms of English irregular verbs was Vincent F. Hopper, whose list of 123 irregular verbs in *English Verb Conjugations* (Barron's, 1975) was both an inspiration and a starting point for the 501 verbs here. I have attempted to determine all of the irregular verbs in English. Most sources refer to over 200. Dictionaries, grammars, and handbooks provided a list of almost 300—although that included several compounds, such as "reread," "underwrite," and so forth. I consulted the word frequency lists for the spoken language *Word Frequencies of Spoken American English* (1979), by Hartvig Dahl, who notes that "only 848 words account for 90% of spoken usage" (p. vii). I have included all verbs found in the first 1,000 words of the spoken sample.

Similarly I have included verbs in the first 2,000 words of written speech as determined by the Brown corpus in W. Nelson Francis and Henry Kucera's *Frequency Analysis of English Usage* (Boston: Houghton Mifflin, 1982). At the final stage I carefully compared my list to the entire body of the *American Heritage Dictionary of the English Language* (Third Edition, 1992) to seek out forms that might cause difficulty for learners and native speakers alike. For all of the entries, I have compared the *American Heritage* entries to those of the *Oxford Modern English Dictionary* (Second Edition, 1996), *Merriam Webster's Collegiate Dictionary* (Tenth Edition, 1993), and *Webster's New World Dictionary* (Third Edition, 1990).

In the course of my work it became clear that there are several accepted forms and some disagreements. This is as it should be. English has resisted most efforts to prescribe "correct" usage. A living language spoken natively by hundreds of millions living in the United States, Great Britain, Australia, New Zealand, and Canada, it is also spoken by hundreds of millions who learn English in addition to their native languages. I have relied on two of the most recent grammars in English for guidance: Randolf Quirk, Sidney Greenbaum, et al., *A Comprehensive Grammar of the English Language* (1985) and Sidney Greenbaum, *The Oxford English Grammar* (1996). I have also consulted Kenneth G. Wilson, *The Columbia Guide to Standard American English* (1993).

My purpose has been to describe what can and may occur. I make no claim that each and every form of the verbs presented here has or will actually occur in speech or writing. They are all potential forms, and even when one must imagine possible situations or figurative usages for some of them, the forms are here for your information.

I have also become convinced of how complex the entire verbal system is, and how much work is required by native speakers and learners alike to master all the forms. *501 English Verbs* is itself a pioneering attempt and I look forward to your comments and suggestions for the next edition.

Thomas R. Beyer, Jr.
Middlebury College
Middlebury, Vermont
U.S.A.

abide
(active voice)

be abided/abode
(passive voice)

Infinitive: **to abide**
Perfect Infinitive: **to have abided**
Present Participle: **abiding**
Past Participle: **abided**

Infinitive: **to be abided**
Perfect Infinitive: **to have been abided**
Present Participle: **being abided**
Past Participle: **been abided**

INDICATIVE MOOD

Pres.	I, we, you, they **abide**	I **am abided** we, you, they **are abided**
	he, she, it **abides**	he, she, it **is abided**
Pres. *Prog.*	I **am abiding** we, you, they **are abiding** he, she, it **is abiding**	I **am being abided** we, you, they **are being abided** he, she, it **is being abided**
Pres. *Int.*	I, we, you, they **do abide** he, she, it **does abide**	I, we, you, they **do get abided** he, she, it **does get abided**
Fut.	I, he, she, it, we, you, they **will abide**	I, he, she, it, we, you, they **will be abided**
Past	I, he, she, it, we, you, they **abode**	I, he, she, it **was abided** we, you, they **were abided**
Past *Prog.*	I, he, she, it **was abiding** we, you, they **were abiding**	I, he, she, it **was being abided** we, you, they **were being abided**
Past *Int.*	I, he, she, it, we, you, they **did abide**	I, he, she, it, we, you, they **did get abided**
Pres. *Perf.*	I, we, you, they **have abided** he, she, it **has abided**	I, we, you, they **have been abided** he, she, it **has been abided**
Past *Perf.*	I, he, she, it, we, you, they **had abided**	I, he, she, it, we, you, they **had been abided**
Fut. *Perf.*	I, he, she, it, we, you, they **will have abided**	I, he, she, it, we, you, they **will have been abided**

IMPERATIVE MOOD

abide **be abided**

SUBJUNCTIVE MOOD

Pres.	if I, he, she, it, we, you, they **abide**	if I, he, she, it, we, you, they **be abided**
Past	if I, he, she, it, we, you, they **abode**	if I, he, she, it, we, you, they **were abided**
Fut.	if I, he, she, it, we, you, they **should abide**	if I, he, she, it, we, you, they **should be abided**

Transitive and intransitive. In the past tense ABODE and ABIDED are acceptable. For the past participle, ABIDED is now more frequently used. ABODE has a "literary" ring. As an intransitive verb ABODE means "to dwell or live somewhere." The *Oxford Modern English Dictionary* prefers "**abided** or rarely **abode**."

1

accept
(active voice)

be accepted
(passive voice)

Infinitive: **to accept**
Perfect Infinitive: **to have accepted**
Present Participle: **accepting**
Past Participle: **accepted**

Infinitive: **to be accepted**
Perfect Infinitive: **to have been accepted**
Present Participle: **being accepted**
Past Participle: **been accepted**

INDICATIVE MOOD

Pres.	I, we, you, they **accept**	I **am accepted**
		we, you, they **are accepted**
	he, she, it **accepts**	he, she, it **is accepted**
Pres.	I am accepting	I **am being accepted**
Prog.	we, you, they **are accepting**	we, you, they **are being accepted**
	he, she, it **is accepting**	he, she, it **is being accepted**
Pres.	I, we, you, they **do accept**	I, we, you, they **do get accepted**
Int.	he, she, it **does accept**	he, she, it **does get accepted**
Fut.	I, he, she, it,	I, he, she, it,
	we, you, they **will accept**	we, you, they **will be accepted**
Past	I, he, she, it,	I, he, she, it **was accepted**
	we, you, they **accepted**	we, you, they **were accepted**
Past	I, he, she, it **was accepting**	I, he, she, it **was being accepted**
Prog.	we, you, they **were accepting**	we, you, they **were being accepted**
Past	I, he, she, it,	I, he, she, it,
Int.	we, you, they **did accept**	we, you, they **did get accepted**
Pres.	I, we, you, they **have accepted**	I, we, you, they **have been accepted**
Perf.	he, she, it **has accepted**	he, she, it **has been accepted**
Past	I, he, she, it,	I, he, she, it,
Perf.	we, you, they **had accepted**	we, you, they **had been accepted**
Fut.	I, he, she, it, we, you, they	I, he, she, it, we, you, they
Perf.	**will have accepted**	**will have been accepted**

IMPERATIVE MOOD

accept

be accepted

SUBJUNCTIVE MOOD

Pres.	if I, he, she, it,	if I, he, she, it,
	we, you, they **accept**	we, you, they **be accepted**
Past	if I, he, she, it,	if I, he, she, it,
	we, you, they **accepted**	we, you, they **were accepted**
Fut.	if I, he, she, it,	if I, he, she, it,
	we, you, they **should accept**	we, you, they **should be accepted**

Transitive and intransitive.

achieve
(active voice)

PRINCIPAL PARTS: **achieves, achieving, achieved, achieved**

be achieved
(passive voice)

Infinitive: **to achieve**
Perfect Infinitive: **to have achieved**
Present Participle: **achieving**
Past Participle: **achieved**

Infinitive: **to be achieved**
Perfect Infinitive: **to have been achieved**
Present Participle: **being achieved**
Past Participle: **been achieved**

INDICATIVE MOOD

Pres.	I, we, you, they **achieve**	I **am achieved**
		we, you, they **are achieved**
	he, she, it **achieves**	he, she, it **is achieved**
Pres.	I **am achieving**	I **am being achieved**
Prog.	we, you, they **are achieving**	we, you, they **are being achieved**
	he, she, it **is achieving**	he, she, it **is being achieved**
Pres.	I, we, you, they **do achieve**	I, we, you, they **do get achieved**
Int.	he, she, it **does achieve**	he, she, it **does get achieved**
Fut.	I, he, she, it, we, you, they **will achieve**	I, he, she, it, we, you, they **will be achieved**
Past	I, he, she, it, we, you, they **achieved**	I, he, she, it **was achieved** we, you, they **were achieved**
Past	I, he, she, it **was achieving**	I, he, she, it **was being achieved**
Prog.	we, you, they **were achieving**	we, you, they **were being achieved**
Past	I, he, she, it, we, you, they **did achieve**	I, he, she, it, we, you, they **did get achieved**
Int.		
Pres.	I, we, you, they **have achieved**	I, we, you, they **have been achieved**
Perf.	he, she, it **has achieved**	he, she, it **has been achieved**
Past	I, he, she, it, we, you, they **had achieved**	I, he, she, it, we, you, they **had been achieved**
Perf.		
Fut.	I, he, she, it, we, you, they **will have achieved**	I, he, she, it, we, you, they **will have been achieved**
Perf.		

IMPERATIVE MOOD

achieve

be achieved

SUBJUNCTIVE MOOD

Pres.	if I, he, she, it, we, you, they **achieve**	if I, he, she, it we, you, they **be achieved**
Past	if I, he, she, it, we, you, they **achieved**	if I, he, she, it, we, you, they **were achieved**
Fut.	if I, he, she, it, we, you, they **should achieve**	if I, he, she, it, we, you, they **should be achieved**

Transitive and intransitive.

Infinitive: **to act**
Perfect Infinitive: **to have acted**
Present Participle: **acting**
Past Participle: **acted**

Infinitive: **to be acted**
Perfect Infinitive: **to have been acted**
Present Participle: **being acted**
Past Participle: **been acted**

INDICATIVE MOOD

	Active	Passive
Pres.	I, we, you, they **act** he, she, it **acts**	I **am acted** we, you, they **are acted** he, she, it **is acted**
Pres. Prog.	I **am acting** we, you, they **are acting** he, she, it **is acting**	I **am being acted** we, you, they **are being acted** he, she, it **is being acted**
Pres. Int.	I, we, you, they **do act** he, she, it **does act**	I, we, you, they **do get acted** he, she, it **does get acted**
Fut.	I, he, she, it, we, you, they **will act**	I, he, she, it, we, you, they **will be acted**
Past	I, he, she, it, we, you, they **acted**	I, he, she, it **was acted** we, you, they **were acted**
Past Prog.	I, he, she, it **was acting** we, you, they **were acting**	I, he, she, it **was being acted** we, you, they **were being acted**
Past Int.	I, he, she, it, we, you, they **did act**	I, he, she, it, we, you, they **did get acted**
Pres. Perf.	I, we, you, they **have acted** he, she, it **has acted**	I, we, you, they **have been acted** he, she, it **has been acted**
Past Perf.	I, he, she, it, we, you, they **had acted**	I, he, she, it, we, you, they **had been acted**
Fut. Perf.	I, he, she, it, we, you, they **will have acted**	I, he, she, it, we, you, they **will have been acted**

IMPERATIVE MOOD

act

be acted

SUBJUNCTIVE MOOD

	Active	Passive
Pres.	if I, he, she, it, we, you, they **act**	if I, he, she, it, we, you, they **be acted**
Past	if I, he, she, it, we, you, they **acted**	if I, he, she, it, we, you, they **were acted**
Fut.	if I, he, she, it, we, you, they **should act**	if I, he, she, it, we, you, they **should be acted**

Transitive and intransitive.

add
(active voice)

PRINCIPAL PARTS: **adds, adding, added, added**

be added
(passive voice)

Infinitive: **to add**
Perfect Infinitive: **to have added**
Present Participle: **adding**
Past Participle: **added**

Infinitive: **to be added**
Perfect Infinitive: **to have been added**
Present Participle: **being added**
Past Participle: **been added**

INDICATIVE MOOD

Pres.	I, we, you, they **add**	I **am added**
		we, you, they **are added**
	he, she, it **adds**	he, she, it **is added**
Pres. *Prog.*	I **am adding**	I **am being added**
	we, you, they **are adding**	we, you, they **are being added**
	he, she, it **is adding**	he, she, it **is being added**
Pres. *Int.*	I, we, you, they **do add**	I, we, you, they **do get added**
	he, she, it **does add**	he, she, it **does get added**
Fut.	I, he, she, it,	I, he, she, it,
	we, you, they **will add**	we, you, they **will be added**
Past	I, he, she, it,	I, he, she, it **was added**
	we, you, they **added**	we, you, they **were added**
Past *Prog.*	I, he, she, it **was adding**	I, he, she, it **was being added**
	we, you, they **were adding**	we, you, they **were being added**
Past *Int.*	I, he, she, it,	I, he, she, it,
	we, you, they **did add**	we, you, they **did get added**
Pres. *Perf.*	I, we, you, they **have added**	I, we, you, they **have been added**
	he, she, it **has added**	he, she, it **has been added**
Past *Perf.*	I, he, she, it,	I, he, she, it,
	we, you, they **had added**	we, you, they **had been added**
Fut. *Perf.*	I, he, she, it, we, you, they	I, he, she, it, we, you, they
	will have added	**will have been added**

IMPERATIVE MOOD

add

be added

SUBJUNCTIVE MOOD

Pres.	if I, he, she, it,	if I, he, she, it,
	we, you, they **add**	we, you, they **be added**
Past	if I, he, she, it,	if I, he, she, it,
	we, you, they **added**	we, you, they **were added**
Fut.	if I, he, she, it,	if I, he, she, it,
	we, you, they **should add**	we, you, they **should be added**

Transitive and intransitive.

admit
(active voice)

PRINCIPAL PARTS: **admits, admitting,
admitted, admitted**

be admitted
(passive voice)

Infinitive: **to admit**
Perfect Infinitive: **to have admitted**
Present Participle: **admitting**
Past Participle: **admitted**

Infinitive: **to be admitted**
Perfect Infinitive: **to have been admitted**
Present Participle: **being admitted**
Past Participle: **been admitted**

INDICATIVE MOOD

Pres.	I, we, you, they **admit**	I **am admitted**
		we, you, they **are admitted**
	he, she, it **admits**	he, she, it **is admitted**
Pres.	I **am admitting**	I **am being admitted**
Prog.	we, you, they **are admitting**	we, you, they **are being admitted**
	he, she, it **is admitting**	he, she, it **is being admitted**
Pres.	I, we, you, they **do admit**	I, we, you, they **do get admitted**
Int.	he, she, it **does admit**	he, she, it **does get admitted**
Fut.	I, he, she, it,	I, he, she, it,
	we, you, they **will admit**	we, you, they **will be admitted**
Past	I, he, she, it,	I, he, she, it **was admitted**
	we, you, they **admitted**	we, you, they **were admitted**
Past	I, he, she, it **was admitting**	I, he, she, it **was being admitted**
Prog.	we, you, they **were admitting**	we, you, they **were being admitted**
Past	I, he, she, it,	I, he, she, it,
Int.	we, you, they **did admit**	we, you, they **did get admitted**
Pres.	I, we, you, they **have admitted**	I, we, you, they **have been admitted**
Perf.	he, she, it **has admitted**	he, she, it **has been admitted**
Past	I, he, she, it,	I, he, she, it,
Perf.	we, you, they **had admitted**	we, you, they **had been admitted**
Fut.	I, he, she, it, we, you, they	I, he, she, it, we, you, they
Perf.	**will have admitted**	**will have been admitted**

IMPERATIVE MOOD

admit   **be admitted**

SUBJUNCTIVE MOOD

Pres.	if I, he, she, it,	if I, he, she, it,
	we, you, they **admit**	we, you, they **be admitted**
Past	if I, he, she, it,	if I, he, she, it,
	we, you, they **admitted**	we, you, they **were admitted**
Fut.	if I, he, she, it,	if I, he, she, it,
	we, you, they **should admit**	we, you, they **should be admitted**

Transitive and intransitive.

agree
(active voice)

PRINCIPAL PARTS: **agrees, agreeing, agreed, agreed**

be agreed
(passive voice)

Infinitive: **to agree**
Perfect Infinitive: **to have agreed**
Present Participle: **agreeing**
Past Participle: **agreed**

Infinitive: **to be agreed**
Perfect Infinitive: **to have been agreed**
Present Participle: **being agreed**
Past Participle: **been agreed**

INDICATIVE MOOD

Pres.	I, we, you, they **agree** he, she, it **agrees**	I am **agreed** we, you, they **are agreed** he, she, it **is agreed**
Pres. *Prog.*	I **am agreeing** we, you, they **are agreeing** he, she, it **is agreeing**	I am **being agreed** we, you, they **are being agreed** he, she, it **is being agreed**
Pres. *Int.*	I, we, you, they **do agree** he, she, it **does agree**	I, we, you, they **do get agreed** he, she, it **does get agreed**
Fut.	I, he, she, it, we, you, they **will agree**	I, he, she, it, we, you, they **will be agreed**
Past	I, he, she, it, we, you, they **agreed**	I, he, she, it **was agreed** we, you, they **were agreed**
Past *Prog.*	I, he, she, it **was agreeing** we, you, they **were agreeing**	I, he, she, it **was being agreed** we, you, they **were being agreed**
Past *Int.*	I, he, she, it, we, you, they **did agree**	I, he, she, it, we, you, they **did get agreed**
Pres. *Perf.*	I, we, you, they **have agreed** he, she, it **has agreed**	I, we, you, they **have been agreed** he, she, it **has been agreed**
Past *Perf.*	I, he, she, it, we, you, they **had agreed**	I, he, she, it, we, you, they **had been agreed**
Fut. *Perf.*	I, he, she, it, we, you, they **will have agreed**	I, he, she, it, we, you, they **will have been agreed**

IMPERATIVE MOOD

agree　　　　　　　　　　　　**be agreed**

SUBJUNCTIVE MOOD

Pres.	if I, he, she, it, we, you, they **agree**	if I, he, she, it, we, you, they **be agreed**
Past	if I, he, she, it, we, you, they **agreed**	if I, he, she, it, we, you, they **were agreed**
Fut.	if I, he, she, it, we, you, they **should agree**	if I, he, she, it, we, you, they **should be agreed**

Intransitive and transitive.

allow
(active voice)

PRINCIPAL PARTS: **allows, allowing, allowed, allowed**

be allowed
(passive voice)

Infinitive: **to allow**
Perfect Infinitive: **to have allowed**
Present Participle: **allowing**
Past Participle: **allowed**

Infinitive: **to be allowed**
Perfect Infinitive: **to have been allowed**
Present Participle: **being allowed**
Past Participle: **been allowed**

INDICATIVE MOOD

Pres.	I, we, you, they **allow**	I **am allowed**
		we, you, they **are allowed**
	he, she, it **allows**	he, she, it **is allowed**
Pres.	I **am allowing**	I **am being allowed**
Prog.	we, you, they **are allowing**	we, you, they **are being allowed**
	he, she, it **is allowing**	he, she, it **is being allowed**
Pres.	I, we, you, they **do allow**	I, we, you, they **do get allowed**
Int.	he, she, it **does allow**	he, she, it **does get allowed**
Fut.	I, he, she, it,	I, he, she, it,
	we, you, they **will allow**	we, you, they **will be allowed**
Past	I, he, she, it,	I, he, she, it **was allowed**
	we, you, they **allowed**	we, you, they **were allowed**
Past	I, he, she, it **was allowing**	I, he, she, it **was being allowed**
Prog.	we, you, they **were allowing**	we, you, they **were being allowed**
Past	I, he, she, it,	I, he, she, it,
Int.	we, you, they **did allow**	we, you, they **did get allowed**
Pres.	I, we, you, they **have allowed**	I, we, you, they **have been allowed**
Perf.	he, she, it **has allowed**	he, she, it **has been allowed**
Past	I, he, she, it,	I, he, she, it,
Perf.	we, you, they **had allowed**	we, you, they **had been allowed**
Fut.	I, he, she, it, we, you, they	I, he, she, it, we, you, they
Perf.	**will have allowed**	**will have been allowed**

IMPERATIVE MOOD

allow

be allowed

SUBJUNCTIVE MOOD

Pres.	if I, he, she, it,	if I, he, she, it,
	we, you, they **allow**	we, you, they **be allowed**
Past	if I, he, she, it,	if I, he, she, it,
	we, you, they **allowed**	we, you, they **were allowed**
Fut.	if I, he, she, it,	if I, he, she, it,
	we, you, they **should allow**	we, you, they **should be allowed**

Transitive and intransitive.

announce
(active voice)

be announced
(passive voice)

Infinitive: **to announce**
Perfect Infinitive: **to have announced**
Present Participle: **announcing**
Past Participle: **announced**

Infinitive: **to be announced**
Perfect Infinitive: **to have been announced**
Present Participle: **being announced**
Past Participle: **been announced**

INDICATIVE MOOD

Pres.	I, we, you, they **announce**	I **am announced**
		we, you, they **are announced**
	he, she, it **announces**	he, she, it **is announced**
Pres.	I **am announcing**	I **am being announced**
Prog.	we, you, they **are announcing**	we, you, they **are being announced**
	he, she, it **is announcing**	he, she, it **is being announced**
Pres.	I, we, you, they **do announce**	I, we, you, they **do get announced**
Int.	he, she, it **does announce**	he, she, it **does get announced**
Fut.	I, he, she, it,	I, he, she, it,
	we, you, they **will announce**	we, you, they **will be announced**
Past	I, he, she, it,	I, he, she, it **was announced**
	we, you, they **announced**	we, you, they **were announced**
Past	I, he, she, it **was announcing**	I, he, she, it **was being announced**
Prog.	we, you, they **were announcing**	we, you, they **were being announced**
Past	I, he, she, it,	I, he, she, it,
Int.	we, you, they **did announce**	we, you, they **did get announced**
Pres.	I, we, you, they **have announced**	I, we, you, they **have been announced**
Perf.	he, she, it **has announced**	he, she, it **has been announced**
Past	I, he, she, it,	I, he, she, it,
Perf.	we, you, they **had announced**	we, you, they **had been announced**
Fut.	I, he, she, it, we, you, they	I, he, she, it, we, you, they
Perf.	**will have announced**	**will have been announced**

IMPERATIVE MOOD

announce   **be announced**

SUBJUNCTIVE MOOD

Pres.	if I, he, she, it,	if I, he, she, it,
	we, you, they **announce**	we, you, they **be announced**
Past	if I, he, she, it,	if I, he, she, it,
	we, you, they **announced**	we, you, they **were announced**
Fut.	if I, he, she, it,	if I, he, she, it,
	we, you, they **should announce**	we, you, they **should be announced**

Transitive and intransitive.

annoy
(active voice)

be annoyed
(passive voice)

Infinitive: **to annoy**
Perfect Infinitive: **to have annoyed**
Present Participle: **annoying**
Past Participle: **annoyed**

Infinitive: **to be annoyed**
Perfect Infinitive: **to have been annoyed**
Present Participle: **being annoyed**
Past Participle: **been annoyed**

INDICATIVE MOOD

Pres.	I, we, you, they **annoy**	I **am annoyed**
		we, you, they **are annoyed**
	he, she, it **annoys**	he, she, it **is annoyed**
Pres.	I **am annoying**	I **am being annoyed**
Prog.	we, you, they **are annoying**	we, you, they **are being annoyed**
	he, she, it **is annoying**	he, she, it **is being annoyed**
Pres.	I, we, you, they **do annoy**	I, we, you, they **do get annoyed**
Int.	he, she, it **does annoy**	he, she, it **does get annoyed**
Fut.	I, he, she, it,	I, he, she, it,
	we, you, they **will annoy**	we, you, they **will be annoyed**
Past	I, he, she, it,	I, he, she, it **was annoyed**
	we, you, they **annoyed**	we, you, they **were annoyed**
Past	I, he, she, it **was annoying**	I, he, she, it **was being annoyed**
Prog.	we, you, they **were annoying**	we, you, they **were being annoyed**
Past	I, he, she, it,	I, he, she, it,
Int.	we, you, they **did annoy**	we, you, they **did get annoyed**
Pres.	I, we, you, they **have annoyed**	I, we, you, they **have been annoyed**
Perf.	he, she, it **has annoyed**	he, she, it **has been annoyed**
Past	I, he, she, it,	I, he, she, it,
Perf.	we, you, they **had annoyed**	we, you, they **had been annoyed**
Fut.	I, he, she, it, we, you, they	I, he, she, it, we, you, they
Perf.	**will have annoyed**	**will have been annoyed**

IMPERATIVE MOOD

annoy   **be annoyed**

SUBJUNCTIVE MOOD

Pres.	if I, he, she, it,	if I, he, she, it,
	we, you, they **annoy**	we, you, they **be annoyed**
Past	if I, he, she, it,	if I, he, she, it,
	we, you, they **annoyed**	we, you, they **were annoyed**
Fut.	if I, he, she, it,	if I, he, she, it,
	we, you, they **should annoy**	we, you, they **should be annoyed**

Transitive and intransitive.

appear   PRINCIPAL PARTS: **appears, appearing, appeared, appeared**

Infinitive: **to appear**
Perfect Infinitive: **to have appeared**
Present Participle: **appearing**
Past Participle: **appeared**

INDICATIVE MOOD

Pres. I, we, you, they **appear**

 he, she, it **appears**

Pres. **I am appearing**
Prog. we, you, they **are appearing**
 he, she, it **is appearing**

Pres. I, we, you, they **do appear**
Int. he, she, it **does appear**

Fut. I, he, she, it,
 we, you, they **will appear**

Past I, he, she, it,
 we, you, they **appeared**

Past I, he, she, it **was appearing**
Prog. we, you, they **were appearing**

Past I, he, she, it,
Int. we, you, they **did appear**

Pres. I, we, you, they **have appeared**
Perf. he, she, it **has appeared**

Past I, he, she, it,
Perf. we, you, they **had appeared**

Fut. I, he, she, it, we, you, they
Perf. **will have appeared**

IMPERATIVE MOOD

 appear

SUBJUNCTIVE MOOD

Pres. if I, he, she, it,
 we, you, they **appear**

Past if I, he, she, it,
 we, you, they **appeared**

Fut. if I, he, she, it,
 we, you, they **should appear**

apply
(active voice)

PRINCIPAL PARTS: **applies, applying, applied, applied**

be applied
(passive voice)

Infinitive: **to apply**
Perfect Infinitive: **to have applied**
Present Participle: **applying**
Past Participle: **applied**

Infinitive: **to be applied**
Perfect Infinitive: **to have been applied**
Present Participle: **being applied**
Past Participle: **been applied**

INDICATIVE MOOD

Pres.	I, we, you, they **apply**	I **am applied**
		we, you, they **are applied**
	he, she, it **applies**	he, she, it **is applied**
Pres.	I **am applying**	I **am being applied**
Prog.	we, you, they **are applying**	we, you, they **are being applied**
	he, she, it **is applying**	he, she, it **is being applied**
Pres.	I, we, you, they **do apply**	I, we, you, they **do get applied**
Int.	he, she, it **does apply**	he, she, it **does get applied**
Fut.	I, he, she, it,	I, he, she, it,
	we, you, they **will apply**	we, you, they **will be applied**
Past	I, he, she, it,	I, he, she, it **was applied**
	we, you, they **applied**	we, you, they **were applied**
Past	I, he, she, it **was applying**	I, he, she, it **was being applied**
Prog.	we, you, they **were applying**	we, you, they **were being applied**
Past	I, he, she, it,	I, he, she, it,
Int.	we, you, they **did apply**	we, you, they **did get applied**
Pres.	I, we, you, they **have applied**	I, we, you, they **have been applied**
Perf.	he, she, it **has applied**	he, she, it **has been applied**
Past	I, he, she, it,	I, he, she, it,
Perf.	we, you, they **had applied**	we, you, they **had been applied**
Fut.	I, he, she, it, we, you, they	I, he, she, it, we, you, they
Perf.	**will have applied**	**will have been applied**

IMPERATIVE MOOD

apply

be applied

SUBJUNCTIVE MOOD

Pres.	if I, he, she, it,	if I, he, she, it,
	we, you, they **apply**	we, you, they **be applied**
Past	if I, he, she, it,	if I, he, she, it,
	we, you, they **applied**	we, you, they **were applied**
Fut.	if I, he, she, it,	if I, he, she, it,
	we, you, they **should apply**	we, you, they **should be applied**

Transitive and intransitive.

arise

Infinitive: **to arise**
Perfect Infinitive: **to have arisen**
Present Participle: **arising**
Past Participle: **arisen**

INDICATIVE MOOD

Pres. I, we, you, they **arise**

he, she, it **arises**

Pres. I **am arising**
Prog. we, you, they **are arising**
he, she, it **is arising**

Pres. I, we, you, they **do arise**
Int. he, she, it **does arise**

Fut. I, he, she, it,
we, you, they **will arise**

Past I, he, she, it,
we, you, they **arose**

Past I, he, she, it **was arising**
Prog. we, you, they **were arising**

Past I, he, she, it,
Int. we, you, they **did arise**

Pres. I, we, you, they **have arisen**
Perf. he, she, it **has arisen**

Past I, he, she, it,
Perf. we, you, they **had arisen**

Fut. I, he, she, it, we, you, they
Perf. **will have arisen**

IMPERATIVE MOOD

arise

SUBJUNCTIVE MOOD

Pres. if I, he, she, it,
we, you, they **arise**

Past if I, he, she, it,
we, you, they **arose**

Fut. if I, he, she, it,
we, you, they **should arise**

ask
(active voice)

be asked
(passive voice)

Infinitive: **to ask**
Perfect Infinitive: **to have asked**
Present Participle: **asking**
Past Participle: **asked**

Infinitive: **to be asked**
Perfect Infinitive: **to have been asked**
Present Participle: **being asked**
Past Participle: **been asked**

INDICATIVE MOOD

Pres.	I, we, you, they **ask**	I am **asked**
		we, you, they **are asked**
	he, she, it **asks**	he, she, it **is asked**
Pres. *Prog.*	I **am asking**	I **am being asked**
	we, you, they **are asking**	we, you, they **are being asked**
	he, she, it **is asking**	he, she, it **is being asked**
Pres. *Int.*	I, we, you, they **do ask**	I, we, you, they **do get asked**
	he, she, it **does ask**	he, she, it **does get asked**
Fut.	I, he, she, it, we, you, they **will ask**	I, he, she, it, we, you, they **will be asked**
Past	I, he, she, it, we, you, they **asked**	I, he, she, it **was asked** we, you, they **were asked**
Past *Prog.*	I, he, she, it **was asking** we, you, they **were asking**	I, he, she, it **was being asked** we, you, they **were being asked**
Past *Int.*	I, he, she, it, we, you, they **did ask**	I, he, she, it, we, you, they **did get asked**
Pres. *Perf.*	I, we, you, they **have asked** he, she, it **has asked**	I, we, you, they **have been asked** he, she, it **has been asked**
Past *Perf.*	I, he, she, it, we, you, they **had asked**	I, he, she, it, we, you, they **had been asked**
Fut. *Perf.*	I, he, she, it, we, you, they **will have asked**	I, he, she, it, we, you, they **will have been asked**

IMPERATIVE MOOD

ask
be asked

SUBJUNCTIVE MOOD

Pres.	if I, he, she, it, we, you, they **ask**	if I, he, she, it, we, you, they **be asked**
Past	if I, he, she, it, we, you, they **asked**	if I, he, she, it, we, you, they **were asked**
Fut.	if I, he, she, it, we, you, they **should ask**	if I, he, she, it, we, you, they **should be asked**

Transitive and intransitive.

assume
(active voice)

be assumed
(passive voice)

Infinitive: **to assume**
Perfect Infinitive: **to have assumed**
Present Participle: **assuming**
Past Participle: **assumed**

Infinitive: **to be assumed**
Perfect Infinitive: **to have been assumed**
Present Participle: **being assumed**
Past Participle: **been assumed**

INDICATIVE MOOD

Pres.	I, we, you, they **assume**	I am assumed
		we, you, they **are assumed**
	he, she, it **assumes**	he, she, it **is assumed**
Pres. *Prog.*	I am assuming	I am being assumed
	we, you, they **are assuming**	we, you, they **are being assumed**
	he, she, it **is assuming**	he, she, it **is being assumed**
Pres. *Int.*	I, we, you, they **do assume**	I, we, you, they **do get assumed**
	he, she, it **does assume**	he, she, it **does get assumed**
Fut.	I, he, she, it, we, you, they **will assume**	I, he, she, it, we, you, they **will be assumed**
Past	I, he, she, it, we, you, they **assumed**	I, he, she, it **was assumed** we, you, they **were assumed**
Past *Prog.*	I, he, she, it **was assuming** we, you, they **were assuming**	I, he, she, it **was being assumed** we, you, they **were being assumed**
Past *Int.*	I, he, she, it, we, you, they **did assume**	I, he, she, it, we, you, they **did get assumed**
Pres. *Perf.*	I, we, you, they **have assumed** he, she, it **has assumed**	I, we, you, they **have been assumed** he, she, it **has been assumed**
Past *Perf.*	I, he, she, it, we, you, they **had assumed**	I, he, she, it, we, you, they **had been assumed**
Fut. *Perf.*	I, he, she, it, we, you, they **will have assumed**	I, he, she, it, we, you, they **will have been assumed**

IMPERATIVE MOOD

assume   **be assumed**

SUBJUNCTIVE MOOD

Pres.	if I, he, she, it, we, you, they **assume**	if I, he, she, it, we, you, they **be assumed**
Past	if I, he, she, it, we, you, they **assumed**	if I, he, she, it, we, you, they **were assumed**
Fut.	if I, he, she, it, we, you, they **should assume**	if I, he, she, it, we, you, they **should be assumed**

attack
(active voice)

be attacked
(passive voice)

Infinitive: **to attack**
Perfect Infinitive: **to have attacked**
Present Participle: **attacking**
Past Participle: **attacked**

Infinitive: **to be attacked**
Perfect Infinitive: **to have been attacked**
Present Participle: **being attacked**
Past Participle: **been attacked**

INDICATIVE MOOD

Pres.	I, we, you, they **attack**	I am attacked
		we, you, they **are attacked**
	he, she, it **attacks**	he, she, it **is attacked**
Pres.	I am attacking	I am being attacked
Prog.	we, you, they **are attacking**	we, you, they **are being attacked**
	he, she, it **is attacking**	he, she, it **is being attacked**
Pres.	I, we, you, they **do attack**	I, we, you, they **do get attacked**
Int.	he, she, it **does attack**	he, she, it **does get attacked**
Fut.	I, he, she, it,	I, he, she, it,
	we, you, they **will attack**	we, you, they **will be attacked**
Past	I, he, she, it,	I, he, she, it **was attacked**
	we, you, they **attacked**	we, you, they **were attacked**
Past	I, he, she, it **was attacking**	I, he, she, it **was being attacked**
Prog.	we, you, they **were attacking**	we, you, they **were being attacked**
Past	I, he, she, it,	I, he, she, it,
Int.	we, you, they **did attack**	we, you, they **did get attacked**
Pres.	I, we, you, they **have attacked**	I, we, you, they **have been attacked**
Perf.	he, she, it **has attacked**	he, she, it **has been attacked**
Past	I, he, she, it,	I, he, she, it,
Perf.	we, you, they **had attacked**	we, you, they **had been attacked**
Fut.	I, he, she, it, we, you, they	I, he, she, it, we, you, they
Perf.	**will have attacked**	**will have been attacked**

IMPERATIVE MOOD

attack

be attacked

SUBJUNCTIVE MOOD

Pres.	if I, he, she, it,	if I, he, she, it,
	we, you, they **attack**	we, you, they **be attacked**
Past	if I, he, she, it,	if I, he, she, it,
	we, you, they **attacked**	we, you, they **were attacked**
Fut.	if I, he, she, it,	if I, he, she, it,
	we, you, they **should attack**	we, you, they **should be attacked**

Transitive and intransitive.

attend
(active voice)

be attended
(passive voice)

Infinitive: **to attend**
Perfect Infinitive: **to have attended**
Present Participle: **attending**
Past Participle: **attended**

Infinitive: **to be attended**
Perfect Infinitive: **to have been attended**
Present Participle: **being attended**
Past Participle: **been attended**

INDICATIVE MOOD

Pres.	I, we, you, they **attend**	I **am attended** we, you, they **are attended**
	he, she, it **attends**	he, she, it **is attended**
Pres. *Prog.*	I **am attending** we, you, they **are attending** he, she, it **is attending**	I **am being attended** we, you, they **are being attended** he, she, it **is being attended**
Pres. *Int.*	I, we, you, they **do attend** he, she, it **does attend**	I, we, you, they **do get attended** he, she, it **does get attended**
Fut.	I, he, she, it, we, you, they **will attend**	I, he, she, it, we, you, they **will be attended**
Past	I, he, she, it, we, you, they **attended**	I, he, she, it **was attended** we, you, they **were attended**
Past *Prog.*	I, he, she, it **was attending** we, you, they **were attending**	I, he, she, it **was being attended** we, you, they **were being attended**
Past *Int.*	I, he, she, it, we, you, they **did attend**	I, he, she, it, we, you, they **did get attended**
Pres. *Perf.*	I, we, you, they **have attended** he, she, it **has attended**	I, we, you, they **have been attended** he, she, it **has been attended**
Past *Perf.*	I, he, she, it, we, you, they **had attended**	I, he, she, it, we, you, they **had been attended**
Fut. *Perf.*	I, he, she, it, we, you, they **will have attended**	I, he, she, it, we, you, they **will have been attended**

IMPERATIVE MOOD

attend   **be attended**

SUBJUNCTIVE MOOD

Pres.	if I, he, she, it, we, you, they **attend**	if I, he, she, it, we, you, they **be attended**
Past	if I, he, she, it, we, you, they **attended**	if I, he, she, it, we, you, they **were attended**
Fut.	if I, he, she, it, we, you, they **should attend**	if I, he, she, it, we, you, they **should be attended**

Transitive and intransitive.

avoid
(active voice)

be avoided
(passive voice)

Infinitive: **to avoid**
Perfect Infinitive: **to have avoided**
Present Participle: **avoiding**
Past Participle: **avoided**

Infinitive: **to be avoided**
Perfect Infinitive: **to have been avoided**
Present Participle: **being avoided**
Past Participle: **been avoided**

INDICATIVE MOOD

Pres.	I, we, you, they **avoid**	I **am avoided**
		we, you, they **are avoided**
	he, she, it **avoids**	he, she, it **is avoided**
Pres.	I **am avoiding**	I **am being avoided**
Prog.	we, you, they **are avoiding**	we, you, they **are being avoided**
	he, she, it **is avoiding**	he, she, it **is being avoided**
Pres.	I, we, you, they **do avoid**	I, we, you, they **do get avoided**
Int.	he, she, it **does avoid**	he, she, it **does get avoided**
Fut.	I, he, she, it,	I, he, she, it,
	we, you, they **will avoid**	we, you, they **will be avoided**
Past	I, he, she, it,	I, he, she, it **was avoided**
	we, you, they **avoided**	we, you, they **were avoided**
Past	I, he, she, it **was avoiding**	I, he, she, it **was being avoided**
Prog.	we, you, they **were avoiding**	we, you, they **were being avoided**
Past	I, he, she, it,	I, he, she, it,
Int.	we, you, they **did avoid**	we, you, they **did get avoided**
Pres.	I, we, you, they **have avoided**	I, we, you, they **have been avoided**
Perf.	he, she, it **has avoided**	he, she, it **has been avoided**
Past	I, he, she, it,	I, he, she, it,
Perf.	we, you, they **had avoided**	we, you, they **had been avoided**
Fut.	I, he, she, it, we, you, they	I, he, she, it, we, you, they
Perf.	**will have avoided**	**will have been avoided**

IMPERATIVE MOOD

avoid   **be avoided**

SUBJUNCTIVE MOOD

Pres.	if I, he, she, it,	if I, he, she, it,
	we, you, they **avoid**	we, you, they **be avoided**
Past	if I, he, she, it,	if I, he, she, it,
	we, you, they **avoided**	we, you, they **were avoided**
Fut.	if I, he, she, it,	if I, he, she, it,
	we, you, they **should avoid**	we, you, they **should be avoided**

PRINCIPAL PARTS: **awakes, awaking,**
awoke/awaked, awaked/awoken

be awaked
(passive voice)

Infinitive: **to awake**
Perfect Infinitive: **to have awaked**
Present Participle: **awaking**
Past Participle: **awaked**

Infinitive: **to be awaked**
Perfect Infinitive: **to have been awaked**
Present Participle: **being awaked**
Past Participle: **been awaked**

INDICATIVE MOOD

Pres.	I, we, you, they **awake**	I **am awaked**
		we, you, they **are awaked**
	he, she, it **awakes**	he, she, it **is awaked**
Pres.	I **am awaking**	I **am being awaked**
Prog.	we, you, they **are awaking**	we, you, they **are being awaked**
	he, she, it **is awaking**	he, she, it **is being awaked**
Pres.	I, we, you, they **do awake**	I, we, you, they **do get awaked**
Int.	he, she, it **does awake**	he, she, it **does get awaked**
Fut.	I, he, she, it,	I, he, she, it,
	we, you, they **will awake**	we, you, they **will be awaked**
Past	I, he, she, it,	I, he, she, it **was awaked**
	we, you, they **awoke**	we, you, they **were awaked**
Past	I, he, she, it **was awaking**	I, he, she, it **was being awaked**
Prog.	we, you, they **were awaking**	we, you, they **were being awaked**
Past	I, he, she, it,	I, he, she, it,
Int.	we, you, they **did awake**	we, you, they **did get awaked**
Pres.	I, we, you, they **have awaked**	I, we, you, they **have been awaked**
Perf.	he, she, it **has awaked**	he, she, it **has been awaked**
Past	I, he, she, it,	I, he, she, it,
Perf.	we, you, they **had awaked**	we, you, they **had been awaked**
Fut.	I, he, she, it, we, you, they	I, he, she, it, we, you, they
Perf.	**will have awaked**	**will have been awaked**

IMPERATIVE MOOD

awake

be awaked

SUBJUNCTIVE MOOD

Pres.	if I, he, she, it,	if I, he, she, it,
	we, you, they **awake**	we, you, they **be awaked**
Past	if I, he, she, it,	if I, he, she, it,
	we, you, they **awoke**	we, you, they **were awaked**
Fut.	if I, he, she, it,	if I, he, she, it,
	we, you, they **should awake**	we, you, they **should be awaked**

Transitive and intransitive. Both forms of the past, AWOKE and AWAKED, are standard as are the past participles AWAKED and AWOKEN. The verb AWAKE and the related AWAKEN are synonymous with WAKE and WAKEN, but the former are more often used figuratively. The *Oxford Modern English Dictionary* lists only AWOKE for the past tense and AWOKEN for the past participle. *Merriam-Webster's Collegiate Dictionary* accepts AWOKE as a past participle.

Infinitive: **to awaken**
Perfect Infinitive: **to have awakened**
Present Participle: **awakening**
Past Participle: **awakened**

Infinitive: **to be awakened**
Perfect Infinitive: **to have been awakened**
Present Participle: **being awakened**
Past Participle: **been awakened**

INDICATIVE MOOD

Pres.	I, we, you, they **awaken**	I **am awakened**
		we, you, they **are awakened**
	he, she, it **awakens**	he, she, it **is awakened**
Pres.	I **am awakening**	I **am being awakened**
Prog.	we, you, they **are awakening**	we, you, they **are being awakened**
	he, she, it **is awakening**	he, she, it **is being awakened**
Pres.	I, we, you, they **do awaken**	I, we, you, they **do get awakened**
Int.	he, she, it **does awaken**	he, she, it **does get awakened**
Fut.	I, he, she, it,	I, he, she, it,
	we, you, they **will awaken**	we, you, they **will be awakened**
Past	I, he, she, it,	I, he, she, it **was awakened**
	we, you, they **awakened**	we, you, they **were awakened**
Past	I, he, she, it **was awakening**	I, he, she, it **was being awakened**
Prog.	we, you, they **were awakening**	we, you, they **were being awakened**
Past	I, he, she, it,	I, he, she, it,
Int.	we, you, they **did awaken**	we, you, they **did get awakened**
Pres.	I, we, you, they **have awakened**	I, we, you, they **have been awakened**
Perf.	he, she, it **has awakened**	he, she, it **has been awakened**
Past	I, he, she, it,	I, he, she, it,
Perf.	we, you, they **had awakened**	we, you, they **had been awakened**
Fut.	I, he, she, it, we, you, they	I, he, she, it, we, you, they
Perf.	**will have awakened**	**will have been awakened**

IMPERATIVE MOOD

awaken

be awakened

SUBJUNCTIVE MOOD

Pres.	if I, he, she, it,	if I, he, she, it,
	we, you, they **awaken**	we, you, they **be awakened**
Past	if I, he, she, it,	if I, he, she, it,
	we, you, they **awakened**	we, you, they **were awakened**
Fut.	if I, he, she, it,	if I, he, she, it,
	we, you, they **should awaken**	we, you, they **should be awakened**

Transitive and intransitive.

bar
(active voice)

be barred
(passive voice)

Infinitive: **to bar**
Perfect Infinitive: **to have barred**
Present Participle: **barring**
Past Participle: **barred**

Infinitive: **to be barred**
Perfect Infinitive: **to have been barred**
Present Participle: **being barred**
Past Participle: **been barred**

INDICATIVE MOOD

Pres.	I, we, you, they **bar**	I **am barred**
		we, you, they **are barred**
	he, she, it **bars**	he, she, it **is barred**
Pres.	I **am barring**	I **am being barred**
Prog.	we, you, they **are barring**	we, you, they **are being barred**
	he, she, it **is barring**	he, she, it **is being barred**
Pres.	I, we, you, they **do bar**	I, we, you, they **do get barred**
Int.	he, she, it **does bar**	he, she, it **does get barred**
Fut.	I, he, she, it,	I, he, she, it,
	we, you, they **will bar**	we, you, they **will be barred**
Past	I, he, she, it,	I, he, she, it **was barred**
	we, you, they **barred**	we, you, they **were barred**
Past	I, he, she, it **was barring**	I, he, she, it **was being barred**
Prog.	we, you, they **were barring**	we, you, they **were being barred**
Past	I, he, she, it,	I, he, she, it,
Int.	we, you, they **did bar**	we, you, they **did get barred**
Pres.	I, we, you, they **have barred**	I, we, you, they **have been barred**
Perf.	he, she, it **has barred**	he, she, it **has been barred**
Past	I, he, she, it,	I, he, she, it,
Perf.	we, you, they **had barred**	we, you, they **had been barred**
Fut.	I, he, she, it, we, you, they	I, he, she, it, we, you, they
Perf.	**will have barred**	**will have been barred**

IMPERATIVE MOOD

bar   **be barred**

SUBJUNCTIVE MOOD

Pres.	if I, he, she, it,	if I, he, she, it,
	we, you, they **bar**	we, you, they **be barred**
Past	if I, he, she, it,	if I, he, she, it,
	we, you, they **barred**	we, you, they **were barred**
Fut.	if I, he, she, it,	if I, he, she, it,
	we, you, they **should bar**	we, you, they **should be barred**

bare
(active voice)

be bared
(passive voice)

Infinitive: **to bare**
Perfect Infinitive: **to have bared**
Present Participle: **baring**
Past Participle: **bared**

Infinitive: **to be bared**
Perfect Infinitive: **to have been bared**
Present Participle: **being bared**
Past Participle: **been bared**

INDICATIVE MOOD

Pres.	I, we, you, they **bare**	I **am bared**
		we, you, they **are bared**
	he, she, it **bares**	he, she, it **is bared**
Pres.	I **am baring**	I **am being bared**
Prog.	we, you, they **are baring**	we, you, they **are being bared**
	he, she, it **is baring**	he, she, it **is being bared**
Pres.	I, we, you, they **do bare**	I, we, you, they **do get bared**
Int.	he, she, it **does bare**	he, she, it **does get bared**
Fut.	I, he, she, it,	I, he, she, it,
	we, you, they **will bare**	we, you, they **will be bared**
Past	I, he, she, it,	I, he, she, it **was bared**
	we, you, they **bared**	we, you, they **were bared**
Past	I, he, she, it **was baring**	I, he, she, it **was being bared**
Prog.	we, you, they **were baring**	we, you, they **were being bared**
Past	I, he, she, it,	I, he, she, it,
Int.	we, you, they **did bare**	we, you, they **did get bared**
Pres.	I, we, you, they **have bared**	I, we, you, they **have been bared**
Perf.	he, she, it **has bared**	he, she, it **has been bared**
Past	I, he, she, it,	I, he, she, it,
Perf.	we, you, they **had bared**	we, you, they **had been bared**
Fut.	I, he, she, it, we, you, they	I, he, she, it, we, you, they
Perf.	**will have bared**	**will have been bared**

IMPERATIVE MOOD

bare　　　　　　　　**be bared**

SUBJUNCTIVE MOOD

Pres.	if I, he, she, it,	if I, he, she, it,
	we, you, they **bare**	we, you, they **be bared**
Past	if I, he, she, it,	if I, he, she, it,
	we, you, they **bared**	we, you, they **were bared**
Fut.	if I, he, she, it,	if I, he, she, it,
	we, you, they **should bare**	we, you, they **should be bared**

BARE meaning "uncover" is pronounced like the verb BEAR meaning "carry."

PRINCIPAL PARTS: **bases, basing,
based, based**

Infinitive: **to base**
Perfect Infinitive: **to have based**
Present Participle: **basing**
Past Participle: **based**

Infinitive: **to be based**
Perfect Infinitive: **to have been based**
Present Participle: **being based**
Past Participle: **been based**

INDICATIVE MOOD

Pres.	I, we, you, they **base**	I **am based**
		we, you, they **are based**
	he, she, it **bases**	he, she, it **is based**
Pres.	I **am basing**	I **am being based**
Prog.	we, you, they **are basing**	we, you, they **are being based**
	he, she, it **is basing**	he, she, it **is being based**
Pres.	I, we, you, they **do base**	I, we, you, they **do get based**
Int.	he, she, it **does base**	he, she, it **does get based**
Fut.	I, he, she, it,	I, he, she, it,
	we, you, they **will base**	we, you, they **will be based**
Past	I, he, she, it,	I, he, she, it **was based**
	we, you, they **based**	we, you, they **were based**
Past	I, he, she, it **was basing**	I, he, she, it **was being based**
Prog.	we, you, they **were basing**	we, you, they **were being based**
Past	I, he, she, it,	I, he, she, it,
Int.	we, you, they **did base**	we, you, they **did get based**
Pres.	I, we, you, they **have based**	I, we, you, they **have been based**
Perf.	he, she, it **has based**	he, she, it **has been based**
Past	I, he, she, it,	I, he, she, it,
Perf.	we, you, they **had based**	we, you, they **had been based**
Fut.	I, he, she, it, we, you, they	I, he, she, it, we, you, they
Perf.	**will have based**	**will have been based**

IMPERATIVE MOOD

base   **be based**

SUBJUNCTIVE MOOD

Pres.	if I, he, she, it,	if I, he, she, it,
	we, you, they **base**	we, you, they **be based**
Past	if I, he, she, it,	if I, he, she, it,
	we, you, they **based**	we, you, they **were based**
Fut.	if I, he, she, it,	if I, he, she, it,
	we, you, they **should base**	we, you, they **should be based**

Infinitive: **to be**
Perfect Infinitive: **to have been**
Present Participle: **being**
Past Participle: **been**

INDICATIVE MOOD

Pres.	I **am** we, you, they **are** he, she, it **is**
Pres. *Prog.*	I **am being** we, you, they **are being** he, she, it **is being**
Fut.	I, he, she, it, we, you, they **will be**
Past	I, he, she, it, **was** we, you, they **were**
Past *Prog.*	I, he, she, it **was being** we, you, they **were being**
Pres. *Perf.*	I, we, you, they **have been** he, she, it **has been**
Past *Perf.*	I, he, she, it, we, you, they **had been**
Fut. *Perf.*	I, he, she, it, we, you, they **will have been**

IMPERATIVE MOOD

be

SUBJUNCTIVE MOOD

Pres.	if I, he, she, it, we, you, they **be**
Past	if I, he, she, it, we, you, they **were**
Fut.	if I, he, she, it, we, you, they **should be**

BE is the only English verb with a distinct form for the first person singular present, I AM, and two forms for the past, WAS and WERE. BE is often contracted: I am = I'm, he is = he's, you are = you're. It is also contracted in the negative forms: they aren't, he isn't. There is no correct contraction for "I am not" or "Am I not." The colloquial and substandard **ain't** is often heard for "I am not," "he is not," "we are not," etc. "Aren't I" is more often heard in British English.
BE is also used as an auxiliary verb for the progressive tenses and the passive voice. The forms THOU ART and THOU WERT are archaic.

bear
(active voice)

be borne/born
(passive voice)

Infinitive: **to bear**
Perfect Infinitive: **to have borne**
Present Participle: **bearing**
Past Participle: **borne**

Infinitive: **to be borne**
Perfect Infinitive: **to have been borne**
Present Participle: **being borne**
Past Participle: **been borne**

INDICATIVE MOOD

Pres.	I, we, you, they **bear**	I am borne
		we, you, they **are borne**
	he, she, it **bears**	he, she, it **is borne**
Pres. *Prog.*	I am bearing	I am being borne
	we, you, they **are bearing**	we, you, they **are being borne**
	he, she, it **is bearing**	he, she, it **is being borne**
Pres. *Int.*	I, we, you, they **do bear**	I, we, you, they **do get borne**
	he, she, it **does bear**	he, she, it **does get borne**
Fut.	I, he, she, it, we, you, they **will bear**	I, he, she, it, we, you, they **will be borne**
Past	I, he, she, it, we, you, they **bore**	I, he, she, it **was borne** we, you, they **were borne**
Past *Prog.*	I, he, she, it **was bearing** we, you, they **were bearing**	I, he, she, it **was being borne** we, you, they **were being borne**
Past *Int.*	I, he, she, it, we, you, they **did bear**	I, he, she, it, we, you, they **did get borne**
Pres. *Perf.*	I, we, you, they **have borne**	I, we, you, they **have been borne**
	he, she, it **has borne**	he, she, it **has been borne**
Past *Perf.*	I, he, she, it, we, you, they **had borne**	I, he, she, it, we, you, they **had been borne**
Fut. *Perf.*	I, he, she, it, we, you, they **will have borne**	I, he, she, it, we, you, they **will have been borne**

IMPERATIVE MOOD

bear   **be borne**

SUBJUNCTIVE MOOD

Pres.	if I, he, she, it, we, you, they **bear**	if I, he, she, it, we, you, they **be borne**
Past	if I, he, she, it, we, you, they **bore**	if I, he, she, it, we, you, they **were borne**
Fut.	if I, he, she, it, we, you, they **should bear**	if I, he, she, it, we, you, they **should be borne**

Transitive and intransitive. The participle has two acceptable forms: BORNE relates to being "carried," while BORN relates to "birth."
"The little girl was being borne on her father's shoulders. She was born just a year ago."

beat
(active voice)

be beaten/beat
(passive voice)

Infinitive: **to beat**
Perfect Infinitive: **to have beaten**
Present Participle: **beating**
Past Participle: **beaten**

Infinitive: **to be beaten**
Perfect Infinitive: **to have been beaten**
Present Participle: **being beaten**
Past Participle: **been beaten**

INDICATIVE MOOD

Pres.	I, we, you, they **beat**	I am beaten
		we, you, they **are beaten**
	he, she, it **beats**	he, she, it **is beaten**
Pres. *Prog.*	I am beating	I am being beaten
	we, you, they **are beating**	we, you, they **are being beaten**
	he, she, it **is beating**	he, she, it **is being beaten**
Pres. *Int.*	I, we, you, they **do beat**	I, we, you, they **do get beaten**
	he, she, it **does beat**	he, she, it **does get beaten**
Fut.	I, he, she, it, we, you, they **will beat**	I, he, she, it, we, you, they **will be beaten**
Past	I, he, she, it, we, you, they **beat**	I, he, she, it **was beaten** we, you, they **were beaten**
Past *Prog.*	I, he, she, it, we, you, they **were beating**	I, he, she, it **was being beaten** we, you, they **were being beaten**
Past *Int.*	I, he, she, it, we, you, they **did beat**	I, he, she, it, we, you, they **did get beaten**
Pres. *Perf.*	I, we, you, they **have beaten** he, she, it **has beaten**	I, we, you, they **have been beaten** he, she, it **has been beaten**
Past *Perf.*	I, he, she, it, we, you, they **had beaten**	I, he, she, it, we, you, they **had been beaten**
Fut. *Perf.*	I, he, she, it, we, you, they **will have beaten**	I, he, she, it, we, you, they **will have been beaten**

IMPERATIVE MOOD

beat   **be beaten**

SUBJUNCTIVE MOOD

Pres.	if I, he, she, it, we, you, they **beat**	if I, he, she, it, we, you, they **be beaten**
Past	if I, he, she, it, we, you, they **beat**	if I, he, she, it, we, you, they **were beaten**
Fut.	if I, he, she, it, we, you, they **should beat**	if I, he, she, it, we, you, they **should be beaten**

Transitive and intransitive.

26

become
(active voice)

be become
(passive voice)

Infinitive: **to become**
Perfect Infinitive: **to have become**
Present Participle: **becoming**
Past Participle: **become**

Infinitive: **to be become**
Perfect Infinitive: **to have been become**
Present Participle: **being become**
Past Participle: **been become**

INDICATIVE MOOD

Pres.	I, we, you, they **become**	I **am become**
		we, you, they **are become**
	he, she, it **becomes**	he, she, it **is become**
Pres.	I **am becoming**	I am being **become**
Prog.	we, you, they **are becoming**	we, you, they **are being become**
	he, she, it **is becoming**	he, she, it **is being become**
Pres.	I, we, you, they **do become**	I, we, you, they **do get become**
Int.	he, she, it **does become**	he, she, it **does get become**
Fut.	I, he, she, it,	I, he, she, it,
	we, you, they **will become**	we, you, they **will be become**
Past	I, he, she, it,	I, he, she, it **was become**
	we, you, they **became**	we, you, they **were become**
Past	I, he, she, it **was becoming**	I, he, she, it **was being become**
Prog.	we, you, they **were becoming**	we, you, they **were being become**
Past	I, he, she, it,	I, he, she, it,
Int.	we, you, they **did become**	we, you, they **did get become**
Pres.	I, we, you, they **have become**	I, we, you, they **have been become**
Perf.	he, she, it **has become**	he, she, it **has been become**
Past	I, he, she, it,	I, he, she, it,
Perf.	we, you, they **had become**	we, you, they **had been become**
Fut.	I, he, she, it, we, you, they	I, he, she, it, we, you, they
Perf.	**will have become**	**will have been become**

IMPERATIVE MOOD

become   **be become**

SUBJUNCTIVE MOOD

Pres.	if I, he, she, it,	if I, he, she, it,
	we, you, they **become**	we, you, they **be become**
Past	if I, he, she, it,	if I, he, she, it,
	we, you, they **became**	we, you, they **were become**
Fut.	if I, he, she, it,	if I, he, she, it,
	we, you, they **should become**	we, you, they **should be become**

Intransitive and transitive.

beg
(active voice)

be begged
(passive voice)

Infinitive: **to beg**
Perfect Infinitive: **to have begged**
Present Participle: **begging**
Past Participle: **begged**

Infinitive: **to be begged**
Perfect Infinitive: **to have been begged**
Present Participle: **being begged**
Past Participle: **been begged**

INDICATIVE MOOD

Pres.	I, we, you, they **beg**	I **am begged**
		we, you, they **are begged**
	he, she, it **begs**	he, she, it **is begged**
Pres.	I **am begging**	I **am being begged**
Prog.	we, you, they **are begging**	we, you, they **are being begged**
	he, she, it **is begging**	he, she, it **is being begged**
Pres.	I, we, you, they **do beg**	I, we, you, they **do get begged**
Int.	he, she, it **does beg**	he, she, it **does get begged**
Fut.	I, he, she, it,	I, he, she, it,
	we, you, they **will beg**	we, you, they **will be begged**
Past	I, he, she, it,	I, he, she, it **was begged**
	we, you, they **begged**	we, you, they **were begged**
Past	I, he, she, it **was begging**	I, he, she, it **was being begged**
Prog.	we, you, they **were begging**	we, you, they **were being begged**
Past	I, he, she, it,	I, he, she, it,
Int.	we, you, they **did beg**	we, you, they **did get begged**
Pres.	I, we, you, they **have begged**	I, we, you, they **have been begged**
Perf.	he, she, it **has begged**	he, she, it **has been begged**
Past	I, he, she, it,	I, he, she, it,
Perf.	we, you, they **had begged**	we, you, they **had been begged**
Fut.	I, he, she, it, we, you, they	I, he, she, it, we, you, they
Perf.	**will have begged**	**will have been begged**

IMPERATIVE MOOD

beg **be begged**

SUBJUNCTIVE MOOD

Pres.	if I, he, she, it,	if I, he, she, it,
	we, you, they **beg**	we, you, they **be begged**
Past	if I, he, she, it,	if I, he, she, it,
	we, you, they **begged**	we, you, they **were begged**
Fut.	if I, he, she, it,	if I, he, she, it,
	we, you, they **should beg**	we, you, they **should be begged**

Transitive and intransitive.

beget
(active voice)

be begotten/begot
(passive voice)

Infinitive: **to beget**
Perfect Infinitive: **to have begotten**
Present Participle: **begetting**
Past Participle: **begotten**

Infinitive: **to be begotten**
Perfect Infinitive: **to have been begotten**
Present Participle: **being begotten**
Past Participle: **been begotten**

INDICATIVE MOOD

Pres.	I, we, you, they **beget** he, she, it **begets**	I **am begotten** we, you, they **are begotten** he, she, it **is begotten**
Pres. *Prog.*	I **am begetting** we, you, they **are begetting** he, she, it **is begetting**	I **am being begotten** we, you, they **are being begotten** he, she, it **is being begotten**
Pres. *Int.*	I, we, you, they **do beget** he, she, it **does beget**	I, we, you, they **do get begotten** he, she, it **does get begotten**
Fut.	I, he, she, it, we, you, they **will beget**	I, he, she, it, we, you, they **will be begotten**
Past	I, he, she, it, we, you, they **begot**	I, he, she, it **was begotten** we, you, they **were begotten**
Past *Prog.*	I, he, she, it **was begetting** we, you, they **were begetting**	I, he, she, it **was being begotten** we, you, they **were being begotten**
Past *Int.*	I, he, she, it, we, you, they **did beget**	I, he, she, it, we, you, they **did get begotten**
Pres. *Perf.*	I, we, you, they **have begotten** he, she, it **has begotten**	I, we, you, they **have been begotten** he, she, it **has been begotten**
Past *Perf.*	I, he, she, it, we, you, they **had begotten**	I, he, she, it, we, you, they **had been begotten**
Fut. *Perf.*	I, he, she, it, we, you, they **will have begotten**	I, he, she, it, we, you, they **will have been begotten**

IMPERATIVE MOOD

beget   **be begotten**

SUBJUNCTIVE MOOD

Pres.	if I, he, she, it, we, you, they **beget**	if I, he, she, it, we, you, they **be begotten**
Past	if I, he, she, it, we, you, they **begot**	if I, he, she, it, we, you, they **were begotten**
Fut.	if I, he, she, it, we, you, they **should beget**	if I, he, she, it, we, you, they **should be begotten**

The past tense form BEGAT is considered archaic.

begin
(active voice)

be begun
(passive voice)

Infinitive: **to begin**
Perfect Infinitive: **to have begun**
Present Participle: **beginning**
Past Participle: **begun**

Infinitive: **to be begun**
Perfect Infinitive: **to have been begun**
Present Participle: **being begun**
Past Participle: **been begun**

INDICATIVE MOOD

Pres.	I, we, you, they **begin**	I **am begun**
		we, you, they **are begun**
	he, she, it **begins**	he, she, it **is begun**
Pres.	I **am beginning**	I **am being begun**
Prog.	we, you, they **are beginning**	we, you, they **are being begun**
	he, she, it **is beginning**	he, she, it **is being begun**
Pres.	I, we, you, they **do begin**	I, we, you, they **do get begun**
Int.	he, she, it **does begin**	he, she, it **does get begun**
Fut.	I, he, she, it, we, you, they **will begin**	I, he, she, it, we, you, they **will be begun**
Past	I, he, she, it, we, you, they **began**	I, he, she, it **was begun** we, you, they **were begun**
Past *Prog.*	I, he, she, it **was beginning** we, you, they **were beginning**	I, he, she, it **was being begun** we, you, they **were being begun**
Past *Int.*	I, he, she, it, we, you, they **did begin**	I, he, she, it, we, you, they **did get begun**
Pres. *Perf.*	I, we, you, they **have begun** he, she, it **has begun**	I, we, you, they **have been begun** he, she, it **has been begun**
Past *Perf.*	I, he, she, it, we, you, they **had begun**	I, he, she, it, we, you, they **had been begun**
Fut. *Perf.*	I, he, she, it, we, you, they **will have begun**	I, he, she, it, we, you, they **will have been begun**

IMPERATIVE MOOD

begin   **be begun**

SUBJUNCTIVE MOOD

Pres.	if I, he, she, it, we, you, they **begin**	if I, he, she, it, we, you, they **be begun**
Past	if I, he, she, it, we, you, they **began**	if I, he, she, it, we, you, they **were begun**
Fut.	if I, he, she, it, we, you, they **should begin**	if I, he, she, it, we, you, they **should be begun**

Intransitive and transitive.

behold
(active voice)

be beheld
(passive voice)

Infinitive: **to behold**
Perfect Infinitive: **to have beheld**
Present Participle: **beholding**
Past Participle: **beheld**

Infinitive: **to be beheld**
Perfect Infinitive: **to have been beheld**
Present Participle: **being beheld**
Past Participle: **been beheld**

INDICATIVE MOOD

Pres.	I, we, you, they **behold**	I **am beheld**
		we, you, they **are beheld**
	he, she, it **beholds**	he, she, it **is beheld**
Pres. *Prog.*	I **am beholding**	I **am being beheld**
	we, you, they **are beholding**	we, you, they **are being beheld**
	he, she, it **is beholding**	he, she, it **is being beheld**
Pres. *Int.*	I, we, you, they **do behold**	I, we, you, they **do get beheld**
	he, she, it **does behold**	he, she, it **does get beheld**
Fut.	I, he, she, it, we, you, they **will behold**	I, he, she, it, we, you, they **will be beheld**
Past	I, he, she, it, we, you, they **beheld**	I, he, she, it **was beheld** we, you, they **were beheld**
Past *Prog.*	I, he, she, it **was beholding** we, you, they **were beholding**	I, he, she, it **was being beheld** we, you, they **were being beheld**
Past *Int.*	I, he, she, it, we, you, they **did behold**	I, he, she, it, we, you, they **did get beheld**
Pres. *Perf.*	I, we, you, they **have beheld**	I, we, you, they **have been beheld**
	he, she, it **has beheld**	he, she, it **has been beheld**
Past *Perf.*	I, he, she, it, we, you, they **had beheld**	I, he, she, it, we, you, they **had been beheld**
Fut. *Perf.*	I, he, she, it, we, you, they **will have beheld**	I, he, she, it, we, you, they **will have been beheld**

IMPERATIVE MOOD

behold

be beheld

SUBJUNCTIVE MOOD

Pres.	if I, he, she, it, we, you, they **behold**	if I, he, she, it, we, you, they **be beheld**
Past	if I, he, she, it, we, you, they **beheld**	if I, he, she, it, we, you, they **were beheld**
Fut.	if I, he, she, it, we, you, they **should behold**	if I, he, she, it, we, you, they **should be beheld**

Transitive and intransitive.

31

believe
(active voice)

PRINCIPAL PARTS: **believes, believing, believed, believed**

be believed
(passive voice)

Infinitive: **to believe**
Perfect Infinitive: **to have believed**
Present Participle: **believing**
Past Participle: **believed**

Infinitive: **to be believed**
Perfect Infinitive: **to have been believed**
Present Participle: **being believed**
Past Participle: **been believed**

INDICATIVE MOOD

Pres.	I, we, you, they **believe**	I **am believed**
		we, you, they **are believed**
	he, she, it **believes**	he, she, it **is believed**
Pres. *Prog.*	I **am believing**	I **am being believed**
	we, you, they **are believing**	we, you, they **are being believed**
	he, she, it **is believing**	he, she, it **is being believed**
Pres. *Int.*	I, we, you, they **do believe**	I, we, you, they **do get believed**
	he, she, it **does believe**	he, she, it **does get believed**
Fut.	I, he, she, it, we, you, they **will believe**	I, he, she, it, we, you, they **will be believed**
Past	I, he, she, it, we, you, they **believed**	I, he, she, it **was believed** we, you, they **were believed**
Past *Prog.*	I, he, she, it **was believing** we, you, they **were believing**	I, he, she, it **was being believed** we, you, they **were being believed**
Past *Int.*	I, he, she, it, we, you, they **did believe**	I, he, she, it, we, you, they **did get believed**
Pres. *Perf.*	I, we, you, they **have believed** he, she, it **has believed**	I, we, you, they **have been believed** he, she, it **has been believed**
Past *Perf.*	I, he, she, it, we, you, they **had believed**	I, he, she, it, we, you, they **had been believed**
Fut. *Perf.*	I, he, she, it, we, you, they **will have believed**	I, he, she, it, we, you, they **will have been believed**

IMPERATIVE MOOD

believe

be believed

SUBJUNCTIVE MOOD

Pres.	if I, he, she, it, we, you, they **believe**	if I, he, she, it, we, you, they **be believed**
Past	if I, he, she, it, we, you, they **believed**	if I, he, she, it, we, you, they **were believed**
Fut.	if I, he, she, it, we, you, they **should believe**	if I, he, she, it, we, you, they **should be believed**

Transitive and intransitive.

bend
(active voice)

PRINCIPAL PARTS: **bends, bending, bent, bent**

be bent
(passive voice)

Infinitive: **to bend**
Perfect Infinitive: **to have bent**
Present Participle: **bending**
Past Participle: **bent**

Infinitive: **to be bent**
Perfect Infinitive: **to have been bent**
Present Participle: **being bent**
Past Participle: **been bent**

INDICATIVE MOOD

Pres.	I, we, you, they **bend**	I **am bent**
		we, you, they **are bent**
	he, she, it **bends**	he, she, it **is bent**
Pres. *Prog.*	I **am bending**	I **am being bent**
	we, you, they **are bending**	we, you, they **are being bent**
	he, she, it **is bending**	he, she, it **is being bent**
Pres. *Int.*	I, we, you, they **do bend**	I, we, you, they **do get bent**
	he, she, it **does bend**	he, she, it **does get bent**
Fut.	I, he, she, it, we, you, they **will bend**	I, he, she, it, we, you, they **will be bent**
Past	I, he, she, it, we, you, they **bent**	I, he, she, it **was bent** we, you, they **were bent**
Past *Prog.*	I, he, she, it **was bending** we, you, they **were bending**	I, he, she, it **was being bent** we, you, they **were being bent**
Past *Int.*	I, he, she, it, we, you, they **did bend**	I, he, she, it, we, you, they **did get bent**
Pres. *Perf.*	I, we, you, they **have bent** he, she, it **has bent**	I, we, you, they **have been bent** he, she, it **has been bent**
Past *Perf.*	I, he, she, it, we, you, they **had bent**	I, he, she, it, we, you, they **had been bent**
Fut. *Perf.*	I, he, she, it, we, you, they **will have bent**	I, he, she, it, we, you, they **will have been bent**

IMPERATIVE MOOD

bend

be bent

SUBJUNCTIVE MOOD

Pres.	if I, he, she, it, we, you, they **bend**	if I, he, she, it, we, you, they **be bent**
Past	if I, he, she, it, we, you, they **bent**	if I, he, she, it, we, you, they **were bent**
Fut.	if I, he, she, it, we, you, they **should bend**	if I, he, she, it, we, you, they **should be bent**

Transitive and intransitive.

bereave
(active voice)

PRINCIPAL PARTS: **bereaves, bereaving, bereaved/bereft, bereaved/bereft**

be bereaved/bereft
(passive voice)

Infinitive: **to bereave**
Perfect Infinitive: **to have bereaved**
Present Participle: **bereaving**
Past Participle: **bereaved**

Infinitive: **to be bereaved**
Perfect Infinitive: **to have been bereaved**
Present Participle: **being bereaved**
Past Participle: **been bereaved**

INDICATIVE MOOD

Pres.	I, we, you, they **bereave**	I **am bereaved** we, you, they **are bereaved**
	he, she, it **bereaves**	he, she, it **is bereaved**
Pres. *Prog.*	I **am bereaving** we, you, they **are bereaving** he, she, it **is bereaving**	I **am being bereaved** we, you, they **are being bereaved** he, she, it **is being bereaved**
Pres. *Int.*	I, we, you, they **do bereave** he, she, it **does bereave**	I, we, you, they **do get bereaved** he, she, it **does get bereaved**
Fut.	I, he, she, it, we, you, they **will bereave**	I, he, she, it, we, you, they **will be bereaved**
Past	I, he, she, it, we, you, they **bereaved**	I, he, she, it **was bereaved** we, you, they **were bereaved**
Past *Prog.*	I, he, she, it **was bereaving** we, you, they **were bereaving**	I, he, she, it **was being bereaved** we, you, they **were being bereaved**
Past *Int.*	I, he, she, it, we, you, they **did bereave**	I, he, she, it, we, you, they **did get bereaved**
Pres. *Perf.*	I, we, you, they **have bereaved** he, she, it **has bereaved**	I, we, you, they **have been bereaved** he, she, it **has been bereaved**
Past *Perf.*	I, he, she, it, we, you, they **had bereaved**	I, he, she, it, we, you, they **had been bereaved**
Fut. *Perf.*	I, he, she, it, we, you, they **will have bereaved**	I, he, she, it, we, you, they **will have been bereaved**

IMPERATIVE MOOD

bereave

be bereaved

SUBJUNCTIVE MOOD

Pres.	if I, he, she, it, we, you, they **bereave**	if I, he, she, it we, you, they **be bereaved**
Past	if I, he, she, it, we, you, they **bereaved**	if I, he, she, it, we, you, they **were bereaved**
Fut.	if I, he, she, it, we, you, they **should bereave**	if I, he, she, it, we, you, they **should be bereaved**

Past tense and past participle may be either BEREAVED or BEREFT.

beseech
(active voice)

be besought/ beseeched
(passive voice)

Infinitive: **to beseech**
Perfect Infinitive: **to have besought**
Present Participle: **beseeching**
Past Participle: **besought**

Infinitive: **to be besought**
Perfect Infinitive: **to have been besought**
Present Participle: **being besought**
Past Participle: **been besought**

INDICATIVE MOOD

Pres.	I, we, you, they **beseech**	I **am besought**
		we, you, they **are besought**
	he, she, it **beseeches**	he, she, it **is besought**
Pres.	I **am beseeching**	I **am being besought**
Prog.	we, you, they **are beseeching**	we, you, they **are being besought**
	he, she, it **is beseeching**	he, she, it **is being besought**
Pres.	I, we, you, they **do beseech**	I, we, you, they **do get besought**
Int.	he, she, it **does beseech**	he, she, it **does get besought**
Fut.	I, he, she, it,	I, he, she, it,
	we, you, they **will beseech**	we, you, they **will be besought**
Past	I, he, she, it,	I, he, she, it **was besought**
	we, you, they **besought**	we, you, they **were besought**
Past	I, he, she, it **was beseeching**	I, he, she, it **was being besought**
Prog.	we, you, they **were beseeching**	we, you, they **were being besought**
Past	I, he, she, it,	I, he, she, it,
Int.	we, you, they **did beseech**	we, you, they **did get besought**
Pres.	I, we, you, they **have besought**	I, we, you, they **have been besought**
Perf.	he, she, it **has besought**	he, she, it **has been besought**
Past	I, he, she, it,	I, he, she, it,
Perf.	we, you, they **had besought**	we, you, they **had been besought**
Fut.	I, he, she, it, we, you, they	I, he, she, it, we, you, they
Perf.	**will have besought**	**will have been besought**

IMPERATIVE MOOD

beseech

be besought

SUBJUNCTIVE MOOD

Pres.	if I, he, she, it,	if I, he, she, it,
	we, you, they **beseech**	we, you, they **be besought**
Past	if I, he, she, it,	if I, he, she, it,
	we, you, they **besought**	we, you, they **were besought**
Fut.	if I, he, she, it,	if I, he, she, it,
	we, you, they **should beseech**	we, you, they **should be besought**

Transitive and intransitive. The past tense and the past participle are BESOUGHT or BESEECHED.

beset
(active voice)

be beset
(passive voice)

Infinitive: **to beset**
Perfect Infinitive: **to have beset**
Present Participle: **besetting**
Past Participle: **beset**

Infinitive: **to be beset**
Perfect Infinitive: **to have been beset**
Present Participle: **being beset**
Past Participle: **been beset**

INDICATIVE MOOD

Pres.	I, we, you, they **beset**	I **am beset**
		we, you, they **are beset**
	he, she, it **besets**	he, she, it **is beset**
Pres.	I **am besetting**	I **am being beset**
Prog.	we, you, they **are besetting**	we, you, they **are being beset**
	he, she, it **is besetting**	he, she, it **is being beset**
Pres.	I, we, you, they **do beset**	I, we, you, they **do get beset**
Int.	he, she, it **does beset**	he, she, it **does get beset**
Fut.	I, he, she, it,	I, he, she, it,
	we, you, they **will beset**	we, you, they **will be beset**
Past	I, he, she, it,	I, he, she, it **was beset**
	we, you, they **beset**	we, you, they **were beset**
Past	I, he, she, it **was besetting**	I, he, she, it **was being beset**
Prog.	we, you, they **were besetting**	we, you, they **were being beset**
Past	I, he, she, it,	I, he, she, it,
Int.	we, you, they **did beset**	we, you, they **did get beset**
Pres.	I, we, you, they **have beset**	I, we, you, they **have been beset**
Perf.	he, she, it **has beset**	he, she, it **has been beset**
Past	I, he, she, it,	I, he, she, it,
Perf.	we, you, they **had beset**	we, you, they **had been beset**
Fut.	I, he, she, it, we, you, they	I, he, she, it, we, you, they
Perf.	**will have beset**	**will have been beset**

IMPERATIVE MOOD

beset   **be beset**

SUBJUNCTIVE MOOD

Pres.	if I, he, she, it,	if I, he, she, it,
	we, you, they **beset**	we, you, they **be beset**
Past	if I, he, she, it,	if I, he, she, it,
	we, you, they **beset**	we, you, they **were beset**
Fut.	if I, he, she, it,	if I, he, she, it,
	we, you, they **should beset**	we, you, they **should be beset**

---

bestride

(active voice)

PRINCIPAL PARTS: **bestrides, bestriding, bestrode, bestridden**

be bestridden

(passive voice)

Infinitive: **to bestride**
Perfect Infinitive: **to have bestridden**
Present Participle: **bestriding**
Past Participle: **bestridden**

Infinitive: **to be bestridden**
Perfect Infinitive: **to have been bestridden**
Present Participle: **being bestridden**
Past Participle: **been bestridden**

INDICATIVE MOOD

Pres.	I, we, you, they **bestride**	I **am bestridden**
		we, you, they **are bestridden**
	he, she, it **bestrides**	he, she, it **is bestridden**
Pres.	I **am bestriding**	I **am being bestridden**
Prog.	we, you, they **are bestriding**	we, you, they **are being bestridden**
	he, she, it **is bestriding**	he, she, it **is being bestridden**
Pres.	I, we, you, they **do bestride**	I, we, you, they **do get bestridden**
Int.	he, she, it **does bestride**	he, she, it **does get bestridden**
Fut.	I, he, she, it,	I, he, she, it,
	we, you, they **will bestride**	we, you, they **will be bestridden**
Past	I, he, she, it,	I, he, she, it **was bestridden**
	we, you, they **bestrode**	we, you, they **were bestridden**
Past	I, he, she, it **was bestriding**	I, he, she, it **was being bestridden**
Prog.	we, you, they **were bestriding**	we, you, they **were being bestridden**
Past	I, he, she, it,	I, he, she, it,
Int.	we, you, they **did bestride**	we, you, they **did get bestridden**
Pres.	I, we, you, they **have bestridden**	I, we, you, they **have been bestridden**
Perf.	he, she, it **has bestridden**	he, she, it **has been bestridden**
Past	I, he, she, it,	I, he, she, it,
Perf.	we, you, they **had bestridden**	we, you, they **had been bestridden**
Fut.	I, he, she, it, we, you, they	I, he, she, it, we, you, they
Perf.	**will have bestridden**	**will have been bestridden**

IMPERATIVE MOOD

bestride	**be bestridden**

SUBJUNCTIVE MOOD

Pres.	if I, he, she, it,	if I, he, she, it,
	we, you, they **bestride**	we, you, they **be bestridden**
Past	if I, he, she, it,	if I, he, she, it,
	we, you, they **bestrode**	we, you, they **were bestridden**
Fut.	if I, he, she, it,	if I, he, she, it,
	we, you, they **should bestride**	we, you, they **should be bestridden**

(active voice)

PRINCIPAL PARTS: **bets, betting,
bet/betted, bet/betted**

be bet/betted
(passive voice)

Infinitive: **to bet**
Perfect Infinitive: **to have bet**
Present Participle: **betting**
Past Participle: **bet**

Infinitive: **to be bet**
Perfect Infinitive: **to have been bet**
Present Participle: **being bet**
Past Participle: **been bet**

INDICATIVE MOOD

Pres.	I, we, you, they **bet**	I **am bet**
		we, you, they **are bet**
	he, she, it **bets**	he, she, it **is bet**
Pres.	I **am betting**	I **am being bet**
Prog.	we, you, they **are betting**	we, you, they **are being bet**
	he, she, it **is betting**	he, she, it **is being bet**
Pres.	I, we, you, they **do bet**	I, we, you, they **do get bet**
Int.	he, she, it **does bet**	he, she, it **does get bet**
Fut.	I, he, she, it,	I, he, she, it,
	we, you, they **will bet**	we, you, they **will be bet**
Past	I, he, she, it,	I, he, she, it **was bet**
	we, you, they **bet**	we, you, they **were bet**
Past	I, he, she, it **was betting**	I, he, she, it **was being bet**
Prog.	we, you, they **were betting**	we, you, they **were being bet**
Past	I, he, she, it,	I, he, she, it,
Int.	we, you, they **did bet**	we, you, they **did get bet**
Pres.	I, we, you, they **have bet**	I, we, you, they **have been bet**
Perf.	he, she, it **has bet**	he, she, it **has been bet**
Past	I, he, she, it,	I, he, she, it,
Perf.	we, you, they **had bet**	we, you, they **had been bet**
Fut.	I, he, she, it, we, you, they	I, he, she, it, we, you, they
Perf.	**will have bet**	**will have been bet**

IMPERATIVE MOOD

bet

be bet

SUBJUNCTIVE MOOD

Pres.	if I, he, she, it,	if I, he, she, it,
	we, you, they **bet**	we, you, they **be bet**
Past	if I, he, she, it,	if I, he, she, it,
	we, you, they **bet**	we, you, they **were bet**
Fut.	if I, he, she, it,	if I, he, she, it,
	we, you, they **should bet**	we, you, they **should be bet**

Transitive and intransitive. BETTED is becoming rare. Use BET for the past tense and past participle.

bid
(active voice)

be bid
(passive voice)

Infinitive: **to bid**
Perfect Infinitive: **to have bid**
Present Participle: **bidding**
Past Participle: **bid**

Infinitive: **to be bid**
Perfect Infinitive: **to have been bid**
Present Participle: **being bid**
Past Participle: **been bid**

INDICATIVE MOOD

Pres.	I, we, you, they **bid**	I **am bid**
		we, you, they **are bid**
	he, she, it **bids**	he, she, it **is bid**
Pres.	I **am bidding**	I **am being bid**
Prog.	we, you, they **are bidding**	we, you, they **are being bid**
	he, she, it **is bidding**	he, she, it **is being bid**
Pres.	I, we, you, they **do bid**	I, we, you, they **do get bid**
Int.	he, she, it **does bid**	he, she, it **does get bid**
Fut.	I, he, she, it, we, you, they **will bid**	I, he, she, it, we, you, they **will be bid**
Past	I, he, she, it, we, you, they **bid**	I, he, she, it **was bid** we, you, they **were bid**
Past	I, he, she, it **was bidding**	I, he, she, it **was being bid**
Prog.	we, you, they **were bidding**	we, you, they **were being bid**
Past	I, he, she, it, we, you, they **did bid**	I, he, she, it, we, you, they **did get bid**
Int.		
Pres.	I, we, you, they **have bid**	I, we, you, they **have been bid**
Perf.	he, she, it **has bid**	he, she, it **has been bid**
Past	I, he, she, it, we, you, they **had bid**	I, he, she, it, we, you, they **had been bid**
Perf.		
Fut.	I, he, she, it, we, you, they	I, he, she, it, we, you, they
Perf.	**will have bid**	**will have been bid**

IMPERATIVE MOOD

bid

be bid

SUBJUNCTIVE MOOD

Pres.	if I, he, she, it, we, you, they **bid**	if I, he, she, it, we, you, they **be bid**
Past	if I, he, she, it, we, you, they **bid**	if I, he, she, it, we, you, they **were bid**
Fut.	if I, he, she, it, we, you, they **should bid**	if I, he, she, it, we, you, they **should be bid**

Transitive and intransitive. BID has the past tense and participle from BID when it means "offering."

bid
(active voice)

be bidden
(passive voice)

Infinitive: **to bid**
Perfect Infinitive: **to have bidden**
Present Participle: **bidding**
Past Participle: **bidden**

Infinitive: **to be bidden**
Perfect Infinitive: **to have been bidden**
Present Participle: **being bidden**
Past Participle: **been bidden**

INDICATIVE MOOD

Pres.	I, we, you, they **bid**	I **am bidden**
		we, you, they **are bidden**
	he, she, it **bids**	he, she, it **is bidden**
Pres.	I **am bidding**	I **am being bidden**
Prog.	we, you, they **are bidding**	we, you, they **are being bidden**
	he, she, it **is bidding**	he, she, it **is being bidden**
Pres.	I, we, you, they **do bid**	I, we, you, they **do get bidden**
Int.	he, she, it **does bid**	he, she, it **does get bidden**
Fut.	I, he, she, it,	I, he, she, it,
	we, you, they **will bid**	we, you, they **will be bidden**
Past	I, he, she, it,	I, he, she, it **was bidden**
	we, you, they **bade**	we, you, they **were bidden**
Past	I, he, she, it **was bidding**	I, he, she, it **was being bidden**
Prog.	we, you, they **were bidding**	we, you, they **were being bidden**
Past	I, he, she, it,	I, he, she, it,
Int.	we, you, they **did bid**	we, you, they **did get bidden**
Pres.	I, we, you, they **have bidden**	I, we, you, they **have been bidden**
Perf.	he, she, it **has bidden**	he, she, it **has been bidden**
Past	I, he, she, it,	I, he, she, it,
Perf.	we, you, they **had bidden**	we, you, they **had been bidden**
Fut.	I, he, she, it, we, you, they	I, he, she, it, we, you, they
Perf.	**will have bidden**	**will have been bidden**

IMPERATIVE MOOD

bid   **be bidden**

SUBJUNCTIVE MOOD

Pres.	if I, he, she, it,	if I, he, she, it,
	we, you, they **bid**	we, you, they **be bidden**
Past	if I, he, she, it,	if I, he, she, it,
	we, you, they **bade**	we, you, they **were bidden**
Fut.	if I, he, she, it,	if I, he, she, it,
	we, you, they **should bid**	we, you, they **should be bidden**

BID has the past tense BADE and participle form BIDDEN when it means "directing" or "inviting." The *Oxford Modern English Dictionary* considers the past tense form BADE and past participle BIDDEN archaic.

bide
(active voice)

be bided
(passive voice)

Infinitive: **to bide**
Perfect Infinitive: **to have bided**
Present Participle: **biding**
Past Participle: **bided**

Infinitive: **to be bided**
Perfect Infinitive: **to have been bided**
Present Participle: **being bided**
Past Participle: **been bided**

INDICATIVE MOOD

Pres.	I, we, you, they **bide**	I **am bided**
		we, you, they **are bided**
	he, she, it **bides**	he, she, it **is bided**
Pres.	I **am biding**	I **am being bided**
Prog.	we, you, they **are biding**	we, you, they **are being bided**
	he, she, it **is biding**	he, she, it **is being bided**
Pres.	I, we, you, they **do bide**	I, we, you, they **do get bided**
Int.	he, she, it **does bide**	he, she, it **does get bided**
Fut.	I, he, she, it,	I, he, she, it,
	we, you, they **will bide**	we, you, they **will be bided**
Past	I, he, she, it,	I, he, she, it **was bided**
	we, you, they **bided**	we, you, they **were bided**
Past	I, he, she, it **was biding**	I, he, she, it **was being bided**
Prog.	we, you, they **were biding**	we, you, they **were being bided**
Past	I, he, she, it,	I, he, she, it,
Int.	we, you, they **did bide**	we, you, they **did get bided**
Pres.	I, we, you, they **have bided**	I, we, you, they **have been bided**
Perf.	he, she, it **has bided**	he, she, it **has been bided**
Past	I, he, she, it,	I, he, she, it,
Perf.	we, you, they **had bided**	we, you, they **had been bided**
Fut.	I, he, she, it, we, you, they	I, he, she, it, we, you, they
Perf.	**will have bided**	**will have been bided**

IMPERATIVE MOOD

bide

be bided

SUBJUNCTIVE MOOD

Pres.	if I, he, she, it,	if I, he, she, it,
	we, you, they **bide**	we, you, they **be bided**
Past	if I, he, she, it,	if I, he, she, it,
	we, you, they **bided**	we, you, they **were bided**
Fut.	if I, he, she, it,	if I, he, she, it,
	we, you, they **should bide**	we, you, they **should be bided**

Intransitive and transitive. In the past tense, BIDED and BODE are acceptable. For the past participle, only BIDED is now used.

bind
(active voice)

be bound
(passive voice)

Infinitive: **to bind**
Perfect Infinitive: **to have bound**
Present Participle: **binding**
Past Participle: **bound**

Infinitive: **to be bound**
Perfect Infinitive: **to have been bound**
Present Participle: **being bound**
Past Participle: **been bound**

INDICATIVE MOOD

Pres.	I, we, you, they **bind**	I **am bound**
		we, you, they **are bound**
	he, she, it **binds**	he, she, it **is bound**
Pres. *Prog.*	I **am binding**	I **am being bound**
	we, you, they **are binding**	we, you, they **are being bound**
	he, she, it **is binding**	he, she, it **is being bound**
Pres. *Int.*	I, we, you, they **do bind**	I, we, you, **do get bound**
	he, she, it **does bind**	he, she, it **does get bound**
Fut.	I, he, she, it, we, you, they **will bind**	I, he, she, it, we, you, they **will be bound**
Past	I, he, she, it, we, you, they **bound**	I, he, she, it **was bound** we, you, they **were bound**
Past *Prog.*	I, he, she, it **was binding** we, you, they **were binding**	I, he, she, it **was being bound** we, you, they **were being bound**
Past *Int.*	I, he, she, it, we, you, they **did bind**	I, he, she, it, we, you, they **did get bound**
Pres. *Perf.*	I, we, you, they **have bound** he, she, it **has bound**	I, we, you, **have been bound** he, she, it **has been bound**
Past *Perf.*	I, he, she, it, we, you, they **had bound**	I, he, she, it, we, you, they **had been bound**
Fut. *Perf.*	I, he, she, it, we, you, they **will have bound**	I, he, she, it, we, you, they **will have been bound**

IMPERATIVE MOOD

bind

be bound

SUBJUNCTIVE MOOD

Pres.	if I, he, she, it, we, you, they **bind**	if I, he, she, it, we, you, they **be bound**
Past	if I, he, she, it, we, you, they **bound**	if I, he, she, it, we, you, they **were bound**
Fut.	if I, he, she, it, we, you, they **should bind**	if I, he, she, it, we, you, they **should be bound**

Transitive and intransitive.

bite
(active voice)

PRINCIPAL PARTS: **bites, biting,
bit, bitten/bit**

be bitten/bit
(passive voice)

Infinitive: **to bite**
Perfect Infinitive: **to have bitten**
Present Participle: **biting**
Past Participle: **bitten**

Infinitive: **to be bitten**
Perfect Infinitive: **to have been bitten**
Present Participle: **being bitten**
Past Participle: **been bitten**

INDICATIVE MOOD

Pres.	I, we, you, they **bite**	I **am bitten**
		we, you, they **are bitten**
	he, she, it **bites**	he, she, it **is bitten**
Pres.	I **am biting**	I **am being bitten**
Prog.	we, you, they **are biting**	we, you, they **are being bitten**
	he, she, it **is biting**	he, she, it **is being bitten**
Pres.	I, we, you, they **do bite**	I, we, you, they **do get bitten**
Int.	he, she, it **does bite**	he, she, it **does get bitten**
Fut.	I, he, she, it,	I, he, she, it,
	we, you, they **will bite**	we, you, they **will be bitten**
Past	I, he, she, it,	I, he, she, it **was bitten**
	we, you, they **bit**	we, you, they **were bitten**
Past	I, he, she, it **was biting**	I, he, she, it **was being bitten**
Prog.	we, you, they **were biting**	we, you, they **were being bitten**
Past	I, he, she, it,	I, he, she, it,
Int.	we, you, they **did bite**	we, you, they **did get bitten**
Pres.	I, we, you, they **have bitten**	I, we, you, they **have been bitten**
Perf.	he, she, it **has bitten**	he, she, it **has been bitten**
Past	I, he, she, it,	I, he, she, it,
Perf.	we, you, they **had bitten**	we, you, they **had been bitten**
Fut.	I, he, she, it, we, you, they	I, he, she, it, we, you, they
Perf.	**will have bitten**	**will have been bitten**

IMPERATIVE MOOD

bite   **be bitten**

SUBJUNCTIVE MOOD

Pres.	if I, he, she, it,	if I, he, she, it,
	we, you, they **bite**	we, you, they **be bitten**
Past	if I, he, she, it,	if I, he, she, it,
	we, you, they **bit**	we, you, they **were bitten**
Fut.	if I, he, she, it,	if I, he, she, it,
	we, you, they **should bite**	we, you, they **should be bitten**

The past participle may be either BITTEN or BIT.

bleed
(active voice)

be bled
(passive voice)

Infinitive: **to bleed**
Perfect Infinitive: **to have bled**
Present Participle: **bleeding**
Past Participle: **bled**

Infinitive: **to be bled**
Perfect Infinitive: **to have been bled**
Present Participle: **being bled**
Past Participle: **been bled**

INDICATIVE MOOD

Pres.	I, we, you, they **bleed**	I **am bled**
		we, you, they **are bled**
	he, she, it **bleeds**	he, she, it **is bled**
Pres.	I **am bleeding**	I **am being bled**
Prog.	we, you, they **are bleeding**	we, you, they **are being bled**
	he, she, it **is bleeding**	he, she, it **is being bled**
Pres.	I, we, you, they **do bleed**	I, we, you, they **do get bled**
Int.	he, she, it **does bleed**	he, she, it **does get bled**
Fut.	I, he, she, it,	I, he, she, it,
	we, you, they **will bleed**	we, you, they **will be bled**
Past	I, he, she, it,	I, he, she, it **was bled**
	we, you, they **bled**	we, you, they **were bled**
Past	I, he, she, it **was bleeding**	I, he, she, it **was being bled**
Prog.	we, you, they **were bleeding**	we, you, they **were being bled**
Past	I, he, she, it,	I, he, she, it,
Int.	we, you, they **did bleed**	we, you, they **did get bled**
Pres.	I, we, you, they **have bled**	I, we, you, they **have been bled**
Perf.	he, she, it **has bled**	he, she, it **has been bled**
Past	I, he, she, it,	I, he, she, it,
Perf.	we, you, they **had bled**	we, you, they **had been bled**
Fut.	I, he, she, it, we, you, they	I, he, she, it, we, you, they
Perf.	**will have bled**	**will have been bled**

IMPERATIVE MOOD

bleed   **be bled**

SUBJUNCTIVE MOOD

Pres.	if I, he, she, it,	if I, he, she, it,
	we, you, they **bleed**	we, you, they **be bled**
Past	if I, he, she, it,	if I, he, she, it,
	we, you, they **bled**	we, you, they **were bled**
Fut.	if I, he, she, it,	if I, he, she, it,
	we, you, they **should bleed**	we, you, they **should be bled**

Intransitive and transitive.

blend
(active voice)

be blended/blent
(passive voice)

Infinitive: **to blend**
Perfect Infinitive: **to have blended**
Present Participle: **blending**
Past Participle: **blended**

Infinitive: **to be blended**
Perfect Infinitive: **to have been blended**
Present Participle: **being blended**
Past Participle: **been blended**

INDICATIVE MOOD

Pres.	I, we, you, they **blend**	I **am blended**
		we, you, they **are blended**
	he, she, it **blends**	he, she, it **is blended**
Pres.	I **am blending**	I **am being blended**
Prog.	we, you, they **are blending**	we, you, they **are being blended**
	he, she, it **is blending**	he, she, it **is being blended**
Pres.	I, we, you, they **do blend**	I, we, you, they **do get blended**
Int.	he, she, it **does blend**	he, she, it **does get blended**
Fut.	I, he, she, it,	I, he, she, it,
	we, you, they **will blend**	we, you, they **will be blended**
Past	I, he, she, it,	I, he, she, it **was blended**
	we, you, they **blended**	we, you, they **were blended**
Past	I, he, she, it **was blending**	I, he, she, it **was being blended**
Prog.	we, you, they **were blending**	we, you, they **were being blended**
Past	I, he, she, it,	I, he, she, it,
Int.	we, you, they **did blend**	we, you, they **did get blended**
Pres.	I, we, you, they **have blended**	I, we, you, they **have been blended**
Perf.	he, she, it **has blended**	he, she, it **has been blended**
Past	I, he, she, it,	I, he, she, it,
Perf.	we, you, they **had blended**	we, you, they **had been blended**
Fut.	I, he, she, it, we, you, they	I, he, she, it, we, you, they
Perf.	**will have blended**	**will have been blended**

IMPERATIVE MOOD

blend　　　　　　　　　　**be blended**

SUBJUNCTIVE MOOD

Pres.	if I, he, she, it,	if I, he, she, it,
	we, you, they **blend**	we, you, they **be blended**
Past	if I, he, she, it,	if I, he, she, it,
	we, you, they **blended**	we, you, they **were blended**
Fut.	if I, he, she, it,	if I, he, she, it,
	we, you, they **should blend**	we, you, they **should be blended**

Transitive and intransitive. The past tense and participle forms BLENDED and BLENT are both acceptable. The *Oxford Dictionary* lists BLENT as poetic for the past tense and past participle.

bless
(active voice)

PRINCIPAL PARTS: blesses, blessing, blessed/blest, blessed/blest

be blessed
(passive voice)

Infinitive: **to bless**
Perfect Infinitive: **to have blessed**
Present Participle: **blessing**
Past Participle: **blessed**

Infinitive: **to be blessed**
Perfect Infinitive: **to have been blessed**
Present Participle: **being blessed**
Past Participle: **been blessed**

INDICATIVE MOOD

Pres.	I, we, you, they **bless**	I **am blessed**
		we, you, they **are blessed**
	he, she, it **blesses**	he, she, it **is blessed**
Pres.	I **am blessing**	I **am being blessed**
Prog.	we, you, they **are blessing**	we, you, they **are being blessed**
	he, she, it **is blessing**	he, she, it **is being blessed**
Pres.	I, we, you, they **do bless**	I, we, you, they **do get blessed**
Int.	he, she, it **does bless**	he, she, it **does get blessed**
Fut.	I, he, she, it,	I, he, she, it,
	we, you, they **will bless**	we, you, they **will be blessed**
Past	I, he, she, it,	I, he, she, it **was blessed**
	we, you, they **blessed**	we, you, they **were blessed**
Past	I, he, she, it **was blessing**	I, he, she, it **was being blessed**
Prog.	we, you, they **were blessing**	we, you, they **were being blessed**
Past	I, he, she, it,	I, he, she, it,
Int.	we, you, they **did bless**	we, you, they **did get blessed**
Pres.	I, we, you, they **have blessed**	I, we, you, they **have been blessed**
Perf.	he, she, it **has blessed**	he, she, it **has been blessed**
Past	I, he, she, it,	I, he, she, it,
Perf.	we, you, they **had blessed**	we, you, they **had been blessed**
Fut.	I, he, she, it, we, you, they	I, he, she, it, we, you, they
Perf.	**will have blessed**	**will have been blessed**

IMPERATIVE MOOD

bless

be blessed

SUBJUNCTIVE MOOD

Pres.	if I, he, she, it,	if I, he, she, it,
	we, you, they **bless**	we, you, they **be blessed**
Past	if I, he, she, it,	if I, he, she, it,
	we, you, they **blessed**	we, you, they **were blessed**
Fut.	if I, he, she, it,	if I, he, she, it,
	we, you, they **should bless**	we, you, they **should be blessed**

According to the *Oxford Dictionary*, BLEST is the poetic form of the past tense and past participle.

blow
(active voice)

be blown
(passive voice)

Infinitive: **to blow**
Perfect Infinitive: **to have blown**
Present Participle: **blowing**
Past Participle: **blown**

Infinitive: **to be blown**
Perfect Infinitive: **to have been blown**
Present Participle: **being blown**
Past Participle: **been blown**

INDICATIVE MOOD

Pres.	I, we, you, they **blow**	I **am blown**
		we, you, they **are blown**
	he, she, it **blows**	he, she, it **is blown**
Pres.	I **am blowing**	I **am being blown**
Prog.	we, you, they **are blowing**	we, you, they **are being blown**
	he, she, it **is blowing**	he, she, it **is being blown**
Pres.	I, we, you, they **do blow**	I, we, you, they **do get blown**
Int.	he, she, it **does blow**	he, she, it **does get blown**
Fut.	I, he, she, it,	I, he, she, it,
	we, you, they **will blow**	we, you, they **will be blown**
Past	I, he, she, it,	I, he, she, it **was blown**
	we, you, they **blew**	we, you, they **were blown**
Past	I, he, she, it **was blowing**	I, he, she, it **was being blown**
Prog.	we, you, they **were blowing**	we, you, they **were being blown**
Past	I, he, she, it,	I, he, she, it,
Int.	we, you, they **did blow**	we, you, they **did get blown**
Pres.	I, we, you, they **have blown**	I, we, you, they **have been blown**
Perf.	he, she, it **has blown**	he, she, it **has been blown**
Past	I, he, she, it,	I, he, she, it,
Perf.	we, you, they **had blown**	we, you, they **had been blown**
Fut.	I, he, she, it, we, you, they	I, he, she, it, we, you, they
Perf.	**will have blown**	**will have been blown**

IMPERATIVE MOOD

blow · **be blown**

SUBJUNCTIVE MOOD

Pres.	if I, he, she, it,	if I, he, she, it,
	we, you, they **blow**	we, you, they **be blown**
Past	if I, he, she, it,	if I, he, she, it,
	we, you, they **blew**	we, you, they **were blown**
Fut.	if I, he, she, it,	if I, he, she, it,
	we, you, they **should blow**	we, you, they **should be blown**

Intransitive and transitive.

bother
(active voice)

be bothered
(passive voice)

Infinitive: **to bother**
Perfect Infinitive: **to have bothered**
Present Participle: **bothering**
Past Participle: **bothered**

Infinitive: **to be bothered**
Perfect Infinitive: **to have been bothered**
Present Participle: **being bothered**
Past Participle: **been bothered**

INDICATIVE MOOD

Pres.	I, we, you, they **bother** he, she, it **bothers**	I **am bothered** we, you, they **are bothered** he, she, it **is bothered**
Pres. Prog.	I **am bothering** we, you, they **are bothering** he, she, it **is bothering**	I **am being bothered** we, you, they **are being bothered** he, she, it **is being bothered**
Pres. Int.	I, we, you, they **do bother** he, she, it **does bother**	I, we, you, they **do get bothered** he, she, it **does get bothered**
Fut.	I, he, she, it, we, you, they **will bother**	I, he, she, it, we, you, they **will be bothered**
Past	I, he, she, it, we, you, they **bothered**	I, he, she, it **was bothered** we, you, they **were bothered**
Past Prog.	I, he, she, it **was bothering** we, you, they **were bothering**	I, he, she, it **was being bothered** we, you, they **were being bothered**
Past Int.	I, he, she, it, we, you, they **did bother**	I, he, she, it, we, you, they **did get bothered**
Pres. Perf.	I, we, you, they **have bothered** he, she, it **has bothered**	I, we, you, they **have been bothered** he, she, it **has been bothered**
Past Perf.	I, he, she, it, we, you, they **had bothered**	I, he, she, it, we, you, they **had been bothered**
Fut. Perf.	I, he, she, it, we, you, they **will have bothered**	I, he, she, it, we, you, they **will have been bothered**

IMPERATIVE MOOD

bother

be bothered

SUBJUNCTIVE MOOD

Pres.	if I, he, she, it, we, you, they **bother**	if I, he, she, it, we, you, they **be bothered**
Past	if I, he, she, it, we, you, they **bothered**	if I, he, she, it, we, you, they **were bothered**
Fut.	if I, he, she, it, we, you, they **should bother**	if I, he, she, it, we, you, they **should be bothered**

Transitive and intransitive.

break
(active voice)

PRINCIPAL PARTS: **breaks, breaking, broke, broken**

be broken
(passive voice)

Infinitive: **to break**
Perfect Infinitive: **to have broken**
Present Participle: **breaking**
Past Participle: **broken**

Infinitive: **to be broken**
Perfect Infinitive: **to have been broken**
Present Participle: **being broken**
Past Participle: **been broken**

INDICATIVE MOOD

Pres.	I, we, you, they **break**	I **am broken**
		we, you, they **are broken**
	he, she, it **breaks**	he, she, it **is broken**
Pres.	I **am breaking**	I **am being broken**
Prog.	we, you, they **are breaking**	we, you, they **are being broken**
	he, she, it **is breaking**	he, she, it **is being broken**
Pres.	I, we, you, they **do break**	I, we, you, they **do get broken**
Int.	he, she, it **does break**	he, she, it **does get broken**
Fut.	I, he, she, it,	I, he, she, it,
	we, you, they **will break**	we, you, they **will be broken**
Past	I, he, she, it,	I, he, she, it **was broken**
	we, you, they **broke**	we, you, they **were broken**
Past	I, he, she, it **was breaking**	I, he, she, it **was being broken**
Prog.	we, you, they **were breaking**	we, you, they **were being broken**
Past	I, he, she, it,	I, he, she, it,
Int.	we, you, they **did break**	we, you, they **did get broken**
Pres.	I, we, you, they **have broken**	I, we, you, they **have been broken**
Perf.	he, she, it **has broken**	he, she, it **has been broken**
Past	I, he, she, it,	I, he, she, it,
Perf.	we, you, they **had broken**	we, you, they **had been broken**
Fut.	I, he, she, it, we, you, they	I, he, she, it, we, you, they
Perf.	**will have broken**	**will have been broken**

IMPERATIVE MOOD

break

be broken

SUBJUNCTIVE MOOD

Pres.	if I, he, she, it,	if I, he, she, it,
	we, you, they **break**	we, you, they **be broken**
Past	if I, he, she, it,	if I, he, she, it,
	we, you, they **broke**	we, you, they **were broken**
Fut.	if I, he, she, it,	if I, he, she, it,
	we, you, they **should break**	we, you, they **should be broken**

Transitive and intransitive. The past tense BRAKE and past participle BROKE are archaic.

breed
(active voice)

be bred
(passive voice)

Infinitive: **to breed**
Perfect Infinitive: **to have bred**
Present Participle: **breeding**
Past Participle: **bred**

Infinitive: **to be bred**
Perfect Infinitive: **to have been bred**
Present Participle: **being bred**
Past Participle: **been bred**

INDICATIVE MOOD

Pres.	I, we, you, they **breed**	I **am bred**
		we, you, they **are bred**
	he, she, it **breeds**	he, she, it **is bred**
Pres. *Prog.*	I **am breeding**	I **am being bred**
	we, you, they **are breeding**	we, you, they **are being bred**
	he, she, it **is breeding**	he, she, it **is being bred**
Pres. *Int.*	I, we, you, they **do breed**	I, we, you, they **do get bred**
	he, she, it **does breed**	he, she, it **does get bred**
Fut.	I, he, she, it, we, you, they **will breed**	I, he, she, it, we, you, they **will be bred**
Past	I, he, she, it, we, you, they **bred**	I, he, she, it **was bred** we, you, they **were bred**
Past *Prog.*	I, he, she, it **was breeding** we, you, they **were breeding**	I, he, she, it **was being bred** we, you, they **were being bred**
Past *Int.*	I, he, she, it, we, you, they **did breed**	I, he, she, it, we, you, they **did get bred**
Pres. *Perf.*	I, we, you, they **have bred**	I, we, you, they **have been bred**
	he, she, it **has bred**	he, she, it **has been bred**
Past *Perf.*	I, he, she, it, we, you, they **had bred**	I, he, she, it, we, you, they **had been bred**
Fut. *Perf.*	I, he, she, it, we, you, they **will have bred**	I, he, she, it, we, you, they **will have been bred**

IMPERATIVE MOOD

breed   **be bred**

SUBJUNCTIVE MOOD

Pres.	if I, he, she, it, we, you, they **breed**	if I, he, she, it, we, you, they **be bred**
Past	if I, he, she, it, we, you, they **bred**	if I, he, she, it, we, you, they **were bred**
Fut.	if I, he, she, it, we, you, they **should breed**	if I, he, she, it, we, you, they **should be bred**

Transitive and intransitive.

bring
(active voice)

be brought
(passive voice)

Infinitive: **to bring**
Perfect Infinitive: **to have brought**
Present Participle: **bringing**
Past Participle: **brought**

Infinitive: **to be brought**
Perfect Infinitive: **to have been brought**
Present Participle: **being brought**
Past Participle: **been brought**

INDICATIVE MOOD

Pres.	I, we, you, they **bring**		I am **brought**
			we, you, they **are brought**
	he, she, it **brings**		he, she, it **is brought**
Pres.	I am **bringing**		I am **being brought**
Prog.	we, you, they **are bringing**		we, you, they **are being brought**
	he, she, it **is bringing**		he, she, it **is being brought**
Pres.	I, we, you, they **do bring**		I, we, you, they **do get brought**
Int.	he, she, it **does bring**		he, she, it **does get brought**
Fut.	I, he, she, it,		I, he, she, it,
	we, you, they **will bring**		we, you, they **will be brought**
Past	I, he, she, it,		I, he, she, it **was brought**
	we, you, they **brought**		we, you, they **were brought**
Past	I, he, she, it **was bringing**		I, he, she, it **was being brought**
Prog.	we, you, they **were bringing**		we, you, they **were being brought**
Past	I, he, she, it,		I, he, she, it,
Int.	we, you, they **did bring**		we, you, they **did get brought**
Pres.	I, we, you, they **have brought**		I, we, you, they **have been brought**
Perf.	he, she, it **has brought**		he, she, it **has been brought**
Past	I, he, she, it,		I, he, she, it,
Perf.	we, you, they **had brought**		we, you, they **had been brought**
Fut.	I, he, she, it, we, you, they		I, he, she, it, we, you, they
Perf.	**will have brought**		**will have been brought**

IMPERATIVE MOOD

bring   **be brought**

SUBJUNCTIVE MOOD

Pres.	if I, he, she, it, we, you, they **bring**	if I, he, she, it, we, you, they **be brought**
Past	if I, he, she, it, we, you, they **brought**	if I, he, she, it, we, you, they **were brought**
Fut.	if I, he, she, it, we, you, they **should bring**	if I, he, she, it, we, you, they **should be brought**

Transitive and intransitive.

broadcast
(active voice)

PRINCIPAL PARTS: **broadcasts, broadcasting, broadcast/broadcasted, broadcast/broadcasted**

be broadcast/ broadcasted
(passive voice)

Infinitive: **to broadcast**
Perfect Infinitive: **to have broadcast**
Present Participle: **broadcasting**
Past Participle: **broadcast**

Infinitive: **to be broadcast**
Perfect Infinitive: **to have been broadcast**
Present Participle: **being broadcast**
Past Participle: **been broadcast**

INDICATIVE MOOD

Pres.	I, we, you, they **broadcast**	I **am broadcast** we, you, they **are broadcast**
	he, she, it **broadcasts**	he, she, it **is broadcast**
Pres. *Prog.*	I **am broadcasting** we, you, they **are broadcasting** he, she, it **is broadcasting**	I **am being broadcast** we, you, they **are being broadcast** he, she, it is **being broadcast**
Pres. *Int.*	I, we, you, they **do broadcast** he, she, it **does broadcast**	I, we, you, they **do get broadcast** he, she, it **does get broadcast**
Fut.	I, he, she, it, we, you, they **will broadcast**	I, he, she, it, we, you, they **will be broadcast**
Past	I, he, she, it, we, you, they **broadcast**	I, he, she, it **was broadcast** we, you, they **were broadcast**
Past *Prog.*	I, he, she, it **was broadcasting** we, you, they **were broadcasting**	I, he, she, it **was being broadcast** we, you, they **were being broadcast**
Past *Int.*	I, he, she, it, we, you, they **did broadcast**	I, he, she, it, we, you, they **did get broadcast**
Pres. *Perf.*	I, we, you, they **have broadcast** he, she, it **has broadcast**	I, we, you, they **have been broadcast** he, she, it **has been broadcast**
Past *Perf.*	I, he, she, it, we, you, they **had broadcast**	I, he, she, it, we, you, they **had been broadcast**
Fut. *Perf.*	I, he, she, it, we, you, they **will have broadcast**	I, he, she, it, we, you, they **will have been broadcast**

IMPERATIVE MOOD

broadcast   **be broadcast**

SUBJUNCTIVE MOOD

Pres.	if I, he, she, it, we, you, they **broadcast**	if I, he, she, it, we, you, they **be broadcast**
Past	if I, he, she, it, we, you, they **broadcast**	if I, he, she, it, we, you, they **were broadcast**
Fut.	if I, he, she, it, we, you, they **should broadcast**	if I, he, she, it, we, you, they **should be broadcast**

Transitive and intransitive. The past tense and past participle may be BROADCAST or BROADCASTED. The *Oxford Dictionary* recognizes BROADCASTED only as a past participle.

build
(active voice)

PRINCIPAL PARTS: builds, building, built, built

be built
(passive voice)

Infinitive: **to build**
Perfect Infinitive: **to have built**
Present Participle: **building**
Past Participle: **built**

Infinitive: **to be built**
Perfect Infinitive: **to have been built**
Present Participle: **being built**
Past Participle: **been built**

INDICATIVE MOOD

Pres.	I, we, you, they **build**	I **am built**
		we, you, they **are built**
	he, she, it **builds**	he, she, it **is built**
Pres.	I **am building**	I **am being built**
Prog.	we, you, they **are building**	we, you, they **are being built**
	he, she, it **is building**	he, she, it **is being built**
Pres.	I, we, you, they **do build**	I, we, you, they **do get built**
Int.	he, she, it **does build**	he, she, it **does get built**
Fut.	I, he, she, it,	I, he, she, it,
	we, you, they **will build**	we, you, they **will be built**
Past	I, he, she, it,	I, he, she, it **was built**
	we, you, they **built**	we, you, they **were built**
Past	I, he, she, it **was building**	I, he, she, it **was being built**
Prog.	we, you, they **were building**	we, you, they **were being built**
Past	I, he, she, it,	I, he, she, it,
Int.	we, you, they **did build**	we, you, they **did get built**
Pres.	I, we, you, they **have built**	I, we, you, they **have been built**
Perf.	he, she, it **has built**	he, she, it **has been built**
Past	I, he, she, it,	I, he, she, it,
Perf.	we, you, they **had built**	we, you, they **had been built**
Fut.	I, he, she, it, we, you, they	I, he, she, it, we, you, they
Perf.	**will have built**	**will have been built**

IMPERATIVE MOOD

build

be built

SUBJUNCTIVE MOOD

Pres.	if I, he, she, it,	if I, he, she, it,
	we, you, they **build**	we, you, they **be built**
Past	if I, he, she, it,	if I, he, she, it,
	we, you, they **built**	we, you, they **were built**
Fut.	if I, he, she, it,	if I, he, she, it,
	we, you, they **should build**	we, you, they **should be built**

Transitive and intransitive. *Webster's New World Dictionary* lists BUILDED as an archaic form of the past tense and past participle.

burn
(active voice)

be burned/burnt
(passive voice)

Infinitive: **to burn**
Perfect Infinitive: **to have burned**
Present Participle: **burning**
Past Participle: **burned**

Infinitive: **to be burned**
Perfect Infinitive: **to have been burned**
Present Participle: **being burned**
Past Participle: **been burned**

INDICATIVE MOOD

Pres.	I, we, you, they **burn**	I **am burned**
		we, you, they **are burned**
	he, she, it **burns**	he, she, it **is burned**
Pres.	I **am burning**	I **am being burned**
Prog.	we, you, they **are burning**	we, you, they **are being burned**
	he, she, it **is burning**	he, she, it **is being burned**
Pres.	I, we, you, they **do burn**	I, we, you, they **do get burned**
Int.	he, she, it **does burn**	he, she, it **does get burned**
Fut.	I, he, she, it,	I, he, she, it,
	we, you, they **will burn**	we, you, they **will be burned**
Past	I, he, she, it,	I, he, she, it **was burned**
	we, you, they **burned**	we, you, they **were burned**
Past	I, he, she, it **was burning**	I, he, she, it **was being burned**
Prog.	we, you, they **were burning**	we, you, they **were being burned**
Past	I, he, she, it,	I, he, she, it,
Int.	we, you, they **did burn**	we, you, they **did get burned**
Pres.	I, we, you, they **have burned**	I, we, you, they **have been burned**
Perf.	he, she, it **has burned**	he, she, it **has been burned**
Past	I, he, she, it,	I, he, she, it,
Perf.	we, you, they **had burned**	we, you, they **had been burned**
Fut.	I, he, she, it, we, you, they	I, he, she, it, we, you, they
Perf.	**will have burned**	**will have been burned**

IMPERATIVE MOOD

burn   **be burned**

SUBJUNCTIVE MOOD

Pres.	if I, he, she, it,	if I, he, she, it,
	we, you, they **burn**	we, you, they **be burned**
Past	if I, he, she, it,	if I, he, she, it,
	we, you, they **burned**	we, you, they **were burned**
Fut.	if I, he, she, it,	if I, he, she, it,
	we, you, they **should burn**	we, you, they **should be burned**

Transitive and intransitive. The past tense and past participle are BURNED and BURNT. The _Oxford Dictionary_ lists BURNT before BURNED.

54

burst
(active voice)

PRINCIPAL PARTS: **bursts, bursting, burst, burst**

be burst
(passive voice)

Infinitive: **to burst**
Perfect Infinitive: **to have burst**
Present Participle: **bursting**
Past Participle: **burst**

Infinitive: **to be burst**
Perfect Infinitive: **to have been burst**
Present Participle: **being burst**
Past Participle: **been burst**

INDICATIVE MOOD

Pres.	I, we, you, they **burst**	I **am burst**
		we, you, they **are burst**
	he, she, it **bursts**	he, she, it **is burst**
Pres.	I **am bursting**	I **am being burst**
Prog.	we, you, they **are bursting**	we, you, they **are being burst**
	he, she, it **is bursting**	he, she, it **is being burst**
Pres.	I, we, you, they **do burst**	I, we, you, they **do get burst**
Int.	he, she, it **does burst**	he, she, it **does get burst**
Fut.	I, he, she, it,	I, he, she, it,
	we, you, they **will burst**	we, you, they **will be burst**
Past	I, he, she, it,	I, he, she, it **was burst**
	we, you, they **burst**	we, you, they **were burst**
Past	I, he, she, it **was bursting**	I, he, she, it **was being burst**
Prog.	we, you, they **were bursting**	we, you, they **were being burst**
Past	I, he, she, it,	I, he, she, it,
Int.	we, you, they **did burst**	we, you, they **did get burst**
Pres.	I, we, you, they **have burst**	I, we, you, they **have been burst**
Perf.	he, she, it **has burst**	he, she, it **has been burst**
Past	I, he, she, it,	I, he, she, it,
Perf.	we, you, they **had burst**	we, you, they **had been burst**
Fut.	I, he, she, it, we, you, they	I, he, she, it, we, you, they
Perf.	**will have burst**	**will have been burst**

IMPERATIVE MOOD

burst

be burst

SUBJUNCTIVE MOOD

Pres.	if I, he, she, it,	if I, he, she, it,
	we, you, they **burst**	we, you, they **be burst**
Past	if I, he, she, it,	if I, he, she, it,
	we, you, they **burst**	we, you, they **were burst**
Fut.	if I, he, she, it,	if I, he, she, it,
	we, you, they **should burst**	we, you, they **should be burst**

Intransitive and transitive. *Merriam Webster's* lists BURSTED as an alternative past tense and past participle.

bust
(active voice)

be busted
(passive voice)

Infinitive: **to bust**
Perfect Infinitive: **to have busted**
Present Participle: **busting**
Past Participle: **busted**

Infinitive: **to be busted**
Perfect Infinitive: **to have been busted**
Present Participle: **being busted**
Past Participle: **been busted**

INDICATIVE MOOD

Pres.	I, we, you, they **bust**	I **am busted**
		we, you, they **are busted**
	he, she, it **busts**	he, she, it **is busted**
Pres.	I **am busting**	I **am being busted**
Prog.	we, you, they **are busting**	we, you, they **are being busted**
	he, she, it **is busting**	he, she, it **is being busted**
Pres.	I, we, you, they **do bust**	I, we, you, they **do get busted**
Int.	he, she, it **does bust**	he, she, it **does get busted**
Fut.	I, he, she, it,	I, he, she, it,
	we, you, they **will bust**	we, you, they **will be busted**
Past	I, he, she, it,	I, he, she, it **was busted**
	we, you, they **busted**	we, you, they **were busted**
Past	I, he, she, it **was busting**	I, he, she, it **was being busted**
Prog.	we, you, they **were busting**	we, you, they **were being busted**
Past	I, he, she, it,	I, he, she, it,
Int.	we, you, they **did bust**	we, you, they **did get busted**
Pres.	I, we, you, they **have busted**	I, we, you, they **have been busted**
Perf.	he, she, it **has busted**	he, she, it **has been busted**
Past	I, he, she, it,	I, he, she, it,
Perf.	we, you, they **had busted**	we, you, they **had been busted**
Fut.	I, he, she, it, we, you, they	I, he, she, it, we, you, they
Perf.	**will have busted**	**will have been busted**

IMPERATIVE MOOD

bust   **be busted**

SUBJUNCTIVE MOOD

Pres.	if I, he, she, it,	if I, he, she, it,
	we, you, they **bust**	we, you, they **be busted**
Past	if I, he, she, it,	if I, he, she, it,
	we, you, they **busted**	we, you, they **were busted**
Fut.	if I, he, she, it,	if I, he, she, it,
	we, you, they **should bust**	we, you, they **should be busted**

Considered slang in many instances, BUST can often be found in standard speech "bust the budget" or "bust a union." *Merriam Webster's* and the *Oxford Dictionary* recognize BUST as an alternate past tense and past participle form.

buy
(active voice)

be bought
(passive voice)

Infinitive: **to buy**
Perfect Infinitive: **to have bought**
Present Participle: **buying**
Past Participle: **bought**

Infinitive: **to be bought**
Perfect Infinitive: **to have been bought**
Present Participle: **being bought**
Past Participle: **been bought**

INDICATIVE MOOD

Pres.	I, we, you, they **buy**	I am **bought**
		we, you, they **are bought**
	he, she, it **buys**	he, she, it **is bought**
Pres.	I **am buying**	I **am being bought**
Prog.	we, you, they **are buying**	we, you, they **are being bought**
	he, she, it **is buying**	he, she, it **is being bought**
Pres.	I, we, you, they **do buy**	I, we, you, they **do get bought**
Int.	he, she, it **does buy**	he, she, it **does get bought**
Fut.	I, he, she, it,	I, he, she, it,
	we, you, they **will buy**	we, you, they **will be bought**
Past	I, he, she, it,	I, he, she, it **was bought**
	we, you, they **bought**	we, you, they **were bought**
Past	I, he, she, it **was buying**	I, he, she, it **was being bought**
Prog.	we, you, they **were buying**	we, you, they **were being bought**
Past	I, he, she, it,	I, he, she, it,
Int.	we, you, they **did buy**	we, you, they **did get bought**
Pres.	I, we, you, they **have bought**	I, we, you, they **have been bought**
Perf.	he, she, it **has bought**	he, she, it **has been bought**
Past	I, he, she, it,	I, he, she, it,
Perf.	we, you, they **had bought**	we, you, they **had been bought**
Fut.	I, he, she, it, we, you, they	I, he, she, it, we, you, they
Perf.	**will have bought**	**will have been bought**

IMPERATIVE MOOD

buy   **be bought**

SUBJUNCTIVE MOOD

Pres.	if I, he, she, it,	if I, he, she, it,
	we, you, they **buy**	we, you, they **be bought**
Past	if I, he, she, it,	if I, he, she, it,
	we, you, they **bought**	we, you, they **were bought**
Fut.	if I, he, she, it,	if I, he, she, it,
	we, you, they **should buy**	we, you, they **should be bought**

Transitive and intransitive.

call
(active voice)

be called
(passive voice)

Infinitive: **to call**
Perfect Infinitive: **to have called**
Present Participle: **calling**
Past Participle: **called**

Infinitive: **to be called**
Perfect Infinitive: **to have been called**
Present Participle: **being called**
Past Participle: **been called**

INDICATIVE MOOD

Pres.	I, we, you, they **call**	I am called
		we, you, they **are called**
	he, she, it **calls**	he, she, it **is called**
Pres.	I **am calling**	I **am being called**
Prog.	we, you, they **are calling**	we, you, they **are being called**
	he, she, it **is calling**	he, she, it **is being called**
Pres.	I, we, you, they **do call**	I, we, you, they **do get called**
Int.	he, she, it **does call**	he, she, it **does get called**
Fut.	I, he, she, it,	I, he, she, it,
	we, you, they **will call**	we, you, they **will be called**
Past	I, he, she, it,	I, he, she, it **was called**
	we, you, they **called**	we, you, they **were called**
Past	I, he, she, it **was calling**	I, he, she, it **was being called**
Prog.	we, you, they **were calling**	we, you, they **were being called**
Past	I, he, she, it,	I, he, she, it,
Int.	we, you, they **did call**	we, you, they **did get called**
Pres.	I, we, you, they **have called**	I, we, you, they **have been called**
Perf.	he, she, it **has called**	he, she, it **has been called**
Past	I, he, she, it,	I, he, she, it,
Perf.	we, you, they **had called**	we, you, they **had been called**
Fut.	I, he, she, it, we, you, they	I, he, she, it, we, you, they
Perf.	**will have called**	**will have been called**

IMPERATIVE MOOD

call

be called

SUBJUNCTIVE MOOD

Pres.	if I, he, she, it,	if I, he, she, it,
	we, you, they **call**	we, you, they **be called**
Past	if I, he, she, it,	if I, he, she, it,
	we, you, they **called**	we, you, they **were called**
Fut.	if I, he, she, it,	if I, he, she, it,
	we, you, they **should call**	we, you, they **should be called**

Transitive and intransitive.

can[*]
(active voice)

PRINCIPAL PARTS: **cans, canning,
canned, canned**

be canned
(passive voice)

Infinitive: **to can**
Perfect Infinitive: **to have canned**
Present Participle: **canning**
Past Participle: **canned**

Infinitive: **to be canned**
Perfect Infinitive: **to have been canned**
Present Participle: **being canned**
Past Participle: **been canned**

INDICATIVE MOOD

Pres.	I, we, you, they **can**	I am **canned**
		we, you, they **are canned**
	he, she, it **cans**	he, she, it **is canned**
Pres.	I am **canning**	I am **being canned**
Prog.	we, you, they **are canning**	we, you, they **are being canned**
	he, she, it **is canning**	he, she, it **is being canned**
Pres.	I, we, you, they **do can**	I, we, you, they **do get canned**
Int.	he, she, it **does can**	he, she, it **does get canned**
Fut.	I, he, she, it,	I, he, she, it,
	we, you, they **will can**	we, you, they **will be canned**
Past	I, he, she, it,	I, he, she, it **was canned**
	we, you, they **canned**	we, you, they **were canned**
Past	I, he, she, it **was canning**	I, he, she, it **was being canned**
Prog.	we, you, they **were canning**	we, you, they **were being canned**
Past	I, he, she, it,	I, he, she, it,
Int.	we, you, they **did can**	we, you, they **did get canned**
Pres.	I, we, you, they **have canned**	I, we, you, they **have been canned**
Perf.	he, she, it **has canned**	he, she, it **has been canned**
Past	I, he, she, it,	I, he, she, it,
Perf.	we, you, they **had canned**	we, you, they **had been canned**
Fut.	I, he, she, it, we, you, they	I, he, she, it, we, you, they
Perf.	**will have canned**	**will have been canned**

IMPERATIVE MOOD

can

be canned

SUBJUNCTIVE MOOD

Pres.	if I, he, she, it,	if I, he, she, it,
	we, you, they **can**	we, you, they **be canned**
Past	if I, he, she, it,	if I, he, she, it,
	we, you, they **canned**	we, you, they **were canned**
Fut.	if I, he, she, it,	if I, he, she, it,
	we, you, they **should can**	we, you, they **should be canned**

*Meaning to place in a container for preservation.

care
(active voice)

PRINCIPAL PARTS: **cares, caring,
cared, cared**

be cared
(passive voice)

Infinitive: **to care**
Perfect Infinitive: **to have cared**
Present Participle: **caring**
Past Participle: **cared**

Infinitive: **to be cared**
Perfect Infinitive: **to have been cared**
Present Participle: **being cared**
Past Participle: **been cared**

INDICATIVE MOOD

Pres.	I, we, you, they **care**	I **am cared** we, you, they **are cared**
	he, she, it **cares**	he, she, it **is cared**
Pres. *Prog.*	I **am caring** we, you, they **are caring** he, she, it **is caring**	I **am being cared** we, you, they **are being cared** he, she, it **is being cared**
Pres. *Int.*	I, we, you, they **do care** he, she, it **does care**	I, we, you, they **do get cared** he, she, it **does get cared**
Fut.	I, he, she, it, we, you, they **will care**	I, he, she, it, we, you, they **will be cared**
Past	I, he, she, it, we, you, they **cared**	I, he, she, it **was cared** we, you, they **were cared**
Past *Prog.*	I, he, she, it **was caring** we, you, they **were caring**	I, he, she, it **was being cared** we, you, they **were being cared**
Past *Int.*	I, he, she, it, we, you, they **did care**	I, he, she, it, we, you, they **did get cared**
Pres. *Perf.*	I, we, you, they **have cared** he, she, it **has cared**	I, we, you, they **have been cared** he, she, it **has been cared**
Past *Perf.*	I, he, she, it, we, you, they **had cared**	I, he, she, it, we, you, they **had been cared**
Fut. *Perf.*	I, he, she, it, we, you, they **will have cared**	I, he, she, it, we, you, they **will have been cared**

IMPERATIVE MOOD

care

be cared

SUBJUNCTIVE MOOD

Pres.	if I, he, she, it, we, you, they **care**	if I, he, she, it, we, you, they **be cared**
Past	if I, he, she, it, we, you, they **cared**	if I, he, she, it, we, you, they **were cared**
Fut.	if I, he, she, it, we, you, they **should care**	if I, he, she, it, we, you, they **should be cared**

Transitive and intransitive.

carry
(active voice)

be carried
(passive voice)

Infinitive: **to carry**
Perfect Infinitive: **to have carried**
Present Participle: **carrying**
Past Participle: **carried**

Infinitive: **to be carried**
Perfect Infinitive: **to have been carried**
Present Participle: **being carried**
Past Participle: **been carried**

INDICATIVE MOOD

Pres.	I, we, you, they **carry**	I **am carried**
		we, you, they **are carried**
	he, she, it **carries**	he, she, it **is carried**
Pres.	I **am carrying**	I **am being carried**
Prog.	we, you, they **are carrying**	we, you, they **are being carried**
	he, she, it **is carrying**	he, she, it **is being carried**
Pres.	I, we, you, they **do carry**	I, we, you, they **do get carried**
Int.	he, she, it **does carry**	he, she, it **does get carried**
Fut.	I, he, she, it,	I, he, she, it,
	we, you, they **will carry**	we, you, they **will be carried**
Past	I, he, she, it,	I, he, she, it **was carried**
	we, you, they **carried**	we, you, they **were carried**
Past	I, he, she, it **was carrying**	I, he, she, it **was being carried**
Prog.	we, you, they **were carrying**	we, you, they **were being carried**
Past	I, he, she, it,	I, he, she, it,
Int.	we, you, they **did carry**	we, you, they **did get carried**
Pres.	I, we, you, they **have carried**	I, we, you, they **have been carried**
Perf.	he, she, it **has carried**	he, she, it **has been carried**
Past	I, he, she, it,	I, he, she, it,
Perf.	we, you, they **had carried**	we, you, they **had been carried**
Fut.	I, he, she, it, we, you, they	I, he, she, it, we, you, they
Perf.	**will have carried**	**will have been carried**

IMPERATIVE MOOD

carry **be carried**

SUBJUNCTIVE MOOD

Pres.	if I, he, she, it,	if I, he, she, it,
	we, you, they **carry**	we, you, they **be carried**
Past	if I, he, she, it,	if I, he, she, it,
	we, you, they **carried**	we, you, they **were carried**
Fut.	if I, he, she, it,	if I, he, she, it,
	we, you, they **should carry**	we, you, they **should be carried**

Transitive and intransitive.

cast
(active voice)

be cast
(passive voice)

Infinitive: **to cast**
Perfect Infinitive: **to have cast**
Present Participle: **casting**
Past Participle: **cast**

Infinitive: **to be cast**
Perfect Infinitive: **to have been cast**
Present Participle: **being cast**
Past Participle: **been cast**

INDICATIVE MOOD

Pres.	I, we, you, they **cast**	I am cast
		we, you, they **are cast**
	he, she, it **casts**	he, she, it **is cast**
Pres.	I am casting	I am being cast
Prog.	we, you, they **are casting**	we, you, they **are being cast**
	he, she, it **is casting**	he, she, it **is being cast**
Pres.	I, we, you, they **do cast**	I, we, you, they **do get cast**
Int.	he, she, it **does cast**	he, she, it **does get cast**
Fut.	I, he, she, it,	I, he, she, it,
	we, you, they **will cast**	we, you, they **will be cast**
Past	I, he, she, it,	I, he, she, it **was cast**
	we, you, they **cast**	we, you, they **were cast**
Past	I, he, she, it **was casting**	I, he, she, it **was being cast**
Prog.	we, you, they **were casting**	we, you, they **were being cast**
Past	I, he, she, it,	I, he, she, it,
Int.	we, you, they **did cast**	we, you, they **did get cast**
Pres.	I, we, you, they **have cast**	I, we, you, they **have been cast**
Perf.	he, she, it **has cast**	he, she, it **has been cast**
Past	I, he, she, it,	I, he, she, it,
Perf.	we, you, they **had cast**	we, you, they **had been cast**
Fut.	I, he, she, it, we, you, they	I, he, she, it, we, you, they
Perf.	**will have cast**	**will have been cast**

IMPERATIVE MOOD

cast   **be cast**

SUBJUNCTIVE MOOD

Pres.	if I, he, she, it,	if I, he, she, it,
	we, you, they **cast**	we, you, they **be cast**
Past	if I, he, she, it,	if I, he, she, it,
	we, you, they **cast**	we, you, they **were cast**
Fut.	if I, he, she, it,	if I, he, she, it,
	we, you, they **should cast**	we, you, they **should be cast**

Transitive and intransitive.

catch
(active voice)

PRINCIPAL PARTS: **catches, catching, caught, caught**

be caught
(passive voice)

Infinitive: **to catch**
Perfect Infinitive: **to have caught**
Present Participle: **catching**
Past Participle: **caught**

Infinitive: **to be caught**
Perfect Infinitive: **to have been caught**
Present Participle: **being caught**
Past Participle: **been caught**

INDICATIVE MOOD

Pres.	I, we, you, they **catch**	I **am caught**
		we, you, they **are caught**
	he, she, it **catches**	he, she, it **is caught**
Pres.	I **am catching**	I **am being caught**
Prog.	we, you, they **are catching**	we, you, they **are being caught**
	he, she, it **is catching**	he, she, it **is being caught**
Pres.	I, we, you, they **do catch**	I, we, you, they **do get caught**
Int.	he, she, it **does catch**	he, she, it **does get caught**
Fut.	I, he, she, it,	I, he, she, it,
	we, you, they **will catch**	we, you, they **will be caught**
Past	I, he, she, it,	I, he, she, it **was caught**
	we, you, they **caught**	we, you, they **were caught**
Past	I, he, she, it **was catching**	I, he, she, it **was being caught**
Prog.	we, you, they **were catching**	we, you, they **were being caught**
Past	I, he, she, it,	I, he, she, it,
Int.	we, you, they **did catch**	we, you, they **did get caught**
Pres.	I, we, you, they **have caught**	I, we, you, they **have been caught**
Perf.	he, she, it **has caught**	he, she, it **has been caught**
Past	I, he, she, it,	I, he, she, it,
Perf.	we, you, they **had caught**	we, you, they **had been caught**
Fut.	I, he, she, it, we, you, they	I, he, she, it, we, you, they
Perf.	**will have caught**	**will have been caught**

IMPERATIVE MOOD

catch   **be caught**

SUBJUNCTIVE MOOD

Pres.	if I, he, she, it,	if I, he, she, it,
	we, you, they **catch**	we, you, they **be caught**
Past	if I, he, she, it,	if I, he, she, it,
	we, you, they **caught**	we, you, they **were caught**
Fut.	if I, he, she, it,	if I, he, she, it,
	we, you, they **should catch**	we, you, they **should be caught**

Transitive and intransitive.

cause
(active voice)

be caused
(passive voice)

Infinitive: **to cause**
Perfect Infinitive: **to have caused**
Present Participle: **causing**
Past Participle: **caused**

Infinitive: **to be caused**
Perfect Infinitive: **to have been caused**
Present Participle: **being caused**
Past Participle: **been caused**

INDICATIVE MOOD

Pres.	I, we, you, they **cause**	I **am caused**
		we, you, they **are caused**
	he, she, it **causes**	he, she, it **is caused**
Pres.	I **am causing**	I **am being caused**
Prog.	we, you, they **are causing**	we, you, they **are being caused**
	he, she, it **is causing**	he, she, it **is being caused**
Pres.	I, we, you, they **do cause**	I, we, you, they **do get caused**
Int.	he, she, it **does cause**	he, she, it **does get caused**
Fut.	I, he, she, it,	I, he, she, it,
	we, you, they **will cause**	we, you, they **will be caused**
Past	I, he, she, it,	I, he, she, it **was caused**
	we, you, they **caused**	we, you, they **were caused**
Past	I, he, she, it **was causing**	I, he, she, it **was being caused**
Prog.	we, you, they **were causing**	we, you, they **were being caused**
Past	I, he, she, it,	I, he, she, it,
Int.	we, you, they **did cause**	we, you, they **did get caused**
Pres.	I, we, you, they **have caused**	I, we, you, they **have been caused**
Perf.	he, she, it **has caused**	he, she, it **has been caused**
Past	I, he, she, it,	I, he, she, it,
Perf.	we, you, they **had caused**	we, you, they **had been caused**
Fut.	I, he, she, it, we, you, they	I, he, she, it, we, you, they
Perf.	**will have caused**	**will have been caused**

IMPERATIVE MOOD

cause
be caused

SUBJUNCTIVE MOOD

Pres.	if I, he, she, it,	if I, he, she, it,
	we, you, they **cause**	we, you, they **be caused**
Past	if I, he, she, it,	if I, he, she, it,
	we, you, they **caused**	we, you, they **were caused**
Fut.	if I, he, she, it,	if I, he, she, it,
	we, you, they **should cause**	we, you, they **should be caused**

---

change
(active voice)

be changed
(passive voice)

Infinitive: **to change**
Perfect Infinitive: **to have changed**
Present Participle: **changing**
Past Participle: **changed**

Infinitive: **to be changed**
Perfect Infinitive: **to have been changed**
Present Participle: **being changed**
Past Participle: **been changed**

INDICATIVE MOOD

Pres.	I, we, you, they **change**	I **am changed**
		we, you, they **are changed**
	he, she, it **changes**	he, she, it **is changed**
Pres.	I **am changing**	I **am being changed**
Prog.	we, you, they **are changing**	we, you, they **are being changed**
	he, she, it **is changing**	he, she, it **is being changed**
Pres.	I, we, you, they **do change**	I, we, you, they **do get changed**
Int.	he, she, it **does change**	he, she, it **does get changed**
Fut.	I, he, she, it,	I, he, she, it,
	we, you, they **will change**	we, you, they **will be changed**
Past	I, he, she, it,	I, he, she, it **was changed**
	we, you, they **changed**	we, you, they **were changed**
Past	I, he, she, it **was changing**	I, he, she, it **was being changed**
Prog.	we, you, they **were changing**	we, you, they **were being changed**
Past	I, he, she, it,	I, he, she, it,
Int.	we, you, they **did change**	we, you, they **did get changed**
Pres.	I, we, you, they **have changed**	I, we, you, they **have been changed**
Perf.	he, she, it **has changed**	he, she, it **has been changed**
Past	I, he, she, it,	I, he, she, it,
Perf.	we, you, they **had changed**	we, you, they **had been changed**
Fut.	I, he, she, it, we, you, they	I, he, she, it, we, you, they
Perf.	**will have changed**	**will have been changed**

IMPERATIVE MOOD

change   **be changed**

SUBJUNCTIVE MOOD

Pres.	if I, he, she, it,	if I, he, she, it,
	we, you, they **change**	we, you, they **be changed**
Past	if I, he, she, it,	if I, he, she, it,
	we, you, they **changed**	we, you, they **were changed**
Fut.	if I, he, she, it,	if I, he, she, it,
	we, you, they **should change**	we, you, they **should be changed**

Transitive and intransitive.

chide
(active voice)

PRINCIPAL PARTS: **chides, chiding, chided/chid, chided/chid/ chidden**

be chided/chid/ chidden
(passive voice)

Infinitive: **to chide**
Perfect Infinitive: **to have chided**
Present Participle: **chiding**
Past Participle: **chided**

Infinitive: **to be chided**
Perfect Infinitive: **to have been chided**
Present Participle: **being chided**
Past Participle: **been chided**

INDICATIVE MOOD

Pres.	I, we, you, they **chide**	I am **chided**
		we, you, they **are chided**
	he, she, it **chides**	he, she, it **is chided**
Pres.	I **am chiding**	I **am being chided**
Prog.	we, you, they **are chiding**	we, you, they **are being chided**
	he, she, it **is chiding**	he, she, it **is being chided**
Pres.	I, we, you, they **do chide**	I, we, you, they **do get chided**
Int.	he, she, it **does chide**	he, she, it **does get chided**
Fut.	I, he, she, it,	I, he, she, it,
	we, you, they **will chide**	we, you, they **will be chided**
Past	I, he, she, it,	I, he, she, it **was chided**
	we, you, they **chided**	we, you, they **were chided**
Past	I, he, she, it **was chiding**	I, he, she, it **was being chided**
Prog.	we, you, they **were chiding**	we, you, they **were being chided**
Past	I, he, she, it,	I, he, she, it,
Int.	we, you, they **did chide**	we, you, they **did get chided**
Pres.	I, we, you, they **have chided**	I, we, you, they **have been chided**
Perf.	he, she, it **has chided**	he, she, it **has been chided**
Past	I, he, she, it,	I, he, she, it,
Perf.	we, you, they **had chided**	we, you, they **had been chided**
Fut.	I, he, she, it, we, you, they	I, he, she, it, we, you, they
Perf.	**will have chided**	**will have been chided**

IMPERATIVE MOOD

chide   **be chided**

SUBJUNCTIVE MOOD

Pres.	if I, he, she, it,	if I, he, she, it,
	we, you, they **chide**	we, you, they **be chided**
Past	if I, he, she, it,	if I, he, she, it,
	we, you, they **chided**	we, you, they **were chided**
Fut.	if I, he, she, it,	if I, he, she, it,
	we, you, they **should chide**	we, you, they **should be chided**

Transitive and intransitive. American English prefers CHIDED for the past tense and past participle.

choose
(active voice)

PRINCIPAL PARTS: **chooses, choosing, chose, chosen**

be chosen
(passive voice)

Infinitive: **to choose**
Perfect Infinitive: **to have chosen**
Present Participle: **choosing**
Past Participle: **chosen**

Infinitive: **to be chosen**
Perfect Infinitive: **to have been chosen**
Present Participle: **being chosen**
Past Participle: **been chosen**

INDICATIVE MOOD

Pres.	I, we, you, they **choose** he, she, it **chooses**	I **am chosen** we, you, they **are chosen** he, she, it **is chosen**
Pres. *Prog.*	I **am choosing** we, you, they **are choosing** he, she, it **is choosing**	I **am being chosen** we, you, they **are being chosen** he, she, it **is being chosen**
Pres. *Int.*	I, we, you, they **do choose** he, she, it **does choose**	I, we, you, they **do get chosen** he, she, it **does get chosen**
Fut.	I, he, she, it, we, you, they **will choose**	I, he, she, it, we, you, they **will be chosen**
Past	I, he, she, it, we, you, they **chose**	I, he, she, it **was chosen** we, you, they **were chosen**
Past *Prog.*	I, he, she, it **was choosing** we, you, they **were choosing**	I, he, she, it **was being chosen** we, you, they **were being chosen**
Past *Int.*	I, he, she, it, we, you, they **did choose**	I, he, she, it, we, you, they **did get chosen**
Pres. *Perf.*	I, we, you, they **have chosen** he, she, it **has chosen**	I, we, you, they **have been chosen** he, she, it **has been chosen**
Past *Perf.*	I, he, she, it, we, you, they **had chosen**	I, he, she, it, we, you, they **had been chosen**
Fut. *Perf.*	I, he, she, it, we, you, they **will have chosen**	I, he, she, it, we, you, they **will have been chosen**

IMPERATIVE MOOD

choose

be chosen

SUBJUNCTIVE MOOD

Pres.	if I, he, she, it, we, you, they **choose**	if I, he, she, it, we, you, they **be chosen**
Past	if I, he, she, it, we, you, they **chose**	if I, he, she, it, we, you, they **were chosen**
Fut.	if I, he, she, it, we, you, they **should choose**	if I, he, she, it, we, you, they **should be chosen**

Transitive and intransitive.

cleave
(active voice)

PRINCIPAL PARTS: **cleaves, cleaving, cleft/cleaved/clove, cleft/cleaved/ cloven**

be cleft/cleaved/ cloven
(passive voice)

Infinitive: **to cleave**
Perfect Infinitive: **to have cleft**
Present Participle: **cleaving**
Past Participle: **cleft**

Infinitive: **to be cleft**
Perfect Infinitive: **to have been cleft**
Present Participle: **being cleft**
Past Participle: **been cleft**

INDICATIVE MOOD

Pres.	I, we, you, they **cleave**	I **am cleft**
		we, you, they **are cleft**
	he, she, it **cleaves**	he, she, it **is cleft**
Pres. *Prog.*	I **am cleaving**	I **am being cleft**
	we, you, they **are cleaving**	we, you, they **are being cleft**
	he, she, it **is cleaving**	he, she, it **is being cleft**
Pres. *Int.*	I, we, you, they **do cleave**	I, we, you, they **do get cleft**
	he, she, it **does cleave**	he, she, it **does get cleft**
Fut.	I, he, she, it, we, you, they **will cleave**	I, he, she, it, we, you, they **will be cleft**
Past	I, he, she, it, we, you, they **cleft**	I, he, she, it **was cleft** we, you, they **were cleft**
Past *Prog.*	I, he, she, it **was cleaving** we, you, they **were cleaving**	I, he, she, it **was being cleft** we, you, they **were being cleft**
Past *Int.*	I, he, she, it, we, you, they **did cleave**	I, he, she, it, we, you, they **did get cleft**
Pres. *Perf.*	I, we, you, they **have cleft** he, she, it **has cleft**	I, we, you, they **have been cleft** he, she, it **has been cleft**
Past *Perf.*	I, he, she, it, we, you, they **had cleft**	I, he, she, it, we, you, they **had been cleft**
Fut. *Perf.*	I, he, she, it, we, you, they **will have cleft**	I, he, she, it, we, you, they **will have been cleft**

IMPERATIVE MOOD

cleave　　　　　　**be cleft**

SUBJUNCTIVE MOOD

Pres.	if I, he, she, it, we, you, they **cleave**	if I, he, she, it, we, you, they **be cleft**
Past	if I, he, she, it, we, you, they **cleft**	if I, he, she, it, we, you, they **were cleft**
Fut.	if I, he, she, it, we, you, they **should cleave**	if I, he, she, it, we, you, they **should be cleft**

CLEAVE is a transitive verb meaning to "cut, penetrate." The *Oxford Dictionary* prefers the CLOVE and CLOVEN forms. *Merriam Webster's* and *Webster's* list CLEAVED as the initial forms over CLEFT. There is also an intransitive verb CLEAVE that has CLEAVED as both its past and past participle, and that means "clinging fast, being faithful."

cling PRINCIPAL PARTS: **clings, clinging, clung, clung**

Infinitive: **to cling**
Perfect Infinitive: **to have clung**
Present Participle: **clinging**
Past Participle: **clung**

INDICATIVE MOOD

Pres. I, we, you, they **cling**

he, she, it **clings**

Pres. I **am clinging**
Prog. we, you, they **are clinging**
he, she, it **is clinging**

Pres. I, we, you, they **do cling**
Int. he, she, it **does cling**

Fut. I, he, she, it,
we, you, they **will cling**

Past I, he, she, it,
we, you, they **clung**

Past I, he, she, it **was clinging**
Prog. we, you, they **were clinging**

Past I, he, she, it,
Int. we, you, they **did cling**

Pres. I, we, you, they **have clung**
Perf. he, she, it **has clung**

Past I, he, she, it,
Perf. we, you, they **had clung**

Fut. I, he, she, it, we, you, they
Perf. **will have clung**

IMPERATIVE MOOD

cling

SUBJUNCTIVE MOOD

Pres. if I, he, she, it,
we, you, they **cling**

Past if I, he, she, it,
we, you, they **clung**

Fut. if I, he, she, it,
we, you, they **should cling**

close
(active voice)

be closed
(passive voice)

Infinitive: **to close**
Perfect Infinitive: **to have closed**
Present Participle: **closing**
Past Participle: **closed**

Infinitive: **to be closed**
Perfect Infinitive: **to have been closed**
Present Participle: **being closed**
Past Participle: **been closed**

INDICATIVE MOOD

Pres.	I, we, you, they **close**	I **am closed**
		we, you, they **are closed**
	he, she, it **closes**	he, she, it **is closed**
Pres.	I **am closing**	I **am being closed**
Prog.	we, you, they **are closing**	we, you, they **are being closed**
	he, she, it **is closing**	he, she, it **is being closed**
Pres.	I, we, you, they **do close**	I, we, you, they **do get closed**
Int.	he, she, it **does close**	he, she, it **does get closed**
Fut.	I, he, she, it,	I, he, she, it,
	we, you, they **will close**	we, you, they **will be closed**
Past	I, he, she, it,	I, he, she, it **was closed**
	we, you, they **closed**	we, you, they **were closed**
Past	I, he, she, it **was closing**	I, he, she, it **was being closed**
Prog.	we, you, they **were closing**	we, you, they **were being closed**
Past	I, he, she, it,	I, he, she, it,
Int.	we, you, they **did close**	we, you, they **did get closed**
Pres.	I, we, you, they **have closed**	I, we, you, they **have been closed**
Perf.	he, she, it **has closed**	he, she, it **has been closed**
Past	I, he, she, it,	I, he, she, it,
Perf.	we, you, they **had closed**	we, you, they **had been closed**
Fut.	I, he, she, it, we, you, they	I, he, she, it, we, you, they
Perf.	**will have closed**	**will have been closed**

IMPERATIVE MOOD

close

be closed

SUBJUNCTIVE MOOD

Pres.	if I, he, she, it,	if I, he, she, it,
	we, you, they **close**	we, you, they **be closed**
Past	if I, he, she, it,	if I, he, she, it,
	we, you, they **closed**	we, you, they **were closed**
Fut.	if I, he, she, it,	if I, he, she, it,
	we, you, they **should close**	we, you, they **should be closed**

Transitive and intransitive.

PRINCIPAL PARTS: **clothes, clothing,
clothed/clad, clothed/clad**

be clothed/clad
(passive voice)

Infinitive: **to clothe**
Perfect Infinitive: **to have clothed**
Present Participle: **clothing**
Past Participle: **clothed**

Infinitive: **to be clothed**
Perfect Infinitive: **to have been clothed**
Present Participle: **being clothed**
Past Participle: **been clothed**

INDICATIVE MOOD

Pres.	I, we, you, they **clothe**	I **am clothed**
		we, you, they **are clothed**
	he, she, it **clothes**	he, she, it **is clothed**
Pres.	I **am clothing**	I **am being clothed**
Prog.	we, you, they **are clothing**	we, you, they **are being clothed**
	he, she, it **is clothing**	he, she, it **is being clothed**
Pres.	I, we, you, they **do clothe**	I, we, you, they **do get clothed**
Int.	he, she, it **does clothe**	he, she, it **does get clothed**
Fut.	I, he, she, it,	I, he, she, it,
	we, you, they **will clothe**	we, you, they **will be clothed**
Past	I, he, she, it,	I, he, she, it **was clothed**
	we, you, they **clothed**	we, you, they **were clothed**
Past	I, he, she, it **was clothing**	I, he, she, it **was being clothed**
Prog.	we, you, they **were clothing**	we, you, they **were being clothed**
Past	I, he, she, it,	I, he, she, it,
Int.	we, you, they **did clothe**	we, you, they **did get clothed**
Pres.	I, we, you, they **have clothed**	I, we, you, they **have been clothed**
Perf.	he, she, it **has clothed**	he, she, it **has been clothed**
Past	I, he, she, it,	I, he, she, it,
Perf.	we, you, they **had clothed**	we, you, they **had been clothed**
Fut.	I, he, she, it, we, you, they	I, he, she, it, we, you, they
Perf.	**will have clothed**	**will have been clothed**

IMPERATIVE MOOD

clothe

be clothed

SUBJUNCTIVE MOOD

Pres.	if I, he, she, it,	if I, he, she, it,
	we, you, they **clothe**	we, you, they **be clothed**
Past	if I, he, she, it,	if I, he, she, it,
	we, you, they **clothed**	we, you, they **were clothed**
Fut.	if I, he, she, it,	if I, he, she, it,
	we, you, they **should clothe**	we, you, they **should be clothed**

The *Oxford Dictionary* lists CLAD as the poetic or archaic past and past participle.

Infinitive: **to come**
Perfect Infinitive: **to have come**
Present Participle: **coming**
Past Participle: **come**

INDICATIVE MOOD

Pres.	I, we, you, they **come** he, she, it **comes**
Pres. *Prog.*	**I am coming** we, you, they **are coming** he, she, it **is coming**
Pres. *Int.*	I, we, you, they **do come** he, she, it **does come**
Fut.	I, he, she, it, we, you, they **will come**
Past	I, he, she, it, we, you, they **came**
Past *Prog.*	I, he, she, it **was coming** we, you, they **were coming**
Past *Int.*	I, he, she, it, we, you, they **did come**
Pres. *Perf.*	I, we, you, they **have come** he, she, it **has come**
Past *Perf.*	I, he, she, it, we, you, they **had come**
Fut. *Perf.*	I, he, she, it, we, you, they **will have come**

IMPERATIVE MOOD

come

SUBJUNCTIVE MOOD

Pres.	if I, he, she, it, we, you, they **come**
Past	if I, he, she, it, we, you, they **came**
Fut.	if I, he, she, it we, you, they **should come**

compare
(active voice)

PRINCIPAL PARTS: **compares, comparing, compared, compared**

be compared
(passive voice)

Infinitive: **to compare**
Perfect Infinitive: **to have compared**
Present Participle: **comparing**
Past Participle: **compared**

Infinitive: **to be compared**
Perfect Infinitive: **to have been compared**
Present Participle: **being compared**
Past Participle: **been compared**

INDICATIVE MOOD

Pres.	I, we, you, they **compare**	I **am compared**
		we, you, they **are compared**
	he, she, it **compares**	he, she, it **is compared**
Pres.	I **am comparing**	I **am being compared**
Prog.	we, you, they **are comparing**	we, you, they **are being compared**
	he, she, it **is comparing**	he, she, it **is being compared**
Pres.	I, we, you, they **do compare**	I, we, you, they **do get compared**
Int.	he, she, it **does compare**	he, she, it **does get compared**
Fut.	I, he, she, it,	I, he, she, it,
	we, you, they **will compare**	we, you, they **will be compared**
Past	I, he, she, it,	I, he, she, it **was compared**
	we, you, they **compared**	we, you, they **were compared**
Past	I, he, she, it **was comparing**	I, he, she, it **was being compared**
Prog.	we, you, they **were comparing**	we, you, they **were being compared**
Past	I, he, she, it,	I, he, she, it,
Int.	we, you, they **did compare**	we, you, they **did get compared**
Pres.	I, we, you, they **have compared**	I, we, you, they **have been compared**
Perf.	he, she, it **has compared**	he, she, it **has been compared**
Past	I, he, she, it,	I, he, she, it,
Perf.	we, you, they **had compared**	we, you, they **had been compared**
Fut.	I, he, she, it, we, you, they	I, he, she, it, we, you, they
Perf.	**will have compared**	**will have been compared**

IMPERATIVE MOOD

compare   **be compared**

SUBJUNCTIVE MOOD

Pres.	if I, he, she, it,	if I, he, she, it,
	we, you, they **compare**	we, you, they **be compared**
Past	if I, he, she, it,	if I, he, she, it,
	we, you, they **compared**	we, you, they **were compared**
Fut.	if I, he, she, it,	if I, he, she, it,
	we, you, they **should compare**	we, you, they **should be compared**

Transitive and intransitive.

concern
(active voice)

PRINCIPAL PARTS: **concerns, concerning, concerned, concerned**

be concerned
(passive voice)

Infinitive: **to concern**
Perfect Infinitive: **to have concerned**
Present Participle: **concerning**
Past Participle: **concerned**

Infinitive: **to be concerned**
Perfect Infinitive: **to have been concerned**
Present Participle: **being concerned**
Past Participle: **been concerned**

INDICATIVE MOOD

Pres.	I, we, you, they **concern**	I **am concerned**
		we, you, they **are concerned**
	he, she, it **concerns**	he, she, it **is concerned**
Pres.	I **am concerning**	I **am being concerned**
Prog.	we, you, they **are concerning**	we, you, they **are being concerned**
	he, she, it **is concerning**	he, she, it **is being concerned**
Pres.	I, we, you, they **do concern**	I, we, you, they **do get concerned**
Int.	he, she, it **does concern**	he, she, it **does get concerned**
Fut.	I, he, she, it,	I, he, she, it,
	we, you, they **will concern**	we, you, they **will be concerned**
Past	I, he, she, it,	I, he, she, it **was concerned**
	we, you, they **concerned**	we, you, they **were concerned**
Past	I, he, she, it **was concerning**	I, he, she, it **was being concerned**
Prog.	we, you, they **were concerning**	we, you, they **were being concerned**
Past	I, he, she, it,	I, he, she, it,
Int.	we, you, they **did concern**	we, you, they **did get concerned**
Pres.	I, we, you, they **have concerned**	I, we, you, they **have been concerned**
Perf.	he, she, it **has concerned**	he, she, it **has been concerned**
Past	I, he, she, it,	I, he, she, it,
Perf.	we, you, they **had concerned**	we, you, they **had been concerned**
Fut.	I, he, she, it, we, you, they	I, he, she, it, we, you, they
Perf.	**will have concerned**	**will have been concerned**

IMPERATIVE MOOD

concern

be concerned

SUBJUNCTIVE MOOD

Pres.	if I, he, she, it,	if I, he, she, it,
	we, you, they **concern**	we, you, they **be concerned**
Past	if I, he, she, it,	if I, he, she, it,
	we, you, they **concerned**	we, you, they **were concerned**
Fut.	if I, he, she, it,	if I, he, she, it,
	we, you, they **should concern**	we, you, they **should be concerned**

74

confuse
(active voice)

PRINCIPAL PARTS: **confuses, confusing, confused, confused**

be confused
(passive voice)

Infinitive: **to confuse**
Perfect Infinitive: **to have confused**
Present Participle: **confusing**
Past Participle: **confused**

Infinitive: **to be confused**
Perfect Infinitive: **to have been confused**
Present Participle: **being confused**
Past Participle: **been confused**

INDICATIVE MOOD

Pres.	I, we, you, they **confuse**	I **am confused**
		we, you, they **are confused**
	he, she, it **confuses**	he, she, it **is confused**
Pres.	I **am confusing**	I **am being confused**
Prog.	we, you, they **are confusing**	we, you, they **are being confused**
	he, she, it **is confusing**	he, she, it **is being confused**
Pres.	I, we, you, they **do confuse**	I, we, you, they **do get confused**
Int.	he, she, it **does confuse**	he, she, it **does get confused**
Fut.	I, he, she, it,	I, he, she, it,
	we, you, they **will confuse**	we, you, they **will be confused**
Past	I, he, she, it,	I, he, she, it **was confused**
	we, you, they **confused**	we, you, they **were confused**
Past	I, he, she, it **was confusing**	I, he, she, it **was being confused**
Prog.	we, you, they **were confusing**	we, you, they **were being confused**
Past	I, he, she, it,	I, he, she, it,
Int.	we, you, they **did confuse**	we, you, they **did get confused**
Pres.	I, we, you, they **have confused**	I, we, you, they **have been confused**
Perf.	he, she, it **has confused**	he, she, it **has been confused**
Past	I, he, she, it,	I, he, she, it,
Perf.	we, you, they **had confused**	we, you, they **had been confused**
Fut.	I, he, she, it, we, you, they	I, he, she, it, we, you, they
Perf.	**will have confused**	**will have been confused**

IMPERATIVE MOOD

confuse   **be confused**

SUBJUNCTIVE MOOD

Pres.	if I, he, she, it,	if I, he, she, it,
	we, you, they **confuse**	we, you, they **be confused**
Past	if I, he, she, it,	if I, he, she, it,
	we, you, they **confused**	we, you, they **were confused**
Fut.	if I, he, she, it,	if I, he, she, it,
	we, you, they **should confuse**	we, you, they **should be confused**

connect
(active voice)

be connected
(passive voice)

Infinitive: **to connect**
Perfect Infinitive: **to have connected**
Present Participle: **connecting**
Past Participle: **connected**

Infinitive: **to be connected**
Perfect Infinitive: **to have been connected**
Present Participle: **being connected**
Past Participle: **been connected**

INDICATIVE MOOD

Pres.	I, we, you, they **connect**	I **am connected**
		we, you, they **are connected**
	he, she, it **connects**	he, she, it **is connected**
Pres.	I **am connecting**	I **am being connected**
Prog.	we, you, they **are connecting**	we, you, they **are being connected**
	he, she, it **is connecting**	he, she, it **is being connected**
Pres.	I, we, you, they **do connect**	I, we, you, they **do get connected**
Int.	he, she, it **does connect**	he, she, it **does get connected**
Fut.	I, he, she, it,	I, he, she, it,
	we, you, they **will connect**	we, you, they **will be connected**
Past	I, he, she, it,	I, he, she, it **was connected**
	we, you, they **connected**	we, you, they **were connected**
Past	I, he, she, it **was connecting**	I, he, she, it **was being connected**
Prog.	we, you, they **were connecting**	we, you, they **were being connected**
Past	I, he, she, it,	I, he, she, it,
Int.	we, you, they **did connect**	we, you, they **did get connected**
Pres.	I, we, you, they **have connected**	I, we, you, they **have been connected**
Perf.	he, she, it **has connected**	he, she, it **has been connected**
Past	I, he, she, it,	I, he, she, it,
Perf.	we, you, they **had connected**	we, you, they **had been connected**
Fut.	I, he, she, it, we, you, they	I, he, she, it, we, you, they
Perf.	**will have connected**	**will have been connected**

IMPERATIVE MOOD

connect **be connected**

SUBJUNCTIVE MOOD

Pres.	if I, he, she, it,	if I, he, she, it,
	we, you, they **connect**	we, you, they **be connected**
Past	if I, he, she, it,	if I, he, she, it,
	we, you, they **connected**	we, you, they **were connected**
Fut.	if I, he, she, it,	if I, he, she, it,
	we, you, they **should connect**	we, you, they **should be connected**

Transitive and intransitive.

consider
(active voice)

be considered
(passive voice)

Infinitive: **to consider**
Perfect Infinitive: **to have considered**
Present Participle: **considering**
Past Participle: **considered**

Infinitive: **to be considered**
Perfect Infinitive: **to have been considered**
Present Participle: **being considered**
Past Participle: **been considered**

INDICATIVE MOOD

Pres.	I, we, you, they **consider**	I **am considered**
		we, you, they **are considered**
	he, she, it **considers**	he, she, it **is considered**
Pres.	I **am considering**	I **am being considered**
Prog.	we, you, they **are considering**	we, you, they **are being considered**
	he, she, it **is considering**	he, she, it **is being considered**
Pres.	I, we, you, they **do consider**	I, we, you, they **do get considered**
Int.	he, she, it **does consider**	he, she, it **does get considered**
Fut.	I, he, she, it,	I, he, she, it,
	we, you, they **will consider**	we, you, they **will be considered**
Past	I, he, she, it,	I, he, she, it **was considered**
	we, you, they **considered**	we, you, they **were considered**
Past	I, he, she, it **was considering**	I, he, she, it **was being considered**
Prog.	we, you, they **were considering**	we, you, they **were being considered**
Past	I, he, she, it,	I, he, she, it,
Int.	we, you, they **did consider**	we, you, they **did get considered**
Pres.	I, we, you, they **have considered**	I, we, you, they **have been considered**
Perf.	he, she, it **has considered**	he, she, it **has been considered**
Past	I, he, she, it,	I, he, she, it,
Perf.	we, you, they **had considered**	we, you, they **had been considered**
Fut.	I, he, she, it, we, you, they	I, he, she, it, we, you, they
Perf.	**will have considered**	**will have been considered**

IMPERATIVE MOOD

consider **be considered**

SUBJUNCTIVE MOOD

Pres.	if I, he, she, it,	if I, he, she, it,
	we, you, they **consider**	we, you, they **be considered**
Past	if I, he, she, it,	if I, he, she, it,
	we, you, they **considered**	we, you, they **were considered**
Fut.	if I, he, she, it,	if I, he, she, it,
	we, you, they **should consider**	we, you, they **should be considered**

Transitive and intransitive.

contain
(active voice)

be contained
(passive voice)

Infinitive: **to contain**
Perfect Infinitive: **to have contained**
Present Participle: **containing**
Past Participle: **contained**

Infinitive: **to be contained**
Perfect Infinitive: **to have been contained**
Present Participle: **being contained**
Past Participle: **been contained**

INDICATIVE MOOD

Pres.	I, we, you, they **contain** he, she, it **contains**	I **am contained** we, you, they **are contained** he, she, it **is contained**
Pres. *Prog.*	I **am containing** we, you, they **are containing** he, she, it **is containing**	I **am being contained** we, you, they **are being contained** he, she, it **is being contained**
Pres. *Int.*	I, we, you, they **do contain** he, she, it **does contain**	I, we, you, they **do get contained** he, she, it **does get contained**
Fut.	I, he, she, it, we, you, they **will contain**	I, he, she, it, we, you, they **will be contained**
Past	I, he, she, it, we, you, they **contained**	I, he, she, it **was contained** we, you, they **were contained**
Past *Prog.*	I, he, she, it **was containing** we, you, they **were containing**	I, he, she, it **was being contained** we, you, they **were being contained**
Past *Int.*	I, he, she, it, we, you, they **did contain**	I, he, she, it, we, you, they **did get contained**
Pres. *Perf.*	I, we, you, they **have contained** he, she, it **has contained**	I, we, you, they **have been contained** he, she, it **has been contained**
Past *Perf.*	I, he, she, it, we, you, they **had contained**	I, he, she, it, we, you, they **had been contained**
Fut. *Perf.*	I, he, she, it, we, you, they **will have contained**	I, he, she, it, we, you, they **will have been contained**

IMPERATIVE MOOD

contain　　　　　　　　　　**be contained**

SUBJUNCTIVE MOOD

Pres.	if I, he, she, it, we, you, they **contain**	if I, he, she, it, we, you, they **be contained**
Past	if I, he, she, it, we, you, they **contained**	if I, he, she, it, we, you, they **were contained**
Fut.	if I, he, she, it, we, you, they **should contain**	if I, he, she, it, we, you, they **should be contained**

Transitive and intransitive.

continue
(active voice)

PRINCIPAL PARTS: **continues, continuing,
continued, continued**

be continued
(passive voice)

Infinitive: **to continue**
Perfect Infinitive: **to have continued**
Present Participle: **continuing**
Past Participle: **continued**

Infinitive: **to be continued**
Perfect Infinitive: **to have been continued**
Present Participle: **being continued**
Past Participle: **been continued**

INDICATIVE MOOD

Pres.	I, we, you, they **continue**	I **am continued**
		we, you, they **are continued**
	he, she, it **continues**	he, she, it **is continued**
Pres.	I **am continuing**	I **am being continued**
Prog.	we, you, they **are continuing**	we, you, they **are being continued**
	he, she, it **is continuing**	he, she, it **is being continued**
Pres.	I, we, you, they **do continue**	I, we, you, they **do get continued**
Int.	he, she, it **does continue**	he, she, it **does get continued**
Fut.	I, he, she, it,	I, he, she, it,
	we, you, they **will continue**	we, you, they **will be continued**
Past	I, he, she, it,	I, he, she, it **was continued**
	we, you, they **continued**	we, you, they **were continued**
Past	I, he, she, it **was continuing**	I, he, she, it **was being continued**
Prog.	we, you, they **were continuing**	we, you, they **were being continued**
Past	I, he, she, it,	I, he, she, it,
Int.	we, you, they **did continue**	we, you, they **did get continued**
Pres.	I, we, you, they **have continued**	I, we, you, they **have been continued**
Perf.	he, she, it **has continued**	he, she, it **has been continued**
Past	I, he, she, it,	I, he, she, it,
Perf.	we, you, they **had continued**	we, you, they **had been continued**
Fut.	I, he, she, it, we, you, they	I, he, she, it, we, you, they
Perf.	**will have continued**	**will have been continued**

IMPERATIVE MOOD

continue   **be continued**

SUBJUNCTIVE MOOD

Pres.	if I, he, she, it,	if I, he, she, it,
	we, you, they **continue**	we, you, they **be continued**
Past	if I, he, she, it,	if I, he, she, it,
	we, you, they **continued**	we, you, they **were continued**
Fut.	if I, he, she, it,	if I, he, she, it,
	we, you, they **should continue**	we, you, they **should be continued**

Intransitive and transitive.

cost
(active voice)

be cost
(passive voice)

Infinitive: **to cost**
Perfect Infinitive: **to have cost**
Present Participle: **costing**
Past Participle: **cost**

Infinitive: **to be cost**
Perfect Infinitive: **to have been cost**
Present Participle: **being cost**
Past Participle: **been cost**

INDICATIVE MOOD

Pres.	I, we, you, they **cost** he, she, it **costs**	I **am cost** we, you, they **are cost** he, she, it **is cost**
Pres. *Prog.*	I am **costing** we, you, they **are costing** he, she, it **is costing**	I am **being cost** we, you, they **are being cost** he, she, it **is being cost**
Pres. *Int.*	I, we, you, they **do cost** he, she, it **does cost**	I, we, you, they **do get cost** he, she, it **does get cost**
Fut.	I, he, she, it, we, you, they **will cost**	I, he, she, it, we, you, they **will be cost**
Past	I, he, she, it, we, you, they **cost**	I, he, she, it **was cost** we, you, they **were cost**
Past *Prog.*	I, he, she, it **was costing** we, you, they **were costing**	I, he, she, it **was being cost** we, you, they **were being cost**
Past *Int.*	I, he, she, it, we, you, they **did cost**	I, he, she, it, we, you, they **did get cost**
Pres. *Perf.*	I, we, you, they **have cost** he, she, it **has cost**	I, we, you, they **have been cost** he, she, it **has been cost**
Past *Perf.*	I, he, she, it, we, you, they **had cost**	I, he, she, it, we, you, they **had been cost**
Fut. *Perf.*	I, he, she, it, we, you, they **will have cost**	I, he, she, it, we, you, they **will have been cost**

IMPERATIVE MOOD

cost

be cost

SUBJUNCTIVE MOOD

Pres.	if I, he, she, it, we, you, they **cost**	if I, he, she, it, we, you, they **be cost**
Past	if I, he, she, it, we, you, they **cost**	if I, he, she, it, we, you, they **were cost**
Fut.	if I, he, she, it, we, you, they **should cost**	if I, he, she, it, we, you, they **should be cost**

Intransitive and transitive. The forms COSTED, especially with the preposition OUT for the past tense and past participle, are used when referring to "estimating or determining the price of something."

cover
(active voice)

PRINCIPAL PARTS: **covers, covering, covered, covered**

be covered
(passive voice)

Infinitive: **to cover**
Perfect Infinitive: **to have covered**
Present Participle: **covering**
Past Participle: **covered**

Infinitive: **to be covered**
Perfect Infinitive: **to have been covered**
Present Participle: **being covered**
Past Participle: **been covered**

INDICATIVE MOOD

Pres.	I, we, you, they **cover**	I **am covered**
		we, you, they **are covered**
	he, she, it **covers**	he, she, it **is covered**
Pres. _Prog._	I **am covering**	I **am being covered**
	we, you, they **are covering**	we, you, they **are being covered**
	he, she, it **is covering**	he, she, it **is being covered**
Pres. _Int._	I, we, you, they **do cover**	I, we, you, they **do get covered**
	he, she, it **does cover**	he, she, it **does get covered**
Fut.	I, he, she, it, we, you, they **will cover**	I, he, she, it, we, you, they **will be covered**
Past	I, he, she, it, we, you, they **covered**	I, he, she, it **was covered** we, you, they **were covered**
Past _Prog._	I, he, she, it **was covering** we, you, they **were covering**	I, he, she, it **was being covered** we, you, they **were being covered**
Past _Int._	I, he, she, it, we, you, they **did cover**	I, he, she, it, we, you, they **did get covered**
Pres. _Perf._	I, we, you, they **have covered** he, she, it **has covered**	I, we, you, they **have been covered** he, she, it **has been covered**
Past _Perf._	I, he, she, it, we, you, they **had covered**	I, he, she, it, we, you, they **had been covered**
Fut. _Perf._	I, he, she, it, we, you, they **will have covered**	I, he, she, it, we, you, they **will have been covered**

IMPERATIVE MOOD

cover

be covered

SUBJUNCTIVE MOOD

Pres.	if I, he, she, it, we, you, they **cover**	if I, he, she, it, we, you, they **be covered**
Past	if I, he, she, it, we, you, they **covered**	if I, he, she, it, we, you, they **were covered**
Fut.	if I, he, she, it, we, you, they **should cover**	if I, he, she, it, we, you, they **should be covered**

Transitive and intransitive.

create
(active voice)

be created
(passive voice)

Infinitive: **to create**
Perfect Infinitive: **to have created**
Present Participle: **creating**
Past Participle: **created**

Infinitive: **to be created**
Perfect Infinitive: **to have been created**
Present Participle: **being created**
Past Participle: **been created**

INDICATIVE MOOD

Pres.	I, we, you, they **create**	I **am created**
		we, you, they **are created**
	he, she, it **creates**	he, she, it **is created**
Pres.	I **am creating**	I **am being created**
Prog.	we, you, they **are creating**	we, you, they **are being created**
	he, she, it **is creating**	he, she, it **is being created**
Pres.	I, we, you, they **do create**	I, we, you, they **do get created**
Int.	he, she, it **does create**	he, she, it **does get created**
Fut.	I, he, she, it,	I, he, she, it,
	we, you, they **will create**	we, you, they **will be created**
Past	I, he, she, it,	I, he, she, it **was created**
	we, you, they **created**	we, you, they **were created**
Past	I, he, she, it **was creating**	I, he, she, it **was being created**
Prog.	we, you, they **were creating**	we, you, they **were being created**
Past	I, he, she, it,	I, he, she, it,
Int.	we, you, they **did create**	we, you, they **did get created**
Pres.	I, we, you, they **have created**	I, we, you, they **have been created**
Perf.	he, she, it **has created**	he, she, it **has been created**
Past	I, he, she, it,	I, he, she, it,
Perf.	we, you, they **had created**	we, you, they **had been created**
Fut.	I, he, she, it, we, you, they	I, he, she, it, we, you, they
Perf.	**will have created**	**will have been created**

IMPERATIVE MOOD

create   **be created**

SUBJUNCTIVE MOOD

Pres.	if I, he, she, it,	if I, he, she, it,
	we, you, they **create**	we, you, they **be created**
Past	if I, he, she, it,	if I, he, she, it,
	we, you, they **created**	we, you, they **were created**
Fut.	if I, he, she, it,	if I, he, she, it,
	we, you, they **should create**	we, you, they **should be created**

Transitive and intransitive.

creep PRINCIPAL PARTS: **creeps, creeping, crept, crept**

Infinitive: **to creep**
Perfect Infinitive: **to have crept**
Present Participle: **creeping**
Past Participle: **crept**

INDICATIVE MOOD

Pres. I, we, you, they **creep**

he, she, it **creeps**

Pres. I **am creeping**
Prog. we, you, they **are creeping**
he, she, it **is creeping**

Pres. I, we, you, they **do creep**
Int. he, she, it **does creep**

Fut. I, he, she, it,
we, you, they **will creep**

Past I, he, she, it,
we, you, they **crept**

Past I, he, she, it **was creeping**
Prog. we, you, they **were creeping**

Past I, he, she, it,
Int. we, you, they **did creep**

Pres. I, we, you, they **have crept**
Perf. he, she, it **has crept**

Past I, he, she, it,
Perf. we, you, they **had crept**

Fut. I, he, she, it, we, you, they
Perf. **will have crept**

IMPERATIVE MOOD

creep

SUBJUNCTIVE MOOD

Pres. if I, he, she, it,
we, you, they **creep**

Past if I, he, she, it,
we, you, they **crept**

Fut. if I, he, she, it,
we, you, they **should creep**

---

cry
(active voice)

be cried
(passive voice)

Infinitive: **to cry**
Perfect Infinitive: **to have cried**
Present Participle: **crying**
Past Participle: **cried**

Infinitive: **to be cried**
Perfect Infinitive: **to have been cried**
Present Participle: **being cried**
Past Participle: **been cried**

INDICATIVE MOOD

Pres.	I, we, you, they **cry** he, she, it **cries**	I **am cried** we, you, they **are cried** he, she, it **is cried**	
Pres. *Prog.*	I am **crying** we, you, they **are crying** he, she, it **is crying**	I **am being cried** we, you, they **are being cried** he, she, it **is being cried**	
Pres. *Int.*	I, we, you, they **do cry** he, she, it **does cry**	I, we, you, they **do get cried** he, she, it **does get cried**	
Fut.	I, he, she, it, we, you, they **will cry**	I, he, she, it, we, you, they **will be cried**	
Past	I, he, she, it, we, you, they **cried**	I, he, she, it **was cried** we, you, they **were cried**	
Past *Prog.*	I, he, she, it **was crying** we, you, they **were crying**	I, he, she, it **was being cried** we, you, they **were being cried**	
Past *Int.*	I, he, she, it, we, you, they **did cry**	I, he, she, it, we, you, they **did get cried**	
Pres. *Perf.*	I, we, you, they **have cried** he, she, it **has cried**	I, we, you, they **have been cried** he, she, it **has been cried**	
Past *Perf.*	I, he, she, it, we, you, they **had cried**	I, he, she, it, we, you, they **had been cried**	
Fut. *Perf.*	I, he, she, it, we, you, they **will have cried**	I, he, she, it, we, you, they **will have been cried**	

IMPERATIVE MOOD

cry   **be cried**

SUBJUNCTIVE MOOD

Pres.	if I, he, she, it, we, you, they **cry**	if I, he, she, it, we, you, they **be cried**
Past	if I, he, she, it, we, you, they **cried**	if I, he, she, it, we, you, they **were cried**
Fut.	if I, he, she, it, we, you, they **should cry**	if I, he, she, it, we, you, they **should be cried**

Intransitive and transitive.

cut
(active voice)

PRINCIPAL PARTS: **cuts, cutting, cut, cut**

be cut
(passive voice)

Infinitive: **to cut**
Perfect Infinitive: **to have cut**
Present Participle: **cutting**
Past Participle: **cut**

Infinitive: **to be cut**
Perfect Infinitive: **to have been cut**
Present Participle: **being cut**
Past Participle: **been cut**

INDICATIVE MOOD

Pres.	I, we, you, they **cut**	I **am cut**
		we, you, they **are cut**
	he, she, it **cuts**	he, she, it **is cut**
Pres. *Prog.*	I **am cutting**	I **am being cut**
	we, you, they **are cutting**	we, you, they **are being cut**
	he, she, it **is cutting**	he, she, it **is being cut**
Pres. *Int.*	I, we, you, they **do cut**	I, we, you, they **do get cut**
	he, she, it **does cut**	he, she, it **does get cut**
Fut.	I, he, she, it, we, you, they **will cut**	I, he, she, it, we, you, they **will be cut**
Past	I, he, she, it, we, you, they **cut**	I, he, she, it **was cut** we, you, they **were cut**
Past *Prog.*	I, he, she, it **was cutting** we, you, they **were cutting**	I, he, she, it **was being cut** we, you, they **were being cut**
Past *Int.*	I, he, she, it, we, you, they **did cut**	I, he, she, it, we, you, they **did get cut**
Pres. *Perf.*	I, we, you, they **have cut** he, she, it **has cut**	I, we, you, they **have been cut** he, she, it **has been cut**
Past *Perf.*	I, he, she, it, we, you, they **had cut**	I, he, she, it, we, you, they **had been cut**
Fut. *Perf.*	I, he, she, it, we, you, they **will have cut**	I, he, she, it, we, you, they **will have been cut**

IMPERATIVE MOOD

cut

be cut

SUBJUNCTIVE MOOD

Pres.	if I, he, she, it, we, you, they **cut**	if I, he, she, it, we, you, they **be cut**
Past	if I, he, she, it, we, you, they **cut**	if I, he, she, it, we, you, they **were cut**
Fut.	if I, he, she, it, we, you, they **should cut**	if I, he, she, it, we, you, they **should be cut**

Transitive and intransitive.

dare
(active voice)

PRINCIPAL PARTS: **dares/dare, daring, dared, dared**

be dared
(passive voice)

Infinitive: **to dare**
Perfect Infinitive: **to have dared**
Present Participle: **daring**
Past Participle: **dared**

Infinitive: **to be dared**
Perfect Infinitive: **to have been dared**
Present Participle: **being dared**
Past Participle: **been dared**

INDICATIVE MOOD

Pres.	I, we, you, they **dare**	I **am dared**
		we, you, they **are dared**
	he, she, it **dares/dare**	he, she, it **is dared**
Pres.	I **am daring**	I **am being dared**
Prog.	we, you, they **are daring**	we, you, they **are being dared**
	he, she, it **is daring**	he, she, it **is being dared**
Pres.	I, we, you, they **do dare**	I, we, you, they **do get dared**
Int.	he, she, it **does dare**	he, she, it **does get dared**
Fut.	I, he, she, it,	I, he, she, it,
	we, you, they **will dare**	we, you, they **will be dared**
Past	I, he, she, it,	I, he, she, it **was dared**
	we, you, they **dared**	we, you, they **were dared**
Past	I, he, she, it **was daring**	I, he, she, it **was being dared**
Prog.	we, you, they **were daring**	we, you, they **were being dared**
Past	I, he, she, it,	I, he, she, it,
Int.	we, you, they **did dare**	we, you, they **did get dared**
Pres.	I, we, you, they **have dared**	I, we, you, they **have been dared**
Perf.	he, she, it **has dared**	he, she, it **has been dared**
Past	I, he, she, it,	I, he, she, it,
Perf.	we, you, they **had dared**	we, you, they **had been dared**
Fut.	I, he, she, it, we, you, they	I, he, she, it, we, you, they
Perf.	**will have dared**	**will have been dared**

IMPERATIVE MOOD

dare   **be dared**

SUBJUNCTIVE MOOD

Pres.	if I, he, she, it,	if I, he, she, it,
	we, you, they **dare**	we, you, they **be dared**
Past	if I, he, she, it,	if I, he, she, it,
	we, you, they **dared**	we, you, they **were dared**
Fut.	if I, he, she, it,	if I, he, she, it,
	we, you, they **should dare**	we, you, they **should be dared**

Intransitive and transitive. DARE can behave like an auxiliary verb (may, can) and then has the third person singular form DARE: "How dare he?" In this usage it does not need "do" in questions. There is also no "to" after this verb and before another: "Don't you dare break your promise."

86

deal
(active voice)

be dealt
(passive voice)

Infinitive: **to deal**
Perfect Infinitive: **to have dealt**
Present Participle: **dealing**
Past Participle: **dealt**

Infinitive: **to be dealt**
Perfect Infinitive: **to have been dealt**
Present Participle: **being dealt**
Past Participle: **been dealt**

INDICATIVE MOOD

Pres.	I, we, you, they **deal**	I **am dealt**
		we, you, they **are dealt**
	he, she, it **deals**	he, she, it **is dealt**
Pres. Prog.	I **am dealing**	I **am being dealt**
	we, you, they **are dealing**	we, you, they **are being dealt**
	he, she, it **is dealing**	he, she, it **is being dealt**
Pres. Int.	I, we, you, they **do deal**	I, we, you, they **do get dealt**
	he, she, it **does deal**	he, she, it **does get dealt**
Fut.	I, he, she, it, we, you, they **will deal**	I, he, she, it, we, you, they **will be dealt**
Past	I, he, she, it, we, you, they **dealt**	I, he, she, it **was dealt**
		we, you, they **were dealt**
Past Prog.	I, he, she, it **was dealing**	I, he, she, it **was being dealt**
	we, you, they **were dealing**	we, you, they **were being dealt**
Past Int.	I, he, she, it, we, you, they **did deal**	I, he, she, it, we, you, they **did get dealt**
Pres. Perf.	I, we, you, they **have dealt**	I, we, you, they **have been dealt**
	he, she, it **has dealt**	he, she, it **has been dealt**
Past Perf.	I, he, she, it, we, you, they **had dealt**	I, he, she, it, we, you, they **had been dealt**
Fut. Perf.	I, he, she, it, we, you, they **will have dealt**	I, he, she, it, we, you, they **will have been dealt**

IMPERATIVE MOOD

deal **be dealt**

SUBJUNCTIVE MOOD

Pres.	if I, he, she, it, we, you, they **deal**	if I, he, she, it, we, you, they **be dealt**
Past	if I, he, she, it, we, you, they **dealt**	if I, he, she, it, we, you, they **were dealt**
Fut.	if I, he, she, it, we, you, they **should deal**	if I, he, she, it, we, you, they **should be dealt**

Transitive and intransitive.

decide
(active voice)

be decided
(passive voice)

Infinitive: **to decide**
Perfect Infinitive: **to have decided**
Present Participle: **deciding**
Past Participle: **decided**

Infinitive: **to be decided**
Perfect Infinitive: **to have been decided**
Present Participle: **being decided**
Past Participle: **been decided**

INDICATIVE MOOD

Pres.	I, we, you, they **decide**	I **am decided** we, you, they **are decided**
	he, she, it **decides**	he, she, it **is decided**
Pres. *Prog.*	I **am deciding** we, you, they **are deciding** he, she, it **is deciding**	I **am being decided** we, you, they **are being decided** he, she, it **is being decided**
Pres. *Int.*	I, we, you, they **do decide** he, she, it **does decide**	I, we, you, they **do get decided** he, she, it **does get decided**
Fut.	I, he, she, it, we, you, they **will decide**	I, he, she, it, we, you, they **will be decided**
Past	I, he, she, it, we, you, they **decided**	I, he, she, it **was decided** we, you, they **were decided**
Past *Prog.*	I, he, she, it **was deciding** we, you, they **were deciding**	I, he, she, it **was being decided** we, you, they **were being decided**
Past *Int.*	I, he, she, it, we, you, they **did decide**	I, he, she, it, we, you, they **did get decided**
Pres. *Perf.*	I, we, you, they **have decided** he, she, it **has decided**	I, we, you, they **have been decided** he, she, it **has been decided**
Past *Perf.*	I, he, she, it, we, you, they **had decided**	I, he, she, it, we, you, they **had been decided**
Fut. *Perf.*	I, he, she, it, we, you, they **will have decided**	I, he, she, it, we, you, they **will have been decided**

IMPERATIVE MOOD

decide   **be decided**

SUBJUNCTIVE MOOD

Pres.	if I, he, she, it, we, you, they **decide**	if I, he, she, it, we, you, they **be decided**
Past	if I, he, she, it, we, you, they **decided**	if I, he, she, it, we, you, they **were decided**
Fut.	if I, he, she, it, we, you, they **should decide**	if I, he, she, it, we, you, they **should be decided**

Transitive and intransitive.

88

deep-freeze
(active voice)

be deep-frozen
(passive voice)

Infinitive: **to deep-freeze**
Perfect Infinitive: **to have deep-frozen**
Present Participle: **deep-freezing**
Past Participle: **deep-frozen**

Infinitive: **to be deep-frozen**
Perfect Infinitive: **to have been deep-frozen**
Present Participle: **being deep-frozen**
Past Participle: **been deep-frozen**

INDICATIVE MOOD

Pres.	I, we, you, they **deep-freeze**	I am deep-frozen
		we, you, they **are deep-frozen**
	he, she, it **deep-freezes**	he, she, it **is deep-frozen**
Pres.	I **am deep-freezing**	I **am being deep-frozen**
Prog.	we, you, they **are deep-freezing**	we, you, they **are being deep-frozen**
	he, she, it **is deep-freezing**	he, she, it **is being deep-frozen**
Pres.	I, we, you, they **do deep-freeze**	I, we, you, they **do get deep-frozen**
Int.	he, she, it **does deep-freeze**	he, she, it **does get deep-frozen**
Fut.	I, he, she, it, we, you, they **will deep-freeze**	I, he, she, it, we, you, they **will be deep-frozen**
Past	I, he, she, it, we, you, they **deep-froze**	I, he, she, it **was deep-frozen** we, you, they **were deep-frozen**
Past	I, he, she, it **was deep-freezing**	I, he, she, it **was being deep-frozen**
Prog.	we, you, they **were deep-freezing**	we, you, they **were being deep-frozen**
Past	I, he, she, it,	I, he, she, it,
Int.	we, you, they **did deep-freeze**	we, you, they **did get deep-frozen**
Pres.	I, we, you, they **have deep-frozen**	I, we, you, they **have been deep-frozen**
Perf.	he, she, it **has deep-frozen**	he, she, it **has been deep-frozen**
Past	I, he, she, it,	I, he, she, it,
Perf.	we, you, they **had deep-frozen**	we, you, they **had been deep-frozen**
Fut.	I, he, she, it, we, you, they	I, he, she, it, we, you, they
Perf.	**will have deep-frozen**	**will have been deep-frozen**

IMPERATIVE MOOD

deep-freeze   **be deep-frozen**

SUBJUNCTIVE MOOD

Pres.	if I, he, she, it, we, you, they **deep-freeze**	if I, he, she, it, we, you, they **be deep-frozen**
Past	if I, he, she, it, we, you, they **deep-froze**	if I, he, she, it, we, you, they **were deep-frozen**
Fut.	if I, he, she, it, we, you, they **should deep-freeze**	if I, he, she, it, we, you, they **should be deep-frozen**

describe
(active voice)

PRINCIPAL PARTS: **describes, describing, described, described**

be described
(passive voice)

Infinitive: **to describe**
Perfect Infinitive: **to have described**
Present Participle: **describing**
Past Participle: **described**

Infinitive: **to be described**
Perfect Infinitive: **to have been described**
Present Participle: **being described**
Past Participle: **been described**

INDICATIVE MOOD

Pres.	I, we, you, they **describe**	I **am described**
		we, you, they **are described**
	he, she, it **describes**	he, she, it **is described**
Pres.	I **am describing**	I **am being described**
Prog.	we, you, they **are describing**	we, you, they **are being described**
	he, she, it **is describing**	he, she, it **is being described**
Pres.	I, we, you, they **do describe**	I, we, you, they **do get described**
Int.	he, she, it **does describe**	he, she, it **does get described**
Fut.	I, he, she, it,	I, he, she, it,
	we, you, they **will describe**	we, you, they **will be described**
Past	I, he, she, it,	I, he, she, it **was described**
	we, you, they **described**	we, you, they **were described**
Past	I, he, she, it **was describing**	I, he, she, it **was being described**
Prog.	we, you, they **were describing**	we, you, they **were being described**
Past	I, he, she, it,	I, he, she, it,
Int.	we, you, they **did describe**	we, you, they **did get described**
Pres.	I, we, you, they **have described**	I, we, you, they **have been described**
Perf.	he, she, it **has described**	he, she, it **has been described**
Past	I, he, she, it,	I, he, she, it,
Perf.	we, you, they **had described**	we, you, they **had been described**
Fut.	I, he, she, it, we, you, they	I, he, she, it, we, you, they
Perf.	**will have described**	**will have been described**

IMPERATIVE MOOD

describe

be described

SUBJUNCTIVE MOOD

Pres.	if I, he, she, it,	if I, he, she, it,
	we, you, they **describe**	we, you, they **be described**
Past	if I, he, she, it,	if I, he, she, it,
	we, you, they **described**	we, you, they **were described**
Fut.	if I, he, she, it,	if I, he, she, it,
	we, you, they **should describe**	we, you, they **should be described**

design
(active voice)

be designed
(passive voice)

Infinitive: **to design**
Perfect Infinitive: **to have designed**
Present Participle: **designing**
Past Participle: **designed**

Infinitive: **to be designed**
Perfect Infinitive: **to have been designed**
Present Participle: **being designed**
Past Participle: **been designed**

INDICATIVE MOOD

Pres.	I, we, you, they **design** he, she, it **designs**	I **am designed** we, you, they **are designed** he, she, it **is designed**	
Pres. *Prog.*	I **am designing** we, you, they **are designing** he, she, it **is designing**	I **am being designed** we, you, they **are being designed** he, she, it **is being designed**	
Pres. *Int.*	I, we, you, they **do design** he, she, it **does design**	I, we, you, they **do get designed** he, she, it **does get designed**	
Fut.	I, he, she, it, we, you, they **will design**	I, he, she, it, we, you, they **will be designed**	
Past	I, he, she, it, we, you, they **designed**	I, he, she, it **was designed** we, you, they **were designed**	
Past *Prog.*	I, he, she, it **was designing** we, you, they **were designing**	I, he, she, it **was being designed** we, you, they **were being designed**	
Past *Int.*	I, he, she, it, we, you, they **did design**	I, he, she, it, we, you, they **did get designed**	
Pres. *Perf.*	I, we, you, they **have designed** he, she, it **has designed**	I, we, you, they **have been designed** he, she, it **has been designed**	
Past *Perf.*	I, he, she, it, we, you, they **had designed**	I, he, she, it, we, you, they **had been designed**	
Fut. *Perf.*	I, he, she, it, we, you, they **will have designed**	I, he, she, it, we, you, they **will have been designed**	

IMPERATIVE MOOD

design be designed

SUBJUNCTIVE MOOD

Pres.	if I, he, she, it, we, you, they **design**	if I, he, she, it, we, you, they **be designed**
Past	if I, he, she, it, we, you, they **designed**	if I, he, she, it, we, you, they **were designed**
Fut.	if I, he, she, it, we, you, they **should design**	if I, he, she, it, we, you, they **should be designed**

Transitive and intransitive.

determine
(active voice)

be determined
(passive voice)

Infinitive: **to determine**
Perfect Infinitive: **to have determined**
Present Participle: **determining**
Past Participle: **determined**

Infinitive: **to be determined**
Perfect Infinitive: **to have been determined**
Present Participle: **being determined**
Past Participle: **been determined**

INDICATIVE MOOD

Pres.	I, we, you, they **determine**	I **am determined**
		we, you, they **are determined**
	he, she, it **determines**	he, she, it **is determined**
Pres.	I **am determining**	I **am being determined**
Prog.	we, you, they **are determining**	we, you, they **are being determined**
	he, she, it **is determining**	he, she, it **is being determined**
Pres.	I, we, you, they **do determine**	I, we, you, they **do get determined**
Int.	he, she, it **does determine**	he, she, it **does get determined**
Fut.	I, he, she, it, we, you, they **will determine**	I, he, she, it, we, you, they **will be determined**
Past	I, he, she, it, we, you, they **determined**	I, he, she, it **was determined** we, you, they **were determined**
Past *Prog.*	I, he, she, it **was determining** we, you, they **were determining**	I, he, she, it **was being determined** we, you, they **were being determined**
Past *Int.*	I, he, she, it, we, you, they **did determine**	I, he, she, it, we, you, they **did get determined**
Pres. *Perf.*	I, we, you, they **have determined** he, she, it **has determined**	I, we, you, they **have been determined** he, she, it **has been determined**
Past *Perf.*	I, he, she, it, we, you, they **had determined**	I, he, she, it, we, you, they **had been determined**
Fut. *Perf.*	I, he, she, it, we, you, they **will have determined**	I, he, she, it, we, you, they **will have been determined**

IMPERATIVE MOOD

determine   **be determined**

SUBJUNCTIVE MOOD

Pres.	if I, he, she, it, we, you, they **determine**	if I, he, she, it, we, you, they **be determined**
Past	if I, he, she, it, we, you, they **determined**	if I, he, she, it, we, you, they **were determined**
Fut.	if I, he, she, it, we, you, they **should determine**	if I, he, she, it, we, you, they **should be determined**

Transitive and intransitive.

develop
(active voice)

be developed
(passive voice)

Infinitive: **to develop**
Perfect Infinitive: **to have developed**
Present Participle: **developing**
Past Participle: **developed**

Infinitive: **to be developed**
Perfect Infinitive: **to have been developed**
Present Participle: **being developed**
Past Participle: **been developed**

INDICATIVE MOOD

Pres.	I, we, you, they **develop**	I **am developed**
		we, you, they **are developed**
	he, she, it **develops**	he, she, it **is developed**
Pres.	I **am developing**	I **am being developed**
Prog.	we, you, they **are developing**	we, you, they **are being developed**
	he, she, it **is developing**	he, she, it **is being developed**
Pres.	I, we, you, they **do develop**	I, we, you, they **do get developed**
Int.	he, she, it **does develop**	he, she, it **does get developed**
Fut.	I, he, she, it,	I, he, she, it,
	we, you, they **will develop**	we, you, they **will be developed**
Past	I, he, she, it,	I, he, she, it **was developed**
	we, you, they **developed**	we, you, they **were developed**
Past	I, he, she, it **was developing**	I, he, she, it **was being developed**
Prog.	we, you, they **were developing**	we, you, they **were being developed**
Past	I, he, she, it,	I, he, she, it,
Int.	we, you, they **did develop**	we, you, they **did get developed**
Pres.	I, we, you, they **have developed**	I, we, you, they **have been developed**
Perf.	he, she, it **has developed**	he, she, it **has been developed**
Past	I, he, she, it,	I, he, she, it,
Perf.	we, you, they **had developed**	we, you, they **had been developed**
Fut.	I, he, she, it, we, you, they	I, he, she, it, we, you, they
Perf.	**will have developed**	**will have been developed**

IMPERATIVE MOOD

develop　　　　　　　　　　**be developed**

SUBJUNCTIVE MOOD

Pres.	if I, he, she, it,	if I, he, she, it,
	we, you, they **develop**	we, you, they **be developed**
Past	if I, he, she, it,	if I, he, she, it,
	we, you, they **developed**	we, you, they **were developed**
Fut.	if I, he, she, it,	if I, he, she, it,
	we, you, they **should develop**	we, you, they **should be developed**

Transitive and intransitive. The *Oxford Dictionary* lists DEVELOP with no final *e*. While the spellings DEVELOPE and DEVELOPES can be found, the *Columbia Guide to Standard American English* declares that there is no *e* after the *p*.

dial
(active voice)

be dialed/dialled
(passive voice)

Infinitive: **to dial**
Perfect Infinitive: **to have dialed**
Present Participle: **dialing**
Past Participle: **dialed**

Infinitive: **to be dialed**
Perfect Infinitive: **to have been dialed**
Present Participle: **being dialed**
Past Participle: **been dialed**

INDICATIVE MOOD

Pres.	I, we, you, they **dial**	I **am dialed**
		we, you, they **are dialed**
	he, she, it **dials**	he, she, it **is dialed**
Pres.	I **am dialing**	I **am being dialed**
Prog.	we, you, they **are dialing**	we, you, they **are being dialed**
	he, she, it **is dialing**	he, she, it **is being dialed**
Pres.	I, we, you, they **do dial**	I, we, you, they **do get dialed**
Int.	he, she, it **does dial**	he, she, it **does get dialed**
Fut.	I, he, she, it, we, you, they **will dial**	I, he, she, it, we, you, they **will be dialed**
Past	I, he, she, it, we, you, they **dialed**	I, he, she, it **was dialed** we, you, they **were dialed**
Past	I, he, she, it **was dialing**	I, he, she, it **was being dialed**
Prog.	we, you, they **were dialing**	we, you, they **were being dialed**
Past	I, he, she, it,	I, he, she, it,
Int.	we, you, they **did dial**	we, you, they **did get dialed**
Pres.	I, we, you, they **have dialed**	I, we, you, they **have been dialed**
Perf.	he, she, it **has dialed**	he, she, it **has been dialed**
Past	I, he, she, it,	I, he, she, it,
Perf.	we, you, they **had dialed**	we, you, they **had been dialed**
Fut.	I, he, she, it, we, you, they	I, he, she, it, we, you, they
Perf.	**will have dialed**	**will have been dialed**

IMPERATIVE MOOD

dial   **be dialed**

SUBJUNCTIVE MOOD

Pres.	if I, he, she, it, we, you, they **dial**	if I, he, she, it, we, you, they **be dialed**
Past	if I, he, she, it, we, you, they **dialed**	if I, he, she, it, we, you, they **were dialed**
Fut.	if I, he, she, it, we, you, they **should dial**	if I, he, she, it, we, you, they **should be dialed**

Transitive and intransitive. In the present participle DIALING and DIALLING are acceptable, just as in the past tense and past participle are DIALED and DIALLED. The *Oxford Dictionary* prefers the DIALLED as British, noting DIALING-DIALED as American.

die

Infinitive: **to die**
Perfect Infinitive: **to have died**
Present Participle: **dying**
Past Participle: **died**

INDICATIVE MOOD

Pres.	I, we, you, they **die**
	he, she, it **dies**
Pres.	I **am dying**
Prog.	we, you, they **are dying**
	he, she, it **is dying**
Pres.	I, we, you, they **do die**
Int.	he, she, it **does die**
Fut.	I, he, she, it,
	we, you, they **will die**
Past	I, he, she, it,
	we, you, they **died**
Past	I, he, she, it **was dying**
Prog.	we, you, they **were dying**
Past	I, he, she, it,
Int.	we, you, they **did die**
Pres.	I, we, you, they **have died**
Perf.	he, she, it **has died**
Past	I, he, she, it,
Perf.	we, you, they **had died**
Fut.	I, he, she, it, we, you, they
Perf.	**will have died**

IMPERATIVE MOOD

die

SUBJUNCTIVE MOOD

Pres.	if I, he, she, it,
	we, you, they **die**
Past	if I, he, she, it,
	we, you, they **died**
Fut.	if I, he, she, it,
	we, you, they **should die**

DIE/DYING means to lose one's life. Another verb, DIE, DIEING, DIED, DIED, means to stamp out or mold.

die
(active voice)

be died
(passive voice)

Infinitive: **to die**
Perfect Infinitive: **to have died**
Present Participle: **dieing**
Past Participle: **died**

Infinitive: **to be died**
Perfect Infinitive: **to have been died**
Present Participle: **being died**
Past Participle: **been died**

INDICATIVE MOOD

Pres.	I, we, you, they **die**	I **am died**
		we, you, they **are died**
	he, she, it **dies**	he, she, it **is died**
Pres.	I **am dieing**	I **am being died**
Prog.	we, you, they **are dieing**	we, you, they **are being died**
	he, she, it **is dieing**	he, she, it **is being died**
Pres.	I, we, you, they **do die**	I, we, you, they **do get died**
Int.	he, she, it **does die**	he, she, it **does get died**
Fut.	I, he, she, it,	I, he, she, it,
	we, you, they **will die**	we, you, they **will be died**
Past	I, he, she, it,	I, he, she, it **was died**
	we, you, they **died**	we, you, they **were died**
Past	I, he, she, it **was dieing**	I, he, she, it **was being died**
Prog.	we, you, they **were dieing**	we, you, they **were being died**
Past	I, he, she, it,	I, he, she, it,
Int.	we, you, they **did die**	we, you, they **did get died**
Pres.	I, we, you, they **have died**	I, we, you, they **have been died**
Perf.	he, she, it **has died**	he, she, it **has been died**
Past	I, he, she, it,	I, he, she, it,
Perf.	we, you, they **had died**	we, you, they **had been died**
Fut.	I, he, she, it, we, you, they	I, he, she, it, we, you, they
Perf.	**will have died**	**will have been died**

IMPERATIVE MOOD

die

be died

SUBJUNCTIVE MOOD

Pres.	if I, he, she, it,	if I, he, she, it,
	we, you, they **die**	we, you, they **be died**
Past	if I, he, she, it,	if I, he, she, it,
	we, you, they **died**	we, you, they **were died**
Fut.	if I, he, she, it,	if I, he, she, it,
	we, you, they **should die**	we, you, they **should be died**

This verb means to "cut or form as with a die."

dig
(active voice)

PRINCIPAL PARTS: **digs, digging, dug, dug**

be dug
(passive voice)

Infinitive: **to dig**
Perfect Infinitive: **to have dug**
Present Participle: **digging**
Past Participle: **dug**

Infinitive: **to be dug**
Perfect Infinitive: **to have been dug**
Present Participle: **being dug**
Past Participle: **been dug**

INDICATIVE MOOD

Pres.	I, we, you, they **dig**	I **am dug**
		we, you, they **are dug**
	he, she, it **digs**	he, she, it **is dug**
Pres.	I **am digging**	I **am being dug**
Prog.	we, you, they **are digging**	we, you, they **are being dug**
	he, she, it **is digging**	he, she, it **is being dug**
Pres.	I, we, you, they **do dig**	I, we, you, they **do get dug**
Int.	he, she, it **does dig**	he, she, it **does get dug**
Fut.	I, he, she, it,	I, he, she, it,
	we, you, they **will dig**	we, you, they **will be dug**
Past	I, he, she, it,	I, he, she, it **was dug**
	we, you, they **dug**	we, you, they **were dug**
Past	I, he, she, it **was digging**	I, he, she, it **was being dug**
Prog.	we, you, they **were digging**	we, you, they **were being dug**
Past	I, he, she, it,	I, he, she, it,
Int.	we, you, they **did dig**	we, you, they **did get dug**
Pres.	I, we, you, they **have dug**	I, we, you, they **have been dug**
Perf.	he, she, it **has dug**	he, she, it **has been dug**
Past	I, he, she, it,	I, he, she, it,
Perf.	we, you, they **had dug**	we, you, they **had been dug**
Fut.	I, he, she, it, we, you, they	I, he, she, it, we, you, they
Perf.	**will have dug**	**will have been dug**

IMPERATIVE MOOD

dig

be dug

SUBJUNCTIVE MOOD

Pres.	if I, he, she, it,	if I, he, she, it,
	we, you, they **dig**	we, you, they **be dug**
Past	if I, he, she, it,	if I, he, she, it,
	we, you, they **dug**	we, you, they **were dug**
Fut.	if I, he, she, it,	if I, he, she, it,
	we, you, they **should dig**	we, you, they **should be dug**

Transitive and intransitive.

discover
(active voice)

PRINCIPAL PARTS: **discovers, discovering, discovered, discovered**

be discovered
(passive voice)

Infinitive: **to discover**
Perfect Infinitive: **to have discovered**
Present Participle: **discovering**
Past Participle: **discovered**

Infinitive: **to be discovered**
Perfect Infinitive: **to have been discovered**
Present Participle: **being discovered**
Past Participle: **been discovered**

INDICATIVE MOOD

Pres.	I, we, you, they **discover**	I **am discovered** we, you, they **are discovered**
	he, she, it **discovers**	he, she, it **is discovered**
Pres. *Prog.*	I **am discovering** we, you, they **are discovering** he, she, it **is discovering**	I **am being discovered** we, you, they **are being discovered** he, she, it **is being discovered**
Pres. *Int.*	I, we, you, they **do discover** he, she, it **does discover**	I, we, you, they **do get discovered** he, she, it **does get discovered**
Fut.	I, he, she, it, we, you, they **will discover**	I, he, she, it, we, you, they **will be discovered**
Past	I, he, she, it, we, you, they **discovered**	I, he, she, it **was discovered** we, you, they **were discovered**
Past *Prog.*	I, he, she, it **was discovering** we, you, they **were discovering**	I, he, she, it **was being discovered** we, you, they **were being discovered**
Past *Int.*	I, he, she, it, we, you, they **did discover**	I, he, she, it, we, you, they **did get discovered**
Pres. *Perf.*	I, we, you, they **have discovered** he, she, it **has discovered**	I, we, you, they **have been discovered** he, she, it **has been discovered**
Past *Perf.*	I, he, she, it, we, you, they **had discovered**	I, he, she, it, we, you, they **had been discovered**
Fut. *Perf.*	I, he, she, it, we, you, they **will have discovered**	I, he, she, it, we, you, they **will have been discovered**

IMPERATIVE MOOD

discover   **be discovered**

SUBJUNCTIVE MOOD

Pres.	if I, he, she, it, we, you, they **discover**	if I, he, she, it, we, you, they **be discovered**
Past	if I, he, she, it, we, you, they **discovered**	if I, he, she, it, we, you, they **were discovered**
Fut.	if I, he, she, it, we, you, they **should discover**	if I, he, she, it, we, you, they **should be discovered**

Transitive and intransitive.

98

discuss
(active voice)

PRINCIPAL PARTS: **discusses, discussing,
discussed, discussed**

be discussed
(passive voice)

Infinitive: **to discuss**
Perfect Infinitive: **to have discussed**
Present Participle: **discussing**
Past Participle: **discussed**

Infinitive: **to be discussed**
Perfect Infinitive: **to have been discussed**
Present Participle: **being discussed**
Past Participle: **been discussed**

INDICATIVE MOOD

Pres.	I, we, you, they **discuss**	I **am discussed**
		we, you, they **are discussed**
	he, she, it **discusses**	he, she, it **is discussed**
Pres.	I **am discussing**	I **am being discussed**
Prog.	we, you, they **are discussing**	we, you, they **are being discussed**
	he, she, it **is discussing**	he, she, it **is being discussed**
Pres.	I, we, you, they **do discuss**	I, we, you, they **do get discussed**
Int.	he, she, it **does discuss**	he, she, it **does get discussed**
Fut.	I, he, she, it,	I, he, she, it,
	we, you, they **will discuss**	we, you, they **will be discussed**
Past	I, he, she, it,	I, he, she, it **was discussed**
	we, you, they **discussed**	we, you, they **were discussed**
Past	I, he, she, it **was discussing**	I, he, she, it **was being discussed**
Prog.	we, you, they **were discussing**	we, you, they **were being discussed**
Past	I, he, she, it,	I, he, she, it,
Int.	we, you, they **did discuss**	we, you, they **did get discussed**
Pres.	I, we, you, they **have discussed**	I, we, you, they **have been discussed**
Perf.	he, she, it **has discussed**	he, she, it **has been discussed**
Past	I, he, she, it,	I, he, she, it,
Perf.	we, you, they **had discussed**	we, you, they **had been discussed**
Fut.	I, he, she, it, we, you, they	I, he, she, it, we, you, they
Perf.	**will have discussed**	**will have been discussed**

IMPERATIVE MOOD

discuss   **be discussed**

SUBJUNCTIVE MOOD

Pres.	if I, he, she, it,	if I, he, she, it,
	we, you, they **discuss**	we, you, they **be discussed**
Past	if I, he, she, it,	if I, he, she, it,
	we, you, they **discussed**	we, you, they **were discussed**
Fut.	if I, he, she, it,	if I, he, she, it,
	we, you, they **should discuss**	we, you, they **should be discussed**

dive
(active voice)

PRINCIPAL PARTS: **dives, diving, dived/dove, dived**

be dived
(passive voice)

Infinitive: **to dive**
Perfect Infinitive: **to have dived**
Present Participle: **dived/dove**
Past Participle: **dived**

Infinitive: **to be dived**
Perfect Infinitive: **to have been dived**
Present Participle: **being dived**
Past Participle: **been dived**

INDICATIVE MOOD

Pres.	I, we, you, they **dive**	I **am dived**
		we, you, they **are dived**
	he, she, it **dives**	he, she, it **is dived**
Pres.	I **am diving**	I **am being dived**
Prog.	we, you, they **are diving**	we, you, they **are being dived**
	he, she, it **is diving**	he, she, it **is being dived**
Pres.	I, we, you, they **do dive**	I, we, you, they **do get dived**
Int.	he, she, it **does dive**	he, she, it **does get dived**
Fut.	I, he, she, it,	I, he, she, it,
	we, you, they **will dive**	we, you, they **will be dived**
Past	I, he, she, it,	I, he, she, it **was dived**
	we, you, they **dived/dove**	we, you, they **were dived**
Past	I, he, she, it **was diving**	I, he, she, it **was being dived**
Prog.	we, you, they **were diving**	we, you, they **were being dived**
Past	I, he, she, it,	I, he, she, it,
Int.	we, you, they **did dive**	we, you, they **did get dived**
Pres.	I, we, you, they **have dived**	I, we, you, they **have been dived**
Perf.	he, she, it **has dived**	he, she, it **has been dived**
Past	I, he, she, it,	I, he, she, it,
Perf.	we, you, they **had dived**	we, you, they **had been dived**
Fut.	I, he, she, it, we, you, they	I, he, she, it, we, you, they
Perf.	**will have dived**	**will have been dived**

IMPERATIVE MOOD

dive **be dived**

SUBJUNCTIVE MOOD

Pres.	if I, he, she, it,	if I, he, she, it,
	we, you, they **dive**	we, you, they **be dived**
Past	if I, he, she, it,	if I, he, she, it,
	we, you, they **dived/dove**	we, you, they **were dived**
Fut.	if I, he, she, it,	if I, he, she, it,
	we, you, they **should dive**	we, you, they **should be dived**

This is normally an intransitive verb, but it can be transitive and thus have a passive voice when it means someone forcing something down, such as, "The pilot dived the plane." The past tense forms DIVED and DOVE are both accepted in American English.

do
(active voice)

be done
(passive voice)

Infinitive: **to do**
Perfect Infinitive: **to have done**
Present Participle: **doing**
Past Participle: **done**

Infinitive: **to be done**
Perfect Infinitive: **to have been done**
Present Participle: **being done**
Past Participle: **been done**

INDICATIVE MOOD

Pres.	I, we, you, they **do**		I **am done**
			we, you, they **are done**
	he, she, it **does**		he, she, it **is done**
Pres.	I **am doing**		I am being **done**
Prog.	we, you, they **are doing**		we, you, they **are being done**
	he, she, it **is doing**		he, she, it **is being done**
Pres.	I, we, you, they **do do**		I, we, you, they **do get done**
Int.	he, she, it **does do**		he, she, it **does get done**
Fut.	I, he, she, it,		I, he, she, it,
	we, you, they **will do**		we, you, they **will be done**
Past	I, he, she, it,		I, he, she, it **was done**
	we, you, they **did**		we, you, they **were done**
Past	I, he, she, it **was doing**		I, he, she, it **was being done**
Prog.	we, you, they **were doing**		we, you, they **were being done**
Past	I, he, she, it,		I, he, she, it,
Int.	we, you, they **did do**		we, you, they **did get done**
Pres.	I, we, you, they **have done**		I, we, you, they **have been done**
Perf.	he, she, it **has done**		he, she, it **has been done**
Past	I, he, she, it,		I, he, she, it,
Perf.	we, you, they **had done**		we, you, they **had been done**
Fut.	I, he, she, it, we, you, they		I, he, she, it, we, you, they
Perf.	**will have done**		**will have been done**

IMPERATIVE MOOD

do

be done

SUBJUNCTIVE MOOD

Pres.	if I, he, she, it,	if I, he, she, it,
	we, you, they **do**	we, you, they **be done**
Past	if I, he, she, it,	if I, he, she, it,
	we, you, they **did**	we, you, they **were done**
Fut.	if I, he, she, it,	if I, he, she, it,
	we, you, they **should do**	we, you, they **should be done**

As a transitive verb, DO means "performing, fulfilling." As an intransitive verb, it means "behaving." DO is also an auxiliary verb used to form the intensive tenses. It can be contracted in the negative forms: do not = don't, does not = doesn't, did not = didn't.

drag
(active voice)

be dragged
(passive voice)

Infinitive: **to drag**
Perfect Infinitive: **to have dragged**
Present Participle: **dragging**
Past Participle: **dragged**

Infinitive: **to be dragged**
Perfect Infinitive: **to have been dragged**
Present Participle: **being dragged**
Past Participle: **been dragged**

INDICATIVE MOOD

Pres.	I, we, you, they **drag**	I **am dragged** we, you, they **are dragged**
	he, she, it **drags**	he, she, it **is dragged**
Pres. *Prog.*	I **am dragging** we, you, they **are dragging** he, she, it **is dragging**	I **am being dragged** we, you, they **are being dragged** he, she, it **is being dragged**
Pres. *Int.*	I, we, you, they **do drag** he, she, it **does drag**	I, we, you, they **do get dragged** he, she, it **does get dragged**
Fut.	I, he, she, it, we, you, they **will drag**	I, he, she, it, we, you, they **will be dragged**
Past	I, he, she, it we, you, they **dragged**	I, he, she, it **was dragged** we, you, they **were dragged**
Past *Prog.*	I, he, she, it **was dragging** we, you, they **were dragging**	I, he, she, it **was being dragged** we, you, they **were being dragged**
Past *Int.*	I, he, she, it, we, you, they **did drag**	I, he, she, it, we, you, they **did get dragged**
Pres. *Perf.*	I, we, you, they **have dragged** he, she, it **has dragged**	I, we, you, they **have been dragged** he, she, it **has been dragged**
Past *Perf.*	I, he, she, it, we, you, they **had dragged**	I, he, she, it, we, you, they **had been dragged**
Fut. *Perf.*	I, he, she, it, we, you, they **will have dragged**	I, he, she, it, we, you, they **will have been dragged**

IMPERATIVE MOOD

drag   **be dragged**

SUBJUNCTIVE MOOD

Pres.	if I, he, she, it, we, you, they **drag**	if I, he, she, it, we, you, they **be dragged**
Past	if I, he, she, it, we, you, they **dragged**	if I, he, she, it, we, you, they **were dragged**
Fut.	if I, he, she, it, we, you, they **should drag**	if I, he, she, it, we, you, they **should be dragged**

Transitive and intransitive.

draw
(active voice)

be drawn
(passive voice)

Infinitive: **to draw**
Perfect Infinitive: **to have drawn**
Present Participle: **drawing**
Past Participle: **drawn**

Infinitive: **to be drawn**
Perfect Infinitive: **to have been drawn**
Present Participle: **being drawn**
Past Participle: **been drawn**

INDICATIVE MOOD

Pres.	I, we, you, they **draw**	I **am drawn**
		we, you, they **are drawn**
	he, she, it **draws**	he, she, it **is drawn**
Pres.	I **am drawing**	I **am being drawn**
Prog.	we, you, they **are drawing**	we, you, they **are being drawn**
	he, she, it **is drawing**	he, she, it **is being drawn**
Pres.	I, we, you, they **do draw**	I, we, you, they **do get drawn**
Int.	he, she, it **does draw**	he, she, it **does get drawn**
Fut.	I, he, she, it, we, you, they **will draw**	I, he, she, it, we, you, they **will be drawn**
Past	I, he, she, it, we, you, they **drew**	I, he, she, it **was drawn** we, you, they **were drawn**
Past	I, he, she, it **was drawing**	I, he, she, it **was being drawn**
Prog.	we, you, they **were drawing**	we, you, they **were being drawn**
Past	I, he, she, it, we, you, they **did draw**	I, he, she, it, we, you, they **did get drawn**
Int.		
Pres.	I, we, you, they **have drawn**	I, we, you, they **have been drawn**
Perf.	he, she, it **has drawn**	he, she, it **has been drawn**
Past	I, he, she, it, we, you, they **had drawn**	I, he, she, it, we, you, they **had been drawn**
Perf.		
Fut.	I, he, she, it, we, you, they	I, he, she, it, we, you, they
Perf.	**will have drawn**	**will have been drawn**

IMPERATIVE MOOD

draw   **be drawn**

SUBJUNCTIVE MOOD

Pres.	if I, he, she, it, we, you, they **draw**	if I, he, she, it, we, you, they **be drawn**
Past	if I, he, she, it, we, you, they **drew**	if I, he, she, it, we, you, they **were drawn**
Fut.	if I, he, she, it, we, you, they **should draw**	if I, he, she, it, we, you, they **should be drawn**

Transitive and intransitive.

dream
(active voice)

be dreamed/dreamt
(passive voice)

Infinitive: **to dream**
Perfect Infinitive: **to have dreamed**
Present Participle: **dreaming**
Past Participle: **dreamed**

Infinitive: **to be dreamed**
Perfect Infinitive: **to have been dreamed**
Present Participle: **being dreamed**
Past Participle: **been dreamed**

INDICATIVE MOOD

Pres.	I, we, you, they **dream**	I **am dreamed**
		we, you, they **are dreamed**
	he, she, it **dreams**	he, she, it **is dreamed**
Pres. *Prog.*	I **am dreaming** we, you, they **are dreaming** he, she, it **is dreaming**	I **am being dreamed** we, you, they **are being dreamed** he, she, it **is being dreamed**
Pres. *Int.*	I, we, you, they **do dream** he, she, it **does dream**	I, we, you, they **do get dreamed** he, she, it **does get dreamed**
Fut.	I, he, she, it, we, you, they **will dream**	I, he, she, it, we, you, they **will be dreamed**
Past	I, he, she, it, we, you, they **dreamed**	I, he, she, it **was dreamed** we, you, they **were dreamed**
Past *Prog.*	I, he, she, it **was dreaming** we, you, they **were dreaming**	I, he, she, it **was being dreamed** we, you, they **were being dreamed**
Past *Int.*	I, he, she, it, we, you, they **did dream**	I, he, she, it, we, you, they **did get dreamed**
Pres. *Perf.*	I, we, you, they **have dreamed** he, she, it **has dreamed**	I, we, you, they **have been dreamed** he, she, it **has been dreamed**
Past *Perf.*	I, he, she, it, we, you, they **had dreamed**	I, he, she, it, we, you, they **had been dreamed**
Fut. *Perf.*	I, he, she, it, we, you, they **will have dreamed**	I, he, she, it, we, you, they **will have been dreamed**

IMPERATIVE MOOD

dream	**be dreamed**

SUBJUNCTIVE MOOD

Pres.	if I, he, she, it, we, you, they **dream**	if I, he, she, it, we, you, they **be dreamed**
Past	if I, he, she, it, we, you, they **dreamed**	if I, he, she, it, we, you, they **were dreamed**
Fut.	if I, he, she, it, we, you, they **should dream**	if I, he, she, it, we, you, they **should be dreamed**

Intransitive and transitive. Both DREAMED and DREAMT are acceptable past and past participle forms. DREAMED is more popular in American English.

drink
(active voice)

be drunk
(passive voice)

Infinitive: **to drink**
Perfect Infinitive: **to have drunk**
Present Participle: **drinking**
Past Participle: **drunk**

Infinitive: **to be drunk**
Perfect Infinitive: **to have been drunk**
Present Participle: **being drunk**
Past Participle: **been drunk**

INDICATIVE MOOD

Pres.	I, we, you, they **drink**	I **am drunk**
		we, you, they **are drunk**
	he, she, it **drinks**	he, she, it **is drunk**
Pres.	I **am drinking**	I **am being drunk**
Prog.	we, you, they **are drinking**	we, you, they **are being drunk**
	he, she, it **is drinking**	he, she, it **is being drunk**
Pres.	I, we, you, they **do drink**	I, we, you, they **do get drunk**
Int.	he, she, it **does drink**	he, she, it **does get drunk**
Fut.	I, he, she, it,	I, he, she, it,
	we, you, they **will drink**	we, you, they **will be drunk**
Past	I, he, she, it,	I, he, she, it **was drunk**
	we, you, they **drank**	we, you, they **were drunk**
Past	I, he, she, it **was drinking**	I, he, she, it **was being drunk**
Prog.	we, you, they **were drinking**	we, you, they **were being drunk**
Past	I, he, she, it,	I, he, she, it,
Int.	we, you, they **did drink**	we, you, they **did get drunk**
Pres.	I, we, you, they **have drunk**	I, we, you, they **have been drunk**
Perf.	he, she, it **has drunk**	he, she, it **has been drunk**
Past	I, he, she, it,	I, he, she, it,
Perf.	we, you, they **had drunk**	we, you, they **had been drunk**
Fut.	I, he, she, it, we, you, they	I, he, she, it, we, you, they
Perf.	**will have drunk**	**will have been drunk**

IMPERATIVE MOOD

drink   **be drunk**

SUBJUNCTIVE MOOD

Pres.	if I, he, she, it,	if I, he, she, it,
	we, you, they **drink**	we, you, they **be drunk**
Past	if I, he, she, it,	if I, he, she, it,
	we, you, they **drank**	we, you, they **were drunk**
Fut.	if I, he, she, it,	if I, he, she, it,
	we, you, they **should drink**	we, you, they **should be drunk**

Transitive and intransitive. *Merriam Webster's* lists DRANK as an alternate past participle. *Webster's* characterizes that form as colloquial.

drive
(active voice)

PRINCIPAL PARTS: **drives, driving, drove, driven**

be driven
(passive voice)

Infinitive: **to drive**
Perfect Infinitive: **to have driven**
Present Participle: **driven**
Past Participle: **driven**

Infinitive: **to be driven**
Perfect Infinitive: **to have been driven**
Present Participle: **being driven**
Past Participle: **been driven**

INDICATIVE MOOD

Pres.	I, we, you, they **drive**	I **am driven**
		we, you, they **are driven**
	he, she, it **drives**	he, she, it **is driven**
Pres.	I **am driving**	I **am being driven**
Prog.	we, you, they **are driving**	we, you, they **are being driven**
	he, she, it **is driving**	he, she, it **is being driven**
Pres.	I, we, you, they **do drive**	I, we, you, they **do get driven**
Int.	he, she, it **does drive**	he, she, it **does get driven**
Fut.	I, he, she, it,	I, he, she, it,
	we, you, they **will drive**	we, you, they **will be driven**
Past	I, he, she, it,	I, he, she, it **was driven**
	we, you, they **drove**	we, you, they **were driven**
Past	I, he, she, it **was driving**	I, he, she, it **was being driven**
Prog.	we, you, they **were driving**	we, you, they **were being driven**
Past	I, he, she, it,	I, he, she, it,
Int.	we, you, they **did drive**	we, you, they **did get driven**
Pres.	I, we, you, they **have driven**	I, we, you, they **have been driven**
Perf.	he, she, it **has driven**	he, she, it **has been driven**
Past	I, he, she, it,	I, he, she, it,
Perf.	we, you, they **had driven**	we, you, they **had been driven**
Fut.	I, he, she, it, we, you, they	I, he, she, it, we, you, they
Perf.	**will have driven**	**will have been driven**

IMPERATIVE MOOD

drive

be driven

SUBJUNCTIVE MOOD

Pres.	if I, he, she, it,	if I, he, she, it,
	we, you, they **drive**	we, you, they **be driven**
Past	if I, he, she, it,	if I, he, she, it,
	we, you, they **drove**	we, you, they **were driven**
Fut.	if I, he, she, it,	if I, he, she, it,
	we, you, they **should drive**	we, you, they **should be driven**

Transitive and intransitive.

drop
(active voice)

PRINCIPAL PARTS: **drops, dropping, dropped, dropped**

be dropped
(passive voice)

Infinitive: **to drop**
Perfect Infinitive: **to have dropped**
Present Participle: **dropping**
Past Participle: **dropped**

Infinitive: **to be dropped**
Perfect Infinitive: **to have been dropped**
Present Participle: **being dropped**
Past Participle: **been dropped**

INDICATIVE MOOD

Pres.	I, we, you, they **drop**	I **am dropped**
		we, you, they **are dropped**
	he, she, it **drops**	he, she, it **is dropped**
Pres.	I **am dropping**	I **am being dropped**
Prog.	we, you, they **are dropping**	we, you, they **are being dropped**
	he, she, it **is dropping**	he, she, it **is being dropped**
Pres.	I, we, you, they **do drop**	I, we, you, they **do get dropped**
Int.	he, she, it **does drop**	he, she, it **does get dropped**
Fut.	I, he, she, it, we, you, they **will drop**	I, he, she, it, we, you, they **will be dropped**
Past	I, he, she, it, we, you, they **dropped**	I, he, she, it **was dropped** we, you, they **were dropped**
Past	I, he, she, it **was dropping**	I, he, she, it **was being dropped**
Prog.	we, you, they **were dropping**	we, you, they **were being dropped**
Past	I, he, she, it, we, you, they **did drop**	I, he, she, it, we, you, they **did get dropped**
Int.		
Pres.	I, we, you, they **have dropped**	I, we, you, they **have been dropped**
Perf.	he, she, it **has dropped**	he, she, it **has been dropped**
Past	I, he, she, it, we, you, they **had dropped**	I, he, she, it, we, you, they **had been dropped**
Perf.		
Fut.	I, he, she, it, we, you, they	I, he, she, it, we, you, they
Perf.	**will have dropped**	**will have been dropped**

IMPERATIVE MOOD

drop   **be dropped**

SUBJUNCTIVE MOOD

Pres.	if I, he, she, it, we, you, they **drop**	if I, he, she, it, we, you, they **be dropped**
Past	if I, he, she, it, we, you, they **dropped**	if I, he, she, it, we, you, they **were dropped**
Fut.	if I, he, she, it, we, you, they **should drop**	if I, he, she, it, we, you, they **should be dropped**

Intransitive and transitive.

Infinitive: **to dwell**
Perfect Infinitive: **to have dwelt**
Present Participle: **dwelling**
Past Participle: **dwelt**

INDICATIVE MOOD

Pres. I, we, you, they **dwell**

   he, she, it **dwells**

Pres. **I am dwelling**
Prog. we, you, they **are dwelling**
   he, she, it **is dwelling**

Pres. I, we, you, they **do dwell**
Int.   he, she, it **does dwell**

Fut.   I, he, she, it,
   we, you, they **will dwell**

Past   I, he, she, it,
   we, you, they **dwelt**

Past   I, he, she, it **was dwelling**
Prog. we, you, they **were dwelling**

Past   I, he, she, it,
Int.   we, you, they **did dwell**

Pres. I, we, you, they **have dwelt**
Perf. he, she, it **has dwelt**

Past   I, he, she, it,
Perf. we, you, they **had dwelt**

Fut.   I, he, she, it, we, you, they
Perf. **will have dwelt**

IMPERATIVE MOOD

   dwell

SUBJUNCTIVE MOOD

Pres. if I, he, she, it,
   we, you, they **dwell**

Past   if I, he, she, it,
   we, you, they **dwelt**

Fut.   if I, he, she, it,
   we, you, they **should dwell**

The past tense and past participle may be DWELT or DWELLED.

108

dye
(active voice)

PRINCIPAL PARTS: dyes, dyeing, dyed, dyed

be dyed
(passive voice)

Infinitive: **to dye**
Perfect Infinitive: **to have dyed**
Present Participle: **dyeing**
Past Participle: **dyed**

Infinitive: **to be dyed**
Perfect Infinitive: **to have been dyed**
Present Participle: **being dyed**
Past Participle: **been dyed**

INDICATIVE MOOD

Pres.	I, we, you, they **dye**	I **am dyed**
		we, you, they **are dyed**
	he, she, it **dyes**	he, she, it **is dyed**
Pres.	I **am dyeing**	I **am being dyed**
Prog.	we, you, they **are dyeing**	we, you, they **are being dyed**
	he, she, it **is dyeing**	he, she, it **is being dyed**
Pres.	I, we, you, they **do dye**	I, we, you, they **do get dyed**
Int.	he, she, it **does dye**	he, she, it **does get dyed**
Fut.	I, he, she, it,	I, he, she, it,
	we, you, they **will dye**	we, you, they **will be dyed**
Past	I, he, she, it,	I, he, she, it **was dyed**
	we, you, they **dyed**	we, you, they **were dyed**
Past	I, he, she, it **was dyeing**	I, he, she, it **was being dyed**
Prog.	we, you, they **were dyeing**	we, you, they **were being dyed**
Past	I, he, she, it,	I, he, she, it,
Int.	we, you, they **did dye**	we, you, they **did get dyed**
Pres.	I, we, you, they **have dyed**	I, we, you, they **have been dyed**
Perf.	he, she, it **has dyed**	he, she, it **has been dyed**
Past	I, he, she, it,	I, he, she, it,
Perf.	we, you, they **had dyed**	we, you, they **had been dyed**
Fut.	I, he, she, it, we, you, they	I, he, she, it, we, you, they
Perf.	**will have dyed**	**will have been dyed**

IMPERATIVE MOOD

dye   **be dyed**

SUBJUNCTIVE MOOD

Pres.	if I, he, she, it,	if I, he, she, it,
	we, you, they **dye**	we, you, they **be dyed**
Past	if I, he, she, it,	if I, he, she, it,
	we, you, they **dyed**	we, you, they **were dyed**
Fut.	if I, he, she, it,	if I, he, she, it,
	we, you, they **should dye**	we, you, they **should be dyed**

Transitive and intransitive.

earn
(active voice)

be earned
(passive voice)

Infinitive: **to earn**
Perfect Infinitive: **to have earned**
Present Participle: **earning**
Past Participle: **earned**

Infinitive: **to be earned**
Perfect Infinitive: **to have been earned**
Present Participle: **being earned**
Past Participle: **been earned**

INDICATIVE MOOD

Pres.	I, we, you, they **earn**	I **am earned**
		we, you, they **are earned**
	he, she, it **earns**	he, she, it **is earned**
Pres.	I **am earning**	I **am being earned**
Prog.	we, you, they **are earning**	we, you, they **are being earned**
	he, she, it **is earning**	he, she, it **is being earned**
Pres.	I, we, you, they **do earn**	I, we, you, they **do get earned**
Int.	he, she, it **does earn**	he, she, it **does get earned**
Fut.	I, he, she, it,	I, he, she, it,
	we, you, they **will earn**	we, you, they **will be earned**
Past	I, he, she, it,	I, he, she, it **was earned**
	we, you, they **earned**	we, you, they **were earned**
Past	I, he, she, it **was earning**	I, he, she, it **was being earned**
Prog.	we, you, they **were earning**	we, you, they **were being earned**
Past	I, he, she, it,	I, he, she, it,
Int.	we, you, they **did earn**	we, you, they **did get earned**
Pres.	I, we, you, they **have earned**	I, we, you, they **have been earned**
Perf.	he, she, it **has earned**	he, she, it **has been earned**
Past	I, he, she, it,	I, he, she, it,
Perf.	we, you, they **had earned**	we, you, they **had been earned**
Fut.	I, he, she, it, we, you, they	I, he, she, it, we, you, they
Perf.	**will have earned**	**will have been earned**

IMPERATIVE MOOD

earn   **be earned**

SUBJUNCTIVE MOOD

Pres.	if I, he, she, it,	if I, he, she, it,
	we, you, they **earn**	we, you, they **be earned**
Past	if I, he, she, it,	if I, he, she, it,
	we, you, they **earned**	we, you, they **were earned**
Fut.	if I, he, she, it,	if I, he, she, it,
	we, you, they **should earn**	we, you, they **should be earned**

eat
(active voice)

be eaten
(passive voice)

Infinitive: **to eat**
Perfect Infinitive: **to have eaten**
Present Participle: **eating**
Past Participle: **eaten**

Infinitive: **to be eaten**
Perfect Infinitive: **to have been eaten**
Present Participle: **being eaten**
Past Participle: **been eaten**

INDICATIVE MOOD

Pres.	I, we, you, they **eat**	I **am eaten**
		we, you, they **are eaten**
	he, she, it **eats**	he, she, it **is eaten**
Pres.	I **am eating**	I **am being eaten**
Prog.	we, you, they **are eating**	we, you, they **are being eaten**
	he, she, it **is eating**	he, she, it **is being eaten**
Pres.	I, we, you, they **do eat**	I, we, you, they **do get eaten**
Int.	he, she, it **does eat**	he, she, it **does get eaten**
Fut.	I, he, she, it,	I, he, she, it,
	we, you, they **will eat**	we, you, they **will be eaten**
Past	I, he, she, it,	I, he, she, it **was eaten**
	we, you, they **ate**	we, you, they **were eaten**
Past	I, he, she, it **was eating**	I, he, she, it **was being eaten**
Prog.	we, you, they **were eating**	we, you, they **were being eaten**
Past	I, he, she, it,	I, he, she, it,
Int.	we, you, they **did eat**	we, you, they **did get eaten**
Pres.	I, we, you, they **have eaten**	I, we, you, they **have been eaten**
Perf.	he, she, it **has eaten**	he, she, it **has been eaten**
Past	I, he, she, it,	I, he, she, it,
Perf.	we, you, they **had eaten**	we, you, they **had been eaten**
Fut.	I, he, she, it, we, you, they	I, he, she, it, we, you, they
Perf.	**will have eaten**	**will have been eaten**

IMPERATIVE MOOD

eat   **be eaten**

SUBJUNCTIVE MOOD

Pres.	if I, he, she, it,	if I, he, she, it,
	we, you, they **eat**	we, you, they **be eaten**
Past	if I, he, she, it,	if I, he, she, it,
	we, you, they **ate**	we, you, they **were eaten**
Fut.	if I, he, she, it,	if I, he, she, it,
	we, you, they **should eat**	we, you, they **should be eaten**

Transitive and intransitive.

echo
(active voice)

be echoed
(passive voice)

Infinitive: **to echo**
Perfect Infinitive: **to have echoed**
Present Participle: **echoing**
Past Participle: **echoed**

Infinitive: **to be echoed**
Perfect Infinitive: **to have been echoed**
Present Participle: **being echoed**
Past Participle: **been echoed**

INDICATIVE MOOD

Pres.	I, we, you, they **echo**	I **am echoed**
		we, you, they **are echoed**
	he, she, it **echoes**	he, she, it **is echoed**
Pres.	I **am echoing**	I **am being echoed**
Prog.	we, you, they **are echoing**	we, you, they **are being echoed**
	he, she, it **is echoing**	he, she, it **is being echoed**
Pres.	I, we, you, they **do echo**	I, we, you, they **do get echoed**
Int.	he, she, it **does echo**	he, she, it **does get echoed**
Fut.	I, he, she, it,	I, he, she, it,
	we, you, they **will echo**	we, you, they **will be echoed**
Past	I, he, she, it,	I, he, she, it **was echoed**
	we, you, they **echoed**	we, you, they **were echoed**
Past	I, he, she, it **was echoing**	I, he, she, it **was being echoed**
Prog.	we, you, they **were echoing**	we, you, they **were being echoed**
Past	I, he, she, it,	I, he, she, it,
Int.	we, you, they **did echo**	we, you, they **did get echoed**
Pres.	I, we, you, they **have echoed**	I, we, you, they **have been echoed**
Perf.	he, she, it **has echoed**	he, she, it **has been echoed**
Past	I, he, she, it,	I, he, she, it,
Perf.	we, you, they **had echoed**	we, you, they **had been echoed**
Fut.	I, he, she, it, we, you, they	I, he, she, it, we, you, they
Perf.	**will have echoed**	**will have been echoed**

IMPERATIVE MOOD

echo

be echoed

SUBJUNCTIVE MOOD

Pres.	if I, he, she, it,	if I, he, she, it,
	we, you, they **echo**	we, you, they **be echoed**
Past	if I, he, she, it,	if I, he, she, it,
	we, you, they **echoed**	we, you, they **were echoed**
Fut.	if I, he, she, it,	if I, he, she, it,
	we, you, they **should echo**	we, you, they **should be echoed**

Transitive and intransitive.

PRINCIPAL PARTS: **embarrasses, embarrassing, embarrassed, embarrassed**

Infinitive: **to embarrass**
Perfect Infinitive: **to have embarrassed**
Present Participle: **embarrassing**
Past Participle: **embarrassed**

Infinitive: **to be embarrassed**
Perfect Infinitive: **to have been embarrassed**
Present Participle: **being embarrassed**
Past Participle: **been embarrassed**

INDICATIVE MOOD

Pres.	I, we, you, they **embarrass**	I **am embarrassed**
		we, you, they **are embarrassed**
	he, she, it **embarrasses**	he, she, it **is embarrassed**
Pres.	I **am embarrassing**	I **am being embarrassed**
Prog.	we, you, they **are embarrassing**	we, you, they **are being embarrassed**
	he, she, it **is embarrassing**	he, she, it **is being embarrassed**
Pres.	I, we, you, they **do embarrass**	I, we, you, they **do get embarrassed**
Int.	he, she, it **does embarrass**	he, she, it **does get embarrassed**
Fut.	I, he, she, it,	I, he, she, it,
	we, you, they **will embarrass**	we, you, they **will be embarrassed**
Past	I, he, she, it,	I, he, she, it **was embarrassed**
	we, you, they **embarrassed**	we, you, they **were embarrassed**
Past	I, he, she, it **was embarrassing**	I, he, she, it **was being embarrassed**
Prog.	we, you, they **were embarrassing**	we, you, they **were being embarrassed**
Past	I, he, she, it,	I, he, she, it,
Int.	we, you, they **did embarrass**	we, you, they **did get embarrassed**
Pres.	I, we, you, they **have embarrassed**	I, we, you, they **have been embarrassed**
Perf.	he, she, it **has embarrassed**	he, she, it **has been embarrassed**
Past	I, he, she, it,	I, he, she, it, we, you, they
Perf.	we, you, they **had embarrassed**	**had been embarrassed**
Fut.	I, he, she, it, we, you, they	I, he, she, it, we, you, they
Perf.	**will have embarrassed**	**will have been embarrassed**

IMPERATIVE MOOD

embarrass   **be embarrassed**

SUBJUNCTIVE MOOD

Pres.	if I, he, she, it,	if I, he, she, it,
	we, you, they **embarrass**	we, you, they **be embarrassed**
Past	if I, he, she, it,	if I, he, she, it,
	we, you, they **embarrassed**	we, you, they **were embarrassed**
Fut.	if I, he, she, it,	if I, he, she, it,
	we, you, they **should embarrass**	we, you, they **should be embarrassed**

end
(active voice)

be ended
(passive voice)

Infinitive: **to end**
Perfect Infinitive: **to have ended**
Present Participle: **ending**
Past Participle: **ended**

Infinitive: **to be ended**
Perfect Infinitive: **to have been ended**
Present Participle: **being ended**
Past Participle: **been ended**

INDICATIVE MOOD

Pres.	I, we, you, they **end**	I **am ended**
		we, you, they **are ended**
	he, she, it **ends**	he, she, it **is ended**
Pres.	I **am ending**	I **am being ended**
Prog.	we, you, they **are ending**	we, you, they **are being ended**
	he, she, it **is ending**	he, she, it **is being ended**
Pres.	I, we, you, they **do end**	I, we, you, they **do get ended**
Int.	he, she, it **does end**	he, she, it **does get ended**
Fut.	I, he, she, it,	I, he, she, it,
	we, you, they **will end**	we, you, they **will be ended**
Past	I, he, she, it,	I, he, she, it **was ended**
	we, you, they **ended**	we, you, they **were ended**
Past	I, he, she, it **was ending**	I, he, she, it **was being ended**
Prog.	we, you, they **were ending**	we, you, they **were being ended**
Past	I, he, she, it,	I, he, she, it,
Int.	we, you, they **did end**	we, you, they **did get ended**
Pres.	I, we, you, they **have ended**	I, we, you, they **have been ended**
Perf.	he, she, it **has ended**	he, she, it **has been ended**
Past	I, he, she, it,	I, he, she, it,
Perf.	we, you, they **had ended**	we, you, they **had been ended**
Fut.	I, he, she, it, we, you, they	I, he, she, it, we, you, they
Perf.	**will have ended**	**will have been ended**

IMPERATIVE MOOD

end

be ended

SUBJUNCTIVE MOOD

Pres.	if I, he, she, it,	if I, he, she, it,
	we, you, they **end**	we, you, they **be ended**
Past	if I, he, she, it,	if I, he, she, it,
	we, you, they **ended**	we, you, they **were ended**
Fut.	if I, he, she, it,	if I, he, she, it,
	we, you, they **should end**	we, you, they **should be ended**

Transitive and intransitive.

enjoy
(active voice)

PRINCIPAL PARTS: **enjoys, enjoying, enjoyed, enjoyed**

be enjoyed
(passive voice)

Infinitive: **to enjoy**
Perfect Infinitive: **to have enjoyed**
Present Participle: **enjoying**
Past Participle: **enjoyed**

Infinitive: **to be enjoyed**
Perfect Infinitive: **to have been enjoyed**
Present Participle: **being enjoyed**
Past Participle: **been enjoyed**

INDICATIVE MOOD

Pres.	I, we, you, they **enjoy**	I **am enjoyed**
		we, you, they **are enjoyed**
	he, she, it **enjoys**	he, she, it **is enjoyed**
Pres.	I **am enjoying**	I **am being enjoyed**
Prog.	we, you, they **are enjoying**	we, you, they **are being enjoyed**
	he, she, it **is enjoying**	he, she, it **is being enjoyed**
Pres.	I, we, you, they **do enjoy**	I, we, you, they **do get enjoyed**
Int.	he, she, it **does enjoy**	he, she, it **does get enjoyed**
Fut.	I, he, she, it,	I, he, she, it,
	we, you, they **will enjoy**	we, you, they **will be enjoyed**
Past	I, he, she, it,	I, he, she, it **was enjoyed**
	we, you, they **enjoyed**	we, you, they **were enjoyed**
Past	I, he, she, it **was enjoying**	I, he, she, it **was being enjoyed**
Prog.	we, you, they **were enjoying**	we, you, they **were being enjoyed**
Past	I, he, she, it,	I, he, she, it,
Int.	we, you, they **did enjoy**	we, you, they **did get enjoyed**
Pres.	I, we, you, they **have enjoyed**	I, we, you, they **have been enjoyed**
Perf.	he, she, it **has enjoyed**	he, she, it **has been enjoyed**
Past	I, he, she, it,	I, he, she, it,
Perf.	we, you, they **had enjoyed**	we, you, they **had been enjoyed**
Fut.	I, he, she, it, we, you, they	I, he, she, it, we, you, they
Perf.	**will have enjoyed**	**will have been enjoyed**

IMPERATIVE MOOD

enjoy   **be enjoyed**

SUBJUNCTIVE MOOD

Pres.	if I, he, she, it,	if I, he, she, it,
	we, you, they **enjoy**	we, you, they **be enjoyed**
Past	if I, he, she, it,	if I, he, she, it,
	we, you, they **enjoyed**	we, you, they **were enjoyed**
Fut.	if I, he, she, it,	if I, he, she, it,
	we, you, they **should enjoy**	we, you, they **should be enjoyed**

Transitive and intransitive.

enter
(active voice)

PRINCIPAL PARTS: **enters, entering,
entered, entered**

be entered
(passive voice)

Infinitive: **to enter**
Perfect Infinitive: **to have entered**
Present Participle: **entering**
Past Participle: **entered**

Infinitive: **to be entered**
Perfect Infinitive: **to have been entered**
Present Participle: **being entered**
Past Participle: **been entered**

INDICATIVE MOOD

Pres.	I, we, you, they **enter**	I **am entered**
		we, you, they **are entered**
	he, she, it **enters**	he, she, it **is entered**
Pres.	I **am entering**	I **am being entered**
Prog.	we, you, they **are entering**	we, you, they **are being entered**
	he, she, it **is entering**	he, she, it **is being entered**
Pres.	I, we, you, they **do enter**	I, we, you, they **do get entered**
Int.	he, she, it **does enter**	he, she, it **does get entered**
Fut.	I, he, she, it,	I, he, she, it,
	we, you, they **will enter**	we, you, they **will be entered**
Past	I, he, she, it,	I, he, she, it **was entered**
	we, you, they **entered**	we, you, they **were entered**
Past	I, he, she, it **was entering**	I, he, she, it **was being entered**
Prog.	we, you, they **were entering**	we, you, they **were being entered**
Past	I, he, she, it,	I, he, she, it,
Int.	we, you, they **did enter**	we, you, they **did get entered**
Pres.	I, we, you, they **have entered**	I, we, you, they **have been entered**
Perf.	he, she, it **has entered**	he, she, it **has been entered**
Past	I, he, she, it,	I, he, she, it,
Perf.	we, you, they **had entered**	we, you, they **had been entered**
Fut.	I, he, she, it, we, you, they	I, he, she, it, we, you, they
Perf.	**will have entered**	**will have been entered**

IMPERATIVE MOOD

enter   **be entered**

SUBJUNCTIVE MOOD

Pres.	if I, he, she, it,	if I, he, she, it,
	we, you, they **enter**	we, you, they **be entered**
Past	if I, he, she, it,	if I, he, she, it,
	we, you, they **entered**	we, you, they **were entered**
Fut.	if I, he, she, it,	if I, he, she, it,
	we, you, they **should enter**	we, you, they **should be entered**

Transitive and intransitive.

envelop
(active voice)

be enveloped
(passive voice)

Infinitive: **to envelop**
Perfect Infinitive: **to have enveloped**
Present Participle: **enveloping**
Past Participle: **enveloped**

Infinitive: **to be enveloped**
Perfect Infinitive: **to have been enveloped**
Present Participle: **being enveloped**
Past Participle: **been enveloped**

INDICATIVE MOOD

Pres.	I, we, you, they **envelop**	I am **enveloped**
		we, you, they **are enveloped**
	he, she, it **envelops**	he, she, it **is enveloped**
Pres.	I **am enveloping**	I **am being enveloped**
Prog.	we, you, they **are enveloping**	we, you, they **are being enveloped**
	he, she, it **is enveloping**	he, she, it **is being enveloped**
Pres.	I, we, you, they **do envelop**	I, we, you, they **do get enveloped**
Int.	he, she, it **does envelop**	he, she, it **does get enveloped**
Fut.	I, he, she, it,	I, he, she, it,
	we, you, they **will envelop**	we, you, they **will be enveloped**
Past	I, he, she, it,	I, he, she, it **was enveloped**
	we, you, they **enveloped**	we, you, they **were enveloped**
Past	I, he, she, it **was enveloping**	I, he, she, it **was being enveloped**
Prog.	we, you, they **were enveloping**	we, you, they **were being enveloped**
Past	I, he, she, it,	I, he, she, it,
Int.	we, you, they **did envelop**	we, you, they **did get enveloped**
Pres.	I, we, you, they **have enveloped**	I, we, you, they **have been enveloped**
Perf.	he, she, it **has enveloped**	he, she, it **has been enveloped**
Past	I, he, she, it,	I, he, she, it,
Perf.	we, you, they **had enveloped**	we, you, they **had been enveloped**
Fut.	I, he, she, it, we, you, they	I, he, she, it, we, you, they
Perf.	**will have enveloped**	**will have been enveloped**

IMPERATIVE MOOD

envelop   **be enveloped**

SUBJUNCTIVE MOOD

Pres.	if I, he, she, it,	if I, he, she, it,
	we, you, they **envelop**	we, you, they **be enveloped**
Past	if I, he, she, it,	if I, he, she, it,
	we, you, they **enveloped**	we, you, they **were enveloped**
Fut.	if I, he, she, it,	if I, he, she, it,
	we, you, they **should envelop**	we, you, they **should be enveloped**

establish
(active voice)

be established
(passive voice)

Infinitive: **to establish**
Perfect Infinitive: **to have established**
Present Participle: **establishing**
Past Participle: **established**

Infinitive: **to be established**
Perfect Infinitive: **to have been established**
Present Participle: **being established**
Past Participle: **been established**

INDICATIVE MOOD

Pres.	I, we, you, they **establish**	I **am established**
		we, you, they **are established**
	he, she, it **establishes**	he, she, it **is established**
Pres.	I **am establishing**	I **am being established**
Prog.	we, you, they **are establishing**	we, you, they **are being established**
	he, she, it **is establishing**	he, she, it **is being established**
Pres.	I, we, you, they **do establish**	I, we, you, they **do get established**
Int.	he, she, it **does establish**	he, she, it **does get established**
Fut.	I, he, she, it,	I, he, she, it,
	we, you, they **will establish**	we, you, they **will be established**
Past	I, he, she, it,	I, he, she, it **was established**
	we, you, they **established**	we, you, they **were established**
Past	I, he, she, it **was establishing**	I, he, she, it **was being established**
Prog.	we, you, they **were establishing**	we, you, they **were being established**
Past	I, he, she, it,	I, he, she, it,
Int.	we, you, they **did establish**	we, you, they **did get established**
Pres.	I, we, you, they **have established**	I, we, you, they **have been established**
Perf.	he, she, it **has established**	he, she, it **has been established**
Past	I, he, she, it,	I, he, she, it,
Perf.	we, you, they **had established**	we, you, they **had been established**
Fut.	I, he, she, it, we, you, they	I, he, she, it, we, you, they
Perf.	**will have established**	**will have been established**

IMPERATIVE MOOD

establish

be established

SUBJUNCTIVE MOOD

Pres.	if I, he, she, it,	if I, he, she, it,
	we, you, they **establish**	we, you, they **be established**
Past	if I, he, she, it,	if I, he, she, it,
	we, you, they **established**	we, you, they **were established**
Fut.	if I, he, she, it,	if I, he, she, it,
	we, you, they **should establish**	we, you, they **should be established**

excuse
(active voice)

PRINCIPAL PARTS: **excuses, excusing, excused, excused**

be excused
(passive voice)

Infinitive: **to excuse**
Perfect Infinitive: **to have excused**
Present Participle: **excusing**
Past Participle: **excused**

Infinitive: **to be excused**
Perfect Infinitive: **to have been excused**
Present Participle: **being excused**
Past Participle: **been excused**

INDICATIVE MOOD

Pres.	I, we, you, they **excuse**	I **am excused**
		we, you, they **are excused**
	he, she, it **excuses**	he, she, it **is excused**
Pres.	I **am excusing**	I **am being excused**
Prog.	we, you, they **are excusing**	we, you, they **are being excused**
	he, she, it **is excusing**	he, she, it **is being excused**
Pres.	I, we, you, they **do excuse**	I, we, you, they **do get excused**
Int.	he, she, it **does excuse**	he, she, it **does get excused**
Fut.	I, he, she, it,	I, he, she, it,
	we, you, they **will excuse**	we, you, they **will be excused**
Past	I, he, she, it,	I, he, she, it **was excused**
	we, you, they **excused**	we, you, they **were excused**
Past	I, he, she, it **was excusing**	I, he, she, it **was being excused**
Prog.	we, you, they **were excusing**	we, you, they **were being excused**
Past	I, he, she, it,	I, he, she, it,
Int.	we, you, they **did excuse**	we, you, they **did get excused**
Pres.	I, we, you, they **have excused**	I, we, you, they **have been excused**
Perf.	he, she, it **has excused**	he, she, it **has been excused**
Past	I, he, she, it,	I, he, she, it,
Perf.	we, you, they **had excused**	we, you, they **had been excused**
Fut.	I, he, she, it, we, you, they	I, he, she, it, we, you, they
Perf.	**will have excused**	**will have been excused**

IMPERATIVE MOOD

excuse   **be excused**

SUBJUNCTIVE MOOD

Pres.	if I, he, she, it,	if I, he, she, it,
	we, you, they **excuse**	we, you, they **be excused**
Past	if I, he, she, it,	if I, he, she, it,
	we, you, they **excused**	we, you, they **were excused**
Fut.	if I, he, she, it,	if I, he, she, it,
	we, you, they **should excuse**	we, you, they **should be excused**

Infinitive: **to exist**
Perfect Infinitive: **to have existed**
Present Participle: **existing**
Past Participle: **existed**

INDICATIVE MOOD

Pres.	I, we, you, they **exist**
	he, she, it **exists**
Pres. *Prog.*	I **am existing** we, you, they **are existing** he, she, it **is existing**
Pres. *Int.*	I, we, you, they **do exist** he, she, it **does exist**
Fut.	I, he, she, it, we, you, they **will exist**
Past	I, he, she, it, we, you, they **existed**
Past *Prog.*	I, he, she, it **was existing** we, you, they **were existing**
Past *Int.*	I, he, she, it, we, you, they **did exist**
Pres. *Perf.*	I, we, you, they **have existed** he, she, it **has existed**
Past *Perf.*	I, he, she, it, we, you, they **had existed**
Fut. *Perf.*	I, he, she, it, we, you, they **will have existed**

IMPERATIVE MOOD

exist

SUBJUNCTIVE MOOD

Pres.	if I, he, she, it, we, you, they **exist**
Past	if I, he, she, it, we, you, they **existed**
Fut.	if I, he, she, it, we, you, they **should exist**

expect
(active voice)

PRINCIPAL PARTS: **expects, expecting, expected, expected**

be expected
(passive voice)

Infinitive: **to expect**
Perfect Infinitive: **to have expected**
Present Participle: **expecting**
Past Participle: **expected**

Infinitive: **to be expected**
Perfect Infinitive: **to have been expected**
Present Participle: **being expected**
Past Participle: **been expected**

INDICATIVE MOOD

Pres.	I, we, you, they **expect**	I **am expected**
		we, you, they **are expected**
	he, she, it **expects**	he, she, it **is expected**
Pres.	I **am expecting**	I **am being expected**
Prog.	we, you, they **are expecting**	we, you, they **are being expected**
	he, she, it **is expecting**	he, she, it **is being expected**
Pres.	I, we, you, they **do expect**	I, we, you, they **do get expected**
Int.	he, she, it **does expect**	he, she, it **does get expected**
Fut.	I, he, she, it,	I, he, she, it,
	we, you, they **will expect**	we, you, they **will be expected**
Past	I, he, she, it,	I, he, she, it **was expected**
	we, you, they **expected**	we, you, they **were expected**
Past	I, he, she, it **was expecting**	I, he, she, it **was being expected**
Prog.	we, you, they **were expecting**	we, you, they **were being expected**
Past	I, he, she, it,	I, he, she, it,
Int.	we, you, they **did expect**	we, you, they **did get expected**
Pres.	I, we, you, they **have expected**	I, we, you, they **have been expected**
Perf.	he, she, it **has expected**	he, she, it **has been expected**
Past	I, he, she, it,	I, he, she, it,
Perf.	we, you, they **had expected**	we, you, they **had been expected**
Fut.	I, he, she, it, we, you, they	I, he, she, it, we, you, they
Perf.	**will have expected**	**will have been expected**

IMPERATIVE MOOD

expect   **be expected**

SUBJUNCTIVE MOOD

Pres.	if I, he, she, it,	if I, he, she, it,
	we, you, they **expect**	we, you, they **be expected**
Past	if I, he, she, it,	if I, he, she, it,
	we, you, they **expected**	we, you, they **were expected**
Fut.	if I, he, she, it,	if I, he, she, it,
	we, you, they **should expect**	we, you, they **should be expected**

Transitive and intransitive. As an intransitive verb used with the progressive tenses, this verb means to "be pregnant" or "looking forward to the birth of a child."

explain
(active voice)

be explained
(passive voice)

Infinitive: **to explain**
Perfect Infinitive: **to have explained**
Present Participle: **explaining**
Past Participle: **explained**

Infinitive: **to be explained**
Perfect Infinitive: **to have been explained**
Present Participle: **being explained**
Past Participle: **been explained**

INDICATIVE MOOD

Pres.	I, we, you, they **explain**	I **am explained**
		we, you, they **are explained**
	he, she, it **explains**	he, she, it **is explained**
Pres.	I **am explaining**	I **am being explained**
Prog.	we, you, they **are explaining**	we, you, they **are being explained**
	he, she, it **is explaining**	he, she, it **is being explained**
Pres.	I, we, you, they **do explain**	I, we, you, they **do get explained**
Int.	he, she, it **does explain**	he, she, it **does get explained**
Fut.	I, he, she, it,	I, he, she, it,
	we, you, they **will explain**	we, you, they **will be explained**
Past	I, he, she, it,	I, he, she, it **was explained**
	we, you, they **explained**	we, you, they **were explained**
Past	I, he, she, it **was explaining**	I, he, she, it **was being explained**
Prog.	we, you, they **were explaining**	we, you, they **were being explained**
Past	I, he, she, it,	I, he, she, it,
Int.	we, you, they **did explain**	we, you, they **did get explained**
Pres.	I, we, you, they **have explained**	I, we, you, they **have been explained**
Perf.	he, she, it **has explained**	he, she, it **has been explained**
Past	I, he, she, it,	I, he, she, it,
Perf.	we, you, they **had explained**	we, you, they **had been explained**
Fut.	I, he, she, it, we, you, they	I, he, she, it, we, you, they
Perf.	**will have explained**	**will have been explained**

IMPERATIVE MOOD

explain   **be explained**

SUBJUNCTIVE MOOD

Pres.	if I, he, she, it,	if I, he, she, it,
	we, you, they **explain**	we, you, they **be explained**
Past	if I, he, she, it,	if I, he, she, it,
	we, you, they **explained**	we, you, they **were explained**
Fut.	if I, he, she, it,	if I, he, she, it,
	we, you, they **should explain**	we, you, they **should be explained**

Transitive and intransitive.

express
(active voice)

be expressed
(passive voice)

Infinitive: **to express**
Perfect Infinitive: **to have expressed**
Present Participle: **expressing**
Past Participle: **expressed**

Infinitive: **to be expressed**
Perfect Infinitive: **to have been expressed**
Present Participle: **being expressed**
Past Participle: **been expressed**

INDICATIVE MOOD

Pres.	I, we, you, they **express**	I **am expressed** we, you, they **are expressed**
	he, she, it **expresses**	he, she, it **is expressed**
Pres. *Prog.*	I **am expressing** we, you, they **are expressing** he, she, it **is expressing**	I **am being expressed** we, you, they **are being expressed** he, she, it **is being expressed**
Pres. *Int.*	I, we, you, they **do express** he, she, it **does express**	I, we, you, they **do get expressed** he, she, it **does get expressed**
Fut.	I, he, she, it, we, you, they **will express**	I, he, she, it, we, you, they **will be expressed**
Past	I, he, she, it, we, you, they **expressed**	I, he, she, it **was expressed** we, you, they **were expressed**
Past *Prog.*	I, he, she, it **was expressing** we, you, they **were expressing**	I, he, she, it **was being expressed** we, you, they **were being expressed**
Past *Int.*	I, he, she, it, we, you, they **did express**	I, he, she, it, we, you, they **did get expressed**
Pres. *Perf.*	I, we, you, they **have expressed** he, she, it **has expressed**	I, we, you, they **have been expressed** he, she, it **has been expressed**
Past *Perf.*	I, he, she, it, we, you, they **had expressed**	I, he, she, it, we, you, they **had been expressed**
Fut. *Perf.*	I, he, she, it, we, you, they **will have expressed**	I, he, she, it, we, you, they **will have been expressed**

IMPERATIVE MOOD

express   **be expressed**

SUBJUNCTIVE MOOD

Pres.	if I, he, she, it, we, you, they **express**	if I, he, she, it, we, you, they **be expressed**
Past	if I, he, she, it, we, you, they **expressed**	if I, he, she, it, we, you, they **were expressed**
Fut.	if I, he, she, it, we, you, they **should express**	if I, he, she, it, we, you, they **should be expressed**

extend
(active voice)

PRINCIPAL PARTS: extends, extending, extended, extended

be extended
(passive voice)

Infinitive: **to extend**
Perfect Infinitive: **to have extended**
Present Participle: **extending**
Past Participle: **extended**

Infinitive: **to be extended**
Perfect Infinitive: **to have been extended**
Present Participle: **being extended**
Past Participle: **been extended**

INDICATIVE MOOD

Pres.	I, we, you, they **extend**	I **am extended**
		we, you, they **are extended**
	he, she, it **extends**	he, she, it **is extended**
Pres. *Prog.*	I **am extending**	I **am being extended**
	we, you, they **are extending**	we, you, they **are being extended**
	he, she, it **is extending**	he, she, it **is being extended**
Pres. *Int.*	I, we, you, they **do extend**	I, we, you, they **do get extended**
	he, she, it **does extend**	he, she, it **does get extended**
Fut.	I, he, she, it, we, you, they **will extend**	I, he, she, it, we, you, they **will be extended**
Past	I, he, she, it, we, you, they **extended**	I, he, she, it **was extended** we, you, they **were extended**
Past *Prog.*	I, he, she, it **was extending** we, you, they **were extending**	I, he, she, it **was being extended** we, you, they **were being extended**
Past *Int.*	I, he, she, it, we, you, they **did extend**	I, he, she, it, we, you, they **did get extended**
Pres. *Perf.*	I, we, you, they **have extended** he, she, it **has extended**	I, we, you, they **have been extended** he, she, it **has been extended**
Past *Perf.*	I, he, she, it, we, you, they **had extended**	I, he, she, it, we, you, they **had been extended**
Fut. *Perf.*	I, he, she, it, we, you, they **will have extended**	I, he, she, it, we, you, they **will have been extended**

IMPERATIVE MOOD

extend   **be extended**

SUBJUNCTIVE MOOD

Pres.	if I, he, she, it, we, you, they **extend**	if I, he, she, it, we, you, they **be extended**
Past	if I, he, she, it, we, you, they **extended**	if I, he, she, it, we, you, they **were extended**
Fut.	if I, he, she, it, we, you, they **should extend**	if I, he, she, it, we, you, they **should be extended**

Transitive and intransitive.

face
(active voice)

be faced
(passive voice)

Infinitive: **to face**
Perfect Infinitive: **to have faced**
Present Participle: **facing**
Past Participle: **faced**

Infinitive: **to be faced**
Perfect Infinitive: **to have been faced**
Present Participle: **being faced**
Past Participle: **been faced**

INDICATIVE MOOD

Pres.	I, we, you, they **face**	I **am faced**
		we, you, they **are faced**
	he, she, it **faces**	he, she, it **is faced**
Pres.	I **am facing**	I **am being faced**
Prog.	we, you, they **are facing**	we, you, they **are being faced**
	he, she, it **is facing**	he, she, it **is being faced**
Pres.	I, we, you, they **do face**	I, we, you, they **do get faced**
Int.	he, she, it **does face**	he, she, it **does get faced**
Fut.	I, he, she, it,	I, he, she, it,
	we, you, they **will face**	we, you, they **will be faced**
Past	I, he, she, it,	I, he, she, it **was faced**
	we, you, they **faced**	we, you, they **were faced**
Past	I, he, she, it **was facing**	I, he, she, it **was being faced**
Prog.	we, you, they **were facing**	we, you, they **were being faced**
Past	I, he, she, it,	I, he, she, it,
Int.	we, you, they **did face**	we, you, they **did get faced**
Pres.	I, we, you, they **have faced**	I, we, you, they **have been faced**
Perf.	he, she, it **has faced**	he, she, it **has been faced**
Past	I, he, she, it,	I, he, she, it,
Perf.	we, you, they **had faced**	we, you, they **had been faced**
Fut.	I, he, she, it, we, you, they	I, he, she, it, we, you, they
Perf.	**will have faced**	**will have been faced**

IMPERATIVE MOOD

face   **be faced**

SUBJUNCTIVE MOOD

Pres.	if I, he, she, it,	if I, he, she, it,
	we, you, they **face**	we, you, they **be faced**
Past	if I, he, she, it,	if I, he, she, it,
	we, you, they **faced**	we, you, they **were faced**
Fut.	if I, he, she, it,	if I, he, she, it,
	we, you, they **should face**	we, you, they **should be faced**

Transitive and intransitive.

fail
(active voice)

**PRINCIPAL PARTS: fails, failing,
failed, failed**

be failed
(passive voice)

Infinitive: **to fail**
Perfect Infinitive: **to have failed**
Present Participle: **failing**
Past Participle: **failed**

Infinitive: **to be failed**
Perfect Infinitive: **to have been failed**
Present Participle: **being failed**
Past Participle: **been failed**

INDICATIVE MOOD

Pres.	I, we, you, they **fail**	I **am failed**
		we, you, they **are failed**
	he, she, it **fails**	he, she, it **is failed**
Pres.	I **am failing**	I **am being failed**
Prog.	we, you, they **are failing**	we, you, they **are being failed**
	he, she, it **is failing**	he, she, it **is being failed**
Pres.	I, we, you, they **do fail**	I, we, you, they **do get failed**
Int.	he, she, it **does fail**	he, she, it **does get failed**
Fut.	I, he, she, it,	I, he, she, it,
	we, you, they **will fail**	we, you, they **will be failed**
Past	I, he, she, it,	I, he, she, it **was failed**
	we, you, they **failed**	we, you, they **were failed**
Past	I, he, she, it **was failing**	I, he, she, it **was being failed**
Prog.	we, you, they **were failing**	we, you, they **were being failed**
Past	I, he, she, it,	I, he, she, it,
Int.	we, you, they **did fail**	we, you, they **did get failed**
Pres.	I, we, you, they **have failed**	I, we, you, they **have been failed**
Perf.	he, she, it **has failed**	he, she, it **has been failed**
Past	I, he, she, it,	I, he, she, it,
Perf.	we, you, they **had failed**	we, you, they **had been failed**
Fut.	I, he, she, it, we, you, they	I, he, she, it, we, you, they
Perf.	**will have failed**	**will have been failed**

IMPERATIVE MOOD

fail

be failed

SUBJUNCTIVE MOOD

Pres.	if I, he, she, it,	if I, he, she, it,
	we, you, they **fail**	we, you, they **be failed**
Past	if I, he, she, it,	if I, he, she, it,
	we, you, they **failed**	we, you, they **were failed**
Fut.	if I, he, she, it,	if I, he, she, it,
	we, you, they **should fail**	we, you, they **should be failed**

Intransitive and transitive.

fall

Infinitive: **to fall**
Perfect Infinitive: **to have fallen**
Present Participle: **falling**
Past Participle: **fallen**

INDICATIVE MOOD

Pres.	I, we, you, they **fall**
	he, she, it **falls**
Pres. *Prog.*	**I am falling** we, you, they **are falling** he, she, it **is falling**
Pres. *Int.*	I, we, you, they **do fall** he, she, it **does fall**
Fut.	I, he, she, it, we, you, they **will fall**
Past	I, he, she, it, we, you, they **fell**
Past *Prog.*	I, he, she, it **was falling** we, you, they **were falling**
Past *Int.*	I, he, she, it, we, you, they **did fall**
Pres. *Perf.*	I, we, you, they **have fallen** he, she, it **has fallen**
Past *Perf.*	I, he, she, it, we, you, they **had fallen**
Fut. *Perf.*	I, he, she, it, we, you, they **will have fallen**

IMPERATIVE MOOD

fall

SUBJUNCTIVE MOOD

Pres.	if I, he, she, it, we, you, they **fall**
Past	if I, he, she, it, we, you, they **fell**
Fut.	if I, he, she, it, we, you, they **should fall**

Intransitive. In the meaning of to "fell a tree," this verb can be transitive.

feed
(active voice)

be fed
(passive voice)

Infinitive: **to feed**
Perfect Infinitive: **to have fed**
Present Participle: **feeding**
Past Participle: **fed**

Infinitive: **to be fed**
Perfect Infinitive: **to have been fed**
Present Participle: **being fed**
Past Participle: **been fed**

INDICATIVE MOOD

Pres.	I, we, you, they **feed**	I **am fed**
		we, you, they **are fed**
	he, she, it **feeds**	he, she, it **is fed**
Pres.	I **am feeding**	I **am being fed**
Prog.	we, you, they **are feeding**	we, you, they **are being fed**
	he, she, it **is feeding**	he, she, it **is being fed**
Pres.	I, we, you, they **do feed**	I, we, you, they **do get fed**
Int.	he, she, it **does feed**	he, she, it **does get fed**
Fut.	I, he, she, it,	I, he, she, it,
	we, you, they **will feed**	we, you, they **will be fed**
Past	I, he, she, it,	I, he, she, it **was fed**
	we, you, they **fed**	we, you, they **were fed**
Past	I, he, she, it **was feeding**	I, he, she, it **was being fed**
Prog.	we, you, they **were feeding**	we, you, they **were being fed**
Past	I, he, she, it,	I, he, she, it,
Int.	we, you, they **did feed**	we, you, they **did get fed**
Pres.	I, we, you, they **have fed**	I, we, you, they **have been fed**
Perf.	he, she, it **has fed**	he, she, it **has been fed**
Past	I, he, she, it,	I, he, she, it,
Perf.	we, you, they **had fed**	we, you, they **had been fed**
Fut.	I, he, she, it, we, you, they	I, he, she, it, we, you, they
Perf.	**will have fed**	**will have been fed**

IMPERATIVE MOOD

feed

be fed

SUBJUNCTIVE MOOD

Pres.	if I, he, she, it,	if I, he, she, it,
	we, you, they **feed**	we, you, they **be fed**
Past	if I, he, she, it,	if I, he, she, it,
	we, you, they **fed**	we, you, they **were fed**
Fut.	if I, he, she, it,	if I, he, she, it,
	we, you, they **should feed**	we, you, they **should be fed**

Transitive and intransitive.

feel
(active voice)

PRINCIPAL PARTS: **feels, feeling, felt, felt**

be felt
(passive voice)

Infinitive: **to feel**
Perfect Infinitive: **to have felt**
Present Participle: **feeling**
Past Participle: **felt**

Infinitive: **to be felt**
Perfect Infinitive: **to have been felt**
Present Participle: **being felt**
Past Participle: **been felt**

INDICATIVE MOOD

Pres.	I, we, you, they **feel**	I **am felt**
		we, you, they **are felt**
	he, she, it **feels**	he, she, it **is felt**
Pres. *Prog.*	I **am feeling**	I **am being felt**
	we, you, they **are feeling**	we, you, they **are being felt**
	he, she, it **is feeling**	he, she, it **is being felt**
Pres. *Int.*	I, we, you, they **do feel**	I, we, you, they **do get felt**
	he, she, it **does feel**	he, she, it **does get felt**
Fut.	I, he, she, it, we, you, they **will feel**	I, he, she, it, we, you, they **will be felt**
Past	I, he, she, it, we, you, they **felt**	I, he, she, it **was felt** we, you, they **were felt**
Past *Prog.*	I, he, she, it **was feeling** we, you, they **were feeling**	I, he, she, it **was being felt** we, you, they **were being felt**
Past *Int.*	I, he, she, it, we, you, they **did feel**	I, he, she, it, we, you, they **did get felt**
Pres. *Perf.*	I, we, you, they **have felt** he, she, it **has felt**	I, we, you, they **have been felt** he, she, it **has been felt**
Past *Perf.*	I, he, she, it, we, you, they **had felt**	I, he, she, it, we, you, they **had been felt**
Fut. *Perf.*	I, he, she, it, we, you, they **will have felt**	I, he, she, it, we, you, they **will have been felt**

IMPERATIVE MOOD

feel

be felt

SUBJUNCTIVE MOOD

Pres.	if I, he, she, it, we, you, they **feel**	if I, he, she, it, we, you, they **be felt**
Past	if I, he, she, it, we, you, they **felt**	if I, he, she, it, we, you, they **were felt**
Fut.	if I, he, she, it, we, you, they **should feel**	if I, he, she, it, we, you, they **should be felt**

Transitive and intransitive.

fell
(active voice)

be felled
(passive voice)

Infinitive: **to fell**
Perfect Infinitive: **to have felled**
Present Participle: **felling**
Past Participle: **felled**

Infinitive: **to be felled**
Perfect Infinitive: **to have been felled**
Present Participle: **being felled**
Past Participle: **been felled**

INDICATIVE MOOD

Pres.	I, we, you, they **fell**	I **am felled**
		we, you, they **are felled**
	he, she, it **fells**	he, she, it **is felled**
Pres.	I **am felling**	I **am being felled**
Prog.	we, you, they **are felling**	we, you, they **are being felled**
	he, she, it **is felling**	he, she, it **is being felled**
Pres.	I, we, you, they **do fell**	I, we, you, they **do get felled**
Int.	he, she, it **does fell**	he, she, it **does get felled**
Fut.	I, he, she, it,	I, he, she, it,
	we, you, they **will fell**	we, you, they **will be felled**
Past	I, he, she, it,	I, he, she, it **was felled**
	we, you, they **felled**	we, you, they **were felled**
Past	I, he, she, it **was felling**	I, he, she, it **was being felled**
Prog.	we, you, they **were felling**	we, you, they **were being felled**
Past	I, he, she, it,	I, he, she, it,
Int.	we, you, they **did fell**	we, you, they **did get felled**
Pres.	I, we, you, they **have felled**	I, we, you, they **have been felled**
Perf.	he, she, it **has felled**	he, she, it **has been felled**
Past	I, he, she, it,	I, he, she, it,
Perf.	we, you, they **had felled**	we, you, they **had been felled**
Fut.	I, he, she, it, we, you, they	I, he, she, it, we, you, they
Perf.	**will have felled**	**will have been felled**

IMPERATIVE MOOD

fell

be felled

SUBJUNCTIVE MOOD

Pres.	if I, he, she, it,	if I, he, she, it,
	we, you, they **fell**	we, you, they **be felled**
Past	if I, he, she, it,	if I, he, she, it,
	we, you, they **felled**	we, you, they **were felled**
Fut.	if I, he, she, it,	if I, he, she, it,
	we, you, they **should fell**	we, you, they **should be felled**

fight
(active voice)

be fought
(passive voice)

Infinitive: **to fight**
Perfect Infinitive: **to have fought**
Present Participle: **fighting**
Past Participle: **fought**

Infinitive: **to be fought**
Perfect Infinitive: **to have been fought**
Present Participle: **being fought**
Past Participle: **been fought**

INDICATIVE MOOD

Pres.	I, we, you, they **fight**	I am **fought**
		we, you, they **are fought**
	he, she, it **fights**	he, she, it **is fought**
Pres.	I **am fighting**	I **am being fought**
Prog.	we, you, they **are fighting**	we, you, they **are being fought**
	he, she, it **is fighting**	he, she, it **is being fought**
Pres.	I, we, you, they **do fight**	I, we, you, they **do get fought**
Int.	he, she, it **does fight**	he, she, it **does get fought**
Fut.	I, he, she, it,	I, he, she, it,
	we, you, they **will fight**	we, you, they **will be fought**
Past	I, he, she, it,	I, he, she, it **was fought**
	we, you, they **fought**	we, you, they **were fought**
Past	I, he, she, it **was fighting**	I, he, she, it **was being fought**
Prog.	we, you, they **were fighting**	we, you, they **were being fought**
Past	I, he, she, it,	I, he, she, it,
Int.	we, you, they **did fight**	we, you, they **did get fought**
Pres.	I, we, you, they **have fought**	I, we, you, they **have been fought**
Perf.	he, she, it **has fought**	he, she, it **has been fought**
Past	I, he, she, it,	I, he, she, it,
Perf.	we, you, they **had fought**	we, you, they **had been fought**
Fut.	I, he, she, it, we, you, they	I, he, she, it, we, you, they
Perf.	**will have fought**	**will have been fought**

IMPERATIVE MOOD

fight   **be fought**

SUBJUNCTIVE MOOD

Pres.	if I, he, she, it,	if I, he, she, it,
	we, you, they **fight**	we, you, they **be fought**
Past	if I, he, she, it,	if I, he, she, it,
	we, you, they **fought**	we, you, they **were fought**
Fut.	if I, he, she, it,	if I, he, she, it,
	we, you, they **should fight**	we, you, they **should be fought**

Intransitive and transitive.

figure
(active voice)

be figured
(passive voice)

Infinitive: **to figure**
Perfect Infinitive: **to have figured**
Present Participle: **figuring**
Past Participle: **figured**

Infinitive: **to be figured**
Perfect Infinitive: **to have been figured**
Present Participle: **being figured**
Past Participle: **been figured**

INDICATIVE MOOD

Pres.	I, we, you, they **figure**	I **am figured**
		we, you, they **are figured**
	he, she, it **figures**	he, she, it **is figured**
Pres.	I **am figuring**	I **am being figured**
Prog.	we, you, they **are figuring**	we, you, they **are being figured**
	he, she, it **is figuring**	he, she, it **is being figured**
Pres.	I, we, you, they **do figure**	I, we, you, they **do get figured**
Int.	he, she, it **does figure**	he, she, it **does get figured**
Fut.	I, he, she, it,	I, he, she, it,
	we, you, they **will figure**	we, you, they **will be figured**
Past	I, he, she, it,	I, he, she, it **was figured**
	we, you, they **figured**	we, you, they **were figured**
Past	I, he, she, it **was figuring**	I, he, she, it **was being figured**
Prog.	we, you, they **were figuring**	we, you, they **were being figured**
Past	I, he, she, it,	I, he, she, it,
Int.	we, you, they **did figure**	we, you, they **did get figured**
Pres.	I, we, you, they **have figured**	I, we, you, they **have been figured**
Perf.	he, she, it **has figured**	he, she, it **has been figured**
Past	I, he, she, it,	I, he, she, it,
Perf.	we, you, they **had figured**	we, you, they **had been figured**
Fut.	I, he, she, it, we, you, they	I, he, she, it, we, you, they
Perf.	**will have figured**	**will have been figured**

IMPERATIVE MOOD

figure   **be figured**

SUBJUNCTIVE MOOD

Pres.	if I, he, she, it,	if I, he, she, it,
	we, you, they **figure**	we, you, they **be figured**
Past	if I, he, she, it,	if I, he, she, it,
	we, you, they **figured**	we, you, they **were figured**
Fut.	if I, he, she, it,	if I, he, she, it,
	we, you, they **should figure**	we, you, they **should be figured**

Transitive and intransitive.

fill
(active voice)

PRINCIPAL PARTS: **fills, filling, filled, filled**

be filled
(passive voice)

Infinitive: **to fill**
Perfect Infinitive: **to have filled**
Present Participle: **filling**
Past Participle: **filled**

Infinitive: **to be filled**
Perfect Infinitive: **to have been filled**
Present Participle: **being filled**
Past Participle: **been filled**

INDICATIVE MOOD

Pres.	I, we, you, they **fill**	I **am filled**
		we, you, they **are filled**
	he, she, it **fills**	he, she, it **is filled**
Pres.	I **am filling**	I **am being filled**
Prog.	we, you, they **are filling**	we, you, they **are being filled**
	he, she, it **is filling**	he, she, it **is being filled**
Pres.	I, we, you, they **do fill**	I, we, you, they **do get filled**
Int.	he, she, it **does fill**	he, she, it **does get filled**
Fut.	I, he, she, it,	I, he, she, it,
	we, you, they **will fill**	we, you, they **will be filled**
Past	I, he, she, it,	I, he, she, it **was filled**
	we, you, they **filled**	we, you, they **were filled**
Past	I, he, she, it **was filling**	I, he, she, it **was being filled**
Prog.	we, you, they **were filling**	we, you, they **were being filled**
Past	I, he, she, it,	I, he, she, it,
Int.	we, you, they **did fill**	we, you, they **did get filled**
Pres.	I, we, you, they **have filled**	I, we, you, they **have been filled**
Perf.	he, she, it **has filled**	he, she, it **has been filled**
Past	I, he, she, it,	I, he, she, it,
Perf.	we, you, they **had filled**	we, you, they **had been filled**
Fut.	I, he, she, it, we, you, they	I, he, she, it, we, you, they
Perf.	**will have filled**	**will have been filled**

IMPERATIVE MOOD

fill

be filled

SUBJUNCTIVE MOOD

Pres.	if I, he, she, it,	if I, he, she, it,
	we, you, they **fill**	we, you, they **be filled**
Past	if I, he, she, it,	if I, he, she, it,
	we, you, they **filled**	we, you, they **were filled**
Fut.	if I, he, she, it,	if I, he, she, it,
	we, you, they **should fill**	we, you, they **should be filled**

Transitive and intransitive.

find
(active voice)

be found
(passive voice)

Infinitive: **to find**
Perfect Infinitive: **to have found**
Present Participle: **finding**
Past Participle: **found**

Infinitive: **to be found**
Perfect Infinitive: **to have been found**
Present Participle: **being found**
Past Participle: **been found**

INDICATIVE MOOD

Pres.	I, we, you, they **find**	I **am found**
		we, you, they **are found**
	he, she, it **finds**	he, she, it **is found**
Pres.	I **am finding**	I **am being found**
Prog.	we, you, they **are finding**	we, you, they **are being found**
	he, she, it **is finding**	he, she, it **is being found**
Pres.	I, we, you, they **do find**	I, we, you, they **do get found**
Int.	he, she, it **does find**	he, she, it **does get found**
Fut.	I, he, she, it,	I, he, she, it,
	we, you, they **will find**	we, you, they **will be found**
Past	I, he, she, it,	I, he, she, it **was found**
	we, you, they **found**	we, you, they **were found**
Past	I, he, she, it **was finding**	I, he, she, it **was being found**
Prog.	we, you, they **were finding**	we, you, they **were being found**
Past	I, he, she, it,	I, he, she, it,
Int.	we, you, they **did find**	we, you, they **did get found**
Pres.	I, we, you, they **have found**	I, we, you, they **have been found**
Perf.	he, she, it **has found**	he, she, it **has been found**
Past	I, he, she, it,	I, he, she, it,
Perf.	we, you, they **had found**	we, you, they **had been found**
Fut.	I, he, she, it, we, you, they	I, he, she, it, we, you, they
Perf.	**will have found**	**will have been found**

IMPERATIVE MOOD

find　　　　　　　　　**be found**

SUBJUNCTIVE MOOD

Pres.	if I, he, she, it,	if I, he, she, it,
	we, you, they **find**	we, you, they **be found**
Past	if I, he, she, it,	if I, he, she, it,
	we, you, they **found**	we, you, they **were found**
Fut.	if I, he, she, it,	if I, he, she, it,
	we, you, they **should find**	we, you, they **should be found**

This verb is normally transitive, except for the legal meaning, which uses the intransitive as in the following: "They **found** for the plaintiff, or the defendant."

finish
(active voice)

be finished
(passive voice)

Infinitive: **to finish**
Perfect Infinitive: **to have finished**
Present Participle: **finishing**
Past Participle: **finished**

Infinitive: **to be finished**
Perfect Infinitive: **to have been finished**
Present Participle: **being finished**
Past Participle: **been finished**

INDICATIVE MOOD

Pres.	I, we, you, they **finish**	I **am finished**
		we, you, they **are finished**
	he, she, it **finishes**	he, she, it **is finished**
Pres.	I **am finishing**	I **am being finished**
Prog.	we, you, they **are finishing**	we, you, they **are being finished**
	he, she, it **is finishing**	he, she, it **is being finished**
Pres.	I, we, you, they **do finish**	I, we, you, they **do get finished**
Int.	he, she, it **does finish**	he, she, it **does get finished**
Fut.	I, he, she, it,	I, he, she, it,
	we, you, they **will finish**	we, you, they **will be finished**
Past	I, he, she, it,	I, he, she, it **was finished**
	we, you, they **finished**	we, you, they **were finished**
Past	I, he, she, it **was finishing**	I, he, she, it **was being finished**
Prog.	we, you, they **were finishing**	we, you, they **were being finished**
Past	I, he, she, it,	I, he, she, it,
Int.	we, you, they **did finish**	we, you, they **did get finished**
Pres.	I, we, you, they **have finished**	I, we, you, they **have been finished**
Perf.	he, she, it **has finished**	he, she, it **has been finished**
Past	I, he, she, it,	I, he, she, it,
Perf.	we, you, they **had finished**	we, you, they **had been finished**
Fut.	I, he, she, it, we, you, they	I, he, she, it, we, you, they
Perf.	**will have finished**	**will have been finished**

IMPERATIVE MOOD

finish

be finished

SUBJUNCTIVE MOOD

Pres.	if I, he, she, it,	if I, he, she, it,
	we, you, they **finish**	we, you, they **be finished**
Past	if I, he, she, it,	if I, he, she, it,
	we, you, they **finished**	we, you, they **were finished**
Fut.	if I, he, she, it,	if I, he, she, it,
	we, you, they **should finish**	we, you, they **should be finished**

Transitive and intransitive.

fit
(active voice)

PRINCIPAL PARTS: **fits, fitting,
fitted/fit, fitted**

be fitted
(passive voice)

Infinitive: **to fit**
Perfect Infinitive: **to have fitted**
Present Participle: **fitting**
Past Participle: **fitted**

Infinitive: **to be fitted**
Perfect Infinitive: **to have been fitted**
Present Participle: **being fitted**
Past Participle: **been fitted**

INDICATIVE MOOD

Pres.	I, we, you, they **fit**	I **am fitted**
		we, you, they **are fitted**
	he, she, it **fits**	he, she, it **is fitted**
Pres.	I **am fitting**	I **am being fitted**
Prog.	we, you, they **are fitting**	we, you, they **are being fitted**
	he, she, it **is fitting**	he, she, it **is being fitted**
Pres.	I, we, you, they **do fit**	I, we, you, they **do get fitted**
Int.	he, she, it **does fit**	he, she, it **does get fitted**
Fut.	I, he, she, it,	I, he, she, it,
	we, you, they **will fit**	we, you, they **will be fitted**
Past	I, he, she, it,	I, he, she, it **was fitted**
	we, you, they **fitted/fit**	we, you, they **were fitted**
Past	I, he, she, it **was fitting**	I, he, she, it **was being fitted**
Prog.	we, you, they **were fitting**	we, you, they **were being fitted**
Past	I, he, she, it,	I, he, she, it,
Int.	we, you, they **did fit**	we, you, they **did get fitted**
Pres.	I, we, you, they **have fitted**	I, we, you, they **have been fitted**
Perf.	he, she, it **has fitted**	he, she, it **has been fitted**
Past	I, he, she, it,	I, he, she, it,
Perf.	we, you, they **had fitted**	we, you, they **had been fitted**
Fut.	I, he, she, it, we, you, they	I, he, she, it, we, you, they
Perf.	**will have fitted**	**will have been fitted**

IMPERATIVE MOOD

fit   **be fitted**

SUBJUNCTIVE MOOD

Pres.	if I, he, she, it,	if I, he, she, it,
	we, you, they **fit**	we, you, they **be fitted**
Past	if I, he, she, it,	if I, he, she, it,
	we, you, they **fitted/fit**	we, you, they **were fitted**
Fut.	if I, he, she, it,	if I, he, she, it,
	we, you, they **should fit**	we, you, they **should be fitted**

The past tense has two forms, FITTED and FIT: "They fitted him for a suit"; "The shoes fit nicely."

flee
(active voice)

be fled
(passive voice)

Infinitive: **to flee**
Perfect Infinitive: **to have fled**
Present Participle: **fleeing**
Past Participle: **fled**

Infinitive: **to be fled**
Perfect Infinitive: **to have been fled**
Present Participle: **being fled**
Past Participle: **been fled**

INDICATIVE MOOD

Pres.	I, we, you, they **flee**	I **am fled**
		we, you, they **are fled**
	he, she, it **flees**	he, she, it **is fled**
Pres.	I **am fleeing**	I **am being fled**
Prog.	we, you, they **are fleeing**	we, you, they **are being fled**
	he, she, it **is fleeing**	he, she, it **is being fled**
Pres.	I, we, you, they **do flee**	I, we, you, they **do get fled**
Int.	he, she, it **does flee**	he, she, it **does get fled**
Fut.	I, he, she, it,	I, he, she, it,
	we, you, they **will flee**	we, you, they **will be fled**
Past	I, he, she, it,	I, he, she, it **was fled**
	we, you, they **fled**	we, you, they **were fled**
Past	I, he, she, it **was fleeing**	I, he, she, it **was being fled**
Prog.	we, you, they **were fleeing**	we, you, they **were being fled**
Past	I, he, she, it,	I, he, she, it,
Int.	we, you, they **did flee**	we, you, they **did get fled**
Pres.	I, we, you, they **have fled**	I, we, you, they **have been fled**
Perf.	he, she, it **has fled**	he, she, it **has been fled**
Past	I, he, she, it,	I, he, she, it,
Perf.	we, you, they **had fled**	we, you, they **had been fled**
Fut.	I, he, she, it, we, you, they	I, he, she, it, we, you, they
Perf.	**will have fled**	**will have been fled**

IMPERATIVE MOOD

flee   **be fled**

SUBJUNCTIVE MOOD

Pres.	if I, he, she, it,	if I, he, she, it,
	we, you, they **flee**	we, you, they **be fled**
Past	if I, he, she, it,	if I, he, she, it,
	we, you, they **fled**	we, you, they **were fled**
Fut.	if I, he, she, it,	if I, he, she, it,
	we, you, they **should flee**	we, you, they **should be fled**

Intransitive and transitive.

fling
(active voice)

be flung
(passive voice)

Infinitive: **to fling**
Perfect Infinitive: **to have flung**
Present Participle: **flinging**
Past Participle: **flung**

Infinitive: **to be flung**
Perfect Infinitive: **to have been flung**
Present Participle: **being flung**
Past Participle: **been flung**

INDICATIVE MOOD

Pres.	I, we, you, they **fling**	I **am flung**
		we, you, they **are flung**
	he, she, it **flings**	he, she, it **is flung**
Pres.	I **am flinging**	I **am being flung**
Prog.	we, you, they **are flinging**	we, you, they **are being flung**
	he, she, it **is flinging**	he, she, it **is being flung**
Pres.	I, we, you, they **do fling**	I, we, you, they **do get flung**
Int.	he, she, it **does fling**	he, she, it **does get flung**
Fut.	I, he, she, it,	I, he, she, it,
	we, you, they **will fling**	we, you, they **will be flung**
Past	I, he, she, it,	I, he, she, it **was flung**
	we, you, they **flung**	we, you, they **were flung**
Past	I, he, she, it **was flinging**	I, he, she, it **was being flung**
Prog.	we, you, they **were flinging**	we, you, they **were being flung**
Past	I, he, she, it,	I, he, she, it,
Int.	we, you, they **did fling**	we, you, they **did get flung**
Pres.	I, we, you, they **have flung**	I, we, you, they **have been flung**
Perf.	he, she, it **has flung**	he, she, it **has been flung**
Past	I, he, she, it,	I, he, she, it,
Perf.	we, you, they **had flung**	we, you, they **had been flung**
Fut.	I, he, she, it, we, you, they	I, he, she, it, we, you, they
Perf.	**will have flung**	**will have been flung**

IMPERATIVE MOOD

fling **be flung**

SUBJUNCTIVE MOOD

Pres.	if I, he, she, it,	if I, he, she, it,
	we, you, they **fling**	we, you, they **be flung**
Past	if I, he, she, it,	if I, he, she, it,
	we, you, they **flung**	we, you, they **were flung**
Fut.	if I, he, she, it,	if I, he, she, it,
	we, you, they **should fling**	we, you, they **should be flung**

Transitive and intransitive.

fly
(active voice)

PRINCIPAL PARTS: **flies, flying, flew, flown**

be flown
(passive voice)

Infinitive: **to fly**
Perfect Infinitive: **to have flown**
Present Participle: **flying**
Past Participle: **flown**

Infinitive: **to be flown**
Perfect Infinitive: **to have been flown**
Present Participle: **being flown**
Past Participle: **been flown**

INDICATIVE MOOD

Pres.	I, we, you, they **fly**	I **am flown**
		we, you, they **are flown**
	he, she, it **flies**	he, she, it **is flown**
Pres. Prog.	I **am flying**	I **am being flown**
	we, you, they **are flying**	we, you, they **are being flown**
	he, she, it **is flying**	he, she, it **is being flown**
Pres. Int.	I, we, you, they **do fly**	I, we, you, they **do get flown**
	he, she, it **does fly**	he, she, it **does get flown**
Fut.	I, he, she, it, we, you, they **will fly**	I, he, she, it, we, you, they **will be flown**
Past	I, he, she, it, we, you, they **flew**	I, he, she, it **was flown** we, you, they **were flown**
Past Prog.	I, he, she, it **was flying** we, you, they **were flying**	I, he, she, it **was being flown** we, you, they **were being flown**
Past Int.	I, he, she, it, we, you, they **did fly**	I, he, she, it, we, you, they **did get flown**
Pres. Perf.	I, we, you, they **have flown** he, she, it **has flown**	I, we, you, they **have been flown** he, she, it **has been flown**
Past Perf.	I, he, she, it, we, you, they **had flown**	I, he, she, it, we, you, they **had been flown**
Fut. Perf.	I, he, she, it, we, you, they **will have flown**	I, he, she, it, we, you, they **will have been flown**

IMPERATIVE MOOD

fly

be flown

SUBJUNCTIVE MOOD

Pres.	if I, he, she, it, we, you, they **fly**	if I, he, she, it, we, you, they **be flown**
Past	if I, he, she, it, we, you, they **flew**	if I, he, she, it, we, you, they **were flown**
Fut.	if I, he, she, it, we, you, they **should fly**	if I, he, she, it, we, you, they **should be flown**

Intransitive and transitive. In baseball, the past tense is FLIED meaning "to hit a ball to the outfield": "He flied to center, left, or right."

focus
(active voice)

be focused/ focussed
(passive voice)

Infinitive: **to focus**
Perfect Infinitive: **to have focused**
Present Participle: **focusing**
Past Participle: **focused**

Infinitive: **to be focused**
Perfect Infinitive: **to have been focused**
Present Participle: **being focused**
Past Participle: **been focused**

INDICATIVE MOOD

Pres.	I, we, you, they **focus**	I **am focused**
		we, you, they **are focused**
	he, she, it **focuses**	he, she, it **is focused**
Pres. *Prog.*	I **am focusing**	I **am being focused**
	we, you, they **are focusing**	we, you, they **are being focused**
	he, she, it **is focusing**	he, she, it **is being focused**
Pres. *Int.*	I, we, you, they **do focus**	I, we, you, they **do get focused**
	he, she, it **does focus**	he, she, it **does get focused**
Fut.	I, he, she, it, we, you, they **will focus**	I, he, she, it, we, you, they **will be focused**
Past	I, he, she, it, we, you, they **focused**	I, he, she, it **was focused** we, you, they **were focused**
Past *Prog.*	I, he, she, it **was focusing** we, you, they **were focusing**	I, he, she, it **was being focused** we, you, they **were being focused**
Past *Int.*	I, he, she, it, we, you, they **did focus**	I, he, she, it, we, you, they **did get focused**
Pres. *Perf.*	I, we, you, they **have focused** he, she, it **has focused**	I, we, you, they **have been focused** he, she, it **has been focused**
Past *Perf.*	I, he, she, it, we, you, they **had focused**	I, he, she, it, we, you, they **had been focused**
Fut. *Perf.*	I, he, she, it, we, you, they **will have focused**	I, he, she, it, we, you, they **will have been focused**

IMPERATIVE MOOD

focus   **be focused**

SUBJUNCTIVE MOOD

Pres.	if I, he, she, it, we, you, they **focus**	if I, he, she, it, we, you, they **be focused**
Past	if I, he, she, it, we, you, they **focused**	if I, he, she, it, we, you, they **were focused**
Fut.	if I, he, she, it, we, you, they **should focus**	if I, he, she, it, we, you, they **should be focused**

Transitive and intransitive. The past tense and participle forms may have either a single or double "s."

follow
(active voice)

be followed
(passive voice)

Infinitive: **to follow**
Perfect Infinitive: **to have followed**
Present Participle: **following**
Past Participle: **followed**

Infinitive: **to be followed**
Perfect Infinitive: **to have been followed**
Present Participle: **being followed**
Past Participle: **been followed**

INDICATIVE MOOD

Pres.	I, we, you, they **follow**	I **am followed**
		we, you, they **are followed**
	he, she, it **follows**	he, she, it **is followed**
Pres. *Prog.*	I **am following**	I **am being followed**
	we, you, they **are following**	we, you, they **are being followed**
	he, she, it **is following**	he, she, it **is being followed**
Pres. *Int.*	I, we, you, they **do follow**	I, we, you, they **do get followed**
	he, she, it **does follow**	he, she, it **does get followed**
Fut.	I, he, she, it, we, you, they **will follow**	I, he, she, it, we, you, they **will be followed**
Past	I, he, she, it, we, you, they **followed**	I, he, she, it **was followed** we, you, they **were followed**
Past *Prog.*	I, he, she, it **was following** we, you, they **were following**	I, he, she, it **was being followed** we, you, they **were being followed**
Past *Int.*	I, he, she, it, we, you, they **did follow**	I, he, she, it, we, you, they **did get followed**
Pres. *Perf.*	I, we, you, they **have followed** he, she, it **has followed**	I, we, you, they **have been followed** he, she, it **has been followed**
Past *Perf.*	I, he, she, it, we, you, they **had followed**	I, he, she, it, we, you, they **had been followed**
Fut. *Perf.*	I, he, she, it, we, you, they **will have followed**	I, he, she, it, we, you, they **will have been followed**

IMPERATIVE MOOD

follow   **be followed**

SUBJUNCTIVE MOOD

Pres.	if I, he, she, it, we, you, they **follow**	if I, he, she, it, we, you, they **be followed**
Past	if I, he, she, it, we, you, they **followed**	if I, he, she, it, we, you, they **were followed**
Fut.	if I, he, she, it, we, you, they **should follow**	if I, he, she, it, we, you, they **should be followed**

Transitive and intransitive.

forbear
(active voice)

be forborne
(passive voice)

Infinitive: **to forbear**
Perfect Infinitive: **to have forborne**
Present Participle: **forbearing**
Past Participle: **forborne**

Infinitive: **to be forborne**
Perfect Infinitive: **to have been forborne**
Present Participle: **being forborne**
Past Participle: **been forborne**

INDICATIVE MOOD

Pres.	I, we, you, they **forbear**	I **am forborne**
		we, you, they **are forborne**
	he, she, it **forbears**	he, she, it **is forborne**
Pres.	I **am forbearing**	I **am being forborne**
Prog.	we, you, they **are forbearing**	we, you, they **are being forborne**
	he, she, it **is forbearing**	he, she, it **is being forborne**
Pres.	I, we, you, they **do forbear**	I, we, you, they **do get forborne**
Int.	he, she, it **does forbear**	he, she, it **does get forborne**
Fut.	I, he, she, it,	I, he, she, it,
	we, you, they **will forbear**	we, you, they **will be forborne**
Past	I, he, she, it,	I, he, she, it **was forborne**
	we, you, they **forbore**	we, you, they **were forborne**
Past	I, he, she, it **was forbearing**	I, he, she, it **was being forborne**
Prog.	we, you, they **were forbearing**	we, you, they **were being forborne**
Past	I, he, she, it,	I, he, she, it,
Int.	we, you, they **did forbear**	we, you, they **did get forborne**
Pres.	I, we, you, they **have forborne**	I, we, you, they **have been forborne**
Perf.	he, she, it **has forborne**	he, she, it **has been forborne**
Past	I, he, she, it,	I, he, she, it,
Perf.	we, you, they **had forborne**	we, you, they **had been forborne**
Fut.	I, he, she, it, we, you, they	I, he, she, it, we, you, they
Perf.	**will have forborne**	**will have been forborne**

IMPERATIVE MOOD

forbear   **be forborne**

SUBJUNCTIVE MOOD

Pres.	if I, he, she, it,	if I, he, she, it,
	we, you, they **forbear**	we, you, they **be forborne**
Past	if I, he, she, it,	if I, he, she, it,
	we, you, they **forbore**	we, you, they **were forborne**
Fut.	if I, he, she, it,	if I, he, she, it,
	we, you, they **should forbear**	we, you, they **should be forborne**

142

forbid
(active voice)

PRINCIPAL PARTS: **forbids, forbidding, forbade/forbad, forbidden/forbid**

be forbidden/forbid
(passive voice)

Infinitive: **to forbid**
Perfect Infinitive: **to have forbidden**
Present Participle: **forbidding**
Past Participle: **forbidden**

Infinitive: **to be forbidden**
Perfect Infinitive: **to have been forbidden**
Present Participle: **being forbidden**
Past Participle: **been forbidden**

INDICATIVE MOOD

Pres.	I, we, you, they **forbid**	I **am forbidden**
		we, you, they **are forbidden**
	he, she, it **forbids**	he, she, it **is forbidden**
Pres. *Prog.*	I **am forbidding**	I **am being forbidden**
	we, you, they **are forbidding**	we, you, they **are being forbidden**
	he, she, it **is forbidding**	he, she, it **is being forbidden**
Pres. *Int.*	I, we, you, they **do forbid**	I, we, you, they **do get forbidden**
	he, she, it **does forbid**	he, she, it **does get forbidden**
Fut.	I, he, she, it, we, you, they **will forbid**	I, he, she, it, we, you, they **will be forbidden**
Past	I, he, she, it, we, you, they **forbade/forbad**	I, he, she, it **was forbidden** we, you, they **were forbidden**
Past *Prog.*	I, he, she, it **was forbidding** we, you, they **were forbidding**	I, he, she, it **was being forbidden** we, you, they **were being forbidden**
Past *Int.*	I, he, she, it, we, you, they **did forbid**	I, he, she, it, we, you, they **did get forbidden**
Pres. *Perf.*	I, we, you, they **have forbidden** he, she, it **has forbidden**	I, we, you, they **have been forbidden** he, she, it **has been forbidden**
Past *Perf.*	I, he, she, it, we, you, they **had forbidden**	I, he, she, it, we, you, they **had been forbidden**
Fut. *Perf.*	I, he, she, it, we, you, they **will have forbidden**	I, he, she, it, we, you, they **will have been forbidden**

IMPERATIVE MOOD

forbid   **be forbidden**

SUBJUNCTIVE MOOD

Pres.	if I, he, she, it, we, you, they **forbid**	if I, he, she, it, we, you, they **be forbidden**
Past	if I, he, she, it, we, you, they **forbade/forbad**	if I, he, she, it, we, you, they **were forbidden**
Fut.	if I, he, she, it, we, you, they **should forbid**	if I, he, she, it, we, you, they **should be forbidden**

In the past tense FORBADE and FORBAD are acceptable. The past participle may be FORBIDDEN or FORBID.

force
(active voice)

PRINCIPAL PARTS: **forces, forcing, forced, forced**

be forced
(passive voice)

Infinitive: **to force**
Perfect Infinitive: **to have forced**
Present Participle: **forcing**
Past Participle: **forced**

Infinitive: **to be forced**
Perfect Infinitive: **to have been forced**
Present Participle: **being forced**
Past Participle: **been forced**

INDICATIVE MOOD

Pres.	I, we, you, they **force** he, she, it **forces**	I **am forced** we, you, they **are forced** he, she, it **is forced**	
Pres. *Prog.*	I **am forcing** we, you, they **are forcing** he, she, it **is forcing**	I **am being forced** we, you, they **are being forced** he, she, it **is being forced**	
Pres. *Int.*	I, we, you, they **do force** he, she, it **does force**	I, we, you, they **do get forced** he, she, it **does get forced**	
Fut.	I, he, she, it, we, you, they **will force**	I, he, she, it, we, you, they **will be forced**	
Past	I, he, she, it, we, you, they **forced**	I, he, she, it **was forced** we, you, they **were forced**	
Past *Prog.*	I, he, she, it **was forcing** we, you, they **were forcing**	I, he, she, it **was being forced** we, you, they **were being forced**	
Past *Int.*	I, he, she, it, we, you, they **did force**	I, he, she, it, we, you, they **did get forced**	
Pres. *Perf.*	I, we, you, they **have forced** he, she, it **has forced**	I, we, you, they **have been forced** he, she, it **has been forced**	
Past *Perf.*	I, he, she, it, we, you, they **had forced**	I, he, she, it, we, you, they **had been forced**	
Fut. *Perf.*	I, he, she, it, we, you, they **will have forced**	I, he, she, it, we, you, they **will have been forced**	

IMPERATIVE MOOD

force   **be forced**

SUBJUNCTIVE MOOD

Pres.	if I, he, she, it, we, you, they **force**	if I, he, she, it, we, you, they **be forced**
Past	if I, he, she, it, we, you, they **forced**	if I, he, she, it, we, you, they **were forced**
Fut.	if I, he, she, it, we, you, they **should force**	if I, he, she, it, we, you, they **should be forced**

forecast
(active voice)

PRINCIPAL PARTS: **forecasts, forecasting, forecast/forecasted, forecast/forecasted**

be forecast/ forecasted
(passive voice)

Infinitive: **to forecast**
Perfect Infinitive: **to have forecast**
Present Participle: **forecasting**
Past Participle: **forecast**

Infinitive: **to be forecast**
Perfect Infinitive: **to have been forecast**
Present Participle: **being forecast**
Past Participle: **been forecast**

INDICATIVE MOOD

Pres.	I, we, you, they **forecast**	I **am forecast**
		we, you, they **are forecast**
	he, she, it **forecasts**	he, she, it **is forecast**
Pres. *Prog.*	I **am forecasting**	I **am being forecast**
	we, you, they **are forecasting**	we, you, they **are being forecast**
	he, she, it **is forecasting**	he, she, it **is being forecast**
Pres. *Int.*	I, we, you, they **do forecast**	I, we, you, they **do get forecast**
	he, she, it **does forecast**	he, she, it **does get forecast**
Fut.	I, he, she, it, we, you, they **will forecast**	I, he, she, it, we, you, they **will be forecast**
Past	I, he, she, it, we, you, they **forecast**	I, he, she, it **was forecast** we, you, they **were forecast**
Past *Prog.*	I, he, she, it **was forecasting** we, you, they **were forecasting**	I, he, she, it **was being forecast** we, you, they **were being forecast**
Past *Int.*	I, he, she, it, we, you, they **did forecast**	I, he, she, it, we, you, they **did get forecast**
Pres. *Perf.*	I, we, you, they **have forecast** he, she, it **has forecast**	I, we, you, they **have been forecast** he, she, it **has been forecast**
Past *Perf.*	I, he, she, it, we, you, they **had forecast**	I, he, she, it, we, you, they **had been forecast**
Fut. *Perf.*	I, he, she, it, we, you, they **will have forecast**	I, he, she, it, we, you, they **will have been forecast**

IMPERATIVE MOOD

forecast   **be forecast**

SUBJUNCTIVE MOOD

Pres.	if I, he, she, it, we, you, they **forecast**	if I, he, she, it, we, you, they **be forecast**
Past	if I, he, she, it, we, you, they **forecast**	if I, he, she, it, we, you, they **were forecast**
Fut.	if I, he, she, it, we, you, they **should forecast**	if I, he, she, it, we, you, they **should be forecast**

Transitive and intransitive. In the past and past participle forms, both FORECAST and FORECASTED are acceptable.

foresee
(active voice)

be foreseen
(passive voice)

Infinitive: **to foresee**
Perfect Infinitive: **to have foreseen**
Present Participle: **foreseeing**
Past Participle: **foreseen**

Infinitive: **to be foreseen**
Perfect Infinitive: **to have been foreseen**
Present Participle: **being foreseen**
Past Participle: **been foreseen**

INDICATIVE MOOD

Pres. I, we, you, they **foresee**

he, she, it **foresees**

I **am foreseen**
we, you, they **are foreseen**
he, she, it **is foreseen**

Pres. **I am foreseeing**
Prog. we, you, they **are foreseeing**
he, she, it **is foreseeing**

I **am being foreseen**
we, you, they **are being foreseen**
he, she, it **is being foreseen**

Pres. I, we, you, they **do foresee**
Int. he, she, it **does foresee**

I, we, you, they **do get foreseen**
he, she, it **does get foreseen**

Fut. I, he, she, it,
we, you, they **will foresee**

I, he, she, it,
we, you, they **will be foreseen**

Past I, he, she, it,
we, you, they **foresaw**

I, he, she, it **was foreseen**
we, you, they **were foreseen**

Past I, he, she, it **was foreseeing**
Prog. we, you, they **were foreseeing**

I, he, she, it **was being foreseen**
we, you, they **were being foreseen**

Past I, he, she, it,
Int. we, you, they **did foresee**

I, he, she, it,
we, you, they **did get foreseen**

Pres. I, we, you, they **have foreseen**
Perf. he, she, it **has foreseen**

I, we, you, they **have been foreseen**
he, she, it **has been foreseen**

Past I, he, she, it,
Perf. we, you, they **had foreseen**

I, he, she, it,
we, you, they **had been foreseen**

Fut. I, he, she, it, we, you, they
Perf. **will have foreseen**

I, he, she, it, we, you, they
will have been foreseen

IMPERATIVE MOOD

foresee

be foreseen

SUBJUNCTIVE MOOD

Pres. if I, he, she, it,
we, you, they **foresee**

if I, he, she, it,
we, you, they **be foreseen**

Past if I, he, she, it,
we, you, they **foresaw**

if I, he, she, it,
we, you, they **were foreseen**

Fut. if I, he, she, it,
we, you, they **should foresee**

if I, he, she, it,
we, you, they **should be foreseen**

foretell
(active voice)

be foretold
(passive voice)

Infinitive: **to foretell**
Perfect Infinitive: **to have foretold**
Present Participle: **foretelling**
Past Participle: **foretold**

Infinitive: **to be foretold**
Perfect Infinitive: **to have been foretold**
Present Participle: **being foretold**
Past Participle: **been foretold**

INDICATIVE MOOD

Pres.	I, we, you, they **foretell**	I **am foretold**
		we, you, they **are foretold**
	he, she, it **foretells**	he, she, it **is foretold**
Pres.	I **am foretelling**	I **am being foretold**
Prog.	we, you, they **are foretelling**	we, you, they **are being foretold**
	he, she, it **is foretelling**	he, she, it **is being foretold**
Pres.	I, we, you, they **do foretell**	I, we, you, they **do get foretold**
Int.	he, she, it **does foretell**	he, she, it **does get foretold**
Fut.	I, he, she, it,	I, he, she, it,
	we, you, they **will foretell**	we, you, they **will be foretold**
Past	I, he, she, it,	I, he, she, it **was foretold**
	we, you, they **foretold**	we, you, they **were foretold**
Past	I, he, she, it **was foretelling**	I, he, she, it **was being foretold**
Prog.	we, you, they **were foretelling**	we, you, they **were being foretold**
Past	I, he, she, it,	I, he, she, it,
Int.	we, you, they **did foretell**	we, you, they **did get foretold**
Pres.	I, we, you, they **have foretold**	I, we, you, they **have been foretold**
Perf.	he, she, it **has foretold**	he, she, it **has been foretold**
Past	I, he, she, it,	I, he, she, it,
Perf.	we, you, they **had foretold**	we, you, they **had been foretold**
Fut.	I, he, she, it, we, you, they	I, he, she, it, we, you, they
Perf.	**will have foretold**	**will have been foretold**

IMPERATIVE MOOD

foretell

be foretold

SUBJUNCTIVE MOOD

Pres.	if I, he, she, it,	if I, he, she, it,
	we, you, they **foretell**	we, you, they **be foretold**
Past	if I, he, she, it,	if I, he, she, it,
	we, you, they **foretold**	we, you, they **were foretold**
Fut.	if I, he, she, it,	if I, he, she, it,
	we, you, they **should foretell**	we, you, they **should be foretold**

forget
(active voice)

PRINCIPAL PARTS: forgets, forgetting, forgot, forgotten/forgot

be forgotten/forgot
(passive voice)

Infinitive: **to forget**
Perfect Infinitive: **to have forgotten**
Present Participle: **forgetting**
Past Participle: **forgotten**

Infinitive: **to be forgotten**
Perfect Infinitive: **to have been forgotten**
Present Participle: **being forgotten**
Past Participle: **been forgotten**

INDICATIVE MOOD

Pres.	I, we, you, they **forget**	I **am forgotten**
		we, you, they **are forgotten**
	he, she, it **forgets**	he, she, it **is forgotten**
Pres.	I **am forgetting**	I **am being forgotten**
Prog.	we, you, they **are forgetting**	we, you, they **are being forgotten**
	he, she, it **is forgetting**	he, she, it **is being forgotten**
Pres.	I, we, you, they **do forget**	I, we, you, **do get forgotten**
Int.	he, she, it **does forget**	he, she, it **does get forgotten**
Fut.	I, he, she, it,	I, he, she, it,
	we, you, they **will forget**	we, you, they **will be forgotten**
Past	I, he, she, it,	I, he, she, it **was forgotten**
	we, you, they **forgot**	we, you, they **were forgotten**
Past	I, he, she, it **was forgetting**	I, he, she, it **was being forgotten**
Prog.	we, you, they **were forgetting**	we, you, they **were being forgotten**
Past	I, he, she, it,	I, he, she, it,
Int.	we, you, they **did forget**	we, you, they **did get forgotten**
Pres.	I, we, you, they **have forgotten**	I, we, you, they **have been forgotten**
Perf.	he, she, it **has forgotten**	he, she, it **has been forgotten**
Past	I, he, she, it,	I, he, she, it,
Perf.	we, you, they **had forgotten**	we, you, they **had been forgotten**
Fut.	I, he, she, it, we, you, they	I, he, she, it, we, you, they
Perf.	**will have forgotten**	**will have been forgotten**

IMPERATIVE MOOD

forget

be forgotten

SUBJUNCTIVE MOOD

Pres.	if I, he, she, it,	if I, he, she, it,
	we, you, they **forget**	we, you, they **be forgotten**
Past	if I, he, she, it,	if I, he, she, it,
	we, you, they **forgot**	we, you, they **were forgotten**
Fut.	if I, he, she, it,	if I, he, she, it,
	we, you, they **should forget**	we, you, they **should be forgotten**

Transitive and intransitive. The past participle form may be either FORGOTTEN or FORGOT.

forgive
(active voice)

be forgiven
(passive voice)

Infinitive: **to forgive**
Perfect Infinitive: **to have forgiven**
Present Participle: **forgiving**
Past Participle: **forgiven**

Infinitive: **to be forgiven**
Perfect Infinitive: **to have been forgiven**
Present Participle: **being forgiven**
Past Participle: **been forgiven**

INDICATIVE MOOD

Pres.	I, we, you, they **forgive** he, she, it **forgives**	I **am forgiven** we, you, they **are forgiven** he, she, it **is forgiven**
Pres. *Prog.*	I **am forgiving** we, you, they **are forgiving** he, she, it **is forgiving**	I **am being forgiven** we, you, they **are being forgiven** he, she, it **is being forgiven**
Pres. *Int.*	I, we, you, they **do forgive** he, she, it **does forgive**	I, we, you, they **do get forgiven** he, she, it **does get forgiven**
Fut.	I, he, she, it, we, you, they **will forgive**	I, he, she, it, we, you, they **will be forgiven**
Past	I, he, she, it, we, you, they **forgave**	I, he, she, it **was forgiven** we, you, they **were forgiven**
Past *Prog.*	I, he, she, it **was forgiving** we, you, they **were forgiving**	I, he, she, it **was being forgiven** we, you, they **were being forgiven**
Past *Int.*	I, he, she, it, we, you, they **did forgive**	I, he, she, it, we, you, they **did get forgiven**
Pres. *Perf.*	I, we, you, they **have forgiven** he, she, it **has forgiven**	I, we, you, they **have been forgiven** he, she, it **has been forgiven**
Past *Perf.*	I, he, she, it, we, you, they **had forgiven**	I, he, she, it, we, you, they **had been forgiven**
Fut. *Perf.*	I, he, she, it, we, you, they **will have forgiven**	I, he, she, it, we, you, they **will have been forgiven**

IMPERATIVE MOOD

forgive   **be forgiven**

SUBJUNCTIVE MOOD

Pres.	if I, he, she, it, we, you, they **forgive**	if I, he, she, it, we, you, they **be forgiven**
Past	if I, he, she, it, we, you, they **forgave**	if I, he, she, it, we, you, they **were forgiven**
Fut.	if I, he, she, it, we, you, they **should forgive**	if I, he, she, it, we, you, they **should be forgiven**

Transitive and intransitive.

forgo
(active voice)

PRINCIPAL PARTS: **forgoes, forgoing, forwent, forgone**

be forgone
(passive voice)

Infinitive: **to forgo**
Perfect Infinitive: **to have forgone**
Present Participle: **forgoing**
Past Participle: **forgone**

Infinitive: **to be forgone**
Perfect Infinitive: **to have been forgone**
Present Participle: **being forgone**
Past Participle: **been forgone**

INDICATIVE MOOD

Pres.	I, we, you, they **forgo**	I **am forgone**
		we, you, they **are forgone**
	he, she, it **forgoes**	he, she, it **is forgone**
Pres.	I **am forgoing**	I **am being forgone**
Prog.	we, you, they **are forgoing**	we, you, they **are being forgone**
	he, she, it **is forgoing**	he, she, it **is being forgone**
Pres.	I, we, you, they **do forgo**	I, we, you, they **do get forgone**
Int.	he, she, it **does forgo**	he, she, it **does get forgone**
Fut.	I, he, she, it, we, you, they **will forgo**	I, he, she, it, we, you, they **will be forgone**
Past	I, he, she, it, we, you, they **forwent**	I, he, she, it **was forgone** we, you, they **were forgone**
Past	I, he, she, it **was forgoing**	I, he, she, it **was being forgone**
Prog.	we, you, they **were forgoing**	we, you, they **were being forgone**
Past	I, he, she, it, we, you, they **did forgo**	I, he, she, it, we, you, they **did get forgone**
Int.		
Pres.	I, we, you, they **have forgone**	I, we, you, they **have been forgone**
Perf.	he, she, it **has forgone**	he, she, it **has been forgone**
Past	I, he, she, it, we, you, they **had forgone**	I, he, she, it, we, you, they **had been forgone**
Perf.		
Fut.	I, he, she, it, we, you, they **will have forgone**	I, he, she, it, we, you, they **will have been forgone**
Perf.		

IMPERATIVE MOOD

forgo   **be forgone**

SUBJUNCTIVE MOOD

Pres.	if I, he, she, it, we, you, they **forgo**	if I, he, she, it, we, you, they **be forgone**
Past	if I, he, she, it, we, you, they **forwent**	if I, he, she, it, we, you, they **were forgone**
Fut.	if I, he, she, it, we, you, they **should forgo**	if I, he, she, it, we, you, they **should be forgone**

An alternate spelling of this verb, meaning "to abstain," is FOREGO, its past and past participle FOREWENT and FOREGONE. There is another verb FOREGO (past and past participle FOREWENT, FOREWENT), which means "to precede, come before something."

Infinitive: **to form**
Perfect Infinitive: **to have formed**
Present Participle: **forming**
Past Participle: **formed**

Infinitive: **to be formed**
Perfect Infinitive: **to have been formed**
Present Participle: **being formed**
Past Participle: **been formed**

INDICATIVE MOOD

Pres.	I, we, you, they **form**	I **am formed**
		we, you, they **are formed**
	he, she, it **forms**	he, she, it **is formed**
Pres.	I **am forming**	I **am being formed**
Prog.	we, you, they **are forming**	we, you, they **are being formed**
	he, she, it **is forming**	he, she, it **is being formed**
Pres.	I, we, you, they **do form**	I, we, you, they **do get formed**
Int.	he, she, it **does form**	he, she, it **does get formed**
Fut.	I, he, she, it, we, you, they **will form**	I, he, she, it, we, you, they **will be formed**
Past	I, he, she, it, we, you, they **formed**	I, he, she, it **was formed** we, you, they **were formed**
Past	I, he, she, it **was forming**	I, he, she, it **was being formed**
Prog.	we, you, they **were forming**	we, you, they **were being formed**
Past	I, he, she, it, we, you, they **did form**	I, he, she, it, we, you, they **did get formed**
Int.		
Pres.	I, we, you, they **have formed**	I, we, you, they **have been formed**
Perf.	he, she, it **has formed**	he, she, it **has been formed**
Past	I, he, she, it, we, you, they **had formed**	I, he, she, it, we, you, they **had been formed**
Perf.		
Fut.	I, he, she, it, we, you, they	I, he, she, it, we, you, they
Perf.	**will have formed**	**will have been formed**

IMPERATIVE MOOD

form

be formed

SUBJUNCTIVE MOOD

Pres.	if I, he, she, it, we, you, they **form**	if I, he, she, it, we, you, they **be formed**
Past	if I, he, she, it, we, you, they **formed**	if I, he, she, it, we, you, they **were formed**
Fut.	if I, he, she, it, we, you, they **should form**	if I, he, she, it, we, you, they **should be formed**

Transitive and intransitive.

forsake
(active voice)

PRINCIPAL PARTS: **forsakes, forsaking, forsook, forsaken**

be forsaken
(passive voice)

Infinitive: **to forsake**
Perfect Infinitive: **to have forsaken**
Present Participle: **forsaking**
Past Participle: **forsaken**

Infinitive: **to be forsaken**
Perfect Infinitive: **to have been forsaken**
Present Participle: **being forsaken**
Past Participle: **been forsaken**

INDICATIVE MOOD

Pres.	I, we, you, they **forsake**	I **am forsaken**
		we, you, they **are forsaken**
	he, she, it **forsakes**	he, she, it **is forsaken**
Pres. *Prog.*	I **am forsaking**	I **am being forsaken**
	we, you, they **are forsaking**	we, you, they **are being forsaken**
	he, she, it **is forsaking**	he, she, it **is being forsaken**
Pres. *Int.*	I, we, you, they **do forsake**	I, we, you, they **do get forsaken**
	he, she, it **does forsake**	he, she, it **does get forsaken**
Fut.	I, he, she, it, we, you, they **will forsake**	I, he, she, it, we, you, they **will be forsaken**
Past	I, he, she, it, we, you, they **foresook**	I, he, she, it **was forsaken** we, you, they **were forsaken**
Past *Prog.*	I, he, she, it **was forsaking** we, you, they **were forsaking**	I, he, she, it **was being forsaken** we, you, they **were being forsaken**
Past *Int.*	I, he, she, it, we, you, they **did forsake**	I, he, she, it, we, you, they **did get forsaken**
Pres. *Perf.*	I, we, you, they **have forsaken** he, she, it **has forsaken**	I, we, you, they **have been forsaken** he, she, it **has been forsaken**
Past *Perf.*	I, he, she, it, we, you, they **had forsaken**	I, he, she, it, we, you, they **had been forsaken**
Fut. *Perf.*	I, he, she, it, we, you, they **will have forsaken**	I, he, she, it, we, you, they **will have been forsaken**

IMPERATIVE MOOD

forsake

be forsaken

SUBJUNCTIVE MOOD

Pres.	if I, he, she, it, we, you, they **forsake**	if I, he, she, it, we, you, they **be forsaken**
Past	if I, he, she, it, we, you, they **foresook**	if I, he, she, it, we, you, they **were forsaken**
Fut.	if I, he, she, it, we, you, they **should forsake**	if I, he, she, it, we, you, they **should be forsaken**

forswear
(active voice)

PRINCIPAL PARTS: **forswears, forswearing, forswore, forsworn**

be forsworn
(passive voice)

Infinitive: **to forswear**
Perfect Infinitive: **to have forsworn**
Present Participle: **forswearing**
Past Participle: **forsworn**

Infinitive: **to be forsworn**
Perfect Infinitive: **to have been forsworn**
Present Participle: **being forsworn**
Past Participle: **been forsworn**

INDICATIVE MOOD

Pres.	I, we, you, they **forswear**	I **am forsworn**
		we, you, they **are forsworn**
	he, she, it **forswears**	he, she, it **is forsworn**
Pres.	I **am forswearing**	I **am being forsworn**
Prog.	we, you, they **are forswearing**	we, you, they **are being forsworn**
	he, she, it **is forswearing**	he, she, it **is being forsworn**
Pres.	I, we, you, they **do forswear**	I, we, you, they **do get forsworn**
Int.	he, she, it **does forswear**	he, she, it **does get forsworn**
Fut.	I, he, she, it,	I, he, she, it,
	we, you, they **will forswear**	we, you, they **will be forsworn**
Past	I, he, she, it,	I, he, she, it **was forsworn**
	we, you, they **forswore**	we, you, they **were forsworn**
Past	I, he, she, it **was forswearing**	I, he, she, it **was being forsworn**
Prog.	we, you, they **were forswearing**	we, you, they **were being forsworn**
Past	I, he, she, it,	I, he, she, it,
Int.	we, you, they **did forswear**	we, you, they **did get forsworn**
Pres.	I, we, you, they **have forsworn**	I, we, you, they **have been forsworn**
Perf.	he, she, it **has forsworn**	he, she, it **has been forsworn**
Past	I, he, she, it,	I, he, she, it,
Perf.	we, you, they **had forsworn**	we, you, they **had been forsworn**
Fut.	I, he, she, it, we, you, they	I, he, she, it, we, you, they
Perf.	**will have forsworn**	**will have been forsworn**

IMPERATIVE MOOD

forswear   **be forsworn**

SUBJUNCTIVE MOOD

Pres.	if I, he, she, it,	if I, he, she, it,
	we, you, they **forswear**	we, you, they **be forsworn**
Past	if I, he, she, it,	if I, he, she, it,
	we, you, they **forswore**	we, you, they **were forsworn**
Fut.	if I, he, she, it,	if I, he, she, it,
	we, you, they **should forswear**	we, you, they **should be forsworn**

Transitive and intransitive. The spellings FORESWEAR, FORESWORE, and FORESWORN are also acceptable.

found
(active voice)

be founded
(passive voice)

Infinitive: **to found**
Perfect Infinitive: **to have founded**
Present Participle: **founding**
Past Participle: **founded**

Infinitive: **to be founded**
Perfect Infinitive: **to have been founded**
Present Participle: **being founded**
Past Participle: **been founded**

INDICATIVE MOOD

Pres.	I, we, you, they **found** he, she, it **founds**	I **am founded** we, you, they **are founded** he, she, it **is founded**
Pres. *Prog.*	I **am founding** we, you, they **are founding** he, she, it **is founding**	I **am being founded** we, you, they **are being founded** he, she, it **is being founded**
Pres. *Int.*	I, we, you, they **do found** he, she, it **does found**	I, we, you, they **do get founded** he, she, it **does get founded**
Fut.	I, he, she, it, we, you, they **will found**	I, he, she, it, we, you, they **will be founded**
Past	I, he, she, it, we, you, they **founded**	I, he, she, it **was founded** we, you, they **were founded**
Past *Prog.*	I, he, she, it **was founding** we, you, they **were founding**	I, he, she, it **was being founded** we, you, they **were being founded**
Past *Int.*	I, he, she, it, we, you, they **did found**	I, he, she, it, we, you, they **did get founded**
Pres. *Perf.*	I, we, you, they **have founded** he, she, it **has founded**	I, we, you, they **have been founded** he, she, it **has been founded**
Past *Perf.*	I, he, she, it, we, you, they **had founded**	I, he, she, it, we, you, they **had been founded**
Fut. *Perf.*	I, he, she, it, we, you, they **will have founded**	I, he, she, it, we, you, they **will have been founded**

IMPERATIVE MOOD

found   **be founded**

SUBJUNCTIVE MOOD

Pres.	if I, he, she, it, we, you, they **found**	if I, he, she, it, we, you, they **be founded**
Past	if I, he, she, it, we, you, they **founded**	if I, he, she, it, we, you, they **were founded**
Fut.	if I, he, she, it, we, you, they **should found**	if I, he, she, it, we, you, they **should be founded**

Transitive and intransitive.

free
(active voice)

PRINCIPAL PARTS: **frees, freeing, freed, freed**

be freed
(passive voice)

Infinitive: **to free**
Perfect Infinitive: **to have freed**
Present Participle: **freeing**
Past Participle: **freed**

Infinitive: **to be freed**
Perfect Infinitive: **to have been freed**
Present Participle: **being freed**
Past Participle: **been freed**

INDICATIVE MOOD

Pres.	I, we, you, they **free**	I **am freed**
		we, you, they **are freed**
	he, she, it **frees**	he, she, it **is freed**
Pres. *Prog.*	I **am freeing**	I **am being freed**
	we, you, they **are freeing**	we, you, they **are being freed**
	he, she, it **is freeing**	he, she, it **is being freed**
Pres. *Int.*	I, we, you, they **do free**	I, we, you, they **do get freed**
	he, she, it **does free**	he, she, it **does get freed**
Fut.	I, he, she, it, we, you, they **will free**	I, he, she, it, we, you, they **will be freed**
Past	I, he, she, it, we, you, they **freed**	I, he, she, it **was freed** we, you, they **were freed**
Past *Prog.*	I, he, she, it **was freeing** we, you, they **were freeing**	I, he, she, it **was being freed** we, you, they **were being freed**
Past *Int.*	I, he, she, it, we, you, they **did free**	I, he, she, it, we, you, they **did get freed**
Pres. *Perf.*	I, we, you, they **have freed** he, she, it **has freed**	I, we, you, they **have been freed** he, she, it **has been freed**
Past *Perf.*	I, he, she, it, we, you, they **had freed**	I, he, she, it, we, you, they **had been freed**
Fut. *Perf.*	I, he, she, it, we, you, they **will have freed**	I, he, she, it, we, you, they **will have been freed**

IMPERATIVE MOOD

free **be freed**

SUBJUNCTIVE MOOD

Pres.	if I, he, she, it, we, you, they **free**	if I, he, she, it, we, you, they **be freed**
Past	if I, he, she, it, we, you, they **freed**	if I, he, she, it, we, you, they **were freed**
Fut.	if I, he, she, it, we, you, they **should free**	if I, he, she, it, we, you, they **should be freed**

freeze
(active voice)

be frozen
(passive voice)

Infinitive: **to freeze**
Perfect Infinitive: **to have frozen**
Present Participle: **freezing**
Past Participle: **frozen**

Infinitive: **to be frozen**
Perfect Infinitive: **to have been frozen**
Present Participle: **being frozen**
Past Participle: **been frozen**

INDICATIVE MOOD

Pres.	I, we, you, they **freeze**	I **am frozen** we, you, they **are frozen**
	he, she, it **freezes**	he, she, it **is frozen**
Pres. *Prog.*	I **am freezing** we, you, they **are freezing** he, she, it **is freezing**	I **am being frozen** we, you, they **are being frozen** he, she, it **is being frozen**
Pres. *Int.*	I, we, you, they **do freeze** he, she, it **does freeze**	I, we, you, they **do get frozen** he, she, it **does get frozen**
Fut.	I, he, she, it, we, you, they **will freeze**	I, he, she, it, we, you, they **will be frozen**
Past	I, he, she, it, we, you, they **froze**	I, he, she, it **was frozen** we, you, they **were frozen**
Past *Prog.*	I, he, she, it **was freezing** we, you, they **were freezing**	I, he, she, it **was being frozen** we, you, they **were being frozen**
Past *Int.*	I, he, she, it, we, you, they **did freeze**	I, he, she, it, we, you, they **did get frozen**
Pres. *Perf.*	I, we, you, they **have frozen** he, she, it **has frozen**	I, we, you, they **have been frozen** he, she, it **has been frozen**
Past *Perf.*	I, he, she, it, we, you, they **had frozen**	I, he, she, it, we, you, they **had been frozen**
Fut. *Perf.*	I, he, she, it, we, you, they **will have frozen**	I, he, she, it, we, you, they **will have been frozen**

IMPERATIVE MOOD

freeze   **be frozen**

SUBJUNCTIVE MOOD

Pres.	if I, he, she, it, we, you, they **freeze**	if I, he, she, it, we, you, they **be frozen**
Past	if I, he, she, it, we, you, they **froze**	if I, he, she, it, we, you, they **were frozen**
Fut.	if I, he, she, it, we, you, they **should freeze**	if I, he, she, it, we, you, they **should be frozen**

Intransitive and transitive.

frighten
(active voice)

PRINCIPAL PARTS: **frightens, frightening, frightened, frightened**

be frightened
(passive voice)

Infinitive: **to frighten**
Perfect Infinitive: **to have frightened**
Present Participle: **frightening**
Past Participle: **frightened**

Infinitive: **to be frightened**
Perfect Infinitive: **to have been frightened**
Present Participle: **being frightened**
Past Participle: **been frightened**

INDICATIVE MOOD

Pres.	I, we, you, they **frighten** he, she, it **frightens**	I **am frightened** we, you, they **are frightened** he, she, it **is frightened**
Pres. Prog.	I **am frightening** we, you, they **are frightening** he, she, it **is frightening**	I **am being frightened** we, you, they **are being frightened** he, she, it **is being frightened**
Pres. Int.	I, we, you, they **do frighten** he, she, it **does frighten**	I, we, you, they **do get frightened** he, she, it **does get frightened**
Fut.	I, he, she, it, we, you, they **will frighten**	I, he, she, it, we, you, they **will be frightened**
Past	I, he, she, it, we, you, they **frightened**	I, he, she, it **was frightened** we, you, they **were frightened**
Past Prog.	I, he, she, it **was frightening** we, you, they **were frightening**	I, he, she, it **was being frightened** we, you, they **were being frightened**
Past Int.	I, he, she, it, we, you, they **did frighten**	I, he, she, it, we, you, they **did get frightened**
Pres. Perf.	I, we, you, they **have frightened** he, she, it **has frightened**	I, we, you, they **have been frightened** he, she, it **has been frightened**
Past Perf.	I, he, she, it, we, you, they **had frightened**	I, he, she, it, we, you, they **had been frightened**
Fut. Perf.	I, he, she, it, we, you, they **will have frightened**	I, he, she, it, we, you, they **will have been frightened**

IMPERATIVE MOOD

frighten

be frightened

SUBJUNCTIVE MOOD

Pres.	if I, he, she, it, we, you, they **frighten**	if I, he, she, it, we, you, they **be frightened**
Past	if I, he, she, it, we, you, they **frightened**	if I, he, she, it, we, you, they **were frightened**
Fut.	if I, he, she, it, we, you, they **should frighten**	if I, he, she, it, we, you, they **should be frightened**

gamble
(active voice)

gambled
(passive voice)

Infinitive: **to gamble**
Perfect Infinitive: **to have gambled**
Present Participle: **gambling**
Past Participle: **gambled**

Infinitive: **to be gambled**
Perfect Infinitive: **to have been gambled**
Present Participle: **being gambled**
Past Participle: **been gambled**

INDICATIVE MOOD

Pres.	I, we, you, they **gamble**	I **am gambled**
		we, you, they **are gambled**
	he, she, it **gambles**	he, she, it **is gambled**
Pres.	I am **gambling**	I **am being gambled**
Prog.	we, you, they **are gambling**	we, you, they **are being gambled**
	he, she, it **is gambling**	he, she, it **is being gambled**
Pres.	I, we, you, they **do gamble**	I, we, you, they **do get gambled**
Int.	he, she, it **does gamble**	he, she, it **does get gambled**
Fut.	I, he, she, it,	I, he, she, it,
	we, you, they **will gamble**	we, you, they **will be gambled**
Past	I, he, she, it,	I, he, she, it **was gambled**
	we, you, they **gambled**	we, you, they **were gambled**
Past	I, he, she, it **was gambling**	I, he, she, it **was being gambled**
Prog.	we, you, they **were gambling**	we, you, they **were being gambled**
Past	I, he, she, it,	I, he, she, it,
Int.	we, you, they **did gamble**	we, you, they **did get gambled**
Pres.	I, we, you, they **have gambled**	I, we, you, they **have been gambled**
Perf.	he, she, it **has gambled**	he, she, it **has been gambled**
Past	I, he, she, it,	I, he, she, it,
Perf.	we, you, they **had gambled**	we, you, they **had been gambled**
Fut.	I, he, she, it, we, you, they	I, he, she, it, we, you, they
Perf.	**will have gambled**	**will have been gambled**

IMPERATIVE MOOD

gamble   **be gambled**

SUBJUNCTIVE MOOD

Pres.	if I, he, she, it,	if I, he, she, it,
	we, you, they **gamble**	we, you, they **be gambled**
Past	if I, he, she, it,	if I, he, she, it,
	we, you, they **gambled**	we, you, they **were gambled**
Fut.	if I, he, she, it,	if I, he, she, it,
	we, you, they **should gamble**	we, you, they **should be gambled**

get
(active voice)

be gotten/got
(passive voice)

Infinitive: **to get**
Perfect Infinitive: **to have gotten**
Present Participle: **getting**
Past Participle: **gotten**

Infinitive: **to be gotten**
Perfect Infinitive: **to have been gotten**
Present Participle: **being gotten**
Past Participle: **been gotten**

INDICATIVE MOOD

Pres.	I, we, you, they **get**	I **am gotten**
		we, you, they **are gotten**
	he, she, it **gets**	he, she, it **is gotten**
Pres.	I **am getting**	I **am being gotten**
Prog.	we, you, they **are getting**	we, you, they **are being gotten**
	he, she, it **is getting**	he, she, it **is being gotten**
Pres.	I, we, you, they **do get**	I, we, you, they **do get gotten**
Int.	he, she, it **does get**	he, she, it **does get gotten**
Fut.	I, he, she, it, we, you, they **will get**	I, he, she, it, we, you, they **will be gotten**
Past	I, he, she, it, we, you, they **got**	I, he, she, it **was gotten**
		we, you, they **were gotten**
Past	I, he, she, it **was getting**	I, he, she, it **was being gotten**
Prog.	we, you, they **were getting**	we, you, they **were being gotten**
Past	I, he, she, it, we, you, they **did get**	I, he, she, it, we, you, they **did get gotten**
Int.		
Pres.	I, we, you, they **have gotten**	I, we, you, they **have been gotten**
Perf.	he, she, it **has gotten**	he, she, it **has been gotten**
Past	I, he, she, it, we, you, they **had gotten**	I, he, she, it, we, you, they **had been gotten**
Perf.		
Fut.	I, he, she, it, we, you, they	I, he, she, it, we, you, they
Perf.	**will have gotten**	**will have been gotten**

IMPERATIVE MOOD

get

be gotten

SUBJUNCTIVE MOOD

Pres.	if I, he, she, it, we, you, they **get**	if I, he, she, it, we, you, they **be gotten**
Past	if I, he, she, it, we, you, they **got**	if I, he, she, it, we, you, they **were gotten**
Fut.	if I, he, she, it, we, you, they **should get**	if I, he, she, it, we, you, they **should be gotten**

Transitive and intransitive. The past participle form may be either GOTTEN or GOT. The verb is used to make a passive statement, such as "I got elected." American English has both past participles, with GOT meaning "have" and GOTTEN meaning "obtained." The *Oxford Dictionary* prefers the past participle GOT. The archaic form of the past tense is GAT.

gild
(active voice)

be gilded/gilt
(passive voice)

Infinitive: **to gild**
Perfect Infinitive: **to have gilded**
Present Participle: **gilding**
Past Participle: **gilded**

Infinitive: **to be gilded**
Perfect Infinitive: **to have been gilded**
Present Participle: **being gilded**
Past Participle: **been gilded**

INDICATIVE MOOD

Pres.	I, we, you, they **gild**	I **am gilded**
		we, you, they **are gilded**
	he, she, it **gilds**	he, she, it **is gilded**
Pres.	I **am gilding**	I **am being gilded**
Prog.	we, you, they **are gilding**	we, you, they **are being gilded**
	he, she, it **is gilding**	he, she, it **is being gilded**
Pres.	I, we, you, they **do gild**	I, we, you, they **do get gilded**
Int.	he, she, it **does gild**	he, she, it **does get gilded**
Fut.	I, he, she, it,	I, he, she, it,
	we, you, they **will gild**	we, you, they **will be gilded**
Past	I, he, she, it,	I, he, she, it **was gilded**
	we, you, they **gilded**	we, you, they **were gilded**
Past	I, he, she, it **was gilding**	I, he, she, it **was being gilded**
Prog.	we, you, they **were gilding**	we, you, they **were being gilded**
Past	I, he, she, it,	I, he, she, it,
Int.	we, you, they **did gild**	we, you, they **did get gilded**
Pres.	I, we, you, they **have gilded**	I, we, you, they **have been gilded**
Perf.	he, she, it **has gilded**	he, she, it **has been gilded**
Past	I, he, she, it,	I, he, she, it,
Perf.	we, you, they **had gilded**	we, you, they **had been gilded**
Fut.	I, he, she, it, we, you, they	I, he, she, it, we, you, they
Perf.	**will have gilded**	**will have been gilded**

IMPERATIVE MOOD

gild

be gilded

SUBJUNCTIVE MOOD

Pres.	if I, he, she, it,	if I, he, she, it,
	we, you, they **gild**	we, you, they **be gilded**
Past	if I, he, she, it,	if I, he, she, it,
	we, you, they **gilded**	we, you, they **were gilded**
Fut.	if I, he, she, it,	if I, he, she, it,
	we, you, they **should gild**	we, you, they **should be gilded**

gird
(active voice)

be girded/girt
(passive voice)

Infinitive: **to gird**
Perfect Infinitive: **to have girded**
Present Participle: **girding**
Past Participle: **girded**

Infinitive: **to be girded**
Perfect Infinitive: **to have been girded**
Present Participle: **being girded**
Past Participle: **been girded**

INDICATIVE MOOD

Pres.	I, we, you, they **gird**	I **am girded**
		we, you, they **are girded**
	he, she, it **girds**	he, she, it **is girded**
Pres.	I **am girding**	I **am being girded**
Prog.	we, you, they **are girding**	we, you, they **are being girded**
	he, she, it **is girding**	he, she, it **is being girded**
Pres.	I, we, you, they **do gird**	I, we, you, they **do get girded**
Int.	he, she, it **does gird**	he, she, it **does get girded**
Fut.	I, he, she, it,	I, he, she, it,
	we, you, they **will gird**	we, you, they **will be girded**
Past	I, he, she, it,	I, he, she, it **was girded**
	we, you, they **girded**	we, you, they **were girded**
Past	I, he, she, it **was girding**	I, he, she, it **was being girded**
Prog.	we, you, they **were girding**	we, you, they **were being girded**
Past	I, he, she, it,	I, he, she, it,
Int.	we, you, they **did gird**	we, you, they **did get girded**
Pres.	I, we, you, they **have girded**	I, we, you, they **have been girded**
Perf.	he, she, it **has girded**	he, she, it **has been girded**
Past	I, he, she, it,	I, he, she, it,
Perf.	we, you, they **had girded**	we, you, they **had been girded**
Fut.	I, he, she, it, we, you, they	I, he, she, it, we, you, they
Perf.	**will have girded**	**will have been girded**

IMPERATIVE MOOD

gird   **be girded**

SUBJUNCTIVE MOOD

Pres.	if I, he, she, it,	if I, he, she, it,
	we, you, they **gird**	we, you, they **be girded**
Past	if I, he, she, it,	if I, he, she, it,
	we, you, they **girded**	we, you, they **were girded**
Fut.	if I, he, she, it,	if I, he, she, it,
	we, you, they **should gird**	we, you, they **should be girded**

Transitive and intransitive. Both forms GIRDED and GIRT are acceptable.

give
(active voice)

be given
(passive voice)

Infinitive: **to give**
Perfect Infinitive: **to have given**
Present Participle: **giving**
Past Participle: **given**

Infinitive: **to be given**
Perfect Infinitive: **to have been given**
Present Participle: **being given**
Past Participle: **been given**

INDICATIVE MOOD

Pres.	I, we, you, they **give**	I **am given**
		we, you, they **are given**
	he, she, it **gives**	he, she, it **is given**
Pres.	I **am giving**	I **am being given**
Prog.	we, you, they **are giving**	we, you, they **are being given**
	he, she, it **is giving**	he, she, it **is being given**
Pres.	I, we, you, they **do give**	I, we, you, they **do get given**
Int.	he, she, it **does give**	he, she, it **does get given**
Fut.	I, he, she, it,	I, he, she, it,
	we, you, they **will give**	we, you, they **will be given**
Past	I, he, she, it,	I, he, she, it **was given**
	we, you, they **gave**	we, you, they **were given**
Past	I, he, she, it **was giving**	I, he, she, it **was being given**
Prog.	we, you, they **were giving**	we, you, they **were being given**
Past	I, he, she, it,	I, he, she, it,
Int.	we, you, they **did give**	we, you, they **did get given**
Pres.	I, we, you, they **have given**	I, we, you, they **have been given**
Perf.	he, she, it **has given**	he, she, it **has been given**
Past	I, he, she, it,	I, he, she, it,
Perf.	we, you, they **had given**	we, you, they **had been given**
Fut.	I, he, she, it, we, you, they	I, he, she, it, we, you, they
Perf.	**will have given**	**will have been given**

IMPERATIVE MOOD

give   **be given**

SUBJUNCTIVE MOOD

Pres.	if I, he, she, it,	if I, he, she, it,
	we, you, they **give**	we, you, they **be given**
Past	if I, he, she, it,	if I, he, she, it,
	we, you, they **gave**	we, you, they **were given**
Fut.	if I, he, she, it,	if I, he, she, it,
	we, you, they **should give**	we, you, they **should be given**

Transitive and intransitive.

go
(active voice)

be gone
(passive voice)

Infinitive: **to go**
Perfect Infinitive: **to have gone**
Present Participle: **going**
Past Participle: **gone**

Infinitive: **to be gone**
Perfect Infinitive: **to have been gone**
Present Participle: **being gone**
Past Participle: **been gone**

INDICATIVE MOOD

Pres.	I, we, you, they **go** he, she, it **goes**	I **am gone** we, you, they **are gone** he, she, it **is gone**
Pres. *Prog.*	I **am going** we, you, they **are going** he, she, it **is going**	I **am being gone** we, you, they **are being gone** he, she, it **is being gone**
Pres. *Int.*	I, we, you, they **do go** he, she, it **does go**	I, we, you, they **do get gone** he, she, it **does get gone**
Fut.	I, he, she, it, we, you, they **will go**	I, he, she, it, we, you, they **will be gone**
Past	I, he, she, it, we, you, they **went**	I, he, she, it **was gone** we, you, they **were gone**
Past *Prog.*	I, he, she, it **was going** we, you, they **were going**	I, he, she, it **was being gone** we, you, they **were being gone**
Past *Int.*	I, he, she, it, we, you, they **did go**	I, he, she, it, we, you, they **did get gone**
Pres. *Perf.*	I, we, you, they **have gone** he, she, it **has gone**	I, we, you, they **have been gone** he, she, it **has been gone**
Past *Perf.*	I, he, she, it, we, you, they **had gone**	I, he, she, it, we, you, they **had been gone**
Fut. *Perf.*	I, he, she, it, we, you, they **will have gone**	I, he, she, it, we, you, they **will have been gone**

IMPERATIVE MOOD

go

be gone

SUBJUNCTIVE MOOD

Pres.	if I, he, she, it, we, you, they **go**	if I, he, she, it, we, you, they **be gone**
Past	if I, he, she, it, we, you, they **went**	if I, he, she, it, we, you, they **were gone**
Fut.	if I, he, she, it, we, you, they **should go**	if I, he, she, it, we, you, they **should be gone**

Intransitive and transitive.

grind
(active voice)

PRINCIPAL PARTS: **grinds, grinding,
ground, ground**

be ground
(passive voice)

Infinitive: **to grind**
Perfect Infinitive: **to have ground**
Present Participle: **grinding**
Past Participle: **ground**

Infinitive: **to be ground**
Perfect Infinitive: **to have been ground**
Present Participle: **being ground**
Past Participle: **been ground**

INDICATIVE MOOD

Pres.	I, we, you, they **grind**	I **am ground** we, you, they **are ground**
	he, she, it **grinds**	he, she, it **is ground**
Pres. *Prog.*	I **am grinding** we, you, they **are grinding** he, she, it **is grinding**	I **am being ground** we, you, they **are being ground** he, she, it **is being ground**
Pres. *Int.*	I, we, you, they **do grind** he, she, it **does grind**	I, we, you, they **do get ground** he, she, it **does get ground**
Fut.	I, he, she, it, we, you, they **will grind**	I, he, she, it, we, you, they **will be ground**
Past	I, he, she, it, we, you, they **ground**	I, he, she, it **was ground** we, you, they **were ground**
Past *Prog.*	I, he, she, it **was grinding** we, you, they **were grinding**	I, he, she, it **was being ground** we, you, they **were being ground**
Past *Int.*	I, he, she, it, we, you, they **did grind**	I, he, she, it, we, you, they **did get ground**
Pres. *Perf.*	I, we, you, they **have ground** he, she, it **has ground**	I, we, you, they **have been ground** he, she, it **has been ground**
Past *Perf.*	I, he, she, it, we, you, they **had ground**	I, he, she, it, we, you, they **had been ground**
Fut. *Perf.*	I, he, she, it, we, you, they **will have ground**	I, he, she, it, we, you, they **will have been ground**

IMPERATIVE MOOD

grind   **be ground**

SUBJUNCTIVE MOOD

Pres.	if I, he, she, it, we, you, they **grind**	if I, he, she, it, we, you, they **be ground**
Past	if I, he, she, it, we, you, they **ground**	if I, he, she, it, we, you, they **were ground**
Fut.	if I, he, she, it, we, you, they **should grind**	if I, he, she, it, we, you, they **should be ground**

Transitive and intransitive.

grow
(active voice)

PRINCIPAL PARTS: **grows, growing, grew, grown**

be grown
(passive voice)

Infinitive: **to grow**
Perfect Infinitive: **to have grown**
Present Participle: **growing**
Past Participle: **grown**

Infinitive: **to be grown**
Perfect Infinitive: **to have been grown**
Present Participle: **being grown**
Past Participle: **been grown**

INDICATIVE MOOD

Pres.	I, we, you, they **grow**	I **am grown**
		we, you, they **are grown**
	he, she, it **grows**	he, she, it **is grown**
Pres.	I **am growing**	I **am being grown**
Prog.	we, you, they **are growing**	we, you, they **are being grown**
	he, she, it **is growing**	he, she, it **is being grown**
Pres.	I, we, you, they **do grow**	I, we, you, they **do get grown**
Int.	he, she, it **does grow**	he, she, it **does get grown**
Fut.	I, he, she, it,	I, he, she, it,
	we, you, they **will grow**	we, you, they **will be grown**
Past	I, he, she, it,	I, he, she, it **was grown**
	we, you, they **grew**	we, you, they **were grown**
Past	I, he, she, it **was growing**	I, he, she, it **was being grown**
Prog.	we, you, they **were growing**	we, you, they **were being grown**
Past	I, he, she, it,	I, he, she, it,
Int.	we, you, they **did grow**	we, you, they **did get grown**
Pres.	I, we, you, they **have grown**	I, we, you, they **have been grown**
Perf.	he, she, it **has grown**	he, she, it **has been grown**
Past	I, he, she, it,	I, he, she, it,
Perf.	we, you, they **had grown**	we, you, they **had been grown**
Fut.	I, he, she, it, we, you, they	I, he, she, it, we, you, they
Perf.	**will have grown**	**will have been grown**

IMPERATIVE MOOD

grow

be grown

SUBJUNCTIVE MOOD

Pres.	if I, he, she, it,	if I, he, she, it,
	we, you, they **grow**	we, you, they **be grown**
Past	if I, he, she, it,	if I, he, she, it,
	we, you, they **grew**	we, you, they **were grown**
Fut.	if I, he, she, it,	if I, he, she, it,
	we, you, they **should grow**	we, you, they **should be grown**

Intransitive and transitive.

guess
(active voice)

be guessed
(passive voice)

Infinitive: **to guess**
Perfect Infinitive: **to have guessed**
Present Participle: **guessing**
Past Participle: **guessed**

Infinitive: **to be guessed**
Perfect Infinitive: **to have been guessed**
Present Participle: **being guessed**
Past Participle: **been guessed**

INDICATIVE MOOD

Pres.	I, we, you, they **guess**	I **am guessed**
		we, you, they **are guessed**
	he, she, it **guesses**	he, she, it **is guessed**
Pres.	I **am guessing**	I **am being guessed**
Prog.	we, you, they **are guessing**	we, you, they **are being guessed**
	he, she, it **is guessing**	he, she, it **is being guessed**
Pres.	I, we, you, they **do guess**	I, we, you, they **do get guessed**
Int.	he, she, it **does guess**	he, she, it **does get guessed**
Fut.	I, he, she, it,	I, he, she, it,
	we, you, they **will guess**	we, you, they **will be guessed**
Past	I, he, she, it,	I, he, she, it **was guessed**
	we, you, they **guessed**	we, you, they **were guessed**
Past	I, he, she, it **was guessing**	I, he, she, it **was being guessed**
Prog.	we, you, they **were guessing**	we, you, they **were being guessed**
Past	I, he, she, it,	I, he, she, it,
Int.	we, you, they **did guess**	we, you, they **did get guessed**
Pres.	I, we, you, they **have guessed**	I, we, you, they **have been guessed**
Perf.	he, she, it **has guessed**	he, she, it **has been guessed**
Past	I, he, she, it,	I, he, she, it,
Perf.	we, you, they **had guessed**	we, you, they **had been guessed**
Fut.	I, he, she, it, we, you, they	I, he, she, it, we, you, they
Perf.	**will have guessed**	**will have been guessed**

IMPERATIVE MOOD

guess   **be guessed**

SUBJUNCTIVE MOOD

Pres.	if I, he, she, it,	if I, he, she, it,
	we, you, they **guess**	we, you, they **be guessed**
Past	if I, he, she, it,	if I, he, she, it,
	we, you, they **guessed**	we, you, they **were guessed**
Fut.	if I, he, she, it,	if I, he, she, it,
	we, you, they **should guess**	we, you, they **should be guessed**

Transitive and intransitive.

hamstring
(active voice)

be hamstrung
(passive voice)

Infinitive: **to hamstring**
Perfect Infinitive: **to have hamstrung**
Present Participle: **hamstringing**
Past Participle: **hamstrung**

Infinitive: **to be hamstrung**
Perfect Infinitive: **to have been hamstrung**
Present Participle: **being hamstrung**
Past Participle: **been hamstrung**

INDICATIVE MOOD

Pres.	I, we, you, they **hamstring**	I am **hamstrung**
		we, you, they **are hamstrung**
	he, she, it **hamstrings**	he, she, it **is hamstrung**
Pres.	I am **hamstringing**	I **am being hamstrung**
Prog.	we, you, they **are hamstringing**	we, you, they **are being hamstrung**
	he, she, it **is hamstringing**	he, she, it **is being hamstrung**
Pres.	I, we, you, they **do hamstring**	I, we, you, they **do get hamstrung**
Int.	he, she, it **does hamstring**	he, she, it **does get hamstrung**
Fut.	I, he, she, it,	I, he, she, it,
	we, you, they **will hamstring**	we, you, they **will be hamstrung**
Past	I, he, she, it,	I, he, she, it **was hamstrung**
	we, you, they **hamstrung**	we, you, they **were hamstrung**
Past	I, he, she, it **was hamstringing**	I, he, she, it **was being hamstrung**
Prog.	we, you, they **were hamstringing**	we, you, they **were being hamstrung**
Past	I, he, she, it,	I, he, she, it,
Int.	we, you, they **did hamstring**	we, you, they **did get hamstrung**
Pres.	I, we, you, they **have hamstrung**	I, we, you, they **have been hamstrung**
Perf.	he, she, it **has hamstrung**	he, she, it **has been hamstrung**
Past	I, he, she, it,	I, he, she, it,
Perf.	we, you, they **had hamstrung**	we, you, they **had been hamstrung**
Fut.	I, he, she, it, we, you, they	I, he, she, it, we, you, they
Perf.	**will have hamstrung**	**will have been hamstrung**

IMPERATIVE MOOD

hamstring

be hamstrung

SUBJUNCTIVE MOOD

Pres.	if I, he, she, it,	if I, he, she, it,
	we, you, they **hamstring**	we, you, they **be hamstrung**
Past	if I, he, she, it,	if I, he, she, it,
	we, you, they **hamstrung**	we, you, they **were hamstrung**
Fut.	if I, he, she, it,	if I, he, she, it,
	we, you, they **should hamstring**	we, you, they **should be hamstrung**

handle
(active voice)

be handled
(passive voice)

Infinitive: **to handle**
Perfect Infinitive: **to have handled**
Present Participle: **handling**
Past Participle: **handled**

Infinitive: **to be handled**
Perfect Infinitive: **to have been handled**
Present Participle: **being handled**
Past Participle: **been handled**

INDICATIVE MOOD

Pres.	I, we, you, they **handle**	I **am handled**
		we, you, they **are handled**
	he, she, it **handles**	he, she, it **is handled**
Pres.	I **am handling**	I **am being handled**
Prog.	we, you, they **are handling**	we, you, they **are being handled**
	he, she, it **is handling**	he, she, it **is being handled**
Pres.	I, we, you, they **do handle**	I, we, you, they **do get handled**
Int.	he, she, it **does handle**	he, she, it **does get handled**
Fut.	I, he, she, it,	I, he, she, it,
	we, you, they **will handle**	we, you, they **will be handled**
Past	I, he, she, it,	I, he, she, it **was handled**
	we, you, they **handled**	we, you, they **were handled**
Past	I, he, she, it **was handling**	I, he, she, it **was being handled**
Prog.	we, you, they **were handling**	we, you, they **were being handled**
Past	I, he, she, it,	I, he, she, it,
Int.	we, you, they **did handle**	we, you, they **did get handled**
Pres.	I, we, you, they **have handled**	I, we, you, they **have been handled**
Perf.	he, she, it **has handled**	he, she, it **has been handled**
Past	I, he, she, it,	I, he, she, it,
Perf.	we, you, they **had handled**	we, you, they **had been handled**
Fut.	I, he, she, it, we, you, they	I, he, she, it, we, you, they
Perf.	**will have handled**	**will have been handled**

IMPERATIVE MOOD

handle

be handled

SUBJUNCTIVE MOOD

Pres.	if I, he, she, it,	if I, he, she, it,
	we, you, they **handle**	we, you, they **be handled**
Past	if I, he, she, it,	if I, he, she, it,
	we, you, they **handled**	we, you, they **were handled**
Fut.	if I, he, she, it,	if I, he, she, it,
	we, you, they **should handle**	we, you, they **should be handled**

Transitive and intransitive.

hang
(active voice)

PRINCIPAL PARTS: **hangs, hanging,
hung, hung**

be hung
(passive voice)

Infinitive: **to hang**
Perfect Infinitive: **to have hung**
Present Participle: **hanging**
Past Participle: **hung**

Infinitive: **to be hung**
Perfect Infinitive: **to have been hung**
Present Participle: **being hung**
Past Participle: **been hung**

INDICATIVE MOOD

Pres.	I, we, you, they **hang** he, she, it **hangs**	I **am hung** we, you, they **are hung** he, she, it **is hung**
Pres. *Prog.*	I **am hanging** we, you, they **are hanging** he, she, it **is hanging**	I **am being hung** we, you, they **are being hung** he, she, it **is being hung**
Pres. *Int.*	I, we, you, they **do hang** he, she, it **does hang**	I, we, you, they **do get hung** he, she, it **does get hung**
Fut.	I, he, she, it, we, you, they **will hang**	I, he, she, it, we, you, they **will be hung**
Past	I, he, she, it, we, you, they **hung**	I, he, she, it **was hung** we, you, they **were hung**
Past *Prog.*	I, he, she, it **was hanging** we, you, they **were hanging**	I, he, she, it **was being hung** we, you, they **were being hung**
Past *Int.*	I, he, she, it, we, you, they **did hang**	I, he, she, it, we, you, they **did get hung**
Pres. *Perf.*	I, we, you, they **have hung** he, she, it **has hung**	I, we, you, they **have been hung** he, she, it **has been hung**
Past *Perf.*	I, he, she, it, we, you, they **had hung**	I, he, she, it, we, you, they **had been hung**
Fut. *Perf.*	I, he, she, it, we, you, they **will have hung**	I, he, she, it, we, you, they **will have been hung**

IMPERATIVE MOOD

hang

be hung

SUBJUNCTIVE MOOD

Pres.	if I, he, she, it, we, you, they **hang**	if I, he, she, it, we, you, they **be hung**
Past	if I, he, she, it, we, you, they **hung**	if I, he, she, it, we, you, they **were hung**
Fut.	if I, he, she, it, we, you, they **should hang**	if I, he, she, it, we, you, they **should be hung**

Transitive and intransitive. This means to "hang an object, fasten something."

hang
(active voice)

be hanged
(passive voice)

Infinitive: **to hang**
Perfect Infinitive: **to have hanged**
Present Participle: **hanging**
Past Participle: **hanged**

Infinitive: **to be hanged**
Perfect Infinitive: **to have been hanged**
Present Participle: **being hanged**
Past Participle: **been hanged**

INDICATIVE MOOD

Pres.	I, we, you, they **hang** he, she, it **hangs**		I **am hanged** we, you, they **are hanged** he, she, it **is hanged**
Pres. *Prog.*	I **am hanging** we, you, they **are hanging** he, she, it **is hanging**		I **am being hanged** we, you, they **are being hanged** he, she, it **is being hanged**
Pres. *Int.*	I, we, you, they **do hang** he, she, it **does hang**		I, we, you, they **do get hanged** he, she, it **does get hanged**
Fut.	I, he, she, it, we, you, they **will hang**		I, he, she, it, we, you, they **will be hanged**
Past	I, he, she, it we, you, they **hanged**		I, he, she, it **was hanged** we, you, they **were hanged**
Past *Prog.*	I, he, she, it **was hanging** we, you, they **were hanging**		I, he, she, it **was being hanged** we, you, they **were being hanged**
Past *Int.*	I, he, she, it, we, you, they **did hang**		I, he, she, it, we, you, they **did get hanged**
Pres. *Perf.*	I, we, you, they **have hanged** he, she, it **has hanged**		I, we, you, they **have been hanged** he, she, it **has been hanged**
Past *Perf.*	I, he, she, it, we, you, they **had hanged**		I, he, she, it, we, you, they **had been hanged**
Fut. *Perf.*	I, he, she, it, we, you, they **will have hanged**		I, he, she, it, we, you, they **will have been hanged**

IMPERATIVE MOOD

hang   **be hanged**

SUBJUNCTIVE MOOD

Pres.	if I, he, she, it, we, you, they **hang**		if I, he, she, it, we, you, they **be hanged**
Past	if I, he, she, it, we, you, they **hanged**		if I, he, she, it, we, you, they **were hanged**
Fut.	if I, he, she, it, we, you, they **should hang**		if I, he, she, it, we, you, they **should be hanged**

Transitive and intransitive. This means to "execute a person by hanging" or to "express exasperation."

170

happen

Infinitive: **to happen**
Perfect Infinitive: **to have happened**
Present Participle: **happening**
Past Participle: **happened**

INDICATIVE MOOD

Pres.	I, we, you, they **happen**
	he, she, it **happens**
Pres.	**I am happening**
Prog.	we, you, they **are happening**
	he, she, it **is happening**
Pres.	I, we, you, they **do happen**
Int.	he, she, it **does happen**
Fut.	I, he, she, it,
	we, you, they **will happen**
Past	I, he, she, it,
	we, you, they **happened**
Past	I, he, she, it **was happening**
Prog.	we, you, they **were happening**
Past	I, he, she, it,
Int.	we, you, they **did happen**
Pres.	I, we, you, they **have happened**
Perf.	he, she, it **has happened**
Past	I, he, she, it,
Perf.	we, you, they **had happened**
Fut.	I, he, she, it, we, you, they
Perf.	**will have happened**

IMPERATIVE MOOD

happen

SUBJUNCTIVE MOOD

Pres.	if I, he, she, it,
	we, you, they **happen**
Past	if I, he, she, it,
	we, you, they **happened**
Fut.	if I, he, she, it,
	we, you, they **should happen**

PRINCIPAL PARTS: **hates, hating,
hated, hated**

Infinitive: **to hate**
Perfect Infinitive: **to have hated**
Present Participle: **hating**
Past Participle: **hated**

Infinitive: **to be hated**
Perfect Infinitive: **to have been hated**
Present Participle: **being hated**
Past Participle: **been hated**

INDICATIVE MOOD

Pres.	I, we, you, they **hate**	I **am hated**
		we, you, they **are hated**
	he, she, it **hates**	he, she, it **is hated**
Pres.	I **am hating**	I **am being hated**
Prog.	we, you, they **are hating**	we, you, they **are being hated**
	he, she, it **is hating**	he, she, it **is being hated**
Pres.	I, we, you, they **do hate**	I, we, you, they **do get hated**
Int.	he, she, it **does hate**	he, she, it **does get hated**
Fut.	I, he, she, it,	I, he, she, it,
	we, you, they **will hate**	we, you, they **will be hated**
Past	I, he, she, it,	I, he, she, it **was hated**
	we, you, they **hated**	we, you, they **were hated**
Past	I, he, she, it **was hating**	I, he, she, it **was being hated**
Prog.	we, you, they **were hating**	we, you, they **were being hated**
Past	I, he, she, it,	I, he, she, it,
Int.	we, you, they **did hate**	we, you, they **did get hated**
Pres.	I, we, you, they **have hated**	I, we, you, they **have been hated**
Perf.	he, she, it **has hated**	he, she, it **has been hated**
Past	I, he, she, it,	I, he, she, it,
Perf.	we, you, they **had hated**	we, you, they **had been hated**
Fut.	I, he, she, it, we, you, they	I, he, she, it, we, you, they
Perf.	**will have hated**	**will have been hated**

IMPERATIVE MOOD

hate

be hated

SUBJUNCTIVE MOOD

Pres.	if I, he, she, it,	if I, he, she, it,
	we, you, they **hate**	we, you, they **be hated**
Past	if I, he, she, it,	if I, he, she, it,
	we, you, they **hated**	we, you, they **were hated**
Fut.	if I, he, she, it,	if I, he, she, it,
	we, you, they **should hate**	we, you, they **should be hated**

Transitive and intransitive.

have
(active voice)

PRINCIPAL PARTS: **has, having, had, had**

be had
(passive voice)

Infinitive: **to have**
Perfect Infinitive: **to have had**
Present Participle: **having**
Past Participle: **had**

Infinitive: **to be had**
Perfect Infinitive: **to have been had**
Present Participle: **being had**
Past Participle: **been had**

INDICATIVE MOOD

Pres.	I, we, you, they **have**	I **am had** we, you, they **are had**
	he, she, it **has**	he, she, it **is had**
Pres. *Prog.*	I **am having** we, you, they **are having**	I **am being had** we, you, they **are being had**
	he, she, it **is having**	he, she, it **is being had**
Pres. *Int.*	I, we, you, they **do have**	I, we, you, they **do get had**
	he, she, it **does have**	he, she, it **does get had**
Fut.	I, he, she, it, we, you, they **will have**	I, he, she, it, we, you, they **will be had**
Past	I, he, she, it, we, you, they **had**	I, he, she, it **was had** we, you, they **were had**
Past *Prog.*	I, he, she, it **was having** we, you, they **were having**	I, he, she, it **was being had** we, you, they **were being had**
Past *Int.*	I, he, she, it, we, you, they **did have**	I, he, she, it, we, you, they **did get had**
Pres. *Perf.*	I, we, you, they **have had** he, she, it **has had**	I, we, you, they **have been had** he, she, it **has been had**
Past *Perf.*	I, he, she, it, we, you, they **had had**	I, he, she, it, we, you, they **had been had**
Fut. *Perf.*	I, he, she, it, we, you, they **will have had**	I, he, she, it, we, you, they **will have been had**

IMPERATIVE MOOD

have   **be had**

SUBJUNCTIVE MOOD

Pres.	if I, he, she, it, we, you, they **have**	if I, he, she, it, we, you, they **be had**
Past	if I, he, she, it, we, you, they **had**	if I, he, she, it, we, you, they **were had**
Fut.	if I, he, she, it, we, you, they **should have**	if I, he, she, it, we, you, they **should be had**

As a transitive verb, HAVE means "possessing." It is also an auxiliary verb used to form the perfect tenses. It can be contracted: I have = I've, you have = you've, she has = she's, he has = he's, she had = she'd, he had = he'd; the negative contractions are haven't, hasn't, hadn't.

hear
(active voice)

be heard
(passive voice)

Infinitive: **to hear**
Perfect Infinitive: **to have heard**
Present Participle: **hearing**
Past Participle: **heard**

Infinitive: **to be heard**
Perfect Infinitive: **to have been heard**
Present Participle: **being heard**
Past Participle: **been heard**

INDICATIVE MOOD

Pres.	I, we, you, they **hear**	I **am heard**
		we, you, they **are heard**
	he, she, it **hears**	he, she, it **is heard**
Pres.	I **am hearing**	I **am being heard**
Prog.	we, you, they **are hearing**	we, you, they **are being heard**
	he, she, it **is hearing**	he, she, it **is being heard**
Pres.	I, we, you, they **do hear**	I, we, you, they **do get heard**
Int.	he, she, it **does hear**	he, she, it **does get heard**
Fut.	I, he, she, it,	I, he, she, it,
	we, you, they **will hear**	we, you, they **will be heard**
Past	I, he, she, it,	I, he, she, it **was heard**
	we, you, they **heard**	we, you, they **were heard**
Past	I, he, she, it **was hearing**	I, he, she, it **was being heard**
Prog.	we, you, they **were hearing**	we, you, they **were being heard**
Past	I, he, she, it,	I, he, she, it,
Int.	we, you, they **did hear**	we, you, they **did get heard**
Pres.	I, we, you, they **have heard**	I, we, you, they **have been heard**
Perf.	he, she, it **has heard**	he, she, it **has been heard**
Past	I, he, she, it,	I, he, she, it,
Perf.	we, you, they **had heard**	we, you, they **had been heard**
Fut.	I, he, she, it, we, you, they	I, he, she, it, we, you, they
Perf.	**will have heard**	**will have been heard**

IMPERATIVE MOOD

hear
be heard

SUBJUNCTIVE MOOD

Pres.	if I, he, she, it,	if I, he, she, it,
	we, you, they **hear**	we, you, they **be heard**
Past	if I, he, she, it,	if I, he, she, it,
	we, you, they **heard**	we, you, they **were heard**
Fut.	if I, he, she, it,	if I, he, she, it,
	we, you, they **should hear**	we, you, they **should be heard**

Transitive and intransitive.

heave
(active voice)

PRINCIPAL PARTS: heaves, heaving, heaved, heaved

be heaved
(passive voice)

Infinitive: **to heave**
Perfect Infinitive: **to have heaved**
Present Participle: **heaving**
Past Participle: **heaved**

Infinitive: **to be heaved**
Perfect Infinitive: **to have been heaved**
Present Participle: **being heaved**
Past Participle: **been heaved**

INDICATIVE MOOD

Pres.	I, we, you, they **heave**	I **am heaved**
		we, you, they **are heaved**
	he, she, it **heaves**	he, she, it **is heaved**
Pres.	I **am heaving**	I **am being heaved**
Prog.	we, you, they **are heaving**	we, you, they **are being heaved**
	he, she, it **is heaving**	he, she, it **is being heaved**
Pres.	I, we, you, they **do heave**	I, we, you, they **do get heaved**
Int.	he, she, it **does heave**	he, she, it **does get heaved**
Fut.	I, he, she, it,	I, he, she, it,
	we, you, they **will heave**	we, you, they **will be heaved**.
Past	I, he, she, it,	I, he, she, it **was heaved**
	we, you, they **heaved**	we, you, they **were heaved**
Past	I, he, she, it **was heaving**	I, he, she, it **was being heaved**
Prog.	we, you, they **were heaving**	we, you, they **were being heaved**
Past	I, he, she, it,	I, he, she, it,
Int.	we, you, they **did heave**	we, you, they **did get heaved**
Pres.	I, we, you, they **have heaved**	I, we, you, they **have been heaved**
Perf.	he, she, it **has heaved**	he, she, it **has been heaved**
Past	I, he, she, it,	I, he, she, it,
Perf.	we, you, they **had heaved**	we, you, they **had been heaved**
Fut.	I, he, she, it, we, you, they	I, he, she, it, we, you, they
Perf.	**will have heaved**	**will have been heaved**

IMPERATIVE MOOD

heave   **be heaved**

SUBJUNCTIVE MOOD

Pres.	if I, he, she, it,	if I, he, she, it,
	we, you, they **heave**	we, you, they **be heaved**
Past	if I, he, she, it,	if I, he, she, it,
	we, you, they **heaved**	we, you, they **were heaved**
Fut.	if I, he, she, it,	if I, he, she, it,
	we, you, they **should heave**	we, you, they **should be heaved**

Transitive and intransitive. The past tense and past participle HOVE is used in nautical terminology meaning "move alongside, pull, or haul in rope or cable."

help
(active voice)

be helped
(passive voice)

Infinitive: **to help**
Perfect Infinitive: **to have helped**
Present Participle: **helping**
Past Participle: **helped**

Infinitive: **to be helped**
Perfect Infinitive: **to have been helped**
Present Participle: **being helped**
Past Participle: **been helped**

INDICATIVE MOOD

Pres.	I, we, you, they **help**		I **am helped**
			we, you, they **are helped**
	he, she, it **helps**		he, she, it **is helped**
Pres.	I **am helping**		I **am being helped**
Prog.	we, you, they **are helping**		we, you, they **are being helped**
	he, she, it **is helping**		he, she, it **is being helped**
Pres.	I, we, you, they **do help**		I, we, you, they **do get helped**
Int.	he, she, it **does help**		he, she, it **does get helped**
Fut.	I, he, she, it,		I, he, she, it,
	we, you, they **will help**		we, you, they **will be helped**
Past	I, he, she, it,		I, he, she, it **was helped**
	we, you, they **helped**		we, you, they **were helped**
Past	I, he, she, it **was helping**		I, he, she, it **was being helped**
Prog.	we, you, they **were helping**		we, you, they **were being helped**
Past	I, he, she, it,		I, he, she, it,
Int.	we, you, they **did help**		we, you, they **did get helped**
Pres.	I, we, you, they **have helped**		I, we, you, they **have been helped**
Perf.	he, she, it **has helped**		he, she, it **has been helped**
Past	I, he, she, it,		I, he, she, it,
Perf.	we, you, they **had helped**		we, you, they **had been helped**
Fut.	I, he, she, it, we, you, they		I, he, she, it, we, you, they
Perf.	**will have helped**		**will have been helped**

IMPERATIVE MOOD

help   **be helped**

SUBJUNCTIVE MOOD

Pres.	if I, he, she, it,		if I, he, she, it,
	we, you, they **help**		we, you, they **be helped**
Past	if I, he, she, it,		if I, he, she, it,
	we, you, they **helped**		we, you, they **were helped**
Fut.	if I, he, she, it,		if I, he, she, it,
	we, you, they **should help**		we, you, they **should be helped**

Transitive and intransitive.

hem
(active voice)

be hemmed
(passive voice)

Infinitive: **to hem**
Perfect Infinitive: **to have hemmed**
Present Participle: **hemming**
Past Participle: **hemmed**

Infinitive: **to be hemmed**
Perfect Infinitive: **to have been hemmed**
Present Participle: **being hemmed**
Past Participle: **been hemmed**

INDICATIVE MOOD

Pres.	I, we, you, they **hem**	I **am hemmed**
		we, you, they **are hemmed**
	he, she, it **hems**	he, she, it **is hemmed**
Pres.	I **am hemming**	I **am being hemmed**
Prog.	we, you, they **are hemming**	we, you, they **are being hemmed**
	he, she, it **is hemming**	he, she, it **is being hemmed**
Pres.	I, we, you, they **do hem**	I, we, you, they **do get hemmed**
Int.	he, she, it **does hem**	he, she, it **does get hemmed**
Fut.	I, he, she, it,	I, he, she, it,
	we, you, they **will hem**	we, you, they **will be hemmed**
Past	I, he, she, it,	I, he, she, it **was hemmed**
	we, you, they **hemmed**	we, you, they **were hemmed**
Past	I, he, she, it **was hemming**	I, he, she, it **was being hemmed**
Prog.	we, you, they **were hemming**	we, you, they **were being hemmed**
Past	I, he, she, it,	I, he, she, it,
Int.	we, you, they **did hem**	we, you, they **did get hemmed**
Pres.	I, we, you, they **have hemmed**	I, we, you, they **have been hemmed**
Perf.	he, she, it **has hemmed**	he, she, it **has been hemmed**
Past	I, he, she, it,	I, he, she, it,
Perf.	we, you, they **had hemmed**	we, you, they **had been hemmed**
Fut.	I, he, she, it, we, you, they	I, he, she, it, we, you, they
Perf.	**will have hemmed**	**will have been hemmed**

IMPERATIVE MOOD

hem

be hemmed

SUBJUNCTIVE MOOD

Pres.	if I, he, she, it,	if I, he, she, it,
	we, you, they **hem**	we, you, they **be hemmed**
Past	if I, he, she, it,	if I, he, she, it,
	we, you, they **hemmed**	we, you, they **were hemmed**
Fut.	if I, he, she, it,	if I, he, she, it,
	we, you, they **should hem**	we, you, they **should be hemmed**

As a transitive verb, this means stitching an edge or border on a piece of cloth. As an intransitive verb, it means to give a short cough or mark a hesitation in speech.

hew
(active voice)

be hewn/hewed
(passive voice)

Infinitive: **to hew**
Perfect Infinitive: **to have hewn**
Present Participle: **hewing**
Past Participle: **hewn**

Infinitive: **to be hewn**
Perfect Infinitive: **to have been hewn**
Present Participle: **being hewn**
Past Participle: **been hewn**

INDICATIVE MOOD

Pres.	I, we, you, they **hew**	I **am hewn**
		we, you, they **are hewn**
	he, she, it **hews**	he, she, it **is hewn**
Pres.	I **am hewing**	I **am being hewn**
Prog.	we, you, they **are hewing**	we, you, they **are being hewn**
	he, she, it **is hewing**	he, she, it **is being hewn**
Pres.	I, we, you, they **do hew**	I, we, you, they **do get hewn**
Int.	he, she, it **does hew**	he, she, it **does get hewn**
Fut.	I, he, she, it,	I, he, she, it,
	we, you, they **will hew**	we, you, they **will be hewn**
Past	I, he, she, it,	I, he, she, it **was hewn**
	we, you, they **hewed**	we, you, they **were hewn**
Past	I, he, she, it **was hewing**	I, he, she, it **was being hewn**
Prog.	we, you, they **were hewing**	we, you, they **were being hewn**
Past	I, he, she, it,	I, he, she, it,
Int.	we, you, they **did hew**	we, you, they **did get hewn**
Pres.	I, we, you, they **have hewn**	I, we, you, they **have been hewn**
Perf.	he, she, it **has hewn**	he, she, it **has been hewn**
Past	I, he, she, it,	I, he, she, it,
Perf.	we, you, they **had hewn**	we, you, they **had been hewn**
Fut.	I, he, she, it, we, you, they	I, he, she, it, we, you, they
Perf.	**will have hewn**	**will have been hewn**

IMPERATIVE MOOD

hew   **be hewn**

SUBJUNCTIVE MOOD

Pres.	if I, he, she, it,	if I, he, she, it,
	we, you, they **hew**	we, you, they **be hewn**
Past	if I, he, she, it,	if I, he, she, it,
	we, you, they **hewed**	we, you, they **were hewn**
Fut.	if I, he, she, it,	if I, he, she, it,
	we, you, they **should hew**	we, you, they **should be hewn**

Transitive and intransitive.

hide
(active voice)

be hidden/hid
(passive voice)

Infinitive: **to hide**
Perfect Infinitive: **to have hidden**
Present Participle: **hiding**
Past Participle: **hidden**

Infinitive: **to be hidden**
Perfect Infinitive: **to have been hidden**
Present Participle: **being hidden**
Past Participle: **been hidden**

INDICATIVE MOOD

Pres.	I, we, you, they **hide**	I **am hidden**
		we, you, they **are hidden**
	he, she, it **hides**	he, she, it **is hidden**
Pres.	I **am hiding**	I **am being hidden**
Prog.	we, you, they **are hiding**	we, you, they **are being hidden**
	he, she, it **is hiding**	he, she, it **is being hidden**
Pres.	I, we, you, they **do hide**	I, we, you, they **do get hidden**
Int.	he, she, it **does hide**	he, she, it **does get hidden**
Fut.	I, he, she, it,	I, he, she, it,
	we, you, they **will hide**	we, you, they **will be hidden**
Past	I, he, she, it,	I, he, she, it **was hidden**
	we, you, they **hid**	we, you, they **were hidden**
Past	I, he, she, it **was hiding**	I, he, she, it **was being hidden**
Prog.	we, you, they **were hiding**	we, you, they **were being hidden**
Past	I, he, she, it,	I, he, she, it,
Int.	we, you, they **did hide**	we, you, they **did get hidden**
Pres.	I, we, you, they **have hidden**	I, we, you, they **have been hidden**
Perf.	he, she, it **has hidden**	he, she, it **has been hidden**
Past	I, he, she, it,	I, he, she, it,
Perf.	we, you, they **had hidden**	we, you, they **had been hidden**
Fut.	I, he, she, it, we, you, they	I, he, she, it, we, you, they
Perf.	**will have hidden**	**will have been hidden**

IMPERATIVE MOOD

hide

be hidden

SUBJUNCTIVE MOOD

Pres.	if I, he, she, it,	if I, he, she, it,
	we, you, they **hide**	we, you, they **be hidden**
Past	if I, he, she, it,	if I, he, she, it,
	we, you, they **hid**	we, you, they **were hidden**
Fut.	if I, he, she, it,	if I, he, she, it,
	we, you, they **should hide**	we, you, they **should be hidden**

Transitive and intransitive. The verb means to "be or put out of sight." The past participle may be either HIDDEN or HID. The *Oxford Dictionary* considers the past participle HID archaic.

hide
(active voice)

be hided
(passive voice)

Infinitive: **to hide**
Perfect Infinitive: **to have hided**
Present Participle: **hiding**
Past Participle: **hided**

Infinitive: **to be hided**
Perfect Infinitive: **to have been hided**
Present Participle: **being hided**
Past Participle: **been hided**

INDICATIVE MOOD

Pres.	I, we, you, they **hide** he, she, it **hides**	I **am hided** we, you, they **are hided** he, she, it **is hided**
Pres. *Prog.*	I **am hiding** we, you, they **are hiding** he, she, it **is hiding**	I **am being hided** we, you, they **are being hided** he, she, it **is being hided**
Pres. *Int.*	I, we, you, they **do hide** he, she, it **does hide**	I, we, you, they **do get hided** he, she, it **does get hided**
Fut.	I, he, she, it, we, you, they **will hide**	I, he, she, it, we, you, they **will be hided**
Past	I, he, she, it, we, you, they **hided**	I, he, she, it **was hided** we, you, they **were hided**
Past *Prog.*	I, he, she, it **was hiding** we, you, they **were hiding**	I, he, she, it **was being hided** we, you, they **were being hided**
Past *Int.*	I, he, she, it, we, you, they **did hide**	I, he, she, it, we, you, they **did get hided**
Pres. *Perf.*	I, we, you, they **have hided** he, she, it **has hided**	I, we, you, they **have been hided** he, she, it **has been hided**
Past *Perf.*	I, he, she, it, we, you, they **had hided**	I, he, she, it, we, you, they **had been hided**
Fut. *Perf.*	I, he, she, it, we, you, they **will have hided**	I, he, she, it, we, you, they **will have been hided**

IMPERATIVE MOOD

hide　　　　　　　　　**be hided**

SUBJUNCTIVE MOOD

Pres.	if I, he, she, it, we, you, they **hide**	if I, he, she, it, we, you, they **be hided**
Past	if I, he, she, it, we, you, they **hided**	if I, he, she, it, we, you, they **were hided**
Fut.	if I, he, she, it, we, you, they **should hide**	if I, he, she, it, we, you, they **should be hided**

This verb means to "beat or flog."

hit
(active voice)

be hit
(passive voice)

Infinitive: **to hit**
Perfect Infinitive: **to have hit**
Present Participle: **hitting**
Past Participle: **hit**

Infinitive: **to be hit**
Perfect Infinitive: **to have been hit**
Present Participle: **being hit**
Past Participle: **been hit**

INDICATIVE MOOD

Pres.	I, we, you, they **hit**	I **am hit**
		we, you, they **are hit**
	he, she, it **hits**	he, she, it **is hit**
Pres. *Prog.*	I **am hitting**	I **am being hit**
	we, you, they **are hitting**	we, you, they **are being hit**
	he, she, it **is hitting**	he, she, it **is being hit**
Pres. *Int.*	I, we, you, they **do hit**	I, we, you, they **do get hit**
	he, she, it **does hit**	he, she, it **does get hit**
Fut.	I, he, she, it, we, you, they **will hit**	I, he, she, it, we, you, they **will be hit**
Past	I, he, she, it, we, you, they **hit**	I, he, she, it **was hit** we, you, they **were hit**
Past *Prog.*	I, he, she, it **was hitting** we, you, they **were hitting**	I, he, she, it **was being hit** we, you, they **were being hit**
Past *Int.*	I, he, she, it, we, you, they **did hit**	I, he, she, it, we, you, they **did get hit**
Pres. *Perf.*	I, we, you, they **have hit** he, she, it **has hit**	I, we, you, they **have been hit** he, she, it **has been hit**
Past *Perf.*	I, he, she, it, we, you, they **had hit**	I, he, she, it, we, you, they **had been hit**
Fut. *Perf.*	I, he, she, it, we, you, they **will have hit**	I, he, she, it, we, you, they **will have been hit**

IMPERATIVE MOOD

hit

be hit

SUBJUNCTIVE MOOD

Pres.	if I, he, she, it, we, you, they **hit**	if I, he, she, it, we, you, they **be hit**
Past	if I, he, she, it, we, you, they **hit**	if I, he, she, it, we, you, they **were hit**
Fut.	if I, he, she, it, we, you, they **should hit**	if I, he, she, it, we, you, they **should be hit**

Transitive and intransitive.

hold
(active voice)

be held
(passive voice)

Infinitive: **to hold**
Perfect Infinitive: **to have held**
Present Participle: **holding**
Past Participle: **held**

Infinitive: **to be held**
Perfect Infinitive: **to have been held**
Present Participle: **being held**
Past Participle: **been held**

INDICATIVE MOOD

Pres.	I, we, you, they **hold**	I **am held**
		we, you, they **are held**
	he, she, it **holds**	he, she, it **is held**
Pres.	I **am holding**	I **am being held**
Prog.	we, you, they **are holding**	we, you, they **are being held**
	he, she, it **is holding**	he, she, it **is being held**
Pres.	I, we, you, they **do hold**	I, we, you, they **do get held**
Int.	he, she, it **does hold**	he, she, it **does get held**
Fut.	I, he, she, it,	I, he, she, it,
	we, you, they **will hold**	we, you, they **will be held**
Past	I, he, she, it,	I, he, she, it **was held**
	we, you, they **held**	we, you, they **were held**
Past	I, he, she, it **was holding**	I, he, she, it **was being held**
Prog.	we, you, they **were holding**	we, you, they **were being held**
Past	I, he, she, it,	I, he, she, it,
Int.	we, you, they **did hold**	we, you, they **did get held**
Pres.	I, we, you, they **have held**	I, we, you, they **have been held**
Perf.	he, she, it **has held**	he, she, it **has been held**
Past	I, he, she, it,	I, he, she, it,
Perf.	we, you, they **had held**	we, you, they **had been held**
Fut.	I, he, she, it, we, you, they	I, he, she, it, we, you, they
Perf.	**will have held**	**will have been held**

IMPERATIVE MOOD

hold   **be held**

SUBJUNCTIVE MOOD

Pres.	if I, he, she, it,	if I, he, she, it,
	we, you, they **hold**	we, you, they **be held**
Past	if I, he, she, it,	if I, he, she, it,
	we, you, they **held**	we, you, they **were held**
Fut.	if I, he, she, it,	if I, he, she, it,
	we, you, they **should hold**	we, you, they **should be held**

Transitive and intransitive.

hop
(active voice)

be hopped
(passive voice)

Infinitive: **to hop**
Perfect Infinitive: **to have hopped**
Present Participle: **hopping**
Past Participle: **hopped**

Infinitive: **to be hopped**
Perfect Infinitive: **to have been hopped**
Present Participle: **being hopped**
Past Participle: **been hopped**

INDICATIVE MOOD

Pres.	I, we, you, they **hop**	I **am hopped**
		we, you, they **are hopped**
	he, she, it **hops**	he, she, it **is hopped**
Pres.	I **am hopping**	I **am being hopped**
Prog.	we, you, they **are hopping**	we, you, they **are being hopped**
	he, she, it **is hopping**	he, she, it **is being hopped**
Pres.	I, we, you, they **do hop**	I, we, you, they **do get hopped**
Int.	he, she, it **does hop**	he, she, it **does get hopped**
Fut.	I, he, she, it,	I, he, she, it,
	we, you, they **will hop**	we, you, they **will be hopped**
Past	I, he, she, it,	I, he, she, it **was hopped**
	we, you, they **hopped**	we, you, they **were hopped**
Past	I, he, she, it **was hopping**	I, he, she, it **was being hopped**
Prog.	we, you, they **were hopping**	we, you, they **were being hopped**
Past	I, he, she, it,	I, he, she, it,
Int.	we, you, they **did hop**	we, you, they **did get hopped**
Pres.	I, we, you, they **have hopped**	I, we, you, they **have been hopped**
Perf.	he, she, it **has hopped**	he, she, it **has been hopped**
Past	I, he, she, it,	I, he, she, it,
Perf.	we, you, they **had hopped**	we, you, they **had been hopped**
Fut.	I, he, she, it, we, you, they	I, he, she, it, we, you, they
Perf.	**will have hopped**	**will have been hopped**

IMPERATIVE MOOD

hop **be hopped**

SUBJUNCTIVE MOOD

Pres.	if I, he, she, it,	if I, he, she, it,
	we, you, they **hop**	we, you, they **be hopped**
Past	if I, he, she, it,	if I, he, she, it,
	we, you, they **hopped**	we, you, they **were hopped**
Fut.	if I, he, she, it,	if I, he, she, it,
	we, you, they **should hop**	we, you, they **should be hopped**

Intransitive and transitive.

hope
(active voice)

be hoped
(passive voice)

Infinitive: **to hope**
Perfect Infinitive: **to have hoped**
Present Participle: **hoping**
Past Participle: **hoped**

Infinitive: **to be hoped**
Perfect Infinitive: **to have been hoped**
Present Participle: **being hoped**
Past Participle: **been hoped**

INDICATIVE MOOD

Pres.	I, we, you, they **hope** he, she, it **hopes**	I **am hoped** we, you, they **are hoped** he, she, it **is hoped**
Pres. *Prog.*	I **am hoping** we, you, they **are hoping** he, she, it **is hoping**	I **am being hoped** we, you, they **are being hoped** he, she, it **is being hoped**
Pres. *Int.*	I, we, you, they **do hope** he, she, it **does hope**	I, we, you, they **do get hoped** he, she, it **does get hoped**
Fut.	I, he, she, it, we, you, they **will hope**	I, he, she, it, we, you, they **will be hoped**
Past	I, he, she, it, we, you, they **hoped**	I, he, she, it **was hoped** we, you, they **were hoped**
Past *Prog.*	I, he, she, it **was hoping** we, you, they **were hoping**	I, he, she, it **was being hoped** we, you, they **were being hoped**
Past *Int.*	I, he, she, it, we, you, they **did hope**	I, he, she, it, we, you, they **did get hoped**
Pres. *Perf.*	I, we, you, they **have hoped** he, she, it **has hoped**	I, we, you, they **have been hoped** he, she, it **has been hoped**
Past *Perf.*	I, he, she, it, we, you, they **had hoped**	I, he, she, it, we, you, they **had been hoped**
Fut. *Perf.*	I, he, she, it, we, you, they **will have hoped**	I, he, she, it, we, you, they **will have been hoped**

IMPERATIVE MOOD

hope   **be hoped**

SUBJUNCTIVE MOOD

Pres.	ïf I, he, she, it, we, you, they **hope**	if I, he, she, it, we, you, they **be hoped**
Past	if I, he, she, it, we, you, they **hoped**	if I, he, she, it, we, you, they **were hoped**
Fut.	if I, he, she, it, we, you, they **should hope**	if I, he, she, it, we, you, they **should be hoped**

Intransitive and transitive.

hurt
(active voice)

PRINCIPAL PARTS: **hurts, hurting, hurt, hurt**

be hurt
(passive voice)

Infinitive: **to hurt**
Perfect Infinitive: **to have hurt**
Present Participle: **hurting**
Past Participle: **hurt**

Infinitive: **to be hurt**
Perfect Infinitive: **to have been hurt**
Present Participle: **being hurt**
Past Participle: **been hurt**

INDICATIVE MOOD

Pres.	I, we, you, they **hurt**	I **am hurt**
		we, you, they **are hurt**
	he, she, it **hurts**	he, she, it **is hurt**
Pres.	I **am hurting**	I **am being hurt**
Prog.	we, you, they **are hurting**	we, you, they **are being hurt**
	he, she, it **is hurting**	he, she, it **is being hurt**
Pres.	I, we, you, they **do hurt**	I, we, you, they **do get hurt**
Int.	he, she, it **does hurt**	he, she, it **does get hurt**
Fut.	I, he, she, it,	I, he, she, it,
	we, you, they **will hurt**	we, you, they **will be hurt**
Past	I, he, she, it,	I, he, she, it **was hurt**
	we, you, they **hurt**	we, you, they **were hurt**
Past	I, he, she, it **was hurting**	I, he, she, it **was being hurt**
Prog.	we, you, they **were hurting**	we, you, they **were being hurt**
Past	I, he, she, it,	I, he, she, it,
Int.	we, you, they **did hurt**	we, you, they **did get hurt**
Pres.	I, we, you, they **have hurt**	I, we, you, they **have been hurt**
Perf.	he, she, it **has hurt**	he, she, it **has been hurt**
Past	I, he, she, it,	I, he, she, it,
Perf.	we, you, they **had hurt**	we, you, they **had been hurt**
Fut.	I, he, she, it, we, you, they	I, he, she, it, we, you, they
Perf.	**will have hurt**	**will have been hurt**

IMPERATIVE MOOD

hurt

be hurt

SUBJUNCTIVE MOOD

Pres.	if I, he, she, it,	if I, he, she, it,
	we, you, they **hurt**	we, you, they **be hurt**
Past	if I, he, she, it,	if I, he, she, it,
	we, you, they **hurt**	we, you, they **were hurt**
Fut.	if I, he, she, it,	if I, he, she, it,
	we, you, they **should hurt**	we, you, they **should be hurt**

Transitive and intransitive.

imagine
(active voice)

PRINCIPAL PARTS: **imagines, imagining, imagined, imagined**

be imagined
(passive voice)

Infinitive: **to imagine**
Perfect Infinitive: **to have imagined**
Present Participle: **imagining**
Past Participle: **imagined**

Infinitive: **to be imagined**
Perfect Infinitive: **to have been imagined**
Present Participle: **being imagined**
Past Participle: **been imagined**

INDICATIVE MOOD

Pres.	I, we, you, they **imagine**	I **am imagined**
		we, you, they **are imagined**
	he, she, it **imagines**	he, she, it **is imagined**
Pres.	I **am imagining**	I **am being imagined**
Prog.	we, you, they **are imagining**	we, you, they **are being imagined**
	he, she, it **is imagining**	he, she, it **is being imagined**
Pres.	I, we, you, they **do imagine**	I, we, you, they **do get imagined**
Int.	he, she, it **does imagine**	he, she, it **does get imagined**
Fut.	I, he, she, it,	I, he, she, it,
	we, you, they **will imagine**	we, you, they **will be imagined**
Past	I, he, she, it,	I, he, she, it **was imagined**
	we, you, they **imagined**	we, you, they **were imagined**
Past	I, he, she, it **was imagining**	I, he, she, it **was being imagined**
Prog.	we, you, they **were imagining**	we, you, they **were being imagined**
Past	I, he, she, it,	I, he, she, it,
Int.	we, you, they **did imagine**	we, you, they **did get imagined**
Pres.	I, we, you, they **have imagined**	I, we, you, they **have been imagined**
Perf.	he, she, it **has imagined**	he, she, it **has been imagined**
Past	I, he, she, it,	I, he, she, it,
Perf.	we, you, they **had imagined**	we, you, they **had been imagined**
Fut.	I, he, she, it, we, you, they	I, he, she, it, we, you, they
Perf.	**will have imagined**	**will have been imagined**

IMPERATIVE MOOD

imagine   **be imagined**

SUBJUNCTIVE MOOD

Pres.	if I, he, she, it,	if I, he, she, it,
	we, you, they **imagine**	we, you, they **be imagined**
Past	if I, he, she, it,	if I, he, she, it,
	we, you, they **imagined**	we, you, they **were imagined**
Fut.	if I, he, she, it,	if I, he, she, it,
	we, you, they **should imagine**	we, you, they **should be imagined**

Transitive and intransitive.

186

improve
(active voice)

PRINCIPAL PARTS: **improves, improving, improved, improved**

be improved
(passive voice)

Infinitive: **to improve**
Perfect Infinitive: **to have improved**
Present Participle: **improving**
Past Participle: **improved**

Infinitive: **to be improved**
Perfect Infinitive: **to have been improved**
Present Participle: **being improved**
Past Participle: **been improved**

INDICATIVE MOOD

Pres.	I, we, you, they **improve**	I **am improved** we, you, they **are improved**
	he, she, it **improves**	he, she, it **is improved**
Pres. *Prog.*	I **am improving** we, you, they **are improving** he, she, it **is improving**	I **am being improved** we, you, they **are being improved** he, she, it **is being improved**
Pres. *Int.*	I, we, you, they **do improve** he, she, it **does improve**	I, we, you, they **do get improved** he, she, it **does get improved**
Fut.	I, he, she, it, we, you, they **will improve**	I, he, she, it, we, you, they **will be improved**
Past	I, he, she, it, we, you, they **improved**	I, he, she, it **was improved** we, you, they **were improved**
Past *Prog.*	I, he, she, it **was improving** we, you, they **were improving**	I, he, she, it **was being improved** we, you, they **were being improved**
Past *Int.*	I, he, she, it, we, you, they **did improve**	I, he, she, it, we, you, they **did get improved**
Pres. *Perf.*	I, we, you, they **have improved** he, she, it **has improved**	I, we, you, they **have been improved** he, she, it **has been improved**
Past *Perf.*	I, he, she, it, we, you, they **had improved**	I, he, she, it, we, you, they **had been improved**
Fut. *Perf.*	I, he, she, it, we, you, they **will have improved**	I, he, she, it, we, you, they **will have been improved**

IMPERATIVE MOOD

improve

be improved

SUBJUNCTIVE MOOD

Pres.	if I, he, she, it, we, you, they **improve**	if I, he, she, it, we, you, they **be improved**
Past	if I, he, she, it, we, you, they **improved**	if I, he, she, it, we, you, they **were improved**
Fut.	if I, he, she, it, we, you, they **should improve**	if I, he, she, it, we, you, they **should be improved**

Transitive and intransitive.

include
(active voice)

be included
(passive voice)

Infinitive: **to include**
Perfect Infinitive: **to have included**
Present Participle: **including**
Past Participle: **included**

Infinitive: **to be included**
Perfect Infinitive: **to have been included**
Present Participle: **being included**
Past Participle: **been included**

INDICATIVE MOOD

Pres.	I, we, you, they **include**	I **am included**
		we, you, they **are included**
	he, she, it **includes**	he, she, it **is included**
Pres.	I **am including**	I **am being included**
Prog.	we, you, they **are including**	we, you, they **are being included**
	he, she, it **is including**	he, she, it **is being included**
Pres.	I, we, you, they **do include**	I, we, you, they **do get included**
Int.	he, she, it **does include**	he, she, it **does get included**
Fut.	I, he, she, it,	I, he, she, it,
	we, you, they **will include**	we, you, they **will be included**
Past	I, he, she, it,	I, he, she, it **was included**
	we, you, they **included**	we, you, they **were included**
Past	I, he, she, it **was including**	I, he, she, it **was being included**
Prog.	we, you, they **were including**	we, you, they **were being included**
Past	I, he, she, it,	I, he, she, it,
Int.	we, you, they **did include**	we, you, they **did get included**
Pres.	I, we, you, they **have included**	I, we, you, they **have been included**
Perf.	he, she, it **has included**	he, she, it **has been included**
Past	I, he, she, it,	I, he, she, it,
Perf.	we, you, they **had included**	we, you, they **had been included**
Fut.	I, he, she, it, we, you, they	I, he, she, it, we, you, they
Perf.	**will have included**	**will have been included**

IMPERATIVE MOOD

include

be included

SUBJUNCTIVE MOOD

Pres.	if I, he, she, it,	if I, he, she, it,
	we, you, they **include**	we, you, they **be included**
Past	if I, he, she, it,	if I, he, she, it,
	we, you, they **included**	we, you, they **were included**
Fut.	if I, he, she, it,	if I, he, she, it,
	we, you, they **should include**	we, you, they **should be included**

increase
(active voice)

PRINCIPAL PARTS: **increases, increasing, increased, increased**

be increased
(passive voice)

Infinitive: **to increase**
Perfect Infinitive: **to have increased**
Present Participle: **increasing**
Past Participle: **increased**

Infinitive: **to be increased**
Perfect Infinitive: **to have been increased**
Present Participle: **being increased**
Past Participle: **been increased**

INDICATIVE MOOD

Pres.	I, we, you, they **increase**	I **am increased**
		we, you, they **are increased**
	he, she, it **increases**	he, she, it **is increased**
Pres.	I **am increasing**	I **am being increased**
Prog.	we, you, they **are increasing**	we, you, they **are being increased**
	he, she, it **is increasing**	he, she, it **is being increased**
Pres.	I, we, you, they **do increase**	I, we, you, they **do get increased**
Int.	he, she, it **does increase**	he, she, it **does get increased**
Fut.	I, he, she, it,	I, he, she, it,
	we, you, they **will increase**	we, you, they **will be increased**
Past	I, he, she, it,	I, he, she, it **was increased**
	we, you, they **increased**	we, you, they **were increased**
Past	I, he, she, it **was increasing**	I, he, she, it **was being increased**
Prog.	we, you, they **were increasing**	we, you, they **were being increased**
Past	I, he, she, it,	I, he, she, it,
Int.	we, you, they **did increase**	we, you, they **did get increased**
Pres.	I, we, you, they **have increased**	I, we, you, they **have been increased**
Perf.	he, she, it **has increased**	he, she, it **has been increased**
Past	I, he, she, it,	I, he, she, it,
Perf.	we, you, they **had increased**	we, you, they **had been increased**
Fut.	I, he, she, it, we, you, they	I, he, she, it, we, you, they
Perf.	**will have increased**	**will have been increased**

IMPERATIVE MOOD

increase

be increased

SUBJUNCTIVE MOOD

Pres.	if I, he, she, it,	if I, he, she, it,
	we, you, they **increase**	we, you, they **be increased**
Past	if I, he, she, it,	if I, he, she, it,
	we, you, they **increased**	we, you, they **were increased**
Fut.	if I, he, she, it,	if I, he, she, it,
	we, you, they **should increase**	we, you, they **should be increased**

Intransitive and transitive.

indicate
(active voice)

be indicated
(passive voice)

Infinitive: **to indicate**
Perfect Infinitive: **to have indicated**
Present Participle: **indicating**
Past Participle: **indicated**

Infinitive: **to be indicated**
Perfect Infinitive: **to have been indicated**
Present Participle: **being indicated**
Past Participle: **been indicated**

INDICATIVE MOOD

Pres.	I, we, you, they **indicate**	I **am indicated**
		we, you, they **are indicated**
	he, she, it **indicates**	he, she, it **is indicated**
Pres.	I **am indicating**	I **am being indicated**
Prog.	we, you, they **are indicating**	we, you, they **are being indicated**
	he, she, it **is indicating**	he, she, it **is being indicated**
Pres.	I, we, you, they **do indicate**	I, we, you, they **do get indicated**
Int.	he, she, it **does indicate**	he, she, it **does get indicated**
Fut.	I, he, she, it,	I, he, she, it,
	we, you, they **will indicate**	we, you, they **will be indicated**
Past	I, he, she, it,	I, he, she, it **was indicated**
	we, you, they **indicated**	we, you, they **were indicated**
Past	I, he, she, it **was indicating**	I, he, she, it **was being indicated**
Prog.	we, you, they **were indicating**	we, you, they **were being indicated**
Past	I, he, she, it,	I, he, she, it,
Int.	we, you, they **did indicate**	we, you, they **did get indicated**
Pres.	I, we, you, they **have indicated**	I, we, you, they **have been indicated**
Perf.	he, she, it **has indicated**	he, she, it **has been indicated**
Past	I, he, she, it,	I, he, she, it,
Perf.	we, you, they **had indicated**	we, you, they **had been indicated**
Fut.	I, he, she, it, we, you, they	I, he, she, it, we, you, they
Perf.	**will have indicated**	**will have been indicated**

IMPERATIVE MOOD

indicate

be indicated

SUBJUNCTIVE MOOD

Pres.	if I, he, she, it,	if I, he, she, it,
	we, you, they **indicate**	we, you, they **be indicated**
Past	if I, he, she, it,	if I, he, she, it,
	we, you, they **indicated**	we, you, they **were indicated**
Fut.	if I, he, she, it,	if I, he, she, it,
	we, you, they **should indicate**	we, you, they **should be indicated**

inset
(active voice)

be inset
(passive voice)

Infinitive: **to inset**
Perfect Infinitive: **to have inset**
Present Participle: **insetting**
Past Participle: **inset**

Infinitive: **to be inset**
Perfect Infinitive: **to have been inset**
Present Participle: **being inset**
Past Participle: **been inset**

INDICATIVE MOOD

Pres.	I, we, you, they **inset**	I **am inset**
		we, you, they **are inset**
	he, she, it **insets**	he, she, it **is inset**
Pres.	I **am insetting**	I **am being inset**
Prog.	we, you, they **are insetting**	we, you, they **are being inset**
	he, she, it **is insetting**	he, she, it **is being inset**
Pres.	I, we, you, they **do inset**	I, we, you, they **do get inset**
Int.	he, she, it **does inset**	he, she, it **does get inset**
Fut.	I, he, she, it,	I, he, she, it,
	we, you, they **will inset**	we, you, they **will be inset**
Past	I, he, she, it,	I, he, she, it **was inset**
	we, you, they **inset**	we, you, they **were inset**
Past	I, he, she, it **was insetting**	I, he, she, it **was being inset**
Prog.	we, you, they **were insetting**	we, you, they **were being inset**
Past	I, he, she, it,	I, he, she, it,
Int.	we, you, they **did inset**	we, you, they **did get inset**
Pres.	I, we, you, they **have inset**	I, we, you, they **have been inset**
Perf.	he, she, it **has inset**	he, she, it **has been inset**
Past	I, he, she, it,	I, he, she, it,
Perf.	we, you, they **had inset**	we, you, they **had been inset**
Fut.	I, he, she, it, we, you, they	I, he, she, it, we, you, they
Perf.	**will have inset**	**will have been inset**

IMPERATIVE MOOD

inset **be inset**

SUBJUNCTIVE MOOD

Pres.	if I, he, she, it,	if I, he, she, it,
	we, you, they **inset**	we, you, they **be inset**
Past	if I, he, she, it,	if I, he, she, it,
	we, you, they **inset**	we, you, they **were inset**
Fut.	if I, he, she, it,	if I, he, she, it,
	we, you, they **should inset**	we, you, they **should be inset**

The *Oxford Dictionary* and *Merriam Webster's* recognize INSETTED as an alternate past tense and past participle.

involve
(active voice)

PRINCIPAL PARTS: **involves, involving, involved, involved**

be involved
(passive voice)

Infinitive: **to involve**
Perfect Infinitive: **to have involved**
Present Participle: **involving**
Past Participle: **involved**

Infinitive: **to be involved**
Perfect Infinitive: **to have been involved**
Present Participle: **being involved**
Past Participle: **been involved**

INDICATIVE MOOD

Pres.	I, we, you, they **involve**	I **am involved**
		we, you, they **are involved**
	he, she, it **involves**	he, she, it **is involved**
Pres.	I **am involving**	I **am being involved**
Prog.	we, you, they **are involving**	we, you, they **are being involved**
	he, she, it **is involving**	he, she, it **is being involved**
Pres.	I, we, you, they **do involve**	I, we, you, they **do get involved**
Int.	he, she, it **does involve**	he, she, it **does get involved**
Fut.	I, he, she, it,	I, he, she, it,
	we, you, they **will involve**	we, you, they **will be involved**
Past	I, he, she, it,	I, he, she, it **was involved**
	we, you, they **involved**	we, you, they **were involved**
Past	I, he, she, it **was involving**	I, he, she, it **was being involved**
Prog.	we, you, they **were involving**	we, you, they **were being involved**
Past	I, he, she, it,	I, he, she, it,
Int.	we, you, they **did involve**	we, you, they **did get involved**
Pres.	I, we, you, they **have involved**	I, we, you, they **have been involved**
Perf.	he, she, it **has involved**	he, she, it **has been involved**
Past	I, he, she, it,	I, he, she, it,
Perf.	we, you, they **had involved**	we, you, they **had been involved**
Fut.	I, he, she, it, we, you, they	I, he, she, it, we, you, they
Perf.	**will have involved**	**will have been involved**

IMPERATIVE MOOD

involve

be involved

SUBJUNCTIVE MOOD

Pres.	if I, he, she, it,	if I, he, she, it,
	we, you, they **involve**	we, you, they **be involved**
Past	if I, he, she, it,	if I, he, she, it,
	we, you, they **involved**	we, you, they **were involved**
Fut.	if I, he, she, it,	if I, he, she, it,
	we, you, they **should involve**	we, you, they **should be involved**

join
(active voice)

PRINCIPAL PARTS: **joins, joining,
joined, joined**

be joined
(passive voice)

Infinitive: **to join**
Perfect Infinitive: **to have joined**
Present Participle: **joining**
Past Participle: **joined**

Infinitive: **to be joined**
Perfect Infinitive: **to have been joined**
Present Participle: **being joined**
Past Participle: **been joined**

INDICATIVE MOOD

Pres.	I, we, you, they **join**	I **am joined**
		we, you, they **are joined**
	he, she, it **joins**	he, she, it **is joined**
Pres.	I **am joining**	I **am being joined**
Prog.	we, you, they **are joining**	we, you, they **are being joined**
	he, she, it **is joining**	he, she, it **is being joined**
Pres.	I, we, you, they **do join**	I, we, you, they **do get joined**
Int.	he, she, it **does join**	he, she, it **does get joined**
Fut.	I, he, she, it,	I, he, she, it,
	we, you, they **will join**	we, you, they **will be joined**
Past	I, he, she, it,	I, he, she, it **was joined**
	we, you, they **joined**	we, you, they **were joined**
Past	I, he, she, it **was joining**	I, he, she, it **was being joined**
Prog.	we, you, they **were joining**	we, you, they **were being joined**
Past	I, he, she, it,	I, he, she, it,
Int.	we, you, they **did join**	we, you, they **did get joined**
Pres.	I, we, you, they **have joined**	I, we, you, they **have been joined**
Perf.	he, she, it **has joined**	he, she, it **has been joined**
Past	I, he, she, it,	I, he, she, it,
Perf.	we, you, they **had joined**	we, you, they **had been joined**
Fut.	I, he, she, it, we, you, they	I, he, she, it, we, you, they
Perf.	**will have joined**	**will have been joined**

IMPERATIVE MOOD

join   **be joined**

SUBJUNCTIVE MOOD

Pres.	if I, he, she, it,	if I, he, she, it,
	we, you, they **join**	we, you, they **be joined**
Past	if I, he, she, it,	if I, he, she, it,
	we, you, they **joined**	we, you, they **were joined**
Fut.	if I, he, she, it,	if I, he, she, it,
	we, you, they **should join**	we, you, they **should be joined**

Transitive and intransitive.

keep
(active voice)

be kept
(passive voice)

Infinitive: **to keep**
Perfect Infinitive: **to have kept**
Present Participle: **keeping**
Past Participle: **kept**

Infinitive: **to be kept**
Perfect Infinitive: **to have been kept**
Present Participle: **being kept**
Past Participle: **been kept**

INDICATIVE MOOD

Pres.	I, we, you, they **keep**	I **am kept**
		we, you, they **are kept**
	he, she, it **keeps**	he, she, it **is kept**
Pres.	I **am keeping**	I **am being kept**
Prog.	we, you, they **are keeping**	we, you, they **are being kept**
	he, she, it **is keeping**	he, she, it **is being kept**
Pres.	I, we, you, they **do keep**	I, we, you, they **do get kept**
Int.	he, she, it **does keep**	he, she, it **does get kept**
Fut.	I, he, she, it, we, you, they **will keep**	I, he, she, it, we, you, they **will be kept**
Past	I, he, she, it, we, you, they **kept**	I, he, she, it **was kept** we, you, they **were kept**
Past	I, he, she, it **was keeping**	I, he, she, it **was being kept**
Prog.	we, you, they **were keeping**	we, you, they **were being kept**
Past	I, he, she, it, we, you, they **did keep**	I, he, she, it, we, you, they **did get kept**
Int.		
Pres.	I, we, you, they **have kept**	I, we, you, they **have been kept**
Perf.	he, she, it **has kept**	he, she, it **has been kept**
Past	I, he, she, it, we, you, they **had kept**	I, he, she, it, we, you, they **had been kept**
Perf.		
Fut.	I, he, she, it, we, you, they **will have kept**	I, he, she, it, we, you, they **will have been kept**
Perf.		

IMPERATIVE MOOD

keep   **be kept**

SUBJUNCTIVE MOOD

Pres.	if I, he, she, it, we, you, they **keep**	if I, he, she, it, we, you, they **be kept**
Past	if I, he, she, it, we, you, they **kept**	if I, he, she, it, we, you, they **were kept**
Fut.	if I, he, she, it, we, you, they **should keep**	if I, he, she, it, we, you, they **should be kept**

Transitive and intransitive.

194

kill
(active voice)

be killed
(passive voice)

Infinitive: **to kill**
Perfect Infinitive: **to have killed**
Present Participle: **killing**
Past Participle: **killed**

Infinitive: **to be killed**
Perfect Infinitive: **to have been killed**
Present Participle: **being killed**
Past Participle: **been killed**

INDICATIVE MOOD

Pres.	I, we, you, they **kill**	I **am killed**
		we, you, they **are killed**
	he, she, it **kills**	he, she, it **is killed**
Pres.	I **am killing**	I **am being killed**
Prog.	we, you, they **are killing**	we, you, they **are being killed**
	he, she, it **is killing**	he, she, it **is being killed**
Pres.	I, we, you, they **do kill**	I, we, you, they **do get killed**
Int.	he, she, it **does kill**	he, she, it **does get killed**
Fut.	I, he, she, it,	I, he, she, it,
	we, you, they **will kill**	we, you, they **will be killed**
Past	I, he, she, it,	I, he, she, it **was killed**
	we, you, they **killed**	we, you, they **were killed**
Past	I, he, she, it **was killing**	I, he, she, it **was being killed**
Prog.	we, you, they **were killing**	we, you, they **were being killed**
Past	I, he, she, it,	I, he, she, it,
Int.	we, you, they **did kill**	we, you, they **did get killed**
Pres.	I, we, you, they **have killed**	I, we, you, they **have been killed**
Perf.	he, she, it **has killed**	he, she, it **has been killed**
Past	I, he, she, it,	I, he, she, it,
Perf.	we, you, they **had killed**	we, you, they **had been killed**
Fut.	I, he, she, it, we, you, they	I, he, she, it, we, you, they
Perf.	**will have killed**	**will have been killed**

IMPERATIVE MOOD

kill **be killed**

SUBJUNCTIVE MOOD

Pres.	if I, he, she, it,	if I, he, she, it,
	we, you, they **kill**	we, you, they **be killed**
Past	if I, he, she, it,	if I, he, she, it,
	we, you, they **killed**	we, you, they **were killed**
Fut.	if I, he, she, it,	if I, he, she, it,
	we, you, they **should kill**	we, you, they **should be killed**

Transitive and intransitive.

kneel

Infinitive: **to kneel**
Perfect Infinitive: **to have knelt**
Present Participle: **kneeling**
Past Participle: **knelt**

INDICATIVE MOOD

Pres.   I, we, you, they **kneel**

he, she, it **kneels**

Pres. **I am kneeling**
Prog. we, you, they **are kneeling**
he, she, it **is kneeling**

Pres. I, we, you, they **do kneel**
Int. he, she, it **does kneel**

Fut. I, he, she, it,
we, you, they **will kneel**

Past I, he, she, it,
we, you, they **knelt**

Past I, he, she, it **was kneeling**
Prog. we, you, they **were kneeling**

Past I, he, she, it,
Int. we, you, they **did kneel**

Pres. I, we, you, they **have knelt**
Perf. he, she, it **has knelt**

Past I, he, she, it,
Perf. we, you, they **had knelt**

Fut. I, he, she, it, we, you, they
Perf. **will have knelt**

IMPERATIVE MOOD

kneel

SUBJUNCTIVE MOOD

Pres. if I, he, she, it,
we, you, they **kneel**

Past if I, he, she, it,
we, you, they **knelt**

Fut. if I, he, she, it,
we, you, they **should kneel**

knit
(active voice)

PRINCIPAL PARTS: **knits, knitting,
knit/knitted, knit/knitted**

be knit/knitted
(passive voice)

Infinitive: **to knit**
Perfect Infinitive: **to have knit**
Present Participle: **knitting**
Past Participle: **knit**

Infinitive: **to be knit**
Perfect Infinitive: **to have been knit**
Present Participle: **being knit**
Past Participle: **been knit**

INDICATIVE MOOD

Pres.	I, we, you, they **knit**	I **am knit** we, you, they **are knit**
	he, she, it **knits**	he, she, it **is knit**
Pres. *Prog.*	I **am knitting** we, you, they **are knitting**	I **am being knit** we, you, they **are being knit**
	he, she, it **is knitting**	he, she, it **is being knit**
Pres. *Int.*	I, we, you, they **do knit**	I, we, you, they **do get knit**
	he, she, it **does knit**	he, she, it **does get knit**
Fut.	I, he, she, it, we, you, they **will knit**	I, he, she, it, we, you, they **will be knit**
Past	I, he, she, it, we, you, they **knit**	I, he, she, it **was knit** we, you, they **were knit**
Past *Prog.*	I, he, she, it **was knitting** we, you, they **were knitting**	I, he, she, it **was being knit** we, you, they **were being knit**
Past *Int.*	I, he, she, it, we, you, they **did knit**	I, he, she, it, we, you, they **did get knit**
Pres. *Perf.*	I, we, you, they **have knit** he, she, it **has knit**	I, we, you, they **have been knit** he, she, it **has been knit**
Past *Perf.*	I, he, she, it, we, you, they **had knit**	I, he, she, it, we, you, they **had been knit**
Fut. *Perf.*	I, he, she, it, we, you, they **will have knit**	I, he, she, it, we, you, they **will have been knit**

IMPERATIVE MOOD

knit   **be knit**

SUBJUNCTIVE MOOD

Pres.	if I, he, she, it, we, you, they **knit**	if I, he, she, it, we, you, they **be knit**
Past	if I, he, she, it, we, you, they **knit**	if I, he, she, it, we, you, they **were knit**
Fut.	if I, he, she, it, we, you, they **should knit**	if I, he, she, it, we, you, they **should be knit**

Transitive and intransitive. *Webster's* and the *Oxford Dictionary* list KNITTED as the first form for the past tense and past participle.

knock
(active voice)

PRINCIPAL PARTS: **knocks, knocking, knocked, knocked**

be knocked
(passive voice)

Infinitive: **to knock**
Perfect Infinitive: **to have knocked**
Present Participle: **knocking**
Past Participle: **knocked**

Infinitive: **to be knocked**
Perfect Infinitive: **to have been knocked**
Present Participle: **being knocked**
Past Participle: **been knocked**

INDICATIVE MOOD

Pres.	I, we, you, they **knock**	I **am knocked**
		we, you, they **are knocked**
	he, she, it **knocks**	he, she, it **is knocked**
Pres.	I **am knocking**	I **am being knocked**
Prog.	we, you, they **are knocking**	we, you, they **are being knocked**
	he, she, it **is knocking**	he, she, it **is being knocked**
Pres.	I, we, you, they **do knock**	I, we, you, they **do get knocked**
Int.	he, she, it **does knock**	he, she, it **does get knocked**
Fut.	I, he, she, it,	I, he, she, it,
	we, you, they **will knock**	we, you, they **will be knocked**
Past	I, he, she, it,	I, he, she, it **was knocked**
	we, you, they **knocked**	we, you, they **were knocked**
Past	I, he, she, it **was knocking**	I, he, she, it **was being knocked**
Prog.	we, you, they **were knocking**	we, you, they **were being knocked**
Past	I, he, she, it,	I, he, she, it,
Int.	we, you, they **did knock**	we, you, they **did get knocked**
Pres.	I, we, you, they **have knocked**	I, we, you, they **have been knocked**
Perf.	he, she, it **has knocked**	he, she, it **has been knocked**
Past	I, he, she, it,	I, he, she, it,
Perf.	we, you, they **had knocked**	we, you, they **had been knocked**
Fut.	I, he, she, it, we, you, they	I, he, she, it, we, you, they
Perf.	**will have knocked**	**will have been knocked**

IMPERATIVE MOOD

knock

be knocked

SUBJUNCTIVE MOOD

Pres.	if I, he, she, it,	if I, he, she, it,
	we, you, they **knock**	we, you, they **be knocked**
Past	if I, he, she, it,	if I, he, she, it,
	we, you, they **knocked**	we, you, they **were knocked**
Fut.	if I, he, she, it,	if I, he, she, it,
	we, you, they **should knock**	we, you, they **should be knocked**

Transitive and intransitive. In idiomatic expressions, the American and British variants differ significantly. To avoid embarrassment use this verb with caution. See Phrasal Verbs.

know
(active voice)

be known
(passive voice)

Infinitive: **to know**
Perfect Infinitive: **to have known**
Present Participle: **knowing**
Past Participle: **known**

Infinitive: **to be known**
Perfect Infinitive: **to have been known**
Present Participle: **being known**
Past Participle: **been known**

INDICATIVE MOOD

Pres.	I, we, you, they **know**	I **am known**
		we, you, they **are known**
	he, she, it **knows**	he, she, it **is known**
Pres.	I **am knowing**	I **am being known**
Prog.	we, you, they **are knowing**	we, you, they **are being known**
	he, she, it **is knowing**	he, she, it **is being known**
Pres.	I, we, you, they **do know**	I, we, you, they **do get known**
Int.	he, she, it **does know**	he, she, it **does get known**
Fut.	I, he, she, it,	I, he, she, it,
	we, you, they **will know**	we, you, they **will be known**
Past	I, he, she, it,	I, he, she, it **was known**
	we, you, they **knew**	we, you, they **were known**
Past	I, he, she, it **was knowing**	I, he, she, it **was being known**
Prog.	we, you, they **were knowing**	we, you, they **were being known**
Past	I, he, she, it,	I, he, she, it,
Int.	we, you, they **did know**	we, you, they **did get known**
Pres.	I, we, you, they **have known**	I, we, you, they **have been known**
Perf.	he, she, it **has known**	he, she, it **has been known**
Past	I, he, she, it,	I, he, she, it,
Perf.	we, you, they **had known**	we, you, they **had been known**
Fut.	I, he, she, it, we, you, they	I, he, she, it, we, you, they
Perf.	**will have known**	**will have been known**

IMPERATIVE MOOD

know

be known

SUBJUNCTIVE MOOD

Pres.	if I, he, she, it,	if I, he, she, it,
	we, you, they **know**	we, you, they **be known**
Past	if I, he, she, it,	if I, he, she, it,
	we, you, they **knew**	we, you, they **were known**
Fut.	if I, he, she, it,	if I, he, she, it,
	we, you, they **should know**	we, you, they **should be known**

Transitive and intransitive.

lade
(active voice)

PRINCIPAL PARTS: **lades, lading, laded, laden/laded**

be laden/laded
(passive voice)

Infinitive: **to lade**
Perfect Infinitive: **to have laden**
Present Participle: **lading**
Past Participle: **laden**

Infinitive: **to be laden**
Perfect Infinitive: **to have been laden**
Present Participle: **being laden**
Past Participle: **been laden**

INDICATIVE MOOD

Pres.	I, we, you, they **lade**	I **am laden**
		we, you, they **are laden**
	he, she, it **lades**	he, she, it **is laden**
Pres. *Prog.*	I **am lading**	I **am being laden**
	we, you, they **are lading**	we, you, they **are being laden**
	he, she, it **is lading**	he, she, it **is being laden**
Pres. *Int.*	I, we, you, they **do lade**	I, we, you, they **do get laden**
	he, she, it **does lade**	he, she, it **does get laden**
Fut.	I, he, she, it, we, you, they **will lade**	I, he, she, it, we, you, they **will be laden**
Past	I, he, she, it, we, you, they **laded**	I, he, she, it **was laden** we, you, they **were laden**
Past *Prog.*	I, he, she, it **was lading** we, you, they **were lading**	I, he, she, it **was being laden** we, you, they **were being laden**
Past *Int.*	I, he, she, it, we, you, they **did lade**	I, he, she, it, we, you, they **did get laden**
Pres. *Perf.*	I, we, you, they **have laden** he, she, it **has laden**	I, we, you, they **have been laden** he, she, it **has been laden**
Past *Perf.*	I, he, she, it, we, you, they **had laden**	I, he, she, it, we, you, they **had been laden**
Fut. *Perf.*	I, he, she, it, we, you, they **will have laden**	I, he, she, it, we, you, they **will have been laden**

IMPERATIVE MOOD

lade   **be laden**

SUBJUNCTIVE MOOD

Pres.	if I, he, she, it, we, you, they **lade**	if I, he, she, it, we, you, they **be laden**
Past	if I, he, she, it, we, you, they **laded**	if I, he, she, it, we, you, they **were laden**
Fut.	if I, he, she, it, we, you, they **should lade**	if I, he, she, it, we, you, they **should be laden**

Transitive and intransitive.

lay
(active voice)

PRINCIPAL PARTS: lays, laying, laid, laid

be laid
(passive voice)

Infinitive: **to lay**
Perfect Infinitive: **to have laid**
Present Participle: **laying**
Past Participle: **laid**

Infinitive: **to be laid**
Perfect Infinitive: **to have been laid**
Present Participle: **being laid**
Past Participle: **been laid**

INDICATIVE MOOD

Pres.	I, we, you, they **lay** he, she, it **lays**	I **am laid** we, you, they **are laid** he, she, it **is laid**
Pres. *Prog.*	I **am laying** we, you, they **are laying** he, she, it **is laying**	I **am being laid** we, you, they **are being laid** he, she, it **is being laid**
Pres. *Int.*	I, we, you, they **do lay** he, she, it **does lay**	I, we, you, they **do get laid** he, she, it **does get laid**
Fut.	I, he, she, it, we, you, they **will lay**	I, he, she, it, we, you, they **will be laid**
Past	I, he, she, it, we, you, they **laid**	I, he, she, it **was laid** we, you, they **were laid**
Past *Prog.*	I, he, she, it **was laying** we, you, they **were laying**	I, he, she, it **was being laid** we, you, they **were being laid**
Past *Int.*	I, he, she, it, we, you, they **did lay**	I, he, she, it, we, you, they **did get laid**
Pres. *Perf.*	I, we, you, they **have laid** he, she, it **has laid**	I, we, you, they **have been laid** he, she, it **has been laid**
Past *Perf.*	I, he, she, it, we, you, they **had laid**	I, he, she, it, we, you, they **had been laid**
Fut. *Perf.*	I, he, she, it, we, you, they **will have laid**	I, he, she, it, we, you, they **will have been laid**

IMPERATIVE MOOD

lay

be laid

SUBJUNCTIVE MOOD

Pres.	if I, he, she, it, we, you, they **lay**	if I, he, she, it, we, you, they **be laid**
Past	if I, he, she, it, we, you, they **laid**	if I, he, she, it, we, you, they **were laid**
Fut.	if I, he, she, it, we, you, they **should lay**	if I, he, she, it, we, you, they **should be laid**

Transitive and intransitive. Do not confuse the verb LAY with the verb LIE.

lead
(active voice)

be led
(passive voice)

Infinitive: **to lead**
Perfect Infinitive: **to have led**
Present Participle: **leading**
Past Participle: **led**

Infinitive: **to be led**
Perfect Infinitive: **to have been led**
Present Participle: **being led**
Past Participle: **been led**

INDICATIVE MOOD

Pres.	I, we, you, they **lead**	I **am led**
		we, you, they **are led**
	he, she, it **leads**	he, she, it **is led**
Pres.	I **am leading**	I **am being led**
Prog.	we, you, they **are leading**	we, you, they **are being led**
	he, she, it **is leading**	he, she, it **is being led**
Pres.	I, we, you, they **do lead**	I, we, you, they **do get led**
Int.	he, she, it **does lead**	he, she, it **does get led**
Fut.	I, he, she, it,	I, he, she, it,
	we, you, they **will lead**	we, you, they **will be led**
Past	I, he, she, it,	I, he, she, it **was led**
	we, you, they **led**	we, you, they **were led**
Past	I, he, she, it **was leading**	I, he, she, it **was being led**
Prog.	we, you, they **were leading**	we, you, they **were being led**
Past	I, he, she, it,	I, he, she, it,
Int.	we, you, they **did lead**	we, you, they **did get led**
Pres.	I, we, you, they **have led**	I, we, you, they **have been led**
Perf.	he, she, it **has led**	he, she, it **has been led**
Past	I, he, she, it,	I, he, she, it,
Perf.	we, you, they **had led**	we, you, they **had been led**
Fut.	I, he, she, it, we, you, they	I, he, she, it, we, you, they
Perf.	**will have led**	**will have been led**

IMPERATIVE MOOD

lead

be led

SUBJUNCTIVE MOOD

Pres.	if I, he, she, it,	if I, he, she, it,
	we, you, they **lead**	we, you, they **be led**
Past	if I, he, she, it,	if I, he, she, it,
	we, you, they **led**	we, you, they **were led**
Fut.	if I, he, she, it,	if I, he, she, it,
	we, you, they **should lead**	we, you, they **should be led**

Transitive and intransitive.

lean
(active voice)

PRINCIPAL PARTS: **leans, leaning, leaned, leaned**

be leaned
(passive voice)

Infinitive: **to lean**
Perfect Infinitive: **to have leaned**
Present Participle: **leaning**
Past Participle: **leaned**

Infinitive: **to be leaned**
Perfect Infinitive: **to have been leaned**
Present Participle: **being leaned**
Past Participle: **been leaned**

INDICATIVE MOOD

Pres.	I, we, you, they **lean**	I **am leaned**
		we, you, they **are leaned**
	he, she, it **leans**	he, she, it **is leaned**
Pres.	I **am leaning**	I **am being leaned**
Prog.	we, you, they **are leaning**	we, you, they **are being leaned**
	he, she, it **is leaning**	he, she, it **is being leaned**
Pres.	I, we, you, they **do lean**	I, we, you, they **do get leaned**
Int.	he, she, it **does lean**	he, she, it **does get leaned**
Fut.	I, he, she, it, we, you, they **will lean**	I, he, she, it, we, you, they **will be leaned**
Past	I, he, she, it, we, you, they **leaned**	I, he, she, it **was leaned** we, you, they **were leaned**
Past	I, he, she, it **was leaning**	I, he, she, it **was being leaned**
Prog.	we, you, they **were leaning**	we, you, they **were being leaned**
Past	I, he, she, it,	I, he, she, it,
Int.	we, you, they **did lean**	we, you, they **did get leaned**
Pres.	I, we, you, they **have leaned**	I, we, you, they **have been leaned**
Perf.	he, she, it **has leaned**	he, she, it **has been leaned**
Past	I, he, she, it,	I, he, she, it,
Perf.	we, you, they **had leaned**	we, you, they **had been leaned**
Fut.	I, he, she, it, we, you, they	I, he, she, it, we, you, they
Perf.	**will have leaned**	**will have been leaned**

IMPERATIVE MOOD

lean

be leaned

SUBJUNCTIVE MOOD

Pres.	if I, he, she, it, we, you, they **lean**	if I, he, she, it, we, you, they **be leaned**
Past	if I, he, she, it, we, you, they **leaned**	if I, he, she, it, we, you, they **were leaned**
Fut.	if I, he, she, it, we, you, they **should lean**	if I, he, she, it, we, you, they **should be leaned**

Intransitive and transitive. *Webster's* and the *Oxford Dictionary* recognize LEANT as an alternate past tense and past participle form, especially in British English.

leap
(active voice)

be leaped/leapt
(passive voice)

Infinitive: **to leap**
Perfect Infinitive: **to have leaped**
Present Participle: **leaping**
Past Participle: **leaped**

Infinitive: **to be leaped**
Perfect Infinitive: **to have been leaped**
Present Participle: **being leaped**
Past Participle: **been leaped**

INDICATIVE MOOD

Pres.	I, we, you, they **leap**	I **am leaped**
		we, you, they **are leaped**
	he, she, it **leaps**	he, she, it **is leaped**
Pres.	I **am leaping**	I **am being leaped**
Prog.	we, you, they **are leaping**	we, you, they **are being leaped**
	he, she, it **is leaping**	he, she, it **is being leaped**
Pres.	I, we, you, they **do leap**	I, we, you, they **do get leaped**
Int.	he, she, it **does leap**	he, she, it **does get leaped**
Fut.	I, he, she, it,	I, he, she, it,
	we, you, they **will leap**	we, you, they **will be leaped**
Past	I, he, she, it,	I, he, she, it **was leaped**
	we, you, they **leaped**	we, you, they **were leaped**
Past	I, he, she, it **was leaping**	I, he, she, it **was being leaped**
Prog.	we, you, they **were leaping**	we, you, they **were being leaped**
Past	I, he, she, it,	I, he, she, it,
Int.	we, you, they **did leap**	we, you, they **did get leaped**
Pres.	I, we, you, they **have leaped**	I, we, you, they **have been leaped**
Perf.	he, she, it **has leaped**	he, she, it **has been leaped**
Past	I, he, she, it,	I, he, she, it,
Perf.	we, you, they **had leaped**	we, you, they **had been leaped**
Fut.	I, he, she, it, we, you, they	I, he, she, it, we, you, they
Perf.	**will have leaped**	**will have been leaped**

IMPERATIVE MOOD

leap   **be leaped**

SUBJUNCTIVE MOOD

Pres.	if I, he, she, it,	if I, he, she, it,
	we, you, they **leap**	we, you, they **be leaped**
Past	if I, he, she, it,	if I, he, she, it,
	we, you, they **leaped**	we, you, they **were leaped**
Fut.	if I, he, she, it,	if I, he, she, it,
	we, you, they **should leap**	we, you, they **should be leaped**

Intransitive and transitive. _Webster's_ lists LEAPT as the first form for the past tense and past participle and also recognizes the spelling LEPT.

learn
(active voice)

be learned/learnt
(passive voice)

Infinitive: **to learn**
Perfect Infinitive: **to have learned**
Present Participle: **learning**
Past Participle: **learned**

Infinitive: **to be learned**
Perfect Infinitive: **to have been learned**
Present Participle: **being learned**
Past Participle: **been learned**

INDICATIVE MOOD

Pres.	I, we, you, they **learn**	I **am learned**
		we, you, they **are learned**
	he, she, it **learns**	he, she, it **is learned**
Pres. *Prog.*	I **am learning**	I **am being learned**
	we, you, they **are learning**	we, you, they **are being learned**
	he, she, it **is learning**	he, she, it **is being learned**
Pres. *Int.*	I, we, you, they **do learn**	I, we, you, they **do get learned**
	he, she, it **does learn**	he, she, it **does get learned**
Fut.	I, he, she, it,	I, he, she, it,
	we, you, they **will learn**	we, you, they **will be learned**
Past	I, he, she, it,	I, he, she, it **was learned**
	we, you, they **learned**	we, you, they **were learned**
Past *Prog.*	I, he, she, it **was learning**	I, he, she, it **was being learned**
	we, you, they **were learning**	we, you, they **were being learned**
Past *Int.*	I, he, she, it,	I, he, she, it,
	we, you, they **did learn**	we, you, they **did get learned**
Pres. *Perf.*	I, we, you, they **have learned**	I, we, you, they **have been learned**
	he, she, it **has learned**	he, she, it **has been learned**
Past *Perf.*	I, he, she, it,	I, he, she, it,
	we, you, they **had learned**	we, you, they **had been learned**
Fut. *Perf.*	I, he, she, it, we, you, they	I, he, she, it, we, you, they
	will have learned	**will have been learned**

IMPERATIVE MOOD

learn   **be learned**

SUBJUNCTIVE MOOD

Pres.	if I, he, she, it,	if I, he, she, it,
	we, you, they **learn**	we, you, they **be learned**
Past	if I, he, she, it,	if I, he, she, it,
	we, you, they **learned**	we, you, they **were learned**
Fut.	if I, he, she, it,	if I, he, she, it,
	we, you, they **should learn**	we, you, they **should be learned**

Transitive and intransitive. The past tense and past participle have the forms LEARNED and LEARNT.

leave
(active voice)

be left
(passive voice)

Infinitive: **to leave**
Perfect Infinitive: **to have left**
Present Participle: **leaving**
Past Participle: **left**

Infinitive: **to be left**
Perfect Infinitive: **to have been left**
Present Participle: **being left**
Past Participle: **been left**

INDICATIVE MOOD

Pres.	I, we, you, they **leave** he, she, it **leaves**	I **am left** we, you, they **are left** he, she, it **is left**
Pres. Prog.	I **am leaving** we, you, they **are leaving** he, she, it **is leaving**	I **am being left** we, you, they **are being left** he, she, it **is being left**
Pres. Int.	I, we, you, they **do leave** he, she, it **does leave**	I, we, you, they **do get left** he, she, it **does get left**
Fut.	I, he, she, it, we, you, they **will leave**	I, he, she, it, we, you, they **will be left**
Past	I, he, she, it, we, you, they **left**	I, he, she, it **was left** we, you, they **were left**
Past Prog.	I, he, she, it **was leaving** we, you, they **were leaving**	I, he, she, it **was being left** we, you, they **were being left**
Past Int.	I, he, she, it, we, you, they **did leave**	I, he, she, it, we, you, they **did get left**
Pres. Perf.	I, we, you, they **have left** he, she, it **has left**	I, we, you, they **have been left** he, she, it **has been left**
Past Perf.	I, he, she, it, we, you, they **had left**	I, he, she, it, we, you, they **had been left**
Fut. Perf.	I, he, she, it, we, you, they **will have left**	I, he, she, it, we, you, they **will have been left**

IMPERATIVE MOOD

leave

be left

SUBJUNCTIVE MOOD

Pres.	if I, he, she, it, we, you, they **leave**	if I, he, she, it, we, you, they **be left**
Past	if I, he, she, it, we, you, they **left**	if I, he, she, it, we, you, they **were left**
Fut.	if I, he, she, it, we, you, they **should leave**	if I, he, she, it, we, you, they **should be left**

Transitive and intransitive. There is an intransitive verb LEAVE, with past and past participle LEAVED, meaning to bear leaves.

lend
(active voice)

be lent
(passive voice)

Infinitive: **to lend**
Perfect Infinitive: **to have lent**
Present Participle: **lending**
Past Participle: **lent**

Infinitive: **to be lent**
Perfect Infinitive: **to have been lent**
Present Participle: **being lent**
Past Participle: **been lent**

INDICATIVE MOOD

Pres.	I, we, you, they **lend**	I **am lent**	
	he, she, it **lends**	we, you, they **are lent**	
		he, she, it **is lent**	
Pres.	I **am lending**	I **am being lent**	
Prog.	we, you, they **are lending**	we, you, they **are being lent**	
	he, she, it **is lending**	he, she, it **is being lent**	
Pres.	I, we, you, they **do lend**	I, we, you, they **do get lent**	
Int.	he, she, it **does lend**	he, she, it **does get lent**	
Fut.	I, he, she, it,	I, he, she, it,	
	we, you, they **will lend**	we, you, they **will be lent**	
Past	I, he, she, it,	I, he, she, it **was lent**	
	we, you, they **lent**	we, you, they **were lent**	
Past	I, he, she, it **was lending**	I, he, she, it **was being lent**	
Prog.	we, you, they **were lending**	we, you, they **were being lent**	
Past	I, he, she, it,	I, he, she, it,	
Int.	we, you, they **did lend**	we, you, they **did get lent**	
Pres.	I, we, you, they **have lent**	I, we, you, they **have been lent**	
Perf.	he, she, it **has lent**	he, she, it **has been lent**	
Past	I, he, she, it,	I, he, she, it,	
Perf.	we, you, they **had lent**	we, you, they **had been lent**	
Fut.	I, he, she, it, we, you, they	I, he, she, it, we, you, they	
Perf.	**will have lent**	**will have been lent**	

IMPERATIVE MOOD

lend   **be lent**

SUBJUNCTIVE MOOD

Pres.	if I, he, she, it,	if I, he, she, it,
	we, you, they **lend**	we, you, they **be lent**
Past	if I, he, she, it,	if I, he, she, it,
	we, you, they **lent**	we, you, they **were lent**
Fut.	if I, he, she, it,	if I, he, she, it,
	we, you, they **should lend**	we, you, they **should be lent**

Transitive and intransitive.

let
(active voice)

be let
(passive voice)

Infinitive: **to let**
Perfect Infinitive: **to have let**
Present Participle: **letting**
Past Participle: **let**

Infinitive: **to be let**
Perfect Infinitive: **to have been let**
Present Participle: **being let**
Past Participle: **been let**

INDICATIVE MOOD

Pres.	I, we, you, they **let**		I **am let**
			we, you, they **are let**
	he, she, it **lets**		he, she, it **is let**
Pres.	I **am letting**		I **am being let**
Prog.	we, you, they **are letting**		we, you, they **are being let**
	he, she, it **is letting**		he, she, it **is being let**
Pres.	I, we, you, they **do let**		I, we, you, they **do get let**
Int.	he, she, it **does let**		he, she, it **does get let**
Fut.	I, he, she, it,		I, he, she, it,
	we, you, they **will let**		we, you, they **will be let**
Past	I, he, she, it,		I, he, she, it **was let**
	we, you, they **let**		we, you, they **were let**
Past	I, he, she, it **was letting**		I, he, she, it **was being let**
Prog.	we, you, they **were letting**		we, you, they **were being let**
Past	I, he, she, it,		I, he, she, it,
Int.	we, you, they **did let**		we, you, they **did get let**
Pres.	I, we, you, they **have let**		I, we, you, they **have been let**
Perf.	he, she, it **has let**		he, she, it **has been let**
Past	I, he, she, it,		I, he, she, it,
Perf.	we, you, they **had let**		we, you, they **had been let**
Fut.	I, he, she, it, we, you, they		I, he, she, it, we, you, they
Perf.	**will have let**		**will have been let**

IMPERATIVE MOOD

let   **be let**

SUBJUNCTIVE MOOD

Pres.	if I, he, she, it,	if I, he, she, it,
	we, you, they **let**	we, you, they **be let**
Past	if I, he, she, it,	if I, he, she, it,
	we, you, they **let**	we, you, they **were let**
Fut.	if I, he, she, it,	if I, he, she, it,
	we, you, they **should let**	we, you, they **should be let**

Transitive and intransitive.

PRINCIPAL PARTS: **lies, lying, lay, lain**

Infinitive: **to lie**
Perfect Infinitive: **to have lain**
Present Participle: **lying**
Past Participle: **lain**

INDICATIVE MOOD

Pres.	I, we, you, they **lie**
	he, she, it **lies**
Pres. Prog.	I **am lying**
	we, you, they **are lying**
	he, she, it **is lying**
Pres. Int.	I, we, you, they **do lie**
	he, she, it **does lie**
Fut.	I, he, she, it, we, you, they **will lie**
Past	I, he, she, it, we, you, they **lay**
Past Prog.	I, he, she, it **was lying**
	we, you, they **were lying**
Past Int.	I, he, she, it, we, you, they **did lie**
Pres. Perf.	I, we, you, they **have lain**
	he, she, it **has lain**
Past Perf.	I, he, she, it, we, you, they **had lain**
Fut. Perf.	I, he, she, it, we, you, they **will have lain**

IMPERATIVE MOOD

lie

SUBJUNCTIVE MOOD

Pres.	if I, he, she, it, we, you, they **lie**
Past	if I, he, she, it, we, you, they **lay**
Fut.	if I, he, she, it, we, you, they **should lie**

The intransitive verb meaning to "be or place flat."

lie
(active voice)

PRINCIPAL PARTS: **lies, lying,
lied, lied**

be lied
(passive voice)

Infinitive: **to lie**
Perfect Infinitive: **to have lied**
Present Participle: **lying**
Past Participle: **lied**

Infinitive: **to be lied**
Perfect Infinitive: **to have been lied**
Present Participle: **being lied**
Past Participle: **been lied**

INDICATIVE MOOD

Pres.	I, we, you, they **lie**	I **am lied**
		we, you, they **are lied**
	he, she, it **lies**	he, she, it **is lied**
Pres.	I **am lying**	I **am being lied**
Prog.	we, you, they **are lying**	we, you, they **are being lied**
	he, she, it **is lying**	he, she, it **is being lied**
Pres.	I, we, you, they **do lie**	I, we, you, they **do get lied**
Int.	he, she, it **does lie**	he, she, it **does get lied**
Fut.	I, he, she, it,	I, he, she, it,
	we, you, they **will lie**	we, you, they **will be lied**
Past	I, he, she, it,	I, he, she, it **was lied**
	we, you, they **lied**	we, you, they **were lied**
Past	I, he, she, it **was lying**	I, he, she, it **was being lied**
Prog.	we, you, they **were lying**	we, you, they **were being lied**
Past	I, he, she, it,	I, he, she, it,
Int.	we, you, they **did lie**	we, you, they **did get lied**
Pres.	I, we, you, they **have lied**	I, we, you, they **have been lied**
Perf.	he, she, it **has lied**	he, she, it **has been lied**
Past	I, he, she, it,	I, he, she, it,
Perf.	we, you, they **had lied**	we, you, they **had been lied**
Fut.	I, he, she, it, we, you, they	I, he, she, it, we, you, they
Perf.	**will have lied**	**will have been lied**

IMPERATIVE MOOD

lie   **be lied**

SUBJUNCTIVE MOOD

Pres.	if I, he, she, it,	if I, he, she, it,
	we, you, they **lie**	we, you, they **be lied**
Past	if I, he, she, it,	if I, he, she, it,
	we, you, they **lied**	we, you, they **were lied**
Fut.	if I, he, she, it,	if I, he, she, it,
	we, you, they **should lie**	we, you, they **should be lied**

Intransitive and transitive. This verb means to "tell something that is not true."

light
(active voice)

be lighted/lit
(passive voice)

Infinitive: **to light**
Perfect Infinitive: **to have lighted**
Present Participle: **lighting**
Past Participle: **lighted**

Infinitive: **to be lighted**
Perfect Infinitive: **to have been lighted**
Present Participle: **being lighted**
Past Participle: **been lighted**

INDICATIVE MOOD

Pres.	I, we, you, they **light**	I **am lighted**
		we, you, they **are lighted**
	he, she, it **lights**	he, she, it **is lighted**
Pres. Prog.	I **am lighting**	I **am being lighted**
	we, you, they **are lighting**	we, you, they **are being lighted**
	he, she, it **is lighting**	he, she, it **is being lighted**
Pres. Int.	I, we, you, they **do light**	I, we, you, they **do get lighted**
	he, she, it **does light**	he, she, it **does get lighted**
Fut.	I, he, she, it, we, you, they **will light**	I, he, she, it, we, you, they **will be lighted**
Past	I, he, she, it, we, you, they **lighted**	I, he, she, it **was lighted** we, you, they **were lighted**
Past Prog.	I, he, she, it **was lighting** we, you, they **were lighting**	I, he, she, it **was being lighted** we, you, they **were being lighted**
Past Int.	I, he, she, it, we, you, they **did light**	I, he, she, it, we, you, they **did get lighted**
Pres. Perf.	I, we, you, they **have lighted**	I, we, you, they **have been lighted**
	he, she, it **has lighted**	he, she, it **has been lighted**
Past Perf.	I, he, she, it, we, you, they **had lighted**	I, he, she, it, we, you, they **had been lighted**
Fut. Perf.	I, he, she, it, we, you, they **will have lighted**	I, he, she, it, we, you, they **will have been lighted**

IMPERATIVE MOOD

light   **be lighted**

SUBJUNCTIVE MOOD

Pres.	if I, he, she, it, we, you, they **light**	if I, he, she, it, we, you, they **be lighted**
Past	if I, he, she, it, we, you, they **lighted**	if I, he, she, it, we, you, they **were lighted**
Fut.	if I, he, she, it, we, you, they **should light**	if I, he, she, it, we, you, they **should be lighted**

Transitive and intransitive. *Merriam Webster's* and the *Oxford Dictionary* list LIT as the first form for the past tense and past participle.

lighten
(active voice)

PRINCIPAL PARTS: **lightens, lightening, lightened, lightened**

be lightened
(passive voice)

Infinitive: **to lighten**
Perfect Infinitive: **to have lightened**
Present Participle: **lightening**
Past Participle: **lightened**

Infinitive: **to be lightened**
Perfect Infinitive: **to have been lightened**
Present Participle: **being lightened**
Past Participle: **been lightened**

INDICATIVE MOOD

Pres.	I, we, you, they **lighten**	I **am lightened**
		we, you, they **are lightened**
	he, she, it **lightens**	he, she, it **is lightened**
Pres.	I **am lightening**	I **am being lightened**
Prog.	we, you, they **are lightening**	we, you, they **are being lightened**
	he, she, it **is lightening**	he, she, it **is being lightened**
Pres.	I, we, you, they **do lighten**	I, we, you, they **do get lightened**
Int.	he, she, it **does lighten**	he, she, it **does get lightened**
Fut.	I, he, she, it,	I, he, she, it,
	we, you, they **will lighten**	we, you, they **will be lightened**
Past	I, he, she, it,	I, he, she, it **was lightened**
	we, you, they **lightened**	we, you, they **were lightened**
Past	I, he, she, it **was lightening**	I, he, she, it **was being lightened**
Prog.	we, you, they **were lightening**	we, you, they **were being lightened**
Past	I, he, she, it,	I, he, she, it,
Int.	we, you, they **did lighten**	we, you, they **did get lightened**
Pres.	I, we, you, they **have lightened**	I, we, you, they **have been lightened**
Perf.	he, she, it **has lightened**	he, she, it **has been lightened**
Past	I, he, she, it,	I, he, she, it,
Perf.	we, you, they **had lightened**	we, you, they **had been lightened**
Fut.	I, he, she, it, we, you, they	I, he, she, it, we, you, they
Perf.	**will have lightened**	**will have been lightened**

IMPERATIVE MOOD

lighten

be lightened

SUBJUNCTIVE MOOD

Pres.	if I, he, she, it,	if I, he, she, it,
	we, you, they **lighten**	we, you, they **be lightened**
Past	if I, he, she, it,	if I, he, she, it,
	we, you, they **lightened**	we, you, they **were lightened**
Fut.	if I, he, she, it,	if I, he, she, it,
	we, you, they **should lighten**	we, you, they **should be lightened**

Transitive and intransitive.

212

like
(active voice)

be liked
(passive voice)

Infinitive: **to like**
Perfect Infinitive: **to have liked**
Present Participle: **liking**
Past Participle: **liked**

Infinitive: **to be liked**
Perfect Infinitive: **to have been liked**
Present Participle: **being liked**
Past Participle: **been liked**

INDICATIVE MOOD

Pres.	I, we, you, they **like**	I **am liked**
		we, you, they **are liked**
	he, she, it **likes**	he, she, it **is liked**
Pres.	I **am liking**	I **am being liked**
Prog.	we, you, they **are liking**	we, you, they **are being liked**
	he, she, it **is liking**	he, she, it **is being liked**
Pres.	I, we, you, they **do like**	I, we, you, they **do get liked**
Int.	he, she, it **does like**	he, she, it **does get liked**
Fut.	I, he, she, it,	I, he, she, it,
	we, you, they **will like**	we, you, they **will be liked**
Past	I, he, she, it,	I, he, she, it **was liked**
	we, you, they **liked**	we, you, they **were liked**
Past	I, he, she, it **was liking**	I, he, she, it **was being liked**
Prog.	we, you, they **were liking**	we, you, they **were being liked**
Past	I, he, she, it,	I, he, she, it,
Int.	we, you, they **did like**	we, you, they **did get liked**
Pres.	I, we, you, they **have liked**	I, we, you, they **have been liked**
Perf.	he, she, it **has liked**	he, she, it **has been liked**
Past	I, he, she, it,	I, he, she, it,
Perf.	we, you, they **had liked**	we, you, they **had been liked**
Fut.	I, he, she, it, we, you, they	I, he, she, it, we, you, they
Perf.	**will have liked**	**will have been liked**

IMPERATIVE MOOD

like   **be liked**

SUBJUNCTIVE MOOD

Pres.	if I, he, she, it,	if I, he, she, it,
	we, you, they **like**	we, you, they **be liked**
Past	if I, he, she, it,	if I, he, she, it,
	we, you, they **liked**	we, you, they **were liked**
Fut.	if I, he, she, it,	if I, he, she, it,
	we, you, they **should like**	we, you, they **should be liked**

Transitive and intransitive.

limit
(active voice)

be limited
(passive voice)

Infinitive: **to limit**
Perfect Infinitive: **to have limited**
Present Participle: **limiting**
Past Participle: **limited**

Infinitive: **to be limited**
Perfect Infinitive: **to have been limited**
Present Participle: **being limited**
Past Participle: **been limited**

INDICATIVE MOOD

Pres.	I, we, you, they **limit**	I **am limited**
		we, you, they **are limited**
	he, she, it **limits**	he, she, it **is limited**
Pres.	I **am limiting**	I **am being limited**
Prog.	we, you, they **are limiting**	we, you, they **are being limited**
	he, she, it **is limiting**	he, she, it **is being limited**
Pres.	I, we, you, they **do limit**	I, we, you, they **do get limited**
Int.	he, she, it **does limit**	he, she, it **does get limited**
Fut.	I, he, she, it,	I, he, she, it,
	we, you, they **will limit**	we, you, they **will be limited**
Past	I, he, she, it,	I, he, she, it **was limited**
	we, you, they **limited**	we, you, they **were limited**
Past	I, he, she, it **was limiting**	I, he, she, it **was being limited**
Prog.	we, you, they **were limiting**	we, you, they **were being limited**
Past	I, he, she, it,	I, he, she, it,
Int.	we, you, they **did limit**	we, you, they **did get limited**
Pres.	I, we, you, they **have limited**	I, we, you, they **have been limited**
Perf.	he, she, it **has limited**	he, she, it **has been limited**
Past	I, he, she, it,	I, he, she, it,
Perf.	we, you, they **had limited**	we, you, they **had been limited**
Fut.	I, he, she, it, we, you, they	I, he, she, it, we, you, they
Perf.	**will have limited**	**will have been limited**

IMPERATIVE MOOD

limit   **be limited**

SUBJUNCTIVE MOOD

Pres.	if I, he, she, it,	if I, he, she, it,
	we, you, they **limit**	we, you, they **be limited**
Past	if I, he, she, it,	if I, he, she, it,
	we, you, they **limited**	we, you, they **were limited**
Fut.	if I, he, she, it,	if I, he, she, it,
	we, you, they **should limit**	we, you, they **should be limited**

Transitive and intransitive.

listen

Infinitive: **to listen**
Perfect Infinitive: **to have listened**
Present Participle: **listening**
Past Participle: **listened**

INDICATIVE MOOD

Pres.	I, we, you, they **listen**
	he, she, it **listens**
Pres. *Prog.*	I **am listening**
	we, you, they **are listening**
	he, she, it **is listening**
Pres. *Int.*	I, we, you, they **do listen**
	he, she, it **does listen**
Fut.	I, he, she, it, we, you, they **will listen**
Past	I, he, she, it, we, you, they **listened**
Past *Prog.*	I, he, she, it **was listening**
	we, you, they **were listening**
Past *Int.*	I, he, she, it, we, you, they **did listen**
Pres. *Perf.*	I, we, you, they **have listened**
	he, she, it **has listened**
Past *Perf.*	I, he, she, it, we, you, they **had listened**
Fut. *Perf.*	I, he, she, it, we, you, they **will have listened**

IMPERATIVE MOOD

listen

SUBJUNCTIVE MOOD

Pres.	if I, he, she, it, we, you, they **listen**
Past	if I, he, she, it, we, you, they **listened**
Fut.	if I, he, she, it, we, you, they **should listen**

live
(active voice)

be lived
(passive voice)

Infinitive: **to live**
Perfect Infinitive: **to have lived**
Present Participle: **living**
Past Participle: **lived**

Infinitive: **to be lived**
Perfect Infinitive: **to have been lived**
Present Participle: **being lived**
Past Participle: **been lived**

INDICATIVE MOOD

Pres.	I, we, you, they **live**	I **am lived**
		we, you, they **are lived**
	he, she, it **lives**	he, she, it **is lived**
Pres.	I **am living**	I **am being lived**
Prog.	we, you, they **are living**	we, you, they **are being lived**
	he, she, it **is living**	he, she, it **is being lived**
Pres.	I, we, you, they **do live**	I, we, you, they **do get lived**
Int.	he, she, it **does live**	he, she, it **does get lived**
Fut.	I, he, she, it,	I, he, she, it,
	we, you, they **will live**	we, you, they **will be lived**
Past	I, he, she, it,	I, he, she, it **was lived**
	we, you, they **lived**	we, you, they **were lived**
Past	I, he, she, it **was living**	I, he, she, it **was being lived**
Prog.	we, you, they **were living**	we, you, they **were being lived**
Past	I, he, she, it,	I, he, she, it,
Int.	we, you, they **did live**	we, you, they **did get lived**
Pres.	I, we, you, they **have lived**	I, we, you, they **have been lived**
Perf.	he, she, it **has lived**	he, she, it **has been lived**
Past	I, he, she, it,	I, he, she, it,
Perf.	we, you, they **had lived**	we, you, they **had been lived**
Fut.	I, he, she, it, we, you, they	I, he, she, it, we, you, they
Perf.	**will have lived**	**will have been lived**

IMPERATIVE MOOD

live   **be lived**

SUBJUNCTIVE MOOD

Pres.	if I, he, she, it,	if I, he, she, it,
	we, you, they **live**	we, you, they **be lived**
Past	if I, he, she, it,	if I, he, she, it,
	we, you, they **lived**	we, you, they **were lived**
Fut.	if I, he, she, it,	if I, he, she, it,
	we, you, they **should live**	we, you, they **should be lived**

Transitive and intransitive.

load
(active voice)

be loaded
(passive voice)

Infinitive: **to load**
Perfect Infinitive: **to have loaded**
Present Participle: **loading**
Past Participle: **loaded**

Infinitive: **to be loaded**
Perfect Infinitive: **to have been loaded**
Present Participle: **being loaded**
Past Participle: **been loaded**

INDICATIVE MOOD

	Active	Passive
Pres.	I, we, you, they **load** he, she, it **loads**	I **am loaded** we, you, they **are loaded** he, she, it **is loaded**
Pres. Prog.	I **am loading** we, you, they **are loading** he, she, it **is loading**	I **am being loaded** we, you, they **are being loaded** he, she, it **is being loaded**
Pres. Int.	I, we, you, they **do load** he, she, it **does load**	I, we, you, they **do get loaded** he, she, it **does get loaded**
Fut.	I, he, she, it, we, you, they **will load**	I, he, she, it, we, you, they **will be loaded**
Past	I, he, she, it, we, you, they **loaded**	I, he, she, it **was loaded** we, you, they **were loaded**
Past Prog.	I, he, she, it **was loading** we, you, they **were loading**	I, he, she, it **was being loaded** we, you, they **were being loaded**
Past Int.	I, he, she, it, we, you, they **did load**	I, he, she, it, we, you, they **did get loaded**
Pres. Perf.	I, we, you, they **have loaded** he, she, it **has loaded**	I, we, you, they **have been loaded** he, she, it **has been loaded**
Past Perf.	I, he, she, it, we, you, they **had loaded**	I, he, she, it, we, you, they **had been loaded**
Fut. Perf.	I, he, she, it, we, you, they **will have loaded**	I, he, she, it, we, you, they **will have been loaded**

IMPERATIVE MOOD

load   **be loaded**

SUBJUNCTIVE MOOD

	Active	Passive
Pres.	if I, he, she, it, we, you, they **load**	if I, he, she, it, we, you, they **be loaded**
Past	if I, he, she, it, we, you, they **loaded**	if I, he, she, it, we, you, they **were loaded**
Fut.	if I, he, she, it, we, you, they **should load**	if I, he, she, it, we, you, they **should be loaded**

Transitive and intransitive.

look
(active voice)

be looked
(passive voice)

Infinitive: **to look**
Perfect Infinitive: **to have looked**
Present Participle: **looking**
Past Participle: **looked**

Infinitive: **to be looked**
Perfect Infinitive: **to have been looked**
Present Participle: **being looked**
Past Participle: **been looked**

INDICATIVE MOOD

Pres.	I, we, you, they **look**	I **am looked**
		we, you, they **are looked**
	he, she, it **looks**	he, she, it **is looked**
Pres.	I **am looking**	I **am being looked**
Prog.	we, you, they **are looking**	we, you, they **are being looked**
	he, she, it **is looking**	he, she, it **is being looked**
Pres.	I, we, you, they **do look**	I, we, you, they **do get looked**
Int.	he, she, it **does look**	he, she, it **does get looked**
Fut.	I, he, she, it,	I, he, she, it,
	we, you, they **will look**	we, you, they **will be looked**
Past	I, he, she, it,	I, he, she, it **was looked**
	we, you, they **looked**	we, you, they **were looked**
Past	I, he, she, it **was looking**	I, he, she, it **was being looked**
Prog.	we, you, they **were looking**	we, you, they **were being looked**
Past	I, he, she, it,	I, he, she, it,
Int.	we, you, they **did look**	we, you, they **did get looked**
Pres.	I, we, you, they **have looked**	I, we, you, they **have been looked**
Perf.	he, she, it **has looked**	he, she, it **has been looked**
Past	I, he, she, it,	I, he, she, it,
Perf.	we, you, they **had looked**	we, you, they **had been looked**
Fut.	I, he, she, it, we, you, they	I, he, she, it, we, you, they
Perf.	**will have looked**	**will have been looked**

IMPERATIVE MOOD

look

be looked

SUBJUNCTIVE MOOD

Pres.	if I, he, she, it,	if I, he, she, it,
	we, you, they **look**	we, you, they **be looked**
Past	if I, he, she, it,	if I, he, she, it,
	we, you, they **looked**	we, you, they **were looked**
Fut.	if I, he, she, it,	if I, he, she, it,
	we, you, they **should look**	we, you, they **should be looked**

Intransitive and transitive.

loose
(active voice)

PRINCIPAL PARTS: **looses, loosing, loosed, loosed**

be loosed
(passive voice)

Infinitive: **to loose**
Perfect Infinitive: **to have loosed**
Present Participle: **loosing**
Past Participle: **loosed**

Infinitive: **to be loosed**
Perfect Infinitive: **to have been loosed**
Present Participle: **being loosed**
Past Participle: **been loosed**

INDICATIVE MOOD

Pres.	I, we, you, they **loose**	I am **loosed**
		we, you, they **are loosed**
	he, she, it **looses**	he, she, it **is loosed**
Pres.	I am **loosing**	I am **being loosed**
Prog.	we, you, they **are loosing**	we, you, they **are being loosed**
	he, she, it **is loosing**	he, she, it **is being loosed**
Pres.	I, we, you, they **do loose**	I, we, you, they **do get loosed**
Int.	he, she, it **does loose**	he, she, it **does get loosed**
Fut.	I, he, she, it,	I, he, she, it,
	we, you, they **will loose**	we, you, they **will be loosed**
Past	I, he, she, it	I, he, she, it **was loosed**
	we, you, they **loosed**	we, you, they **were loosed**
Past	I, he, she, it **was loosing**	I, he, she, it **was being loosed**
Prog.	we, you, they **were loosing**	we, you, they **were being loosed**
Past	I, he, she, it,	I, he, she, it,
Int.	we, you, they **did loose**	we, you, they **did get loosed**
Pres.	I, we, you, they **have loosed**	I, we, you, they **have been loosed**
Perf.	he, she, it **has loosed**	he, she, it **has been loosed**
Past	I, he, she, it,	I, he, she, it,
Perf.	we, you, they **had loosed**	we, you, they **had been loosed**
Fut.	I, he, she, it, we, you, they	I, he, she, it, we, you, they
Perf.	**will have loosed**	**will have been loosed**

IMPERATIVE MOOD

loose　　　　　　**be loosed**

SUBJUNCTIVE MOOD

Pres.	if I, he, she, it,	if I, he, she, it,
	we, you, they **loose**	we, you, they **be loosed**
Past	if I, he, she, it,	if I, he, she, it,
	we, you, they **loosed**	we, you, they **were loosed**
Fut.	if I, he, she, it,	if I, he, she, it,
	we, you, they **should loose**	we, you, they **should be loosed**

Transitive and intransitive.

loosen
(active voice)

be loosened
(passive voice)

Infinitive: **to loosen**
Perfect Infinitive: **to have loosened**
Present Participle: **loosened**
Past Participle: **loosened**

Infinitive: **to be loosened**
Perfect Infinitive: **to have been loosened**
Present Participle: **being loosened**
Past Participle: **been loosened**

INDICATIVE MOOD

Pres.	I, we, you, they **loosen**	I **am loosened**
		we, you, they **are loosened**
	he, she, it **loosens**	he, she, it **is loosened**
Pres.	I **am loosening**	I **am being loosened**
Prog.	we, you, they **are loosening**	we, you, they **are being loosened**
	he, she, it **is loosening**	he, she, it **is being loosened**
Pres.	I, we, you, they **do loosen**	I, we, you, they **do get loosened**
Int.	he, she, it **does loosen**	he, she, it **does get loosened**
Fut.	I, he, she, it,	I, he, she, it,
	we, you, they **will loosen**	we, you, they **will be loosened**
Past	I, he, she, it,	I, he, she, it **was loosened**
	we, you, they **loosened**	we, you, they **were loosened**
Past	I, he, she, it **was loosening**	I, he, she, it **was being loosened**
Prog.	we, you, they **were loosening**	we, you, they **were being loosened**
Past	I, he, she, it,	I, he, she, it,
Int.	we, you, they **did loosen**	we, you, they **did get loosened**
Pres.	I, we, you, they **have loosened**	I, we, you, they **have been loosened**
Perf.	he, she, it **has loosened**	he, she, it **has been loosened**
Past	I, he, she, it,	I, he, she, it,
Perf.	we, you, they **had loosened**	we, you, they **had been loosened**
Fut.	I, he, she, it, we, you, they	I, he, she, it, we, you, they
Perf.	**will have loosened**	**will have been loosened**

IMPERATIVE MOOD

loosen **be loosened**

SUBJUNCTIVE MOOD

Pres.	if I, he, she, it,	if I, he, she, it,
	we, you, they **loosen**	we, you, they **be loosened**
Past	if I, he, she, it,	if I, he, she, it,
	we, you, they **loosened**	we, you, they **were loosened**
Fut.	if I, he, she, it,	if I, he, she, it,
	we, you, they **should loosen**	we, you, they **should be loosened**

Transitive and intransitive.

lose
(active voice)

PRINCIPAL PARTS: **loses, losing, lost, lost**

be lost
(passive voice)

Infinitive: **to lose**
Perfect Infinitive: **to have lost**
Present Participle: **losing**
Past Participle: **lost**

Infinitive: **to be lost**
Perfect Infinitive: **to have been lost**
Present Participle: **being lost**
Past Participle: **been lost**

INDICATIVE MOOD

Pres.	I, we, you, they **lose**	I **am lost**
		we, you, they **are lost**
	he, she, it **loses**	he, she, it **is lost**
Pres.	I **am losing**	I **am being lost**
Prog.	we, you, they **are losing**	we, you, they **are being lost**
	he, she, it **is losing**	he, she, it **is being lost**
Pres.	I, we, you, they **do lose**	I, we, you, they **do get lost**
Int.	he, she, it **does lose**	he, she, it **does get lost**
Fut.	I, he, she, it, we, you, they **will lose**	I, he, she, it, we, you, they **will be lost**
Past	I, he, she, it, we, you, they **lost**	I, he, she, it **was lost** we, you, they **were lost**
Past	I, he, she, it **was losing**	I, he, she, it **was being lost**
Prog.	we, you, they **were losing**	we, you, they **were being lost**
Past	I, he, she, it, we, you, they **did lose**	I, he, she, it, we, you, they **did get lost**
Int.		
Pres.	I, we, you, they **have lost**	I, we, you, they **have been lost**
Perf.	he, she, it **has lost**	he, she, it **has been lost**
Past	I, he, she, it, we, you, they **had lost**	I, he, she, it, we, you, they **had been lost**
Perf.		
Fut.	I, he, she, it, we, you, they **will have lost**	I, he, she, it, we, you, they **will have been lost**
Perf.		

IMPERATIVE MOOD

lose

be lost

SUBJUNCTIVE MOOD

Pres.	if I, he, she, it, we, you, they **lose**	if I, he, she, it, we, you, they **be lost**
Past	if I, he, she, it, we, you, they **lost**	if I, he, she, it, we, you, they **were lost**
Fut.	if I, he, she, it, we, you, they **should lose**	if I, he, she, it, we, you, they **should be lost**

Transitive and intransitive.

love
(active voice)

PRINCIPAL PARTS: **loves, loving, loved, loved**

be loved
(passive voice)

Infinitive: **to love**
Perfect Infinitive: **to have loved**
Present Participle: **loving**
Past Participle: **loved**

Infinitive: **to be loved**
Perfect Infinitive: **to have been loved**
Present Participle: **being loved**
Past Participle: **been loved**

INDICATIVE MOOD

Pres.	I, we, you, they **love**	I **am loved**
		we, you, they **are loved**
	he, she, it **loves**	he, she, it **is loved**
Pres.	I **am loving**	I **am being loved**
Prog.	we, you, they **are loving**	we, you, they **are being loved**
	he, she, it **is loving**	he, she, it **is being loved**
Pres.	I, we, you, they **do love**	I, we, you, they **do get loved**
Int.	he, she, it **does love**	he, she, it **does get loved**
Fut.	I, he, she, it,	I, he, she, it,
	we, you, they **will love**	we, you, they **will be loved**
Past	I, he, she, it,	I, he, she, it **was loved**
	we, you, they **loved**	we, you, they **were loved**
Past	I, he, she, it **was loving**	I, he, she, it **was being loved**
Prog.	we, you, they **were loving**	we, you, they **were being loved**
Past	I, he, she, it,	I, he, she, it,
Int.	we, you, they **did love**	we, you, they **did get loved**
Pres.	I, we, you, they **have loved**	I, we, you, they **have been loved**
Perf.	he, she, it **has loved**	he, she, it **has been loved**
Past	I, he, she, it,	I, he, she, it,
Perf.	we, you, they **had loved**	we, you, they **had been loved**
Fut.	I, he, she, it, we, you, they	I, he, she, it, we, you, they
Perf.	**will have loved**	**will have been loved**

IMPERATIVE MOOD

love   **be loved**

SUBJUNCTIVE MOOD

Pres.	if I, he, she, it,	if I, he, she, it,
	we, you, they **love**	we, you, they **be loved**
Past	if I, he, she, it,	if I, he, she, it,
	we, you, they **loved**	we, you, they **were loved**
Fut.	if I, he, she, it,	if I, he, she, it,
	we, you, they **should love**	we, you, they **should be loved**

Transitive and intransitive.

maintain
(active voice)

(passive voice)

Infinitive: **to maintain**
Perfect Infinitive: **to have maintained**
Present Participle: **maintaining**
Past Participle: **maintained**

Infinitive: **to be maintained**
Perfect Infinitive: **to have been maintained**
Present Participle: **being maintained**
Past Participle: **been maintained**

INDICATIVE MOOD

Pres.	I, we, you, they **maintain**	I am maintained
		we, you, they **are maintained**
	he, she, it **maintains**	he, she, it **is maintained**
Pres.	I **am maintaining**	I **am being maintained**
Prog.	we, you, they **are maintaining**	we, you, they **are being maintained**
	he, she, it **is maintaining**	he, she, it **is being maintained**
Pres.	I, we, you, they **do maintain**	I, we, you, they **do get maintained**
Int.	he, she, it **does maintain**	he, she, it **does get maintained**
Fut.	I, he, she, it,	I, he, she, it,
	we, you, they **will maintain**	we, you, they **will be maintained**
Past	I, he, she, it,	I, he, she, it **was maintained**
	we, you, they **maintained**	we, you, they **were maintained**
Past	I, he, she, it **was maintaining**	I, he, she, it **was being maintained**
Prog.	we, you, they **were maintaining**	we, you, they **were being maintained**
Past	I, he, she, it,	I, he, she, it, we, you, they
Int.	we, you, they **did maintain**	**did get maintained**
Pres.	I, we, you, they **have maintained**	I, we, you, they **have been maintained**
Perf.	he, she, it **has maintained**	he, she, it **has been maintained**
Past	I, he, she, it,	I, he, she, it,
Perf.	we, you, they **had maintained**	we, you, they **had been maintained**
Fut.	I, he, she, it, we, you, they	I, he, she, it, we, you, they
Perf.	**will have maintained**	**will have been maintained**

IMPERATIVE MOOD

maintain

be maintained

SUBJUNCTIVE MOOD

Pres.	if I, he, she, it,	if I, he, she, it,
	we, you, they **maintain**	we, you, they **be maintained**
Past	if I, he, she, it,	if I, he, she, it,
	we, you, they **maintained**	we, you, they **were maintained**
Fut.	if I, he, she, it,	if I, he, she, it,
	we, you, they **should maintain**	we, you, they **should be maintained**

make
(active voice)

be made
(passive voice)

Infinitive: **to make**
Perfect Infinitive: **to have made**
Present Participle: **making**
Past Participle: **made**

Infinitive: **to be made**
Perfect Infinitive: **to have been made**
Present Participle: **being made**
Past Participle: **been made**

INDICATIVE MOOD

Pres.	I, we, you, they **make**	I **am made**
		we, you, they **are made**
	he, she, it **makes**	he, she, it **is made**
Pres.	I **am making**	I **am being made**
Prog.	we, you, they **are making**	we, you, they **are being made**
	he, she, it **is making**	he, she, it **is being made**
Pres.	I, we, you, they **do make**	I, we, you, they **do get made**
Int.	he, she, it **does make**	he, she, it **does get made**
Fut.	I, he, she, it,	I, he, she, it,
	we, you, they **will make**	we, you, they **will be made**
Past	I, he, she, it,	I, he, she, it **was made**
	we, you, they **made**	we, you, they **were made**
Past	I, he, she, it **was making**	I, he, she, it **was being made**
Prog.	we, you, they **were making**	we, you, they **were being made**
Past	I, he, she, it,	I, he, she, it,
Int.	we, you, they **did make**	we, you, they **did get made**
Pres.	I, we, you, they **have made**	I, we, you, they **have been made**
Perf.	he, she, it **has made**	he, she, it **has been made**
Past	I, he, she, it,	I, he, she, it,
Perf.	we, you, they **had made**	we, you, they **had been made**
Fut.	I, he, she, it, we, you, they	I, he, she, it, we, you, they
Perf.	**will have made**	**will have been made**

IMPERATIVE MOOD

make　　　　　　　　**be made**

SUBJUNCTIVE MOOD

Pres.	if I, he, she, it,	if I, he, she, it,
	we, you, they **make**	we, you, they **be made**
Past	if I, he, she, it,	if I, he, she, it,
	we, you, they **made**	we, you, they **were made**
Fut.	if I, he, she, it,	if I, he, she, it,
	we, you, they **should make**	we, you, they **should be made**

Transitive and intransitive.

manage
(active voice)

be managed
(passive voice)

Infinitive: **to manage**
Perfect Infinitive: **to have managed**
Present Participle: **managing**
Past Participle: **managed**

Infinitive: **to be managed**
Perfect Infinitive: **to have been managed**
Present Participle: **being managed**
Past Participle: **been managed**

INDICATIVE MOOD

Pres.	I, we, you, they **manage**	I **am managed**
		we, you, they **are managed**
	he, she, it **manages**	he, she, it **is managed**
Pres.	I **am managing**	I **am being managed**
Prog.	we, you, they **are managing**	we, you, they **are being managed**
	he, she, it **is managing**	he, she, it **is being managed**
Pres.	I, we, you, they **do manage**	I, we, you, they **do get managed**
Int.	he, she, it **does manage**	he, she, it **does get managed**
Fut.	I, he, she, it,	I, he, she, it,
	we, you, they **will manage**	we, you, they **will be managed**
Past	I, he, she, it,	I, he, she, it **was managed**
	we, you, they **managed**	we, you, they **were managed**
Past	I, he, she, it **was managing**	I, he, she, it **was being managed**
Prog.	we, you, they **were managing**	we, you, they **were being managed**
Past	I, he, she, it,	I, he, she, it,
Int.	we, you, they **did manage**	we, you, they **did get managed**
Pres.	I, we, you, they **have managed**	I, we, you, they **have been managed**
Perf.	he, she, it **has managed**	he, she, it **has been managed**
Past	I, he, she, it,	I, he, she, it,
Perf.	we, you, they **had managed**	we, you, they **had been managed**
Fut.	I, he, she, it, we, you, they	I, he, she, it, we, you, they
Perf.	**will have managed**	**will have been managed**

IMPERATIVE MOOD

manage

be managed

SUBJUNCTIVE MOOD

Pres.	if I, he, she, it,	if I, he, she, it,
	we, you, they **manage**	we, you, they **be managed**
Past	if I, he, she, it,	if I, he, she, it,
	we, you, they **managed**	we, you, they **were managed**
Fut.	if I, he, she, it,	if I, he, she, it,
	we, you, they **should manage**	we, you, they **should be managed**

Transitive and intransitive.

mark
(active voice)

be marked
(passive voice)

Infinitive: **to mark**
Perfect Infinitive: **to have marked**
Present Participle: **marking**
Past Participle: **marked**

Infinitive: **to be marked**
Perfect Infinitive: **to have been marked**
Present Participle: **being marked**
Past Participle: **been marked**

INDICATIVE MOOD

Pres.	I, we, you, they **mark**	I **am marked**
		we, you, they **are marked**
	he, she, it **marks**	he, she, it **is marked**
Pres.	I **am marking**	I **am being marked**
Prog.	we, you, they **are marking**	we, you, they **are being marked**
	he, she, it **is marking**	he, she, it **is being marked**
Pres.	I, we, you, they **do mark**	I, we, you, they **do get marked**
Int.	he, she, it **does mark**	he, she, it **does get marked**
Fut.	I, he, she, it,	I, he, she, it,
	we, you, they **will mark**	we, you, they **will be marked**
Past	I, he, she, it,	I, he, she, it **was marked**
	we, you, they **marked**	we, you, they **were marked**
Past	I, he, she, it **was marking**	I, he, she, it **was being marked**
Prog.	we, you, they **were marking**	we, you, they **were being marked**
Past	I, he, she, it,	I, he, she, it,
Int.	we, you, they **did mark**	we, you, they **did get marked**
Pres.	I, we, you, they **have marked**	I, we, you, they **have been marked**
Perf.	he, she, it **has marked**	he, she, it **has been marked**
Past	I, he, she, it,	I, he, she, it,
Perf.	we, you, they **had marked**	we, you, they **had been marked**
Fut.	I, he, she, it, we, you, they	I, he, she, it, we, you, they
Perf.	**will have marked**	**will have been marked**

IMPERATIVE MOOD

mark   **be marked**

SUBJUNCTIVE MOOD

Pres.	if I, he, she, it,	if I, he, she, it,
	we, you, they **mark**	we, you, they **be marked**
Past	if I, he, she, it,	if I, he, she, it,
	we, you, they **marked**	we, you, they **were marked**
Fut.	if I, he, she, it,	if I, he, she, it,
	we, you, they **should mark**	we, you, they **should be marked**

Transitive and intransitive.

marry
(active voice)

PRINCIPAL PARTS: **marries, marrying, married, married**

be married
(passive voice)

Infinitive: **to marry**
Perfect Infinitive: **to have married**
Present Participle: **marrying**
Past Participle: **married**

Infinitive: **to be married**
Perfect Infinitive: **to have been married**
Present Participle: **being married**
Past Participle: **been married**

INDICATIVE MOOD

Pres.	I, we, you, they **marry** he, she, it **marries**	I **am married** we, you, they **are married** he, she, it **is married**
Pres. Prog.	I **am marrying** we, you, they **are marrying** he, she, it **is marrying**	I **am being married** we, you, they **are being married** he, she, it **is being married**
Pres. Int.	I, we, you, they **do marry** he, she, it **does marry**	I, we, you, they **do get married** he, she, it **does get married**
Fut.	I, he, she, it, we, you, they **will marry**	I, he, she, it, we, you, they **will be married**
Past	I, he, she, it, we, you, they **married**	I, he, she, it **was married** we, you, they **were married**
Past Prog.	I, he, she, it **was marrying** we, you, they **were marrying**	I, he, she, it **was being married** we, you, they **were being married**
Past Int.	I, he, she, it, we, you, they **did marry**	I, he, she, it, we, you, they **did get married**
Pres. Perf.	I, we, you, they **have married** he, she, it **has married**	I, we, you, they **have been married** he, she, it **has been married**
Past Perf.	I, he, she, it, we, you, they **had married**	I, he, she, it, we, you, they **had been married**
Fut. Perf.	I, he, she, it, we, you, they **will have married**	I, he, she, it, we, you, they **will have been married**

IMPERATIVE MOOD

marry   **be married**

SUBJUNCTIVE MOOD

Pres.	if I, he, she, it, we, you, they **marry**	if I, he, she, it, we, you, they **be married**
Past	if I, he, she, it, we, you, they **married**	if I, he, she, it, we, you, they **were married**
Fut.	if I, he, she, it, we, you, they **should marry**	if I, he, she, it, we, you, they **should be married**

Transitive and intransitive.

mean
(active voice)

be meant
(passive voice)

Infinitive: **to mean**
Perfect Infinitive: **to have meant**
Present Participle: **meaning**
Past Participle: **meant**

Infinitive: **to be meant**
Perfect Infinitive: **to have been meant**
Present Participle: **being meant**
Past Participle: **been meant**

INDICATIVE MOOD

Pres.	I, we, you, they **mean**	I **am meant**
		we, you, they **are meant**
	he, she, it **means**	he, she, it **is meant**
Pres.	I **am meaning**	I **am being meant**
Prog.	we, you, they **are meaning**	we, you, they **are being meant**
	he, she, it **is meaning**	he, she, it **is being meant**
Pres.	I, we, you, they **do mean**	I, we, you, they **do get meant**
Int.	he, she, it **does mean**	he, she, it **does get meant**
Fut.	I, he, she, it,	I, he, she, it,
	we, you, they **will mean**	we, you, they **will be meant**
Past	I, he, she, it,	I, he, she, it **was meant**
	we, you, they **meant**	we, you, they **were meant**
Past	I, he, she, it **was meaning**	I, he, she, it **was being meant**
Prog.	we, you, they **were meaning**	we, you, they **were being meant**
Past	I, he, she, it,	I, he, she, it,
Int.	we, you, they **did mean**	we, you, they **did get meant**
Pres.	I, we, you, they **have meant**	I, we, you, they **have been meant**
Perf.	he, she, it **has meant**	he, she, it **has been meant**
Past	I, he, she, it,	I, he, she, it,
Perf.	we, you, they **had meant**	we, you, they **had been meant**
Fut.	I, he, she, it, we, you, they	I, he, she, it, we, you, they
Perf.	**will have meant**	**will have been meant**

IMPERATIVE MOOD

mean   **be meant**

SUBJUNCTIVE MOOD

Pres.	if I, he, she, it,	if I, he, she, it,
	we, you, they **mean**	we, you, they **be meant**
Past	if I, he, she, it,	if I, he, she, it,
	we, you, they **meant**	we, you, they **were meant**
Fut.	if I, he, she, it,	if I, he, she, it,
	we, you, they **should mean**	we, you, they **should be meant**

Transitive and intransitive.

228

measure
(active voice)

be measured
(passive voice)

Infinitive: **to measure**
Perfect Infinitive: **to have measured**
Present Participle: **measuring**
Past Participle: **measured**

Infinitive: **to be measured**
Perfect Infinitive: **to have been measured**
Present Participle: **being measured**
Past Participle: **been measured**

INDICATIVE MOOD

Pres.	I, we, you, they **measure**	I **am measured**
		we, you, they **are measured**
	he, she, it **measures**	he, she, it **is measured**
Pres.	I **am measuring**	I **am being measured**
Prog.	we, you, they **are measuring**	we, you, they **are being measured**
	he, she, it **is measuring**	he, she, it **is being measured**
Pres.	I, we, you, they **do measure**	I, we, you, they **do get measured**
Int.	he, she, it **does measure**	he, she, it **does get measured**
Fut.	I, he, she, it,	I, he, she, it,
	we, you, they **will measure**	we, you, they **will be measured**
Past	I, he, she, it,	I, he, she, it **was measured**
	we, you, they **measured**	we, you, they **were measured**
Past	I, he, she, it **was measuring**	I, he, she, it **was being measured**
Prog.	we, you, they **were measuring**	we, you, they **were being measured**
Past	I, he, she, it,	I, he, she, it,
Int.	we, you, they **did measure**	we, you, they **did get measured**
Pres.	I, we, you, they **have measured**	I, we, you, they **have been measured**
Perf.	he, she, it **has measured**	he, she, it **has been measured**
Past	I, he, she, it,	I, he, she, it,
Perf.	we, you, they **had measured**	we, you, they **had been measured**
Fut.	I, he, she, it, we, you, they	I, he, she, it, we, you, they
Perf.	**will have measured**	**will have been measured**

IMPERATIVE MOOD

measure   **be measured**

SUBJUNCTIVE MOOD

Pres.	if I, he, she, it,	if I, he, she, it,
	we, you, they **measure**	we, you, they **be measured**
Past	if I, he, she, it,	if I, he, she, it,
	we, you, they **measured**	we, you, they **were measured**
Fut.	if I, he, she, it,	if I, he, she, it,
	we, you, they **should measure**	we, you, they **should be measured**

Transitive and intransitive.

meet
(active voice)

be met
(passive voice)

Infinitive: **to meet**
Perfect Infinitive: **to have met**
Present Participle: **meeting**
Past Participle: **met**

Infinitive: **to be met**
Perfect Infinitive: **to have been met**
Present Participle: **being met**
Past Participle: **been met**

INDICATIVE MOOD

Pres.	I, we, you, they **meet**	I **am met**
		we, you, they **are met**
	he, she, it **meets**	he, she, it **is met**
Pres.	I **am meeting**	I **am being met**
Prog.	we, you, they **are meeting**	we, you, they **are being met**
	he, she, it **is meeting**	he, she, it **is being met**
Pres.	I, we, you, they **do meet**	I, we, you, they **do get met**
Int.	he, she, it **does meet**	he, she, it **does get met**
Fut.	I, he, she, it,	I, he, she, it,
	we, you, they **will meet**	we, you, they **will be met**
Past	I, he, she, it,	I, he, she, it **was met**
	we, you, they **met**	we, you, they **were met**
Past	I, he, she, it **was meeting**	I, he, she, it **was being met**
Prog.	we, you, they **were meeting**	we, you, they **were being met**
Past	I, he, she, it,	I, he, she, it,
Int.	we, you, they **did meet**	we, you, they **did get met**
Pres.	I, we, you, they **have met**	I, we, you, they **have been met**
Perf.	he, she, it **has met**	he, she, it **has been met**
Past	I, he, she, it,	I, he, she, it,
Perf.	we, you, they **had met**	we, you, they **had been met**
Fut.	I, he, she, it, we, you, they	I, he, she, it, we, you, they
Perf.	**will have met**	**will have been met**

IMPERATIVE MOOD

meet   **be met**

SUBJUNCTIVE MOOD

Pres.	if I, he, she, it,	if I, he, she, it,
	we, you, they **meet**	we, you, they **be met**
Past	if I, he, she, it,	if I, he, she, it,
	we, you, they **met**	we, you, they **were met**
Fut.	if I, he, she, it,	if I, he, she, it,
	we, you, they **should meet**	we, you, they **should be met**

Transitive and intransitive.

mention
(active voice)

PRINCIPAL PARTS: **mentions, mentioning, mentioned, mentioned**

be mentioned
(passive voice)

Infinitive: **to mention**
Perfect Infinitive: **to have mentioned**
Present Participle: **mentioning**
Past Participle: **mentioned**

Infinitive: **to be mentioned**
Perfect Infinitive: **to have been mentioned**
Present Participle: **being mentioned**
Past Participle: **been mentioned**

INDICATIVE MOOD

Pres.	I, we, you, they **mention** he, she, it **mentions**	I am mentioned we, you, they **are mentioned** he, she, it **is mentioned**
Pres. *Prog.*	I am mentioning we, you, they **are mentioning** he, she, it **is mentioning**	I am being mentioned we, you, they **are being mentioned** he, she, it **is being mentioned**
Pres. *Int.*	I, we, you, they **do mention** he, she, it **does mention**	I, we, you, they **do get mentioned** he, she, it **does get mentioned**
Fut.	I, he, she, it, we, you, they **will mention**	I, he, she, it, we, you, they **will be mentioned**
Past	I, he, she, it, we, you, they **mentioned**	I, he, she, it **was mentioned** we, you, they **were mentioned**
Past *Prog.*	I, he, she, it **was mentioning** we, you, they **were mentioning**	I, he, she, it **was being mentioned** we, you, they **were being mentioned**
Past *Int.*	I, he, she, it, we, you, they **did mention**	I, he, she, it, we, you, they **did get mentioned**
Pres. *Perf.*	I, we, you, they **have mentioned** he, she, it **has mentioned**	I, we, you, they **have been mentioned** he, she, it **has been mentioned**
Past *Perf.*	I, he, she, it, we, you, they **had mentioned**	I, he, she, it, we, you, they **had been mentioned**
Fut. *Perf.*	I, he, she, it, we, you, they **will have mentioned**	I, he, she, it, we, you, they **will have been mentioned**

IMPERATIVE MOOD

mention

be mentioned

SUBJUNCTIVE MOOD

Pres.	if I, he, she, it, we, you, they **mention**	if I, he, she, it, we, you, they **be mentioned**
Past	if I, he, she, it, we, you, they **mentioned**	if I, he, she, it, we, you, they **were mentioned**
Fut.	if I, he, she, it, we, you, they **should mention**	if I, he, she, it, we, you, they **should be mentioned**

mete
(active voice)

be meted
(passive voice)

Infinitive: **to mete**
Perfect Infinitive: **to have meted**
Present Participle: **meting**
Past Participle: **meted**

Infinitive: **to be meted**
Perfect Infinitive: **to have been meted**
Present Participle: **being meted**
Past Participle: **been meted**

INDICATIVE MOOD

Pres.	I, we, you, they **mete**	I **am meted**
		we, you, they **are meted**
	he, she, it **metes**	he, she, it **is meted**
Pres.	I **am meting**	I **am being meted**
Prog.	we, you, they **are meting**	we, you, they **are being meted**
	he, she, it **is meting**	he, she, it **is being meted**
Pres.	I, we, you, they **do mete**	I, we, you, they **do get meted**
Int.	he, she, it **does mete**	he, she, it **does get meted**
Fut.	I, he, she, it,	I, he, she, it,
	we, you, they **will mete**	we, you, they **will be meted**
Past	I, he, she, it,	I, he, she, it **was meted**
	we, you, they **meted**	we, you, they **were meted**
Past	I, he, she, it **was meting**	I, he, she, it **was being meted**
Prog.	we, you, they **were meting**	we, you, they **were being meted**
Past	I, he, she, it,	I, he, she, it,
Int.	we, you, they **did mete**	we, you, they **did get meted**
Pres.	I, we, you, they **have meted**	I, we, you, they **have been meted**
Perf.	he, she, it **has meted**	he, she, it **has been meted**
Past	I, he, she, it,	I, he, she, it,
Perf.	we, you, they **had meted**	we, you, they **had been meted**
Fut.	I, he, she, it, we, you, they	I, he, she, it, we, you, they
Perf.	**will have meted**	**will have been meted**

IMPERATIVE MOOD

mete   **be meted**

SUBJUNCTIVE MOOD

Pres.	if I, he, she, it,	if I, he, she, it,
	we, you, they **mete**	we, you, they **be meted**
Past	if I, he, she, it,	if I, he, she, it,
	we, you, they **meted**	we, you, they **were meted**
Fut.	if I, he, she, it,	if I, he, she, it,
	we, you, they **should mete**	we, you, they **should be meted**

mimic
(active voice)

PRINCIPAL PARTS: **mimics, mimicking, mimicked, mimicked**

be mimicked
(passive voice)

Infinitive: **to mimic**
Perfect Infinitive: **to have mimicked**
Present Participle: **mimicking**
Past Participle: **mimicked**

Infinitive: **to be mimicked**
Perfect Infinitive: **to have been mimicked**
Present Participle: **being mimicked**
Past Participle: **been mimicked**

INDICATIVE MOOD

Pres.	I, we, you, they **mimic** he, she, it **mimics**	I **am mimicked** we, you, they **are mimicked** he, she, it **is mimicked**
Pres. *Prog.*	I **am mimicking** we, you, they **are mimicking** he, she, it **is mimicking**	I **am being mimicked** we, you, they **are being mimicked** he, she, it **is being mimicked**
Pres. *Int.*	I, we, you, they **do mimic** he, she, it **does mimic**	I, we, you, they **do get mimicked** he, she, it **does get mimicked**
Fut.	I, he, she, it, we, you, they **will mimic**	I, he, she, it, we, you, they **will be mimicked**
Past	I, he, she, it, we, you, they **mimicked**	I, he, she, it **was mimicked** we, you, they **were mimicked**
Past *Prog.*	I, he, she, it **was mimicking** we, you, they **were mimicking**	I, he, she, it **was being mimicked** we, you, they **were being mimicked**
Past *Int.*	I, he, she, it, we, you, they **did mimic**	I, he, she, it, we, you, they **did get mimicked**
Pres. *Perf.*	I, we, you, they **have mimicked** he, she, it **has mimicked**	I, we, you, they **have been mimicked** he, she, it **has been mimicked**
Past *Perf.*	I, he, she, it, we, you, they **had mimicked**	I, he, she, it, we, you, they **had been mimicked**
Fut. *Perf.*	I, he, she, it, we, you, they **will have mimicked**	I, he, she, it, we, you, they **will have been mimicked**

IMPERATIVE MOOD

mimic

be mimicked

SUBJUNCTIVE MOOD

Pres.	if I, he, she, it, we, you, they **mimic**	if I, he, she, it, we, you, they **be mimicked**
Past	if I, he, she, it, we, you, they **mimicked**	if I, he, she, it, we, you, they **were mimicked**
Fut.	if I, he, she, it, we, you, they **should mimic**	if I, he, she, it, we, you, they **should be mimicked**

mind
(active voice)

be minded
(passive voice)

Infinitive: **to mind**
Perfect Infinitive: **to have minded**
Present Participle: **minding**
Past Participle: **minded**

Infinitive: **to be minded**
Perfect Infinitive: **to have been minded**
Present Participle: **being minded**
Past Participle: **been minded**

INDICATIVE MOOD

Pres.	I, we, you, they **mind**	I **am minded**
		we, you, they **are minded**
	he, she, it **minds**	he, she, it **is minded**
Pres.	I **am minding**	I **am being minded**
Prog.	we, you, they **are minding**	we, you, they **are being minded**
	he, she, it **is minding**	he, she, it **is being minded**
Pres.	I, we, you, they **do mind**	I, we, you, they **do get minded**
Int.	he, she, it **does mind**	he, she, it **does get minded**
Fut.	I, he, she, it,	I, he, she, it,
	we, you, they **will mind**	we, you, they **will be minded**
Past	I, he, she, it,	I, he, she, it **was minded**
	we, you, they **minded**	we, you, they **were minded**
Past	I, he, she, it **was minding**	I, he, she, it **was being minded**
Prog.	we, you, they **were minding**	we, you, they **were being minded**
Past	I, he, she, it,	I, he, she, it,
Int.	we, you, they **did mind**	we, you, they **did get minded**
Pres.	I, we, you, they **have minded**	I, we, you, they **have been minded**
Perf.	he, she, it **has minded**	he, she, it **has been minded**
Past	I, he, she, it,	I, he, she, it,
Perf.	we, you, they **had minded**	we, you, they **had been minded**
Fut.	I, he, she, it, we, you, they	I, he, she, it, we, you, they
Perf.	**will have minded**	**will have been minded**

IMPERATIVE MOOD

mind   **be minded**

SUBJUNCTIVE MOOD

Pres.	if I, he, she, it,	if I, he, she, it,
	we, you, they **mind**	we, you, they **be minded**
Past	if I, he, she, it,	if I, he, she, it,
	we, you, they **minded**	we, you, they **were minded**
Fut.	if I, he, she, it,	if I, he, she, it,
	we, you, they **should mind**	we, you, they **should be minded**

Transitive and intransitive.

mislead
(active voice)

PRINCIPAL PARTS: **misleads, misleading, misled, misled**

be misled
(passive voice)

Infinitive: **to mislead**
Perfect Infinitive: **to have misled**
Present Participle: **misleading**
Past Participle: **misled**

Infinitive: **to be misled**
Perfect Infinitive: **to have been misled**
Present Participle: **being misled**
Past Participle: **been misled**

INDICATIVE MOOD

Pres.	I, we, you, they **mislead** he, she, it **misleads**	I **am misled** we, you, they **are misled** he, she, it **is misled**
Pres. Prog.	I **am misleading** we, you, they **are misleading** he, she, it **is misleading**	I **am being misled** we, you, they **are being misled** he, she, it **is being misled**
Pres. Int.	I, we, you, they **do mislead** he, she, it **does mislead**	I, we, you, they **do get misled** he, she, it **does get misled**
Fut.	I, he, she, it, we, you, they **will mislead**	I, he, she, it, we, you, they **will be misled**
Past	I, he, she, it, we, you, they **misled**	I, he, she, it **was misled** we, you, they **were misled**
Past Prog.	I, he, she, it **was misleading** we, you, they **were misleading**	I, he, she, it **was being misled** we, you, they **were being misled**
Past Int.	I, he, she, it, we, you, they **did mislead**	I, he, she, it, we, you, they **did get misled**
Pres. Perf.	I, we, you, they **have misled** he, she, it **has misled**	I, we, you, they **have been misled** he, she, it **has been misled**
Past Perf.	I, he, she, it, we, you, they **had misled**	I, he, she, it, we, you, they **had been misled**
Fut. Perf.	I, he, she, it, we, you, they **will have misled**	I, he, she, it, we, you, they **will have been misled**

IMPERATIVE MOOD

mislead

be misled

SUBJUNCTIVE MOOD

Pres.	if I, he, she, it, we, you, they **mislead**	if I, he, she, it, we, you, they **be misled**
Past	if I, he, she, it, we, you, they **misled**	if I, he, she, it, we, you, they **were misled**
Fut.	if I, he, she, it, we, you, they **should mislead**	if I, he, she, it, we, you, they **should be misled**

misspeak
(active voice)

be misspoken
(passive voice)

Infinitive: **to misspeak**
Perfect Infinitive: **to have misspoken**
Present Participle: **misspeaking**
Past Participle: **misspoken**

Infinitive: **to be misspoken**
Perfect Infinitive: **to have been misspoken**
Present Participle: **being misspoken**
Past Participle: **been misspoken**

INDICATIVE MOOD

Pres.	I, we, you, they **misspeak**	I **am misspoken**
		we, you, they **are misspoken**
	he, she, it **misspeaks**	he, she, it **is misspoken**
Pres.	I **am misspeaking**	I **am being misspoken**
Prog.	we, you, they **are misspeaking**	we, you, they **are being misspoken**
	he, she, it **is misspeaking**	he, she, it **is being misspoken**
Pres.	I, we, you, they **do misspeak**	I, we, you, they **do get misspoken**
Int.	he, she, it **does misspeak**	he, she, it **does get misspoken**
Fut.	I, he, she, it,	I, he, she, it,
	we, you, they **will misspeak**	we, you, they **will be misspoken**
Past	I, he, she, it,	I, he, she, it **was misspoken**
	we, you, they **misspoke**	we, you, they **were misspoken**
Past	I, he, she, it **was misspeaking**	I, he, she, it **was being misspoken**
Prog.	we, you, they **were misspeaking**	we, you, they **were being misspoken**
Past	I, he, she, it,	I, he, she, it,
Int.	we, you, they **did misspeak**	we, you, they **did get misspoken**
Pres.	I, we, you, they **have misspoken**	I, we, you, they **have been misspoken**
Perf.	he, she, it **has misspoken**	he, she, it **has been misspoken**
Past	I, he, she, it,	I, he, she, it,
Perf.	we, you, they **had misspoken**	we, you, they **had been misspoken**
Fut.	I, he, she, it, we, you, they	I, he, she, it, we, you, they
Perf.	**will have misspoken**	**will have been misspoken**

IMPERATIVE MOOD

misspeak   **be misspoken**

SUBJUNCTIVE MOOD

Pres.	if I, he, she, it,	if I, he, she, it,
	we, you, they **misspeak**	we, you, they **be misspoken**
Past	if I, he, she, it,	if I, he, she, it,
	we, you, they **misspoke**	we, you, they **were misspoken**
Fut.	if I, he, she, it,	if I, he, she, it,
	we, you, they **should misspeak**	we, you, they **should be misspoken**

Transitive and intransitive.

236

misspell
(active voice)

be misspelled/ misspelt
(passive voice)

Infinitive: **to misspell**
Perfect Infinitive: **to have misspelled**
Present Participle: **misspelling**
Past Participle: **misspelled**

Infinitive: **to be misspelled**
Perfect Infinitive: **to have been misspelled**
Present Participle: **being misspelled**
Past Participle: **been misspelled**

INDICATIVE MOOD

Pres.	I, we, you, they **misspell**	I **am misspelled**
		we, you, they **are misspelled**
	he, she, it **misspells**	he, she, it **is misspelled**
Pres.	I **am misspelling**	I **am being misspelled**
Prog.	we, you, they **are misspelling**	we, you, they **are being misspelled**
	he, she, it **is misspelling**	he, she, it **is being misspelled**
Pres.	I, we, you, they **do misspell**	I, we, you, they **do get misspelled**
Int.	he, she, it **does misspell**	he, she, it **does get misspelled**
Fut.	I, he, she, it, we, you, they **will misspell**	I, he, she, it, we, you, they **will be misspelled**
Past	I, he, she, it, we, you, they **misspelled**	I, he, she, it **was misspelled** we, you, they **were misspelled**
Past	I, he, she, it **was misspelling**	I, he, she, it **was being misspelled**
Prog.	we, you, they **were misspelling**	we, you, they **were being misspelled**
Past	I, he, she, it, we, you, they **did misspell**	I, he, she, it, we, you, they **did get misspelled**
Int.		
Pres.	I, we, you, they **have misspelled**	I, we, you, they **have been misspelled**
Perf.	he, she, it **has misspelled**	he, she, it **has been misspelled**
Past	I, he, she, it, we, you, they **had misspelled**	I, he, she, it, we, you, they **had been misspelled**
Perf.		
Fut.	I, he, she, it, we, you, they	I, he, she, it, we, you, they
Perf.	**will have misspelled**	**will have been misspelled**

IMPERATIVE MOOD

misspell

be misspelled

SUBJUNCTIVE MOOD

Pres.	if I, he, she, it, we, you, they **misspell**	if I, he, she, it, we, you, they **be misspelled**
Past	if I, he, she, it, we, you, they **misspelled**	if I, he, she, it, we, you, they **were misspelled**
Fut.	if I, he, she, it, we, you, they **should misspell**	if I, he, she, it, we, you, they **should be misspelled**

The *Oxford Dictionary* lists MISSPELT first for the past tense and past participle forms.

misspend
(active voice)

be misspent
(passive voice)

Infinitive: **to misspend**
Perfect Infinitive: **to have misspent**
Present Participle: **misspending**
Past Participle: **misspent**

Infinitive: **to be misspent**
Perfect Infinitive: **to have been misspent**
Present Participle: **being misspent**
Past Participle: **been misspent**

INDICATIVE MOOD

Pres.	I, we, you, they **misspend**	I **am misspent**
		we, you, they **are misspent**
	he, she, it **misspends**	he, she, it **is misspent**
Pres.	I **am misspending**	I **am being misspent**
Prog.	we, you, they **are misspending**	we, you, they **are being misspent**
	he, she, it **is misspending**	he, she, it **is being misspent**
Pres.	I, we, you, they **do misspend**	I, we, you, they **do get misspent**
Int.	he, she, it **does misspend**	he, she, it **does get misspent**
Fut.	I, he, she, it,	I, he, she, it,
	we, you, they **will misspend**	we, you, they **will be misspent**
Past	I, he, she, it,	I, he, she, it **was misspent**
	we, you, they **misspent**	we, you, they **were misspent**
Past	I, he, she, it **was misspending**	I, he, she, it **was being misspent**
Prog.	we, you, they **were misspending**	we, you, they **were being misspent**
Past	I, he, she, it,	I, he, she, it,
Int.	we, you, they **did misspend**	we, you, they **did get misspent**
Pres.	I, we, you, they **have misspent**	I, we, you, they **have been misspent**
Perf.	he, she, it **has misspent**	he, she, it **has been misspent**
Past	I, he, she, it,	I, he, she, it,
Perf.	we, you, they **had misspent**	we, you, they **had been misspent**
Fut.	I, he, she, it, we, you, they	I, he, she, it, we, you, they
Perf.	**will have misspent**	**will have been misspent**

IMPERATIVE MOOD

misspend

be misspent

SUBJUNCTIVE MOOD

Pres.	if I, he, she, it,	if I, he, she, it,
	we, you, they **misspend**	we, you, they **be misspent**
Past	if I, he, she, it,	if I, he, she, it,
	we, you, they **misspent**	we, you, they **were misspent**
Fut.	if I, he, she, it,	if I, he, she, it,
	we, you, they **should misspend**	we, you, they **should be misspent**

mistake
(active voice)

be mistaken
(passive voice)

Infinitive: **to mistake**
Perfect Infinitive: **to have mistaken**
Present Participle: **mistaking**
Past Participle: **mistaken**

Infinitive: **to be mistaken**
Perfect Infinitive: **to have been mistaken**
Present Participle: **being mistaken**
Past Participle: **been mistaken**

INDICATIVE MOOD

Pres.	I, we, you, they **mistake**	I **am mistaken**
		we, you, they **are mistaken**
	he, she, it **mistakes**	he, she, it **is mistaken**
Pres.	I **am mistaking**	I **am being mistaken**
Prog.	we, you, they **are mistaking**	we, you, they **are being mistaken**
	he, she, it **is mistaking**	he, she, it **is being mistaken**
Pres.	I, we, you, they **do mistake**	I, we, you, they **do get mistaken**
Int.	he, she, it **does mistake**	he, she, it **does get mistaken**
Fut.	I, he, she, it,	I, he, she, it,
	we, you, they **will mistake**	we, you, they **will be mistaken**
Past	I, he, she, it,	I, he, she, it **was mistaken**
	we, you, they **mistook**	we, you, they **were mistaken**
Past	I, he, she, it **was mistaking**	I, he, she, it **was being mistaken**
Prog.	we, you, they **were mistaking**	we, you, they **were being mistaken**
Past	I, he, she, it,	I, he, she, it,
Int.	we, you, they **did mistake**	we, you, they **did get mistaken**
Pres.	I, we, you, they **have mistaken**	I, we, you, they **have been mistaken**
Perf.	he, she, it **has mistaken**	he, she, it **has been mistaken**
Past	I, he, she, it,	I, he, she, it,
Perf.	we, you, they **had mistaken**	we, you, they **had been mistaken**
Fut.	I, he, she, it, we, you, they	I, he, she, it, we, you, they
Perf.	**will have mistaken**	**will have been mistaken**

IMPERATIVE MOOD

mistake   **be mistaken**

SUBJUNCTIVE MOOD

Pres.	if I, he, she, it,	if I, he, she, it,
	we, you, they **mistake**	we, you, they **be mistaken**
Past	if I, he, she, it,	if I, he, she, it,
	we, you, they **mistook**	we, you, they **were mistaken**
Fut.	if I, he, she, it,	if I, he, she, it,
	we, you, they **should mistake**	we, you, they **should be mistaken**

Transitive and intransitive.

move
(active voice)

be moved
(passive voice)

Infinitive: **to move**
Perfect Infinitive: **to have moved**
Present Participle: **moving**
Past Participle: **moved**

Infinitive: **to be moved**
Perfect Infinitive: **to have been moved**
Present Participle: **being moved**
Past Participle: **been moved**

INDICATIVE MOOD

Pres.	I, we, you, they **move**	I **am moved**
		we, you, they **are moved**
	he, she, it **moves**	he, she, it **is moved**
Pres.	I **am moving**	I **am being moved**
Prog.	we, you, they **are moving**	we, you, they **are being moved**
	he, she, it **is moving**	he, she, it **is being moved**
Pres.	I, we, you, they **do move**	I, we, you, they **do get moved**
Int.	he, she, it **does move**	he, she, it **does get moved**
Fut.	I, he, she, it,	I, he, she, it,
	we, you, they **will move**	we, you, they **will be moved**
Past	I, he, she, it,	I, he, she, it **was moved**
	we, you, they **moved**	we, you, they **were moved**
Past	I, he, she, it **was moving**	I, he, she, it **was being moved**
Prog.	we, you, they **were moving**	we, you, they **were being moved**
Past	I, he, she, it,	I, he, she, it,
Int.	we, you, they **did move**	we, you, they **did get moved**
Pres.	I, we, you, they **have moved**	I, we, you, they **have been moved**
Perf.	he, she, it **has moved**	he, she, it **has been moved**
Past	I, he, she, it,	I, he, she, it,
Perf.	we, you, they **had moved**	we, you, they **had been moved**
Fut.	I, he, she, it, we, you, they	I, he, she, it, we, you, they
Perf.	**will have moved**	**will have been moved**

IMPERATIVE MOOD

move

be moved

SUBJUNCTIVE MOOD

Pres.	if I, he, she, it,	if I, he, she, it,
	we, you, they **move**	we, you, they **be moved**
Past	if I, he, she, it,	if I, he, she, it,
	we, you, they **moved**	we, you, they **were moved**
Fut.	if I, he, she, it,	if I, he, she, it,
	we, you, they **should move**	we, you, they **should be moved**

Intransitive and transitive.

mow
(active voice)

be mowed/mown
(passive voice)

Infinitive: **to mow**
Perfect Infinitive: **to have mowed**
Present Participle: **mowing**
Past Participle: **mowed**

Infinitive: **to be mowed**
Perfect Infinitive: **to have been mowed**
Present Participle: **being mowed**
Past Participle: **been mowed**

INDICATIVE MOOD

Pres.	I, we, you, they **mow**	I **am mowed**
		we, you, they **are mowed**
	he, she, it **mows**	he, she, it **is mowed**
Pres.	I **am mowing**	I **am being mowed**
Prog.	we, you, they **are mowing**	we, you, they **are being mowed**
	he, she, it **is mowing**	he, she, it **is being mowed**
Pres.	I, we, you, they **do mow**	I, we, you, they **do get mowed**
Int.	he, she, it **does mow**	he, she, it **does get mowed**
Fut.	I, he, she, it, we, you, they **will mow**	I, he, she, it, we, you, they **will be mowed**
Past	I, he, she, it, we, you, they **mowed**	I, he, she, it **was mowed** we, you, they **were mowed**
Past	I, he, she, it **was mowing**	I, he, she, it **was being mowed**
Prog.	we, you, they **were mowing**	we, you, they **were being mowed**
Past	I, he, she, it, we, you, they **did mow**	I, he, she, it, we, you, they **did get mowed**
Int.		
Pres.	I, we, you, they **have mowed**	I, we, you, they **have been mowed**
Perf.	he, she, it **has mowed**	he, she, it **has been mowed**
Past	I, he, she, it, we, you, they **had mowed**	I, he, she, it, we, you, they **had been mowed**
Perf.		
Fut.	I, he, she, it, we, you, they **will have mowed**	I, he, she, it, we, you, they **will have been mowed**
Perf.		

IMPERATIVE MOOD

mow　　　　　　　　　**be mowed**

SUBJUNCTIVE MOOD

Pres.	if I, he, she, it, we, you, they **mow**	if I, he, she, it, we, you, they **be mowed**
Past	if I, he, she, it, we, you, they **mowed**	if I, he, she, it, we, you, they **were mowed**
Fut.	if I, he, she, it, we, you, they **should mow**	if I, he, she, it, we, you, they **should be mowed**

Transitive and intransitive.

241

need
(active voice)

PRINCIPAL PARTS: **needs/need***, **needing**,
needed, needed

be needed
(passive voice)

Infinitive: **to need**
Perfect Infinitive: **to have needed**
Present Participle: **needing**
Past Participle: **needed**

Infinitive: **to be needed**
Perfect Infinitive: **to have been needed**
Present Participle: **being needed**
Past Participle: **been needed**

INDICATIVE MOOD

Pres.	I, we, you, they **need**	I **am needed**
		we, you, they **are needed**
	he, she, it **needs/need***	he, she, it **is needed**
Pres.	I **am needing**	I **am being needed**
Prog.	we, you, they **are needing**	we, you, they **are being needed**
	he, she, it **is needing**	he, she, it **is being needed**
Pres.	I, we, you, they **do need**	I, we, you, they **do get needed**
Int.	he, she, it **does need**	he, she, it **does get needed**
Fut.	I, he, she, it,	I, he, she, it,
	we, you, they **will need**	we, you, they **will be needed**
Past	I, he, she, it,	I, he, she, it **was needed**
	we, you, they **needed**	we, you, they **were needed**
Past	I, he, she, it **was needing**	I, he, she, it **was being needed**
Prog.	we, you, they **were needing**	we, you, they **were being needed**
Past	I, he, she, it,	I, he, she, it,
Int.	we, you, they **did need**	we, you, they **did get needed**
Pres.	I, we, you, they **have needed**	I, we, you, they **have been needed**
Perf.	he, she, it **has needed**	he, she, it **has been needed**
Past	I, he, she, it,	I, he, she, it,
Perf.	we, you, they **had needed**	we, you, they **had been needed**
Fut.	I, he, she, it, we, you, they	I, he, she, it, we, you, they
Perf.	**will have needed**	**will have been needed**

IMPERATIVE MOOD

need

be needed

SUBJUNCTIVE MOOD

Pres.	if I, he, she, it,	if I, he, she, it,
	we, you, they **need**	we, you, they **be needed**
Past	if I, he, she, it,	if I, he, she, it,
	we, you, they **needed**	we, you, they **were needed**
Fut.	if I, he, she, it,	if I, he, she, it,
	we, you, they **should need**	we, you, they **should be needed**

Transitive and intransitive. When used as an auxiliary verb, NEED has only one form even in the he-she-it form: "He need not apply."

note
(active voice)

be noted
(passive voice)

Infinitive: **to note**
Perfect Infinitive: **to have noted**
Present Participle: **noting**
Past Participle: **noted**

Infinitive: **to be noted**
Perfect Infinitive: **to have been noted**
Present Participle: **being noted**
Past Participle: **been noted**

INDICATIVE MOOD

Pres.	I, we, you, they **note** he, she, it **notes**	I am **noted** we, you, they **are noted** he, she, it **is noted**
Pres. *Prog.*	I **am noting** we, you, they **are noting** he, she, it **is noting**	I **am being noted** we, you, they **are being noted** he, she, it **is being noted**
Pres. *Int.*	I, we, you, they **do note** he, she, it **does note**	I, we, you, they **do get noted** he, she, it **does get noted**
Fut.	I, he, she, it, we, you, they **will note**	I, he, she, it, we, you, they **will be noted**
Past	I, he, she, it, we, you, they **noted**	I, he, she, it **was noted** we, you, they **were noted**
Past *Prog.*	I, he, she, it **was noting** we, you, they **were noting**	I, he, she, it **was being noted** we, you, they **were being noted**
Past *Int.*	I, he, she, it, we, you, they **did note**	I, he, she, it, we, you, they **did get noted**
Pres. *Perf.*	I, we, you, they **have noted** he, she, it **has noted**	I, we, you, they **have been noted** he, she, it **has been noted**
Past *Perf.*	I, he, she, it, we, you, they **had noted**	I, he, she, it, we, you, they **had been noted**
Fut. *Perf.*	I, he, she, it, we, you, they **will have noted**	I, he, she, it, we, you, they **will have been noted**

IMPERATIVE MOOD

note

be noted

SUBJUNCTIVE MOOD

Pres.	if I, he, she, it, we, you, they **note**	if I, he, she, it, we, you, they **be noted**
Past	if I, he, she, it, we, you, they **noted**	if I, he, she, it, we, you, they **were noted**
Fut.	if I, he, she, it, we, you, they **should note**	if I, he, she, it, we, you, they **should be noted**

notice
(active voice)

be noticed
(passive voice)

Infinitive: **to notice**
Perfect Infinitive: **to have noticed**
Present Participle: **noticing**
Past Participle: **noticed**

Infinitive: **to be noticed**
Perfect Infinitive: **to have been noticed**
Present Participle: **being noticed**
Past Participle: **been noticed**

INDICATIVE MOOD

Pres.	I, we, you, they **notice**	I **am noticed**
		we, you, they **are noticed**
	he, she, it **notices**	he, she, it **is noticed**
Pres.	I **am noticing**	I **am being noticed**
Prog.	we, you, they **are noticing**	we, you, they **are being noticed**
	he, she, it **is noticing**	he, she, it **is being noticed**
Pres.	I, we, you, they **do notice**	I, we, you, they **do get noticed**
Int.	he, she, it **does notice**	he, she, it **does get noticed**
Fut.	I, he, she, it,	I, he, she, it,
	we, you, they **will notice**	we, you, they **will be noticed**
Past	I, he, she, it,	I, he, she, it **was noticed**
	we, you, they **noticed**	we, you, they **were noticed**
Past	I, he, she, it **was noticing**	I, he, she, it **was being noticed**
Prog.	we, you, they **were noticing**	we, you, they **were being noticed**
Past	I, he, she, it,	I, he, she, it,
Int.	we, you, they **did notice**	we, you, they **did get noticed**
Pres.	I, we, you, they **have noticed**	I, we, you, they **have been noticed**
Perf.	he, she, it **has noticed**	he, she, it **has been noticed**
Past	I, he, she, it,	I, he, she, it,
Perf.	we, you, they **had noticed**	we, you, they **had been noticed**
Fut.	I, he, she, it, we, you, they	I, he, she, it, we, you, they
Perf.	**will have noticed**	**will have been noticed**

IMPERATIVE MOOD

notice

be noticed

SUBJUNCTIVE MOOD

Pres.	if I, he, she, it,	if I, he, she, it,
	we, you, they **notice**	we, you, they **be noticed**
Past	if I, he, she, it,	if I, he, she, it,
	we, you, they **noticed**	we, you, they **were noticed**
Fut.	if I, he, she, it,	if I, he, she, it,
	we, you, they **should notice**	we, you, they **should be noticed**

observe
(active voice)

be observed
(passive voice)

Infinitive: **to observe**
Perfect Infinitive: **to have observed**
Present Participle: **observing**
Past Participle: **observed**

Infinitive: **to be observed**
Perfect Infinitive: **to have been observed**
Present Participle: **being observed**
Past Participle: **been observed**

INDICATIVE MOOD

Pres.	I, we, you, they **observe**	I **am observed**
		we, you, they **are observed**
	he, she, it **observes**	he, she, it **is observed**
Pres.	I **am observing**	I **am being observed**
Prog.	we, you, they **are observing**	we, you, they **are being observed**
	he, she, it **is observing**	he, she, it **is being observed**
Pres.	I, we, you, they **do observe**	I, we, you, they **do get observed**
Int.	he, she, it **does observe**	he, she, it **does get observed**
Fut.	I, he, she, it,	I, he, she, it,
	we, you, they **will observe**	we, you, they **will be observed**
Past	I, he, she, it,	I, he, she, it **was observed**
	we, you, they **observed**	we, you, they **were observed**
Past	I, he, she, it **was observing**	I, he, she, it **was being observed**
Prog.	we, you, they **were observing**	we, you, they **were being observed**
Past	I, he, she, it,	I, he, she, it,
Int.	we, you, they **did observe**	we, you, they **did get observed**
Pres.	I, we, you, they **have observed**	I, we, you, they **have been observed**
Perf.	he, she, it **has observed**	he, she, it **has been observed**
Past	I, he, she, it,	I, he, she, it,
Perf.	we, you, they **had observed**	we, you, they **had been observed**
Fut.	I, he, she, it, we, you, they	I, he, she, it, we, you, they
Perf.	**will have observed**	**will have been observed**

IMPERATIVE MOOD

observe   **be observed**

SUBJUNCTIVE MOOD

Pres.	if I, he, she, it,	if I, he, she, it,
	we, you, they **observe**	we, you, they **be observed**
Past	if I, he, she, it,	if I, he, she, it,
	we, you, they **observed**	we, you, they **were observed**
Fut.	if I, he, she, it,	if I, he, she, it,
	we, you, they **should observe**	we, you, they **should be observed**

Transitive and intransitive.

obtain
(active voice)

be obtained
(passive voice)

Infinitive: **to obtain**
Perfect Infinitive: **to have obtained**
Present Participle: **obtaining**
Past Participle: **obtained**

Infinitive: **to be obtained**
Perfect Infinitive: **to have been obtained**
Present Participle: **being obtained**
Past Participle: **been obtained**

INDICATIVE MOOD

Pres.	I, we, you, they **obtain**	I **am obtained**
		we, you, they **are obtained**
	he, she, it **obtains**	he, she, it **is obtained**
Pres.	I **am obtaining**	I **am being obtained**
Prog.	we, you, they **are obtaining**	we, you, they **are being obtained**
	he, she, it **is obtaining**	he, she, it **is being obtained**
Pres.	I, we, you, they **do obtain**	I, we, you, they **do get obtained**
Int.	he, she, it **does obtain**	he, she, it **does get obtained**
Fut.	I, he, she, it,	I, he, she, it,
	we, you, they **will obtain**	we, you, they **will be obtained**
Past	I, he, she, it,	I, he, she, it **was obtained**
	we, you, they **obtained**	we, you, they **were obtained**
Past	I, he, she, it **was obtaining**	I, he, she, it **was being obtained**
Prog.	we, you, they **were obtaining**	we, you, they **were being obtained**
Past	I, he, she, it,	I, he, she, it,
Int.	we, you, they **did obtain**	we, you, they **did get obtained**
Pres.	I, we, you, they **have obtained**	I, we, you, they **have been obtained**
Perf.	he, she, it **has obtained**	he, she, it **has been obtained**
Past	I, he, she, it,	I, he, she, it,
Perf.	we, you, they **had obtained**	we, you, they **had been obtained**
Fut.	I, he, she, it, we, you, they	I, he, she, it, we, you, they
Perf.	**will have obtained**	**will have been obtained**

IMPERATIVE MOOD

obtain   **be obtained**

SUBJUNCTIVE MOOD

Pres.	if I, he, she, it,	if I, he, she, it,
	we, you, they **obtain**	we, you, they **be obtained**
Past	if I, he, she, it,	if I, he, she, it,
	we, you, they **obtained**	we, you, they **were obtained**
Fut.	if I, he, she, it,	if I, he, she, it,
	we, you, they **should obtain**	we, you, they **should be obtained**

Transitive and intransitive.

Infinitive: **to occur**
Perfect Infinitive: **to have occurred**
Present Participle: **occurring**
Past Participle: **occurred**

INDICATIVE MOOD

Pres.   I, we, you, they **occur**

         he, she, it **occurs**

Pres.   I **am occurring**
Prog.   we, you, they **are occurring**
         he, she, it **is occurring**

Pres.   I, we, you, they **do occur**
Int.   he, she, it **does occur**

Fut.   I, he, she, it,
         we, you, they **will occur**

Past   I, he, she, it,
         we, you, they **occurred**

Past   I, he, she, it **was occurring**
Prog.   we, you, they **were occurring**

Past   I, he, she, it,
Int.   we, you, they **did occur**

Pres.   I, we, you, they **have occurred**
Perf.   he, she, it **has occurred**

Past   I, he, she, it,
Perf.   we, you, they **had occurred**

Fut.   I, he, she, it, we, you, they
Perf.   **will have occurred**

IMPERATIVE MOOD

         occur

SUBJUNCTIVE MOOD

Pres.   if I, he, she, it,
         we, you, they **occur**

Past   if I, he, she, it,
         we, you, they **occurred**

Fut.   if I, he, she, it,
         we, you, they **should occur**

offer
(active voice)

PRINCIPAL PARTS: **offers, offering,
offered, offered**

be offered
(passive voice)

Infinitive: **to offer**
Perfect Infinitive: **to have offered**
Present Participle: **offering**
Past Participle: **offered**

Infinitive: **to be offered**
Perfect Infinitive: **to have been offered**
Present Participle: **being offered**
Past Participle: **been offered**

INDICATIVE MOOD

Pres.	I, we, you, they **offer**	I **am offered**
		we, you, they **are offered**
	he, she, it **offers**	he, she, it **is offered**
Pres.	I **am offering**	I **am being offered**
Prog.	we, you, they **are offering**	we, you, they **are being offered**
	he, she, it **is offering**	he, she, it **is being offered**
Pres.	I, we, you, they **do offer**	I, we, you, they **do get offered**
Int.	he, she, it **does offer**	he, she, it **does get offered**
Fut.	I, he, she, it,	I, he, she, it,
	we, you, they **will offer**	we, you, they **will be offered**
Past	I, he, she, it,	I, he, she, it **was offered**
	we, you, they **offered**	we, you, they **were offered**
Past	I, he, she, it **was offering**	I, he, she, it **was being offered**
Prog.	we, you, they **were offering**	we, you, they **were being offered**
Past	I, he, she, it,	I, he, she, it,
Int.	we, you, they **did offer**	we, you, they **did get offered**
Pres.	I, we, you, they **have offered**	I, we, you, they **have been offered**
Perf.	he, she, it **has offered**	he, she, it **has been offered**
Past	I, he, she, it,	I, he, she, it,
Perf.	we, you, they **had offered**	we, you, they **had been offered**
Fut.	I, he, she, it, we, you, they	I, he, she, it, we, you, they
Perf.	**will have offered**	**will have been offered**

IMPERATIVE MOOD

offer

be offered

SUBJUNCTIVE MOOD

Pres.	if I, he, she, it,	if I, he, she, it,
	we, you, they **offer**	we, you, they **be offered**
Past	if I, he, she, it,	if I, he, she, it,
	we, you, they **offered**	we, you, they **were offered**
Fut.	if I, he, she, it,	if I, he, she, it,
	we, you, they **should offer**	we, you, they **should be offered**

Transitive and intransitive.

offset
(active voice)

PRINCIPAL PARTS: **offsets, offsetting, offset, offset**

be offset
(passive voice)

Infinitive: **to offset**
Perfect Infinitive: **to have offset**
Present Participle: **offsetting**
Past Participle: **offset**

Infinitive: **to be offset**
Perfect Infinitive: **to have been offset**
Present Participle: **being offset**
Past Participle: **been offset**

INDICATIVE MOOD

Pres.	I, we, you, they **offset**	I **am offset**
		we, you, they **are offset**
	he, she, it **offsets**	he, she, it **is offset**
Pres.	I **am offsetting**	I **am being offset**
Prog.	we, you, they **are offsetting**	we, you, they **are being offset**
	he, she, it **is offsetting**	he, she, it **is being offset**
Pres.	I, we, you, they **do offset**	I, we, you, they **do get offset**
Int.	he, she, it **does offset**	he, she, it **does get offset**
Fut.	I, he, she, it, we, you, they **will offset**	I, he, she, it, we, you, they **will be offset**
Past	I, he, she, it, we, you, they **offset**	I, he, she, it **was offset** we, you, they **were offset**
Past	I, he, she, it **was offsetting**	I, he, she, it **was being offset**
Prog.	we, you, they **were offsetting**	we, you, they **were being offset**
Past	I, he, she, it, we, you, they **did offset**	I, he, she, it, we, you, they **did get offset**
Int.		
Pres.	I, we, you, they **have offset**	I, we, you, they **have been offset**
Perf.	he, she, it **has offset**	he, she, it **has been offset**
Past	I, he, she, it, we, you, they **had offset**	I, he, she, it, we, you, they **had been offset**
Perf.		
Fut.	I, he, she, it, we, you, they **will have offset**	I, he, she, it, we, you, they **will have been offset**
Perf.		

IMPERATIVE MOOD

offset be offset

SUBJUNCTIVE MOOD

Pres.	if I, he, she, it, we, you, they **offset**	if I, he, she, it, we, you, they **be offset**
Past	if I, he, she, it, we, you, they **offset**	if I, he, she, it, we, you, they **were offset**
Fut.	if I, he, she, it, we, you, they **should offset**	if I, he, she, it, we, you, they **should be offset**

Transitive and intransitive.

open
(active voice)

be opened
(passive voice)

Infinitive: **to open**
Perfect Infinitive: **to have opened**
Present Participle: **opening**
Past Participle: **opened**

Infinitive: **to be opened**
Perfect Infinitive: **to have been opened**
Present Participle: **being opened**
Past Participle: **been opened**

INDICATIVE MOOD

Pres.	I, we, you, they **open**	I **am opened**
		we, you, they **are opened**
	he, she, it **opens**	he, she, it **is opened**
Pres.	I **am opening**	I **am being opened**
Prog.	we, you, they **are opening**	we, you, they **are being opened**
	he, she, it **is opening**	he, she, it **is being opened**
Pres.	I, we, you, they **do open**	I, we, you, they **do get opened**
Int.	he, she, it **does open**	he, she, it **does get opened**
Fut.	I, he, she, it,	I, he, she, it,
	we, you, they **will open**	we, you, they **will be opened**
Past	I, he, she, it,	I, he, she, it **was opened**
	we, you, they **opened**	we, you, they **were opened**
Past	I, he, she, it **was opening**	I, he, she, it **was being opened**
Prog.	we, you, they **were opening**	we, you, they **were being opened**
Past	I, he, she, it,	I, he, she, it,
Int.	we, you, they **did open**	we, you, they **did get opened**
Pres.	I, we, you, they **have opened**	I, we, you, they **have been opened**
Perf.	he, she, it **has opened**	he, she, it **has been opened**
Past	I, he, she, it,	I, he, she, it,
Perf.	we, you, they **had opened**	we, you, they **had been opened**
Fut.	I, he, she, it, we, you, they	I, he, she, it, we, you, they
Perf.	**will have opened**	**will have been opened**

IMPERATIVE MOOD

open   **be opened**

SUBJUNCTIVE MOOD

Pres.	if I, he, she, it,	if I, he, she, it,
	we, you, they **open**	we, you, they **be opened**
Past	if I, he, she, it,	if I, he, she, it,
	we, you, they **opened**	we, you, they **were opened**
Fut.	if I, he, she, it,	if I, he, she, it,
	we, you, they **should open**	we, you, they **should be opened**

Transitive and intransitive.

operate
(active voice)

be operated
(passive voice)

Infinitive: **to operate**
Perfect Infinitive: **to have operated**
Present Participle: **operating**
Past Participle: **operated**

Infinitive: **to be operated**
Perfect Infinitive: **to have been operated**
Present Participle: **being operated**
Past Participle: **been operated**

INDICATIVE MOOD

Pres.	I, we, you, they **operate**	I **am operated**
		we, you, they **are operated**
	he, she, it **operates**	he, she, it **is operated**
Pres.	I **am operating**	I **am being operated**
Prog.	we, you, they **are operating**	we, you, they **are being operated**
	he, she, it **is operating**	he, she, it **is being operated**
Pres.	I, we, you, they **do operate**	I, we, you, they **do get operated**
Int.	he, she, it **does operate**	he, she, it **does get operated**
Fut.	I, he, she, it, we, you, they **will operate**	I, he, she, it, we, you, they **will be operated**
Past	I, he, she, it we, you, they **operated**	I, he, she, it **was operated** we, you, they **were operated**
Past	I, he, she, it **was operating**	I, he, she, it **was being operated**
Prog.	we, you, they **were operating**	we, you, they **were being operated**
Past	I, he, she, it, we, you, they **did operate**	I, he, she, it, we, you, they **did get operated**
Int.		
Pres.	I, we, you, they **have operated**	I, we, you, they **have been operated**
Perf.	he, she, it **has operated**	he, she, it **has been operated**
Past	I, he, she, it, we, you, they **had operated**	I, he, she, it, we, you, they **had been operated**
Perf.		
Fut.	I, he, she, it, we, you, they	I, he, she, it, we, you, they
Perf.	**will have operated**	**will have been operated**

IMPERATIVE MOOD

operate   **be operated**

SUBJUNCTIVE MOOD

Pres.	if I, he, she, it, we, you, they **operate**	if I, he, she, it, we, you, they **be operated**
Past	if I, he, she, it, we, you, they **operated**	if I, he, she, it, we, you, they **were operated**
Fut.	if I, he, she, it, we, you, they **should operate**	if I, he, she, it, we, you, they **should be operated**

Intransitive and transitive.

order
(active voice)

be ordered
(passive voice)

Infinitive: **to order**
Perfect Infinitive: **to have ordered**
Present Participle: **ordering**
Past Participle: **ordered**

Infinitive: **to be ordered**
Perfect Infinitive: **to have been ordered**
Present Participle: **being ordered**
Past Participle: **been ordered**

INDICATIVE MOOD

Pres.	I, we, you, they **order**	I **am ordered**
		we, you, they **are ordered**
	he, she, it **orders**	he, she, it **is ordered**
Pres.	I **am ordering**	I **am being ordered**
Prog.	we, you, they **are ordering**	we, you, they **are being ordered**
	he, she, it **is ordering**	he, she, it **is being ordered**
Pres.	I, we, you, they **do order**	I, we, you, they **do get ordered**
Int.	he, she, it **does order**	he, she, it **does get ordered**
Fut.	I, he, she, it,	I, he, she, it,
	we, you, they **will order**	we, you, they **will be ordered**
Past	I, he, she, it,	I, he, she, it **was ordered**
	we, you, they **ordered**	we, you, they **were ordered**
Past	I, he, she, it **was ordering**	I, he, she, it **was being ordered**
Prog.	we, you, they **were ordering**	we, you, they **were being ordered**
Past	I, he, she, it,	I, he, she, it,
Int.	we, you, they **did order**	we, you, they **did get ordered**
Pres.	I, we, you, they **have ordered**	I, we, you, they **have been ordered**
Perf.	he, she, it **has ordered**	he, she, it **has been ordered**
Past	I, he, she, it,	I, he, she, it,
Perf.	we, you, they **had ordered**	we, you, they **had been ordered**
Fut.	I, he, she, it, we, you, they	I, he, she, it, we, you, they
Perf.	**will have ordered**	**will have been ordered**

IMPERATIVE MOOD

order   **be ordered**

SUBJUNCTIVE MOOD

Pres.	if I, he, she, it,	if I, he, she, it,
	we, you, they **order**	we, you, they **be ordered**
Past	if I, he, she, it,	if I, he, she, it,
	we, you, they **ordered**	we, you, they **were ordered**
Fut.	if I, he, she, it,	if I, he, she, it,
	we, you, they **should order**	we, you, they **should be ordered**

Transitive and intransitive.

outbid
(active voice)

be outbidden/outbid
(passive voice)

Infinitive: **to outbid**
Perfect Infinitive: **to have outbid**
Present Participle: **outbidding**
Past Participle: **outbidden**

Infinitive: **to be outbidden**
Perfect Infinitive: **to have been outbidden**
Present Participle: **being outbidden**
Past Participle: **been outbidden**

INDICATIVE MOOD

Pres.	I, we, you, they **outbid**	I **am outbidden**
		we, you, they **are outbidden**
	he, she, it **outbids**	he, she, it **is outbidden**
Pres.	I **am outbidding**	I **am being outbidden**
Prog.	we, you, they **are outbidding**	we, you, they **are being outbidden**
	he, she, it **is outbidding**	he, she, it **is being outbidden**
Pres.	I, we, you, they **do outbid**	I, we, you, they **do get outbidden**
Int.	he, she, it **does outbid**	he, she, it **does get outbidden**
Fut.	I, he, she, it,	I, he, she, it,
	we, you, they **will outbid**	we, you, they **will be outbidden**
Past	I, he, she, it,	I, he, she, it **was outbidden**
	we, you, they **outbid**	we, you, they **were outbidden**
Past	I, he, she, it **was outbidding**	I, he, she, it **was being outbidden**
Prog.	we, you, they **were outbidding**	we, you, they **were being outbidden**
Past	I, he, she, it,	I, he, she, it,
Int.	we, you, they **did outbid**	we, you, they **did get outbidden**
Pres.	I, we, you, they **have outbidden**	I, we, you, they **have been outbidden**
Perf.	he, she, it **has outbidden**	he, she, it **has been outbidden**
Past	I, he, she, it,	I, he, she, it,
Perf.	we, you, they **had outbidden**	we, you, they **had been outbidden**
Fut.	I, he, she, it, we, you, they	I, he, she, it, we, you, they
Perf.	**will have outbidden**	**will have been outbidden**

IMPERATIVE MOOD

outbid   **be outbidden**

SUBJUNCTIVE MOOD

Pres.	if I, he, she, it,	if I, he, she, it,
	we, you, they **outbid**	we, you, they **be outbidden**
Past	if I, he, she, it,	if I, he, she, it,
	we, you, they **outbid**	we, you, they **were outbidden**
Fut.	if I, he, she, it,	if I, he, she, it,
	we, you, they **should outbid**	we, you, they **should be outbidden**

The *Oxford Dictionary* and *Webster's* recognize only OUTBID as the past participle.

outdo
(active voice)

be outdone
(passive voice)

Infinitive: **to outdo**
Perfect Infinitive: **to have outdone**
Present Participle: **outdoing**
Past Participle: **outdone**

Infinitive: **to be outdone**
Perfect Infinitive: **to have been outdone**
Present Participle: **being outdone**
Past Participle: **been outdone**

INDICATIVE MOOD

Pres.	I, we, you, they **outdo** he, she, it **outdoes**	I **am outdone** we, you, they **are outdone** he, she, it **is outdone**
Pres. *Prog.*	I **am outdoing** we, you, they **are outdoing** he, she, it **is outdoing**	I **am being outdone** we, you, they **are being outdone** he, she, it **is being outdone**
Pres. *Int.*	I, we, you, they **do outdo** he, she, it **does outdo**	I, we, you, they **do get outdone** he, she, it **does get outdone**
Fut.	I, he, she, it, we, you, they **will outdo**	I, he, she, it, we, you, they **will be outdone**
Past	I, he, she, it, we, you, they **outdid**	I, he, she, it **was outdone** we, you, they **were outdone**
Past *Prog.*	I, he, she, it **was outdoing** we, you, they **were outdoing**	I, he, she, it **was being outdone** we, you, they **were being outdone**
Past *Int.*	I, he, she, it, we, you, they **did outdo**	I, he, she, it, we, you, they **did get outdone**
Pres. *Perf.*	I, we, you, they **have outdone** he, she, it **has outdone**	I, we, you, they **have been outdone** he, she, it **has been outdone**
Past *Perf.*	I, he, she, it, we, you, they **had outdone**	I, he, she, it, we, you, they **had been outdone**
Fut. *Perf.*	I, he, she, it, we, you, they **will have outdone**	I, he, she, it, we, you, they **will have been outdone**

IMPERATIVE MOOD

outdo   **be outdone**

SUBJUNCTIVE MOOD

Pres.	if I, he, she, it, we, you, they **outdo**	if I, he, she, it, we, you, they **be outdone**
Past	if I, he, she, it, we, you, they **outdid**	if I, he, she, it, we, you, they **were outdone**
Fut.	if I, he, she, it, we, you, they **should outdo**	if I, he, she, it, we, you, they **should be outdone**

outfight
(active voice)

be outfought
(passive voice)

Infinitive: **to outfight**
Perfect Infinitive: **to have outfought**
Present Participle: **outfighting**
Past Participle: **outfought**

Infinitive: **to be outfought**
Perfect Infinitive: **to have been outfought**
Present Participle: **being outfought**
Past Participle: **been outfought**

INDICATIVE MOOD

Pres.	I, we, you, they **outfight**	I **am outfought**
		we, you, they **are outfought**
	he, she, it **outfights**	he, she, it **is outfought**
Pres. *Prog.*	I **am outfighting**	I **am being outfought**
	we, you, they **are outfighting**	we, you, they **are being outfought**
	he, she, it **is outfighting**	he, she, it **is being outfought**
Pres. *Int.*	I, we, you, they **do outfight**	I, we, you, they **do get outfought**
	he, she, it **does outfight**	he, she, it **does get outfought**
Fut.	I, he, she, it, we, you, they **will outfight**	I, he, she, it, we, you, they **will be outfought**
Past	I, he, she, it, we, you, they **outfought**	I, he, she, it **was outfought** we, you, they **were outfought**
Past *Prog.*	I, he, she, it **was outfighting** we, you, they **were outfighting**	I, he, she, it **was being outfought** we, you, they **were being outfought**
Past *Int.*	I, he, she, it, we, you, they **did outfight**	I, he, she, it, we, you, they **did get outfought**
Pres. *Perf.*	I, we, you, they **have outfought** he, she, it **has outfought**	I, we, you, they **have been outfought** he, she, it **has been outfought**
Past *Perf.*	I, he, she, it, we, you, they **had outfought**	I, he, she, it, we, you, they **had been outfought**
Fut. *Perf.*	I, he, she, it, we, you, they **will have outfought**	I, he, she, it, we, you, they **will have been outfought**

IMPERATIVE MOOD

outfight

be outfought

SUBJUNCTIVE MOOD

Pres.	if I, he, she, it, we, you, they **outfight**	if I, he, she, it, we, you, they **be outfought**
Past	if I, he, she, it, we, you, they **outfought**	if I, he, she, it, we, you, they **were outfought**
Fut.	if I, he, she, it, we, you, they **should outfight**	if I, he, she, it, we, you, they **should be outfought**

Intransitive and transitive.

outfit
(active voice)

be outfitted
(passive voice)

Infinitive: **to outfit**
Perfect Infinitive: **to have outfit**
Present Participle: **outfitting**
Past Participle: **outfitted**

Infinitive: **to be outfitted**
Perfect Infinitive: **to have been outfitted**
Present Participle: **being outfitted**
Past Participle: **been outfitted**

INDICATIVE MOOD

Pres. I, we, you, they **outfit**

he, she, it **outfits**

I **am outfitted**
we, you, they **are outfitted**
he, she, it **is outfitted**

Pres. I **am outfitting**
Prog. we, you, they **are outfitting**
he, she, it **is outfitting**

I **am being outfitted**
we, you, they **are being outfitted**
he, she, it **is being outfitted**

Pres. I, we, you, they **do outfit**
Int. he, she, it **does outfit**

I, we, you, they **do get outfitted**
he, she, it **does get outfitted**

Fut. I, he, she, it,
we, you, they **will outfit**

I, he, she, it,
we, you, they **will be outfitted**

Past I, he, she, it,
we, you, they **outfitted**

I, he, she, it **was outfitted**
we, you, they **were outfitted**

Past I, he, she, it **was outfitting**
Prog. we, you, they **were outfitting**

I, he, she, it **was being outfitted**
we, you, they **were being outfitted**

Past I, he, she, it,
Int. we, you, they **did outfit**

I, he, she, it,
we, you, they **did get outfitted**

Pres. I, we, you, they **have outfit**
Perf. he, she, it **has outfit**

I, we, you, they **have been outfitted**
he, she, it **has been outfitted**

Past I, he, she, it,
Perf. we, you, they **had outfit**

I, he, she, it,
we, you, they **had been outfitted**

Fut. I, he, she, it, we, you, they
Perf. **will have outfit**

I, he, she, it, we, you, they
will have been outfitted

IMPERATIVE MOOD
outfit

be outfitted

SUBJUNCTIVE MOOD

Pres. if I, he, she, it,
we, you, they **outfit**

if I, he, she, it,
we, you, they **be outfitted**

Past if I, he, she, it,
we, you, they **outfit**

if I, he, she, it,
we, you, they **were outfitted**

Fut. if I, he, she, it,
we, you, they **should outfit**

if I, he, she, it,
we, you, they **should be outfitted**

outgrow
(active voice)

be outgrown
(passive voice)

Infinitive: **to outgrow**
Perfect Infinitive: **to have outgrown**
Present Participle: **outgrowing**
Past Participle: **outgrown**

Infinitive: **to be outgrown**
Perfect Infinitive: **to have been outgrown**
Present Participle: **being outgrown**
Past Participle: **been outgrown**

INDICATIVE MOOD

Pres.	I, we, you, they **outgrow**	I **am outgrown**
		we, you, they **are outgrown**
	he, she, it **outgrows**	he, she, it **is outgrown**
Pres.	I **am outgrowing**	I **am being outgrown**
Prog.	we, you, they **are outgrowing**	we, you, they **are being outgrown**
	he, she, it **is outgrowing**	he, she, it **is being outgrown**
Pres.	I, we, you, they **do outgrow**	I, we, you, they **do get outgrown**
Int.	he, she, it **does outgrow**	he, she, it **does get outgrown**
Fut.	I, he, she, it,	I, he, she, it,
	we, you, they **will outgrow**	we, you, they **will be outgrown**
Past	I, he, she, it,	I, he, she, it **was outgrown**
	we, you, they **outgrew**	we, you, they **were outgrown**
Past	I, he, she, it **was outgrowing**	I, he, she, it **was being outgrown**
Prog.	we, you, they **were outgrowing**	we, you, they **were being outgrown**
Past	I, he, she, it,	I, he, she, it,
Int.	we, you, they **did outgrow**	we, you, they **did get outgrown**
Pres.	I, we, you, they **have outgrown**	I, we, you, they **have been outgrown**
Perf.	he, she, it **has outgrown**	he, she, it **has been outgrown**
Past	I, he, she, it,	I, he, she, it,
Perf.	we, you, they **had outgrown**	we, you, they **had been outgrown**
Fut.	I, he, she, it, we, you, they	I, he, she, it, we, you, they
Perf.	**will have outgrown**	**will have been outgrown**

IMPERATIVE MOOD

outgrow   **be outgrown**

SUBJUNCTIVE MOOD

Pres.	if I, he, she, it,	if I, he, she, it,
	we, you, they **outgrow**	we, you, they **be outgrown**
Past	if I, he, she, it,	if I, he, she, it,
	we, you, they **outgrew**	we, you, they **were outgrown**
Fut.	if I, he, she, it,	if I, he, she, it,
	we, you, they **should outgrow**	we, you, they **should be outgrown**

outrun
(active voice)

be outrun
(passive voice)

Infinitive: **to outrun**
Perfect Infinitive: **to have outrun**
Present Participle: **outrunning**
Past Participle: **outrun**

Infinitive: **to be outrun**
Perfect Infinitive: **to have been outrun**
Present Participle: **being outrun**
Past Participle: **been outrun**

INDICATIVE MOOD

Pres.	I, we, you, they **outrun**	I **am outrun**
		we, you, they **are outrun**
	he, she, it **outruns**	he, she, it **is outrun**
Pres.	I **am outrunning**	I **am being outrun**
Prog.	we, you, they **are outrunning**	we, you, they **are being outrun**
	he, she, it **is outrunning**	he, she, it **is being outrun**
Pres.	I, we, you, they **do outrun**	I, we, you, they **do get outrun**
Int.	he, she, it **does outrun**	he, she, it **does get outrun**
Fut.	I, he, she, it,	I, he, she, it,
	we, you, they **will outrun**	we, you, they **will be outrun**
Past	I, he, she, it,	I, he, she, it **was outrun**
	we, you, they **outran**	we, you, they **were outrun**
Past	I, he, she, it **was outrunning**	I, he, she, it **was being outrun**
Prog.	we, you, they **were outrunning**	we, you, they **were being outrun**
Past	I, he, she, it,	I, he, she, it,
Int.	we, you, they **did outrun**	we, you, they **did get outrun**
Pres.	I, we, you, they **have outrun**	I, we, you, they **have been outrun**
Perf.	he, she, it **has outrun**	he, she, it **has been outrun**
Past	I, he, she, it,	I, he, she, it,
Perf.	we, you, they **had outrun**	we, you, they **had been outrun**
Fut.	I, he, she, it, we, you, they	I, he, she, it, we, you, they
Perf.	**will have outrun**	**will have been outrun**

IMPERATIVE MOOD

outrun

be outrun

SUBJUNCTIVE MOOD

Pres.	if I, he, she, it,	if I, he, she, it,
	we, you, they **outrun**	we, you, they **be outrun**
Past	if I, he, she, it,	if I, he, she, it,
	we, you, they **outran**	we, you, they **were outrun**
Fut.	if I, he, she, it,	if I, he, she, it,
	we, you, they **should outrun**	we, you, they **should be outrun**

overcast
(active voice)

be overcast
(passive voice)

Infinitive: **to overcast**
Perfect Infinitive: **to have overcast**
Present Participle: **overcasting**
Past Participle: **overcast**

Infinitive: **to be overcast**
Perfect Infinitive: **to have been overcast**
Present Participle: **being overcast**
Past Participle: **been overcast**

INDICATIVE MOOD

Pres. I, we, you, they **overcast**

he, she, it **overcasts**

I **am overcast**
we, you, they **are overcast**
he, she, it **is overcast**

Pres. **I am overcasting**
Prog. we, you, they **are overcasting**
he, she, it **is overcasting**

I **am being overcast**
we, you, they **are being overcast**
he, she, it **is being overcast**

Pres. I, we, you, they **do overcast**
Int. he, she, it **does overcast**

I, we, you, they **do get overcast**
he, she, it **does get overcast**

Fut. I, he, she, it,
we, you, they **will overcast**

I, he, she, it,
we, you, they **will be overcast**

Past I, he, she, it,
we, you, they **overcast**

I, he, she, it **was overcast**
we, you, they **were overcast**

Past I, he, she, it **was overcasting**
Prog. we, you, they **were overcasting**

I, he, she, it **was being overcast**
we, you, they **were being overcast**

Past I, he, she, it,
Int. we, you, they **did overcast**

I, he, she, it,
we, you, they **did get overcast**

Pres. I, we, you, they **have overcast**
Perf. he, she, it **has overcast**

I, we, you, they **have been overcast**
he, she, it **has been overcast**

Past I, he, she, it,
Perf. we, you, they **had overcast**

I, he, she, it,
we, you, they **had been overcast**

Fut. I, he, she, it, we, you, they
Perf. **will have overcast**

I, he, she, it, we, you, they
will have been overcast

IMPERATIVE MOOD

overcast

be overcast

SUBJUNCTIVE MOOD

Pres. if I, he, she, it,
we, you, they **overcast**

if I, he, she, it,
we, you, they **be overcast**

Past if I, he, she, it,
we, you, they **overcast**

if I, he, she, it,
we, you, they **were overcast**

Fut. if I, he, she, it,
we, you, they **should overcast**

if I, he, she, it,
we, you, they **should be overcast**

Transitive and intransitive.

overcome
(active voice)

be overcome
(passive voice)

Infinitive: **to overcome**
Perfect Infinitive: **to have overcome**
Present Participle: **overcoming**
Past Participle: **overcome**

Infinitive: **to be overcome**
Perfect Infinitive: **to have been overcome**
Present Participle: **being overcome**
Past Participle: **been overcome**

INDICATIVE MOOD

Pres.	I, we, you, they **overcome**	I **am overcome**
		we, you, they **are overcome**
	he, she, it **overcomes**	he, she, it **is overcome**
Pres.	I **am overcoming**	I am being **overcome**
Prog.	we, you, they **are overcoming**	we, you, they **are being overcome**
	he, she, it **is overcoming**	he, she, it **is being overcome**
Pres.	I, we, you, they **do overcome**	I, we, you, they **do get overcome**
Int.	he, she, it **does overcome**	he, she, it **does get overcome**
Fut.	I, he, she, it,	I, he, she, it,
	we, you, they **will overcome**	we, you, they **will be overcome**
Past	I, he, she, it,	I, he, she, it **was overcome**
	we, you, they **overcame**	we, you, they **were overcome**
Past	I, he, she, it **was overcoming**	I, he, she, it **was being overcome**
Prog.	we, you, they **were overcoming**	we, you, they **were being overcome**
Past	I, he, she, it,	I, he, she, it,
Int.	we, you, they **did overcome**	we, you, they **did get overcome**
Pres.	I, we, you, they **have overcome**	I, we, you, they **have been overcome**
Perf.	he, she, it **has overcome**	he, she, it **has been overcome**
Past	I, he, she, it,	I, he, she, it,
Perf.	we, you, they **had overcome**	we, you, they **had been overcome**
Fut.	I, he, she, it, we, you, they	I, he, she, it, we, you, they
Perf.	**will have overcome**	**will have been overcome**

IMPERATIVE MOOD

overcome

be overcome

SUBJUNCTIVE MOOD

Pres.	if I, he, she, it,	if I, he, she, it,
	we, you, they **overcome**	we, you, they **be overcome**
Past	if I, he, she, it,	if I, he, she, it,
	we, you, they **overcame**	we, you, they **were overcome**
Fut.	if I, he, she, it,	if I, he, she, it, we, you, they
	we, you, they **should overcome**	**should be overcome**

Transitive and intransitive.

overeat

Infinitive: **to overeat**
Perfect Infinitive: **to have overeaten**
Present Participle: **overeating**
Past Participle: **overeaten**

INDICATIVE MOOD

Pres.	I, we, you, they **overeat**
	he, she, it **overeats**
Pres. Prog.	I **am overeating**
	we, you, they **are overeating**
	he, she, it **is overeating**
Pres. Int.	I, we, you, they **do overeat**
	he, she, it **does overeat**
Fut.	I, he, she, it, we, you, they **will overeat**
Past	I, he, she, it, we, you, they **overate**
Past Prog.	I, he, she, it **was overeating**
	we, you, they **were overeating**
Past Int.	I, he, she, it, we, you, they **did overeat**
Pres. Perf.	I, we, you, they **have overeaten**
	he, she, it **has overeaten**
Past Perf.	I, he, she, it, we, you, they **had overeaten**
Fut. Perf.	I, he, she, it, we, you, they **will have overeaten**

IMPERATIVE MOOD

overeat

SUBJUNCTIVE MOOD

Pres.	if I, he, she, it, we, you, they **overeat**
Past	if I, he, she, it, we, you, they **overate**
Fut.	if I, he, she, it, we, you, they **should overeat**

overfeed
(active voice)

PRINCIPAL PARTS: **overfeeds, overfeeding, overfed, overfed**

be overfed
(passive voice)

Infinitive: **to overfeed**
Perfect Infinitive: **to have overfed**
Present Participle: **overfeeding**
Past Participle: **overfed**

Infinitive: **to be overfed**
Perfect Infinitive: **to have been overfed**
Present Participle: **being overfed**
Past Participle: **been overfed**

INDICATIVE MOOD

Pres.	I, we, you, they **overfeed**	I **am overfed**
		we, you, they **are overfed**
	he, she, it **overfeeds**	he, she, it **is overfed**
Pres. *Prog.*	I **am overfeeding**	I **am being overfed**
	we, you, they **are overfeeding**	we, you, they **are being overfed**
	he, she, it **is overfeeding**	he, she, it **is being overfed**
Pres. *Int.*	I, we, you, they **do overfeed**	I, we, you, they **do get overfed**
	he, she, it **does overfeed**	he, she, it **does get overfed**
Fut.	I, he, she, it, we, you, they **will overfeed**	I, he, she, it, we, you, they **will be overfed**
Past	I, he, she, it, we, you, they **overfed**	I, he, she, it **was overfed** we, you, they **were overfed**
Past *Prog.*	I, he, she, it **was overfeeding** we, you, they **were overfeeding**	I, he, she, it **was being overfed** we, you, they **were being overfed**
Past *Int.*	I, he, she, it, we, you, they **did overfeed**	I, he, she, it, we, you, they **did get overfed**
Pres. *Perf.*	I, we, you, they **have overfed** he, she, it **has overfed**	I, we, you, they **have been overfed** he, she, it **has been overfed**
Past *Perf.*	I, he, she, it, we, you, they **had overfed**	I, he, she, it, we, you, they **had been overfed**
Fut. *Perf.*	I, he, she, it, we, you, they **will have overfed**	I, he, she, it, we, you, they **will have been overfed**

IMPERATIVE MOOD

overfeed   **be overfed**

SUBJUNCTIVE MOOD

Pres.	if I, he, she, it, we, you, they **overfeed**	if I, he, she, it, we, you, they **be overfed**
Past	if I, he, she, it, we, you, they **overfed**	if I, he, she, it, we, you, they **were overfed**
Fut.	if I, he, she, it, we, you, they **should overfeed**	if I, he, she, it, we, you, they **should be overfed**

Transitive and intransitive.

262

override
(active voice)

PRINCIPAL PARTS: **overrides, overriding, overrode, overridden**

be overridden
(passive voice)

Infinitive: **to override**
Perfect Infinitive: **to have overridden**
Present Participle: **overriding**
Past Participle: **overridden**

Infinitive: **to be overridden**
Perfect Infinitive: **to have been overridden**
Present Participle: **being overridden**
Past Participle: **been overridden**

INDICATIVE MOOD

Pres.	I, we, you, they **override** he, she, it **overrides**	I **am overridden** we, you, they **are overridden** he, she, it **is overridden**
Pres. *Prog.*	I **am overriding** we, you, they **are overriding** he, she, it **is overriding**	I **am being overridden** we, you, they **are being overridden** he, she, it **is being overridden**
Pres. *Int.*	I, we, you, they **do override** he, she, it **does override**	I, we, you, they **do get overridden** he, she, it **does get overridden**
Fut.	I, he, she, it, we, you, they **will override**	I, he, she, it, we, you, they **will be overridden**
Past	I, he, she, it, we, you, they **overrode**	I, he, she, it **was overridden** we, you, they **were overridden**
Past *Prog.*	I, he, she, it **was overriding** we, you, they **were overriding**	I, he, she, it **was being overridden** we, you, they **were being overridden**
Past *Int.*	I, he, she, it, we, you, they **did override**	I, he, she, it, we, you, they **did get overridden**
Pres. *Perf.*	I, we, you, they **have overridden** he, she, it **has overridden**	I, we, you, they **have been overridden** he, she, it **has been overridden**
Past *Perf.*	I, he, she, it, we, you, they **had overridden**	I, he, she, it, we, you, they **had been overridden**
Fut. *Perf.*	I, he, she, it, we, you, they **will have overridden**	I, he, she, it, we, you, they **will have been overridden**

IMPERATIVE MOOD

override   **be overridden**

SUBJUNCTIVE MOOD

Pres.	if I, he, she, it, we, you, they **override**	if I, he, she, it, we, you, they **be overridden**
Past	if I, he, she, it, we, you, they **overrode**	if I, he, she, it, we, you, they **were overridden**
Fut.	if I, he, she, it, we, you, they **should override**	if I, he, she, it, we, you, they **should be overridden**

overrun
(active voice)

be overrun
(passive voice)

Infinitive: **to overrun**
Perfect Infinitive: **to have overrun**
Present Participle: **overrunning**
Past Participle: **overrun**

Infinitive: **to be overrun**
Perfect Infinitive: **to have been overrun**
Present Participle: **being overrun**
Past Participle: **been overrun**

INDICATIVE MOOD

Pres.	I, we, you, they **overrun**	I **am overrun**
		we, you, they **are overrun**
	he, she, it **overruns**	he, she, it **is overrun**
Pres.	I **am overrunning**	I **am being overrun**
Prog.	we, you, they **are overrunning**	we, you, they **are being overrun**
	he, she, it **is overrunning**	he, she, it **is being overrun**
Pres.	I, we, you, they **do overrun**	I, we, you, they **do get overrun**
Int.	he, she, it **does overrun**	he, she, it **does get overrun**
Fut.	I, he, she, it,	I, he, she, it,
	we, you, they **will overrun**	we, you, they **will be overrun**
Past	I, he, she, it,	I, he, she, it **was overrun**
	we, you, they **overran**	we, you, they **were overrun**
Past	I, he, she, it **was overrunning**	I, he, she, it **was being overrun**
Prog.	we, you, they **were overrunning**	we, you, they **were being overrun**
Past	I, he, she, it,	I, he, she, it,
Int.	we, you, they **did overrun**	we, you, they **did get overrun**
Pres.	I, we, you, they **have overrun**	I, we, you, they **have been overrun**
Perf.	he, she, it **has overrun**	he, she, it **has been overrun**
Past	I, he, she, it,	I, he, she, it,
Perf.	we, you, they **had overrun**	we, you, they **had been overrun**
Fut.	I, he, she, it, we, you, they	I, he, she, it, we, you, they
Perf.	**will have overrun**	**will have been overrun**

IMPERATIVE MOOD

overrun   **be overrun**

SUBJUNCTIVE MOOD

Pres.	if I, he, she, it,	if I, he, she, it,
	we, you, they **overrun**	we, you, they **be overrun**
Past	if I, he, she, it,	if I, he, she, it,
	we, you, they **overran**	we, you, they **were overrun**
Fut.	if I, he, she, it,	if I, he, she, it,
	we, you, they **should overrun**	we, you, they **should be overrun**

Transitive and intransitive.

264

overshoot
(active voice)

PRINCIPAL PARTS: **overshoots, overshooting, overshot, overshot**

be overshot
(passive voice)

Infinitive: **to overshoot**
Perfect Infinitive: **to have overshot**
Present Participle: **overshooting**
Past Participle: **overshot**

Infinitive: **to be overshot**
Perfect Infinitive: **to have been overshot**
Present Participle: **being overshot**
Past Participle: **been overshot**

INDICATIVE MOOD

Pres.	I, we, you, they **overshoot**		I **am overshot**
			we, you, they **are overshot**
	he, she, it **overshoots**		he, she, it **is overshot**
Pres.	I **am overshooting**		I **am being overshot**
Prog.	we, you, they **are overshooting**		we, you, they **are being overshot**
	he, she, it **is overshooting**		he, she, it **is being overshot**
Pres.	I, we, you, they **do overshoot**		I, we, you, they **do get overshot**
Int.	he, she, it **does overshoot**		he, she, it **does get overshot**
Fut.	I, he, she, it,		I, he, she, it,
	we, you, they **will overshoot**		we, you, they **will be overshot**
Past	I, he, she, it,		I, he, she, it **was overshot**
	we, you, they **overshot**		we, you, they **were overshot**
Past	I, he, she, it **was overshooting**		I, he, she, it **was being overshot**
Prog.	we, you, they **were overshooting**		we, you, they **were being overshot**
Past	I, he, she, it,		I, he, she, it,
Int.	we, you, they **did overshoot**		we, you, they **did get overshot**
Pres.	I, we, you, they **have overshot**		I, we, you, they **have been overshot**
Perf.	he, she, it **has overshot**		he, she, it **has been overshot**
Past	I, he, she, it,		I, he, she, it,
Perf.	we, you, they **had overshot**		we, you, they **had been overshot**
Fut.	I, he, she, it, we, you, they		I, he, she, it, we, you, they
Perf.	**will have overshot**		**will have been overshot**

IMPERATIVE MOOD

overshoot   **be overshot**

SUBJUNCTIVE MOOD

Pres.	if I, he, she, it,		if I, he, she, it,
	we, you, they **overshoot**		we, you, they **be overshot**
Past	if I, he, she, it,		if I, he, she, it,
	we, you, they **overshot**		we, you, they **were overshot**
Fut.	if I, he, she, it,		if I, he, she, it,
	we, you, they **should overshoot**		we, you, they **should be overshot**

Transitive and intransitive.

oversleep
(active voice)

be overslept
(passive voice)

Infinitive: **to oversleep**
Perfect Infinitive: **to have overslept**
Present Participle: **oversleeping**
Past Participle: **overslept**

Infinitive: **to be overslept**
Perfect Infinitive: **to have been overslept**
Present Participle: **being overslept**
Past Participle: **been overslept**

INDICATIVE MOOD

Pres.	I, we, you, they **oversleep**	I **am overslept**
		we, you, they **are overslept**
	he, she, it **oversleeps**	he, she, it **is overslept**
Pres.	I **am oversleeping**	I **am being overslept**
Prog.	we, you, they **are oversleeping**	we, you, they **are being overslept**
	he, she, it **is oversleeping**	he, she, it **is being overslept**
Pres.	I, we, you, they **do oversleep**	I, we, you, they **do get overslept**
Int.	he, she, it **does oversleep**	he, she, it **does get overslept**
Fut.	I, he, she, it,	I, he, she, it,
	we, you, they **will oversleep**	we, you, they **will be overslept**
Past	I, he, she, it,	I, he, she, it **was overslept**
	we, you, they **overslept**	we, you, they **were overslept**
Past	I, he, she, it **was oversleeping**	I, he, she, it **was being overslept**
Prog.	we, you, they **were oversleeping**	we, you, they **were being overslept**
Past	I, he, she, it,	I, he, she, it,
Int.	we, you, they **did oversleep**	we, you, they **did get overslept**
Pres.	I, we, you, they **have overslept**	I, we, you, they **have been overslept**
Perf.	he, she, it **has overslept**	he, she, it **has been overslept**
Past	I, he, she, it,	I, he, she, it,
Perf.	we, you, they **had overslept**	we, you, they **had been overslept**
Fut.	I, he, she, it, we, you, they	I, he, she, it, we, you, they
Perf.	**will have overslept**	**will have been overslept**

IMPERATIVE MOOD

oversleep   **be overslept**

SUBJUNCTIVE MOOD

Pres.	if I, he, she, it,	if I, he, she, it,
	we, you, they **oversleep**	we, you, they **be overslept**
Past	if I, he, she, it,	if I, he, she, it,
	we, you, they **overslept**	we, you, they **were overslept**
Fut.	if I, he, she, it,	if I, he, she, it,
	we, you, they **should oversleep**	we, you, they **should be overslept**

Intransitive and transitive.

overtake
(active voice)

be overtaken
(passive voice)

Infinitive: **to overtake**
Perfect Infinitive: **to have overtaken**
Present Participle: **overtaking**
Past Participle: **overtaken**

Infinitive: **to be overtaken**
Perfect Infinitive: **to have been overtaken**
Present Participle: **being overtaken**
Past Participle: **been overtaken**

INDICATIVE MOOD

Pres.	I, we, you, they **overtake**	I **am overtaken**
		we, you, they **are overtaken**
	he, she, it **overtakes**	he, she, it **is overtaken**
Pres.	I **am overtaking**	I **am being overtaken**
Prog.	we, you, they **are overtaking**	we, you, they **are being overtaken**
	he, she, it **is overtaking**	he, she, it **is being overtaken**
Pres.	I, we, you, they **do overtake**	I, we, you, they **do get overtaken**
Int.	he, she, it **does overtake**	he, she, it **does get overtaken**
Fut.	I, he, she, it,	I, he, she, it,
	we, you, they **will overtake**	we, you, they **will be overtaken**
Past	I, he, she, it,	I, he, she, it **was overtaken**
	we, you, they **overtook**	we, you, they **were overtaken**
Past	I, he, she, it **was overtaking**	I, he, she, it **was being overtaken**
Prog.	we, you, they **were overtaking**	we, you, they **were being overtaken**
Past	I, he, she, it,	I, he, she, it,
Int.	we, you, they **did overtake**	we, you, they **did get overtaken**
Pres.	I, we, you, they **have overtaken**	I, we, you, they **have been overtaken**
Perf.	he, she, it **has overtaken**	he, she, it **has been overtaken**
Past	I, he, she, it,	I, he, she, it,
Perf.	we, you, they **had overtaken**	we, you, they **had been overtaken**
Fut.	I, he, she, it, we, you, they	I, he, she, it, we, you, they
Perf.	**will have overtaken**	**will have been overtaken**

IMPERATIVE MOOD

overtake   be overtaken

SUBJUNCTIVE MOOD

Pres.	if I, he, she, it,	if I, he, she, it,
	we, you, they **overtake**	we, you, they **be overtaken**
Past	if I, he, she, it,	if I, he, she, it,
	we, you, they **overtook**	we, you, they **were overtaken**
Fut.	if I, he, she, it,	if I, he, she, it,
	we, you, they **should overtake**	we, you, they **should be overtaken**

overthrow
(active voice)

PRINCIPAL PARTS: **overthrows,
overthrowing, overthrew, overthrown**

be overthrown
(passive voice)

Infinitive: **to overthrow**
Perfect Infinitive: **to have overthrown**
Present Participle: **overthrowing**
Past Participle: **overthrown**

Infinitive: **to be overthrown**
Perfect Infinitive: **to have been overthrown**
Present Participle: **being overthrown**
Past Participle: **been overthrown**

INDICATIVE MOOD

Pres.	I, we, you, they **overthrow**	I **am overthrown** we, you, they **are overthrown**
	he, she, it **overthrows**	he, she, it **is overthrown**
Pres. *Prog.*	I **am overthrowing** we, you, they **are overthrowing** he, she, it **is overthrowing**	I **am being overthrown** we, you, they **are being overthrown** he, she, it **is being overthrown**
Pres. *Int.*	I, we, you, they **do overthrow** he, she, it **does overthrow**	I, we, you, they **do get overthrown** he, she, it **does get overthrown**
Fut.	I, he, she, it, we, you, they **will overthrow**	I, he, she, it, we, you, they **will be overthrown**
Past	I, he, she, it, we, you, they **overthrew**	I, he, she, it **was overthrown** we, you, they **were overthrown**
Past *Prog.*	I, he, she, it **was overthrowing** we, you, they **were overthrowing**	I, he, she, it **was being overthrown** we, you, they **were being overthrown**
Past *Int.*	I, he, she, it, we, you, they **did overthrow**	I, he, she, it, we, you, they **did get overthrown**
Pres. *Perf.*	I, we, you, they **have overthrown** he, she, it **has overthrown**	I, we, you, they **have been overthrown** he, she, it **has been overthrown**
Past *Perf.*	I, he, she, it, we, you, they **had overthrown**	I, he, she, it, we, you, they **had been overthrown**
Fut. *Perf.*	I, he, she, it, we, you, they **will have overthrown**	I, he, she, it, we, you, they **will have been overthrown**

IMPERATIVE MOOD

overthrow

be overthrown

SUBJUNCTIVE MOOD

Pres.	if I, he, she, it, we, you, they **overthrow**	if I, he, she, it, we, you, they **be overthrown**
Past	if I, he, she, it, we, you, they **overthrew**	if I, he, she, it, we, you, they **were overthrown**
Fut.	if I, he, she, it, we, you, they **should overthrow**	if I, he, she, it, we, you, they **should be overthrown**

PRINCIPAL PARTS: **panics, panicking, panicked, panicked**

Infinitive: **to panic**
Perfect Infinitive: **to have panicked**
Present Participle: **panicking**
Past Participle: **panicked**

Infinitive: **to be panicked**
Perfect Infinitive: **to have been panicked**
Present Participle: **being panicked**
Past Participle: **been panicked**

INDICATIVE MOOD

Pres.	I, we, you, they **panic**	I **am panicked**
		we, you, they **are panicked**
	he, she, it **panics**	he, she, it **is panicked**
Pres.	I **am panicking**	I **am being panicked**
Prog.	we, you, they **are panicking**	we, you, they **are being panicked**
	he, she, it **is panicking**	he, she, it **is being panicked**
Pres.	I, we, you, they **do panic**	I, we, you, they **do get panicked**
Int.	he, she, it **does panic**	he, she, it **does get panicked**
Fut.	I, he, she, it,	I, he, she, it,
	we, you, they **will panic**	we, you, they **will be panicked**
Past	I, he, she, it,	I, he, she, it **was panicked**
	we, you, they **panicked**	we, you, they **were panicked**
Past	I, he, she, it **was panicking**	I, he, she, it **was being panicked**
Prog.	we, you, they **were panicking**	we, you, they **were being panicked**
Past	I, he, she, it,	I, he, she, it,
Int.	we, you, they **did panic**	we, you, they **did get panicked**
Pres.	I, we, you, they **have panicked**	I, we, you, they **have been panicked**
Perf.	he, she, it **has panicked**	he, she, it **has been panicked**
Past	I, he, she, it,	I, he, she, it,
Perf.	we, you, they **had panicked**	we, you, they **had been panicked**
Fut.	I, he, she, it, we, you, they	I, he, she, it, we, you, they
Perf.	**will have panicked**	**will have been panicked**

IMPERATIVE MOOD

panic

be panicked

SUBJUNCTIVE MOOD

Pres.	if I, he, she, it,	if I, he, she, it,
	we, you, they **panic**	we, you, they **be panicked**
Past	if I, he, she, it,	if I, he, she, it,
	we, you, they **panicked**	we, you, they **were panicked**
Fut.	if I, he, she, it,	if I, he, she, it,
	we, you, they **should panic**	we, you, they **should be panicked**

Transitive and intransitive.

partake
(active voice)

PRINCIPAL PARTS: **partakes, partaking, partook, partaken**

be partaken
(passive voice)

Infinitive: **to partake**
Perfect Infinitive: **to have partaken**
Present Participle: **partaking**
Past Participle: **partaken**

Infinitive: **to be partaken**
Perfect Infinitive: **to have been partaken**
Present Participle: **being partaken**
Past Participle: **been partaken**

INDICATIVE MOOD

Pres.	I, we, you, they **partake**	I **am partaken**
		we, you, they **are partaken**
	he, she, it **partakes**	he, she, it **is partaken**
Pres.	I **am partaking**	I **am being partaken**
Prog.	we, you, they **are partaking**	we, you, they **are being partaken**
	he, she, it **is partaking**	he, she, it **is being partaken**
Pres.	I, we, you, they **do partake**	I, we, you, they **do get partaken**
Int.	he, she, it **does partake**	he, she, it **does get partaken**
Fut.	I, he, she, it,	I, he, she, it,
	we, you, they **will partake**	we, you, they **will be partaken**
Past	I, he, she, it,	I, he, she, it **was partaken**
	we, you, they **partook**	we, you, they **were partaken**
Past	I, he, she, it **was partaking**	I, he, she, it **was being partaken**
Prog.	we, you, they **were partaking**	we, you, they **were being partaken**
Past	I, he, she, it,	I, he, she, it,
Int.	we, you, they **did partake**	we, you, they **did get partaken**
Pres.	I, we, you, they **have partaken**	I, we, you, they **have been partaken**
Perf.	he, she, it **has partaken**	he, she, it **has been partaken**
Past	I, he, she, it,	I, he, she, it,
Perf.	we, you, they **had partaken**	we, you, they **had been partaken**
Fut.	I, he, she, it, we, you, they	I, he, she, it, we, you, they
Perf.	**will have partaken**	**will have been partaken**

IMPERATIVE MOOD

partake　　　　　　　　　**be partaken**

SUBJUNCTIVE MOOD

Pres.	if I, he, she, it,	if I, he, she, it,
	we, you, they **partake**	we, you, they **be partaken**
Past	if I, he, she, it,	if I, he, she, it,
	we, you, they **partook**	we, you, they **were partaken**
Fut.	if I, he, she, it,	if I, he, she, it,
	we, you, they **should partake**	we, you, they **should be partaken**

Intransitive and transitive.

pass
(active voice)

be passed
(passive voice)

Infinitive: **to pass**
Perfect Infinitive: **to have passed**
Present Participle: **passing**
Past Participle: **passed**

Infinitive: **to be passed**
Perfect Infinitive: **to have been passed**
Present Participle: **being passed**
Past Participle: **been passed**

INDICATIVE MOOD

Pres.	I, we, you, they **pass**	I am **passed**
		we, you, they **are passed**
	he, she, it **passes**	he, she, it **is passed**
Pres. *Prog.*	**I am passing**	**I am being passed**
	we, you, they **are passing**	we, you, they **are being passed**
	he, she, it **is passing**	he, she, it **is being passed**
Pres. *Int.*	I, we, you, they **do pass**	I, we, you, they **do get passed**
	he, she, it **does pass**	he, she, it **does get passed**
Fut.	I, he, she, it, we, you, they **will pass**	I, he, she, it, we, you, they **will be passed**
Past	I, he, she, it, we, you, they **passed**	I, he, she, it **was passed** we, you, they **were passed**
Past *Prog.*	I, he, she, it **was passing** we, you, they **were passing**	I, he, she, it **was being passed** we, you, they **were being passed**
Past *Int.*	I, he, she, it, we, you, they **did pass**	I, he, she, it, we, you, they **did get passed**
Pres. *Perf.*	I, we, you, they **have passed** he, she, it **has passed**	I, we, you, they **have been passed** he, she, it **has been passed**
Past *Perf.*	I, he, she, it, we, you, they **had passed**	I, he, she, it, we, you, they **had been passed**
Fut. *Perf.*	I, he, she, it, we, you, they **will have passed**	I, he, she, it, we, you, they **will have been passed**

IMPERATIVE MOOD

pass

be passed

SUBJUNCTIVE MOOD

Pres.	if I, he, she, it, we, you, they **pass**	if I, he, she, it, we, you, they **be passed**
Past	if I, he, she, it, we, you, they **passed**	if I, he, she, it, we, you, they **were passed**
Fut.	if I, he, she, it, we, you, they **should pass**	if I, he, she, it, we, you, they **should be passed**

Intransitive and transitive.

pay
(active voice)

PRINCIPAL PARTS: **pays, paying, paid, paid**

be paid
(passive voice)

Infinitive: **to pay**
Perfect Infinitive: **to have paid**
Present Participle: **paying**
Past Participle: **paid**

Infinitive: **to be paid**
Perfect Infinitive: **to have been paid**
Present Participle: **being paid**
Past Participle: **been paid**

INDICATIVE MOOD

Pres.	I, we, you, they **pay** he, she, it **pays**	I **am paid** we, you, they **are paid** he, she, it **is paid**
Pres. Prog.	I **am paying** we, you, they **are paying** he, she, it **is paying**	I **am being paid** we, you, they **are being paid** he, she, it **is being paid**
Pres. Int.	I, we, you, they **do pay** he, she, it **does pay**	I, we, you, they **do get paid** he, she, it **does get paid**
Fut.	I, he, she, it, we, you, they **will pay**	I, he, she, it, we, you, they **will be paid**
Past	I, he, she, it, we, you, they **paid**	I, he, she, it **was paid** we, you, they **were paid**
Past Prog.	I, he, she, it **was paying** we, you, they **were paying**	I, he, she, it **was being paid** we, you, they **were being paid**
Past Int.	I, he, she, it, we, you, they **did pay**	I, he, she, it, we, you, they **did get paid**
Pres. Perf.	I, we, you, they **have paid** he, she, it **has paid**	I, we, you, they **have been paid** he, she, it **has been paid**
Past Perf.	I, he, she, it, we, you, they **had paid**	I, he, she, it, we, you, they **had been paid**
Fut. Perf.	I, he, she, it, we, you, they **will have paid**	I, he, she, it, we, you, they **will have been paid**

IMPERATIVE MOOD

pay   **be paid**

SUBJUNCTIVE MOOD

Pres.	if I, he, she, it, we, you, they **pay**	if I, he, she, it, we, you, they **be paid**
Past	if I, he, she, it, we, you, they **paid**	if I, he, she, it, we, you, they **were paid**
Fut.	if I, he, she, it, we, you, they **should pay**	if I, he, she, it, we, you, they **should be paid**

Transitive and intransitive.

pen
(active voice)

PRINCIPAL PARTS: **pens, penning, penned, penned**

be penned
(passive voice)

Infinitive: **to pen**
Perfect Infinitive: **to have penned**
Present Participle: **penning**
Past Participle: **penned**

Infinitive: **to be penned**
Perfect Infinitive: **to have been penned**
Present Participle: **being penned**
Past Participle: **been penned**

INDICATIVE MOOD

Pres.	I, we, you, they **pen**	I am **penned**
		we, you, they **are penned**
	he, she, it **pens**	he, she, it **is penned**
Pres. *Prog.*	I am **penning**	I am **being penned**
	we, you, they **are penning**	we, you, they **are being penned**
	he, she, it **is penning**	he, she, it **is being penned**
Pres. *Int.*	I, we, you, they **do pen**	I, we, you, they **do get penned**
	he, she, it **does pen**	he, she, it **does get penned**
Fut.	I, he, she, it, we, you, they **will pen**	I, he, she, it, we, you, they **will be penned**
Past	I, he, she, it, we, you, they **penned**	I, he, she, it **was penned** we, you, they **were penned**
Past *Prog.*	I, he, she, it **was penning** we, you, they **were penning**	I, he, she, it **was being penned** we, you, they **were being penned**
Past *Int.*	I, he, she, it, we, you, they **did pen**	I, he, she, it, we, you, they **did get penned**
Pres. *Perf.*	I, we, you, they **have penned**	I, we, you, they **have been penned**
	he, she, it **has penned**	he, she, it **has been penned**
Past *Perf.*	I, he, she, it, we, you, they **had penned**	I, he, she, it, we, you, they **had been penned**
Fut. *Perf.*	I, he, she, it, we, you, they **will have penned**	I, he, she, it, we, you, they **will have been penned**

IMPERATIVE MOOD

pen

be penned

SUBJUNCTIVE MOOD

Pres.	if I, he, she, it, we, you, they **pen**	if I, he, she, it, we, you, they **be penned**
Past	if I, he, she, it, we, you, they **penned**	if I, he, she, it, we, you, they **were penned**
Fut.	if I, he, she, it, we, you, they **should pen**	if I, he, she, it, we, you, they **should be penned**

PEN, PENNED means "write or compose." There is another verb PEN, PENNED, or PENT meaning to "confine in a pen."

permit
(active voice)

be permitted
(passive voice)

Infinitive: **to permit**
Perfect Infinitive: **to have permitted**
Present Participle: **permitting**
Past Participle: **permitted**

Infinitive: **to be permitted**
Perfect Infinitive: **to have been permitted**
Present Participle: **being permitted**
Past Participle: **been permitted**

INDICATIVE MOOD

Pres.	I, we, you, they **permit**	I **am permitted**
		we, you, they **are permitted**
	he, she, it **permits**	he, she, it **is permitted**
Pres.	I **am permitting**	I **am being permitted**
Prog.	we, you, they **are permitting**	we, you, they **are being permitted**
	he, she, it **is permitting**	he, she, it **is being permitted**
Pres.	I, we, you, they **do permit**	I, we, you, they **do get permitted**
Int.	he, she, it **does permit**	he, she, it **does get permitted**
Fut.	I, he, she, it,	I, he, she, it,
	we, you, they **will permit**	we, you, they **will be permitted**
Past	I, he, she, it,	I, he, she, it **was permitted**
	we, you, they **permitted**	we, you, they **were permitted**
Past	I, he, she, it **was permitting**	I, he, she, it **was being permitted**
Prog.	we, you, they **were permitting**	we, you, they **were being permitted**
Past	I, he, she, it,	I, he, she, it,
Int.	we, you, they **did permit**	we, you, they **did get permitted**
Pres.	I, we, you, they **have permitted**	I, we, you, they **have been permitted**
Perf.	he, she, it **has permitted**	he, she, it **has been permitted**
Past	I, he, she, it,	I, he, she, it,
Perf.	we, you, they **had permitted**	we, you, they **had been permitted**
Fut.	I, he, she, it, we, you, they	I, he, she, it, we, you, they
Perf.	**will have permitted**	**will have been permitted**

IMPERATIVE MOOD

permit   **be permitted**

SUBJUNCTIVE MOOD

Pres.	if I, he, she, it,	if I, he, she, it,
	we, you, they **permit**	we, you, they **be permitted**
Past	if I, he, she, it,	if I, he, she, it,
	we, you, they **permitted**	we, you, they **were permitted**
Fut.	if I, he, she, it,	if I, he, she, it,
	we, you, they **should permit**	we, you, they **should be permitted**

Transitive and intransitive.

pick
(active voice)

PRINCIPAL PARTS: **picks, picking, picked, picked**

be picked
(passive voice)

Infinitive: **to pick**
Perfect Infinitive: **to have picked**
Present Participle: **picking**
Past Participle: **picked**

Infinitive: **to be picked**
Perfect Infinitive: **to have been picked**
Present Participle: **being picked**
Past Participle: **been picked**

INDICATIVE MOOD

Pres.	I, we, you, they **pick** he, she, it **picks**	I **am picked** we, you, they **are picked** he, she, it **is picked**
Pres. *Prog.*	I **am picking** we, you, they **are picking** he, she, it **is picking**	I **am being picked** we, you, they **are being picked** he, she, it **is being picked**
Pres. *Int.*	I, we, you, they **do pick** he, she, it **does pick**	I, we, you, they **do get picked** he, she, it **does get picked**
Fut.	I, he, she, it, we, you, they **will pick**	I, he, she, it, we, you, they **will be picked**
Past	I, he, she, it, we, you, they **picked**	I, he, she, it **was picked** we, you, they **were picked**
Past *Prog.*	I, he, she, it **was picking** we, you, they **were picking**	I, he, she, it **was being picked** we, you, they **were being picked**
Past *Int.*	I, he, she, it, we, you, they **did pick**	I, he, she, it, we, you, they **did get picked**
Pres. *Perf.*	I, we, you, they **have picked** he, she, it **has picked**	I, we, you, they **have been picked** he, she, it **has been picked**
Past *Perf.*	I, he, she, it, we, you, they **had picked**	I, he, she, it, we, you, they **had been picked**
Fut. *Perf.*	I, he, she, it, we, you, they **will have picked**	I, he, she, it, we, you, they **will have been picked**

IMPERATIVE MOOD

pick　　　　　　**be picked**

SUBJUNCTIVE MOOD

Pres.	if I, he, she, it, we, you, they **pick**	if I, he, she, it, we, you, they **be picked**
Past	if I, he, she, it, we, you, they **picked**	if I, he, she, it, we, you, they **were picked**
Fut.	if I, he, she, it, we, you, they **should pick**	if I, he, she, it, we, you, they **should be picked**

Transitive and intransitive.

place
(active voice)

be placed
(passive voice)

Infinitive: **to place**
Perfect Infinitive: **to have placed**
Present Participle: **placing**
Past Participle: **placed**

Infinitive: **to be placed**
Perfect Infinitive: **to have been placed**
Present Participle: **being placed**
Past Participle: **been placed**

INDICATIVE MOOD

Pres.	I, we, you, they **place**	I **am placed**
		we, you, they **are placed**
	he, she, it **places**	he, she, it **is placed**
Pres.	I **am placing**	I **am being placed**
Prog.	we, you, they **are placing**	we, you, they **are being placed**
	he, she, it **is placing**	he, she, it **is being placed**
Pres.	I, we, you, they **do place**	I, we, you, they **do get placed**
Int.	he, she, it **does place**	he, she, it **does get placed**
Fut.	I, he, she, it,	I, he, she, it,
	we, you, they **will place**	we, you, they **will be placed**
Past	I, he, she, it,	I, he, she, it **was placed**
	we, you, they **placed**	we, you, they **were placed**
Past	I, he, she, it **was placing**	I, he, she, it **was being placed**
Prog.	we, you, they **were placing**	we, you, they **were being placed**
Past	I, he, she, it,	I, he, she, it,
Int.	we, you, they **did place**	we, you, they **did get placed**
Pres.	I, we, you, they **have placed**	I, we, you, they **have been placed**
Perf.	he, she, it **has placed**	he, she, it **has been placed**
Past	I, he, she, it,	I, he, she, it,
Perf.	we, you, they **had placed**	we, you, they **had been placed**
Fut.	I, he, she, it, we, you, they	I, he, she, it, we, you, they
Perf.	**will have placed**	**will have been placed**

IMPERATIVE MOOD

place   **be placed**

SUBJUNCTIVE MOOD

Pres.	if I, he, she, it,	if I, he, she, it,
	we, you, they **place**	we, you, they **be placed**
Past	if I, he, she, it,	if I, he, she, it,
	we, you, they **placed**	we, you, they **were placed**
Fut.	if I, he, she, it,	if I, he, she, it,
	we, you, they **should place**	we, you, they **should be placed**

Transitive and intransitive.

plan
(active voice)

be planned
(passive voice)

Infinitive: **to plan**
Perfect Infinitive: **to have planned**
Present Participle: **planning**
Past Participle: **planned**

Infinitive: **to be planned**
Perfect Infinitive: **to have been planned**
Present Participle: **being planned**
Past Participle: **been planned**

INDICATIVE MOOD

Pres.	I, we, you, they **plan**	I **am planned**
		we, you, they **are planned**
	he, she, it **plans**	he, she, it **is planned**
Pres.	I **am planning**	I **am being planned**
Prog.	we, you, they **are planning**	we, you, they **are being planned**
	he, she, it **is planning**	he, she, it **is being planned**
Pres.	I, we, you, they **do plan**	I, we, you, they **do get planned**
Int.	he, she, it **does plan**	he, she, it **does get planned**
Fut.	I, he, she, it,	I, he, she, it,
	we, you, they **will plan**	we, you, they **will be planned**
Past	I, he, she, it,	I, he, she, it **was planned**
	we, you, they **planned**	we, you, they **were planned**
Past	I, he, she, it **was planning**	I, he, she, it **was being planned**
Prog.	we, you, they **were planning**	we, you, they **were being planned**
Past	I, he, she, it,	I, he, she, it,
Int.	we, you, they **did plan**	we, you, they **did get planned**
Pres.	I, we, you, they **have planned**	I, we, you, they **have been planned**
Perf.	he, she, it **has planned**	he, she, it **has been planned**
Past	I, he, she, it,	I, he, she, it,
Perf.	we, you, they **had planned**	we, you, they **had been planned**
Fut.	I, he, she, it, we, you, they	I, he, she, it, we, you, they
Perf.	**will have planned**	**will have been planned**

IMPERATIVE MOOD

plan

be planned

SUBJUNCTIVE MOOD

Pres.	if I, he, she, it,	if I, he, she, it,
	we, you, they **plan**	we, you, they **be planned**
Past	if I, he, she, it,	if I, he, she, it,
	we, you, they **planned**	we, you, they **were planned**
Fut.	if I, he, she, it,	if I, he, she, it,
	we, you, they **should plan**	we, you, they **should be planned**

Transitive and intransitive.

plane
(active voice)

be planed
(passive voice)

Infinitive: **to plane**
Perfect Infinitive: **to have planed**
Present Participle: **planing**
Past Participle: **planed**

Infinitive: **to be planed**
Perfect Infinitive: **to have been planed**
Present Participle: **being planed**
Past Participle: **been planed**

INDICATIVE MOOD

Pres.	I, we, you, they **plane**	I **am planed**
		we, you, they **are planed**
	he, she, it **planes**	he, she, it **is planed**
Pres.	I **am planing**	I **am being planed**
Prog.	we, you, they **are planing**	we, you, they **are being planed**
	he, she, it **is planing**	he, she, it **is being planed**
Pres.	I, we, you, they **do plane**	I, we, you, they **do get planed**
Int.	he, she, it **does plane**	he, she, it **does get planed**
Fut.	I, he, she, it,	I, he, she, it,
	we, you, they **will plane**	we, you, they **will be planed**
Past	I, he, she, it,	I, he, she, it **was planed**
	we, you, they **planed**	we, you, they **were planed**
Past	I, he, she, it **was planing**	I, he, she, it **was being planed**
Prog.	we, you, they **were planing**	we, you, they **were being planed**
Past	I, he, she, it,	I, he, she, it,
Int.	we, you, they **did plane**	we, you, they **did get planed**
Pres.	I, we, you, they **have planed**	I, we, you, they **have been planed**
Perf.	he, she, it **has planed**	he, she, it **has been planed**
Past	I, he, she, it,	I, he, she, it,
Perf.	we, you, they **had planed**	we, you, they **had been planed**
Fut.	I, he, she, it, we, you, they	I, he, she, it, we, you, they
Perf.	**will have planed**	**will have been planed**

IMPERATIVE MOOD

plane   **be planed**

SUBJUNCTIVE MOOD

Pres.	if I, he, she, it,	if I, he, she, it,
	we, you, they **plane**	we, you, they **be planed**
Past	if I, he, she, it,	if I, he, she, it,
	we, you, they **planed**	we, you, they **were planed**
Fut.	if I, he, she, it,	if I, he, she, it,
	we, you, they **should plane**	we, you, they **should be planed**

Transitive and intransitive.

play
(active voice)

be played
(passive voice)

Infinitive: **to play**
Perfect Infinitive: **to have played**
Present Participle: **playing**
Past Participle: **played**

Infinitive: **to be played**
Perfect Infinitive: **to have been played**
Present Participle: **being played**
Past Participle: **been played**

INDICATIVE MOOD

Pres.	I, we, you, they **play**	I **am played**
		we, you, they **are played**
	he, she, it **plays**	he, she, it **is played**
Pres. *Prog.*	I **am playing**	I **am being played**
	we, you, they **are playing**	we, you, they **are being played**
	he, she, it **is playing**	he, she, it **is being played**
Pres. *Int.*	I, we, you, they **do play**	I, we, you, they **do get played**
	he, she, it **does play**	he, she, it **does get played**
Fut.	I, he, she, it, we, you, they **will play**	I, he, she, it, we, you, they **will be played**
Past	I, he, she, it, we, you, they **played**	I, he, she, it **was played** we, you, they **were played**
Past *Prog.*	I, he, she, it **was playing** we, you, they **were playing**	I, he, she, it **was being played** we, you, they **were being played**
Past *Int.*	I, he, she, it, we, you, they **did play**	I, he, she, it, we, you, they **did get played**
Pres. *Perf.*	I, we, you, they **have played** he, she, it **has played**	I, we, you, they **have been played** he, she, it **has been played**
Past *Perf.*	I, he, she, it, we, you, they **had played**	I, he, she, it, we, you, they **had been played**
Fut. *Perf.*	I, he, she, it, we, you, they **will have played**	I, he, she, it, we, you, they **will have been played**

IMPERATIVE MOOD

play   **be played**

SUBJUNCTIVE MOOD

Pres.	if I, he, she, it, we, you, they **play**	if I, he, she, it, we, you, they **be played**
Past	if I, he, she, it, we, you, they **played**	if I, he, she, it, we, you, they **were played**
Fut.	if I, he, she, it, we, you, they **should play**	if I, he, she, it, we, you, they **should be played**

Intransitive and transitive.

plead
(active voice)

be pleaded/pled
(passive voice)

Infinitive: **to plead**
Perfect Infinitive: **to have pleaded**
Present Participle: **pleading**
Past Participle: **pleaded**

Infinitive: **to be pleaded**
Perfect Infinitive: **to have been pleaded**
Present Participle: **being pleaded**
Past Participle: **been pleaded**

INDICATIVE MOOD

Pres.	I, we, you, they **plead** he, she, it **pleads**	I **am pleaded** we, you, they **are pleaded** he, she, it **is pleaded**
Pres. *Prog.*	I **am pleading** we, you, they **are pleading** he, she, it **is pleading**	I **am being pleaded** we, you, they **are being pleaded** he, she, it **is being pleaded**
Pres. *Int.*	I, we, you, they **do plead** he, she, it **does plead**	I, we, you, they **do get pleaded** he, she, it **does get pleaded**
Fut.	I, he, she, it, we, you, they **will plead**	I, he, she, it, we, you, they **will be pleaded**
Past	I, he, she, it, we, you, they **pleaded**	I, he, she, it **was pleaded** we, you, they **were pleaded**
Past *Prog.*	I, he, she, it **was pleading** we, you, they **were pleading**	I, he, she, it **was being pleaded** we, you, they **were being pleaded**
Past *Int.*	I, he, she, it, we, you, they **did plead**	I, he, she, it, we, you, they **did get pleaded**
Pres. *Perf.*	I, we, you, they **have pleaded** he, she, it **has pleaded**	I, we, you, they **have been pleaded** he, she, it **has been pleaded**
Past *Perf.*	I, he, she, it, we, you, they **had pleaded**	I, he, she, it, we, you, they **had been pleaded**
Fut. *Perf.*	I, he, she, it, we, you, they **will have pleaded**	I, he, she, it, we, you, they **will have been pleaded**

IMPERATIVE MOOD

plead   **be pleaded**

SUBJUNCTIVE MOOD

Pres.	if I, he, she, it, we, you, they **plead**	if I, he, she, it, we, you, they **be pleaded**
Past	if I, he, she, it, we, you, they **pleaded**	if I, he, she, it, we, you, they **were pleaded**
Fut.	if I, he, she, it, we, you, they **should plead**	if I, he, she, it, we, you, they **should be pleaded**

Intransitive and transitive. The *Oxford Dictionary* accepts the past tense and past participle form PLED as American English. *Merriam Webster's* and *Webster's* recognize the alternate spelling PLEAD.

please
(active voice)

be pleased
(passive voice)

Infinitive: **to please**
Perfect Infinitive: **to have pleased**
Present Participle: **pleasing**
Past Participle: **pleased**

Infinitive: **to be pleased**
Perfect Infinitive: **to have been pleased**
Present Participle: **being pleased**
Past Participle: **been pleased**

INDICATIVE MOOD

Pres.	I, we, you, they **please**	I **am pleased**
		we, you, they **are pleased**
	he, she, it **pleases**	he, she, it **is pleased**
Pres.	I **am pleasing**	I **am being pleased**
Prog.	we, you, they **are pleasing**	we, you, they **are being pleased**
	he, she, it **is pleasing**	he, she, it **is being pleased**
Pres.	I, we, you, they **do please**	I, we, you, they **do get pleased**
Int.	he, she, it **does please**	he, she, it **does get pleased**
Fut.	I, he, she, it, we, you, they **will please**	I, he, she, it, we, you, they **will be pleased**
Past	I, he, she, it, we, you, they **pleased**	I, he, she, it **was pleased** we, you, they **were pleased**
Past	I, he, she, it **was pleasing**	I, he, she, it **was being pleased**
Prog.	we, you, they **were pleasing**	we, you, they **were being pleased**
Past	I, he, she, it, we, you, they **did please**	I, he, she, it, we, you, they **did get pleased**
Int.		
Pres.	I, we, you, they **have pleased**	I, we, you, they **have been pleased**
Perf.	he, she, it **has pleased**	he, she, it **has been pleased**
Past	I, he, she, it, we, you, they **had pleased**	I, he, she, it, we, you, they **had been pleased**
Perf.		
Fut.	I, he, she, it, we, you, they **will have pleased**	I, he, she, it, we, you, they **will have been pleased**
Perf.		

IMPERATIVE MOOD

please　　**be pleased**

SUBJUNCTIVE MOOD

Pres.	if I, he, she, it, we, you, they **please**	if I, he, she, it, we, you, they **be pleased**
Past	if I, he, she, it, we, you, they **pleased**	if I, he, she, it, we, you, they **were pleased**
Fut.	if I, he, she, it, we, you, they **should please**	if I, he, she, it, we, you, they **should be pleased**

Transitive and intransitive.

point
(active voice)

PRINCIPAL PARTS: **points, pointing, pointed, pointed**

be pointed
(passive voice)

Infinitive: **to point**
Perfect Infinitive: **to have pointed**
Present Participle: **pointing**
Past Participle: **pointed**

Infinitive: **to be pointed**
Perfect Infinitive: **to have been pointed**
Present Participle: **being pointed**
Past Participle: **been pointed**

INDICATIVE MOOD

Pres.	I, we, you, they **point** he, she, it **points**	I am **pointed** we, you, they **are pointed** he, she, it **is pointed**
Pres. *Prog.*	I am **pointing** we, you, they **are pointing** he, she, it **is pointing**	I am **being pointed** we, you, they **are being pointed** he, she, it **is being pointed**
Pres. *Int.*	I, we, you, they **do point** he, she, it **does point**	I, we, you, they **do get pointed** he, she, it **does get pointed**
Fut.	I, he, she, it, we, you, they **will point**	I, he, she, it, we, you, they **will be pointed**
Past	I, he, she, it, we, you, they **pointed**	I, he, she, it **was pointed** we, you, they **were pointed**
Past *Prog.*	I, he, she, it **was pointing** we, you, they **were pointing**	I, he, she, it **was being pointed** we, you, they **were being pointed**
Past *Int.*	I, he, she, it, we, you, they **did point**	I, he, she, it, we, you, they **did get pointed**
Pres. *Perf.*	I, we, you, they **have pointed** he, she, it **has pointed**	I, we, you, they **have been pointed** he, she, it **has been pointed**
Past *Perf.*	I, he, she, it, we, you, they **had pointed**	I, he, she, it, we, you, they **had been pointed**
Fut. *Perf.*	I, he, she, it, we, you, they **will have pointed**	I, he, she, it, we, you, they **will have been pointed**

IMPERATIVE MOOD

point **be pointed**

SUBJUNCTIVE MOOD

Pres.	if I, he, she, it, we, you, they **point**	if I, he, she, it, we, you, they **be pointed**
Past	if I, he, she, it, we, you, they **pointed**	if I, he, she, it, we, you, they **were pointed**
Fut.	if I, he, she, it, we, you, they **should point**	if I, he, she, it, we, you, they **should be pointed**

Transitive and intransitive.

precede
(active voice)

PRINCIPAL PARTS: **precedes, preceding, preceded, preceded**

be preceded
(passive voice)

Infinitive: **to precede**
Perfect Infinitive: **to have preceded**
Present Participle: **preceding**
Past Participle: **preceded**

Infinitive: **to be preceded**
Perfect Infinitive: **to have been preceded**
Present Participle: **being preceded**
Past Participle: **been preceded**

INDICATIVE MOOD

Pres.	I, we, you, they **precede** he, she, it **precedes**	I **am preceded** we, you, they **are preceded** he, she, it **is preceded**
Pres. *Prog.*	I **am preceding** we, you, they **are preceding** he, she, it **is preceding**	I **am being preceded** we, you, they **are being preceded** he, she, it **is being preceded**
Pres. *Int.*	I, we, you, they **do precede** he, she, it **does precede**	I, we, you, they **do get preceded** he, she, it **does get preceded**
Fut.	I, he, she, it, we, you, they **will precede**	I, he, she, it, we, you, they **will be preceded**
Past	I, he, she, it, we, you, they **preceded**	I, he, she, it **was preceded** we, you, they **were preceded**
Past *Prog.*	I, he, she, it **was preceding** we, you, they **were preceding**	I, he, she, it **was being preceded** we, you, they **were being preceded**
Past *Int.*	I, he, she, it, we, you, they **did precede**	I, he, she, it, we, you, they **did get preceded**
Pres. *Perf.*	I, we, you, they **have preceded** he, she, it **has preceded**	I, we, you, they **have been preceded** he, she, it **has been preceded**
Past *Perf.*	I, he, she, it, we, you, they **had preceded**	I, he, she, it, we, you, they **had been preceded**
Fut. *Perf.*	I, he, she, it, we, you, they **will have preceded**	I, he, she, it, we, you, they **will have been preceded**

IMPERATIVE MOOD

precede

be preceded

SUBJUNCTIVE MOOD

Pres.	if I, he, she, it, we, you, they **precede**	if I, he, she, it, we, you, they **be preceded**
Past	if I, he, she, it, we, you, they **preceded**	if I, he, she, it, we, you, they **were preceded**
Fut.	if I, he, she, it, we, you, they **should precede**	if I, he, she, it, we, you, they **should be preceded**

Transitive and intransitive.

prefer
(active voice)

PRINCIPAL PARTS: **prefers, preferring, preferred, preferred**

be preferred
(passive voice)

Infinitive: **to prefer**
Perfect Infinitive: **to have preferred**
Present Participle: **preferring**
Past Participle: **preferred**

Infinitive: **to be preferred**
Perfect Infinitive: **to have been preferred**
Present Participle: **being preferred**
Past Participle: **been preferred**

INDICATIVE MOOD

Pres.	I, we, you, they **prefer** he, she, it **prefers**	I **am preferred** we, you, they **are preferred** he, she, it **is preferred**
Pres. *Prog.*	I **am preferring** we, you, they **are preferring** he, she, it **is preferring**	I **am being preferred** we, you, they **are being preferred** he, she, it **is being preferred**
Pres. *Int.*	I, we, you, they **do prefer** he, she, it **does prefer**	I, we, you, they **do get preferred** he, she, it **does get preferred**
Fut.	I, he, she, it, we, you, they **will prefer**	I, he, she, it, we, you, they **will be preferred**
Past	I, he, she, it, we, you, they **preferred**	I, he, she, it **was preferred** we, you, they **were preferred**
Past *Prog.*	I, he, she, it **was preferring** we, you, they **were preferring**	I, he, she, it **was being preferred** we, you, they **were being preferred**
Past *Int.*	I, he, she, it, we, you, they **did prefer**	I, he, she, it, we, you, they **did get preferred**
Pres. *Perf.*	I, we, you, they **have preferred** he, she, it **has preferred**	I, we, you, they **have been preferred** he, she, it **has been preferred**
Past *Perf.*	I, he, she, it, we, you, they **had preferred**	I, he, she, it, we, you, they **had been preferred**
Fut. *Perf.*	I, he, she, it, we, you, they **will have preferred**	I, he, she, it, we, you, they **will have been preferred**

IMPERATIVE MOOD

prefer   **be preferred**

SUBJUNCTIVE MOOD

Pres.	if I, he, she, it, we, you, they **prefer**	if I, he, she, it, we, you, they **be preferred**
Past	if I, he, she, it, we, you, they **preferred**	if I, he, she, it, we, you, they **were preferred**
Fut.	if I, he, she, it, we, you, they **should prefer**	if I, he, she, it, we, you, they **should be preferred**

prepare
(active voice)

PRINCIPAL PARTS: **prepares, preparing, prepared, prepared**

be prepared
(passive voice)

Infinitive: **to prepare**
Perfect Infinitive: **to have prepared**
Present Participle: **preparing**
Past Participle: **prepared**

Infinitive: **to be prepared**
Perfect Infinitive: **to have been prepared**
Present Participle: **being prepared**
Past Participle: **been prepared**

INDICATIVE MOOD

Pres.	I, we, you, they **prepare**	I **am prepared**
		we, you, they **are prepared**
	he, she, it **prepares**	he, she, it **is prepared**
Pres.	I **am preparing**	I **am being prepared**
Prog.	we, you, they **are preparing**	we, you, they **are being prepared**
	he, she, it **is preparing**	he, she, it **is being prepared**
Pres.	I, we, you, they **do prepare**	I, we, you, they **do get prepared**
Int.	he, she, it **does prepare**	he, she, it **does get prepared**
Fut.	I, he, she, it,	I, he, she, it,
	we, you, they **will prepare**	we, you, they **will be prepared**
Past	I, he, she, it,	I, he, she, it **was prepared**
	we, you, they **prepared**	we, you, they **were prepared**
Past	I, he, she, it **was preparing**	I, he, she, it **was being prepared**
Prog.	we, you, they **were preparing**	we, you, they **were being prepared**
Past	I, he, she, it,	I, he, she, it,
Int.	we, you, they **did prepare**	we, you, they **did get prepared**
Pres.	I, we, you, they **have prepared**	I, we, you, they **have been prepared**
Perf.	he, she, it **has prepared**	he, she, it **has been prepared**
Past	I, he, she, it,	I, he, she, it,
Perf.	we, you, they **had prepared**	we, you, they **had been prepared**
Fut.	I, he, she, it, we, you, they	I, he, she, it, we, you, they
Perf.	**will have prepared**	**will have been prepared**

IMPERATIVE MOOD

prepare

be prepared

SUBJUNCTIVE MOOD

Pres.	if I, he, she, it,	if I, he, she, it,
	we, you, they **prepare**	we, you, they **be prepared**
Past	if I, he, she, it,	if I, he, she, it,
	we, you, they **prepared**	we, you, they **were prepared**
Fut.	if I, he, she, it,	if I, he, she, it,
	we, you, they **should prepare**	we, you, they **should be prepared**

Transitive and intransitive.

present
(active voice)

be presented
(passive voice)

Infinitive: **to present**
Perfect Infinitive: **to have presented**
Present Participle: **presenting**
Past Participle: **presented**

Infinitive: **to be presented**
Perfect Infinitive: **to have been presented**
Present Participle: **being presented**
Past Participle: **been presented**

INDICATIVE MOOD

Pres.	I, we, you, they **present**	I **am presented**
		we, you, they **are presented**
	he, she, it **presents**	he, she, it **is presented**
Pres.	I **am presenting**	I **am being presented**
Prog.	we, you, they **are presenting**	we, you, they **are being presented**
	he, she, it **is presenting**	he, she, it **is being presented**
Pres.	I, we, you, they **do present**	I, we, you, they **do get presented**
Int.	he, she, it **does present**	he, she, it **does get presented**
Fut.	I, he, she, it,	I, he, she, it,
	we, you, they **will present**	we, you, they **will be presented**
Past	I, he, she, it,	I, he, she, it **was presented**
	we, you, they **presented**	we, you, they **were presented**
Past	I, he, she, it **was presenting**	I, he, she, it **was being presented**
Prog.	we, you, they **were presenting**	we, you, they **were being presented**
Past	I, he, she, it,	I, he, she, it,
Int.	we, you, they **did present**	we, you, they **did get presented**
Pres.	I, we, you, they **have presented**	I, we, you, they **have been presented**
Perf.	he, she, it **has presented**	he, she, it **has been presented**
Past	I, he, she, it,	I, he, she, it,
Perf.	we, you, they **had presented**	we, you, they **had been presented**
Fut.	I, he, she, it, we, you, they	I, he, she, it, we, you, they
Perf.	**will have presented**	**will have been presented**

IMPERATIVE MOOD

present   **be presented**

SUBJUNCTIVE MOOD

Pres.	if I, he, she, it,	if I, he, she, it,
	we, you, they **present**	we, you, they **be presented**
Past	if I, he, she, it,	if I, he, she, it,
	we, you, they **presented**	we, you, they **were presented**
Fut.	if I, he, she, it,	if I, he, she, it,
	we, you, they **should present**	we, you, they **should be presented**

prevent
(active voice)

be prevented
(passive voice)

Infinitive: **to prevent**
Perfect Infinitive: **to have prevented**
Present Participle: **preventing**
Past Participle: **prevented**

Infinitive: **to be prevented**
Perfect Infinitive: **to have been prevented**
Present Participle: **being prevented**
Past Participle: **been prevented**

INDICATIVE MOOD

Pres.	I, we, you, they **prevent**	I **am prevented**
		we, you, they **are prevented**
	he, she, it **prevents**	he, she, it **is prevented**
Pres.	I **am preventing**	I **am being prevented**
Prog.	we, you, they **are preventing**	we, you, they **are being prevented**
	he, she, it **is preventing**	he, she, it **is being prevented**
Pres.	I, we, you, they **do prevent**	I, we, you, they **do get prevented**
Int.	he, she, it **does prevent**	he, she, it **does get prevented**
Fut.	I, he, she, it,	I, he, she, it,
	we, you, they **will prevent**	we, you, they **will be prevented**
Past	I, he, she, it,	I, he, she, it **was prevented**
	we, you, they **prevented**	we, you, they **were prevented**
Past	I, he, she, it **was preventing**	I, he, she, it **was being prevented**
Prog.	we, you, they **were preventing**	we, you, they **were being prevented**
Past	I, he, she, it,	I, he, she, it,
Int.	we, you, they **did prevent**	we, you, they **did get prevented**
Pres.	I, we, you, they **have prevented**	I, we, you, they **have been prevented**
Perf.	he, she, it **has prevented**	he, she, it **has been prevented**
Past	I, he, she, it,	I, he, she, it,
Perf.	we, you, they **had prevented**	we, you, they **had been prevented**
Fut.	I, he, she, it, we, you, they	I, he, she, it, we, you, they
Perf.	**will have prevented**	**will have been prevented**

IMPERATIVE MOOD

prevent

be prevented

SUBJUNCTIVE MOOD

Pres.	if I, he, she, it,	if I, he, she, it,
	we, you, they **prevent**	we, you, they **be prevented**
Past	if I, he, she, it,	if I, he, she, it,
	we, you, they **prevented**	we, you, they **were prevented**
Fut.	if I, he, she, it,	if I, he, she, it,
	we, you, they **should prevent**	we, you, they **should be prevented**

Transitive and intransitive.

proceed PRINCIPAL PARTS: **proceeds, proceeding, proceeded, proceeded**

Infinitive: **to proceed**
Perfect Infinitive: **to have proceeded**
Present Participle: **proceeding**
Past Participle: **proceeded**

INDICATIVE MOOD

Pres. I, we, you, they **proceed**

he, she, it **proceeds**

Pres. I **am proceeding**
Prog. we, you, they **are proceeding**
he, she, it **is proceeding**

Pres. I, we, you, they **do proceed**
Int. he, she, it **does proceed**

Fut. I, he, she, it,
we, you, they **will proceed**

Past I, he, she, it,
we, you, they **proceeded**

Past I, he, she, it **was proceeding**
Prog. we, you, they **were proceeding**

Past I, he, she, it,
Int. we, you, they **did proceed**

Pres. I, we, you, they **have proceeded**
Perf. he, she, it **has proceeded**

Past I, he, she, it,
Perf. we, you, they **had proceeded**

Fut. I, he, she, it, we, you, they
Perf. **will have proceeded**

IMPERATIVE MOOD

proceed

SUBJUNCTIVE MOOD

Pres. if I, he, she, it,
we, you, they **proceed**

Past if I, he, she, it,
we, you, they **proceeded**

Fut. if I, he, she, it,
we, you, they **should proceed**

produce
(active voice)

PRINCIPAL PARTS: **produces, producing,**
produced, produced

be produced
(passive voice)

Infinitive: **to produce**
Perfect Infinitive: **to have produced**
Present Participle: **producing**
Past Participle: **produced**

Infinitive: **to be produced**
Perfect Infinitive: **to have been produced**
Present Participle: **being produced**
Past Participle: **been produced**

INDICATIVE MOOD

Pres.	I, we, you, they **produce**	I **am produced**
		we, you, they **are produced**
	he, she, it **produces**	he, she, it **is produced**
Pres.	I **am producing**	I **am being produced**
Prog.	we, you, they **are producing**	we, you, they **are being produced**
	he, she, it **is producing**	he, she, it **is being produced**
Pres.	I, we, you, they **do produce**	I, we, you, they **do get produced**
Int.	he, she, it **does produce**	he, she, it **does get produced**
Fut.	I, he, she, it,	I, he, she, it,
	we, you, they **will produce**	we, you, they **will be produced**
Past	I, he, she, it,	I, he, she, it **was produced**
	we, you, they **produced**	we, you, they **were produced**
Past	I, he, she, it **was producing**	I, he, she, it **was being produced**
Prog.	we, you, they **were producing**	we, you, they **were being produced**
Past	I, he, she, it,	I, he, she, it,
Int.	we, you, they **did produce**	we, you, they **did get produced**
Pres.	I, we, you, they **have produced**	I, we, you, they **have been produced**
Perf.	he, she, it **has produced**	he, she, it **has been produced**
Past	I, he, she, it,	I, he, she, it,
Perf.	we, you, they **had produced**	we, you, they **had been produced**
Fut.	I, he, she, it, we, you, they	I, he, she, it, we, you, they
Perf.	**will have produced**	**will have been produced**

IMPERATIVE MOOD

produce   **be produced**

SUBJUNCTIVE MOOD

Pres.	if I, he, she, it,	if I, he, she, it,
	we, you, they **produce**	we, you, they **be produced**
Past	if I, he, she, it,	if I, he, she, it,
	we, you, they **produced**	we, you, they **were produced**
Fut.	if I, he, she, it,	if I, he, she, it,
	we, you, they **should produce**	we, you, they **should be produced**

Transitive and intransitive.

program
(active voice)

be programmed/programed
(passive voice)

Infinitive: **to program**
Perfect Infinitive: **to have programmed**
Present Participle: **programming**
Past Participle: **programmed**

Infinitive: **to be programmed**
Perfect Infinitive: **to have been programmed**
Present Participle: **being programmed**
Past Participle: **been programmed**

INDICATIVE MOOD

Pres.	I, we, you, they **program**	I **am programmed**
		we, you, they **are programmed**
	he, she, it **programs**	he, she, it **is programmed**
Pres.	I **am programming**	I **am being programmed**
Prog.	we, you, they **are programming**	we, you, they **are being programmed**
	he, she, it **is programming**	he, she, it **is being programmed**
Pres.	I, we, you, they **do program**	I, we, you, they **do get programmed**
Int.	he, she, it **does program**	he, she, it **does get programmed**
Fut.	I, he, she, it,	I, he, she, it,
	we, you, they **will program**	we, you, they **will be programmed**
Past	I, he, she, it,	I, he, she, it **was programmed**
	we, you, they **programmed**	we, you, they **were programmed**
Past	I, he, she, it **was programming**	I, he, she, it **was being programmed**
Prog.	we, you, they **were programming**	we, you, they **were being programmed**
Past	I, he, she, it,	I, he, she, it, we, you, they
Int.	we, you, they **did program**	**did get programmed**
Pres.	I, we, you, they **have programmed**	I, we, you, they **have been programmed**
Perf.	he, she, it **has programmed**	he, she, it **has been programmed**
Past	I, he, she, it,	I, he, she, it, we, you, they
Perf.	we, you, they **had programmed**	**had been programmed**
Fut.	I, he, she, it, we, you, they	I, he, she, it, we, you, they
Perf.	**will have programmed**	**will have been programmed**

IMPERATIVE MOOD

program   **be programmed**

SUBJUNCTIVE MOOD

Pres.	if I, he, she, it,	if I, he, she, it,
	we, you, they **program**	we, you, they **be programmed**
Past	if I, he, she, it,	if I, he, she, it,
	we, you, they **programmed**	we, you, they **were programmed**
Fut.	if I, he, she, it,	if I, he, she, it, we, you, they
	we, you, they **should program**	**should be programmed**

The British variant of this word can also be spelled PROGRAMME. The spelling with the single "m" is accepted in American English by *American Heritage* and *Merriam Webster's Dictionaries.*

prove
(active voice)

PRINCIPAL PARTS: **proves, proving, proved, proved/proven**

be proved/proven
(passive voice)

Infinitive: **to prove**
Perfect Infinitive: **to have proved**
Present Participle: **proving**
Past Participle: **proved**

Infinitive: **to be proved**
Perfect Infinitive: **to have been proved**
Present Participle: **being proved**
Past Participle: **been proved**

INDICATIVE MOOD

Pres.	I, we, you, they **prove** he, she, it **proves**	I **am proved** we, you, they **are proved** he, she, it **is proved**
Pres. *Prog.*	I **am proving** we, you, they **are proving** he, she, it **is proving**	I **am being proved** we, you, they **are being proved** he, she, it **is being proved**
Pres. *Int.*	I, we, you, they **do prove** he, she, it **does prove**	I, we, you, they **do get proved** he, she, it **does get proved**
Fut.	I, he, she, it, we, you, they **will prove**	I, he, she, it, we, you, they **will be proved**
Past	I, he, she, it, we, you, they **proved**	I, he, she, it **was proved** we, you, they **were proved**
Past *Prog.*	I, he, she, it **was proving** we, you, they **were proving**	I, he, she, it **was being proved** we, you, they **were being proved**
Past *Int.*	I, he, she, it, we, you, they **did prove**	I, he, she, it, we, you, they **did get proved**
Pres. *Perf.*	I, we, you, they **have proved** he, she, it **has proved**	I, we, you, they **have been proved** he, she, it **has been proved**
Past *Perf.*	I, he, she, it, we, you, they **had proved**	I, he, she, it, we, you, they **had been proved**
Fut. *Perf.*	I, he, she, it, we, you, they **will have proved**	I, he, she, it, we, you, they **will have been proved**

IMPERATIVE MOOD

prove

be proved

SUBJUNCTIVE MOOD

Pres.	if I, he, she, it, we, you, they **prove**	if I, he, she, it, we, you, they **be proved**
Past	if I, he, she, it, we, you, they **proved**	if I, he, she, it, we, you, they **were proved**
Fut.	if I, he, she, it, we, you, they **should prove**	if I, he, she, it, we, you, they **should be proved**

Transitive and intransitive.

provide
(active voice)

PRINCIPAL PARTS: **provides, providing, provided, provided**

be provided
(passive voice)

Infinitive: **to provide**
Perfect Infinitive: **to have provided**
Present Participle: **providing**
Past Participle: **provided**

Infinitive: **to be provided**
Perfect Infinitive: **to have been provided**
Present Participle: **being provided**
Past Participle: **been provided**

INDICATIVE MOOD

Pres.	I, we, you, they **provide**	I **am provided**
		we, you, they **are provided**
	he, she, it **provides**	he, she, it **is provided**
Pres.	I **am providing**	I **am being provided**
Prog.	we, you, they **are providing**	we, you, they **are being provided**
	he, she, it **is providing**	he, she, it **is being provided**
Pres.	I, we, you, they **do provide**	I, we, you, they **do get provided**
Int.	he, she, it **does provide**	he, she, it **does get provided**
Fut.	I, he, she, it,	I, he, she, it,
	we, you, they **will provide**	we, you, they **will be provided**
Past	I, he, she, it,	I, he, she, it **was provided**
	we, you, they **provided**	we, you, they **were provided**
Past	I, he, she, it **was providing**	I, he, she, it **was being provided**
Prog.	we, you, they **were providing**	we, you, they **were being provided**
Past	I, he, she, it,	I, he, she, it,
Int.	we, you, they **did provide**	we, you, they **did get provided**
Pres.	I, we, you, they **have provided**	I, we, you, they **have been provided**
Perf.	he, she, it **has provided**	he, she, it **has been provided**
Past	I, he, she, it,	I, he, she, it,
Perf.	we, you, they **had provided**	we, you, they **had been provided**
Fut.	I, he, she, it, we, you, they	I, he, she, it, we, you, they
Perf.	**will have provided**	**will have been provided**

IMPERATIVE MOOD

provide   **be provided**

SUBJUNCTIVE MOOD

Pres.	if I, he, she, it,	if I, he, she, it,
	we, you, they **provide**	we, you, they **be provided**
Past	if I, he, she, it,	if I, he, she, it,
	we, you, they **provided**	we, you, they **were provided**
Fut.	if I, he, she, it,	if I, he, she, it,
	we, you, they **should provide**	we, you, they **should be provided**

Transitive and intransitive.

pull
(active voice)

be pulled
(passive voice)

Infinitive: **to pull**
Perfect Infinitive: **to have pulled**
Present Participle: **pulling**
Past Participle: **pulled**

Infinitive: **to be pulled**
Perfect Infinitive: **to have been pulled**
Present Participle: **being pulled**
Past Participle: **been pulled**

INDICATIVE MOOD

Pres.	I, we, you, they **pull**	I **am pulled**
		we, you, they **are pulled**
	he, she, it **pulls**	he, she, it **is pulled**
Pres.	I **am pulling**	I **am being pulled**
Prog.	we, you, they **are pulling**	we, you, they **are being pulled**
	he, she, it **is pulling**	he, she, it **is being pulled**
Pres.	I, we, you, they **do pull**	I, we, you, they **do get pulled**
Int.	he, she, it **does pull**	he, she, it **does get pulled**
Fut.	I, he, she, it,	I, he, she, it,
	we, you, they **will pull**	we, you, they **will be pulled**
Past	I, he, she, it,	I, he, she, it **was pulled**
	we, you, they **pulled**	we, you, they **were pulled**
Past	I, he, she, it **was pulling**	I, he, she, it **was being pulled**
Prog.	we, you, they **were pulling**	we, you, they **were being pulled**
Past	I, he, she, it,	I, he, she, it,
Int.	we, you, they **did pull**	we, you, they **did get pulled**
Pres.	I, we, you, they **have pulled**	I, we, you, they **have been pulled**
Perf.	he, she, it **has pulled**	he, she, it **has been pulled**
Past	I, he, she, it,	I, he, she, it,
Perf.	we, you, they **had pulled**	we, you, they **had been pulled**
Fut.	I, he, she, it, we, you, they	I, he, she, it, we, you, they
Perf.	**will have pulled**	**will have been pulled**

IMPERATIVE MOOD

pull   **be pulled**

SUBJUNCTIVE MOOD

Pres.	if I, he, she, it,	if I, he, she, it,
	we, you, they **pull**	we, you, they **be pulled**
Past	if I, he, she, it,	if I, he, she, it,
	we, you, they **pulled**	we, you, they **were pulled**
Fut.	if I, he, she, it,	if I, he, she, it,
	we, you, they **should pull**	we, you, they **should be pulled**

Transitive and intransitive.

put
(active voice)

be put
(passive voice)

Infinitive: **to put**
Perfect Infinitive: **to have put**
Present Participle: **putting**
Past Participle: **put**

Infinitive: **to be put**
Perfect Infinitive: **to have been put**
Present Participle: **being put**
Past Participle: **been put**

INDICATIVE MOOD

Pres.	I, we, you, they **put**	I **am put**
		we, you, they **are put**
	he, she, it **puts**	he, she, it **is put**
Pres.	I **am putting**	I **am being put**
Prog.	we, you, they **are putting**	we, you, they **are being put**
	he, she, it **is putting**	he, she, it **is being put**
Pres.	I, we, you, they **do put**	I, we, you, they **do get put**
Int.	he, she, it **does put**	he, she, it **does get put**
Fut.	I, he, she, it,	I, he, she, it,
	we, you, they **will put**	we, you, they **will be put**
Past	I, he, she, it,	I, he, she, it **was put**
	we, you, they **put**	we, you, they **were put**
Past	I, he, she, it **was putting**	I, he, she, it **was being put**
Prog.	we, you, they **were putting**	we, you, they **were being put**
Past	I, he, she, it,	I, he, she, it,
Int.	we, you, they **did put**	we, you, they **did get put**
Pres.	I, we, you, they **have put**	I, we, you, they **have been put**
Perf.	he, she, it **has put**	he, she, it **has been put**
Past	I, he, she, it,	I, he, she, it,
Perf.	we, you, they **had put**	we, you, they **had been put**
Fut.	I, he, she, it, we, you, they	I, he, she, it, we, you, they
Perf.	**will have put**	**will have been put**

IMPERATIVE MOOD

put   be put

SUBJUNCTIVE MOOD

Pres.	if I, he, she, it,	if I, he, she, it,
	we, you, they **put**	we, you, they **be put**
Past	if I, he, she, it,	if I, he, she, it,
	we, you, they **put**	we, you, they **were put**
Fut.	if I, he, she, it,	if I, he, she, it,
	we, you, they **should put**	we, you, they **should be put**

Transitive and intransitive.

quarrel　　　　　PRINCIPAL PARTS: **quarrels, quarreling/ quarrelling, quarreled/quarrelled, quarreled/quarrelled**

Infinitive: **to quarrel**
Perfect Infinitive: **to have quarreled**
Present Participle: **quarreled**
Past Participle: **quarreled**

INDICATIVE MOOD

Pres.	I, we, you, they **quarrel**
	he, she, it **quarrels**
Pres. *Prog.*	I **am quarreling** we, you, they **are quarreling** he, she, it **is quarreling**
Pres. *Int.*	I, we, you, they **do quarrel** he, she, it **does quarrel**
Fut.	I, he, she, it, we, you, they **will quarrel**
Past	I, he, she, it, we, you, they **quarreled**
Past *Prog.*	I, he, she, it **was quarreling** we, you, they **were quarreling**
Past *Int.*	I, he, she, it, we, you, they **did quarrel**
Pres. *Perf.*	I, we, you, they **have quarreled** he, she, it **has quarreled**
Past *Perf.*	I, he, she, it, we, you, they **had quarreled**
Fut. *Perf.*	I, he, she, it, we, you, they **will have quarreled**

IMPERATIVE MOOD

quarrel

SUBJUNCTIVE MOOD

Pres.	if I, he, she, it, we, you, they **quarrel**
Past	if I, he, she, it, we, you, they **quarreled**
Fut.	if I, he, she, it, we, you, they **should quarrel**

The *Oxford Dictionary* prefers the double "ll" in the present and past participles: QUARRELLING, QUARRELLED.

quit
(active voice)

be quit/quitted
(passive voice)

Infinitive: **to quit**
Perfect Infinitive: **to have quit**
Present Participle: **quitting**
Past Participle: **quit**

Infinitive: **to be quit**
Perfect Infinitive: **to have been quit**
Present Participle: **being quit**
Past Participle: **been quit**

INDICATIVE MOOD

Pres.	I, we, you, they **quit**	I **am quit**
		we, you, they **are quit**
	he, she, it **quits**	he, she, it **is quit**
Pres.	I **am quitting**	I **am being quit**
Prog.	we, you, they **are quitting**	we, you, they **are being quit**
	he, she, it **is quitting**	he, she, it **is being quit**
Pres.	I, we, you, they **do quit**	I, we, you, they **do get quit**
Int.	he, she, it **does quit**	he, she, it **does get quit**
Fut.	I, he, she, it,	I, he, she, it,
	we, you, they **will quit**	we, you, they **will be quit**
Past	I, he, she, it,	I, he, she, it **was quit**
	we, you, they **quit**	we, you, they **were quit**
Past	I, he, she, it **was quitting**	I, he, she, it **was being quit**
Prog.	we, you, they **were quitting**	we, you, they **were being quit**
Past	I, he, she, it,	I, he, she, it,
Int.	we, you, they **did quit**	we, you, they **did get quit**
Pres.	I, we, you, they **have quit**	I, we, you, they **have been quit**
Perf.	he, she, it **has quit**	he, she, it **has been quit**
Past	I, he, she, it,	I, he, she, it,
Perf.	we, you, they **had quit**	we, you, they **had been quit**
Fut.	I, he, she, it, we, you, they	I, he, she, it, we, you, they
Perf.	**will have quit**	**will have been quit**

IMPERATIVE MOOD

quit   **be quit**

SUBJUNCTIVE MOOD

Pres.	if I, he, she, it,	if I, he, she, it,
	we, you, they **quit**	we, you, they **be quit**
Past	if I, he, she, it,	if I, he, she, it,
	we, you, they **quit**	we, you, they **were quit**
Fut.	if I, he, she, it,	if I, he, she, it,
	we, you, they **should quit**	we, you, they **should be quit**

Transitive and intransitive.

quiz
(active voice)

PRINCIPAL PARTS: **quizzes, quizzing, quizzed, quizzed**

be quizzed
(passive voice)

Infinitive: **to quiz**
Perfect Infinitive: **to have quizzed**
Present Participle: **quizzing**
Past Participle: **quizzed**

Infinitive: **to be quizzed**
Perfect Infinitive: **to have been quizzed**
Present Participle: **being quizzed**
Past Participle: **been quizzed**

INDICATIVE MOOD

Pres.	I, we, you, they **quiz**	I **am quizzed**
		we, you, they **are quizzed**
	he, she, it **quizzes**	he, she, it **is quizzed**
Pres.	I **am quizzing**	I **am being quizzed**
Prog.	we, you, they **are quizzing**	we, you, they **are being quizzed**
	he, she, it **is quizzing**	he, she, it **is being quizzed**
Pres.	I, we, you, they **do quiz**	I, we, you, they **do get quizzed**
Int.	he, she, it **does quiz**	he, she, it **does get quizzed**
Fut.	I, he, she, it,	I, he, she, it,
	we, you, they **will quiz**	we, you, they **will be quizzed**
Past	I, he, she, it,	I, he, she, it **was quizzed**
	we, you, they **quizzed**	we, you, they **were quizzed**
Past	I, he, she, it **was quizzing**	I, he, she, it **was being quizzed**
Prog.	we, you, they **were quizzing**	we, you, they **were being quizzed**
Past	I, he, she, it,	I, he, she, it,
Int.	we, you, they **did quiz**	we, you, they **did get quizzed**
Pres.	I, we, you, they **have quizzed**	I, we, you, they **have been quizzed**
Perf.	he, she, it **has quizzed**	he, she, it **has been quizzed**
Past	I, he, she, it,	I, he, she, it,
Perf.	we, you, they **had quizzed**	we, you, they **had been quizzed**
Fut.	I, he, she, it, we, you, they	I, he, she, it, we, you, they
Perf.	**will have quizzed**	**will have been quizzed**

IMPERATIVE MOOD

quiz   **be quizzed**

SUBJUNCTIVE MOOD

Pres.	if I, he, she, it,	if I, he, she, it,
	we, you, they **quiz**	we, you, they **be quizzed**
Past	if I, he, she, it,	if I, he, she, it,
	we, you, they **quizzed**	we, you, they **were quizzed**
Fut.	if I, he, she, it,	if I, he, she, it,
	we, you, they **should quiz**	we, you, they **should be quizzed**

radio
(active voice)

PRINCIPAL PARTS: **radios, radioing, radioed, radioed**

be radioed
(passive voice)

Infinitive: **to radio**
Perfect Infinitive: **to have radioed**
Present Participle: **radioing**
Past Participle: **radioed**

Infinitive: **to be radioed**
Perfect Infinitive: **to have been radioed**
Present Participle: **being radioed**
Past Participle: **been radioed**

INDICATIVE MOOD

Pres.	I, we, you, they **radio** he, she, it **radios**	I **am radioed** we, you, they **are radioed** he, she, it **is radioed**
Pres. *Prog.*	I **am radioing** we, you, they **are radioing** he, she, it **is radioing**	I **am being radioed** we, you, they **are being radioed** he, she, it **is being radioed**
Pres. *Int.*	I, we, you, they **do radio** he, she, it **does radio**	I, we, you, they **do get radioed** he, she, it **does get radioed**
Fut.	I, he, she, it, we, you, they **will radio**	I, he, she, it, we, you, they **will be radioed**
Past	I, he, she, it, we, you, they **radioed**	I, he, she, it **was radioed** we, you, they **were radioed**
Past *Prog.*	I, he, she, it **was radioing** we, you, they **were radioing**	I, he, she, it **was being radioed** we, you, they **were being radioed**
Past *Int.*	I, he, she, it, we, you, they **did radio**	I, he, she, it, we, you, they **did get radioed**
Pres. *Perf.*	I, we, you, they **have radioed** he, she, it **has radioed**	I, we, you, they **have been radioed** he, she, it **has been radioed**
Past *Perf.*	I, he, she, it, we, you, they **had radioed**	I, he, she, it, we, you, they **had been radioed**
Fut. *Perf.*	I, he, she, it, we, you, they **will have radioed**	I, he, she, it, we, you, they **will have been radioed**

IMPERATIVE MOOD

radio

be radioed

SUBJUNCTIVE MOOD

Pres.	if I, he, she, it, we, you, they **radio**	if I, he, she, it, we, you, they **be radioed**
Past	if I, he, she, it, we, you, they **radioed**	if I, he, she, it, we, you, they **were radioed**
Fut.	if I, he, she, it, we, you, they **should radio**	if I, he, she, it, we, you, they **should be radioed**

Transitive and intransitive.

raise
(active voice)

be raised
(passive voice)

Infinitive: **to raise**
Perfect Infinitive: **to have raised**
Present Participle: **raising**
Past Participle: **raised**

Infinitive: **to be raised**
Perfect Infinitive: **to have been raised**
Present Participle: **being raised**
Past Participle: **been raised**

INDICATIVE MOOD

Pres.	I, we, you, they **raise**	I **am raised**
		we, you, they **are raised**
	he, she, it **raises**	he, she, it **is raised**
Pres.	I **am raising**	I **am being raised**
Prog.	we, you, they **are raising**	we, you, they **are being raised**
	he, she, it **is raising**	he, she, it **is being raised**
Pres.	I, we, you, they **do raise**	I, we, you, they **do get raised**
Int.	he, she, it **does raise**	he, she, it **does get raised**
Fut.	I, he, she, it,	I, he, she, it,
	we, you, they **will raise**	we, you, they **will be raised**
Past	I, he, she, it,	I, he, she, it **was raised**
	we, you, they **raised**	we, you, they **were raised**
Past	I, he, she, it **was raising**	I, he, she, it **was being raised**
Prog.	we, you, they **were raising**	we, you, they **were being raised**
Past	I, he, she, it,	I, he, she, it,
Int.	we, you, they **did raise**	we, you, they **did get raised**
Pres.	I, we, you, they **have raised**	I, we, you, they **have been raised**
Perf.	he, she, it **has raised**	he, she, it **has been raised**
Past	I, he, she, it,	I, he, she, it,
Perf.	we, you, they **had raised**	we, you, they **had been raised**
Fut.	I, he, she, it, we, you, they	I, he, she, it, we, you, they
Perf.	**will have raised**	**will have been raised**

IMPERATIVE MOOD

raise　　　　　　**be raised**

SUBJUNCTIVE MOOD

Pres.	if I, he, she, it,	if I, he, she, it,
	we, you, they **raise**	we, you, they **be raised**
Past	if I, he, she, it,	if I, he, she, it,
	we, you, they **raised**	we, you, they **were raised**
Fut.	if I, he, she, it,	if I, he, she, it,
	we, you, they **should raise**	we, you, they **should be raised**

Transitive and intransitive.

rap
(active voice)

PRINCIPAL PARTS: **raps, rapping,
rapped/rapt, rapped/rapt**

be rapped/rapt
(passive voice)

Infinitive: **to rap**
Perfect Infinitive: **to have rapped**
Present Participle: **rapping**
Past Participle: **rapped**

Infinitive: **to be rapped**
Perfect Infinitive: **to have been rapped**
Present Participle: **being rapped**
Past Participle: **been rapped**

INDICATIVE MOOD

Pres.	I, we, you, they **rap**	I **am rapped** we, you, they **are rapped**
	he, she, it **raps**	he, she, it **is rapped**
Pres. _Prog._	I **am rapping** we, you, they **are rapping** he, she, it **is rapping**	I **am being rapped** we, you, they **are being rapped** he, she, it **is being rapped**
Pres. _Int._	I, we, you, they **do rap** he, she, it **does rap**	I, we, you, they **do get rapped** he, she, it **does get rapped**
Fut.	I, he, she, it, we, you, they **will rap**	I, he, she, it, we, you, they **will be rapped**
Past	I, he, she, it, we, you, they **rapped**	I, he, she, it **was rapped** we, you, they **were rapped**
Past _Prog._	I, he, she, it **was rapping** we, you, they **were rapping**	I, he, she, it **was being rapped** we, you, they **were being rapped**
Past _Int._	I, he, she, it, we, you, they **did rap**	I, he, she, it, we, you, they **did get rapped**
Pres. _Perf._	I, we, you, they **have rapped** he, she, it **has rapped**	I, we, you, they **have been rapped** he, she, it **has been rapped**
Past _Perf._	I, he, she, it, we, you, they **had rapped**	I, he, she, it, we, you, they **had been rapped**
Fut. _Perf._	I, he, she, it, we, you, they **will have rapped**	I, he, she, it, we, you, they **will have been rapped**

IMPERATIVE MOOD

rap   **be rapped**

SUBJUNCTIVE MOOD

Pres.	if I, he, she, it, we, you, they **rap**	if I, he, she, it, we, you, they **be rapped**
Past	if I, he, she, it, we, you, they **rapped**	if I, he, she, it, we, you, they **were rapped**
Fut.	if I, he, she, it, we, you, they **should rap**	if I, he, she, it, we, you, they **should be rapped**

Transitive and intransitive. There are actually three verbs. The first RAP, RAPPED means to hit sharply. The second takes the past tense and past participle form RAPT, meaning "seized with rapture." The third is intransitive meaning to RAP, as in music.

reach
(active voice)

be reached
(passive voice)

Infinitive: **to reach**
Perfect Infinitive: **to have reached**
Present Participle: **reaching**
Past Participle: **reached**

Infinitive: **to be reached**
Perfect Infinitive: **to have been reached**
Present Participle: **being reached**
Past Participle: **been reached**

INDICATIVE MOOD

Pres.	I, we, you, they **reach**	I am reached
		we, you, they **are reached**
	he, she, it **reaches**	he, she, it **is reached**
Pres. *Prog.*	I **am reaching** we, you, they **are reaching** he, she, it **is reaching**	I am being reached we, you, they **are being reached** he, she, it **is being reached**
Pres. *Int.*	I, we, you, they **do reach** he, she, it **does reach**	I, we, you, they **do get reached** he, she, it **does get reached**
Fut.	I, he, she, it, we, you, they **will reach**	I, he, she, it, we, you, they **will be reached**
Past	I, he, she, it, we, you, they **reached**	I, he, she, it **was reached** we, you, they **were reached**
Past *Prog.*	I, he, she, it **was reaching** we, you, they **were reaching**	I, he, she, it **was being reached** we, you, they **were being reached**
Past *Int.*	I, he, she, it, we, you, they **did reach**	I, he, she, it, we, you, they **did get reached**
Pres. *Perf.*	I, we, you, they **have reached** he, she, it **has reached**	I, we, you, they **have been reached** he, she, it **has been reached**
Past *Perf.*	I, he, she, it, we, you, they **had reached**	I, he, she, it, we, you, they **had been reached**
Fut. *Perf.*	I, he, she, it, we, you, they **will have reached**	I, he, she, it, we, you, they **will have been reached**

IMPERATIVE MOOD

reach   **be reached**

SUBJUNCTIVE MOOD

Pres.	if I, he, she, it, we, you, they **reach**	if I, he, she, it, we, you, they **be reached**
Past	if I, he, she, it, we, you, they **reached**	if I, he, she, it, we, you, they **were reached**
Fut.	if I, he, she, it, we, you, they **should reach**	if I, he, she, it, we, you, they **should be reached**

Transitive and intransitive.

react
(active voice)

be reacted
(passive voice)

Infinitive: **to react**
Perfect Infinitive: **to have reacted**
Present Participle: **reacting**
Past Participle: **reacted**

Infinitive: **to be reacted**
Perfect Infinitive: **to have been reacted**
Present Participle: **being reacted**
Past Participle: **been reacted**

INDICATIVE MOOD

Pres.	I, we, you, they **react**	I **am reacted** we, you, they **are reacted**
	he, she, it **reacts**	he, she, it **is reacted**
Pres.	I **am reacting**	I **am being reacted**
Prog.	we, you, they **are reacting**	we, you, they **are being reacted**
	he, she, it **is reacting**	he, she, it **is being reacted**
Pres.	I, we, you, they **do react**	I, we, you, they **do get reacted**
Int.	he, she, it **does react**	he, she, it **does get reacted**
Fut.	I, he, she, it, we, you, they **will react**	I, he, she, it, we, you, they **will be reacted**
Past	I, he, she, it, we, you, they **reacted**	I, he, she, it **was reacted** we, you, they **were reacted**
Past	I, he, she, it **was reacting**	I, he, she, it **was being reacted**
Prog.	we, you, they **were reacting**	we, you, they **were being reacted**
Past	I, he, she, it, we, you, they **did react**	I, he, she, it, we, you, they **did get reacted**
Int.		
Pres.	I, we, you, they **have reacted**	I, we, you, they **have been reacted**
Perf.	he, she, it **has reacted**	he, she, it **has been reacted**
Past	I, he, she, it, we, you, they **had reacted**	I, he, she, it, we, you, they **had been reacted**
Perf.		
Fut.	I, he, she, it, we, you, they	I, he, she, it, we, you, they
Perf.	**will have reacted**	**will have been reacted**

IMPERATIVE MOOD

react   **be reacted**

SUBJUNCTIVE MOOD

Pres.	if I, he, she, it, we, you, they **react**	if I, he, she, it, we, you, they **be reacted**
Past	if I, he, she, it, we, you, they **reacted**	if I, he, she, it, we, you, they **were reacted**
Fut.	if I, he, she, it, we, you, they **should react**	if I, he, she, it, we, you, they **should be reacted**

Transitive and intransitive.

read
(active voice)

PRINCIPAL PARTS: **reads, reading,**
read, read

be read
(passive voice)

Infinitive: **to read**
Perfect Infinitive: **to have read**
Present Participle: **reading**
Past Participle: **read**

Infinitive: **to be read**
Perfect Infinitive: **to have been read**
Present Participle: **being read**
Past Participle: **been read**

INDICATIVE MOOD

Pres.	I, we, you, they **read**	I **am read**
		we, you, they **are read**
	he, she, it **reads**	he, she, it **is read**
Pres.	I **am reading**	I **am being read**
Prog.	we, you, they **are reading**	we, you, they **are being read**
	he, she, it **is reading**	he, she, it **is being read**
Pres.	I, we, you, they **do read**	I, we, you, they **do get read**
Int.	he, she, it **does read**	he, she, it **does get read**
Fut.	I, he, she, it,	I, he, she, it,
	we, you, they **will read**	we, you, they **will be read**
Past	I, he, she, it,	I, he, she, it **was read**
	we, you, they **read**	we, you, they **were read**
Past	I, he, she, it **was reading**	I, he, she, it **was being read**
Prog.	we, you, they **were reading**	we, you, they **were being read**
Past	I, he, she, it,	I, he, she, it,
Int.	we, you, they **did read**	we, you, they **did get read**
Pres.	I, we, you, they **have read**	I, we, you, they **have been read**
Perf.	he, she, it **has read**	he, she, it **has been read**
Past	I, he, she, it,	I, he, she, it,
Perf.	we, you, they **had read**	we, you, they **had been read**
Fut.	I, he, she, it, we, you, they	I, he, she, it, we, you, they
Perf.	**will have read**	**will have been read**

IMPERATIVE MOOD

read   **be read**

SUBJUNCTIVE MOOD

Pres.	if I, he, she, it,	if I, he, she, it,
	we, you, they **read**	we, you, they **be read**
Past	if I, he, she, it,	if I, he, she, it,
	we, you, they **read**	we, you, they **were read**
Fut.	if I, he, she, it,	if I, he, she, it,
	we, you, they **should read**	we, you, they **should be read**

Transitive and intransitive. Note the pronunciation of the past tense and past participle as "red."

realize
(active voice)

PRINCIPAL PARTS: **realizes, realizing,
realized, realized**

be realized
(passive voice)

Infinitive: **to realize**
Perfect Infinitive: **to have realized**
Present Participle: **realizing**
Past Participle: **realized**

Infinitive: **to be realized**
Perfect Infinitive: **to have been realized**
Present Participle: **being realized**
Past Participle: **been realized**

INDICATIVE MOOD

Pres.	I, we, you, they **realize**	I **am realized**
		we, you, they **are realized**
	he, she, it **realizes**	he, she, it **is realized**
Pres.	I **am realizing**	I **am being realized**
Prog.	we, you, they **are realizing**	we, you, they **are being realized**
	he, she, it **is realizing**	he, she, it **is being realized**
Pres.	I, we, you, they **do realize**	I, we, you, they **do get realized**
Int.	he, she, it **does realize**	he, she, it **does get realized**
Fut.	I, he, she, it,	I, he, she, it,
	we, you, they **will realize**	we, you, they **will be realized**
Past	I, he, she, it,	I, he, she, it **was realized**
	we, you, they **realized**	we, you, they **were realized**
Past	I, he, she, it **was realizing**	I, he, she, it **was being realized**
Prog.	we, you, they **were realizing**	we, you, they **were being realized**
Past	I, he, she, it,	I, he, she, it,
Int.	we, you, they **did realize**	we, you, they **did get realized**
Pres.	I, we, you, they **have realized**	I, we, you, they **have been realized**
Perf.	he, she, it **has realized**	he, she, it **has been realized**
Past	I, he, she, it,	I, he, she, it,
Perf.	we, you, they **had realized**	we, you, they **had been realized**
Fut.	I, he, she, it, we, you, they	I, he, she, it, we, you, they
Perf.	**will have realized**	**will have been realized**

IMPERATIVE MOOD

realize

be realized

SUBJUNCTIVE MOOD

Pres.	if I, he, she, it,	if I, he, she, it,
	we, you, they **realize**	we, you, they **be realized**
Past	if I, he, she, it,	if I, he, she, it,
	we, you, they **realized**	we, you, they **were realized**
Fut.	if I, he, she, it,	if I, he, she, it,
	we, you, they **should realize**	we, you, they **should be realized**

Transitive and intransitive.

rebind
(active voice)

PRINCIPAL PARTS: **rebinds, rebinding,
rebound, rebound**

be rebound
(passive voice)

Infinitive: **to rebind**
Perfect Infinitive: **to have rebound**
Present Participle: **rebinding**
Past Participle: **rebound**

Infinitive: **to be rebound**
Perfect Infinitive: **to have been rebound**
Present Participle: **being rebound**
Past Participle: **been rebound**

INDICATIVE MOOD

Pres.	I, we, you, they **rebind**	I **am rebound**
		we, you, they **are rebound**
	he, she, it **rebinds**	he, she, it **is rebound**
Pres.	I **am rebinding**	I **am being rebound**
Prog.	we, you, they **are rebinding**	we, you, they **are being rebound**
	he, she, it **is rebinding**	he, she, it **is being rebound**
Pres.	I, we, you, they **do rebind**	I, we, you, they **do get rebound**
Int.	he, she, it **does rebind**	he, she, it **does get rebound**
Fut.	I, he, she, it,	I, he, she, it,
	we, you, they **will rebind**	we, you, they **will be rebound**
Past	I, he, she, it,	I, he, she, it **was rebound**
	we, you, they **rebound**	we, you, they **were rebound**
Past	I, he, she, it **was rebinding**	I, he, she, it **was being rebound**
Prog.	we, you, they **were rebinding**	we, you, they **were being rebound**
Past	I, he, she, it,	I, he, she, it,
Int.	we, you, they **did rebind**	we, you, they **did get rebound**
Pres.	I, we, you, they **have rebound**	I, we, you, they **have been rebound**
Perf.	he, she, it **has rebound**	he, she, it **has been rebound**
Past	I, he, she, it,	I, he, she, it,
Perf.	we, you, they **had rebound**	we, you, they **had been rebound**
Fut.	I, he, she, it, we, you, they	I, he, she, it, we, you, they
Perf.	**will have rebound**	**will have been rebound**

IMPERATIVE MOOD

rebind   **be rebound**

SUBJUNCTIVE MOOD

Pres.	if I, he, she, it,	if I, he, she, it,
	we, you, they **rebind**	we, you, they **be rebound**
Past	if I, he, she, it,	if I, he, she, it,
	we, you, they **rebound**	we, you, they **were rebound**
Fut.	if I, he, she, it,	if I, he, she, it,
	we, you, they **should rebind**	we, you, they **should be rebound**

rebound
(active voice)

be rebounded
(passive voice)

Infinitive: **to rebound**
Perfect Infinitive: **to have rebounded**
Present Participle: **rebounding**
Past Participle: **rebounded**

Infinitive: **to be rebounded**
Perfect Infinitive: **to have been rebounded**
Present Participle: **being rebounded**
Past Participle: **been rebounded**

INDICATIVE MOOD

Pres.	I, we, you, they **rebound**	I **am rebounded**
		we, you, they **are rebounded**
	he, she, it **rebounds**	he, she, it **is rebounded**
Pres.	I **am rebounding**	I **am being rebounded**
Prog.	we, you, they **are rebounding**	we, you, they **are being rebounded**
	he, she, it **is rebounding**	he, she, it **is being rebounded**
Pres.	I, we, you, they **do rebound**	I, we, you, they **do get rebounded**
Int.	he, she, it **does rebound**	he, she, it **does get rebounded**
Fut.	I, he, she, it,	I, he, she, it,
	we, you, they **will rebound**	we, you, they **will be rebounded**
Past	I, he, she, it,	I, he, she, it **was rebounded**
	we, you, they **rebounded**	we, you, they **were rebounded**
Past	I, he, she, it **was rebounding**	I, he, she, it **was being rebounded**
Prog.	we, you, they **were rebounding**	we, you, they **were being rebounded**
Past	I, he, she, it,	I, he, she, it,
Int.	we, you, they **did rebound**	we, you, they **did get rebounded**
Pres.	I, we, you, they **have rebounded**	I, we, you, they **have been rebounded**
Perf.	he, she, it **has rebounded**	he, she, it **has been rebounded**
Past	I, he, she, it,	I, he, she, it,
Perf.	we, you, they **had rebounded**	we, you, they **had been rebounded**
Fut.	I, he, she, it, we, you, they	I, he, she, it, we, you, they
Perf.	**will have rebounded**	**will have been rebounded**

IMPERATIVE MOOD

rebound   **be rebounded**

SUBJUNCTIVE MOOD

Pres.	if I, he, she, it,	if I, he, she, it,
	we, you, they **rebound**	we, you, they **be rebounded**
Past	if I, he, she, it,	if I, he, she, it,
	we, you, they **rebounded**	we, you, they **were rebounded**
Fut.	if I, he, she, it,	if I, he, she, it,
	we, you, they **should rebound**	we, you, they **should be rebounded**

Intransitive and transitive.

rebuild
(active voice)

PRINCIPAL PARTS: **rebuilds, rebuilding, rebuilt, rebuilt**

be rebuilt
(passive voice)

Infinitive: **to rebuild**
Perfect Infinitive: **to have rebuilt**
Present Participle: **rebuilding**
Past Participle: **rebuilt**

Infinitive: **to be rebuilt**
Perfect Infinitive: **to have been rebuilt**
Present Participle: **being rebuilt**
Past Participle: **been rebuilt**

INDICATIVE MOOD

Pres.	I, we, you, they **rebuild**	I **am rebuilt** we, you, they **are rebuilt**
	he, she, it **rebuilds**	he, she, it **is rebuilt**
Pres. *Prog.*	I **am rebuilding** we, you, they **are rebuilding** he, she, it **is rebuilding**	I **am being rebuilt** we, you, they **are being rebuilt** he, she, it **is being rebuilt**
Pres. *Int.*	I, we, you, they **do rebuild** he, she, it **does rebuild**	I, we, you, they **do get rebuilt** he, she, it **does get rebuilt**
Fut.	I, he, she, it, we, you, they **will rebuild**	I, he, she, it, we, you, they **will be rebuilt**
Past	I, he, she, it, we, you, they **rebuilt**	I, he, she, it **was rebuilt** we, you, they **were rebuilt**
Past *Prog.*	I, he, she, it **was rebuilding** we, you, they **were rebuilding**	I, he, she, it **was being rebuilt** we, you, they **were being rebuilt**
Past *Int.*	I, he, she, it, we, you, they **did rebuild**	I, he, she, it, we, you, they **did get rebuilt**
Pres. *Perf.*	I, we, you, they **have rebuilt** he, she, it **has rebuilt**	I, we, you, they **have been rebuilt** he, she, it **has been rebuilt**
Past *Perf.*	I, he, she, it, we, you, they **had rebuilt**	I, he, she, it, we, you, they **had been rebuilt**
Fut. *Perf.*	I, he, she, it, we, you, they **will have rebuilt**	I, he, she, it, we, you, they **will have been rebuilt**

IMPERATIVE MOOD

rebuild

be rebuilt

SUBJUNCTIVE MOOD

Pres.	if I, he, she, it, we, you, they **rebuild**	if I, he, she, it, we, you, they **be rebuilt**
Past	if I, he, she, it, we, you, they **rebuilt**	if I, he, she, it, we, you, they **were rebuilt**
Fut.	if I, he, she, it, we, you, they **should rebuild**	if I, he, she, it, we, you, they **should be rebuilt**

Transitive and intransitive.

receive
(active voice)

be received
(passive voice)

Infinitive: **to receive**
Perfect Infinitive: **to have received**
Present Participle: **receiving**
Past Participle: **received**

Infinitive: **to be received**
Perfect Infinitive: **to have been received**
Present Participle: **being received**
Past Participle: **been received**

INDICATIVE MOOD

Pres.	I, we, you, they **receive**	I **am received**
		we, you, they **are received**
	he, she, it **receives**	he, she, it **is received**
Pres.	I **am receiving**	I **am being received**
Prog.	we, you, they **are receiving**	we, you, they **are being received**
	he, she, it **is receiving**	he, she, it **is being received**
Pres.	I, we, you, they **do receive**	I, we, you, they **do get received**
Int.	he, she, it **does receive**	he, she, it **does get received**
Fut.	I, he, she, it,	I, he, she, it,
	we, you, they **will receive**	we, you, they **will be received**
Past	I, he, she, it,	I, he, she, it **was received**
	we, you, they **received**	we, you, they **were received**
Past	I, he, she, it **was receiving**	I, he, she, it **was being received**
Prog.	we, you, they **were receiving**	we, you, they **were being received**
Past	I, he, she, it,	I, he, she, it,
Int.	we, you, they **did receive**	we, you, they **did get received**
Pres.	I, we, you, they **have received**	I, we, you, they **have been received**
Perf.	he, she, it **has received**	he, she, it **has been received**
Past	I, he, she, it,	I, he, she, it,
Perf.	we, you, they **had received**	we, you, they **had been received**
Fut.	I, he, she, it, we, you, they	I, he, she, it, we, you, they
Perf.	**will have received**	**will have been received**

IMPERATIVE MOOD

receive   **be received**

SUBJUNCTIVE MOOD

Pres.	if I, he, she, it,	if I, he, she, it,
	we, you, they **receive**	we, you, they **be received**
Past	if I, he, she, it,	if I, he, she, it,
	we, you, they **received**	we, you, they **were received**
Fut.	if I, he, she, it,	if I, he, she, it,
	we, you, they **should receive**	we, you, they **should be received**

Transitive and intransitive.

recognize
(active voice)

PRINCIPAL PARTS: **recognizes, recognizing, recognized, recognized**

be recognized
(passive voice)

Infinitive: **to recognize**
Perfect Infinitive: **to have recognized**
Present Participle: **recognizing**
Past Participle: **recognized**

Infinitive: **to be recognized**
Perfect Infinitive: **to have been recognized**
Present Participle: **being recognized**
Past Participle: **been recognized**

INDICATIVE MOOD

Pres.	I, we, you, they **recognize**	I **am recognized**
		we, you, they **are recognized**
	he, she, it **recognizes**	he, she, it **is recognized**
Pres.	I **am recognizing**	I **am being recognized**
Prog.	we, you, they **are recognizing**	we, you, they **are being recognized**
	he, she, it **is recognizing**	he, she, it **is being recognized**
Pres.	I, we, you, they **do recognize**	I, we, you, they **do get recognized**
Int.	he, she, it **does recognize**	he, she, it **does get recognized**
Fut.	I, he, she, it,	I, he, she, it,
	we, you, they **will recognize**	we, you, they **will be recognized**
Past	I, he, she, it,	I, he, she, it **was recognized**
	we, you, they **recognized**	we, you, they **were recognized**
Past	I, he, she, it **was recognizing**	I, he, she, it **was being recognized**
Prog.	we, you, they **were recognizing**	we, you, they **were being recognized**
Past	I, he, she, it,	I, he, she, it,
Int.	we, you, they **did recognize**	we, you, they **did get recognized**
Pres.	I, we, you, they **have recognized**	I, we, you, they **have been recognized**
Perf.	he, she, it **has recognized**	he, she, it **has been recognized**
Past	I, he, she, it,	I, he, she, it,
Perf.	we, you, they **had recognized**	we, you, they **had been recognized**
Fut.	I, he, she, it, we, you, they	I, he, she, it, we, you, they
Perf.	**will have recognized**	**will have been recognized**

IMPERATIVE MOOD

recognize

be recognized

SUBJUNCTIVE MOOD

Pres.	if I, he, she, it,	if I, he, she, it,
	we, you, they **recognize**	we, you, they **be recognized**
Past	if I, he, she, it,	if I, he, she, it,
	we, you, they **recognized**	we, you, they **were recognized**
Fut.	if I, he, she, it,	if I, he, she, it,
	we, you, they **should recognize**	we, you, they **should be recognized**

redo
(active voice)

be redone
(passive voice)

Infinitive: **to redo**
Perfect Infinitive: **to have redone**
Present Participle: **redoing**
Past Participle: **redone**

Infinitive: **to be redone**
Perfect Infinitive: **to have been redone**
Present Participle: **being redone**
Past Participle: **been redone**

INDICATIVE MOOD

Pres.	I, we, you, they **redo**	I **am redone**
		we, you, they **are redone**
	he, she, it **redoes**	he, she, it **is redone**
Pres.	I **am redoing**	I **am being redone**
Prog.	we, you, they **are redoing**	we, you, they **are being redone**
	he, she, it **is redoing**	he, she, it **is being redone**
Pres.	I, we, you, they **do redo**	I, we, you, they **do get redone**
Int.	he, she, it **does redo**	he, she, it **does get redone**
Fut.	I, he, she, it,	I, he, she, it,
	we, you, they **will redo**	we, you, they **will be redone**
Past	I, he, she, it,	I, he, she, it **was redone**
	we, you, they **redid**	we, you, they **were redone**
Past	I, he, she, it **was redoing**	I, he, she, it **was being redone**
Prog.	we, you, they **were redoing**	we, you, they **were being redone**
Past	I, he, she, it,	I, he, she, it,
Int.	we, you, they **did redo**	we, you, they **did get redone**
Pres.	I, we, you, they **have redone**	I, we, you, they **have been redone**
Perf.	he, she, it **has redone**	he, she, it **has been redone**
Past	I, he, she, it,	I, he, she, it,
Perf.	we, you, they **had redone**	we, you, they **had been redone**
Fut.	I, he, she, it, we, you, they	I, he, she, it, we, you, they
Perf.	**will have redone**	**will have been redone**

IMPERATIVE MOOD

redo   **be redone**

SUBJUNCTIVE MOOD

Pres.	if I, he, she, it,	if I, he, she, it,
	we, you, they **redo**	we, you, they **be redone**
Past	if I, he, she, it,	if I, he, she, it,
	we, you, they **redid**	we, you, they **were redone**
Fut.	if I, he, she, it,	if I, he, she, it,
	we, you, they **should redo**	we, you, they **should be redone**

---

reduce
(active voice)

be reduced
(passive voice)

Infinitive: **to reduce**
Perfect Infinitive: **to have reduced**
Present Participle: **reducing**
Past Participle: **reduced**

Infinitive: **to be reduced**
Perfect Infinitive: **to have been reduced**
Present Participle: **being reduced**
Past Participle: **been reduced**

INDICATIVE MOOD

Pres.	I, we, you, they **reduce**	I **am reduced**
		we, you, they **are reduced**
	he, she, it **reduces**	he, she, it **is reduced**
Pres.	I **am reducing**	I **am being reduced**
Prog.	we, you, they **are reducing**	we, you, they **are being reduced**
	he, she, it **is reducing**	he, she, it **is being reduced**
Pres.	I, we, you, they **do reduce**	I, we, you, they **do get reduced**
Int.	he, she, it **does reduce**	he, she, it **does get reduced**
Fut.	I, he, she, it, we, you, they **will reduce**	I, he, she, it, we, you, they **will be reduced**
Past	I, he, she, it, we, you, they **reduced**	I, he, she, it **was reduced** we, you, they **were reduced**
Past	I, he, she, it **was reducing**	I, he, she, it **was being reduced**
Prog.	we, you, they **were reducing**	we, you, they **were being reduced**
Past	I, he, she, it, we, you, they **did reduce**	I, he, she, it, we, you, they **did get reduced**
Int.		
Pres.	I, we, you, they **have reduced**	I, we, you, they **have been reduced**
Perf.	he, she, it **has reduced**	he, she, it **has been reduced**
Past	I, he, she, it, we, you, they **had reduced**	I, he, she, it, we, you, they **had been reduced**
Perf.		
Fut.	I, he, she, it, we, you, they	I, he, she, it, we, you, they
Perf.	**will have reduced**	**will have been reduced**

IMPERATIVE MOOD

reduce   **be reduced**

SUBJUNCTIVE MOOD

Pres.	if I, he, she, it, we, you, they **reduce**	if I, he, she, it, we, you, they **be reduced**
Past	if I, he, she, it, we, you, they **reduced**	if I, he, she, it, we, you, they **were reduced**
Fut.	if I, he, she, it, we, you, they **should reduce**	if I, he, she, it, we, you, they **should be reduced**

Transitive and intransitive.

refer
(active voice)

PRINCIPAL PARTS: **refers, referring, referred, referred**

be referred
(passive voice)

Infinitive: **to refer**
Perfect Infinitive: **to have referred**
Present Participle: **referring**
Past Participle: **referred**

Infinitive: **to be referred**
Perfect Infinitive: **to have been referred**
Present Participle: **being referred**
Past Participle: **been referred**

INDICATIVE MOOD

Pres.	I, we, you, they **refer**	I **am referred**
		we, you, they **are referred**
	he, she, it **refers**	he, she, it **is referred**
Pres.	I **am referring**	I **am being referred**
Prog.	we, you, they **are referring**	we, you, they **are being referred**
	he, she, it **is referring**	he, she, it **is being referred**
Pres.	I, we, you, they **do refer**	I, we, you, they **do get referred**
Int.	he, she, it **does refer**	he, she, it **does get referred**
Fut.	I, he, she, it,	I, he, she, it,
	we, you, they **will refer**	we, you, they **will be referred**
Past	I, he, she, it,	I, he, she, it **was referred**
	we, you, they **referred**	we, you, they **were referred**
Past	I, he, she, it **was referring**	I, he, she, it **was being referred**
Prog.	we, you, they **were referring**	we, you, they **were being referred**
Past	I, he, she, it,	I, he, she, it,
Int.	we, you, they **did refer**	we, you, they **did get referred**
Pres.	I, we, you, they **have referred**	I, we, you, they **have been referred**
Perf.	he, she, it **has referred**	he, she, it **has been referred**
Past	I, he, she, it,	I, he, she, it,
Perf.	we, you, they **had referred**	we, you, they **had been referred**
Fut.	I, he, she, it, we, you, they	I, he, she, it, we, you, they
Perf.	**will have referred**	**will have been referred**

IMPERATIVE MOOD

refer be referred

SUBJUNCTIVE MOOD

Pres.	if I, he, she, it,	if I, he, she, it,
	we, you, they **refer**	we, you, they **be referred**
Past	if I, he, she, it,	if I, he, she, it,
	we, you, they **referred**	we, you, they **were referred**
Fut.	if I, he, she, it,	if I, he, she, it,
	we, you, they **should refer**	we, you, they **should be referred**

Transitive and intransitive.

regret
(active voice)

be regretted
(passive voice)

Infinitive: **to regret**
Perfect Infinitive: **to have regretted**
Present Participle: **regretting**
Past Participle: **regretted**

Infinitive: **to be regretted**
Perfect Infinitive: **to have been regretted**
Present Participle: **being regretted**
Past Participle: **been regretted**

INDICATIVE MOOD

Pres.	I, we, you, they **regret**	I **am regretted**
		we, you, they **are regretted**
	he, she, it **regrets**	he, she, it **is regretted**
Pres.	I **am regretting**	I **am being regretted**
Prog.	we, you, they **are regretting**	we, you, they **are being regretted**
	he, she, it **is regretting**	he, she, it **is being regretted**
Pres.	I, we, you, they **do regret**	I, we, you, they **do get regretted**
Int.	he, she, it **does regret**	he, she, it **does get regretted**
Fut.	I, he, she, it,	I, he, she, it,
	we, you, they **will regret**	we, you, they **will be regretted**
Past	I, he, she, it,	I, he, she, it **was regretted**
	we, you, they **regretted**	we, you, they **were regretted**
Past	I, he, she, it **was regretting**	I, he, she, it **was being regretted**
Prog.	we, you, they **were regretting**	we, you, they **were being regretted**
Past	I, he, she, it,	I, he, she, it,
Int.	we, you, they **did regret**	we, you, they **did get regretted**
Pres.	I, we, you, they **have regretted**	I, we, you, they **have been regretted**
Perf.	he, she, it **has regretted**	he, she, it **has been regretted**
Past	I, he, she, it,	I, he, she, it,
Perf.	we, you, they **had regretted**	we, you, they **had been regretted**
Fut.	I, he, she, it, we, you, they	I, he, she, it, we, you, they
Perf.	**will have regretted**	**will have been regretted**

IMPERATIVE MOOD

regret   **be regretted**

SUBJUNCTIVE MOOD

Pres.	if I, he, she, it,	if I, he, she, it,
	we, you, they **regret**	we, you, they **be regretted**
Past	if I, he, she, it,	if I, he, she, it,
	we, you, they **regretted**	we, you, they **were regretted**
Fut.	if I, he, she, it,	if I, he, she, it,
	we, you, they **should regret**	we, you, they **should be regretted**

Transitive and intransitive.

relate
(active voice)

be related
(passive voice)

Infinitive: **to relate**
Perfect Infinitive: **to have related**
Present Participle: **relating**
Past Participle: **related**

Infinitive: **to be related**
Perfect Infinitive: **to have been related**
Present Participle: **being related**
Past Participle: **been related**

INDICATIVE MOOD

Pres.	I, we, you, they **relate**	I **am related**
		we, you, they **are related**
	he, she, it **relates**	he, she, it **is related**
Pres.	I **am relating**	I **am being related**
Prog.	we, you, they **are relating**	we, you, they **are being related**
	he, she, it **is relating**	he, she, it **is being related**
Pres.	I, we, you, they **do relate**	I, we, you, they **do get related**
Int.	he, she, it **does relate**	he, she, it **does get related**
Fut.	I, he, she, it,	I, he, she, it,
	we, you, they **will relate**	we, you, they **will be related**
Past	I, he, she, it,	I, he, she, it **was related**
	we, you, they **related**	we, you, they **were related**
Past	I, he, she, it **was relating**	I, he, she, it **was being related**
Prog.	we, you, they **were relating**	we, you, they **were being related**
Past	I, he, she, it,	I, he, she, it,
Int.	we, you, they **did relate**	we, you, they **did get related**
Pres.	I, we, you, they **have related**	I, we, you, they **have been related**
Perf.	he, she, it **has related**	he, she, it **has been related**
Past	I, he, she, it,	I, he, she, it,
Perf.	we, you, they **had related**	we, you, they **had been related**
Fut.	I, he, she, it, we, you, they	I, he, she, it, we, you, they
Perf.	**will have related**	**will have been related**

IMPERATIVE MOOD

relate

be related

SUBJUNCTIVE MOOD

Pres.	if I, he, she, it,	if I, he, she, it,
	we, you, they **relate**	we, you, they **be related**
Past	if I, he, she, it,	if I, he, she, it,
	we, you, they **related**	we, you, they **were related**
Fut.	if I, he, she, it,	if I, he, she, it,
	we, you, they **should relate**	we, you, they **should be related**

Transitive and intransitive.

re-lay
(active voice)

be re-laid
(passive voice)

Infinitive: **to re-lay**
Perfect Infinitive: **to have re-laid**
Present Participle: **re-laying**
Past Participle: **re-laid**

Infinitive: **to be re-laid**
Perfect Infinitive: **to have been re-laid**
Present Participle: **being re-laid**
Past Participle: **been re-laid**

INDICATIVE MOOD

Pres.	I, we, you, they **re-lay**	I **am re-laid**
		we, you, they **are re-laid**
	he, she, it **re-lays**	he, she, it **is re-laid**
Pres. *Prog.*	I **am re-laying**	I **am being re-laid**
	we, you, they **are re-laying**	we, you, they **are being re-laid**
	he, she, it **is re-laying**	he, she, it **is being re-laid**
Pres. *Int.*	I, we, you, they **do re-lay**	I, we, you, they **do get re-laid**
	he, she, it **does re-lay**	he, she, it **does get re-laid**
Fut.	I, he, she, it, we, you, they **will re-lay**	I, he, she, it, we, you, they **will be re-laid**
Past	I, he, she, it, we, you, they **re-laid**	I, he, she, it **was re-laid** we, you, they **were re-laid**
Past *Prog.*	I, he, she, it **was re-laying** we, you, they **were re-laying**	I, he, she, it **was being re-laid** we, you, they **were being re-laid**
Past *Int.*	I, he, she, it, we, you, they **did re-lay**	I, he, she, it, we, you, they **did get re-laid**
Pres. *Perf.*	I, we, you, they **have re-laid**	I, we, you, they **have been re-laid**
	he, she, it **has re-laid**	he, she, it **has been re-laid**
Past *Perf.*	I, he, she, it, we, you, they **had re-laid**	I, he, she, it, we, you, they **had been re-laid**
Fut. *Perf.*	I, he, she, it, we, you, they **will have re-laid**	I, he, she, it, we, you, they **will have been re-laid**

IMPERATIVE MOOD

re-lay   **be re-laid**

SUBJUNCTIVE MOOD

Pres.	if I, he, she, it, we, you, they **re-lay**	if I, he, she, it, we, you, they **be re-laid**
Past	if I, he, she, it, we, you, they **re-laid**	if I, he, she, it, we, you, they **were re-laid**
Fut.	if I, he, she, it, we, you, they **should re-lay**	if I, he, she, it, we, you, they **should be re-laid**

Transitive and intransitive. This verb means to "install something again."

relay
(active voice)

be relayed
(passive voice)

Infinitive: **to relay**
Perfect Infinitive: **to have relayed**
Present Participle: **relaying**
Past Participle: **relayed**

Infinitive: **to be relayed**
Perfect Infinitive: **to have been relayed**
Present Participle: **being relayed**
Past Participle: **been relayed**

INDICATIVE MOOD

Pres.	I, we, you, they **relay**	I am **relayed**
		we, you, they **are relayed**
	he, she, it **relays**	he, she, it **is relayed**
Pres.	I am **relaying**	I am **being relayed**
Prog.	we, you, they **are relaying**	we, you, they **are being relayed**
	he, she, it **is relaying**	he, she, it **is being relayed**
Pres.	I, we, you, they **do relay**	I, we, you, they **do get relayed**
Int.	he, she, it **does relay**	he, she, it **does get relayed**
Fut.	I, he, she, it,	I, he, she, it,
	we, you, they **will relay**	we, you, they **will be relayed**
Past	I, he, she, it,	I, he, she, it **was relayed**
	we, you, they **relayed**	we, you, they **were relayed**
Past	I, he, she, it **was relaying**	I, he, she, it **was being relayed**
Prog.	we, you, they **were relaying**	we, you, they **were being relayed**
Past	I, he, she, it,	I, he, she, it,
Int.	we, you, they **did relay**	we, you, they **did get relayed**
Pres.	I, we, you, they **have relayed**	I, we, you, they **have been relayed**
Perf.	he, she, it **has relayed**	he, she, it **has been relayed**
Past	I, he, she, it,	I, he, she, it,
Perf.	we, you, they **had relayed**	we, you, they **had been relayed**
Fut.	I, he, she, it, we, you, they	I, he, she, it, we, you, they
Perf.	**will have relayed**	**will have been relayed**

IMPERATIVE MOOD

relay

be relayed

SUBJUNCTIVE MOOD

Pres.	if I, he, she, it,	if I, he, she, it,
	we, you, they **relay**	we, you, they **be relayed**
Past	if I, he, she, it,	if I, he, she, it,
	we, you, they **relayed**	we, you, they **were relayed**
Fut.	if I, he, she, it,	if I, he, she, it,
	we, you, they **should relay**	we, you, they **should be relayed**

remain PRINCIPAL PARTS: **remains, remaining, remained, remained**

Infinitive: **to remain**
Perfect Infinitive: **to have remained**
Present Participle: **remaining**
Past Participle: **remained**

INDICATIVE MOOD

Pres. I, we, you, they **remain**

he, she, it **remains**

Pres. **I am remaining**
Prog. we, you, they **are remaining**
he, she, it **is remaining**

Pres. I, we, you, they **do remain**
Int. he, she, it **does remain**

Fut. I, he, she, it,
we, you, they **will remain**

Past I, he, she, it,
we, you, they **remained**

Past I, he, she, it **was remaining**
Prog. we, you, they **were remaining**

Past I, he, she, it,
Int. we, you, they **did remain**

Pres. I, we, you, they **have remained**
Perf. he, she, it **has remained**

Past I, he, she, it,
Perf. we, you, they **had remained**

Fut. I, he, she, it, we, you, they
Perf. **will have remained**

IMPERATIVE MOOD

remain

SUBJUNCTIVE MOOD

Pres. if I, he, she, it,
we, you, they **remain**

Past if I, he, she, it,
we, you, they **remained**

Fut. if I, he, she, it,
we, you, they **should remain**

remake
(active voice)

be remade
(passive voice)

Infinitive: **to remake**
Perfect Infinitive: **to have remade**
Present Participle: **remaking**
Past Participle: **remade**

Infinitive: **to be remade**
Perfect Infinitive: **to have been remade**
Present Participle: **being remade**
Past Participle: **been remade**

INDICATIVE MOOD

Pres.	I, we, you, they **remake**	I **am remade**
		we, you, they **are remade**
	he, she, it **remakes**	he, she, it **is remade**
Pres. *Prog.*	I **am remaking** we, you, they **are remaking** he, she, it **is remaking**	I **am being remade** we, you, they **are being remade** he, she, it **is being remade**
Pres. *Int.*	I, we, you, they **do remake** he, she, it **does remake**	I, we, you, they **do get remade** he, she, it **does get remade**
Fut.	I, he, she, it, we, you, they **will remake**	I, he, she, it, we, you, they **will be remade**
Past	I, he, she, it, we, you, they **remade**	I, he, she, it **was remade** we, you, they **were remade**
Past *Prog.*	I, he, she, it **was remaking** we, you, they **were remaking**	I, he, she, it **was being remade** we, you, they **were being remade**
Past *Int.*	I, he, she, it, we, you, they **did remake**	I, he, she, it, we, you, they **did get remade**
Pres. *Perf.*	I, we, you, they **have remade** he, she, it **has remade**	I, we, you, they **have been remade** he, she, it **has been remade**
Past *Perf.*	I, he, she, it, we, you, they **had remade**	I, he, she, it, we, you, they **had been remade**
Fut. *Perf.*	I, he, she, it, we, you, they **will have remade**	I, he, she, it, we, you, they **will have been remade**

IMPERATIVE MOOD

remake

be remade

SUBJUNCTIVE MOOD

Pres.	if I, he, she, it, we, you, they **remake**	if I, he, she, it, we, you, they **be remade**
Past	if I, he, she, it, we, you, they **remade**	if I, he, she, it, we, you, they **were remade**
Fut.	if I, he, she, it, we, you, they **should remake**	if I, he, she, it, we, you, they **should be remade**

remember
(active voice)

be remembered
(passive voice)

Infinitive: **to remember**
Perfect Infinitive: **to have remembered**
Present Participle: **remembering**
Past Participle: **remembered**

Infinitive: **to be remembered**
Perfect Infinitive: **to have been remembered**
Present Participle: **being remembered**
Past Participle: **been remembered**

INDICATIVE MOOD

Pres.	I, we, you, they **remember**	I **am remembered**
		we, you, they **are remembered**
	he, she, it **remembers**	he, she, it **is remembered**
Pres.	I **am remembering**	I **am being remembered**
Prog.	we, you, they **are remembering**	we, you, they **are being remembered**
	he, she, it **is remembering**	he, she, it **is being remembered**
Pres.	I, we, you, they **do remember**	I, we, you, they **do get remembered**
Int.	he, she, it **does remember**	he, she, it **does get remembered**
Fut.	I, he, she, it,	I, he, she, it,
	we, you, they **will remember**	we, you, they **will be remembered**
Past	I, he, she, it,	I, he, she, it **was remembered**
	we, you, they **remembered**	we, you, they **were remembered**
Past	I, he, she, it **was remembering**	I, he, she, it **was being remembered**
Prog.	we, you, they **were remembering**	we, you, they **were being remembered**
Past	I, he, she, it,	I, he, she, it,
Int.	we, you, they **did remember**	we, you, they **did get remembered**
Pres.	I, we, you, they **have remembered**	I, we, you, they **have been remembered**
Perf.	he, she, it **has remembered**	he, she, it **has been remembered**
Past	I, he, she, it,	I, he, she, it,
Perf.	we, you, they **had remembered**	we, you, they **had been remembered**
Fut.	I, he, she, it, we, you, they	I, he, she, it, we, you, they
Perf.	**will have remembered**	**will have been remembered**

IMPERATIVE MOOD

remember

be remembered

SUBJUNCTIVE MOOD

Pres.	if I, he, she, it,	if I, he, she, it,
	we, you, they **remember**	we, you, they **be remembered**
Past	if I, he, she, it,	if I, he, she, it,
	we, you, they **remembered**	we, you, they **were remembered**
Fut.	if I, he, she, it,	if I, he, she, it, we, you, they
	we, you, they **should remember**	**should be remembered**

Transitive and intransitive.

319

remove
(active voice)

be removed
(passive voice)

Infinitive: **to remove**
Perfect Infinitive: **to have removed**
Present Participle: **removing**
Past Participle: **removed**

Infinitive: **to be removed**
Perfect Infinitive: **to have been removed**
Present Participle: **being removed**
Past Participle: **been removed**

INDICATIVE MOOD

Pres.	I, we, you, they **remove** he, she, it **removes**	I **am removed** we, you, they **are removed** he, she, it **is removed**
Pres. *Prog.*	I **am removing** we, you, they **are removing** he, she, it **is removing**	I **am being removed** we, you, they **are being removed** he, she, it **is being removed**
Pres. *Int.*	I, we, you, they **do remove** he, she, it **does remove**	I, we, you, they **do get removed** he, she, it **does get removed**
Fut.	I, he, she, it, we, you, they **will remove**	I, he, she, it, we, you, they **will be removed**
Past	I, he, she, it, we, you, they **removed**	I, he, she, it **was removed** we, you, they **were removed**
Past *Prog.*	I, he, she, it **was removing** we, you, they **were removing**	I, he, she, it **was being removed** we, you, they **were being removed**
Past *Int.*	I, he, she, it, we, you, they **did remove**	I, he, she, it, we, you, they **did get removed**
Pres. *Perf.*	I, we, you, they **have removed** he, she, it **has removed**	I, we, you, they **have been removed** he, she, it **has been removed**
Past *Perf.*	I, he, she, it, we, you, they **had removed**	I, he, she, it, we, you, they **had been removed**
Fut. *Perf.*	I, he, she, it, we, you, they **will have removed**	I, he, she, it, we, you, they **will have been removed**

IMPERATIVE MOOD

remove

be removed

SUBJUNCTIVE MOOD

Pres.	if I, he, she, it, we, you, they **remove**	if I, he, she, it, we, you, they **be removed**
Past	if I, he, she, it, we, you, they **removed**	if I, he, she, it, we, you, they **were removed**
Fut.	if I, he, she, it, we, you, they **should remove**	if I, he, she, it, we, you, they **should be removed**

Transitive and intransitive.

rend
(active voice)

PRINCIPAL PARTS: **rends, rending,
rent/rended, rent/rended**

be rent/rended
(passive voice)

Infinitive: **to rend**
Perfect Infinitive: **to have rent**
Present Participle: **rending**
Past Participle: **rent**

Infinitive: **to be rent**
Perfect Infinitive: **to have been rent**
Present Participle: **being rent**
Past Participle: **been rent**

INDICATIVE MOOD

Pres.	I, we, you, they **rend**	I **am rent**
		we, you, they **are rent**
	he, she, it **rends**	he, she, it **is rent**
Pres.	I **am rending**	I **am being rent**
Prog.	we, you, they **are rending**	we, you, they **are being rent**
	he, she, it **is rending**	he, she, it **is being rent**
Pres.	I, we, you, they **do rend**	I, we, you, they **do get rent**
Int.	he, she, it **does rend**	he, she, it **does get rent**
Fut.	I, he, she, it,	I, he, she, it,
	we, you, they **will rend**	we, you, they **will be rent**
Past	I, he, she, it,	I, he, she, it **was rent**
	we, you, they **rent**	we, you, they **were rent**
Past	I, he, she, it **was rending**	I, he, she, it **was being rent**
Prog.	we, you, they **were rending**	we, you, they **were being rent**
Past	I, he, she, it,	I, he, she, it,
Int.	we, you, they **did rend**	we, you, they **did get rent**
Pres.	I, we, you, they **have rent**	I, we, you, they **have been rent**
Perf.	he, she, it **has rent**	he, she, it **has been rent**
Past	I, he, she, it,	I, he, she, it,
Perf.	we, you, they **had rent**	we, you, they **had been rent**
Fut.	I, he, she, it,we, you, they	I, he, she, it, we, you, they
Perf.	**will have rent**	**will have been rent**

IMPERATIVE MOOD

rend   **be rent**

SUBJUNCTIVE MOOD

Pres.	if I, he, she, it,	if I, he, she, it,
	we, you, they **rend**	we, you, they **be rent**
Past	if I, he, she, it,	if I, he, she, it,
	we, you, they **rent**	we, you, they **were rent**
Fut.	if I, he, she, it,	if I, he, she, it,
	we, you, they **should rend**	we, you, they **should be rent**

Transitive and intransitive. The *American Heritage* and *Merriam Webster's* accept for the past tense and past participle both RENT and RENDED.

rent
(active voice)

be rented
(passive voice)

Infinitive: **to rent**
Perfect Infinitive: **to have rented**
Present Participle: **renting**
Past Participle: **rented**

Infinitive: **to be rented**
Perfect Infinitive: **to have been rented**
Present Participle: **being rented**
Past Participle: **been rented**

INDICATIVE MOOD

Pres.	I, we, you, they **rent**	I **am rented**
		we, you, they **are rented**
	he, she, it **rents**	he, she, it **is rented**
Pres.	I **am renting**	I **am being rented**
Prog.	we, you, they **are renting**	we, you, they **are being rented**
	he, she, it **is renting**	he, she, it **is being rented**
Pres.	I, we, you, they **do rent**	I, we, you, they **do get rented**
Int.	he, she, it **does rent**	he, she, it **does get rented**
Fut.	I, he, she, it,	I, he, she, it,
	we, you, they **will rent**	we, you, they **will be rented**
Past	I, he, she, it,	I, he, she, it **was rented**
	we, you, they **rented**	we, you, they **were rented**
Past	I, he, she, it **was renting**	I, he, she, it **was being rented**
Prog.	we, you, they **were renting**	we, you, they **were being rented**
Past	I, he, she, it,	I, he, she, it,
Int.	we, you, they **did rent**	we, you, they **did get rented**
Pres.	I, we, you, they **have rented**	I, we, you, they **have been rented**
Perf.	he, she, it **has rented**	he, she, it **has been rented**
Past	I, he, she, it,	I, he, she, it,
Perf.	we, you, they **had rented**	we, you, they **had been rented**
Fut.	I, he, she, it, we, you, they	I, he, she, it, we, you, they
Perf.	**will have rented**	**will have been rented**

IMPERATIVE MOOD

rent

be rented

SUBJUNCTIVE MOOD

Pres.	if I, he, she, it,	if I, he, she, it,
	we, you, they **rent**	we, you, they **be rented**
Past	if I, he, she, it,	if I, he, she, it,
	we, you, they **rented**	we, you, they **were rented**
Fut.	if I, he, she, it,	if I, he, she, it,
	we, you, they **should rent**	we, you, they **should be rented**

Transitive and intransitive.

repay
(active voice)

be repaid
(passive voice)

Infinitive: **to repay**
Perfect Infinitive: **to have repaid**
Present Participle: **repaying**
Past Participle: **repaid**

Infinitive: **to be repaid**
Perfect Infinitive: **to have been repaid**
Present Participle: **being repaid**
Past Participle: **been repaid**

INDICATIVE MOOD

Pres.	I, we, you, they **repay** he, she, it **repays**	I **am repaid** we, you, they **are repaid** he, she, it **is repaid**
Pres. *Prog.*	I **am repaying** we, you, they **are repaying** he, she, it **is repaying**	I **am being repaid** we, you, they **are being repaid** he, she, it **is being repaid**
Pres. *Int.*	I, we, you, they **do repay** he, she, it **does repay**	I, we, you, they **do get repaid** he, she, it **does get repaid**
Fut.	I, he, she, it, we, you, they **will repay**	I, he, she, it, we, you, they **will be repaid**
Past	I, he, she, it, we, you, they **repaid**	I, he, she, it **was repaid** we, you, they **were repaid**
Past *Prog.*	I, he, she, it **was repaying** we, you, they **were repaying**	I, he, she, it **was being repaid** we, you, they **were being repaid**
Past *Int.*	I, he, she, it, we, you, they **did repay**	I, he, she, it, we, you, they **did get repaid**
Pres. *Perf.*	I, we, you, they **have repaid** he, she, it **has repaid**	I, we, you, they **have been repaid** he, she, it **has been repaid**
Past *Perf.*	I, he, she, it, we, you, they **had repaid**	I, he, she, it, we, you, they **had been repaid**
Fut. *Perf.*	I, he, she, it, we, you, they **will have repaid**	I, he, she, it, we, you, they **will have been repaid**

IMPERATIVE MOOD

repay

be repaid

SUBJUNCTIVE MOOD

Pres.	if I, he, she, it, we, you, they **repay**	if I, he, she, it, we, you, they **be repaid**
Past	if I, he, she, it, we, you, they **repaid**	if I, he, she, it, we, you, they **were repaid**
Fut.	if I, he, she, it, we, you, they **should repay**	if I, he, she, it, we, you, they **should be repaid**

Transitive and intransitive.

reply
(active voice)

PRINCIPAL PARTS: **replies, replying,
replied, replied**

be replied
(passive voice)

Infinitive: **to reply**	*Infinitive:* **to be replied**
Perfect Infinitive: **to have replied**	*Perfect Infinitive:* **to have been replied**
Present Participle: **replying**	*Present Participle:* **being replied**
Past Participle: **replied**	*Past Participle:* **been replied**

INDICATIVE MOOD

Pres.	I, we, you, they **reply**	I **am replied**
		we, you, they **are replied**
	he, she, it **replies**	he, she, it **is replied**
Pres.	I **am replying**	I **am being replied**
Prog.	we, you, they **are replying**	we, you, they **are being replied**
	he, she, it **is replying**	he, she, it **is being replied**
Pres.	I, we, you, they **do reply**	I, we, you, they **do get replied**
Int.	he, she, it **does reply**	he, she, it **does get replied**
Fut.	I, he, she, it,	I, he, she, it,
	we, you, they **will reply**	we, you, they **will be replied**
Past	I, he, she, it,	I, he, she, it **was replied**
	we, you, they **replied**	we, you, they **were replied**
Past	I, he, she, it **was replying**	I, he, she, it **was being replied**
Prog.	we, you, they **were replying**	we, you, they **were being replied**
Past	I, he, she, it,	I, he, she, it,
Int.	we, you, they **did reply**	we, you, they **did get replied**
Pres.	I, we, you, they **have replied**	I, we, you, they **have been replied**
Perf.	he, she, it **has replied**	he, she, it **has been replied**
Past	I, he, she, it,	I, he, she, it,
Perf.	we, you, they **had replied**	we, you, they **had been replied**
Fut.	I, he, she, it, we, you, they	I, he, she, it, we, you, they
Perf.	**will have replied**	**will have been replied**

IMPERATIVE MOOD

| **reply** | **be replied** |

SUBJUNCTIVE MOOD

Pres.	if I, he, she, it,	if I, he, she, it,
	we, you, they **reply**	we, you, they **be replied**
Past	if I, he, she, it,	if I, he, she, it,
	we, you, they **replied**	we, you, they **were replied**
Fut.	if I, he, she, it,	if I, he, she, it,
	we, you, they **should reply**	we, you, they **should be replied**

Transitive and intransitive.

report
(active voice)

be reported
(passive voice)

Infinitive: **to report**
Perfect Infinitive: **to have reported**
Present Participle: **reporting**
Past Participle: **reported**

Infinitive: **to be reported**
Perfect Infinitive: **to have been reported**
Present Participle: **being reported**
Past Participle: **been reported**

INDICATIVE MOOD

Pres.	I, we, you, they **report**	I **am reported**
		we, you, they **are reported**
	he, she, it **reports**	he, she, it **is reported**
Pres. Prog.	I **am reporting**	I **am being reported**
	we, you, they **are reporting**	we, you, they **are being reported**
	he, she, it **is reporting**	he, she, it **is being reported**
Pres. Int.	I, we, you, they **do report**	I, we, you, they **do get reported**
	he, she, it **does report**	he, she, it **does get reported**
Fut.	I, he, she, it, we, you, they **will report**	I, he, she, it, we, you, they **will be reported**
Past	I, he, she, it, we, you, they **reported**	I, he, she, it **was reported** we, you, they **were reported**
Past Prog.	I, he, she, it **was reporting** we, you, they **were reporting**	I, he, she, it **was being reported** we, you, they **were being reported**
Past Int.	I, he, she, it, we, you, they **did report**	I, he, she, it, we, you, they **did get reported**
Pres. Perf.	I, we, you, they **have reported** he, she, it **has reported**	I, we, you, they **have been reported** he, she, it **has been reported**
Past Perf.	I, he, she, it, we, you, they **had reported**	I, he, she, it, we, you, they **had been reported**
Fut. Perf.	I, he, she, it, we, you, they **will have reported**	I, he, she, it, we, you, they **will have been reported**

IMPERATIVE MOOD

report   **be reported**

SUBJUNCTIVE MOOD

Pres.	if I, he, she, it, we, you, they **report**	if I, he, she, it, we, you, they **be reported**
Past	if I, he, she, it, we, you, they **reported**	if I, he, she, it, we, you, they **were reported**
Fut.	if I, he, she, it, we, you, they **should report**	if I, he, she, it, we, you, they **should be reported**

Transitive and intransitive.

325

represent
(active voice)

be represented
(passive voice)

Infinitive: **to represent**
Perfect Infinitive: **to have represented**
Present Participle: **representing**
Past Participle: **represented**

Infinitive: **to be represented**
Perfect Infinitive: **to have been represented**
Present Participle: **being represented**
Past Participle: **been represented**

INDICATIVE MOOD

Pres.	I, we, you, they **represent**	I **am represented** we, you, they **are represented**
	he, she, it **represents**	he, she, it **is represented**
Pres. *Prog.*	I **am representing** we, you, they **are representing** he, she, it **is representing**	I **am being represented** we, you, they **are being represented** he, she, it **is being represented**
Pres. *Int.*	I, we, you, they **do represent** he, she, it **does represent**	I, we, you, they **do get represented** he, she, it **does get represented**
Fut.	I, he, she, it, we, you, they **will represent**	I, he, she, it, we, you, they **will be represented**
Past	I, he, she, it, we, you, they **represented**	I, he, she, it **was represented** we, you, they **were represented**
Past *Prog.*	I, he, she, it **was representing** we, you, they **were representing**	I, he, she, it **was being represented** we, you, they **were being represented**
Past *Int.*	I, he, she, it, we, you, they **did represent**	I, he, she, it, we, you, they **did get represented**
Pres. *Perf.*	I, we, you, they **have represented** he, she, it **has represented**	I, we, you, they **have been represented** he, she, it **has been represented**
Past *Perf.*	I, he, she, it, we, you, they **had represented**	I, he, she, it, we, you, they **had been represented**
Fut. *Perf.*	I, he, she, it, we, you, they **will have represented**	I, he, she, it, we, you, they **will have been represented**

IMPERATIVE MOOD

represent   **be represented**

SUBJUNCTIVE MOOD

Pres.	if I, he, she, it, we, you, they **represent**	if I, he, she, it, we, you, they **be represented**
Past	if I, he, she, it, we, you, they **represented**	if I, he, she, it, we, you, they **were represented**
Fut.	if I, he, she, it, we, you, they **should represent**	if I, he, she, it, we, you, they **should be represented**

require
(active voice)

PRINCIPAL PARTS: **requires, requiring, required, required**

be required
(passive voice)

Infinitive: **to require**
Perfect Infinitive: **to have required**
Present Participle: **requiring**
Past Participle: **required**

Infinitive: **to be required**
Perfect Infinitive: **to have been required**
Present Participle: **being required**
Past Participle: **been required**

INDICATIVE MOOD

Pres.	I, we, you, they **require**	I am required
		we, you, they **are required**
	he, she, it **requires**	he, she, it **is required**
Pres. _Prog._	I **am requiring**	I am being required
	we, you, they **are requiring**	we, you, they **are being required**
	he, she, it **is requiring**	he, she, it **is being required**
Pres. _Int._	I, we, you, they **do require**	I, we, you, they **do get required**
	he, she, it **does require**	he, she, it **does get required**
Fut.	I, he, she, it,	I, he, she, it,
	we, you, they **will require**	we, you, they **will be required**
Past	I, he, she, it,	I, he, she, it **was required**
	we, you, they **required**	we, you, they **were required**
Past _Prog._	I, he, she, it **was requiring**	I, he, she, it **was being required**
	we, you, they **were requiring**	we, you, they **were being required**
Past _Int._	I, he, she, it,	I, he, she, it,
	we, you, they **did require**	we, you, they **did get required**
Pres. _Perf._	I, we, you, they **have required**	I, we, you, they **have been required**
	he, she, it **has required**	he, she, it **has been required**
Past _Perf._	I, he, she, it,	I, he, she, it,
	we, you, they **had required**	we, you, they **had been required**
Fut. _Perf._	I, he, she, it, we, you, they	I, he, she, it, we, you, they
	will have required	**will have been required**

IMPERATIVE MOOD

require **be required**

SUBJUNCTIVE MOOD

Pres.	if I, he, she, it,	if I, he, she, it,
	we, you, they **require**	we, you, they **be required**
Past	if I, he, she, it,	if I, he, she, it,
	we, you, they **required**	we, you, they **were required**
Fut.	if I, he, she, it,	if I, he, she, it,
	we, you, they **should require**	we, you, they **should be required**

Transitive and intransitive.

reread
(active voice)

PRINCIPAL PARTS: **rereads, rereading, reread, reread**

be reread
(passive voice)

Infinitive: **to reread**
Perfect Infinitive: **to have reread**
Present Participle: **rereading**
Past Participle: **reread**

Infinitive: **to be reread**
Perfect Infinitive: **to have been reread**
Present Participle: **being reread**
Past Participle: **been reread**

INDICATIVE MOOD

Pres.	I, we, you, they **reread**	I **am reread**
		we, you, they **are reread**
	he, she, it **rereads**	he, she, it **is reread**
Pres.	I **am rereading**	I **am being reread**
Prog.	we, you, they **are rereading**	we, you, they **are being reread**
	he, she, it **is rereading**	he, she, it **is being reread**
Pres.	I, we, you, they **do reread**	I, we, you, they **do get reread**
Int.	he, she, it **does reread**	he, she, it **does get reread**
Fut.	I, he, she, it,	I, he, she, it,
	we, you, they **will reread**	we, you, they **will be reread**
Past	I, he, she, it,	I, he, she, it **was reread**
	we, you, they **reread**	we, you, they **were reread**
Past	I, he, she, it **was rereading**	I, he, she, it **was being reread**
Prog.	we, you, they **were rereading**	we, you, they **were being reread**
Past	I, he, she, it,	I, he, she, it,
Int.	we, you, they **did reread**	we, you, they **did get reread**
Pres.	I, we, you, they **have reread**	I, we, you, they **have been reread**
Perf.	he, she, it **has reread**	he, she, it **has been reread**
Past	I, he, she, it,	I, he, she, it,
Perf.	we, you, they **had reread**	we, you, they **had been reread**
Fut.	I, he, she, it, we, you, they	I, he, she, it, we, you, they
Perf.	**will have reread**	**will have been reread**

IMPERATIVE MOOD

reread

be reread

SUBJUNCTIVE MOOD

Pres.	if I, he, she, it,	if I, he, she, it,
	we, you, they **reread**	we, you, they **be reread**
Past	if I, he, she, it,	if I, he, she, it,
	we, you, they **reread**	we, you, they **were reread**
Fut.	if I, he, she, it,	if I, he, she, it,
	we, you, they **should reread**	we, you, they **should be reread**

Note the pronunciation of the past tense and past participle as "re-red."

rescue
(active voice)

be rescued
(passive voice)

Infinitive: **to rescue**
Perfect Infinitive: **to have rescued**
Present Participle: **rescuing**
Past Participle: **rescued**

Infinitive: **to be rescued**
Perfect Infinitive: **to have been rescued**
Present Participle: **being rescued**
Past Participle: **been rescued**

INDICATIVE MOOD

Pres.	I, we, you, they **rescue**	I **am rescued**
		we, you, they **are rescued**
	he, she, it **rescues**	he, she, it **is rescued**
Pres.	I **am rescuing**	I **am being rescued**
Prog.	we, you, they **are rescuing**	we, you, they **are being rescued**
	he, she, it **is rescuing**	he, she, it is being rescued
Pres.	I, we, you, they **do rescue**	I, we, you, they **do get rescued**
Int.	he, she, it **does rescue**	he, she, it **does get rescued**
Fut.	I, he, she, it,	I, he, she, it,
	we, you, they **will rescue**	we, you, they **will be rescued**
Past	I, he, she, it,	I, he, she, it **was rescued**
	we, you, they **rescued**	we, you, they **were rescued**
Past	I, he, she, it **was rescuing**	I, he, she, it **was being rescued**
Prog.	we, you, they **were rescuing**	we, you, they **were being rescued**
Past	I, he, she, it,	I, he, she, it,
Int.	we, you, they **did rescue**	we, you, they **did get rescued**
Pres.	I, we, you, they **have rescued**	I, we, you, they **have been rescued**
Perf.	he, she, it **has rescued**	he, she, it **has been rescued**
Past	I, he, she, it,	I, he, she, it,
Perf.	we, you, they **had rescued**	we, you, they **had been rescued**
Fut.	I, he, she, it, we, you, they	I, he, she, it, we, you, they
Perf.	**will have rescued**	**will have been rescued**

IMPERATIVE MOOD

rescue	**be rescued**

SUBJUNCTIVE MOOD

Pres.	if I, he, she, it,	if I, he, she, it,
	we, you, they **rescue**	we, you, they **be rescued**
Past	if I, he, she, it,	if I, he, she, it,
	we, you, they **rescued**	we, you, they **were rescued**
Fut.	if I, he, she, it,	if I, he, she, it,
	we, you, they **should rescue**	we, you, they **should be rescued**

rest
(active voice)

be rested
(passive voice)

Infinitive: **to rest**
Perfect Infinitive: **to have rested**
Present Participle: **resting**
Past Participle: **rested**

Infinitive: **to be rested**
Perfect Infinitive: **to have been rested**
Present Participle: **being rested**
Past Participle: **been rested**

INDICATIVE MOOD

Pres.	I, we, you, they **rest**	I **am rested**
		we, you, they **are rested**
	he, she, it **rests**	he, she, it **is rested**
Pres.	I **am resting**	I **am being rested**
Prog.	we, you, they **are resting**	we, you, they **are being rested**
	he, she, it **is resting**	he, she, it **is being rested**
Pres.	I, we, you, they **do rest**	I, we, you, they **do get rested**
Int.	he, she, it **does rest**	he, she, it **does get rested**
Fut.	I, he, she, it,	I, he, she, it,
	we, you, they **will rest**	we, you, they **will be rested**
Past	I, he, she, it,	I, he, she, it **was rested**
	we, you, they **rested**	we, you, they **were rested**
Past	I, he, she, it **was resting**	I, he, she, it **was being rested**
Prog.	we, you, they **were resting**	we, you, they **were being rested**
Past	I, he, she, it,	I, he, she, it,
Int.	we, you, they **did rest**	we, you, they **did get rested**
Pres.	I, we, you, they **have rested**	I, we, you, they **have been rested**
Perf.	he, she, it **has rested**	he, she, it **has been rested**
Past	I, he, she, it,	I, he, she, it,
Perf.	we, you, they **had rested**	we, you, they **had been rested**
Fut.	I, he, she, it, we, you, they	I, he, she, it, we, you, they
Perf.	**will have rested**	**will have been rested**

IMPERATIVE MOOD

rest

be rested

SUBJUNCTIVE MOOD

Pres.	if I, he, she, it,	if I, he, she, it,
	we, you, they **rest**	we, you, they **be rested**
Past	if I, he, she, it,	if I, he, she, it,
	we, you, they **rested**	we, you, they **were rested**
Fut.	if I, he, she, it,	if I, he, she, it,
	we, you, they **should rest**	we, you, they **should be rested**

Transitive and intransitive.

result　　　　　　PRINCIPAL PARTS: **results, resulting,**
　　　　　　　　　　　　　　resulted, resulted

Infinitive: **to result**
Perfect Infinitive: **to have resulted**
Present Participle: **resulting**
Past Participle: **resulted**

INDICATIVE MOOD

Pres.　I, we, you, they **result**

　　　　he, she, it **results**

Pres.　**I am resulting**
Prog.　we, you, they **are resulting**
　　　　he, she, it **is resulting**

Pres.　I, we, you, they **do result**
Int.　　he, she, it **does result**

Fut.　　I, he, she, it,
　　　　we, you, they **will result**

Past　　I, he, she, it,
　　　　we, you, they **resulted**

Past　　I, he, she, it **was resulting**
Prog.　we, you, they **were resulting**

Past　　I, he, she, it,
Int.　　we, you, they **did result**

Pres.　I, we, you, they **have resulted**
Perf.　he, she, it **has resulted**

Past　　I, he, she, it,
Perf.　we, you, they **had resulted**

Fut.　　I, he, she, it, we, you, they
Perf.　**will have resulted**

IMPERATIVE MOOD

　　　　result

SUBJUNCTIVE MOOD

Pres.　if I, he, she, it,
　　　　we, you, they **result**

Past　　if I, he, she, it,
　　　　we, you, they **resulted**

Fut.　　if I, he, she, it,
　　　　we, you, they **should result**

---

retell
(active voice)

be retold
(passive voice)

Infinitive: **to retell**
Perfect Infinitive: **to have retold**
Present Participle: **retelling**
Past Participle: **retold**

Infinitive: **to be retold**
Perfect Infinitive: **to have been retold**
Present Participle: **being retold**
Past Participle: **been retold**

INDICATIVE MOOD

Pres.	I, we, you, they **retell**	I **am retold**
		we, you, they **are retold**
	he, she, it **retells**	he, she, it **is retold**
Pres.	I **am retelling**	I **am being retold**
Prog.	we, you, they **are retelling**	we, you, they **are being retold**
	he, she, it **is retelling**	he, she, it **is being retold**
Pres.	I, we, you, they **do retell**	I, we, you, they **do get retold**
Int.	he, she, it **does retell**	he, she, it **does get retold**
Fut.	I, he, she, it,	I, he, she, it,
	we, you, they **will retell**	we, you, they **will be retold**
Past	I, he, she, it,	I, he, she, it **was retold**
	we, you, they **retold**	we, you, they **were retold**
Past	I, he, she, it **was retelling**	I, he, she, it **was being retold**
Prog.	we, you, they **were retelling**	we, you, they **were being retold**
Past	I, he, she, it,	I, he, she, it,
Int.	we, you, they **did retell**	we, you, they **did get retold**
Pres.	I, we, you, they **have retold**	I, we, you, they **have been retold**
Perf.	he, she, it **has retold**	he, she, it **has been retold**
Past	I, he, she, it,	I, he, she, it,
Perf.	we, you, they **had retold**	we, you, they **had been retold**
Fut.	I, he, she, it, we, you, they	I, he, she, it, we, you, they
Perf.	**will have retold**	**will have been retold**

IMPERATIVE MOOD

retell   **be retold**

SUBJUNCTIVE MOOD

Pres.	if I, he, she, it,	if I, he, she, it,
	we, you, they **retell**	we, you, they **be retold**
Past	if I, he, she, it,	if I, he, she, it,
	we, you, they **retold**	we, you, they **were retold**
Fut.	if I, he, she, it,	if I, he, she, it,
	we, you, they **should retell**	we, you, they **should be retold**

rethink
(active voice)

be rethought
(passive voice)

Infinitive: **to rethink**
Perfect Infinitive: **to have rethought**
Present Participle: **rethinking**
Past Participle: **rethought**

Infinitive: **to be rethought**
Perfect Infinitive: **to have been rethought**
Present Participle: **being rethought**
Past Participle: **been rethought**

INDICATIVE MOOD

Pres.	I, we, you, they **rethink**	I **am rethought**
		we, you, they **are rethought**
	he, she, it **rethinks**	he, she, it **is rethought**
Pres.	I **am rethinking**	I **am being rethought**
Prog.	we, you, they **are rethinking**	we, you, they **are being rethought**
	he, she, it **is rethinking**	he, she, it **is being rethought**
Pres.	I, we, you, they **do rethink**	I, we, you, they **do get rethought**
Int.	he, she, it **does rethink**	he, she, it **does get rethought**
Fut.	I, he, she, it,	I, he, she, it,
	we, you, they **will rethink**	we, you, they **will be rethought**
Past	I, he, she, it,	I, he, she, it **was rethought**
	we, you, they **rethought**	we, you, they **were rethought**
Past	I, he, she, it **was rethinking**	I, he, she, it **was being rethought**
Prog.	we, you, they **were rethinking**	we, you, they **were being rethought**
Past	I, he, she, it,	I, he, she, it,
Int.	we, you, they **did rethink**	we, you, they **did get rethought**
Pres.	I, we, you, they **have rethought**	I, we, you, they **have been rethought**
Perf.	he, she, it **has rethought**	he, she, it **has been rethought**
Past	I, he, she, it,	I, he, she, it,
Perf.	we, you, they **had rethought**	we, you, they **had been rethought**
Fut.	I, he, she, it, we, you, they	I, he, she, it, we, you, they
Perf.	**will have rethought**	**will have been rethought**

IMPERATIVE MOOD

rethink	**be rethought**

SUBJUNCTIVE MOOD

Pres.	if I, he, she, it,	if I, he, she, it,
	we, you, they **rethink**	we, you, they **be rethought**
Past	if I, he, she, it,	if I, he, she, it,
	we, you, they **rethought**	we, you, they **were rethought**
Fut.	if I, he, she, it,	if I, he, she, it,
	we, you, they **should rethink**	we, you, they **should be rethought**

Transitive and intransitive.

return
(active voice)

be returned
(passive voice)

Infinitive: **to return**
Perfect Infinitive: **to have returned**
Present Participle: **returning**
Past Participle: **returned**

Infinitive: **to be returned**
Perfect Infinitive: **to have been returned**
Present Participle: **being returned**
Past Participle: **been returned**

INDICATIVE MOOD

Pres.	I, we, you, they **return**	I **am returned**
		we, you, they **are returned**
	he, she, it **returns**	he, she, it **is returned**
Pres. *Prog.*	I **am returning**	I **am being returned**
	we, you, they **are returning**	we, you, they **are being returned**
	he, she, it **is returning**	he, she, it **is being returned**
Pres. *Int.*	I, we, you, they **do return**	I, we, you, they **do get returned**
	he, she, it **does return**	he, she, it **does get returned**
Fut.	I, he, she, it, we, you, they **will return**	I, he, she, it, we, you, they **will be returned**
Past	I, he, she, it, we, you, they **returned**	I, he, she, it **was returned** we, you, they **were returned**
Past *Prog.*	I, he, she, it **was returning** we, you, they **were returning**	I, he, she, it **was being returned** we, you, they **were being returned**
Past *Int.*	I, he, she, it, we, you, they **did return**	I, he, she, it, we, you, they **did get returned**
Pres. *Perf.*	I, we, you, they **have returned**	I, we, you, they **have been returned**
	he, she, it **has returned**	he, she, it **has been returned**
Past *Perf.*	I, he, she, it, we, you, they **had returned**	I, he, she, it, we, you, they **had been returned**
Fut. *Perf.*	I, he, she, it, we, you, they **will have returned**	I, he, she, it, we, you, they **will have been returned**

IMPERATIVE MOOD

return

be returned

SUBJUNCTIVE MOOD

Pres.	if I, he, she, it, we, you, they **return**	if I, he, she, it, we, you, they **be returned**
Past	if I, he, she, it, we, you, they **returned**	if I, he, she, it, we, you, they **were returned**
Fut.	if I, he, she, it, we, you, they **should return**	if I, he, she, it, we, you, they **should be returned**

Intransitive and transitive.

334

rewrite
(active voice)

PRINCIPAL PARTS: **rewrites, rewriting, rewrote, rewritten**

be rewritten
(passive voice)

Infinitive: **to rewrite**
Perfect Infinitive: **to have rewritten**
Present Participle: **rewriting**
Past Participle: **rewritten**

Infinitive: **to be rewritten**
Perfect Infinitive: **to have been rewritten**
Present Participle: **being rewritten**
Past Participle: **been rewritten**

INDICATIVE MOOD

Pres.	I, we, you, they **rewrite**	I **am rewritten**
		we, you, they **are rewritten**
	he, she, it **rewrites**	he, she, it **is rewritten**
Pres.	I **am rewriting**	I **am being rewritten**
Prog.	we, you, they **are rewriting**	we, you, they **are being rewritten**
	he, she, it **is rewriting**	he, she, it **is being rewritten**
Pres.	I, we, you, they **do rewrite**	I, we, you, they **do get rewritten**
Int.	he, she, it **does rewrite**	he, she, it **does get rewritten**
Fut.	I, he, she, it,	I, he, she, it,
	we, you, they **will rewrite**	we, you, they **will be rewritten**
Past	I, he, she, it,	I, he, she, it **was rewritten**
	we, you, they **rewrote**	we, you, they **were rewritten**
Past	I, he, she, it **was rewriting**	I, he, she, it **was being rewritten**
Prog.	we, you, they **were rewriting**	we, you, they **were being rewritten**
Past	I, he, she, it,	I, he, she, it,
Int.	we, you, they **did rewrite**	we, you, they **did get rewritten**
Pres.	I, we, you, they **have rewritten**	I, we, you, they **have been rewritten**
Perf.	he, she, it **has rewritten**	he, she, it **has been rewritten**
Past	I, he, she, it,	I, he, she, it,
Perf.	we, you, they **had rewritten**	we, you, they **had been rewritten**
Fut.	I, he, she, it, we, you, they	I, he, she, it, we, you, they
Perf.	**will have rewritten**	**will have been rewritten**

IMPERATIVE MOOD

rewrite **be rewritten**

SUBJUNCTIVE MOOD

Pres.	if I, he, she, it,	if I, he, she, it,
	we, you, they **rewrite**	we, you, they **be rewritten**
Past	if I, he, she, it,	if I, he, she, it,
	we, you, they **rewrote**	we, you, they **were rewritten**
Fut.	if I, he, she, it,	if I, he, she, it,
	we, you, they **should rewrite**	we, you, they **should be rewritten**

Transitive and intransitive.

rid
(active voice)

be rid/ridded
(passive voice)

Infinitive: **to rid**
Perfect Infinitive: **to have rid**
Present Participle: **ridding**
Past Participle: **rid**

Infinitive: **to be rid**
Perfect Infinitive: **to have been rid**
Present Participle: **being rid**
Past Participle: **been rid**

INDICATIVE MOOD

Pres.	I, we, you, they **rid**	I **am rid**
		we, you, they **are rid**
	he, she, it **rids**	he, she, it **is rid**
Pres.	I **am ridding**	I **am being rid**
Prog.	we, you, they **are ridding**	we, you, they **are being rid**
	he, she, it **is ridding**	he, she, it **is being rid**
Pres.	I, we, you, they **do rid**	I, we, you, they **do get rid**
Int.	he, she, it **does rid**	he, she, it **does get rid**
Fut.	I, he, she, it,	I, he, she, it,
	we, you, they **will rid**	we, you, they **will be rid**
Past	I, he, she, it,	I, he, she, it **was rid**
	we, you, they **rid**	we, you, they **were rid**
Past	I, he, she, it **was ridding**	I, he, she, it **was being rid**
Prog.	we, you, they **were ridding**	we, you, they **were being rid**
Past	I, he, she, it,	I, he, she, it,
Int.	we, you, they **did rid**	we, you, they **did get rid**
Pres.	I, we, you, they **have rid**	I, we, you, they **have been rid**
Perf.	he, she, it **has rid**	he, she, it **has been rid**
Past	I, he, she, it,	I, he, she, it,
Perf.	we, you, they **had rid**	we, you, they **had been rid**
Fut.	I, he, she, it, we, you, they	I, he, she, it, we, you, they
Perf.	**will have rid**	**will have been rid**

IMPERATIVE MOOD

rid   **be rid**

SUBJUNCTIVE MOOD

Pres.	if I, he, she, it,	if I, he, she, it,
	we, you, they **rid**	we, you, they **be rid**
Past	if I, he, she, it,	if I, he, she, it,
	we, you, they **rid**	we, you, they **were rid**
Fut.	if I, he, she, it,	if I, he, she, it,
	we, you, they **should rid**	we, you, they **should be rid**

The *Oxford Dictionary* classifies RIDDED as archaic.

ride
(active voice)

PRINCIPAL PARTS: rides, riding, rode, ridden

be ridden
(passive voice)

Infinitive: **to ride**
Perfect Infinitive: **to have ridden**
Present Participle: **riding**
Past Participle: **ridden**

Infinitive: **to be ridden**
Perfect Infinitive: **to have been ridden**
Present Participle: **being ridden**
Past Participle: **been ridden**

INDICATIVE MOOD

Pres.	I, we, you, they **ride**	I **am ridden**
		we, you, they **are ridden**
	he, she, it **rides**	he, she, it **is ridden**
Pres.	I **am riding**	I **am being ridden**
Prog.	we, you, they **are riding**	we, you, they **are being ridden**
	he, she, it **is riding**	he, she, it **is being ridden**
Pres.	I, we, you, they **do ride**	I, we, you, they **do get ridden**
Int.	he, she, it **does ride**	he, she, it **does get ridden**
Fut.	I, he, she, it,	I, he, she, it,
	we, you, they **will ride**	we, you, they **will be ridden**
Past	I, he, she, it,	I, he, she, it **was ridden**
	we, you, they **rode**	we, you, they **were ridden**
Past	I, he, she, it **was riding**	I, he, she, it **was being ridden**
Prog.	we, you, they **were riding**	we, you, they **were being ridden**
Past	I, he, she, it,	I, he, she, it,
Int.	we, you, they **did ride**	we, you, they **did get ridden**
Pres.	I, we, you, they **have ridden**	I, we, you, they **have been ridden**
Perf.	he, she, it **has ridden**	he, she, it **has been ridden**
Past	I, he, she, it,	I, he, she, it,
Perf.	we, you, they **had ridden**	we, you, they **had been ridden**
Fut.	I, he, she, it, we, you, they	I, he, she, it, we, you, they
Perf.	**will have ridden**	**will have been ridden**

IMPERATIVE MOOD

ride   **be ridden**

SUBJUNCTIVE MOOD

Pres.	if I, he, she, it,	if I, he, she, it,
	we, you, they **ride**	we, you, they **be ridden**
Past	if I, he, she, it,	if I, he, she, it,
	we, you, they **rode**	we, you, they **were ridden**
Fut.	if I, he, she, it,	if I, he, she, it,
	we, you, they **should ride**	we, you, they **should be ridden**

Intransitive and transitive.

rig
(active voice)

be rigged
(passive voice)

Infinitive: **to rig**
Perfect Infinitive: **to have rigged**
Present Participle: **rigging**
Past Participle: **rigged**

Infinitive: **to be rigged**
Perfect Infinitive: **to have been rigged**
Present Participle: **being rigged**
Past Participle: **been rigged**

INDICATIVE MOOD

Pres.	I, we, you, they **rig**	I **am rigged**
		we, you, they **are rigged**
	he, she, it **rigs**	he, she, it **is rigged**
Pres.	I **am rigging**	I **am being rigged**
Prog.	we, you, they **are rigging**	we, you, they **are being rigged**
	he, she, it **is rigging**	he, she, it **is being rigged**
Pres.	I, we, you, they **do rig**	I, we, you, they **do get rigged**
Int.	he, she, it **does rig**	he, she, it **does get rigged**
Fut.	I, he, she, it,	I, he, she, it,
	we, you, they **will rig**	we, you, they **will be rigged**
Past	I, he, she, it,	I, he, she, it **was rigged**
	we, you, they **rigged**	we, you, they **were rigged**
Past	I, he, she, it **was rigging**	I, he, she, it **was being rigged**
Prog.	we, you, they **were rigging**	we, you, they **were being rigged**
Past	I, he, she, it,	I, he, she, it,
Int.	we, you, they **did rig**	we, you, they **did get rigged**
Pres.	I, we, you, they **have rigged**	I, we, you, they **have been rigged**
Perf.	he, she, it **has rigged**	he, she, it **has been rigged**
Past	I, he, she, it,	I, he, she, it,
Perf.	we, you, they **had rigged**	we, you, they **had been rigged**
Fut.	I, he, she, it, we, you, they	I, he, she, it, we, you, they
Perf.	**will have rigged**	**will have been rigged**

IMPERATIVE MOOD

rig **be rigged**

SUBJUNCTIVE MOOD

Pres.	if I, he, she, it,	if I, he, she, it,
	we, you, they **rig**	we, you, they **be rigged**
Past	if I, he, she, it,	if I, he, she, it,
	we, you, they **rigged**	we, you, they **were rigged**
Fut.	if I, he, she, it,	if I, he, she, it,
	we, you, they **should rig**	we, you, they **should be rigged**

ring
(active voice)

be rung
(passive voice)

Infinitive: **to ring**
Perfect Infinitive: **to have rung**
Present Participle: **ringing**
Past Participle: **rung**

Infinitive: **to be rung**
Perfect Infinitive: **to have been rung**
Present Participle: **being rung**
Past Participle: **been rung**

INDICATIVE MOOD

Pres.	I, we, you, they **ring**		I **am rung**
			we, you, they **are rung**
	he, she, it **rings**		he, she, it **is rung**
Pres.	I **am ringing**		I **am being rung**
Prog.	we, you, they **are ringing**		we, you, they **are being rung**
	he, she, it **is ringing**		he, she, it **is being rung**
Pres.	I, we, you, they **do ring**		I, we, you, they **do get rung**
Int.	he, she, it **does ring**		he, she, it **does get rung**
Fut.	I, he, she, it,		I, he, she, it,
	we, you, they **will ring**		we, you, they **will be rung**
Past	I, he, she, it,		I, he, she, it **was rung**
	we, you, they **rang**		we, you, they **were rung**
Past	I, he, she, it **was ringing**		I, he, she, it **was being rung**
Prog.	we, you, they **were ringing**		we, you, they **were being rung**
Past	I, he, she, it,		I, he, she, it,
Int.	we, you, they **did ring**		we, you, they **did get rung**
Pres.	I, we, you, they **have rung**		I, we, you, they **have been rung**
Perf.	he, she, it **has rung**		he, she, it **has been rung**
Past	I, he, she, it,		I, he, she, it,
Perf.	we, you, they **had rung**		we, you, they **had been rung**
Fut.	I, he, she, it, we, you, they		I, he, she, it, we, you, they
Perf.	**will have rung**		**will have been rung**

IMPERATIVE MOOD

ring

be rung

SUBJUNCTIVE MOOD

Pres.	if I, he, she, it,		if I, he, she, it,
	we, you, they **ring**		we, you, they **be rung**
Past	if I, he, she, it,		if I, he, she, it,
	we, you, they **rang**		we, you, they **were rung**
Fut.	if I, he, she, it,		if I, he, she, it,
	we, you, they **should ring**		we, you, they **should be rung**

Intransitive and transitive.

ring
(active voice)

be ringed
(passive voice)

Infinitive: **to ring**
Perfect Infinitive: **to have ringed**
Present Participle: **ringing**
Past Participle: **ringed**

Infinitive: **to be ringed**
Perfect Infinitive: **to have been ringed**
Present Participle: **being ringed**
Past Participle: **been ringed**

INDICATIVE MOOD

Pres.	I, we, you, they **ring**	I **am ringed**
		we, you, they **are ringed**
	he, she, it **rings**	he, she, it **is ringed**
Pres.	I **am ringing**	I **am being ringed**
Prog.	we, you, they **are ringing**	we, you, they **are being ringed**
	he, she, it **is ringing**	he, she, it **is being ringed**
Pres.	I, we, you, they **do ring**	I, we, you, they **do get ringed**
Int.	he, she, it **does ring**	he, she, it **does get ringed**
Fut.	I, he, she, it,	I, he, she, it,
	we, you, they **will ring**	we, you, they **will be ringed**
Past	I, he, she, it,	I, he, she, it **was ringed**
	we, you, they **ringed**	we, you, they **were ringed**
Past	I, he, she, it **was ringing**	I, he, she, it **was being ringed**
Prog.	we, you, they **were ringing**	we, you, they **were being ringed**
Past	I, he, she, it,	I, he, she, it,
Int.	we, you, they **did ring**	we, you, they **did get ringed**
Pres.	I, we, you, they **have ringed**	I, we, you, they **have been ringed**
Perf.	he, she, it **has ringed**	he, she, it **has been ringed**
Past	I, he, she, it,	I, he, she, it,
Perf.	we, you, they **had ringed**	we, you, they **had been ringed**
Fut.	I, he, she, it, we, you, they	I, he, she, it, we, you, they
Perf.	**will have ringed**	**will have been ringed**

IMPERATIVE MOOD

ring **be ringed**

SUBJUNCTIVE MOOD

Pres.	if I, he, she, it,	if I, he, she, it,
	we, you, they **ring**	we, you, they **be ringed**
Past	if I, he, she, it,	if I, he, she, it,
	we, you, they **ringed**	we, you, they **were ringed**
Fut.	if I, he, she, it,	if I, he, she, it,
	we, you, they **should ring**	we, you, they **should be ringed**

Transitive and intransitive. This verb means to "encircle." Do not confuse it with the verb meaning to "ring a bell."

rise
(active voice)

be risen
(passive voice)

Infinitive: **to rise**
Perfect Infinitive: **to have risen**
Present Participle: **rising**
Past Participle: **risen**

Infinitive: **to be risen**
Perfect Infinitive: **to have been risen**
Present Participle: **being risen**
Past Participle: **been risen**

INDICATIVE MOOD

Pres.	I, we, you, they **rise** he, she, it **rises**	I **am risen** we, you, they **are risen** he, she, it **is risen**	
Pres. *Prog.*	I **am rising** we, you, they **are rising** he, she, it **is rising**	I **am being risen** we, you, they **are being risen** he, she, it **is being risen**	
Pres. *Int.*	I, we, you, they **do rise** he, she, it **does rise**	I, we, you, they **do get risen** he, she, it **does get risen**	
Fut.	I, he, she, it, we, you, they **will rise**	I, he, she, it, we, you, they **will be risen**	
Past	I, he, she, it, we, you, they **rose**	I, he, she, it **was risen** we, you, they **were risen**	
Past *Prog.*	I, he, she, it **was rising** we, you, they **were rising**	I, he, she, it **was being risen** we, you, they **were being risen**	
Past *Int.*	I, he, she, it, we, you, they **did rise**	I, he, she, it, we, you, they **did get risen**	
Pres. *Perf.*	I, we, you, they **have risen** he, she, it **has risen**	I, we, you, they **have been risen** he, she, it **has been risen**	
Past *Perf.*	I, he, she, it, we, you, they **had risen**	I, he, she, it, we, you, they **had been risen**	
Fut. *Perf.*	I, he, she, it, we, you, they **will have risen**	I, he, she, it, we, you, they **will have been risen**	

IMPERATIVE MOOD

rise   be risen

SUBJUNCTIVE MOOD

Pres.	if I, he, she, it, we, you, they **rise**	if I, he, she, it, we, you, they **be risen**
Past	if I, he, she, it, we, you, they **rose**	if I, he, she, it, we, you, they **were risen**
Fut.	if I, he, she, it, we, you, they **should rise**	if I, he, she, it, we, you, they **should be risen**

Intransitive and transitive.

rive
(active voice)

be riven/rived
(passive voice)

Infinitive: **to rive**
Perfect Infinitive: **to have riven**
Present Participle: **riving**
Past Participle: **riven**

Infinitive: **to be riven**
Perfect Infinitive: **to have been riven**
Present Participle: **being riven**
Past Participle: **been riven**

INDICATIVE MOOD

Pres.	I, we, you, they **rive**	I **am riven**
		we, you, they **are riven**
	he, she, it **rives**	he, she, it **is riven**
Pres.	I **am riving**	I **am being riven**
Prog.	we, you, they **are riving**	we, you, they **are being riven**
	he, she, it **is riving**	he, she, it **is being riven**
Pres.	I, we, you, they **do rive**	I, we, you, they **do get riven**
Int.	he, she, it **does rive**	he, she, it **does get riven**
Fut.	I, he, she, it,	I, he, she, it,
	we, you, they **will rive**	we, you, they **will be riven**
Past	I, he, she, it,	I, he, she, it **was riven**
	we, you, they **rived**	we, you, they **were riven**
Past	I, he, she, it **was riving**	I, he, she, it **was being riven**
Prog.	we, you, they **were riving**	we, you, they **were being riven**
Past	I, he, she, it,	I, he, she, it,
Int.	we, you, they **did rive**	we, you, they **did get riven**
Pres.	I, we, you, they **have riven**	I, we, you, they **have been riven**
Perf.	he, she, it **has riven**	he, she, it **has been riven**
Past	I, he, she, it,	I, he, she, it,
Perf.	we, you, they **had riven**	we, you, they **had been riven**
Fut.	I, he, she, it, we, you, they	I, he, she, it, we, you, they
Perf.	**will have riven**	**will have been riven**

IMPERATIVE MOOD

rive   **be riven**

SUBJUNCTIVE MOOD

Pres.	if I, he, she, it,	if I, he, she, it,
	we, you, they **rive**	we, you, they **be riven**
Past	if I, he, she, it,	if I, he, she, it,
	we, you, they **rived**	we, you, they **were riven**
Fut.	if I, he, she, it,	if I, he, she, it,
	we, you, they **should rive**	we, you, they **should be riven**

Transitive and intransitive.

rob
(active voice)

be robbed
(passive voice)

Infinitive: **to rob**
Perfect Infinitive: **to have robbed**
Present Participle: **robbing**
Past Participle: **robbed**

Infinitive: **to be robbed**
Perfect Infinitive: **to have been robbed**
Present Participle: **being robbed**
Past Participle: **been robbed**

INDICATIVE MOOD

Pres.	I, we, you, they **rob**	I **am robbed**
		we, you, they **are robbed**
	he, she, it **robs**	he, she, it **is robbed**
Pres.	I **am robbing**	I **am being robbed**
Prog.	we, you, they **are robbing**	we, you, they **are being robbed**
	he, she, it **is robbing**	he, she, it **is being robbed**
Pres.	I, we, you, they **do rob**	I, we, you, they **do get robbed**
Int.	he, she, it **does rob**	he, she, it **does get robbed**
Fut.	I, he, she, it,	I, he, she, it,
	we, you, they **will rob**	we, you, they **will be robbed**
Past	I, he, she, it,	I, he, she, it **was robbed**
	we, you, they **robbed**	we, you, they **were robbed**
Past	I, he, she, it **was robbing**	I, he, she, it **was being robbed**
Prog.	we, you, they **were robbing**	we, you, they **were being robbed**
Past	I, he, she, it,	I, he, she, it,
Int.	we, you, they **did rob**	we, you, they **did get robbed**
Pres.	I, we, you, they **have robbed**	I, we, you, they **have been robbed**
Perf.	he, she, it **has robbed**	he, she, it **has been robbed**
Past	I, he, she, it,	I, he, she, it,
Perf.	we, you, they **had robbed**	we, you, they **had been robbed**
Fut.	I, he, she, it, we, you, they	I, he, she, it, we, you, they
Perf.	**will have robbed**	**will have been robbed**

IMPERATIVE MOOD

rob   **be robbed**

SUBJUNCTIVE MOOD

Pres.	if I, he, she, it,	if I, he, she, it,
	we, you, they **rob**	we, you, they **be robbed**
Past	if I, he, she, it,	if I, he, she, it,
	we, you, they **robbed**	we, you, they **were robbed**
Fut.	if I, he, she, it,	if I, he, she, it,
	we, you, they **should rob**	we, you, they **should be robbed**

Intransitive and transitive.

robe
(active voice)

be robed
(passive voice)

Infinitive: **to robe**
Perfect Infinitive: **to have robed**
Present Participle: **robing**
Past Participle: **robed**

Infinitive: **to be robed**
Perfect Infinitive: **to have been robed**
Present Participle: **being robed**
Past Participle: **been robed**

INDICATIVE MOOD

Pres.	I, we, you, they **robe**	I **am robed**
		we, you, they **are robed**
	he, she, it **robes**	he, she, it **is robed**
Pres.	I **am robing**	I **am being robed**
Prog.	we, you, they **are robing**	we, you, they **are being robed**
	he, she, it **is robing**	he, she, it **is being robed**
Pres.	I, we, you, they **do robe**	I, we, you, they **do get robed**
Int.	he, she, it **does robe**	he, she, it **does get robed**
Fut.	I, he, she, it,	I, he, she, it,
	we, you, they **will robe**	we, you, they **will be robed**
Past	I, he, she, it,	I, he, she, it **was robed**
	we, you, they **robed**	we, you, they **were robed**
Past	I, he, she, it **was robing**	I, he, she, it **was being robed**
Prog.	we, you, they **were robing**	we, you, they **were being robed**
Past	I, he, she, it,	I, he, she, it,
Int.	we, you, they **did robe**	we, you, they **did get robed**
Pres.	I, we, you, they **have robed**	I, we, you, they **have been robed**
Perf.	he, she, it **has robed**	he, she, it **has been robed**
Past	I, he, she, it,	I, he, she, it,
Perf.	we, you, they **had robed**	we, you, they **had been robed**
Fut.	I, he, she, it, we, you, they	I, he, she, it, we, you, they
Perf.	**will have robed**	**will have been robed**

IMPERATIVE MOOD

robe   **be robed**

SUBJUNCTIVE MOOD

Pres.	if I, he, she, it,	if I, he, she, it,
	we, you, they **robe**	we, you, they **be robed**
Past	if I, he, she, it,	if I, he, she, it,
	we, you, they **robed**	we, you, they **were robed**
Fut.	if I, he, she, it,	if I, he, she, it,
	we, you, they **should robe**	we, you, they **should be robed**

Intransitive and transitive.

rout
(active voice)

PRINCIPAL PARTS: **routs, routing, routed, routed**

be routed
(passive voice)

Infinitive: **to rout**
Perfect Infinitive: **to have routed**
Present Participle: **routing**
Past Participle: **routed**

Infinitive: **to be routed**
Perfect Infinitive: **to have been routed**
Present Participle: **being routed**
Past Participle: **been routed**

INDICATIVE MOOD

Pres.	I, we, you, they **rout**	I **am routed**
		we, you, they **are routed**
	he, she, it **routs**	he, she, it **is routed**
Pres.	I **am routing**	I **am being routed**
Prog.	we, you, they **are routing**	we, you, they **are being routed**
	he, she, it **is routing**	he, she, it **is being routed**
Pres.	I, we, you, they **do rout**	I, we, you, they **do get routed**
Int.	he, she, it **does rout**	he, she, it **does get routed**
Fut.	I, he, she, it, we, you, they **will rout**	I, he, she, it, we, you, they **will be routed**
Past	I, he, she, it, we, you, they **routed**	I, he, she, it **was routed**
		we, you, they **were routed**
Past	I, he, she, it **was routing**	I, he, she, it **was being routed**
Prog.	we, you, they **were routing**	we, you, they **were being routed**
Past	I, he, she, it, we, you, they **did rout**	I, he, she, it, we, you, they **did get routed**
Int.		
Pres.	I, we, you, they **have routed**	I, we, you, they **have been routed**
Perf.	he, she, it **has routed**	he, she, it **has been routed**
Past	I, he, she, it, we, you, they **had routed**	I, he, she, it, we, you, they **had been routed**
Perf.		
Fut.	I, he, she, it, we, you, they **will have routed**	I, he, she, it, we, you, they **will have been routed**
Perf.		

IMPERATIVE MOOD

rout   be routed

SUBJUNCTIVE MOOD

Pres.	if I, he, she, it, we, you, they **rout**	if I, he, she, it, we, you, they **be routed**
Past	if I, he, she, it, we, you, they **routed**	if I, he, she, it, we, you, they **were routed**
Fut.	if I, he, she, it, we, you, they **should rout**	if I, he, she, it, we, you, they **should be routed**

The transitive verb ROUT means to "force into retreat or defeat." There is also an intransitive and transitive verb meaning to "dig."

route
(active voice)

be routed
(passive voice)

Infinitive: **to route**
Perfect Infinitive: **to have routed**
Present Participle: **routing**
Past Participle: **routed**

Infinitive: **to be routed**
Perfect Infinitive: **to have been routed**
Present Participle: **being routed**
Past Participle: **been routed**

INDICATIVE MOOD

Pres.	I, we, you, they **route**	I **am routed**
		we, you, they **are routed**
	he, she, it **routes**	he, she, it **is routed**
Pres.	I **am routing**	I **am being routed**
Prog.	we, you, they **are routing**	we, you, they **are being routed**
	he, she, it **is routing**	he, she, it **is being routed**
Pres.	I, we, you, they **do route**	I, we, you, they **do get routed**
Int.	he, she, it **does route**	he, she, it **does get routed**
Fut.	I, he, she, it,	I, he, she, it,
	we, you, they **will route**	we, you, they **will be routed**
Past	I, he, she, it,	I, he, she, it **was routed**
	we, you, they **routed**	we, you, they **were routed**
Past	I, he, she, it **was routing**	I, he, she, it **was being routed**
Prog.	we, you, they **were routing**	we, you, they **were being routed**
Past	I, he, she, it,	I, he, she, it,
Int.	we, you, they **did route**	we, you, they **did get routed**
Pres.	I, we, you, they **have routed**	I, we, you, they **have been routed**
Perf.	he, she, it **has routed**	he, she, it **has been routed**
Past	I, he, she, it,	I, he, she, it,
Perf.	we, you, they **had routed**	we, you, they **had been routed**
Fut.	I, he, she, it, we, you, they	I, he, she, it, we, you, they
Perf.	**will have routed**	**will have been routed**

IMPERATIVE MOOD

route   **be routed**

SUBJUNCTIVE MOOD

Pres.	if I, he, she, it,	if I, he, she, it,
	we, you, they **route**	we, you, they **be routed**
Past	if I, he, she, it,	if I, he, she, it,
	we, you, they **routed**	we, you, they **were routed**
Fut.	if I, he, she, it,	if I, he, she, it,
	we, you, they **should rout**	we, you, they **should be routed**

This verb means to "send by a specific route."

346

ruin
(active voice)

PRINCIPAL PARTS: **ruins, ruining, ruined, ruined**

be ruined
(passive voice)

Infinitive: **to ruin**
Perfect Infinitive: **to have ruined**
Present Participle: **ruining**
Past Participle: **ruined**

Infinitive: **to be ruined**
Perfect Infinitive: **to have been ruined**
Present Participle: **being ruined**
Past Participle: **been ruined**

INDICATIVE MOOD

Pres.	I, we, you, they **ruin**	I **am ruined**
		we, you, they **are ruined**
	he, she, it **ruins**	he, she, it **is ruined**
Pres.	I **am ruining**	I **am being ruined**
Prog.	we, you, they **are ruining**	we, you, they **are being ruined**
	he, she, it **is ruining**	he, she, it **is being ruined**
Pres.	I, we, you, they **do ruin**	I, we, you, they **do get ruined**
Int.	he, she, it **does ruin**	he, she, it **does get ruined**
Fut.	I, he, she, it, we, you, they **will ruin**	I, he, she, it, we, you, they **will be ruined**
Past	I, he, she, it, we, you, they **ruined**	I, he, she, it **was ruined** we, you, they **were ruined**
Past	I, he, she, it **was ruining**	I, he, she, it **was being ruined**
Prog.	we, you, they **were ruining**	we, you, they **were being ruined**
Past	I, he, she, it, we, you, they **did ruin**	I, he, she, it, we, you, they **did get ruined**
Int.		
Pres.	I, we, you, they **have ruined**	I, we, you, they **have been ruined**
Perf.	he, she, it **has ruined**	he, she, it **has been ruined**
Past	I, he, she, it, we, you, they **had ruined**	I, he, she, it, we, you, they **had been ruined**
Perf.		
Fut.	I, he, she, it, we, you, they **will have ruined**	I, he, she, it, we, you, they **will have been ruined**
Perf.		

IMPERATIVE MOOD

ruin   **be ruined**

SUBJUNCTIVE MOOD

Pres.	if I, he, she, it, we, you, they **ruin**	if I, he, she, it, we, you, they **be ruined**
Past	if I, he, she, it, we, you, they **ruined**	if I, he, she, it, we, you, they **were ruined**
Fut.	if I, he, she, it, we, you, they **should ruin**	if I, he, she, it, we, you, they **should be ruined**

Transitive and intransitive.

run
(active voice)

be run
(passive voice)

Infinitive: **to run**
Perfect Infinitive: **to have run**
Present Participle: **running**
Past Participle: **run**

Infinitive: **to be run**
Perfect Infinitive: **to have been run**
Present Participle: **being run**
Past Participle: **been run**

INDICATIVE MOOD

Pres.	I, we, you, they **run**	I **am run**
		we, you, they **are run**
	he, she, it **runs**	he, she, it **is run**
Pres.	I **am running**	I **am being run**
Prog.	we, you, they **are running**	we, you, they **are being run**
	he, she, it **is running**	he, she, it **is being run**
Pres.	I, we, you, they **do run**	I, we, you, they **do get run**
Int.	he, she, it **does run**	he, she, it **does get run**
Fut.	I, he, she, it,	I, he, she, it,
	we, you, they **will run**	we, you, they **will be run**
Past	I, he, she, it,	I, he, she, it **was run**
	we, you, they **ran**	we, you, they **were run**
Past	I, he, she, it **was running**	I, he, she, it **was being run**
Prog.	we, you, they **were running**	we, you, they **were being run**
Past	I, he, she, it,	I, he, she, it,
Int.	we, you, they **did run**	we, you, they **did get run**
Pres.	I, we, you, they **have run**	I, we, you, they **have been run**
Perf.	he, she, it **has run**	he, she, it **has been run**
Past	I, he, she, it,	I, he, she, it,
Perf.	we, you, they **had run**	we, you, they **had been run**
Fut.	I, he, she, it, we, you, they	I, he, she, it, we, you, they
Perf.	**will have run**	**will have been run**

IMPERATIVE MOOD

run　　　　　　　　　　　　　**be run**

SUBJUNCTIVE MOOD

Pres.	if I, he, she, it,	if I, he, she, it,
	we, you, they **run**	we, you, they **be run**
Past	if I, he, she, it,	if I, he, she, it,
	we, you, they **ran**	we, you, they **were run**
Fut.	if I, he, she, it,	if I, he, she, it,
	we, you, they **should run**	we, you, they **should be run**

Intransitive and transitive.

save
(active voice)

be saved
(passive voice)

Infinitive: **to save**
Perfect Infinitive: **to have saved**
Present Participle: **saving**
Past Participle: **saved**

Infinitive: **to be saved**
Perfect Infinitive: **to have been saved**
Present Participle: **being saved**
Past Participle: **been saved**

INDICATIVE MOOD

Pres.	I, we, you, they **save**	I am **saved**
		we, you, they **are saved**
	he, she, it **saves**	he, she, it **is saved**
Pres. *Prog.*	I am **saving**	I am **being saved**
	we, you, they **are saving**	we, you, they **are being saved**
	he, she, it **is saving**	he, she, it **is being saved**
Pres. *Int.*	I, we, you, they **do save**	I, we, you, they **do get saved**
	he, she, it **does save**	he, she, it **does get saved**
Fut.	I, he, she, it,	I, he, she, it,
	we, you, they **will save**	we, you, they **will be saved**
Past	I, he, she, it,	I, he, she, it **was saved**
	we, you, they **saved**	we, you, they **were saved**
Past *Prog.*	I, he, she, it **was saving**	I, he, she, it **was being saved**
	we, you, they **were saving**	we, you, they **were being saved**
Past *Int.*	I, he, she, it,	I, he, she, it,
	we, you, they **did save**	we, you, they **did get saved**
Pres. *Perf.*	I, we, you, they **have saved**	I, we, you, they **have been saved**
	he, she, it **has saved**	he, she, it **has been saved**
Past *Perf.*	I, he, she, it,	I, he, she, it,
	we, you, they **had saved**	we, you, they **had been saved**
Fut. *Perf.*	I, he, she, it, we, you, they	I, he, she, it, we, you, they
	will have saved	**will have been saved**

IMPERATIVE MOOD

save　　　　　**be saved**

SUBJUNCTIVE MOOD

Pres.	if I, he, she, it,	if I, he, she, it,
	we, you, they **save**	we, you, they **be saved**
Past	if I, he, she, it,	if I, he, she, it,
	we, you, they **saved**	we, you, they **were saved**
Fut.	if I, he, she, it,	if I, he, she, it,
	we, you, they **should save**	we, you, they **should be saved**

Transitive and intransitive.

PRINCIPAL PARTS: **saws, sawing,
sawed, sawed/sawn**

Infinitive: **to saw**
Perfect Infinitive: **to have sawed**
Present Participle: **sawing**
Past Participle: **sawed**

Infinitive: **to be sawed**
Perfect Infinitive: **to have been sawed**
Present Participle: **being sawed**
Past Participle: **been sawed**

INDICATIVE MOOD

Pres.	I, we, you, they **saw** he, she, it **saws**	I **am sawed** we, you, they **are sawed** he, she, it **is sawed**
Pres. *Prog.*	I **am sawing** we, you, they **are sawing** he, she, it **is sawing**	I **am being sawed** we, you, they **are being sawed** he, she, it **is being sawed**
Pres. *Int.*	I, we, you, they **do saw** he, she, it **does saw**	I, we, you, they **do get sawed** he, she, it **does get sawed**
Fut.	I, he, she, it, we, you, they **will saw**	I, he, she, it, we, you, they **will be sawed**
Past	I, he, she, it, we, you, they **sawed**	I, he, she, it **was sawed** we, you, they **were sawed**
Past *Prog.*	I, he, she, it **was sawing** we, you, they **were sawing**	I, he, she, it **was being sawed** we, you, they **were being sawed**
Past *Int.*	I, he, she, it, we, you, they **did saw**	I, he, she, it, we, you, they **did get sawed**
Pres. *Perf.*	I, we, you, they **have sawed** he, she, it **has sawed**	I, we, you, they **have been sawed** he, she, it **has been sawed**
Past *Perf.*	I, he, she, it, we, you, they **had sawed**	I, he, she, it, we, you, they **had been sawed**
Fut. *Perf.*	I, he, she, it, we, you, they **will have sawed**	I, he, she, it, we, you, they **will have been sawed**

IMPERATIVE MOOD

saw

be sawed

SUBJUNCTIVE MOOD

Pres.	if I, he, she, it, we, you, they **saw**	if I, he, she, it, we, you, they **be sawed**
Past	if I, he, she, it, we, you, they **sawed**	if I, he, she, it, we, you, they **were sawed**
Fut.	if I, he, she, it, we, you, they **should saw**	if I, he, she, it, we, you, they **should be sawed**

Transitive and intransitive.

say
(active voice)

be said
(passive voice)

Infinitive: **to say**
Perfect Infinitive: **to have said**
Present Participle: **saying**
Past Participle: **said**

Infinitive: **to be said**
Perfect Infinitive: **to have been said**
Present Participle: **being said**
Past Participle: **been said**

INDICATIVE MOOD

Pres.	I, we, you, they **say**		I **am said**
			we, you, they **are said**
	he, she, it **says**		he, she, it **is said**
Pres. *Prog.*	I **am saying**		I **am being said**
	we, you, they **are saying**		we, you, they **are being said**
	he, she, it **is saying**		he, she, it **is being said**
Pres. *Int.*	I, we, you, they **do say**		I, we, you, they **do get said**
	he, she, it **does say**		he, she, it **does get said**
Fut.	I, he, she, it, we, you, they **will say**		I, he, she, it, we, you, they **will be said**
Past	I, he, she, it, we, you, they **said**		I, he, she, it **was said** we, you, they **were said**
Past *Prog.*	I, he, she, it **was saying** we, you, they **were saying**		I, he, she, it **was being said** we, you, they **were being said**
Past *Int.*	I, he, she, it, we, you, they **did say**		I, he, she, it, we, you, they **did get said**
Pres. *Perf.*	I, we, you, they **have said** he, she, it **has said**		I, we, you, they **have been said** he, she, it **has been said**
Past *Perf.*	I, he, she, it, we, you, they **had said**		I, he, she, it, we, you, they **had been said**
Fut. *Perf.*	I, he, she, it, we, you, they **will have said**		I, he, she, it, we, you, they **will have been said**

IMPERATIVE MOOD

say　　　　　**be said**

SUBJUNCTIVE MOOD

Pres.	if I, he, she, it, we, you, they **say**		if I, he, she, it, we, you, they **be said**
Past	if I, he, she, it, we, you, they **said**		if I, he, she, it, we, you, they **were said**
Fut.	if I, he, she, it, we, you, they **should say**		if I, he, she, it, we, you, they **should be said**

Transitive and intransitive.

seat
(active voice)

be seated
(passive voice)

Infinitive: **to seat**
Perfect Infinitive: **to have seated**
Present Participle: **seating**
Past Participle: **seated**

Infinitive: **to be seated**
Perfect Infinitive: **to have been seated**
Present Participle: **being seated**
Past Participle: **been seated**

INDICATIVE MOOD

Pres.	I, we, you, they **seat**	I **am seated**
		we, you, they **are seated**
	he, she, it **seats**	he, she, it **is seated**
Pres.	I **am seating**	I **am being seated**
Prog.	we, you, they **are seating**	we, you, they **are being seated**
	he, she, it **is seating**	he, she, it **is being seated**
Pres.	I, we, you, they **do seat**	I, we, you, they **do get seated**
Int.	he, she, it **does seat**	he, she, it **does get seated**
Fut.	I, he, she, it,	I, he, she, it,
	we, you, they **will seat**	we, you, they **will be seated**
Past	I, he, she, it,	I, he, she, it **was seated**
	we, you, they **seated**	we, you, they **were seated**
Past	I, he, she, it **was seating**	I, he, she, it **was being seated**
Prog.	we, you, they **were seating**	we, you, they **were being seated**
Past	I, he, she, it,	I, he, she, it,
Int.	we, you, they **did seat**	we, you, they **did get seated**
Pres.	I, we, you, they **have seated**	I, we, you, they **have been seated**
Perf.	he, she, it **has seated**	he, she, it **has been seated**
Past	I, he, she, it,	I, he, she, it,
Perf.	we, you, they **had seated**	we, you, they **had been seated**
Fut.	I, he, she, it, we, you, they	I, he, she, it, we, you, they
Perf.	**will have seated**	**will have been seated**

IMPERATIVE MOOD

seat **be seated**

SUBJUNCTIVE MOOD

Pres.	if I, he, she, it,	if I, he, she, it,
	we, you, they **seat**	we, you, they **be seated**
Past	if I, he, she, it,	if I, he, she, it,
	we, you, they **seated**	we, you, they **were seated**
Fut.	if I, he, she, it,	if I, he, she, it,
	we, you, they **should seat**	we, you, they **should be seated**

Transitive and intransitive.

352

see
(active voice)

be seen
(passive voice)

Infinitive: **to see**
Perfect Infinitive: **to have seen**
Present Participle: **seeing**
Past Participle: **seen**

Infinitive: **to be seen**
Perfect Infinitive: **to have been seen**
Present Participle: **being seen**
Past Participle: **been seen**

INDICATIVE MOOD

Pres.	I, we, you, they **see** he, she, it **sees**	I **am seen** we, you, they **are seen** he, she, it **is seen**
Pres. *Prog.*	I **am seeing** we, you, they **are seeing** he, she, it **is seeing**	I **am being seen** we, you, they **are being seen** he, she, it **is being seen**
Pres. *Int.*	I, we, you, they **do see** he, she, it **does see**	I, we, you, they **do get seen** he, she, it **does get seen**
Fut.	I, he, she, it, we, you, they **will see**	I, he, she, it, we, you, they **will be seen**
Past	I, he, she, it, we, you, they **saw**	I, he, she, it **was seen** we, you, they **were seen**
Past *Prog.*	I, he, she, it **was seeing** we, you, they **were seeing**	I, he, she, it **was being seen** we, you, they **were being seen**
Past *Int.*	I, he, she, it, we, you, they **did see**	I, he, she, it, we, you, they **did get seen**
Pres. *Perf.*	I, we, you, they **have seen** he, she, it **has seen**	I, we, you, they **have been seen** he, she, it **has been seen**
Past *Perf.*	I, he, she, it, we, you, they **had seen**	I, he, she, it, we, you, they **had been seen**
Fut. *Perf.*	I, he, she, it, we, you, they **will have seen**	I, he, she, it, we, you, they **will have been seen**

IMPERATIVE MOOD

see

be seen

SUBJUNCTIVE MOOD

Pres.	if I, he, she, it, we, you, they **see**	if I, he, she, it, we, you, they **be seen**
Past	if I, he, she, it, we, you, they **saw**	if I, he, she, it, we, you, they **were seen**
Fut.	if I, he, she, it, we, you, they **should see**	if I, he, she, it, we, you, they **should be seen**

Transitive and intransitive.

seek
(active voice)

be sought
(passive voice)

Infinitive: **to seek**
Perfect Infinitive: **to have sought**
Present Participle: **seeking**
Past Participle: **sought**

Infinitive: **to be sought**
Perfect Infinitive: **to have been sought**
Present Participle: **being sought**
Past Participle: **been sought**

INDICATIVE MOOD

Pres.	I, we, you, they **seek**	I am sought
		we, you, they **are sought**
	he, she, it **seeks**	he, she, it **is sought**
Pres.	I am seeking	I am being sought
Prog.	we, you, they **are seeking**	we, you, they **are being sought**
	he, she, it **is seeking**	he, she, it **is being sought**
Pres.	I, we, you, they **do seek**	I, we, you, they **do get sought**
Int.	he, she, it **does seek**	he, she, it **does get sought**
Fut.	I, he, she, it,	I, he, she, it,
	we, you, they **will seek**	we, you, they **will be sought**
Past	I, he, she, it,	I, he, she, it **was sought**
	we, you, they **sought**	we, you, they **were sought**
Past	I, he, she, it **was seeking**	I, he, she, it **was being sought**
Prog.	we, you, they **were seeking**	we, you, they **were being sought**
Past	I, he, she, it,	I, he, she, it,
Int.	we, you, they **did seek**	we, you, they **did get sought**
Pres.	I, we, you, they **have sought**	I, we, you, they **have been sought**
Perf.	he, she, it **has sought**	he, she, it **has been sought**
Past	I, he, she, it,	I, he, she, it,
Perf.	we, you, they **had sought**	we, you, they **had been sought**
Fut.	I, he, she, it, we, you, they	I, he, she, it, we, you, they
Perf.	**will have sought**	**will have been sought**

IMPERATIVE MOOD

seek   be sought

SUBJUNCTIVE MOOD

Pres.	if I, he, she, it,	if I, he, she, it,
	we, you, they **seek**	we, you, they **be sought**
Past	if I, he, she, it,	if I, he, she, it,
	we, you, they **sought**	we, you, they **were sought**
Fut.	if I, he, she, it,	if I, he, she, it,
	we, you, they **should seek**	we, you, they **should be sought**

Transitive and intransitive.

Infinitive: **to seem**
Perfect Infinitive: **to have seemed**
Present Participle: **seeming**
Past Participle: **seemed**

INDICATIVE MOOD

Pres.   I, we, you, they **seem**

           he, she, it **seems**

Pres.   I **am seeming**
Prog.   we, you, they **are seeming**
           he, she, it **is seeming**

Pres.   I, we, you, they **do seem**
Int.   he, she, it **does seem**

Fut.   I, he, she, it,
           we, you, they **will seem**

Past   I, he, she, it,
           we, you, they **seemed**

Past   I, he, she, it **was seeming**
Prog.   we, you, they **were seeming**

Past   I, he, she, it,
Int.   we, you, they **did seem**

Pres.   I, we, you, they **have seemed**
Perf.   he, she, it **has seemed**

Past   I, he, she, it,
Perf.   we, you, they **had seemed**

Fut.   I, he, she, it, we, you, they
Perf.   **will have seemed**

IMPERATIVE MOOD

         seem

SUBJUNCTIVE MOOD

Pres.   if I, he, she, it,
           we, you, they **seem**

Past   if I, he, she, it,
           we, you, they **seemed**

Fut.   if I, he, she, it,
           we, you, they **should seem**

sell
(active voice)

PRINCIPAL PARTS: **sells, selling, sold, sold**

be sold
(passive voice)

Infinitive: **to sell**
Perfect Infinitive: **to have sold**
Present Participle: **selling**
Past Participle: **sold**

Infinitive: **to be sold**
Perfect Infinitive: **to have been sold**
Present Participle: **being sold**
Past Participle: **been sold**

INDICATIVE MOOD

Pres.	I, we, you, they **sell**	I **am sold**	
		we, you, they **are sold**	
	he, she, it **sells**	he, she, it **is sold**	
Pres.	I **am selling**	I **am being sold**	
Prog.	we, you, they **are selling**	we, you, they **are being sold**	
	he, she, it **is selling**	he, she, it **is being sold**	
Pres.	I, we, you, they **do sell**	I, we, you, they **do get sold**	
Int.	he, she, it **does sell**	he, she, it **does get sold**	
Fut.	I, he, she, it,	I, he, she, it,	
	we, you, they **will sell**	we, you, they **will be sold**	
Past	I, he, she, it,	I, he, she, it **was sold**	
	we, you, they **sold**	we, you, they **were sold**	
Past	I, he, she, it **was selling**	I, he, she, it **was being sold**	
Prog.	we, you, they **were selling**	we, you, they **were being sold**	
Past	I, he, she, it,	I, he, she, it,	
Int.	we, you, they **did sell**	we, you, they **did get sold**	
Pres.	I, we, you, they **have sold**	I, we, you, they **have been sold**	
Perf.	he, she, it **has sold**	he, she, it **has been sold**	
Past	I, he, she, it,	I, he, she, it,	
Perf.	we, you, they **had sold**	we, you, they **had been sold**	
Fut.	I, he, she, it, we, you, they	I, he, she, it, we, you, they	
Perf.	**will have sold**	**will have been sold**	

IMPERATIVE MOOD

sell be sold

SUBJUNCTIVE MOOD

Pres.	if I, he, she, it,	if I, he, she, it,
	we, you, they **sell**	we, you, they **be sold**
Past	if I, he, she, it,	if I, he, she, it,
	we, you, they **sold**	we, you, they **were sold**
Fut.	if I, he, she, it,	if I, he, she, it,
	we, you, they **should sell**	we, you, they **should be sold**

Transitive and intransitive.

send
(active voice)

be sent
(passive voice)

Infinitive: **to send**
Perfect Infinitive: **to have sent**
Present Participle: **sending**
Past Participle: **sent**

Infinitive: **to be sent**
Perfect Infinitive: **to have been sent**
Present Participle: **being sent**
Past Participle: **been sent**

INDICATIVE MOOD

Pres.	I, we, you, they **send**	I **am sent**
		we, you, they **are sent**
	he, she, it **sends**	he, she, it **is sent**
Pres.	I **am sending**	I **am being sent**
Prog.	we, you, they **are sending**	we, you, they **are being sent**
	he, she, it **is sending**	he, she, it **is being sent**
Pres.	I, we, you, they **do send**	I, we, you, they **do get sent**
Int.	he, she, it **does send**	he, she, it **does get sent**
Fut.	I, he, she, it,	I, he, she, it,
	we, you, they **will send**	we, you, they **will be sent**
Past	I, he, she, it,	I, he, she, it **was sent**
	we, you, they **sent**	we, you, they **were sent**
Past	I, he, she, it **was sending**	I, he, she, it **was being sent**
Prog.	we, you, they **were sending**	we, you, they **were being sent**
Past	I, he, she, it,	I, he, she, it,
Int.	we, you, they **did send**	we, you, they **did get sent**
Pres.	I, we, you, they **have sent**	I, we, you, they **have been sent**
Perf.	he, she, it **has sent**	he, she, it **has been sent**
Past	I, he, she, it,	I, he, she, it,
Perf.	we, you, they **had sent**	we, you, they **had been sent**
Fut.	I, he, she, it, we, you, they	I, he, she, it, we, you, they
Perf.	**will have sent**	**will have been sent**

IMPERATIVE MOOD

send　　　　　　　**be sent**

SUBJUNCTIVE MOOD

Pres.	if I, he, she, it,	if I, he, she, it,
	we, you, they **send**	we, you, they **be sent**
Past	if I, he, she, it,	if I, he, she, it,
	we, you, they **sent**	we, you, they **were sent**
Fut.	if I, he, she, it,	if I, he, she, it,
	we, you, they **should send**	we, you, they **should be sent**

Transitive and intransitive.

serve (active voice)	PRINCIPAL PARTS: **serves, serving, served, served**	**be served** (passive voice)

Infinitive: **to serve**	*Infinitive:* **to be served**
Perfect Infinitive: **to have served**	*Perfect Infinitive:* **to have been served**
Present Participle: **serving**	*Present Participle:* **being served**
Past Participle: **served**	*Past Participle:* **been served**

INDICATIVE MOOD

Pres.	I, we, you, they **serve** he, she, it **serves**	I **am served** we, you, they **are served** he, she, it **is served**
Pres. *Prog.*	I **am serving** we, you, they **are serving** he, she, it **is serving**	I **am being served** we, you, they **are being served** he, she, it **is being served**
Pres. *Int.*	I, we, you, they **do serve** he, she, it **does serve**	I, we, you, they **do get served** he, she, it **does get served**
Fut.	I, he, she, it, we, you, they **will serve**	I, he, she, it, we, you, they **will be served**
Past	I, he, she, it, we, you, they **served**	I, he, she, it **was served** we, you, they **were served**
Past *Prog.*	I, he, she, it **was serving** we, you, they **were serving**	I, he, she, it **was being served** we, you, they **were being served**
Past *Int.*	I, he, she, it, we, you, they **did serve**	I, he, she, it, we, you, they **did get served**
Pres. *Perf.*	I, we, you, they **have served** he, she, it **has served**	I, we, you, they **have been served** he, she, it **has been served**
Past *Perf.*	I, he, she, it, we, you, they **had served**	I, he, she, it, we, you, they **had been served**
Fut. *Perf.*	I, he, she, it, we, you, they **will have served**	I, he, she, it, we, you, they **will have been served**

IMPERATIVE MOOD

serve	**be served**

SUBJUNCTIVE MOOD

Pres.	if I, he, she, it, we, you, they **serve**	if I, he, she, it, we, you, they **be served**
Past	if I, he, she, it, we, you, they **served**	if I, he, she, it, we, you, they **were served**
Fut.	if I, he, she, it, we, you, they **should serve**	if I, he, she, it, we, you, they **should be served**

Transitive and intransitive.

set
(active voice)

be set
(passive voice)

Infinitive: **to set**
Perfect Infinitive: **to have set**
Present Participle: **setting**
Past Participle: **set**

Infinitive: **to be set**
Perfect Infinitive: **to have been set**
Present Participle: **being set**
Past Participle: **been set**

INDICATIVE MOOD

Pres.	I, we, you, they **set**	I **am set**
		we, you, they **are set**
	he, she, it **sets**	he, she, it **is set**
Pres.	I **am setting**	I **am being set**
Prog.	we, you, they **are setting**	we, you, they **are being set**
	he, she, it **is setting**	he, she, it **is being set**
Pres.	I, we, you, they **do set**	I, we, you, they **do get set**
Int.	he, she, it **does set**	he, she, it **does get set**
Fut.	I, he, she, it,	I, he, she, it,
	we, you, they **will set**	we, you, they **will be set**
Past	I, he, she, it,	I, he, she, it **was set**
	we, you, they **set**	we, you, they **were set**
Past	I, he, she, it **was setting**	I, he, she, it **was being set**
Prog.	we, you, they **were setting**	we, you, they **were being set**
Past	I, he, she, it,	I, he, she, it,
Int.	we, you, they **did set**	we, you, they **did get set**
Pres.	I, we, you, they **have set**	I, we, you, they **have been set**
Perf.	he, she, it **has set**	he, she, it **has been set**
Past	I, he, she, it,	I, he, she, it,
Perf.	we, you, they **had set**	we, you, they **had been set**
Fut.	I, he, she, it, we, you, they	I, he, she, it, we, you, they
Perf.	**will have set**	**will have been set**

IMPERATIVE MOOD

set   **be set**

SUBJUNCTIVE MOOD

Pres.	if I, he, she, it,	if I, he, she, it,
	we, you, they **set**	we, you, they **be set**
Past	if I, he, she, it,	if I, he, she, it,
	we, you, they **set**	we, you, they **were set**
Fut.	if I, he, she, it,	if I, he, she, it,
	we, you, they **should set**	we, you, they **should be set**

Transitive and intransitive.

sew
(active voice)

PRINCIPAL PARTS: **sews, sewing,**
sewed, sewn/sewed

be sewn/sewed
(passive voice)

Infinitive: **to sew**
Perfect Infinitive: **to have sewn**
Present Participle: **sewing**
Past Participle: **sewn**

Infinitive: **to be sewn**
Perfect Infinitive: **to have been sewn**
Present Participle: **being sewn**
Past Participle: **been sewn**

INDICATIVE MOOD

Pres.	I, we, you, they **sew**	I **am sewn**
		we, you, they **are sewn**
	he, she, it **sews**	he, she, it **is sewn**
Pres.	I **am sewing**	I **am being sewn**
Prog.	we, you, they **are sewing**	we, you, they **are being sewn**
	he, she, it **is sewing**	he, she, it **is being sewn**
Pres.	I, we, you, they **do sew**	I, we, you, they **do get sewn**
Int.	he, she, it **does sew**	he, she, it **does get sewn**
Fut.	I, he, she, it,	I, he, she, it,
	we, you, they **will sew**	we, you, they **will be sewn**
Past	I, he, she, it,	I, he, she, it **was sewn**
	we, you, they **sewed**	we, you, they **were sewn**
Past	I, he, she, it **was sewing**	I, he, she, it **was being sewn**
Prog.	we, you, they **were sewing**	we, you, they **were being sewn**
Past	I, he, she, it,	I, he, she, it,
Int.	we, you, they **did sew**	we, you, they **did get sewn**
Pres.	I, we, you, they **have sewn**	I, we, you, they **have been sewn**
Perf.	he, she, it **has sewn**	he, she, it **has been sewn**
Past	I, he, she, it,	I, he, she, it,
Perf.	we, you, they **had sewn**	we, you, they **had been sewn**
Fut.	I, he, she, it, we, you, they	I, he, she, it, we, you, they
Perf.	**will have sewn**	**will have been sewn**

IMPERATIVE MOOD

sew

be sewn

SUBJUNCTIVE MOOD

Pres.	if I, he, she, it,	if I, he, she, it,
	we, you, they **sew**	we, you, they **be sewn**
Past	if I, he, she, it,	if I, he, she, it,
	we, you, they **sewed**	we, you, they **were sewn**
Fut.	if I, he, she, it,	if I, he, she, it,
	we, you, they **should sew**	we, you, they **should be sewn**

Transitive and intransitive.

shake
(active voice)

be shaken
(passive voice)

Infinitive: **to shake**
Perfect Infinitive: **to have shaken**
Present Participle: **shaking**
Past Participle: **shaken**

Infinitive: **to be shaken**
Perfect Infinitive: **to have been shaken**
Present Participle: **being shaken**
Past Participle: **been shaken**

INDICATIVE MOOD

Pres.	I, we, you, they **shake**	I **am shaken**
		we, you, they **are shaken**
	he, she, it **shakes**	he, she, it **is shaken**
Pres.	I **am shaking**	I **am being shaken**
Prog.	we, you, they **are shaking**	we, you, they **are being shaken**
	he, she, it **is shaking**	he, she, it **is being shaken**
Pres.	I, we, you, they **do shake**	I, we, you, they **do get shaken**
Int.	he, she, it **does shake**	he, she, it **does get shaken**
Fut.	I, he, she, it,	I, he, she, it,
	we, you, they **will shake**	we, you, they **will be shaken**
Past	I, he, she, it,	I, he, she, it **was shaken**
	we, you, they **shook**	we, you, they **were shaken**
Past	I, he, she, it **was shaking**	I, he, she, it **was being shaken**
Prog.	we, you, they **were shaking**	we, you, they **were being shaken**
Past	I, he, she, it,	I, he, she, it,
Int.	we, you, they **did shake**	we, you, they **did get shaken**
Pres.	I, we, you, they **have shaken**	I, we, you, they **have been shaken**
Perf.	he, she, it **has shaken**	he, she, it **has been shaken**
Past	I, he, she, it,	I, he, she, it,
Perf.	we, you, they **had shaken**	we, you, they **had been shaken**
Fut.	I, he, she, it, we, you, they	I, he, she, it, we, you, they
Perf.	**will have shaken**	**will have been shaken**

IMPERATIVE MOOD

shake **be shaken**

SUBJUNCTIVE MOOD

Pres.	if I, he, she, it,	if I, he, she, it,
	we, you, they **shake**	we, you, they **be shaken**
Past	if I, he, she, it,	if I, he, she, it,
	we, you, they **shook**	we, you, they **were shaken**
Fut.	if I, he, she, it,	if I, he, she, it,
	we, you, they **should shake**	we, you, they **should be shaken**

Transitive and intransitive.

shampoo
(active voice)

be shampooed
(passive voice)

Infinitive: **to shampoo**
Perfect Infinitive: **to have shampooed**
Present Participle: **shampooing**
Past Participle: **shampooed**

Infinitive: **to be shampooed**
Perfect Infinitive: **to have been shampooed**
Present Participle: **being shampooed**
Past Participle: **been shampooed**

INDICATIVE MOOD

Pres.	I, we, you, they **shampoo**	I **am shampooed**
		we, you, they **are shampooed**
	he, she, it **shampoos**	he, she, it **is shampooed**
Pres.	I **am shampooing**	I **am being shampooed**
Prog.	we, you, they **are shampooing**	we, you, they **are being shampooed**
	he, she, it **is shampooing**	he, she, it **is being shampooed**
Pres.	I, we, you, they **do shampoo**	I, we, you, they **do get shampooed**
Int.	he, she, it **does shampoo**	he, she, it **does get shampooed**
Fut.	I, he, she, it,	I, he, she, it,
	we, you, they **will shampoo**	we, you, they **will be shampooed**
Past	I, he, she, it,	I, he, she, it **was shampooed**
	we, you, they **shampooed**	we, you, they **were shampooed**
Past	I, he, she, it **was shampooing**	I, he, she, it **was being shampooed**
Prog.	we, you, they **were shampooing**	we, you, they **were being shampooed**
Past	I, he, she, it,	I, he, she, it,
Int.	we, you, they **did shampoo**	we, you, they **did get shampooed**
Pres.	I, we, you, they **have shampooed**	I, we, you, they **have been shampooed**
Perf.	he, she, it **has shampooed**	he, she, it **has been shampooed**
Past	I, he, she, it,	I, he, she, it,
Perf.	we, you, they **had shampooed**	we, you, they **had been shampooed**
Fut.	I, he, she, it, we, you, they	I, he, she, it, we, you, they
Perf.	**will have shampooed**	**will have been shampooed**

IMPERATIVE MOOD

shampoo   **be shampooed**

SUBJUNCTIVE MOOD

Pres.	if I, he, she, it,	if I, he, she, it,
	we, you, they **shampoo**	we, you, they **be shampooed**
Past	if I, he, she, it,	if I, he, she, it,
	we, you, they **shampooed**	we, you, they **were shampooed**
Fut.	if I, he, she, it,	if I, he, she, it,
	we, you, they **should shampoo**	we, you, they **should be shampooed**

Transitive and intransitive.

shape
(active voice)

be shaped
(passive voice)

Infinitive: **to shape**
Perfect Infinitive: **to have shaped**
Present Participle: **shaping**
Past Participle: **shaped**

Infinitive: **to be shaped**
Perfect Infinitive: **to have been shaped**
Present Participle: **being shaped**
Past Participle: **been shaped**

INDICATIVE MOOD

Pres.	I, we, you, they **shape**	I **am shaped**
		we, you, they **are shaped**
	he, she, it **shapes**	he, she, it **is shaped**
Pres.	I **am shaping**	I **am being shaped**
Prog.	we, you, they **are shaping**	we, you, they **are being shaped**
	he, she, it **is shaping**	he, she, it **is being shaped**
Pres.	I, we, you, they **do shape**	I, we, you, they **do get shaped**
Int.	he, she, it **does shape**	he, she, it **does get shaped**
Fut.	I, he, she, it,	I, he, she, it,
	we, you, they **will shape**	we, you, they **will be shaped**
Past	I, he, she, it,	I, he, she, it **was shaped**
	we, you, they **shaped**	we, you, they **were shaped**
Past	I, he, she, it **was shaping**	I, he, she, it **was being shaped**
Prog.	we, you, they **were shaping**	we, you, they **were being shaped**
Past	I, he, she, it,	I, he, she, it,
Int.	we, you, they **did shape**	we, you, they **did get shaped**
Pres.	I, we, you, they **have shaped**	I, we, you, they **have been shaped**
Perf.	he, she, it **has shaped**	he, she, it **has been shaped**
Past	I, he, she, it,	I, he, she, it,
Perf.	we, you, they **had shaped**	we, you, they **had been shaped**
Fut.	I, he, she, it, we, you, they	I, he, she, it, we, you, they
Perf.	**will have shaped**	**will have been shaped**

IMPERATIVE MOOD

shape

be shaped

SUBJUNCTIVE MOOD

Pres.	if I, he, she, it,	if I, he, she, it,
	we, you, they **shape**	we, you, they **be shaped**
Past	if I, he, she, it,	if I, he, she, it,
	we, you, they **shaped**	we, you, they **were shaped**
Fut.	if I, he, she, it,	if I, he, she, it,
	we, you, they **should shape**	we, you, they **should be shaped**

Transitive and intransitive.

shave
(active voice)

be shaved/shaven
(passive voice)

Infinitive: **to shave**
Perfect Infinitive: **to have shaved**
Present Participle: **shaving**
Past Participle: **shaved**

Infinitive: **to be shaved**
Perfect Infinitive: **to have been shaved**
Present Participle: **being shaved**
Past Participle: **been shaved**

INDICATIVE MOOD

Pres.	I, we, you, they **shave**	I **am shaved**
		we, you, they **are shaved**
	he, she, it **shaves**	he, she, it **is shaved**
Pres.	I **am shaving**	I **am being shaved**
Prog.	we, you, they **are shaving**	we, you, they **are being shaved**
	he, she, it **is shaving**	he, she, it **is being shaved**
Pres.	I, we, you, they **do shave**	I, we, you, they **do get shaved**
Int.	he, she, it **does shave**	he, she, it **does get shaved**
Fut.	I, he, she, it,	I, he, she, it,
	we, you, they **will shave**	we, you, they **will be shaved**
Past	I, he, she, it,	I, he, she, it **was shaved**
	we, you, they **shaved**	we, you, they **were shaved**
Past	I, he, she, it **was shaving**	I, he, she, it **was being shaved**
Prog.	we, you, they **were shaving**	we, you, they **were being shaved**
Past	I, he, she, it,	I, he, she, it,
Int.	we, you, they **did shave**	we, you, they **did get shaved**
Pres.	I, we, you, they **have shaved**	I, we, you, they **have been shaved**
Perf.	he, she, it **has shaved**	he, she, it **has been shaved**
Past	I, he, she, it,	I, he, she, it,
Perf.	we, you, they **had shaved**	we, you, they **had been shaved**
Fut.	I, he, she, it, we, you, they	I, he, she, it, we, you, they
Perf.	**will have shaved**	**will have been shaved**

IMPERATIVE MOOD

shave

be shaved

SUBJUNCTIVE MOOD

Pres.	if I, he, she, it,	if I, he, she, it,
	we, you, they **shave**	we, you, they **be shaved**
Past	if I, he, she, it,	if I, he, she, it,
	we, you, they **shaved**	we, you, they **were shaved**
Fut.	if I, he, she, it,	if I, he, she, it,
	we, you, they **should shave**	we, you, they **should be shaved**

Transitive and intransitive.

shear
(active voice)

be sheared/shorn
(passive voice)

Infinitive: **to shear**
Perfect Infinitive: **to have sheared**
Present Participle: **shearing**
Past Participle: **sheared**

Infinitive: **to be sheared**
Perfect Infinitive: **to have been sheared**
Present Participle: **being sheared**
Past Participle: **been sheared**

INDICATIVE MOOD

Pres.	I, we, you, they **shear**	I **am sheared**
		we, you, they **are sheared**
	he, she, it **shears**	he, she, it **is sheared**
Pres.	I **am shearing**	I **am being sheared**
Prog.	we, you, they **are shearing**	we, you, they **are being sheared**
	he, she, it **is shearing**	he, she, it **is being sheared**
Pres.	I, we, you, they **do shear**	I, we, you, they **do get sheared**
Int.	he, she, it **does shear**	he, she, it **does get sheared**
Fut.	I, he, she, it,	I, he, she, it,
	we, you, they **will shear**	we, you, they **will be sheared**
Past	I, he, she, it,	I, he, she, it **was sheared**
	we, you, they **sheared**	we, you, they **were sheared**
Past	I, he, she, it **was shearing**	I, he, she, it **was being sheared**
Prog.	we, you, they **were shearing**	we, you, they **were being sheared**
Past	I, he, she, it,	I, he, she, it,
Int.	we, you, they **did shear**	we, you, they **did get sheared**
Pres.	I, we, you, they **have sheared**	I, we, you, they **have been sheared**
Perf.	he, she, it **has sheared**	he, she, it **has been sheared**
Past	I, he, she, it,	I, he, she, it,
Perf.	we, you, they **had sheared**	we, you, they **had been sheared**
Fut.	I, he, she, it, we, you, they	I, he, she, it, we, you, they
Perf.	**will have sheared**	**will have been sheared**

IMPERATIVE MOOD

shear   **be sheared**

SUBJUNCTIVE MOOD

Pres.	if I, he, she, it,	if I, he, she, it,
	we, you, they **shear**	we, you, they **be sheared**
Past	if I, he, she, it,	if I, he, she, it,
	we, you, they **sheared**	we, you, they **were sheared**
Fut.	if I, he, she, it,	if I, he, she, it,
	we, you, they **should shear**	we, you, they **should be sheared**

Transitive and intransitive. The *Oxford Dictionary* notes the archaic past tense SHORE. The past participle may be either SHEARED or SHORN.

shed
(active voice)

be shed
(passive voice)

Infinitive: **to shed**
Perfect Infinitive: **to have shed**
Present Participle: **shedding**
Past Participle: **shed**

Infinitive: **to be shed**
Perfect Infinitive: **to have been shed**
Present Participle: **being shed**
Past Participle: **been shed**

INDICATIVE MOOD

Pres.	I, we, you, they **shed**	I **am shed**
		we, you, they **are shed**
	he, she, it **sheds**	he, she, it **is shed**
Pres.	I **am shedding**	I **am being shed**
Prog.	we, you, they **are shedding**	we, you, they **are being shed**
	he, she, it **is shedding**	he, she, it **is being shed**
Pres.	I, we, you, they **do shed**	I, we, you, they **do get shed**
Int.	he, she, it **does shed**	he, she, it **does get shed**
Fut.	I, he, she, it,	I, he, she, it,
	we, you, they **will shed**	we, you, they **will be shed**
Past	I, he, she, it,	I, he, she, it **was shed**
	we, you, they **shed**	we, you, they **were shed**
Past	I, he, she, it **was shedding**	I, he, she, it **was being shed**
Prog.	we, you, they **were shedding**	we, you, they **were being shed**
Past	I, he, she, it,	I, he, she, it,
Int.	we, you, they **did shed**	we, you, they **did get shed**
Pres.	I, we, you, they **have shed**	I, we, you, they **have been shed**
Perf.	he, she, it **has shed**	he, she, it **has been shed**
Past	I, he, she, it,	I, he, she, it,
Perf.	we, you, they **had shed**	we, you, they **had been shed**
Fut.	I, he, she, it, we, you, they	I, he, she, it, we, you, they
Perf.	**will have shed**	**will have been shed**

IMPERATIVE MOOD

shed

be shed

SUBJUNCTIVE MOOD

Pres.	if I, he, she, it,	if I, he, she, it,
	we, you, they **shed**	we, you, they **be shed**
Past	if I, he, she, it,	if I, he, she, it,
	we, you, they **shed**	we, you, they **were shed**
Fut.	if I, he, she, it,	if I, he, she, it,
	we, you, they **should shed**	we, you, they **should be shed**

Transitive and intransitive.

sheer
(active voice)

be sheered
(passive voice)

Infinitive: **to sheer**
Perfect Infinitive: **to have sheered**
Present Participle: **sheering**
Past Participle: **sheered**

Infinitive: **to be sheered**
Perfect Infinitive: **to have been sheered**
Present Participle: **being sheered**
Past Participle: **been sheered**

INDICATIVE MOOD

Pres.	I, we, you, they **sheer**	I am sheered
		we, you, they **are sheered**
	he, she, it **sheers**	he, she, it **is sheered**
Pres.	I am sheering	I am being sheered
Prog.	we, you, they **are sheering**	we, you, they **are being sheered**
	he, she, it **is sheering**	he, she, it **is being sheered**
Pres.	I, we, you, they **do sheer**	I, we, you, they **do get sheered**
Int.	he, she, it **does sheer**	he, she, it **does get sheered**
Fut.	I, he, she, it,	I, he, she, it,
	we, you, they **will sheer**	we, you, they **will be sheered**
Past	I, he, she, it,	I, he, she, it **was sheered**
	we, you, they **sheered**	we, you, they **were sheered**
Past	I, he, she, it **was sheering**	I, he, she, it **was being sheered**
Prog.	we, you, they **were sheering**	we, you, they **were being sheered**
Past	I, he, she, it,	I, he, she, it,
Int.	we, you, they **did sheer**	we, you, they **did get sheered**
Pres.	I, we, you, they **have sheered**	I, we, you, they **have been sheered**
Perf.	he, she, it **has sheered**	he, she, it **has been sheered**
Past	I, he, she, it,	I, he, she, it,
Perf.	we, you, they **had sheered**	we, you, they **had been sheered**
Fut.	I, he, she, it, we, you, they	I, he, she, it, we, you, they
Perf.	**will have sheered**	**will have been sheered**

IMPERATIVE MOOD

sheer   **be sheered**

SUBJUNCTIVE MOOD

Pres.	if I, he, she, it,	if I, he, she, it,
	we, you, they **sheer**	we, you, they **be sheered**
Past	if I, he, she, it,	if I, he, she, it,
	we, you, they **sheered**	we, you, they **were sheered**
Fut.	if I, he, she, it,	if I, he, she, it,
	we, you, they **should sheer**	we, you, they **should be sheered**

Transitive and intransitive.

shine
(active voice)

PRINCIPAL PARTS: **shines, shining,**
shone/shined, shone/shined

be shone/shined
(passive voice)

Infinitive: **to shine**
Perfect Infinitive: **to have shone**
Present Participle: **shining**
Past Participle: **shone**

Infinitive: **to be shone**
Perfect Infinitive: **to have been shone**
Present Participle: **being shone**
Past Participle: **been shone**

INDICATIVE MOOD

Pres.	I, we, you, they **shine**	I **am shone**
		we, you, they **are shone**
	he, she, it **shines**	he, she, it **is shone**
Pres.	I **am shining**	I **am being shone**
Prog.	we, you, they **are shining**	we, you, they **are being shone**
	he, she, it **is shining**	he, she, it **is being shone**
Pres.	I, we, you, they **do shine**	I, we, you, they **do get shone**
Int.	he, she, it **does shine**	he, she, it **does get shone**
Fut.	I, he, she, it,	I, he, she, it,
	we, you, they **will shine**	we, you, they **will be shone**
Past	I, he, she, it,	I, he, she, it **was shone**
	we, you, they **shone**	we, you, they **were shone**
Past	I, he, she, it **was shining**	I, he, she, it **was being shone**
Prog.	we, you, they **were shining**	we, you, they **were being shone**
Past	I, he, she, it,	I, he, she, it,
Int.	we, you, they **did shine**	we, you, they **did get shone**
Pres.	I, we, you, they **have shone**	I, we, you, they **have been shone**
Perf.	he, she, it **has shone**	he, she, it **has been shone**
Past	I, he, she, it,	I, he, she, it,
Perf.	we, you, they **had shone**	we, you, they **had been shone**
Fut.	I, he, she, it, we, you, they	I, he, she, it, we, you, they
Perf.	**will have shone**	**will have been shone**

IMPERATIVE MOOD

shine

be shone

SUBJUNCTIVE MOOD

Pres.	if I, he, she, it,	if I, he, she, it,
	we, you, they **shine**	we, you, they **be shone**
Past	if I, he, she, it,	if I, he, she, it,
	we, you, they **shone**	we, you, they **were shone**
Fut.	if I, he, she, it,	if I, he, she, it,
	we, you, they **should shine**	we, you, they **should be shone**

Intransitive or transitive. Past tense and past participle may be either SHONE or SHINED. In the meaning of "polishing" only SHINED is used for the past tense and past participle.

shoe
(active voice)

be shod/shodden
(passive voice)

Infinitive: **to shoe**
Perfect Infinitive: **to have shod**
Present Participle: **shoeing**
Past Participle: **shod**

Infinitive: **to be shod**
Perfect Infinitive: **to have been shod**
Present Participle: **being shod**
Past Participle: **been shod**

INDICATIVE MOOD

Pres.	I, we, you, they **shoe**	I am **shod**
		we, you, they **are shod**
	he, she, it **shoes**	he, she, it **is shod**
Pres.	I am **shoeing**	I am **being shod**
Prog.	we, you, they **are shoeing**	we, you, they **are being shod**
	he, she, it **is shoeing**	he, she, it **is being shod**
Pres.	I, we, you, they **do shoe**	I, we, you, they **do get shod**
Int.	he, she, it **does shoe**	he, she, it **does get shod**
Fut.	I, he, she, it, we, you, they **will shoe**	I, he, she, it, we, you, they **will be shod**
Past	I, he, she, it, we, you, they **shod**	I, he, she, it **was shod** we, you, they **were shod**
Past	I, he, she, it **was shoeing**	I, he, she, it **was being shod**
Prog.	we, you, they **were shoeing**	we, you, they **were being shod**
Past	I, he, she, it, we, you, they **did shoe**	I, he, she, it, we, you, they **did get shod**
Int.		
Pres.	I, we, you, they **have shod**	I, we, you, they **have been shod**
Perf.	he, she, it **has shod**	he, she, it **has been shod**
Past	I, he, she, it, we, you, they **had shod**	I, he, she, it, we, you, they **had been shod**
Perf.		
Fut.	I, he, she, it, we, you, they **will have shod**	I, he, she, it, we, you, they **will have been shod**
Perf.		

IMPERATIVE MOOD

shoe   **be shod**

SUBJUNCTIVE MOOD

Pres.	if I, he, she, it, we, you, they **shoe**	if I, he, she, it, we, you, they **be shod**
Past	if I, he, she, it, we, you, they **shod**	if I, he, she, it, we, you, they **were shod**
Fut.	if I, he, she, it, we, you, they **should shoe**	if I, he, she, it, we, you, they **should be shod**

The past participle may be either SHOD or SHODDEN. *Webster's* lists SHOED as an alternate form for the past tense and past participle.

shoot
(active voice)

PRINCIPAL PARTS: **shoots, shooting, shot, shot**

be shot
(passive voice)

Infinitive: **to shoot**
Perfect Infinitive: **to have shot**
Present Participle: **shooting**
Past Participle: **shot**

Infinitive: **to be shot**
Perfect Infinitive: **to have been shot**
Present Participle: **being shot**
Past Participle: **been shot**

INDICATIVE MOOD

Pres.	I, we, you, they **shoot**	I **am shot**
		we, you, they **are shot**
	he, she, it **shoots**	he, she, it **is shot**
Pres.	I **am shooting**	I **am being shot**
Prog.	we, you, they **are shooting**	we, you, they **are being shot**
	he, she, it **is shooting**	he, she, it **is being shot**
Pres.	I, we, you, they **do shoot**	I, we, you, they **do get shot**
Int.	he, she, it **does shoot**	he, she, it **does get shot**
Fut.	I, he, she, it,	I, he, she, it,
	we, you, they **will shoot**	we, you, they **will be shot**
Past	I, he, she, it,	I, he, she, it **was shot**
	we, you, they **shot**	we, you, they **were shot**
Past	I, he, she, it **was shooting**	I, he, she, it **was being shot**
Prog.	we, you, they **were shooting**	we, you, they **were being shot**
Past	I, he, she, it,	I, he, she, it,
Int.	we, you, they **did shoot**	we, you, they **did get shot**
Pres.	I, we, you, they **have shot**	I, we, you, they **have been shot**
Perf.	he, she, it **has shot**	he, she, it **has been shot**
Past	I, he, she, it,	I, he, she, it,
Perf.	we, you, they **had shot**	we, you, they **had been shot**
Fut.	I, he, she, it, we, you, they	I, he, she, it, we, you, they
Perf.	**will have shot**	**will have been shot**

IMPERATIVE MOOD

shoot   **be shot**

SUBJUNCTIVE MOOD

Pres.	if I, he, she, it,	if I, he, she, it,
	we, you, they **shoot**	we, you, they **be shot**
Past	if I, he, she, it,	if I, he, she, it,
	we, you, they **shot**	we, you, they **were shot**
Fut.	if I, he, she, it,	if I, he, she, it,
	we, you, they **should shoot**	we, you, they **should be shot**

Transitive and intransitive.

shop
(active voice)

be shopped
(passive voice)

Infinitive: **to shop**
Perfect Infinitive: **to have shopped**
Present Participle: **shopping**
Past Participle: **shopped**

Infinitive: **to be shopped**
Perfect Infinitive: **to have been shopped**
Present Participle: **being shopped**
Past Participle: **been shopped**

INDICATIVE MOOD

Pres.	I, we, you, they **shop**	I **am shopped** we, you, they **are shopped**
	he, she, it **shops**	he, she, it **is shopped**
Pres. *Prog.*	I **am shopping** we, you, they **are shopping** he, she, it **is shopping**	I **am being shopped** we, you, they **are being shopped** he, she, it **is being shopped**
Pres. *Int.*	I, we, you, they **do shop** he, she, it **does shop**	I, we, you, they **do get shopped** he, she, it **does get shopped**
Fut.	I, he, she, it, we, you, they **will shop**	I, he, she, it, we, you, they **will be shopped**
Past	I, he, she, it, we, you, they **shopped**	I, he, she, it **was shopped** we, you, they **were shopped**
Past *Prog.*	I, he, she, it **was shopping** we, you, they **were shopping**	I, he, she, it **was being shopped** we, you, they **were being shopped**
Past *Int.*	I, he, she, it, we, you, they **did shop**	I, he, she, it, we, you, they **did get shopped**
Pres. *Perf.*	I, we, you, they **have shopped** he, she, it **has shopped**	I, we, you, they **have been shopped** he, she, it **has been shopped**
Past *Perf.*	I, he, she, it, we, you, they **had shopped**	I, he, she, it, we, you, they **had been shopped**
Fut. *Perf.*	I, he, she, it, we, you, they **will have shopped**	I, he, she, it, we, you, they **will have been shopped**

IMPERATIVE MOOD

shop

be shopped

SUBJUNCTIVE MOOD

Pres.	if I, he, she, it, we, you, they **shop**	if I, he, she, it, we, you, they **be shopped**
Past	if I, he, she, it, we, you, they **shopped**	if I, he, she, it, we, you, they **were shopped**
Fut.	if I, he, she, it, we, you, they **should shop**	if I, he, she, it, we, you, they **should be shopped**

Intransitive and transitive.

short
(active voice)

be shorted
(passive voice)

Infinitive: **to short**
Perfect Infinitive: **to have shorted**
Present Participle: **shorting**
Past Participle: **shorted**

Infinitive: **to be shorted**
Perfect Infinitive: **to have been shorted**
Present Participle: **being shorted**
Past Participle: **been shorted**

INDICATIVE MOOD

Pres.	I, we, you, they **short**	I **am shorted**
		we, you, they **are shorted**
	he, she, it **shorts**	he, she, it **is shorted**
Pres.	I **am shorting**	I **am being shorted**
Prog.	we, you, they **are shorting**	we, you, they **are being shorted**
	he, she, it **is shorting**	he, she, it **is being shorted**
Pres.	I, we, you, they **do short**	I, we, you, they **do get shorted**
Int.	he, she, it **does short**	he, she, it **does get shorted**
Fut.	I, he, she, it,	I, he, she, it,
	we, you, they **will short**	we, you, they **will be shorted**
Past	I, he, she, it,	I, he, she, it **was shorted**
	we, you, they **shorted**	we, you, they **were shorted**
Past	I, he, she, it **was shorting**	I, he, she, it **was being shorted**
Prog.	we, you, they **were shorting**	we, you, they **were being shorted**
Past	I, he, she, it,	I, he, she, it,
Int.	we, you, they **did short**	we, you, they **did get shorted**
Pres.	I, we, you, they **have shorted**	I, we, you, they **have been shorted**
Perf.	he, she, it **has shorted**	he, she, it **has been shorted**
Past	I, he, she, it,	I, he, she, it,
Perf.	we, you, they **had shorted**	we, you, they **had been shorted**
Fut.	I, he, she, it, we, you, they	I, he, she, it, we, you, they
Perf.	**will have shorted**	**will have been shorted**

IMPERATIVE MOOD

short   **be shorted**

SUBJUNCTIVE MOOD

Pres.	if I, he, she, it,	if I, he, she, it,
	we, you, they **short**	we, you, they **be shorted**
Past	if I, he, she, it,	if I, he, she, it,
	we, you, they **shorted**	we, you, they **were shorted**
Fut.	if I, he, she, it,	if I, he, she, it,
	we, you, they **should short**	we, you, they **should be shorted**

Transitive and intransitive.

shorten
(active voice)

be shortened
(passive voice)

Infinitive: **to shorten**
Perfect Infinitive: **to have shortened**
Present Participle: **shortening**
Past Participle: **shortened**

Infinitive: **to be shortened**
Perfect Infinitive: **to have been shortened**
Present Participle: **being shortened**
Past Participle: **been shortened**

INDICATIVE MOOD

Pres.	I, we, you, they **shorten**	I **am shortened**
		we, you, they **are shortened**
	he, she, it **shortens**	he, she, it **is shortened**
Pres. *Prog.*	I **am shortening**	I **am being shortened**
	we, you, they **are shortening**	we, you, they **are being shortened**
	he, she, it **is shortening**	he, she, it **is being shortened**
Pres. *Int.*	I, we, you, they **do shorten**	I, we, you, they **do get shortened**
	he, she, it **does shorten**	he, she, it **does get shortened**
Fut.	I, he, she, it, we, you, they **will shorten**	I, he, she, it, we, you, they **will be shortened**
Past	I, he, she, it, we, you, they **shortened**	I, he, she, it **was shortened** we, you, they **were shortened**
Past *Prog.*	I, he, she, it **was shortening** we, you, they **were shortening**	I, he, she, it **was being shortened** we, you, they **were being shortened**
Past *Int.*	I, he, she, it, we, you, they **did shorten**	I, he, she, it, we, you, they **did get shortened**
Pres. *Perf.*	I, we, you, they **have shortened** he, she, it **has shortened**	I, we, you, they **have been shortened** he, she, it **has been shortened**
Past *Perf.*	I, he, she, it, we, you, they **had shortened**	I, he, she, it, we, you, they **had been shortened**
Fut. *Perf.*	I, he, she, it, we, you, they **will have shortened**	I, he, she, it, we, you, they **will have been shortened**

IMPERATIVE MOOD

shorten   **be shortened**

SUBJUNCTIVE MOOD

Pres.	if I, he, she, it, we, you, they **shorten**	if I, he, she, it, we, you, they **be shortened**
Past	if I, he, she, it, we, you, they **shortened**	if I, he, she, it, we, you, they **were shortened**
Fut.	if I, he, she, it, we, you, they **should shorten**	if I, he, she, it, we, you, they **should be shortened**

Transitive and intransitive.

shovel
(active voice)

be shoveled/ shovelled
(passive voice)

Infinitive: **to shovel**
Perfect Infinitive: **to have shoveled**
Present Participle: **shoveling**
Past Participle: **shoveled**

Infinitive: **to be shoveled**
Perfect Infinitive: **to have been shoveled**
Present Participle: **being shoveled**
Past Participle: **been shoveled**

INDICATIVE MOOD

Pres.	I, we, you, they **shovel**	I **am shoveled**
		we, you, they **are shoveled**
	he, she, it **shovels**	he, she, it **is shoveled**
Pres.	I **am shoveling**	I **am being shoveled**
Prog.	we, you, they **are shoveling**	we, you, they **are being shoveled**
	he, she, it **is shoveling**	he, she, it **is being shoveled**
Pres.	I, we, you, they **do shovel**	I, we, you, they **do get shoveled**
Int.	he, she, it **does shovel**	he, she, it **does get shoveled**
Fut.	I, he, she, it,	I, he, she, it,
	we, you, they **will shovel**	we, you, they **will be shoveled**
Past	I, he, she, it,	I, he, she, it **was shoveled**
	we, you, they **shoveled**	we, you, they **were shoveled**
Past	I, he, she, it **was shoveling**	I, he, she, it **was being shoveled**
Prog.	we, you, they **were shoveling**	we, you, they **were being shoveled**
Past	I, he, she, it,	I, he, she, it,
Int.	we, you, they **did shovel**	we, you, they **did get shoveled**
Pres.	I, we, you, they **have shoveled**	I, we, you, they **have been shoveled**
Perf.	he, she, it **has shoveled**	he, she, it **has been shoveled**
Past	I, he, she, it,	I, he, she, it,
Perf.	we, you, they **had shoveled**	we, you, they **had been shoveled**
Fut.	I, he, she, it, we, you, they	I, he, she, it, we, you, they
Perf.	**will have shoveled**	**will have been shoveled**

IMPERATIVE MOOD

shovel   **be shoveled**

SUBJUNCTIVE MOOD

Pres.	if I, he, she, it,	if I, he, she, it,
	we, you, they **shovel**	we, you, they **be shoveled**
Past	if I, he, she, it,	if I, he, she, it,
	we, you, they **shoveled**	we, you, they **were shoveled**
Fut.	if I, he, she, it,	if I, he, she, it,
	we, you, they **should shovel**	we, you, they **should be shoveled**

Transitive and intransitive. The *Oxford Dictionary* prefers the spellings with "ll": SHOVELLING, SHOVELLED.

374

show
(active voice)

be shown/showed
(passive voice)

Infinitive: **to show**
Perfect Infinitive: **to have shown**
Present Participle: **showing**
Past Participle: **shown**

Infinitive: **to be shown**
Perfect Infinitive: **to have been shown**
Present Participle: **being shown**
Past Participle: **been shown**

INDICATIVE MOOD

Pres.	I, we, you, they **show**	I **am shown**
		we, you, they **are shown**
	he, she, it **shows**	he, she, it **is shown**
Pres. *Prog.*	I **am showing**	I **am being shown**
	we, you, they **are showing**	we, you, they **are being shown**
	he, she, it **is showing**	he, she, it **is being shown**
Pres. *Int.*	I, we, you, they **do show**	I, we, you, they **do get shown**
	he, she, it **does show**	he, she, it **does get shown**
Fut.	I, he, she, it, we, you, they **will show**	I, he, she, it, we, you, they **will be shown**
Past	I, he, she, it, we, you, they **showed**	I, he, she, it **was shown** we, you, they **were shown**
Past *Prog.*	I, he, she, it **was showing** we, you, they **were showing**	I, he, she, it **was being shown** we, you, they **were being shown**
Past *Int.*	I, he, she, it, we, you, they **did show**	I, he, she, it, we, you, they **did get shown**
Pres. *Perf.*	I, we, you, they **have shown** he, she, it **has shown**	I, we, you, they **have been shown** he, she, it **has been shown**
Past *Perf.*	I, he, she, it, we, you, they **had shown**	I, he, she, it, we, you, they **had been shown**
Fut. *Perf.*	I, he, she, it, we, you, they **will have shown**	I, he, she, it, we, you, they **will have been shown**

IMPERATIVE MOOD

show　　　　　**be shown**

SUBJUNCTIVE MOOD

Pres.	if I, he, she, it, we, you, they **show**	if I, he, she, it, we, you, they **be shown**
Past	if I, he, she, it, we, you, they **showed**	if I, he, she, it, we, you, they **were shown**
Fut.	if I, he, she, it, we, you, they **should show**	if I, he, she, it, we, you, they **should be shown**

Transitive and intransitive.

shred
(active voice)

be shredded/shred
(passive voice)

Infinitive: **to shred**
Perfect Infinitive: **to have shredded**
Present Participle: **shredding**
Past Participle: **shredded**

Infinitive: **to be shredded**
Perfect Infinitive: **to have been shredded**
Present Participle: **being shredded**
Past Participle: **been shredded**

INDICATIVE MOOD

Pres.	I, we, you, they **shred**	I **am shredded** we, you, they **are shredded**
	he, she, it **shreds**	he, she, it **is shredded**
Pres. *Prog.*	I **am shredding** we, you, they **are shredding** he, she, it **is shredding**	I **am being shredded** we, you, they **are being shredded** he, she, it **is being shredded**
Pres. *Int.*	I, we, you, they **do shred** he, she, it **does shred**	I, we, you, they **do get shredded** he, she, it **does get shredded**
Fut.	I, he, she, it, we, you, they **will shred**	I, he, she, it, we, you, they **will be shredded**
Past	I, he, she, it, we, you, they **shredded**	I, he, she, it **was shredded** we, you, they **were shredded**
Past *Prog.*	I, he, she, it **was shredding** we, you, they **were shredding**	I, he, she, it **was being shredded** we, you, they **were being shredded**
Past *Int.*	I, he, she, it, we, you, they **did shred**	I, he, she, it, we, you, they **did get shredded**
Pres. *Perf.*	I, we, you, they **have shredded** he, she, it **has shredded**	I, we, you, they **have been shredded** he, she, it **has been shredded**
Past *Perf.*	I, he, she, it, we, you, they **had shredded**	I, he, she, it, we, you, they **had been shredded**
Fut. *Perf.*	I, he, she, it, we, you, they **will have shredded**	I, he, she, it, we, you, they **will have been shredded**

IMPERATIVE MOOD

shred　　　　　　　　　　**be shredded**

SUBJUNCTIVE MOOD

Pres.	if I, he, she, it, we, you, they **shred**	if I, he, she, it, we, you, they **be shredded**
Past	if I, he, she, it, we, you, they **shredded**	if I, he, she, it, we, you, they **were shredded**
Fut.	if I, he, she, it, we, you, they **should shred**	if I, he, she, it, we, you, they **should be shredded**

shrink
(active voice)

PRINCIPAL PARTS: shrinks, shrinking, shrank/shrunk, shrunk/shrunken

be shrunk/shrunken
(passive voice)

Infinitive: **to shrink**
Perfect Infinitive: **to have shrunk**
Present Participle: **shrinking**
Past Participle: **shrunk**

Infinitive: **to be shrunk**
Perfect Infinitive: **to have been shrunk**
Present Participle: **being shrunk**
Past Participle: **been shrunk**

INDICATIVE MOOD

Pres.	I, we, you, they **shrink**	I **am shrunk**
		we, you, they **are shrunk**
	he, she, it **shrinks**	he, she, it **is shrunk**
Pres. *Prog.*	I **am shrinking**	I **am being shrunk**
	we, you, they **are shrinking**	we, you, they **are being shrunk**
	he, she, it **is shrinking**	he, she, it **is being shrunk**
Pres. *Int.*	I, we, you, they **do shrink**	I, we, you, they **do get shrunk**
	he, she, it **does shrink**	he, she, it **does get shrunk**
Fut.	I, he, she, it, we, you, they **will shrink**	I, he, she, it, we, you, they **will be shrunk**
Past	I, he, she, it, we, you, they **shrank**	I, he, she, it **was shrunk** we, you, they **were shrunk**
Past *Prog.*	I, he, she, it **was shrinking** we, you, they **were shrinking**	I, he, she, it **was being shrunk** we, you, they **were being shrunk**
Past *Int.*	I, he, she, it, we, you, they **did shrink**	I, he, she, it, we, you, they **did get shrunk**
Pres. *Perf.*	I, we, you, they **have shrunk**	I, we, you, they **have been shrunk**
	he, she, it **has shrunk**	he, she, it **has been shrunk**
Past *Perf.*	I, he, she, it, we, you, they **had shrunk**	I, he, she, it, we, you, they **had been shrunk**
Fut. *Perf.*	I, he, she, it, we, you, they **will have shrunk**	I, he, she, it, we, you, they **will have been shrunk**

IMPERATIVE MOOD

shrink

be shrunk

SUBJUNCTIVE MOOD

Pres.	if I, he, she, it, we, you, they **shrink**	if I, he, she, it, we, you, they **be shrunk**
Past	if I, he, she, it, we, you, they **shrank**	if I, he, she, it, we, you, they **were shrunk**
Fut.	if I, he, she, it, we, you, they **should shrink**	if I, he, she, it, we, you, they **should be shrunk**

Intransitive and transitive. The past tense may be either SHRANK or SHRUNK. The past participle is either SHRUNK or SHRUNKEN.

shrive
(active voice)

be shriven/shrived
(passive voice)

Infinitive: **to shrive**
Perfect Infinitive: **to have shriven**
Present Participle: **shriving**
Past Participle: **shriven**

Infinitive: **to be shriven**
Perfect Infinitive: **to have been shriven**
Present Participle: **being shriven**
Past Participle: **been shriven**

INDICATIVE MOOD

Pres.	I, we, you, they **shrive**	I **am shriven**
		we, you, they **are shriven**
	he, she, it **shrives**	he, she, it **is shriven**
Pres.	I **am shriving**	I **am being shriven**
Prog.	we, you, they **are shriving**	we, you, they **are being shriven**
	he, she, it **is shriving**	he, she, it **is being shriven**
Pres.	I, we, you, they **do shrive**	I, we, you, they **do get shriven**
Int.	he, she, it **does shrive**	he, she, it **does get shriven**
Fut.	I, he, she, it,	I, he, she, it,
	we, you, they **will shrive**	we, you, they **will be shriven**
Past	I, he, she, it,	I, he, she, it **was shriven**
	we, you, they **shrove**	we, you, they **were shriven**
Past	I, he, she, it **was shriving**	I, he, she, it **was being shriven**
Prog.	we, you, they **were shriving**	we, you, they **were being shriven**
Past	I, he, she, it,	I, he, she, it,
Int.	we, you, they **did shrive**	we, you, they **did get shriven**
Pres.	I, we, you, they **have shriven**	I, we, you, they **have been shriven**
Perf.	he, she, it **has shriven**	he, she, it **has been shriven**
Past	I, he, she, it,	I, he, she, it,
Perf.	we, you, they **had shriven**	we, you, they **had been shriven**
Fut.	I, he, she, it, we, you, they	I, he, she, it, we, you, they
Perf.	**will have shriven**	**will have been shriven**

IMPERATIVE MOOD

shrive   **be shriven**

SUBJUNCTIVE MOOD

Pres.	if I, he, she, it,	if I, he, she, it,
	we, you, they **shrive**	we, you, they **be shriven**
Past	if I, he, she, it,	if I, he, she, it,
	we, you, they **shrove**	we, you, they **were shriven**
Fut.	if I, he, she, it,	if I, he, she, it,
	we, you, they **should shrive**	we, you, they **should be shriven**

The past tense forms are SHROVE or SHRIVED. The past participle is SHRIVEN or SHRIVED.

shut
(active voice)

be shut
(passive voice)

Infinitive: **to shut**
Perfect Infinitive: **to have shut**
Present Participle: **shutting**
Past Participle: **shut**

Infinitive: **to be shut**
Perfect Infinitive: **to have been shut**
Present Participle: **being shut**
Past Participle: **been shut**

INDICATIVE MOOD

Pres.	I, we, you, they **shut**	I **am shut**
		we, you, they **are shut**
	he, she, it **shuts**	he, she, it **is shut**
Pres.	I **am shutting**	I **am being shut**
Prog.	we, you, they **are shutting**	we, you, they **are being shut**
	he, she, it **is shutting**	he, she, it **is being shut**
Pres.	I, we, you, they **do shut**	I, we, you, they **do get shut**
Int.	he, she, it **does shut**	he, she, it **does get shut**
Fut.	I, he, she, it,	I, he, she, it,
	we, you, they **will shut**	we, you, they **will be shut**
Past	I, he, she, it,	I, he, she, it **was shut**
	we, you, they **shut**	we, you, they **were shut**
Past	I, he, she, it **was shutting**	I, he, she, it **was being shut**
Prog.	we, you, they **were shutting**	we, you, they **were being shut**
Past	I, he, she, it,	I, he, she, it,
Int.	we, you, they **did shut**	we, you, they **did get shut**
Pres.	I, we, you, they **have shut**	I, we, you, they **have been shut**
Perf.	he, she, it **has shut**	he, she, it **has been shut**
Past	I, he, she, it,	I, he, she, it,
Perf.	we, you, they **had shut**	we, you, they **had been shut**
Fut.	I, he, she, it, we, you, they	I, he, she, it, we, you, they
Perf.	**will have shut**	**will have been shut**

IMPERATIVE MOOD

shut   **be shut**

SUBJUNCTIVE MOOD

Pres.	if I, he, she, it,	if I, he, she, it,
	we, you, they **shut**	we, you, they **be shut**
Past	if I, he, she, it,	if I, he, she, it,
	we, you, they **shut**	we, you, they **were shut**
Fut.	if I, he, she, it,	if I, he, she, it,
	we, you, they **should shut**	we, you, they **should be shut**

Transitive and intransitive.

sing
(active voice)

be sung
(passive voice)

Infinitive: **to sing**
Perfect Infinitive: **to have sung**
Present Participle: **singing**
Past Participle: **sung**

Infinitive: **to be sung**
Perfect Infinitive: **to have been sung**
Present Participle: **being sung**
Past Participle: **been sung**

INDICATIVE MOOD

Pres.	I, we, you, they **sing** he, she, it **sings**	I **am sung** we, you, they **are sung** he, she, it **is sung**
Pres. *Prog.*	I **am singing** we, you, they **are singing** he, she, it **is singing**	I **am being sung** we, you, they **are being sung** he, she, it **is being sung**
Pres. *Int.*	I, we, you, they **do sing** he, she, it **does sing**	I, we, you, they **do get sung** he, she, it **does get sung**
Fut.	I, he, she, it, we, you, they **will sing**	I, he, she, it, we, you, they **will be sung**
Past	I, he, she, it, we, you, they **sang**	I, he, she, it **was sung** we, you, they **were sung**
Past *Prog.*	I, he, she, it **was singing** we, you, they **were singing**	I, he, she, it **was being sung** we, you, they **were being sung**
Past *Int.*	I, he, she, it, we, you, they **did sing**	I, he, she, it, we, you, they **did get sung**
Pres. *Perf.*	I, we, you, they **have sung** he, she, it **has sung**	I, we, you, they **have been sung** he, she, it **has been sung**
Past *Perf.*	I, he, she, it, we, you, they **had sung**	I, he, she, it, we, you, they **had been sung**
Fut. *Perf.*	I, he, she, it, we, you, they **will have sung**	I, he, she, it, we, you, they **will have been sung**

IMPERATIVE MOOD

sing

be sung

SUBJUNCTIVE MOOD

Pres.	if I, he, she, it, we, you, they **sing**	if I, he, she, it, we, you, they **be sung**
Past	if I, he, she, it, we, you, they **sang**	if I, he, she, it, we, you, they **were sung**
Fut.	if I, he, she, it, we, you, they **should sing**	if I, he, she, it, we, you, they **should be sung**

Intransitive and transitive. The *Oxford Dictionary* and *Webster's* do not list the past tense form SUNG.

singe
(active voice)

PRINCIPAL PARTS: **singes, singeing,
singed, singed**

be singed
(passive voice)

Infinitive: **to singe**
Perfect Infinitive: **to have singed**
Present Participle: **singeing**
Past Participle: **singed**

Infinitive: **to be singed**
Perfect Infinitive: **to have been singed**
Present Participle: **being singed**
Past Participle: **been singed**

INDICATIVE MOOD

Pres.	I, we, you, they **singe**	I **am singed**
		we, you, they **are singed**
	he, she, it **singes**	he, she, it **is singed**
Pres.	I **am singeing**	I **am being singed**
Prog.	we, you, they **are singeing**	we, you, they **are being singed**
	he, she, it **is singeing**	he, she, it **is being singed**
Pres.	I, we, you, they **do singe**	I, we, you, they **do get singed**
Int.	he, she, it **does singe**	he, she, it **does get singed**
Fut.	I, he, she, it,	I, he, she, it,
	we, you, they **will singe**	we, you, they **will be singed**
Past	I, he, she, it,	I, he, she, it **was singed**
	we, you, they **singed**	we, you, they **were singed**
Past	I, he, she, it **was singeing**	I, he, she, it **was being singed**
Prog.	we, you, they **were singeing**	we, you, they **were being singed**
Past	I, he, she, it,	I, he, she, it,
Int.	we, you, they **did singe**	we, you, they **did get singed**
Pres.	I, we, you, they **have singed**	I, we, you, they **have been singed**
Perf.	he, she, it **has singed**	he, she, it **has been singed**
Past	I, he, she, it,	I, he, she, it,
Perf.	we, you, they **had singed**	we, you, they **had been singed**
Fut.	I, he, she, it, we, you, they	I, he, she, it, we, you, they
Perf.	**will have singed**	**will have been singed**

IMPERATIVE MOOD

singe   **be singed**

SUBJUNCTIVE MOOD

Pres.	if I, he, she, it,	if I, he, she, it,
	we, you, they **singe**	we, you, they **be singed**
Past	if I, he, she, it,	if I, he, she, it,
	we, you, they **singed**	we, you, they **were singed**
Fut.	if I, he, she, it,	if I, he, she, it,
	we, you, they **should singe**	we, you, they **should be singed**

sink
(active voice)

PRINCIPAL PARTS: **sinks, sinking, sank/sunk, sunk**

be sunk
(passive voice)

Infinitive: **to sink**
Perfect Infinitive: **to have sunk**
Present Participle: **sinking**
Past Participle: **sunk**

Infinitive: **to be sunk**
Perfect Infinitive: **to have been sunk**
Present Participle: **being sunk**
Past Participle: **been sunk**

INDICATIVE MOOD

Pres.	I, we, you, they **sink**	I **am sunk** we, you, they **are sunk**
	he, she, it **sinks**	he, she, it **is sunk**
Pres. *Prog.*	I **am sinking** we, you, they **are sinking**	I **am being sunk** we, you, they **are being sunk**
	he, she, it **is sinking**	he, she, it **is being sunk**
Pres. *Int.*	I, we, you, they **do sink** he, she, it **does sink**	I, we, you, they **do get sunk** he, she, it **does get sunk**
Fut.	I, he, she, it, we, you, they **will sink**	I, he, she, it, we, you, they **will be sunk**
Past	I, he, she, it, we, you, they **sank**	I, he, she, it **was sunk** we, you, they **were sunk**
Past *Prog.*	I, he, she, it **was sinking** we, you, they **were sinking**	I, he, she, it **was being sunk** we, you, they **were being sunk**
Past *Int.*	I, he, she, it, we, you, they **did sink**	I, he, she, it, we, you, they **did get sunk**
Pres. *Perf.*	I, we, you, they **have sunk** he, she, it **has sunk**	I, we, you, they **have been sunk** he, she, it **has been sunk**
Past *Perf.*	I, he, she, it, we, you, they **had sunk**	I, he, she, it, we, you, they **had been sunk**
Fut. *Perf.*	I, he, she, it, we, you, they **will have sunk**	I, he, she, it, we, you, they **will have been sunk**

IMPERATIVE MOOD

sink　　　　　　　　　**be sunk**

SUBJUNCTIVE MOOD

Pres.	if I, he, she, it, we, you, they **sink**	if I, he, she, it, we, you, they **be sunk**
Past	if I, he, she, it, we, you, they **sank**	if I, he, she, it, we, you, they **were sunk**
Fut.	if I, he, she, it, we, you, they **should sink**	if I, he, she, it, we, you, they **should be sunk**

Intransitive and transitive. The past tense may be either SANK or SUNK.

sit
(active voice)

PRINCIPAL PARTS: **sits, sitting, sat, sat**

be sat
(passive voice)

Infinitive: **to sit**
Perfect Infinitive: **to have sat**
Present Participle: **sitting**
Past Participle: **sat**

Infinitive: **to be sat**
Perfect Infinitive: **to have been sat**
Present Participle: **being sat**
Past Participle: **been sat**

INDICATIVE MOOD

Pres.	I, we, you, they **sit**	I **am sat**
		we, you, they **are sat**
	he, she, it **sits**	he, she, it **is sat**
Pres.	I **am sitting**	I **am being sat**
Prog.	we, you, they **are sitting**	we, you, they **are being sat**
	he, she, it **is sitting**	he, she, it **is being sat**
Pres.	I, we, you, they **do sit**	I, we, you, they **do get sat**
Int.	he, she, it **does sit**	he, she, it **does get sat**
Fut.	I, he, she, it,	I, he, she, it,
	we, you, they **will sit**	we, you, they **will be sat**
Past	I, he, she, it,	I, he, she, it **was sat**
	we, you, they **sat**	we, you, they **were sat**
Past	I, he, she, it **was sitting**	I, he, she, it **was being sat**
Prog.	we, you, they **were sitting**	we, you, they **were being sat**
Past	I, he, she, it,	I, he, she, it,
Int.	we, you, they **did sit**	we, you, they **did get sat**
Pres.	I, we, you, they **have sat**	I, we, you, they **have been sat**
Perf.	he, she, it **has sat**	he, she, it **has been sat**
Past	I, he, she, it,	I, he, she, it,
Perf.	we, you, they **had sat**	we, you, they **had been sat**
Fut.	I, he, she, it, we, you, they	I, he, she, it, we, you, they
Perf.	**will have sat**	**will have been sat**

IMPERATIVE MOOD

sit

be sat

SUBJUNCTIVE MOOD

Pres.	if I, he, she, it,	if I, he, she, it,
	we, you, they **sit**	we, you, they **be sat**
Past	if I, he, she, it,	if I, he, she, it,
	we, you, they **sat**	we, you, they **were sat**
Fut.	if I, he, she, it,	if I, he, she, it,
	we, you, they **should sit**	we, you, they **should be sat**

Intransitive and transitive.

ski
(active voice)

PRINCIPAL PARTS: **skis, skiing,
skied, skied**

be skied
(passive voice)

Infinitive: **to ski**
Perfect Infinitive: **to have skied**
Present Participle: **skiing**
Past Participle: **skied**

Infinitive: **to be skied**
Perfect Infinitive: **to have been skied**
Present Participle: **being skied**
Past Participle: **been skied**

INDICATIVE MOOD

Pres.	I, we, you, they **ski**	I **am skied**
		we, you, they **are skied**
	he, she, it **skis**	he, she, it **is skied**
Pres.	I **am skiing**	I **am being skied**
Prog.	we, you, they **are skiing**	we, you, they **are being skied**
	he, she, it **is skiing**	he, she, it **is being skied**
Pres.	I, we, you, they **do ski**	I, we, you, they **do get skied**
Int.	he, she, it **does ski**	he, she, it **does get skied**
Fut.	I, he, she, it,	I, he, she, it,
	we, you, they **will ski**	we, you, they **will be skied**
Past	I, he, she, it,	I, he, she, it **was skied**
	we, you, they **skied**	we, you, they **were skied**
Past	I, he, she, it **was skiing**	I, he, she, it **was being skied**
Prog.	we, you, they **were skiing**	we, you, they **were being skied**
Past	I, he, she, it,	I, he, she, it,
Int.	we, you, they **did ski**	we, you, they **did get skied**
Pres.	I, we, you, they **have skied**	I, we, you, they **have been skied**
Perf.	he, she, it **has skied**	he, she, it **has been skied**
Past	I, he, she, it,	I, he, she, it,
Perf.	we, you, they **had skied**	we, you, they **had been skied**
Fut.	I, he, she, it, we, you, they	I, he, she, it, we, you, they
Perf.	**will have skied**	**will have been skied**

IMPERATIVE MOOD

ski   **be skied**

SUBJUNCTIVE MOOD

Pres.	if I, he, she, it,	if I, he, she, it,
	we, you, they **ski**	we, you, they **be skied**
Past	if I, he, she, it,	if I, he, she, it,
	we, you, they **skied**	we, you, they **were skied**
Fut.	if I, he, she, it,	if I, he, she, it,
	we, you, they **should ski**	we, you, they **should be skied**

Intransitive and transitive.

slay
(active voice)

PRINCIPAL PARTS: **slays, slaying, slew, slain**

be slain
(passive voice)

Infinitive: **to slay**
Perfect Infinitive: **to have slain**
Present Participle: **slaying**
Past Participle: **slain**

Infinitive: **to be slain**
Perfect Infinitive: **to have been slain**
Present Participle: **being slain**
Past Participle: **been slain**

INDICATIVE MOOD

Pres.	I, we, you, they **slay**	I **am slain**
		we, you, they **are slain**
	he, she, it **slays**	he, she, it **is slain**
Pres.	I **am slaying**	I **am being slain**
Prog.	we, you, they **are slaying**	we, you, they **are being slain**
	he, she, it **is slaying**	he, she, it **is being slain**
Pres.	I, we, you, they **do slay**	I, we, you, they **do get slain**
Int.	he, she, it **does slay**	he, she, it **does get slain**
Fut.	I, he, she, it,	I, he, she, it,
	we, you, they **will slay**	we, you, they **will be slain**
Past	I, he, she, it,	I, he, she, it **was slain**
	we, you, they **slew**	we, you, they **were slain**
Past	I, he, she, it **was slaying**	I, he, she, it **was being slain**
Prog.	we, you, they **were slaying**	we, you, they **were being slain**
Past	I, he, she, it,	I, he, she, it,
Int.	we, you, they **did slay**	we, you, they **did get slain**
Pres.	I, we, you, they **have slain**	I, we, you, they **have been slain**
Perf.	he, she, it **has slain**	he, she, it **has been slain**
Past	I, he, she, it,	I, he, she, it,
Perf.	we, you, they **had slain**	we, you, they **had been slain**
Fut.	I, he, she, it, we, you, they	I, he, she, it, we, you, they
Perf.	**will have slain**	**will have been slain**

IMPERATIVE MOOD

slay   **be slain**

SUBJUNCTIVE MOOD

Pres.	if I, he, she, it,	if I, he, she, it,
	we, you, they **slay**	we, you, they **be slain**
Past	if I, he, she, it,	if I, he, she, it,
	we, you, they **slew**	we, you, they **were slain**
Fut.	if I, he, she, it,	if I, he, she, it,
	we, you, they **should slay**	we, you, they **should be slain**

---

sleep
(active voice)

be slept
(passive voice)

Infinitive: **to sleep**
Perfect Infinitive: **to have slept**
Present Participle: **sleeping**
Past Participle: **slept**

Infinitive: **to be slept**
Perfect Infinitive: **to have been slept**
Present Participle: **being slept**
Past Participle: **been slept**

INDICATIVE MOOD

Pres.	I, we, you, they **sleep**	I **am slept**
		we, you, they **are slept**
	he, she, it **sleeps**	he, she, it **is slept**
Pres.	I **am sleeping**	I **am being slept**
Prog.	we, you, they **are sleeping**	we, you, they **are being slept**
	he, she, it **is sleeping**	he, she, it **is being slept**
Pres.	I, we, you, they **do sleep**	I, we, you, they **do get slept**
Int.	he, she, it **does sleep**	he, she, it **does get slept**
Fut.	I, he, she, it,	I, he, she, it,
	we, you, they **will sleep**	we, you, they **will be slept**
Past	I, he, she, it,	I, he, she, it **was slept**
	we, you, they **slept**	we, you, they **were slept**
Past	I, he, she, it **was sleeping**	I, he, she, it **was being slept**
Prog.	we, you, they **were sleeping**	we, you, they **were being slept**
Past	I, he, she, it,	I, he, she, it,
Int.	we, you, they **did sleep**	we, you, they **did get slept**
Pres.	I, we, you, they **have slept**	I, we, you, they **have been slept**
Perf.	he, she, it **has slept**	he, she, it **has been slept**
Past	I, he, she, it,	I, he, she, it,
Perf.	we, you, they **had slept**	we, you, they **had been slept**
Fut.	I, he, she, it, we, you, they	I, he, she, it, we, you, they
Perf.	**will have slept**	**will have been slept**

IMPERATIVE MOOD

sleep be slept

SUBJUNCTIVE MOOD

Pres.	if I, he, she, it,	if I, he, she, it,
	we, you, they **sleep**	we, you, they **be slept**
Past	if I, he, she, it,	if I, he, she, it,
	we, you, they **slept**	we, you, they **were slept**
Fut.	if I, he, she, it,	if I, he, she, it,
	we, you, they **should sleep**	we, you, they **should be slept**

Intransitive and transitive.

slide
(active voice)

be slid
(passive voice)

Infinitive: **to slide**
Perfect Infinitive: **to have slid**
Present Participle: **sliding**
Past Participle: **slid**

Infinitive: **to be slid**
Perfect Infinitive: **to have been slid**
Present Participle: **being slid**
Past Participle: **been slid**

INDICATIVE MOOD

Pres.	I, we, you, they **slide**	I **am slid**
		we, you, they **are slid**
	he, she, it **slides**	he, she, it **is slid**
Pres.	I **am sliding**	I **am being slid**
Prog.	we, you, they **are sliding**	we, you, they **are being slid**
	he, she, it **is sliding**	he, she, it **is being slid**
Pres.	I, we, you, they **do slide**	I, we, you, they **do get slid**
Int.	he, she, it **does slide**	he, she, it **does get slid**
Fut.	I, he, she, it,	I, he, she, it,
	we, you, they **will slide**	we, you, they **will be slid**
Past	I, he, she, it,	I, he, she, it **was slid**
	we, you, they **slid**	we, you, they **were slid**
Past	I, he, she, it **was sliding**	I, he, she, it **was being slid**
Prog.	we, you, they **were sliding**	we, you, they **were being slid**
Past	I, he, she, it,	I, he, she, it,
Int.	we, you, they **did slide**	we, you, they **did get slid**
Pres.	I, we, you, they **have slid**	I, we, you, they **have been slid**
Perf.	he, she, it **has slid**	he, she, it **has been slid**
Past	I, he, she, it,	I, he, she, it,
Perf.	we, you, they **had slid**	we, you, they **had been slid**
Fut.	I, he, she, it, we, you, they	I, he, she, it, we, you, they
Perf.	**will have slid**	**will have been slid**

IMPERATIVE MOOD

slide   be slid

SUBJUNCTIVE MOOD

Pres.	if I, he, she, it,	if I, he, she, it,
	we, you, they **slide**	we, you, they **be slid**
Past	if I, he, she, it,	if I, he, she, it,
	we, you, they **slid**	we, you, they **were slid**
Fut.	if I, he, she, it,	if I, he, she, it,
	we, you, they **should slide**	we, you, they **should be slid**

Intransitive and transitive.

sling
(active voice)

be slung
(passive voice)

Infinitive: **to sling**
Perfect Infinitive: **to have slung**
Present Participle: **slinging**
Past Participle: **slung**

Infinitive: **to be slung**
Perfect Infinitive: **to have been slung**
Present Participle: **being slung**
Past Participle: **been slung**

INDICATIVE MOOD

Pres.	I, we, you, they **sling**	I **am slung**
		we, you, they **are slung**
	he, she, it **slings**	he, she, it **is slung**
Pres.	I **am slinging**	I **am being slung**
Prog.	we, you, they **are slinging**	we, you, they **are being slung**
	he, she, it **is slinging**	he, she, it **is being slung**
Pres.	I, we, you, they **do sling**	I, we, you, they **do get slung**
Int.	he, she, it **does sling**	he, she, it **does get slung**
Fut.	I, he, she, it,	I, he, she, it,
	we, you, they **will sling**	we, you, they **will be slung**
Past	I, he, she, it,	I, he, she, it **was slung**
	we, you, they **slung**	we, you, they **were slung**
Past	I, he, she, it **was slinging**	I, he, she, it **was being slung**
Prog.	we, you, they **were slinging**	we, you, they **were being slung**
Past	I, he, she, it,	I, he, she, it,
Int.	we, you, they **did sling**	we, you, they **did get slung**
Pres.	I, we, you, they **have slung**	I, we, you, they **have been slung**
Perf.	he, she, it **has slung**	he, she, it **has been slung**
Past	I, he, she, it,	I, he, she, it,
Perf.	we, you, they **had slung**	we, you, they **had been slung**
Fut.	I, he, she, it, we, you, they	I, he, she, it, we, you, they
Perf.	**will have slung**	**will have been slung**

IMPERATIVE MOOD

sling   **be slung**

SUBJUNCTIVE MOOD

Pres.	if I, he, she, it,	if I, he, she, it,
	we, you, they **sling**	we, you, they **be slung**
Past	if I, he, she, it,	if I, he, she, it,
	we, you, they **slung**	we, you, they **were slung**
Fut.	if I, he, she, it,	if I, he, she, it,
	we, you, they **should sling**	we, you, they **should be slung**

PRINCIPAL PARTS: **slinks, slinking, slunk/slinked, slunk/slinked**

Infinitive: **to slink**
Perfect Infinitive: **to have slunk**
Present Participle: **slinking**
Past Participle: **slunk**

INDICATIVE MOOD

Pres.	I, we, you, they **slink**
	he, she, it **slinks**
Pres. *Prog.*	**I am slinking** we, you, they **are slinking** he, she, it **is slinking**
Pres. *Int.*	I, we, you, they **do slink** he, she, it **does slink**
Fut.	I, he, she, it, we, you, they **will slink**
Past	I, he, she, it, we, you, they **slunk**
Past *Prog.*	I, he, she, it **was slinking** we, you, they **were slinking**
Past *Int.*	I, he, she, it, we, you, they **did slink**
Pres. *Perf.*	I, we, you, they **have slunk** he, she, it **has slunk**
Past *Perf.*	I, he, she, it, we, you, they **had slunk**
Fut. *Perf.*	I, he, she, it, we, you, they **will have slunk**

IMPERATIVE MOOD

slink

SUBJUNCTIVE MOOD

Pres.	if I, he, she, it, we, you, they **slink**
Past	if I, he, she, it, we, you, they **slunk**
Fut.	if I, he, she, it, we, you, they **should slink**

Intransitive. As a transitive verb SLINK means "for an animal to give birth or be born prematurely."

slip
(active voice)

be slipped
(passive voice)

Infinitive: **to slip**
Perfect Infinitive: **to have slipped**
Present Participle: **slipping**
Past Participle: **slipped**

Infinitive: **to be slipped**
Perfect Infinitive: **to have been slipped**
Present Participle: **being slipped**
Past Participle: **been slipped**

INDICATIVE MOOD

Pres.	I, we, you, they **slip**	I **am slipped**
		we, you, they **are slipped**
	he, she, it **slips**	he, she, it **is slipped**
Pres.	I **am slipping**	I **am being slipped**
Prog.	we, you, they **are slipping**	we, you, they **are being slipped**
	he, she, it **is slipping**	he, she, it **is being slipped**
Pres.	I, we, you, they **do slip**	I, we, you, they **do get slipped**
Int.	he, she, it **does slip**	he, she, it **does get slipped**
Fut.	I, he, she, it,	I, he, she, it,
	we, you, they **will slip**	we, you, they **will be slipped**
Past	I, he, she, it,	I, he, she, it **was slipped**
	we, you, they **slipped**	we, you, they **were slipped**
Past	I, he, she, it **was slipping**	I, he, she, it **was being slipped**
Prog.	we, you, they **were slipping**	we, you, they **were being slipped**
Past	I, he, she, it,	I, he, she, it,
Int.	we, you, they **did slip**	we, you, they **did get slipped**
Pres.	I, we, you, they **have slipped**	I, we, you, they **have been slipped**
Perf.	he, she, it **has slipped**	he, she, it **has been slipped**
Past	I, he, she, it,	I, he, she, it,
Perf.	we, you, they **had slipped**	we, you, they **had been slipped**
Fut.	I, he, she, it, we, you, they	I, he, she, it, we, you, they
Perf.	**will have slipped**	**will have been slipped**

IMPERATIVE MOOD

slip   **be slipped**

SUBJUNCTIVE MOOD

Pres.	if I, he, she, it,	if I, he, she, it,
	we, you, they **slip**	we, you, they **be slipped**
Past	if I, he, she, it,	if I, he, she, it,
	we, you, they **slipped**	we, you, they **were slipped**
Fut.	if I, he, she, it,	if I, he, she, it,
	we, you, they **should slip**	we, you, they **should be slipped**

Intransitive and transitive.

slit
(active voice)

be slit
(passive voice)

Infinitive: **to slit**
Perfect Infinitive: **to have slit**
Present Participle: **slitting**
Past Participle: **slit**

Infinitive: **to be slit**
Perfect Infinitive: **to have been slit**
Present Participle: **being slit**
Past Participle: **been slit**

INDICATIVE MOOD

Pres.	I, we, you, they **slit**	I **am slit**
		we, you, they **are slit**
	he, she, it **slits**	he, she, it **is slit**
Pres.	I **am slitting**	I **am being slit**
Prog.	we, you, they **are slitting**	we, you, they **are being slit**
	he, she, it **is slitting**	he, she, it **is being slit**
Pres.	I, we, you, they **do slit**	I, we, you, they **do get slit**
Int.	he, she, it **does slit**	he, she, it **does get slit**
Fut.	I, he, she, it,	I, he, she, it,
	we, you, they **will slit**	we, you, they **will be slit**
Past	I, he, she, it,	I, he, she, it **was slit**
	we, you, they **slit**	we, you, they **were slit**
Past	I, he, she, it **was slitting**	I, he, she, it **was being slit**
Prog.	we, you, they **were slitting**	we, you, they **were being slit**
Past	I, he, she, it,	I, he, she, it,
Int.	we, you, they **did slit**	we, you, they **did get slit**
Pres.	I, we, you, they **have slit**	I, we, you, they **have been slit**
Perf.	he, she, it **has slit**	he, she, it **has been slit**
Past	I, he, she, it,	I, he, she, it,
Perf.	we, you, they **had slit**	we, you, they **had been slit**
Fut.	I, he, she, it, we, you, they	I, he, she, it, we, you, they
Perf.	**will have slit**	**will have been slit**

IMPERATIVE MOOD

slit

be slit

SUBJUNCTIVE MOOD

Pres.	if I, he, she, it,	if I, he, she, it,
	we, you, they **slit**	we, you, they **be slit**
Past	if I, he, she, it,	if I, he, she, it,
	we, you, they **slit**	we, you, they **were slit**
Fut.	if I, he, she, it,	if I, he, she, it,
	we, you, they **should slit**	we, you, they **should be slit**

smell
(active voice)

be smelled/smelt
(passive voice)

Infinitive: **to smell**
Perfect Infinitive: **to have smelled**
Present Participle: **smelling**
Past Participle: **smelled**

Infinitive: **to be smelled**
Perfect Infinitive: **to have been smelled**
Present Participle: **being smelled**
Past Participle: **been smelled**

INDICATIVE MOOD

Pres.	I, we, you, they **smell**	I **am smelled**
		we, you, they **are smelled**
	he, she, it **smells**	he, she, it **is smelled**
Pres.	I **am smelling**	I **am being smelled**
Prog.	we, you, they **are smelling**	we, you, they **are being smelled**
	he, she, it **is smelling**	he, she, it **is being smelled**
Pres.	I, we, you, they **do smell**	I, we, you, they **do get smelled**
Int.	he, she, it **does smell**	he, she, it **does get smelled**
Fut.	I, he, she, it,	I, he, she, it,
	we, you, they **will smell**	we, you, they **will be smelled**
Past	I, he, she, it,	I, he, she, it **was smelled**
	we, you, they **smelled**	we, you, they **were smelled**
Past	I, he, she, it **was smelling**	I, he, she, it **was being smelled**
Prog.	we, you, they **were smelling**	we, you, they **were being smelled**
Past	I, he, she, it,	I, he, she, it,
Int.	we, you, they **did smell**	we, you, they **did get smelled**
Pres.	I, we, you, they **have smelled**	I, we, you, they **have been smelled**
Perf.	he, she, it **has smelled**	he, she, it **has been smelled**
Past	I, he, she, it,	I, he, she, it,
Perf.	we, you, they **had smelled**	we, you, they **had been smelled**
Fut.	I, he, she, it, we, you, they	I, he, she, it, we, you, they
Perf.	**will have smelled**	**will have been smelled**

IMPERATIVE MOOD

smell   **be smelled**

SUBJUNCTIVE MOOD

Pres.	if I, he, she, it,	if I, he, she, it,
	we, you, they **smell**	we, you, they **be smelled**
Past	if I, he, she, it,	if I, he, she, it,
	we, you, they **smelled**	we, you, they **were smelled**
Fut.	if I, he, she, it,	if I, he, she, it,
	we, you, they **should smell**	we, you, they **should be smelled**

Transitive and intransitive. The *Oxford Dictionary* lists SMELT as the first form for the past tense and past participle.

smile
(active voice)

PRINCIPAL PARTS: **smiles, smiling, smiled, smiled**

be smiled
(passive voice)

Infinitive: **to smile**
Perfect Infinitive: **to have smiled**
Present Participle: **smiling**
Past Participle: **smiled**

Infinitive: **to be smiled**
Perfect Infinitive: **to have been smiled**
Present Participle: **being smiled**
Past Participle: **been smiled**

INDICATIVE MOOD

Pres.	I, we, you, they **smile**	I **am smiled**
		we, you, they **are smiled**
	he, she, it **smiles**	he, she, it **is smiled**
Pres.	I **am smiling**	I **am being smiled**
Prog.	we, you, they **are smiling**	we, you, they **are being smiled**
	he, she, it **is smiling**	he, she, it **is being smiled**
Pres.	I, we, you, they **do smile**	I, we, you, they **do get smiled**
Int.	he, she, it **does smile**	he, she, it **does get smiled**
Fut.	I, he, she, it,	I, he, she, it,
	we, you, they **will smile**	we, you, they **will be smiled**
Past	I, he, she, it,	I, he, she, it **was smiled**
	we, you, they **smiled**	we, you, they **were smiled**
Past	I, he, she, it **was smiling**	I, he, she, it **was being smiled**
Prog.	we, you, they **were smiling**	we, you, they **were being smiled**
Past	I, he, she, it,	I, he, she, it,
Int.	we, you, they **did smile**	we, you, they **did get smiled**
Pres.	I, we, you, they **have smiled**	I, we, you, they **have been smiled**
Perf.	he, she, it **has smiled**	he, she, it **has been smiled**
Past	I, he, she, it,	I, he, she, it,
Perf.	we, you, they **had smiled**	we, you, they **had been smiled**
Fut.	I, he, she, it, we, you, they	I, he, she, it, we, you, they
Perf.	**will have smiled**	**will have been smiled**

IMPERATIVE MOOD

smile

be smiled

SUBJUNCTIVE MOOD

Pres.	if I, he, she, it,	if I, he, she, it,
	we, you, they **smile**	we, you, they **be smiled**
Past	if I, he, she, it,	if I, he, she, it,
	we, you, they **smiled**	we, you, they **were smiled**
Fut.	if I, he, she, it,	if I, he, she, it,
	we, you, they **should smile**	we, you, they **should be smiled**

Intransitive and transitive.

smite
(active voice)

be smitten/smote
(passive voice)

Infinitive: **to smite**
Perfect Infinitive: **to have smitten**
Present Participle: **smiting**
Past Participle: **smitten**

Infinitive: **to be smitten**
Perfect Infinitive: **to have been smitten**
Present Participle: **being smitten**
Past Participle: **been smitten**

INDICATIVE MOOD

Pres.	I, we, you, they **smite**	I **am smitten**
		we, you, they **are smitten**
	he, she, it **smites**	he, she, it **is smitten**
Pres.	I **am smiting**	I **am being smitten**
Prog.	we, you, they **are smiting**	we, you, they **are being smitten**
	he, she, it **is smiting**	he, she, it **is being smitten**
Pres.	I, we, you, they **do smite**	I, we, you, they **do get smitten**
Int.	he, she, it **does smite**	he, she, it **does get smitten**
Fut.	I, he, she, it,	I, he, she, it,
	we, you, they **will smite**	we, you, they **will be smitten**
Past	I, he, she, it,	I, he, she, it **was smitten**
	we, you, they **smote**	we, you, they **were smitten**
Past	I, he, she, it **was smiting**	I, he, she, it **was being smitten**
Prog.	we, you, they **were smiting**	we, you, they **were being smitten**
Past	I, he, she, it,	I, he, she, it,
Int.	we, you, they **did smite**	we, you, they **did get smitten**
Pres.	I, we, you, they **have smitten**	I, we, you, they **have been smitten**
Perf.	he, she, it **has smitten**	he, she, it **has been smitten**
Past	I, he, she, it,	I, he, she, it,
Perf.	we, you, they **had smitten**	we, you, they **had been smitten**
Fut.	I, he, she, it, we, you, they	I, he, she, it, we, you, they
Perf.	**will have smitten**	**will have been smitten**

IMPERATIVE MOOD

smite   **be smitten**

SUBJUNCTIVE MOOD

Pres.	if I, he, she, it,	if I, he, she, it,
	we, you, they **smite**	we, you, they **be smitten**
Past	if I, he, she, it,	if I, he, she, it,
	we, you, they **smote**	we, you, they **were smitten**
Fut.	if I, he, she, it,	if I, he, she, it,
	we, you, they **should smite**	we, you, they **should be smitten**

sneak
(active voice)

be sneaked/snuck
(passive voice)

Infinitive: **to sneak**
Perfect Infinitive: **to have sneaked**
Present Participle: **sneaking**
Past Participle: **sneaked**

Infinitive: **to be sneaked**
Perfect Infinitive: **to have been sneaked**
Present Participle: **being sneaked**
Past Participle: **been sneaked**

INDICATIVE MOOD

Pres.	I, we, you, they **sneak**	I **am sneaked**
		we, you, they **are sneaked**
	he, she, it **sneaks**	he, she, it **is sneaked**
Pres.	I **am sneaking**	I **am being sneaked**
Prog.	we, you, they **are sneaking**	we, you, they **are being sneaked**
	he, she, it **is sneaking**	he, she, it **is being sneaked**
Pres.	I, we, you, they **do sneak**	I, we, you, they **do get sneaked**
Int.	he, she, it **does sneak**	he, she, it **does get sneaked**
Fut.	I, he, she, it,	I, he, she, it,
	we, you, they **will sneak**	we, you, they **will be sneaked**
Past	I, he, she, it,	I, he, she, it **was sneaked**
	we, you, they **sneaked**	we, you, they **were sneaked**
Past	I, he, she, it **was sneaking**	I, he, she, it **was being sneaked**
Prog.	we, you, they **were sneaking**	we, you, they **were being sneaked**
Past	I, he, she, it,	I, he, she, it,
Int.	we, you, they **did sneak**	we, you, they **did get sneaked**
Pres.	I, we, you, they **have sneaked**	I, we, you, they **have been sneaked**
Perf.	he, she, it **has sneaked**	he, she, it **has been sneaked**
Past	I, he, she, it,	I, he, she, it,
Perf.	we, you, they **had sneaked**	we, you, they **had been sneaked**
Fut.	I, he, she, it, we, you, they	I, he, she, it, we, you, they
Perf.	**will have sneaked**	**will have been sneaked**

IMPERATIVE MOOD

sneak   be sneaked

SUBJUNCTIVE MOOD

Pres.	if I, he, she, it,	if I, he, she, it,
	we, you, they **sneak**	we, you, they **be sneaked**
Past	if I, he, she, it,	if I, he, she, it,
	we, you, they **sneaked**	we, you, they **were sneaked**
Fut.	if I, he, she, it,	if I, he, she, it,
	we, you, they **should sneak**	we, you, they **should be sneaked**

Intransitive and transitive. The *Oxford Dictionary* lists as colloquial the past tense and past participle SNUCK.

sound
(active voice)

be sounded
(passive voice)

Infinitive: **to sound**
Perfect Infinitive: **to have sounded**
Present Participle: **sounding**
Past Participle: **sounded**

Infinitive: **to be sounded**
Perfect Infinitive: **to have been sounded**
Present Participle: **being sounded**
Past Participle: **been sounded**

INDICATIVE MOOD

Pres.	I, we, you, they **sound**	I **am sounded**
		we, you, they **are sounded**
	he, she, it **sounds**	he, she, it **is sounded**
Pres.	I **am sounding**	I **am being sounded**
Prog.	we, you, they **are sounding**	we, you, they **are being sounded**
	he, she, it **is sounding**	he, she, it **is being sounded**
Pres.	I, we, you, they **do sound**	I, we, you, they **do get sounded**
Int.	he, she, it **does sound**	he, she, it **does get sounded**
Fut.	I, he, she, it,	I, he, she, it,
	we, you, they **will sound**	we, you, they **will be sounded**
Past	I, he, she, it,	I, he, she, it **was sounded**
	we, you, they **sounded**	we, you, they **were sounded**
Past	I, he, she, it **was sounding**	I, he, she, it **was being sounded**
Prog.	we, you, they **were sounding**	we, you, they **were being sounded**
Past	I, he, she, it,	I, he, she, it,
Int.	we, you, they **did sound**	we, you, they **did get sounded**
Pres.	I, we, you, they **have sounded**	I, we, you, they **have been sounded**
Perf.	he, she, it **has sounded**	he, she, it **has been sounded**
Past	I, he, she, it,	I, he, she, it,
Perf.	we, you, they **had sounded**	we, you, they **had been sounded**
Fut.	I, he, she, it, we, you, they	I, he, she, it, we, you, they
Perf.	**will have sounded**	**will have been sounded**

IMPERATIVE MOOD

sound   **be sounded**

SUBJUNCTIVE MOOD

Pres.	if I, he, she, it,	if I, he, she, it,
	we, you, they **sound**	we, you, they **be sounded**
Past	if I, he, she, it,	if I, he, she, it,
	we, you, they **sounded**	we, you, they **were sounded**
Fut.	if I, he, she, it,	if I, he, she, it,
	we, you, they **should sound**	we, you, they **should be sounded**

Transitive and intransitive.

sow
(active voice)

be sown/sowed
(passive voice)

Infinitive: **to sow**
Perfect Infinitive: **to have sown**
Present Participle: **sowing**
Past Participle: **sown**

Infinitive: **to be sown**
Perfect Infinitive: **to have been sown**
Present Participle: **being sown**
Past Participle: **been sown**

INDICATIVE MOOD

Pres.	I, we, you, they **sow**	I **am sown**
		we, you, they **are sown**
	he, she, it **sows**	he, she, it **is sown**
Pres. *Prog.*	I **am sowing**	I **am being sown**
	we, you, they **are sowing**	we, you, they **are being sown**
	he, she, it **is sowing**	he, she, it **is being sown**
Pres. *Int.*	I, we, you, they **do sow**	I, we, you, they **do get sown**
	he, she, it **does sow**	he, she, it **does get sown**
Fut.	I, he, she, it, we, you, they **will sow**	I, he, she, it, we, you, they **will be sown**
Past	I, he, she, it, we, you, they **sowed**	I, he, she, it **was sown** we, you, they **were sown**
Past *Prog.*	I, he, she, it **was sowing** we, you, they **were sowing**	I, he, she, it **was being sown** we, you, they **were being sown**
Past *Int.*	I, he, she, it, we, you, they **did sow**	I, he, she, it, we, you, they **did get sown**
Pres. *Perf.*	I, we, you, they **have sown** he, she, it **has sown**	I, we, you, they **have been sown** he, she, it **has been sown**
Past *Perf.*	I, he, she, it, we, you, they **had sown**	I, he, she, it, we, you, they **had been sown**
Fut. *Perf.*	I, he, she, it, we, you, they **will have sown**	I, he, she, it, we, you, they **will have been sown**

IMPERATIVE MOOD

sow   be sown

SUBJUNCTIVE MOOD

Pres.	if I, he, she, it, we, you, they **sow**	if I, he, she, it, we, you, they **be sown**
Past	if I, he, she, it, we, you, they **sowed**	if I, he, she, it, we, you, they **were sown**
Fut.	if I, he, she, it, we, you, they **should sow**	if I, he, she, it, we, you, they **should be sown**

Transitive and intransitive.

speak
(active voice)

be spoken
(passive voice)

Infinitive: **to speak**
Perfect Infinitive: **to have spoken**
Present Participle: **speaking**
Past Participle: **spoken**

Infinitive: **to be spoken**
Perfect Infinitive: **to have been spoken**
Present Participle: **being spoken**
Past Participle: **been spoken**

INDICATIVE MOOD

Pres.	I, we, you, they **speak**	I **am spoken**
		we, you, they **are spoken**
	he, she, it **speaks**	he, she, it **is spoken**
Pres.	I **am speaking**	I **am being spoken**
Prog.	we, you, they **are speaking**	we, you, they **are being spoken**
	he, she, it **is speaking**	he, she, it **is being spoken**
Pres.	I, we, you, they **do speak**	I, we, you, they **do get spoken**
Int.	he, she, it **does speak**	he, she, it **does get spoken**
Fut.	I, he, she, it,	I, he, she, it,
	we, you, they **will speak**	we, you, they **will be spoken**
Past	I, he, she, it,	I, he, she, it **was spoken**
	we, you, they **spoke**	we, you, they **were spoken**
Past	I, he, she, it **was speaking**	I, he, she, it **was being spoken**
Prog.	we, you, they **were speaking**	we, you, they **were being spoken**
Past	I, he, she, it,	I, he, she, it,
Int.	we, you, they **did speak**	we, you, they **did get spoken**
Pres.	I, we, you, they **have spoken**	I, we, you, they **have been spoken**
Perf.	he, she, it **has spoken**	he, she, it **has been spoken**
Past	I, he, she, it,	I, he, she, it,
Perf.	we, you, they **had spoken**	we, you, they **had been spoken**
Fut.	I, he, she, it, we, you, they	I, he, she, it, we, you, they
Perf.	**will have spoken**	**will have been spoken**

IMPERATIVE MOOD

speak   **be spoken**

SUBJUNCTIVE MOOD

Pres.	if I, he, she, it,	if I, he, she, it,
	we, you, they **speak**	we, you, they **be spoken**
Past	if I, he, she, it,	if I, he, she, it,
	we, you, they **spoke**	we, you, they **were spoken**
Fut.	if I, he, she, it,	if I, he, she, it,
	we, you, they **should speak**	we, you, they **should be spoken**

Intransitive and transitive.

speed
(active voice)

be sped/speeded
(passive voice)

Infinitive: **to speed**
Perfect Infinitive: **to have sped**
Present Participle: **speeding**
Past Participle: **sped**

Infinitive: **to be sped**
Perfect Infinitive: **to have been sped**
Present Participle: **being sped**
Past Participle: **been sped**

INDICATIVE MOOD

Pres.	I, we, you, they **speed**	I **am sped**
		we, you, they **are sped**
	he, she, it **speeds**	he, she, it **is sped**
Pres.	I **am speeding**	I **am being sped**
Prog.	we, you, they **are speeding**	we, you, they **are being sped**
	he, she, it **is speeding**	he, she, it **is being sped**
Pres.	I, we, you, they **do speed**	I, we, you, they **do get sped**
Int.	he, she, it **does speed**	he, she, it **does get sped**
Fut.	I, he, she, it,	I, he, she, it,
	we, you, they **will speed**	we, you, they **will be sped**
Past	I, he, she, it,	I, he, she, it **was sped**
	we, you, they **sped**	we, you, they **were sped**
Past	I, he, she, it **was speeding**	I, he, she, it **was being sped**
Prog.	we, you, they **were speeding**	we, you, they **were being sped**
Past	I, he, she, it,	I, he, she, it,
Int.	we, you, they **did speed**	we, you, they **did get sped**
Pres.	I, we, you, they **have sped**	I, we, you, they **have been sped**
Perf.	he, she, it **has sped**	he, she, it **has been sped**
Past	I, he, she, it,	I, he, she, it,
Perf.	we, you, they **had sped**	we, you, they **had been sped**
Fut.	I, he, she, it, we, you, they	I, he, she, it, we, you, they
Perf.	**will have sped**	**will have been sped**

IMPERATIVE MOOD

speed

be sped

SUBJUNCTIVE MOOD

Pres.	if I, he, she, it,	if I, he, she, it,
	we, you, they **speed**	we, you, they **be sped**
Past	if I, he, she, it,	if I, he, she, it,
	we, you, they **sped**	we, you, they **were sped**
Fut.	if I, he, she, it,	if I, he, she, it,
	we, you, they **should speed**	we, you, they **should be sped**

Transitive and intransitive.

spell
(active voice)

be spelled/spelt
(passive voice)

Infinitive: **to spell**
Perfect Infinitive: **to have spelled**
Present Participle: **spelling**
Past Participle: **spelled**

Infinitive: **to be spelled**
Perfect Infinitive: **to have been spelled**
Present Participle: **being spelled**
Past Participle: **been spelled**

INDICATIVE MOOD

Pres.	I, we, you, they **spell**	I **am spelled**
		we, you, they **are spelled**
	he, she, it **spells**	he, she, it **is spelled**
Pres.	I **am spelling**	I **am being spelled**
Prog.	we, you, they **are spelling**	we, you, they **are being spelled**
	he, she, it **is spelling**	he, she, it **is being spelled**
Pres.	I, we, you, they **do spell**	I, we, you, they **do get spelled**
Int.	he, she, it **does spell**	he, she, it **does get spelled**
Fut.	I, he, she, it,	I, he, she, it,
	we, you, they **will spell**	we, you, they **will be spelled**
Past	I, he, she, it,	I, he, she, it **was spelled**
	we, you, they **spelled**	we, you, they **were spelled**
Past	I, he, she, it **was spelling**	I, he, she, it **was being spelled**
Prog.	we, you, they **were spelling**	we, you, they **were being spelled**
Past	I, he, she, it,	I, he, she, it,
Int.	we, you, they **did spell**	we, you, they **did get spelled**
Pres.	I, we, you, they **have spelled**	I, we, you, they **have been spelled**
Perf.	he, she, it **has spelled**	he, she, it **has been spelled**
Past	I, he, she, it,	I, he, she, it,
Perf.	we, you, they **had spelled**	we, you, they **had been spelled**
Fut.	I, he, she, it, we, you, they	I, he, she, it, we, you, they
Perf.	**will have spelled**	**will have been spelled**

IMPERATIVE MOOD

spell

be spelled

SUBJUNCTIVE MOOD

Pres.	if I, he, she, it,	if I, he, she, it,
	we, you, they **spell**	we, you, they **be spelled**
Past	if I, he, she, it,	if I, he, she, it,
	we, you, they **spelled**	we, you, they **were spelled**
Fut.	if I, he, she, it,	if I, he, she, it,
	we, you, they **should spell**	we, you, they **should be spelled**

Transitive and intransitive. When the verb refers to "spelling a word" the past tense and past participle may be SPELLED or SPELT. When it means to "relieve someone by taking turns or to cast a spell on someone" only the form SPELLED is permitted.

spend
(active voice)

be spent
(passive voice)

Infinitive: **to spend**
Perfect Infinitive: **to have spent**
Present Participle: **spending**
Past Participle: **spent**

Infinitive: **to be spent**
Perfect Infinitive: **to have been spent**
Present Participle: **being spent**
Past Participle: **been spent**

INDICATIVE MOOD

Pres.	I, we, you, they **spend**	I **am spent**
		we, you, they **are spent**
	he, she, it **spends**	he, she, it **is spent**
Pres.	I **am spending**	I **am being spent**
Prog.	we, you, they **are spending**	we, you, they **are being spent**
	he, she, it **is spending**	he, she, it **is being spent**
Pres.	I, we, you, they **do spend**	I, we, you, they **do get spent**
Int.	he, she, it **does spend**	he, she, it **does get spent**
Fut.	I, he, she, it,	I, he, she, it,
	we, you, they **will spend**	we, you, they **will be spent**
Past	I, he, she, it,	I, he, she, it **was spent**
	we, you, they **spent**	we, you, they **were spent**
Past	I, he, she, it **was spending**	I, he, she, it **was being spent**
Prog.	we, you, they **were spending**	we, you, they **were being spent**
Past	I, he, she, it,	I, he, she, it,
Int.	we, you, they **did spend**	we, you, they **did get spent**
Pres.	I, we, you, they **have spent**	I, we, you, they **have been spent**
Perf.	he, she, it **has spent**	he, she, it **has been spent**
Past	I, he, she, it,	I, he, she, it,
Perf.	we, you, they **had spent**	we, you, they **had been spent**
Fut.	I, he, she, it, we, you, they	I, he, she, it, we, you, they
Perf.	**will have spent**	**will have been spent**

IMPERATIVE MOOD

spend

be spent

SUBJUNCTIVE MOOD

Pres.	if I, he, she, it,	if I, he, she, it,
	we, you, they **spend**	we, you, they **be spent**
Past	if I, he, she, it,	if I, he, she, it,
	we, you, they **spent**	we, you, they **were spent**
Fut.	if I, he, she, it,	if I, he, she, it,
	we, you, they **should spend**	we, you, they **should be spent**

Transitive and intransitive.

spill
(active voice)

be spilled/spilt
(passive voice)

Infinitive: **to spill**
Perfect Infinitive: **to have spilled**
Present Participle: **spilling**
Past Participle: **spilled**

Infinitive: **to be spilled**
Perfect Infinitive: **to have been spilled**
Present Participle: **being spilled**
Past Participle: **been spilled**

INDICATIVE MOOD

Pres.	I, we, you, they **spill** he, she, it **spills**	I **am spilled** we, you, they **are spilled** he, she, it **is spilled**
Pres. *Prog.*	I **am spilling** we, you, they **are spilling** he, she, it **is spilling**	I **am being spilled** we, you, they **are being spilled** he, she, it **is being spilled**
Pres. *Int.*	I, we, you, they **do spill** he, she, it **does spill**	I, we, you, they **do get spilled** he, she, it **does get spilled**
Fut.	I, he, she, it, we, you, they **will spill**	I, he, she, it, we, you, they **will be spilled**
Past	I, he, she, it, we, you, they **spilled**	I, he, she, it **was spilled** we, you, they **were spilled**
Past *Prog.*	I, he, she, it **was spilling** we, you, they **were spilling**	I, he, she, it **was being spilled** we, you, they **were being spilled**
Past *Int.*	I, he, she, it, we, you, they **did spill**	I, he, she, it, we, you, they **did get spilled**
Pres. *Perf.*	I, we, you, they **have spilled** he, she, it **has spilled**	I, we, you, they **have been spilled** he, she, it **has been spilled**
Past *Perf.*	I, he, she, it, we, you, they **had spilled**	I, he, she, it, we, you, they **had been spilled**
Fut. *Perf.*	I, he, she, it, we, you, they **will have spilled**	I, he, she, it, we, you, they **will have been spilled**

IMPERATIVE MOOD

spill   **be spilled**

SUBJUNCTIVE MOOD

Pres.	if I, he, she, it, we, you, they **spill**	if I, he, she, it, we, you, they **be spilled**
Past	if I, he, she, it, we, you, they **spilled**	if I, he, she, it, we, you, they **were spilled**
Fut.	if I, he, she, it, we, you, they **should spill**	if I, he, she, it, we, you, they **should be spilled**

Transitive and intransitive. The *Oxford Dictionary* prefers the form SPILT for the past tense and past participle.

spin
(active voice)

be spun
(passive voice)

Infinitive: **to spin**
Perfect Infinitive: **to have spun**
Present Participle: **spinning**
Past Participle: **spun**

Infinitive: **to be spun**
Perfect Infinitive: **to have been spun**
Present Participle: **being spun**
Past Participle: **been spun**

INDICATIVE MOOD

Pres.	I, we, you, they **spin**	I **am spun**
		we, you, they **are spun**
	he, she, it **spins**	he, she, it **is spun**
Pres.	I **am spinning**	I **am being spun**
Prog.	we, you, they **are spinning**	we, you, they **are being spun**
	he, she, it **is spinning**	he, she, it **is being spun**
Pres.	I, we, you, they **do spin**	I, we, you, they **do get spun**
Int.	he, she, it **does spin**	he, she, it **does get spun**
Fut.	I, he, she, it,	I, he, she, it,
	we, you, they **will spin**	we, you, they **will be spun**
Past	I, he, she, it,	I, he, she, it **was spun**
	we, you, they **spun**	we, you, they **were spun**
Past	I, he, she, it **was spinning**	I, he, she, it **was being spun**
Prog.	we, you, they **were spinning**	we, you, they **were being spun**
Past	I, he, she, it,	I, he, she, it,
Int.	we, you, they **did spin**	we, you, they **did get spun**
Pres.	I, we, you, they **have spun**	I, we, you, they **have been spun**
Perf.	he, she, it **has spun**	he, she, it **has been spun**
Past	I, he, she, it,	I, he, she, it,
Perf.	we, you, they **had spun**	we, you, they **had been spun**
Fut.	I, he, she, it, we, you, they	I, he, she, it, we, you, they
Perf.	**will have spun**	**will have been spun**

IMPERATIVE MOOD

spin

be spun

SUBJUNCTIVE MOOD

Pres.	if I, he, she, it,	if I, he, she, it,
	we, you, they **spin**	we, you, they **be spun**
Past	if I, he, she, it,	if I, he, she, it,
	we, you, they **spun**	we, you, they **were spun**
Fut.	if I, he, she, it,	if I, he, she, it,
	we, you, they **should spin**	we, you, they **should be spun**

Transitive and intransitive. The *Oxford Dictionary* lists SPAN as an alternate past tense form.

spit
(active voice)

PRINCIPAL PARTS: **spits, spitting, spat/spit, spat/spit**

be spat/spit
(passive voice)

Infinitive: **to spit**
Perfect Infinitive: **to have spat**
Present Participle: **spitting**
Past Participle: **spat**

Infinitive: **to be spat**
Perfect Infinitive: **to have been spat**
Present Participle: **being spat**
Past Participle: **been spat**

INDICATIVE MOOD

Pres.	I, we, you, they **spit**	I **am spat**
		we, you, they **are spat**
	he, she, it **spits**	he, she, it **is spat**
Pres.	I **am spitting**	I **am being spat**
Prog.	we, you, they **are spitting**	we, you, they **are being spat**
	he, she, it **is spitting**	he, she, it **is being spat**
Pres.	I, we, you, they **do spit**	I, we, you, they **do get spat**
Int.	he, she, it **does spit**	he, she, it **does get spat**
Fut.	I, he, she, it, we, you, they **will spit**	I, he, she, it, we, you, they **will be spat**
Past	I, he, she, it, we, you, they **spat**	I, he, she, it **was spat** we, you, they **were spat**
Past	I, he, she, it **was spitting**	I, he, she, it **was being spat**
Prog.	we, you, they **were spitting**	we, you, they **were being spat**
Past	I, he, she, it,	I, he, she, it,
Int.	we, you, they **did spit**	we, you, they **did get spat**
Pres.	I, we, you, they **have spat**	I, we, you, they **have been spat**
Perf.	he, she, it **has spat**	he, she, it **has been spat**
Past	I, he, she, it,	I, he, she, it,
Perf.	we, you, they **had spat**	we, you, they **had been spat**
Fut.	I, he, she, it, we, you, they	I, he, she, it, we, you, they
Perf.	**will have spat**	**will have been spat**

IMPERATIVE MOOD

spit   **be spat**

SUBJUNCTIVE MOOD

Pres.	if I, he, she, it, we, you, they **spit**	if I, he, she, it, we, you, they **be spat**
Past	if I, he, she, it, we, you, they **spat**	if I, he, she, it, we, you, they **were spat**
Fut.	if I, he, she, it, we, you, they **should spit**	if I, he, she, it, we, you, they **should be spat**

Transitive or intransitive. For the past and past participle there are two forms, SPAT or SPIT. The verb with the past tense and past participle SPITTED means to "impale on something, as on a spit."

split
(active voice)

be split
(passive voice)

Infinitive: **to split**
Perfect Infinitive: **to have split**
Present Participle: **splitting**
Past Participle: **split**

Infinitive: **to be split**
Perfect Infinitive: **to have been split**
Present Participle: **being split**
Past Participle: **been split**

INDICATIVE MOOD

Pres.	I, we, you, they **split** he, she, it **splits**	I **am split** we, you, they **are split** he, she, it **is split**
Pres. *Prog.*	I **am splitting** we, you, they **are splitting** he, she, it **is splitting**	I **am being split** we, you, they **are being split** he, she, it **is being split**
Pres. *Int.*	I, we, you, they **do split** he, she, it **does split**	I, we, you, they **do get split** he, she, it **does get split**
Fut.	I, he, she, it, we, you, they **will split**	I, he, she, it, we, you, they **will be split**
Past	I, he, she, it, we, you, they **split**	I, he, she, it **was split** we, you, they **were split**
Past *Prog.*	I, he, she, it **was splitting** we, you, they **were splitting**	I, he, she, it **was being split** we, you, they **were being split**
Past *Int.*	I, he, she, it, we, you, they **did split**	I, he, she, it, we, you, they **did get split**
Pres. *Perf.*	I, we, you, they **have split** he, she, it **has split**	I, we, you, they **have been split** he, she, it **has been split**
Past *Perf.*	I, he, she, it, we, you, they **had split**	I, he, she, it, we, you, they **had been split**
Fut. *Perf.*	I, he, she, it, we, you, they **will have split**	I, he, she, it, we, you, they **will have been split**

IMPERATIVE MOOD

split   **be split**

SUBJUNCTIVE MOOD

Pres.	if I, he, she, it, we, you, they **split**	if I, he, she, it, we, you, they **be split**
Past	if I, he, she, it, we, you, they **split**	if I, he, she, it, we, you, they **were split**
Fut.	if I, he, she, it, we, you, they **should split**	if I, he, she, it, we, you, they **should be split**

Transitive and intransitive.

PRINCIPAL PARTS: **spoils, spoiling,
spoiled/spoilt, spoiled/spoilt**

Infinitive: **to spoil**
Perfect Infinitive: **to have spoiled**
Present Participle: **spoiling**
Past Participle: **spoiled**

Infinitive: **to be spoiled**
Perfect Infinitive: **to have been spoiled**
Present Participle: **being spoiled**
Past Participle: **been spoiled**

INDICATIVE MOOD

Pres.	I, we, you, they **spoil**	I **am spoiled**
		we, you, they **are spoiled**
	he, she, it **spoils**	he, she, it **is spoiled**
Pres.	I **am spoiling**	I **am being spoiled**
Prog.	we, you, they **are spoiling**	we, you, they **are being spoiled**
	he, she, it **is spoiling**	he, she, it **is being spoiled**
Pres.	I, we, you, they **do spoil**	I, we, you, they **do get spoiled**
Int.	he, she, it **does spoil**	he, she, it **does get spoiled**
Fut.	I, he, she, it,	I, he, she, it,
	we, you, they **will spoil**	we, you, they **will be spoiled**
Past	I, he, she, it,	I, he, she, it **was spoiled**
	we, you, they **spoiled**	we, you, they **were spoiled**
Past	I, he, she, it **was spoiling**	I, he, she, it **was being spoiled**
Prog.	we, you, they **were spoiling**	we, you, they **were being spoiled**
Past	I, he, she, it,	I, he, she, it,
Int.	we, you, they **did spoil**	we, you, they **did get spoiled**
Pres.	I, we, you, they **have spoiled**	I, we, you, they **have been spoiled**
Perf.	he, she, it **has spoiled**	he, she, it **has been spoiled**
Past	I, he, she, it,	I, he, she, it,
Perf.	we, you, they **had spoiled**	we, you, they **had been spoiled**
Fut.	I, he, she, it, we, you, they	I, he, she, it, we, you, they
Perf.	**will have spoiled**	**will have been spoiled**

IMPERATIVE MOOD

spoil	**be spoiled**

SUBJUNCTIVE MOOD

Pres.	if I, he, she, it,	if I, he, she, it,
	we, you, they **spoil**	we, you, they **be spoiled**
Past	if I, he, she, it,	if I, he, she, it,
	we, you, they **spoiled**	we, you, they **were spoiled**
Fut.	if I, he, she, it,	if I, he, she, it,
	we, you, they **should spoil**	we, you, they **should be spoiled**

Transitive and intransitive. The *Oxford Dictionary* prefers the past tense and past participle form
SPOILT.

spread
(active voice)

be spread
(passive voice)

Infinitive: **to spread**
Perfect Infinitive: **to have spread**
Present Participle: **spreading**
Past Participle: **spread**

Infinitive: **to be spread**
Perfect Infinitive: **to have been spread**
Present Participle: **being spread**
Past Participle: **been spread**

INDICATIVE MOOD

Pres.	I, we, you, they **spread**	I **am spread**
		we, you, they **are spread**
	he, she, it **spreads**	he, she, it **is spread**
Pres.	I **am spreading**	I **am being spread**
Prog.	we, you, they **are spreading**	we, you, they **are being spread**
	he, she, it **is spreading**	he, she, it **is being spread**
Pres.	I, we, you, they **do spread**	I, we, you, they **do get spread**
Int.	he, she, it **does spread**	he, she, it **does get spread**
Fut.	I, he, she, it,	I, he, she, it,
	we, you, they **will spread**	we, you, they **will be spread**
Past	I, he, she, it,	I, he, she, it **was spread**
	we, you, they **spread**	we, you, they **were spread**
Past	I, he, she, it **was spreading**	I, he, she, it **was being spread**
Prog.	we, you, they **were spreading**	we, you, they **were being spread**
Past	I, he, she, it,	I, he, she, it,
Int.	we, you, they **did spread**	we, you, they **did get spread**
Pres.	I, we, you, they **have spread**	I, we, you, they **have been spread**
Perf.	he, she, it **has spread**	he, she, it **has been spread**
Past	I, he, she, it,	I, he, she, it,
Perf.	we, you, they **had spread**	we, you, they **had been spread**
Fut.	I, he, she, it, we, you, they	I, he, she, it, we, you, they
Perf.	**will have spread**	**will have been spread**

IMPERATIVE MOOD

spread   **be spread**

SUBJUNCTIVE MOOD

Pres.	if I, he, she, it,	if I, he, she, it,
	we, you, they **spread**	we, you, they **be spread**
Past	if I, he, she, it,	if I, he, she, it,
	we, you, they **spread**	we, you, they **were spread**
Fut.	if I, he, she, it,	if I, he, she, it,
	we, you, they **should spread**	we, you, they **should be spread**

Transitive and intransitive.

spring
(active voice)

be sprung
(passive voice)

Infinitive: **to spring**
Perfect Infinitive: **to have sprung**
Present Participle: **springing**
Past Participle: **sprung**

Infinitive: **to be sprung**
Perfect Infinitive: **to have been sprung**
Present Participle: **being sprung**
Past Participle: **been sprung**

INDICATIVE MOOD

Pres.	I, we, you, they **spring**		I **am sprung**
			we, you, they **are sprung**
	he, she, it **springs**		he, she, it **is sprung**
Pres.	I **am springing**		I **am being sprung**
Prog.	we, you, they **are springing**		we, you, they **are being sprung**
	he, she, it **is springing**		he, she, it **is being sprung**
Pres.	I, we, you, they **do spring**		I, we, you, they **do get sprung**
Int.	he, she, it **does spring**		he, she, it **does get sprung**
Fut.	I, he, she, it,		I, he, she, it,
	we, you, they **will spring**		we, you, they **will be sprung**
Past	I, he, she, it,		I, he, she, it **was sprung**
	we, you, they **sprang**		we, you, they **were sprung**
Past	I, he, she, it **was springing**		I, he, she, it **was being sprung**
Prog.	we, you, they **were springing**		we, you, they **were being sprung**
Past	I, he, she, it,		I, he, she, it,
Int.	we, you, they **did spring**		we, you, they **did get sprung**
Pres.	I, we, you, they **have sprung**		I, we, you, they **have been sprung**
Perf.	he, she, it **has sprung**		he, she, it **has been sprung**
Past	I, he, she, it,		I, he, she, it,
Perf.	we, you, they **had sprung**		we, you, they **had been sprung**
Fut.	I, he, she, it, we, you, they		I, he, she, it, we, you, they
Perf.	**will have sprung**		**will have been sprung**

IMPERATIVE MOOD

spring

be sprung

SUBJUNCTIVE MOOD

Pres.	if I, he, she, it,		if I, he, she, it,
	we, you, they **spring**		we, you, they **be sprung**
Past	if I, he, she, it,		if I, he, she, it,
	we, you, they **sprang**		we, you, they **were sprung**
Fut.	if I, he, she, it,		if I, he, she, it,
	we, you, they **should spring**		we, you, they **should be sprung**

Intransitive and transitive.

stand
(active voice)

be stood
(passive voice)

Infinitive: **to stand**
Perfect Infinitive: **to have stood**
Present Participle: **standing**
Past Participle: **stood**

Infinitive: **to be stood**
Perfect Infinitive: **to have been stood**
Present Participle: **being stood**
Past Participle: **been stood**

INDICATIVE MOOD

Pres.	I, we, you, they **stand**	I **am stood**
		we, you, they **are stood**
	he, she, it **stands**	he, she, it **is stood**
Pres.	I **am standing**	I **am being stood**
Prog.	we, you, they **are standing**	we, you, they **are being stood**
	he, she, it **is standing**	he, she, it **is being stood**
Pres.	I, we, you, they **do stand**	I, we, you, they **do get stood**
Int.	he, she, it **does stand**	he, she, it **does get stood**
Fut.	I, he, she, it,	I, he, she, it,
	we, you, they **will stand**	we, you, they **will be stood**
Past	I, he, she, it,	I, he, she, it **was stood**
	we, you, they **stood**	we, you, they **were stood**
Past	I, he, she, it **was standing**	I, he, she, it **was being stood**
Prog.	we, you, they **were standing**	we, you, they **were being stood**
Past	I, he, she, it,	I, he, she, it,
Int.	we, you, they **did stand**	we, you, they **did get stood**
Pres.	I, we, you, they **have stood**	I, we, you, they **have been stood**
Perf.	he, she, it **has stood**	he, she, it **has been stood**
Past	I, he, she, it,	I, he, she, it,
Perf.	we, you, they **had stood**	we, you, they **had been stood**
Fut.	I, he, she, it, we, you, they	I, he, she, it, we, you, they
Perf.	**will have stood**	**will have been stood**

IMPERATIVE MOOD

stand

be stood

SUBJUNCTIVE MOOD

Pres.	if I, he, she, it,	if I, he, she, it,
	we, you, they **stand**	we, you, they **be stood**
Past	if I, he, she, it,	if I, he, she, it,
	we, you, they **stood**	we, you, they **were stood**
Fut.	if I, he, she, it,	if I, he, she, it,
	we, you, they **should stand**	we, you, they **should be stood**

Intransitive and transitive.

start
(active voice)

be started
(passive voice)

Infinitive: **to start**
Perfect Infinitive: **to have started**
Present Participle: **starting**
Past Participle: **started**

Infinitive: **to be started**
Perfect Infinitive: **to have been started**
Present Participle: **being started**
Past Participle: **been started**

INDICATIVE MOOD

Pres.	I, we, you, they **start**	I **am started**
		we, you, they **are started**
	he, she, it **starts**	he, she, it **is started**
Pres.	I **am starting**	I **am being started**
Prog.	we, you, they **are starting**	we, you, they **are being started**
	he, she, it **is starting**	he, she, it **is being started**
Pres.	I, we, you, they **do start**	I, we, you, they **do get started**
Int.	he, she, it **does start**	he, she, it **does get started**
Fut.	I, he, she, it,	I, he, she, it,
	we, you, they **will start**	we, you, they **will be started**
Past	I, he, she, it,	I, he, she, it **was started**
	we, you, they **started**	we, you, they **were started**
Past	I, he, she, it **was starting**	I, he, she, it **was being started**
Prog.	we, you, they **were starting**	we, you, they **were being started**
Past	I, he, she, it,	I, he, she, it,
Int.	we, you, they **did start**	we, you, they **did get started**
Pres.	I, we, you, they **have started**	I, we, you, they **have been started**
Perf.	he, she, it **has started**	he, she, it **has been started**
Past	I, he, she, it,	I, he, she, it,
Perf.	we, you, they **had started**	we, you, they **had been started**
Fut.	I, he, she, it, we, you, they	I, he, she, it, we, you, they
Perf.	**will have started**	**will have been started**

IMPERATIVE MOOD

start

be started

SUBJUNCTIVE MOOD

Pres.	if I, he, she, it,	if I, he, she, it,
	we, you, they **start**	we, you, they **be started**
Past	if I, he, she, it,	if I, he, she, it,
	we, you, they **started**	we, you, they **were started**
Fut.	if I, he, she, it,	if I, he, she, it,
	we, you, they **should start**	we, you, they **should be started**

Intransitive and transitive.

410

state
(active voice)

be stated
(passive voice)

Infinitive: **to state**
Perfect Infinitive: **to have stated**
Present Participle: **stating**
Past Participle: **stated**

Infinitive: **to be stated**
Perfect Infinitive: **to have been stated**
Present Participle: **being stated**
Past Participle: **been stated**

INDICATIVE MOOD

Pres.	I, we, you, they **state**	I **am stated**
		we, you, they **are stated**
	he, she, it **states**	he, she, it **is stated**
Pres.	I **am stating**	I **am being stated**
Prog.	we, you, they **are stating**	we, you, they **are being stated**
	he, she, it **is stating**	he, she, it **is being stated**
Pres.	I, we, you, they **do state**	I, we, you, they **do get stated**
Int.	he, she, it **does state**	he, she, it **does get stated**
Fut.	I, he, she, it,	I, he, she, it,
	we, you, they **will state**	we, you, they **will be stated**
Past	I, he, she, it,	I, he, she, it **was stated**
	we, you, they **stated**	we, you, they **were stated**
Past	I, he, she, it **was stating**	I, he, she, it **was being stated**
Prog.	we, you, they **were stating**	we, you, they **were being stated**
Past	I, he, she, it,	I, he, she, it,
Int.	we, you, they **did state**	we, you, they **did get stated**
Pres.	I, we, you, they **have stated**	I, we, you, they **have been stated**
Perf.	he, she, it **has stated**	he, she, it **has been stated**
Past	I, he, she, it,	I, he, she, it,
Perf.	we, you, they **had stated**	we, you, they **had been stated**
Fut.	I, he, she, it, we, you, they	I, he, she, it, we, you, they
Perf.	**will have stated**	**will have been stated**

IMPERATIVE MOOD

state

be stated

SUBJUNCTIVE MOOD

Pres.	if I, he, she, it,	if I, he, she, it,
	we, you, they **state**	we, you, they **be stated**
Past	if I, he, she, it,	if I, he, she, it,
	we, you, they **stated**	we, you, they **were stated**
Fut.	if I, he, she, it,	if I, he, she, it,
	we, you, they **should state**	we, you, they **should be stated**

stave
(active voice)

be staved/stove
(passive voice)

Infinitive: **to stave**
Perfect Infinitive: **to have staved**
Present Participle: **staving**
Past Participle: **staved**

Infinitive: **to be staved**
Perfect Infinitive: **to have been staved**
Present Participle: **being staved**
Past Participle: **been staved**

INDICATIVE MOOD

Pres.	I, we, you, they **stave**	I **am staved**
		we, you, they **are staved**
	he, she, it **staves**	he, she, it **is staved**
Pres.	I **am staving**	I **am being staved**
Prog.	we, you, they **are staving**	we, you, they **are being staved**
	he, she, it **is staving**	he, she, it **is being staved**
Pres.	I, we, you, they **do stave**	I, we, you, they **do get staved**
Int.	he, she, it **does stave**	he, she, it **does get staved**
Fut.	I, he, she, it,	I, he, she, it,
	we, you, they **will stave**	we, you, they **will be staved**
Past	I, he, she, it,	I, he, she, it **was staved**
	we, you, they **staved**	we, you, they **were staved**
Past	I, he, she, it **was staving**	I, he, she, it **was being staved**
Prog.	we, you, they **were staving**	we, you, they **were being staved**
Past	I, he, she, it,	I, he, she, it,
Int.	we, you, they **did stave**	we, you, they **did get staved**
Pres.	I, we, you, they **have staved**	I, we, you, they **have been staved**
Perf.	he, she, it **has staved**	he, she, it **has been staved**
Past	I, he, she, it,	I, he, she, it,
Perf.	we, you, they **had staved**	we, you, they **had been staved**
Fut.	I, he, she, it, we, you, they	I, he, she, it, we, you, they
Perf.	**will have staved**	**will have been staved**

IMPERATIVE MOOD

stave

be staved

SUBJUNCTIVE MOOD

Pres.	if I, he, she, it,	if I, he, she, it,
	we, you, they **stave**	we, you, they **be staved**
Past	if I, he, she, it,	if I, he, she, it,
	we, you, they **staved**	we, you, they **were staved**
Fut.	if I, he, she, it,	if I, he, she, it,
	we, you, they **should stave**	we, you, they **should be staved**

Transitive and intransitive. The *Oxford Dictionary* prefers STOVE for the past tense and past participle.

stay
(active voice)

be stayed
(passive voice)

Infinitive: **to stay**
Perfect Infinitive: **to have stayed**
Present Participle: **staying**
Past Participle: **stayed**

Infinitive: **to be stayed**
Perfect Infinitive: **to have been stayed**
Present Participle: **being stayed**
Past Participle: **been stayed**

INDICATIVE MOOD

Pres.	I, we, you, they **stay**	I **am stayed**
		we, you, they **are stayed**
	he, she, it **stays**	he, she, it **is stayed**
Pres. Prog.	I **am staying**	I **am being stayed**
	we, you, they **are staying**	we, you, they **are being stayed**
	he, she, it **is staying**	he, she, it **is being stayed**
Pres. Int.	I, we, you, they **do stay**	I, we, you, they **do get stayed**
	he, she, it **does stay**	he, she, it **does get stayed**
Fut.	I, he, she, it, we, you, they **will stay**	I, he, she, it, we, you, they **will be stayed**
Past	I, he, she, it, we, you, they **stayed**	I, he, she, it **was stayed** we, you, they **were stayed**
Past Prog.	I, he, she, it **was staying** we, you, they **were staying**	I, he, she, it **was being stayed** we, you, they **were being stayed**
Past Int.	I, he, she, it, we, you, they **did stay**	I, he, she, it, we, you, they **did get stayed**
Pres. Perf.	I, we, you, they **have stayed**	I, we, you, they **have been stayed**
	he, she, it **has stayed**	he, she, it **has been stayed**
Past Perf.	I, he, she, it, we, you, they **had stayed**	I, he, she, it, we, you, they **had been stayed**
Fut. Perf.	I, he, she, it, we, you, they **will have stayed**	I, he, she, it, we, you, they **will have been stayed**

IMPERATIVE MOOD

stay   **be stayed**

SUBJUNCTIVE MOOD

Pres.	if I, he, she, it, we, you, they **stay**	if I, he, she, it, we, you, they **be stayed**
Past	if I, he, she, it, we, you, they **stayed**	if I, he, she, it, we, you, they **were stayed**
Fut.	if I, he, she, it, we, you, they **should stay**	if I, he, she, it, we, you, they **should be stayed**

Intransitive and transitive.

steal
(active voice)

be stolen
(passive voice)

Infinitive: **to steal**
Perfect Infinitive: **to have stolen**
Present Participle: **stealing**
Past Participle: **stolen**

Infinitive: **to be stolen**
Perfect Infinitive: **to have been stolen**
Present Participle: **being stolen**
Past Participle: **been stolen**

INDICATIVE MOOD

Pres.	I, we, you, they **steal**	I am stolen
		we, you, they **are stolen**
	he, she, it **steals**	he, she, it **is stolen**
Pres.	I **am stealing**	I am being stolen
Prog.	we, you, they **are stealing**	we, you, they **are being stolen**
	he, she, it **is stealing**	he, she, it **is being stolen**
Pres.	I, we, you, they **do steal**	I, we, you, they **do get stolen**
Int.	he, she, it **does steal**	he, she, it **does get stolen**
Fut.	I, he, she, it,	I, he, she, it,
	we, you, they **will steal**	we, you, they **will be stolen**
Past	I, he, she, it,	I, he, she, it **was stolen**
	we, you, they **stole**	we, you, they **were stolen**
Past	I, he, she, it **was stealing**	I, he, she, it **was being stolen**
Prog.	we, you, they **were stealing**	we, you, they **were being stolen**
Past	I, he, she, it,	I, he, she, it,
Int.	we, you, they **did steal**	we, you, they **did get stolen**
Pres.	I, we, you, they **have stolen**	I, we, you, they **have been stolen**
Perf.	he, she, it **has stolen**	he, she, it **has been stolen**
Past	I, he, she, it,	I, he, she, it,
Perf.	we, you, they **had stolen**	we, you, they **had been stolen**
Fut.	I, he, she, it, we, you, they	I, he, she, it, we, you, they
Perf.	**will have stolen**	**will have been stolen**

IMPERATIVE MOOD

steal

be stolen

SUBJUNCTIVE MOOD

Pres.	if I, he, she, it,	if I, he, she, it,
	we, you, they **steal**	we, you, they **be stolen**
Past	if I, he, she, it,	if I, he, she, it,
	we, you, they **stole**	we, you, they **were stolen**
Fut.	if I, he, she, it,	if I, he, she, it,
	we, you, they **should steal**	we, you, they **should be stolen**

Transitive and intransitive.

stick
(active voice)

be stuck/sticked
(passive voice)

Infinitive: **to stick**
Perfect Infinitive: **to have stuck**
Present Participle: **sticking**
Past Participle: **stuck**

Infinitive: **to be stuck**
Perfect Infinitive: **to have been stuck**
Present Participle: **being stuck**
Past Participle: **been stuck**

INDICATIVE MOOD

Pres.	I, we, you, they **stick**	I **am stuck**
		we, you, they **are stuck**
	he, she, it **sticks**	he, she, it **is stuck**
Pres.	I **am sticking**	I **am being stuck**
Prog.	we, you, they **are sticking**	we, you, they **are being stuck**
	he, she, it **is sticking**	he, she, it **is being stuck**
Pres.	I, we, you, they **do stick**	I, we, you, they **do get stuck**
Int.	he, she, it **does stick**	he, she, it **does get stuck**
Fut.	I, he, she, it,	I, he, she, it,
	we, you, they **will stick**	we, you, they **will be stuck**
Past	I, he, she, it,	I, he, she, it **was stuck**
	we, you, they **stuck**	we, you, they **were stuck**
Past	I, he, she, it **was sticking**	I, he, she, it **was being stuck**
Prog.	we, you, they **were sticking**	we, you, they **were being stuck**
Past	I, he, she, it,	I, he, she, it,
Int.	we, you, they **did stick**	we, you, they **did get stuck**
Pres.	I, we, you, they **have stuck**	I, we, you, they **have been stuck**
Perf.	he, she, it **has stuck**	he, she, it **has been stuck**
Past	I, he, she, it,	I, he, she, it,
Perf.	we, you, they **had stuck**	we, you, they **had been stuck**
Fut.	I, he, she, it, we, you, they	I, he, she, it, we, you, they
Perf.	**will have stuck**	**will have been stuck**

IMPERATIVE MOOD

stick

be stuck

SUBJUNCTIVE MOOD

Pres.	if I, he, she, it,	if I, he, she, it,
	we, you, they **stick**	we, you, they **be stuck**
Past	if I, he, she, it,	if I, he, she, it,
	we, you, they **stuck**	we, you, they **were stuck**
Fut.	if I, he, she, it,	if I, he, she, it,
	we, you, they **should stick**	we, you, they **should be stuck**

Transitive and intransitive. The past and past participle form STICKED is used in the sense of "propping something up with a stick." It is also used in the printing profession meaning to "set type on a stick."

sting
(active voice)

be stung
(passive voice)

Infinitive: **to sting**
Perfect Infinitive: **to have stung**
Present Participle: **stinging**
Past Participle: **stung**

Infinitive: **to be stung**
Perfect Infinitive: **to have been stung**
Present Participle: **being stung**
Past Participle: **been stung**

INDICATIVE MOOD

Pres.	I, we, you, they **sting**	I **am stung**
		we, you, they **are stung**
	he, she, it **stings**	he, she, it **is stung**
Pres.	I **am stinging**	I **am being stung**
Prog.	we, you, they **are stinging**	we, you, they **are being stung**
	he, she, it **is stinging**	he, she, it **is being stung**
Pres.	I, we, you, they **do sting**	I, we, you, they **do get stung**
Int.	he, she, it **does sting**	he, she, it **does get stung**
Fut.	I, he, she, it,	I, he, she, it,
	we, you, they **will sting**	we, you, they **will be stung**
Past	I, he, she, it,	I, he, she, it **was stung**
	we, you, they **stung**	we, you, they **were stung**
Past	I, he, she, it **was stinging**	I, he, she, it **was being stung**
Prog.	we, you, they **were stinging**	we, you, they **were being stung**
Past	I, he, she, it,	I, he, she, it,
Int.	we, you, they **did sting**	we, you, they **did get stung**
Pres.	I, we, you, they **have stung**	I, we, you, they **have been stung**
Perf.	he, she, it **has stung**	he, she, it **has been stung**
Past	I, he, she, it,	I, he, she, it,
Perf.	we, you, they **had stung**	we, you, they **had been stung**
Fut.	I, he, she, it, we, you, they	I, he, she, it, we, you, they
Perf.	**will have stung**	**will have been stung**

IMPERATIVE MOOD

sting   **be stung**

SUBJUNCTIVE MOOD

Pres.	if I, he, she, it,	if I, he, she, it,
	we, you, they **sting**	we, you, they **be stung**
Past	if I, he, she, it,	if I, he, she, it,
	we, you, they **stung**	we, you, they **were stung**
Fut.	if I, he, she, it,	if I, he, she, it,
	we, you, they **should sting**	we, you, they **should be stung**

Transitive and intransitive.

stink
(active voice)

PRINCIPAL PARTS: **stinks, stinking,**
stank/stunk, stunk

be stunk
(passive voice)

Infinitive: **to stink**
Perfect Infinitive: **to have stunk**
Present Participle: **stinking**
Past Participle: **stunk**

Infinitive: **to be stunk**
Perfect Infinitive: **to have been stunk**
Present Participle: **being stunk**
Past Participle: **been stunk**

INDICATIVE MOOD

Pres.	I, we, you, they **stink**	I **am stunk**
		we, you, they **are stunk**
	he, she, it **stinks**	he, she, it **is stunk**
Pres. *Prog.*	I **am stinking**	I **am being stunk**
	we, you, they **are stinking**	we, you, they **are being stunk**
	he, she, it **is stinking**	he, she, it **is being stunk**
Pres. *Int.*	I, we, you, they **do stink**	I, we, you, they **do get stunk**
	he, she, it **does stink**	he, she, it **does get stunk**
Fut.	I, he, she, it, we, you, they **will stink**	I, he, she, it, we, you, they **will be stunk**
Past	I, he, she, it, we, you, they **stank**	I, he, she, it **was stunk** we, you, they **were stunk**
Past *Prog.*	I, he, she, it **was stinking** we, you, they **were stinking**	I, he, she, it **was being stunk** we, you, they **were being stunk**
Past *Int.*	I, he, she, it, we, you, they **did stink**	I, he, she, it, we, you, they **did get stunk**
Pres. *Perf.*	I, we, you, they **have stunk** he, she, it **has stunk**	I, we, you, they **have been stunk** he, she, it **has been stunk**
Past *Perf.*	I, he, she, it, we, you, they **had stunk**	I, he, she, it, we, you, they **had been stunk**
Fut. *Perf.*	I, he, she, it, we, you, they **will have stunk**	I, he, she, it, we, you, they **will have been stunk**

IMPERATIVE MOOD

stink

be stunk

SUBJUNCTIVE MOOD

Pres.	if I, he, she, it, we, you, they **stink**	if I, he, she, it, we, you, they **be stunk**
Past	if I, he, she, it, we, you, they **stank**	if I, he, she, it, we, you, they **were stunk**
Fut.	if I, he, she, it, we, you, they **should stink**	if I, he, she, it, we, you, they **should be stunk**

Intransitive and transitive.

stop
(active voice)

be stopped
(passive voice)

Infinitive: **to stop**
Perfect Infinitive: **to have stopped**
Present Participle: **stopping**
Past Participle: **stopped**

Infinitive: **to be stopped**
Perfect Infinitive: **to have been stopped**
Present Participle: **being stopped**
Past Participle: **been stopped**

INDICATIVE MOOD

Pres.	I, we, you, they **stop**	I **am stopped**
		we, you, they **are stopped**
	he, she, it **stops**	he, she, it **is stopped**
Pres.	I **am stopping**	I **am being stopped**
Prog.	we, you, they **are stopping**	we, you, they **are being stopped**
	he, she, it **is stopping**	he, she, it **is being stopped**
Pres.	I, we, you, they **do stop**	I, we, you, they **do get stopped**
Int.	he, she, it **does stop**	he, she, it **does get stopped**
Fut.	I, he, she, it,	I, he, she, it,
	we, you, they **will stop**	we, you, they **will be stopped**
Past	I, he, she, it,	I, he, she, it **was stopped**
	we, you, they **stopped**	we, you, they **were stopped**
Past	I, he, she, it **was stopping**	I, he, she, it **was being stopped**
Prog.	we, you, they **were stopping**	we, you, they **were being stopped**
Past	I, he, she, it,	I, he, she, it,
Int.	we, you, they **did stop**	we, you, they **did get stopped**
Pres.	I, we, you, they **have stopped**	I, we, you, they **have been stopped**
Perf.	he, she, it **has stopped**	he, she, it **has been stopped**
Past	I, he, she, it,	I, he, she, it,
Perf.	we, you, they **had stopped**	we, you, they **had been stopped**
Fut.	I, he, she, it, we, you, they	I, he, she, it, we, you, they
Perf.	**will have stopped**	**will have been stopped**

IMPERATIVE MOOD

stop

be stopped

SUBJUNCTIVE MOOD

Pres.	if I, he, she, it,	if I, he, she, it,
	we, you, they **stop**	we, you, they **be stopped**
Past	if I, he, she, it,	if I, he, she, it,
	we, you, they **stopped**	we, you, they **were stopped**
Fut.	if I, he, she, it,	if I, he, she, it,
	we, you, they **should stop**	we, you, they **should be stopped**

Transitive and intransitive.

strew
(active voice)

be strewn/strewed
(passive voice)

Infinitive: **to strew**
Perfect Infinitive: **to have strewn**
Present Participle: **strewing**
Past Participle: **strewn**

Infinitive: **to be strewn**
Perfect Infinitive: **to have been strewn**
Present Participle: **being strewn**
Past Participle: **been strewn**

INDICATIVE MOOD

Pres.	I, we, you, they **strew**	I **am strewn**
		we, you, they **are strewn**
	he, she, it **strews**	he, she, it **is strewn**
Pres.	I **am strewing**	I **am being strewn**
Prog.	we, you, they **are strewing**	we, you, they **are being strewn**
	he, she, it **is strewing**	he, she, it **is being strewn**
Pres.	I, we, you, they **do strew**	I, we, you, they **do get strewn**
Int.	he, she, it **does strew**	he, she, it **does get strewn**
Fut.	I, he, she, it, we, you, they **will strew**	I, he, she, it, we, you, they **will be strewn**
Past	I, he, she, it, we, you, they **strewed**	I, he, she, it **was strewn** we, you, they **were strewn**
Past	I, he, she, it **was strewing**	I, he, she, it **was being strewn**
Prog.	we, you, they **were strewing**	we, you, they **were being strewn**
Past	I, he, she, it, we, you, they **did strew**	I, he, she, it, we, you, they **did get strewn**
Int.		
Pres.	I, we, you, they **have strewn**	I, we, you, they **have been strewn**
Perf.	he, she, it **has strewn**	he, she, it **has been strewn**
Past	I, he, she, it, we, you, they **had strewn**	I, he, she, it, we, you, they **had been strewn**
Perf.		
Fut.	I, he, she, it, we, you, they **will have strewn**	I, he, she, it, we, you, they **will have been strewn**
Perf.		

IMPERATIVE MOOD

strew

be strewn

SUBJUNCTIVE MOOD

Pres.	if I, he, she, it, we, you, they **strew**	if I, he, she, it, we, you, they **be strewn**
Past	if I, he, she, it, we, you, they **strewed**	if I, he, she, it, we, you, they **were strewn**
Fut.	if I, he, she, it, we, you, they **should strew**	if I, he, she, it, we, you, they **should be strewn**

stride
(active voice)

be stridden
(passive voice)

Infinitive: **to stride**
Perfect Infinitive: **to have stridden**
Present Participle: **striding**
Past Participle: **stridden**

Infinitive: **to be stridden**
Perfect Infinitive: **to have been stridden**
Present Participle: **being stridden**
Past Participle: **been stridden**

INDICATIVE MOOD

Pres.	I, we, you, they **stride**	I **am stridden**
		we, you, they **are stridden**
	he, she, it **strides**	he, she, it **is stridden**
Pres.	I **am striding**	I **am being stridden**
Prog.	we, you, they **are striding**	we, you, they **are being stridden**
	he, she, it **is striding**	he, she, it **is being stridden**
Pres.	I, we, you, they **do stride**	I, we, you, they **do get stridden**
Int.	he, she, it **does stride**	he, she, it **does get stridden**
Fut.	I, he, she, it, we, you, they **will stride**	I, he, she, it, we, you, they **will be stridden**
Past	I, he, she, it, we, you, they **strode**	I, he, she, it **was stridden** we, you, they **were stridden**
Past	I, he, she, it **was striding**	I, he, she, it **was being stridden**
Prog.	we, you, they **were striding**	we, you, they **were being stridden**
Past	I, he, she, it, we, you, they **did stride**	I, he, she, it, we, you, they **did get stridden**
Int.		
Pres.	I, we, you, they **have stridden**	I, we, you, they **have been stridden**
Perf.	he, she, it **has stridden**	he, she, it **has been stridden**
Past	I, he, she, it, we, you, they **had stridden**	I, he, she, it, we, you, they **had been stridden**
Perf.		
Fut.	I, he, she, it, we, you, they **will have stridden**	I, he, she, it, we, you, they **will have been stridden**
Perf.		

IMPERATIVE MOOD

stride   **be stridden**

SUBJUNCTIVE MOOD

Pres.	if I, he, she, it, we, you, they **stride**	if I, he, she, it, we, you, they **be stridden**
Past	if I, he, she, it, we, you, they **strode**	if I, he, she, it, we, you, they **were stridden**
Fut.	if I, he, she, it, we, you, they **should stride**	if I, he, she, it, we, you, they **should be stridden**

Intransitive and transitive.

strike
(active voice)

PRINCIPAL PARTS: **strikes, striking, struck, struck/stricken**

be struck/stricken
(passive voice)

Infinitive: **to strike**
Perfect Infinitive: **to have struck**
Present Participle: **striking**
Past Participle: **struck**

Infinitive: **to be struck**
Perfect Infinitive: **to have been struck**
Present Participle: **being struck**
Past Participle: **been struck**

INDICATIVE MOOD

Pres.	I, we, you, they **strike**	I **am struck**
		we, you, they **are struck**
	he, she, it **strikes**	he, she, it **is struck**
Pres.	I **am striking**	I **am being struck**
Prog.	we, you, they **are striking**	we, you, they **are being struck**
	he, she, it **is striking**	he, she, it **is being struck**
Pres.	I, we, you, they **do strike**	I, we, you, they **do get struck**
Int.	he, she, it **does strike**	he, she, it **does get struck**
Fut.	I, he, she, it,	I, he, she, it,
	we, you, they **will strike**	we, you, they **will be struck**
Past	I, he, she, it,	I, he, she, it **was struck**
	we, you, they **struck**	we, you, they **were struck**
Past	I, he, she, it **was striking**	I, he, she, it **was being struck**
Prog.	we, you, they **were striking**	we, you, they **were being struck**
Past	I, he, she, it,	I, he, she, it,
Int.	we, you, they **did strike**	we, you, they **did get struck**
Pres.	I, we, you, they **have struck**	I, we, you, they **have been struck**
Perf.	he, she, it **has struck**	he, she, it **has been struck**
Past	I, he, she, it,	I, he, she, it,
Perf.	we, you, they **had struck**	we, you, they **had been struck**
Fut.	I, he, she, it, we, you, they	I, he, she, it, we, you, they
Perf.	**will have struck**	**will have been struck**

IMPERATIVE MOOD

strike

be struck

SUBJUNCTIVE MOOD

Pres.	if I, he, she, it,	if I, he, she, it,
	we, you, they **strike**	we, you, they **be struck**
Past	if I, he, she, it,	if I, he, she, it,
	we, you, they **struck**	we, you, they **were struck**
Fut.	if I, he, she, it,	if I, he, she, it,
	we, you, they **should strike**	we, you, they **should be struck**

Transitive and intransitive. The *Oxford Dictionary* lists as archaic the past participle form STRICKEN.

string
(active voice)

be strung
(passive voice)

Infinitive: **to string**
Perfect Infinitive: **to have strung**
Present Participle: **stringing**
Past Participle: **strung**

Infinitive: **to be strung**
Perfect Infinitive: **to have been strung**
Present Participle: **being strung**
Past Participle: **been strung**

INDICATIVE MOOD

Pres.	I, we, you, they **string**	I **am strung**
		we, you, they **are strung**
	he, she, it **strings**	he, she, it **is strung**
Pres.	I **am stringing**	I **am being strung**
Prog.	we, you, they **are stringing**	we, you, they **are being strung**
	he, she, it **is stringing**	he, she, it **is being strung**
Pres.	I, we, you, they **do string**	I, we, you, they **do get strung**
Int.	he, she, it **does string**	he, she, it **does get strung**
Fut.	I, he, she, it,	I, he, she, it,
	we, you, they **will string**	we, you, they **will be strung**
Past	I, he, she, it,	I, he, she, it **was strung**
	we, you, they **strung**	we, you, they **were strung**
Past	I, he, she, it **was stringing**	I, he, she, it **was being strung**
Prog.	we, you, they **were stringing**	we, you, they **were being strung**
Past	I, he, she, it,	I, he, she, it,
Int.	we, you, they **did string**	we, you, they **did get strung**
Pres.	I, we, you, they **have strung**	I, we, you, they **have been strung**
Perf.	he, she, it **has strung**	he, she, it **has been strung**
Past	I, he, she, it,	I, he, she, it,
Perf.	we, you, they **had strung**	we, you, they **had been strung**
Fut.	I, he, she, it, we, you, they	I, he, she, it, we, you, they
Perf.	**will have strung**	**will have been strung**

IMPERATIVE MOOD

string   **be strung**

SUBJUNCTIVE MOOD

Pres.	if I, he, she, it,	if I, he, she, it,
	we, you, they **string**	we, you, they **be strung**
Past	if I, he, she, it,	if I, he, she, it,
	we, you, they **strung**	we, you, they **were strung**
Fut.	if I, he, she, it,	if I, he, she, it,
	we, you, they **should string**	we, you, they **should be strung**

Transitive and intransitive.

strive

Infinitive: **to strive**
Perfect Infinitive: **to have strived**
Present Participle: **striving**
Past Participle: **striven**

INDICATIVE MOOD

Pres.	I, we, you, they **strive**
	he, she, it **strives**
Pres. *Prog.*	I **am striving**
	we, you, they **are striving**
	he, she, it **is striving**
Pres. *Int.*	I, we, you, they **do strive**
	he, she, it **does strive**
Fut.	I, he, she, it, we, you, they **will strive**
Past	I, he, she, it, we, you, they **strove**
Past *Prog.*	I, he, she, it **was striving**
	we, you, they **were striving**
Past *Int.*	I, he, she, it, we, you, they **did strive**
Pres. *Perf.*	I, we, you, they **have striven**
	he, she, it **has striven**
Past *Perf.*	I, he, she, it, we, you, they **had striven**
Fut. *Perf.*	I, he, she, it, we, you, they **will have striven**

IMPERATIVE MOOD

strive

SUBJUNCTIVE MOOD

Pres.	if I, he, she, it, we, you, they **strive**
Past	if I, he, she, it, we, you, they **strove**
Fut.	if I, he, she, it, we, you, they **should strive**

The past may be STROVE or STRIVED; the past participle is STRIVEN or STRIVED.

stroke
(active voice)

be stroked
(passive voice)

Infinitive: **to stroke**
Perfect Infinitive: **to have stroked**
Present Participle: **stroking**
Past Participle: **stroked**

Infinitive: **to be stroked**
Perfect Infinitive: **to have been stroked**
Present Participle: **being stroked**
Past Participle: **been stroked**

INDICATIVE MOOD

Pres.	I, we, you, they **stroke**	I **am stroked**
		we, you, they **are stroked**
	he, she, it **strokes**	he, she, it **is stroked**
Pres.	I **am stroking**	I **am being stroked**
Prog.	we, you, they **are stroking**	we, you, they **are being stroked**
	he, she, it **is stroking**	he, she, it **is being stroked**
Pres.	I, we, you, they **do stroke**	I, we, you, they **do get stroked**
Int.	he, she, it **does stroke**	he, she, it **does get stroked**
Fut.	I, he, she, it, we, you, they **will stroke**	I, he, she, it, we, you, they **will be stroked**
Past	I, he, she, it, we, you, they **stroked**	I, he, she, it **was stroked** we, you, they **were stroked**
Past	I, he, she, it **was stroking**	I, he, she, it **was being stroked**
Prog.	we, you, they **were stroking**	we, you, they **were being stroked**
Past	I, he, she, it, we, you, they **did stroke**	I, he, she, it, we, you, they **did get stroked**
Int.		
Pres.	I, we, you, they **have stroked**	I, we, you, they **have been stroked**
Perf.	he, she, it **has stroked**	he, she, it **has been stroked**
Past	I, he, she, it, we, you, they **had stroked**	I, he, she, it, we, you, they **had been stroked**
Perf.		
Fut.	I, he, she, it, we, you, they	I, he, she, it, we, you, they
Perf.	**will have stroked**	**will have been stroked**

IMPERATIVE MOOD

stroke   **be stroked**

SUBJUNCTIVE MOOD

Pres.	if I, he, she, it, we, you, they **stroke**	if I, he, she, it, we, you, they **be stroked**
Past	if I, he, she, it, we, you, they **stroked**	if I, he, she, it, we, you, they **were stroked**
Fut.	if I, he, she, it, we, you, they **should stroke**	if I, he, she, it, we, you, they **should be stroked**

Transitive and intransitive.

study
(active voice)

be studied
(passive voice)

Infinitive: **to study**
Perfect Infinitive: **to have studied**
Present Participle: **studying**
Past Participle: **studied**

Infinitive: **to be studied**
Perfect Infinitive: **to have been studied**
Present Participle: **being studied**
Past Participle: **been studied**

INDICATIVE MOOD

Pres.	I, we, you, they s̲tudy	I **am studied**
		we, you, they **are studied**
	he, she, it **studies**	he, she, it **is studied**
Pres.	I **am studying**	I **am being studied**
Prog.	we, you, they **are studying**	we, you, they **are being studied**
	he, she, it **is studying**	he, she, it **is being studied**
Pres.	I, we, you, they **do study**	I, we, you, they **do get studied**
Int.	he, she, it **does study**	he, she, it **does get studied**
Fut.	I, he, she, it,	I, he, she, it,
	we, you, they **will study**	we, you, they **will be studied**
Past	I, he, she, it,	I, he, she, it **was studied**
	we, you, they **studied**	we, you, they **were studied**
Past	I, he, she, it **was studying**	I, he, she, it **was being studied**
Prog.	we, you, they **were studying**	we, you, they **were being studied**
Past	I, he, she, it,	I, he, she, it,
Int.	we, you, they **did study**	we, you, they **did get studied**
Pres.	I, we, you, they **have studied**	I, we, you, they **have been studied**
Perf.	he, she, it **has studied**	he, she, it **has been studied**
Past	I, he, she, it,	I, he, she, it,
Perf.	we, you, they **had studied**	we, you, they **had been studied**
Fut.	I, he, she, it, we, you, they	I, he, she, it, we, you, they
Perf.	**will have studied**	**will have been studied**

IMPERATIVE MOOD

study

be studied

SUBJUNCTIVE MOOD

Pres.	if I, he, she, it,	if I, he, she, it,
	we, you, they **study**	we, you, they **be studied**
Past	if I, he, she, it,	if I, he, she, it,
	we, you, they **studied**	we, you, they **were studied**
Fut.	if I, he, she, it,	if I, he, she, it,
	we, you, they **should study**	we, you, they **should be studied**

Transitive and intransitive.

suggest
(active voice)

be suggested
(passive voice)

Infinitive: **to suggest**
Perfect Infinitive: **to have suggested**
Present Participle: **suggesting**
Past Participle: **suggested**

Infinitive: **to be suggested**
Perfect Infinitive: **to have been suggested**
Present Participle: **being suggested**
Past Participle: **been suggested**

INDICATIVE MOOD

Pres.	I, we, you, they **suggest**	I **am suggested**
		we, you, they **are suggested**
	he, she, it **suggests**	he, she, it **is suggested**
Pres.	I **am suggesting**	I **am being suggested**
Prog.	we, you, they **are suggesting**	we, you, they **are being suggested**
	he, she, it **is suggesting**	he, she, it **is being suggested**
Pres.	I, we, you, they **do suggest**	I, we, you, they **do get suggested**
Int.	he, she, it **does suggest**	he, she, it **does get suggested**
Fut.	I, he, she, it,	I, he, she, it,
	we, you, they **will suggest**	we, you, they **will be suggested**
Past	I, he, she, it,	I, he, she, it **was suggested**
	we, you, they **suggested**	we, you, they **were suggested**
Past	I, he, she, it **was suggesting**	I, he, she, it **was being suggested**
Prog.	we, you, they **were suggesting**	we, you, they **were being suggested**
Past	I, he, she, it,	I, he, she, it,
Int.	we, you, they **did suggest**	we, you, they **did get suggested**
Pres.	I, we, you, they **have suggested**	I, we, you, they **have been suggested**
Perf.	he, she, it **has suggested**	he, she, it **has been suggested**
Past	I, he, she, it,	I, he, she, it,
Perf.	we, you, they **had suggested**	we, you, they **had been suggested**
Fut.	I, he, she, it, we, you, they	I, he, she, it, we, you, they
Perf.	**will have suggested**	**will have been suggested**

IMPERATIVE MOOD

suggest   **be suggested**

SUBJUNCTIVE MOOD

Pres.	if I, he, she, it,	if I, he, she, it,
	we, you, they **suggest**	we, you, they **be suggested**
Past	if I, he, she, it,	if I, he, she, it,
	we, you, they **suggested**	we, you, they **were suggested**
Fut.	if I, he, she, it,	if I, he, she, it,
	we, you, they **should suggest**	we, you, they **should be suggested**

426

support
(active voice)

PRINCIPAL PARTS: **supports, supporting, supported, supported**

be supported
(passive voice)

Infinitive: **to support**
Perfect Infinitive: **to have supported**
Present Participle: **supporting**
Past Participle: **supported**

Infinitive: **to be supported**
Perfect Infinitive: **to have been supported**
Present Participle: **being supported**
Past Participle: **been supported**

INDICATIVE MOOD

Pres.	I, we, you, they **support** he, she, it **supports**	I **am supported** we, you, they **are supported** he, she, it **is supported**
Pres. *Prog.*	I **am supporting** we, you, they **are supporting** he, she, it **is supporting**	I **am being supported** we, you, they **are being supported** he, she, it **is being supported**
Pres. *Int.*	I, we, you, they **do support** he, she, it **does support**	I, we, you, they **do get supported** he, she, it **does get supported**
Fut.	I, he, she, it, we, you, they **will support**	I, he, she, it, we, you, they **will be supported**
Past	I, he, she, it, we, you, they **supported**	I, he, she, it **was supported** we, you, they **were supported**
Past *Prog.*	I, he, she, it **was supporting** we, you, they **were supporting**	I, he, she, it **was being supported** we, you, they **were being supported**
Past *Int.*	I, he, she, it, we, you, they **did support**	I, he, she, it, we, you, they **did get supported**
Pres. *Perf.*	I, we, you, they **have supported** he, she, it **has supported**	I, we, you, they **have been supported** he, she, it **has been supported**
Past *Perf.*	I, he, she, it, we, you, they **had supported**	I, he, she, it, we, you, they **had been supported**
Fut. *Perf.*	I, he, she, it, we, you, they **will have supported**	I, he, she, it, we, you, they **will have been supported**

IMPERATIVE MOOD

support

be supported

SUBJUNCTIVE MOOD

Pres.	if I, he, she, it, we, you, they **support**	if I, he, she, it, we, you, they **be supported**
Past	if I, he, she, it, we, you, they **supported**	if I, he, she, it, we, you, they **were supported**
Fut.	if I, he, she, it, we, you, they **should support**	if I, he, she, it, we, you, they **should be supported**

suppose
(active voice)

be supposed
(passive voice)

Infinitive: **to suppose**
Perfect Infinitive: **to have supposed**
Present Participle: **supposing**
Past Participle: **supposed**

Infinitive: **to be supposed**
Perfect Infinitive: **to have been supposed**
Present Participle: **being supposed**
Past Participle: **been supposed**

INDICATIVE MOOD

Pres.	I, we, you, they **suppose**	I **am supposed**
		we, you, they **are supposed**
	he, she, it **supposes**	he, she, it **is supposed**
Pres.	I **am supposing**	I **am being supposed**
Prog.	we, you, they **are supposing**	we, you, they **are being supposed**
	he, she, it **is supposing**	he, she, it **is being supposed**
Pres.	I, we, you, they **do suppose**	I, we, you, they **do get supposed**
Int.	he, she, it **does suppose**	he, she, it **does get supposed**
Fut.	I, he, she, it,	I, he, she, it,
	we, you, they **will suppose**	we, you, they **will be supposed**
Past	I, he, she, it,	I, he, she, it **was supposed**
	we, you, they **supposed**	we, you, they **were supposed**
Past	I, he, she, it **was supposing**	I, he, she, it **was being supposed**
Prog.	we, you, they **were supposing**	we, you, they **were being supposed**
Past	I, he, she, it,	I, he, she, it,
Int.	we, you, they **did suppose**	we, you, they **did get supposed**
Pres.	I, we, you, they **have supposed**	I, we, you, they **have been supposed**
Perf.	he, she, it **has supposed**	he, she, it **has been supposed**
Past	I, he, she, it,	I, he, she, it,
Perf.	we, you, they **had supposed**	we, you, they **had been supposed**
Fut.	I, he, she, it, we, you, they	I, he, she, it, we, you, they
Perf.	**will have supposed**	**will have been supposed**

IMPERATIVE MOOD

suppose

be supposed

SUBJUNCTIVE MOOD

Pres.	if I, he, she, it,	if I, he, she, it,
	we, you, they **suppose**	we, you, they **be supposed**
Past	if I, he, she, it,	if I, he, she, it,
	we, you, they **supposed**	we, you, they **were supposed**
Fut.	if I, he, she, it,	if I, he, she, it,
	we, you, they **should suppose**	we, you, they **should be supposed**

Transitive and intransitive.

surprise
(active voice)

PRINCIPAL PARTS: **surprises, surprising, surprised, surprised**

be surprised
(passive voice)

Infinitive: **to surprise**
Perfect Infinitive: **to have surprised**
Present Participle: **surprising**
Past Participle: **surprised**

Infinitive: **to be surprised**
Perfect Infinitive: **to have been surprised**
Present Participle: **being surprised**
Past Participle: **been surprised**

INDICATIVE MOOD

Pres.	I, we, you, they **surprise** he, she, it **surprises**	I **am surprised** we, you, they **are surprised** he, she, it **is surprised**
Pres. *Prog.*	I **am surprising** we, you, they **are surprising** he, she, it **is surprising**	I **am being surprised** we, you, they **are being surprised** he, she, it **is being surprised**
Pres. *Int.*	I, we, you, they **do surprise** he, she, it **does surprise**	I, we, you, they **do get surprised** he, she, it **does get surprised**
Fut.	I, he, she, it, we, you, they **will surprise**	I, he, she, it, we, you, they **will be surprised**
Past	I, he, she, it, we, you, they **surprised**	I, he, she, it **was surprised** we, you, they **were surprised**
Past *Prog.*	I, he, she, it **was surprising** we, you, they **were surprising**	I, he, she, it **was being surprised** we, you, they **were being surprised**
Past *Int.*	I, he, she, it, we, you, they **did surprise**	I, he, she, it, we, you, they **did get surprised**
Pres. *Perf.*	I, we, you, they **have surprised** he, she, it **has surprised**	I, we, you, they **have been surprised** he, she, it **has been surprised**
Past *Perf.*	I, he, she, it, we, you, they **had surprised**	I, he, she, it, we, you, they **had been surprised**
Fut. *Perf.*	I, he, she, it, we, you, they **will have surprised**	I, he, she, it, we, you, they **will have been surprised**

IMPERATIVE MOOD

surprise	**be surprised**

SUBJUNCTIVE MOOD

Pres.	if I, he, she, it, we, you, they **surprise**	if I, he, she, it, we, you, they **be surprised**
Past	if I, he, she, it, we, you, they **surprised**	if I, he, she, it, we, you, they **were surprised**
Fut.	if I, he, she, it, we, you, they **should surprise**	if I, he, she, it, we, you, they **should be surprised**

swear
(active voice)

be sworn
(passive voice)

Infinitive: **to swear**
Perfect Infinitive: **to have sworn**
Present Participle: **swearing**
Past Participle: **sworn**

Infinitive: **to be sworn**
Perfect Infinitive: **to have been sworn**
Present Participle: **being sworn**
Past Participle: **been sworn**

INDICATIVE MOOD

Pres.	I, we, you, they **swear**	I **am sworn**	
		we, you, they **are sworn**	
	he, she, it **swears**	he, she, it **is sworn**	
Pres.	I **am swearing**	I **am being sworn**	
Prog.	we, you, they **are swearing**	we, you, they **are being sworn**	
	he, she, it **is swearing**	he, she, it **is being sworn**	
Pres.	I, we, you, they **do swear**	I, we, you, they **do get sworn**	
Int.	he, she, it **does swear**	he, she, it **does get sworn**	
Fut.	I, he, she, it,	I, he, she, it,	
	we, you, they **will swear**	we, you, they **will be sworn**	
Past	I, he, she, it,	I, he, she, it **was sworn**	
	we, you, they **swore**	we, you, they **were sworn**	
Past	I, he, she, it **was swearing**	I, he, she, it **was being sworn**	
Prog.	we, you, they **were swearing**	we, you, they **were being sworn**	
Past	I, he, she, it,	I, he, she, it,	
Int.	we, you, they **did swear**	we, you, they **did get sworn**	
Pres.	I, we, you, they **have sworn**	I, we, you, they **have been sworn**	
Perf.	he, she, it **has sworn**	he, she, it **has been sworn**	
Past	I, he, she, it,	I, he, she, it,	
Perf.	we, you, they **had sworn**	we, you, they **had been sworn**	
Fut.	I, he, she, it, we, you, they	I, he, she, it, we, you, they	
Perf.	**will have sworn**	**will have been sworn**	

IMPERATIVE MOOD

swear   **be sworn**

SUBJUNCTIVE MOOD

Pres.	if I, he, she, it,	if I, he, she, it,
	we, you, they **swear**	we, you, they **be sworn**
Past	if I, he, she, it,	if I, he, she, it,
	we, you, they **swore**	we, you, they **were sworn**
Fut.	if I, he, she, it,	if I, he, she, it,
	we, you, they **should swear**	we, you, they **should be sworn**

Intransitive and transitive.

sweat
(active voice)

be sweated/sweat
(passive voice)

Infinitive: **to sweat**
Perfect Infinitive: **to have sweated**
Present Participle: **sweating**
Past Participle: **sweated**

Infinitive: **to be sweated**
Perfect Infinitive: **to have been sweated**
Present Participle: **being sweated**
Past Participle: **been sweated**

INDICATIVE MOOD

Pres.	I, we, you, they **sweat**	I **am sweated**
		we, you, they **are sweated**
	he, she, it **sweats**	he, she, it **is sweated**
Pres.	I **am sweating**	I **am being sweated**
Prog.	we, you, they **are sweating**	we, you, they **are being sweated**
	he, she, it **is sweating**	he, she, it **is being sweated**
Pres.	I, we, you, they **do sweat**	I, we, you, they **do get sweated**
Int.	he, she, it **does sweat**	he, she, it **does get sweated**
Fut.	I, he, she, it,	I, he, she, it,
	we, you, they **will sweat**	we, you, they **will be sweated**
Past	I, he, she, it,	I, he, she, it **was sweated**
	we, you, they **sweated**	we, you, they **were sweated**
Past	I, he, she, it **was sweating**	I, he, she, it **was being sweated**
Prog.	we, you, they **were sweating**	we, you, they **were being sweated**
Past	I, he, she, it,	I, he, she, it,
Int.	we, you, they **did sweat**	we, you, they **did get sweated**
Pres.	I, we, you, they **have sweated**	I, we, you, they **have been sweated**
Perf.	he, she, it **has sweated**	he, she, it **has been sweated**
Past	I, he, she, it,	I, he, she, it,
Perf.	we, you, they **had sweated**	we, you, they **had been sweated**
Fut.	I, he, she, it, we, you, they	I, he, she, it, we, you, they
Perf.	**will have sweated**	**will have been sweated**

IMPERATIVE MOOD

sweat be sweated

SUBJUNCTIVE MOOD

Pres.	if I, he, she, it,	if I, he, she, it,
	we, you, they **sweat**	we, you, they **be sweated**
Past	if I, he, she, it,	if I, he, she, it,
	we, you, they **sweated**	we, you, they **were sweated**
Fut.	if I, he, she, it,	if I, he, she, it,
	we, you, they **should sweat**	we, you, they **should be sweated**

Intransitive or transitive. The *Oxford Dictionary* classifies as an Americanism the past tense and past participle SWEAT.

sweep
(active voice)

be swept
(passive voice)

Infinitive: **to sweep**
Perfect Infinitive: **to have swept**
Present Participle: **sweeping**
Past Participle: **swept**

Infinitive: **to be swept**
Perfect Infinitive: **to have been swept**
Present Participle: **being swept**
Past Participle: **been swept**

INDICATIVE MOOD

Pres.	I, we, you, they **sweep**	I **am swept**
		we, you, they **are swept**
	he, she, it **sweeps**	he, she, it **is swept**
Pres. *Prog.*	I **am sweeping** we, you, they **are sweeping** he, she, it **is sweeping**	I **am being swept** we, you, they **are being swept** he, she, it **is being swept**
Pres. *Int.*	I, we, you, they **do sweep** he, she, it **does sweep**	I, we, you, they **do get swept** he, she, it **does get swept**
Fut.	I, he, she, it, we, you, they **will sweep**	I, he, she, it, we, you, they **will be swept**
Past	I, he, she, it, we, you, they **swept**	I, he, she, it **was swept** we, you, they **were swept**
Past *Prog.*	I, he, she, it **was sweeping** we, you, they **were sweeping**	I, he, she, it **was being swept** we, you, they **were being swept**
Past *Int.*	I, he, she, it, we, you, they **did sweep**	I, he, she, it, we, you, they **did get swept**
Pres. *Perf.*	I, we, you, they **have swept** he, she, it **has swept**	I, we, you, they **have been swept** he, she, it **has been swept**
Past *Perf.*	I, he, she, it, we, you, they **had swept**	I, he, she, it, we, you, they **had been swept**
Fut. *Perf.*	I, he, she, it, we, you, they **will have swept**	I, he, she, it, we, you, they **will have been swept**

IMPERATIVE MOOD

sweep   **be swept**

SUBJUNCTIVE MOOD

Pres.	if I, he, she, it, we, you, they **sweep**	if I, he, she, it, we, you, they **be swept**
Past	if I, he, she, it, we, you, they **swept**	if I, he, she, it, we, you, they **were swept**
Fut.	if I, he, she, it, we, you, they **should sweep**	if I, he, she, it, we, you, they **should be swept**

Transitive and intransitive.

swell
(active voice)

PRINCIPAL PARTS: **swells, swelling, swelled, swelled/swollen**

be swelled/swollen
(passive voice)

Infinitive: **to swell**
Perfect Infinitive: **to have swelled**
Present Participle: **swelling**
Past Participle: **swelled**

Infinitive: **to be swelled**
Perfect Infinitive: **to have been swelled**
Present Participle: **being swelled**
Past Participle: **been swelled**

INDICATIVE MOOD

Pres.	I, we, you, they **swell**	I **am swelled**
		we, you, they **are swelled**
	he, she, it **swells**	he, she, it **is swelled**
Pres.	I **am swelling**	I **am being swelled**
Prog.	we, you, they **are swelling**	we, you, they **are being swelled**
	he, she, it **is swelling**	he, she, it **is being swelled**
Pres.	I, we, you, they **do swell**	I, we, you, they **do get swelled**
Int.	he, she, it **does swell**	he, she, it **does get swelled**
Fut.	I, he, she, it,	I, he, she, it,
	we, you, they **will swell**	we, you, they **will be swelled**
Past	I, he, she, it,	I, he, she, it **was swelled**
	we, you, they **swelled**	we, you, they **were swelled**
Past	I, he, she, it **was swelling**	I, he, she, it **was being swelled**
Prog.	we, you, they **were swelling**	we, you, they **were being swelled**
Past	I, he, she, it,	I, he, she, it,
Int.	we, you, they **did swell**	we, you, they **did get swelled**
Pres.	I, we, you, they **have swelled**	I, we, you, they **have been swelled**
Perf.	he, she, it **has swelled**	he, she, it **has been swelled**
Past	I, he, she, it,	I, he, she, it,
Perf.	we, you, they **had swelled**	we, you, they **had been swelled**
Fut.	I, he, she, it, we, you, they	I, he, she, it, we, you, they
Perf.	**will have swelled**	**will have been swelled**

IMPERATIVE MOOD

swell

be swelled

SUBJUNCTIVE MOOD

Pres.	if I, he, she, it,	if I, he, she, it,
	we, you, they **swell**	we, you, they **be swelled**
Past	if I, he, she, it,	if I, he, she, it,
	we, you, they **swelled**	we, you, they **were swelled**
Fut.	if I, he, she, it,	if I, he, she, it,
	we, you, they **should swell**	we, you, they **should be swelled**

Intransitive and transitive. The *Oxford Dictionary* prefers the past participle SWOLLEN.

swim
(active voice)

be swum
(passive voice)

Infinitive: **to swim**
Perfect Infinitive: **to have swum**
Present Participle: **swimming**
Past Participle: **swum**

Infinitive: **to be swum**
Perfect Infinitive: **to have been swum**
Present Participle: **being swum**
Past Participle: **been swum**

INDICATIVE MOOD

Pres.	I, we, you, they **swim** he, she, it **swims**	I **am swum** we, you, they **are swum** he, she, it **is swum**	
Pres. *Prog.*	I **am swimming** we, you, they **are swimming** he, she, it **is swimming**	I **am being swum** we, you, they **are being swum** he, she, it **is being swum**	
Pres. *Int.*	I, we, you, they **do swim** he, she, it **does swim**	I, we, you, they **do get swum** he, she, it **does get swum**	
Fut.	I, he, she, it, we, you, they **will swim**	I, he, she, it, we, you, they **will be swum**	
Past	I, he, she, it, we, you, they **swam**	I, he, she, it **was swum** we, you, they **were swum**	
Past *Prog.*	I, he, she, it **was swimming** we, you, they **were swimming**	I, he, she, it **was being swum** we, you, they **were being swum**	
Past *Int.*	I, he, she, it, we, you, they **did swim**	I, he, she, it, we, you, they **did get swum**	
Pres. *Perf.*	I, we, you, they **have swum** he, she, it **has swum**	I, we, you, they **have been swum** he, she, it **has been swum**	
Past *Perf.*	I, he, she, it, we, you, they **had swum**	I, he, she, it, we, you, they **had been swum**	
Fut. *Perf.*	I, he, she, it, we, you, they **will have swum**	I, he, she, it, we, you, they **will have been swum**	

IMPERATIVE MOOD

swim

be swum

SUBJUNCTIVE MOOD

Pres.	if I, he, she, it, we, you, they **swim**	if I, he, she, it, we, you, they **be swum**
Past	if I, he, she, it, we, you, they **swam**	if I, he, she, it, we, you, they **were swum**
Fut.	if I, he, she, it, we, you, they **should swim**	if I, he, she, it, we, you, they **should be swum**

Intransitive and transitive.

swing
(active voice)

PRINCIPAL PARTS: **swings, swinging, swung, swung**

be swung
(passive voice)

Infinitive: **to swing**
Perfect Infinitive: **to have swung**
Present Participle: **swinging**
Past Participle: **swung**

Infinitive: **to be swung**
Perfect Infinitive: **to have been swung**
Present Participle: **being swung**
Past Participle: **been swung**

INDICATIVE MOOD

Pres.	I, we, you, they **swing**	I **am swung**
		we, you, they **are swung**
	he, she, it **swings**	he, she, it **is swung**
Pres. *Prog.*	I **am swinging**	I **am being swung**
	we, you, they **are swinging**	we, you, they **are being swung**
	he, she, it **is swinging**	he, she, it **is being swung**
Pres. *Int.*	I, we, you, they **do swing**	I, we, you, they **do get swung**
	he, she, it **does swing**	he, she, it **does get swung**
Fut.	I, he, she, it, we, you, they **will swing**	I, he, she, it, we, you, they **will be swung**
Past	I, he, she, it, we, you, they **swung**	I, he, she, it **was swung** we, you, they **were swung**
Past *Prog.*	I, he, she, it **was swinging** we, you, they **were swinging**	I, he, she, it **was being swung** we, you, they **were being swung**
Past *Int.*	I, he, she, it, we, you, they **did swing**	I, he, she, it, we, you, they **did get swung**
Pres. *Perf.*	I, we, you, they **have swung** he, she, it **has swung**	I, we, you, they **have been swung** he, she, it **has been swung**
Past *Perf.*	I, he, she, it, we, you, they **had swung**	I, he, she, it, we, you, they **had been swung**
Fut. *Perf.*	I, he, she, it, we, you, they **will have swung**	I, he, she, it, we, you, they **will have been swung**

IMPERATIVE MOOD

swing   **be swung**

SUBJUNCTIVE MOOD

Pres.	if I, he, she, it, we, you, they **swing**	if I, he, she, it, we, you, they **be swung**
Past	if I, he, she, it, we, you, they **swung**	if I, he, she, it, we, you, they **were swung**
Fut.	if I, he, she, it, we, you, they **should swing**	if I, he, she, it, we, you, they **should be swung**

Intransitive and transitive.

take (active voice)	Principal Parts: **takes, taking, took, taken**	**be taken** (passive voice)

Infinitive: **to take**
Perfect Infinitive: **to have taken**
Present Participle: **taking**
Past Participle: **taken**

Infinitive: **to be taken**
Perfect Infinitive: **to have been taken**
Present Participle: **being taken**
Past Participle: **been taken**

INDICATIVE MOOD

	Active	Passive
Pres.	I, we, you, they **take** he, she, it **takes**	I **am taken** we, you, they **are taken** he, she, it **is taken**
Pres. Prog.	I **am taking** we, you, they **are taking** he, she, it **is taking**	I **am being taken** we, you, they **are being taken** he, she, it **is being taken**
Pres. Int.	I, we, you, they **do take** he, she, it **does take**	I, we, you, they **do get taken** he, she, it **does get taken**
Fut.	I, he, she, it, we, you, they **will take**	I, he, she, it, we, you, they **will be taken**
Past	I, he, she, it, we, you, they **took**	I, he, she, it **was taken** we, you, they **were taken**
Past Prog.	I, he, she, it **was taking** we, you, they **were taking**	I, he, she, it **was being taken** we, you, they **were being taken**
Past Int.	I, he, she, it, we, you, they **did take**	I, he, she, it, we, you, they **did get taken**
Pres. Perf.	I, we, you, they **have taken** he, she, it **has taken**	I, we, you, they **have been taken** he, she, it **has been taken**
Past Perf.	I, he, she, it, we, you, they **had taken**	I, he, she, it, we, you, they **had been taken**
Fut. Perf.	I, he, she, it, we, you, they **will have taken**	I, he, she, it, we, you, they **will have been taken**

IMPERATIVE MOOD

take
be taken

SUBJUNCTIVE MOOD

	Active	Passive
Pres.	if I, he, she, it, we, you, they **take**	if I, he, she, it, we, you, they **be taken**
Past	if I, he, she, it, we, you, they **took**	if I, he, she, it, we, you, they **were taken**
Fut.	if I, he, she, it, we, you, they **should take**	if I, he, she, it, we, you, they **should be taken**

Transitive and intransitive.

436

talk
(active voice)

be talked
(passive voice)

Infinitive: **to talk**
Perfect Infinitive: **to have talked**
Present Participle: **talking**
Past Participle: **talked**

Infinitive: **to be talked**
Perfect Infinitive: **to have been talked**
Present Participle: **being talked**
Past Participle: **been talked**

INDICATIVE MOOD

Pres.	I, we, you, they **talk**	I **am talked**
		we, you, they **are talked**
	he, she, it **talks**	he, she, it **is talked**
Pres.	I **am talking**	I **am being talked**
Prog.	we, you, they **are talking**	we, you, they **are being talked**
	he, she, it **is talking**	he, she, it **is being talked**
Pres.	I, we, you, they **do talk**	I, we, you, they **do get talked**
Int.	he, she, it **does talk**	he, she, it **does get talked**
Fut.	I, he, she, it,	I, he, she, it,
	we, you, they **will talk**	we, you, they **will be talked**
Past	I, he, she, it,	I, he, she, it **was talked**
	we, you, they **talked**	we, you, they **were talked**
Past	I, he, she, it **was talking**	I, he, she, it **was being talked**
Prog.	we, you, they **were talking**	we, you, they **were being talked**
Past	I, he, she, it,	I, he, she, it,
Int.	we, you, they **did talk**	we, you, they **did get talked**
Pres.	I, we, you, they **have talked**	I, we, you, they **have been talked**
Perf.	he, she, it **has talked**	he, she, it **has been talked**
Past	I, he, she, it,	I, he, she, it,
Perf.	we, you, they **had talked**	we, you, they **had been talked**
Fut.	I, he, she, it, we, you, they	I, he, she, it, we, you, they
Perf.	**will have talked**	**will have been talked**

IMPERATIVE MOOD

talk　　　　　　　　　　**be talked**

SUBJUNCTIVE MOOD

Pres.	if I, he, she, it,	if I, he, she, it,
	we, you, they **talk**	we, you, they **be talked**
Past	if I, he, she, it,	if I, he, she, it,
	we, you, they **talked**	we, you, they **were talked**
Fut.	if I, he, she, it,	if I, he, she, it,
	we, you, they **should talk**	we, you, they **should be talked**

Transitive and intransitive.

taxi
(active voice)

be taxied
(passive voice)

Infinitive: **to taxi**
Perfect Infinitive: **to have taxied**
Present Participle: **taxiing**
Past Participle: **taxied**

Infinitive: **to be taxied**
Perfect Infinitive: **to have been taxied**
Present Participle: **being taxied**
Past Participle: **been taxied**

INDICATIVE MOOD

Pres.	I, we, you, they **taxi**	I **am taxied**
		we, you, they **are taxied**
	he, she, it **taxis**	he, she, it **is taxied**
Pres.	I **am taxiing**	I **am being taxied**
Prog.	we, you, they **are taxiing**	we, you, they **are being taxied**
	he, she, it **is taxiing**	he, she, it **is being taxied**
Pres.	I, we, you, they **do taxi**	I, we, you, they **do get taxied**
Int.	he, she, it **does taxi**	he, she, it **does get taxied**
Fut.	I, he, she, it,	I, he, she, it,
	we, you, they **will taxi**	we, you, they **will be taxied**
Past	I, he, she, it,	I, he, she, it **was taxied**
	we, you, they **taxied**	we, you, they **were taxied**
Past	I, he, she, it **was taxiing**	I, he, she, it **was being taxied**
Prog.	we, you, they **were taxiing**	we, you, they **were being taxied**
Past	I, he, she, it,	I, he, she, it,
Int.	we, you, they **did taxi**	we, you, they **did get taxied**
Pres.	I, we, you, they **have taxied**	I, we, you, they **have been taxied**
Perf.	he, she, it **has taxied**	he, she, it **has been taxied**
Past	I, he, she, it,	I, he, she, it,
Perf.	we, you, they **had taxied**	we, you, they **had been taxied**
Fut.	I, he, she, it, we, you, they	I, he, she, it, we, you, they
Perf.	**will have taxied**	**will have been taxied**

IMPERATIVE MOOD

taxi **be taxied**

SUBJUNCTIVE MOOD

Pres.	if I, he, she, it,	if I, he, she, it,
	we, you, they **taxi**	we, you, they **be taxied**
Past	if I, he, she, it,	if I, he, she, it,
	we, you, they **taxied**	we, you, they **were taxied**
Fut.	if I, he, she, it,	if I, he, she, it,
	we, you, they **should taxi**	we, you, they **should be taxied**

Intransitive and transitive.

teach
(active voice)

PRINCIPAL PARTS: **teaches, teaching, taught, taught**

be taught
(passive voice)

Infinitive: **to teach**
Perfect Infinitive: **to have taught**
Present Participle: **teaching**
Past Participle: **taught**

Infinitive: **to be taught**
Perfect Infinitive: **to have been taught**
Present Participle: **being taught**
Past Participle: **been taught**

INDICATIVE MOOD

Pres.	I, we, you, they **teach**	I **am taught** we, you, they **are taught**
	he, she, it **teaches**	he, she, it **is taught**
Pres. *Prog.*	I **am teaching** we, you, they **are teaching** he, she, it **is teaching**	I **am being taught** we, you, they **are being taught** he, she, it **is being taught**
Pres. *Int.*	I, we, you, they **do teach** he, she, it **does teach**	I, we, you, they **do get taught** he, she, it **does get taught**
Fut.	I, he, she, it, we, you, they **will teach**	I, he, she, it, we, you, they **will be taught**
Past	I, he, she, it, we, you, they **taught**	I, he, she, it **was taught** we, you, they **were taught**
Past *Prog.*	I, he, she, it **was teaching** we, you, they **were teaching**	I, he, she, it **was being taught** we, you, they **were being taught**
Past *Int.*	I, he, she, it, we, you, they **did teach**	I, he, she, it, we, you, they **did get taught**
Pres. *Perf.*	I, we, you, they **have taught** he, she, it **has taught**	I, we, you, they **have been taught** he, she, it **has been taught**
Past *Perf.*	I, he, she, it, we, you, they **had taught**	I, he, she, it, we, you, they **had been taught**
Fut. *Perf.*	I, he, she, it, we, you, they **will have taught**	I, he, she, it, we, you, they **will have been taught**

IMPERATIVE MOOD

teach   **be taught**

SUBJUNCTIVE MOOD

Pres.	if I, he, she, it, we, you, they **teach**	if I, he, she, it, we, you, they **be taught**
Past	if I, he, she, it, we, you, they **taught**	if I, he, she, it, we, you, they **were taught**
Fut.	if I, he, she, it, we, you, they **should teach**	if I, he, she, it, we, you, they **should be taught**

Transitive and intransitive.

tear	PRINCIPAL PARTS: **tears, tearing,**	be torn
(active voice)	**tore, torn**	(passive voice)

Infinitive: **to tear**　　　　　　　　　　*Infinitive:* **to be torn**
Perfect Infinitive: **to have torn**　　　　*Perfect Infinitive:* **to have been torn**
Present Participle: **tearing**　　　　　　*Present Participle:* **being torn**
Past Participle: **torn**　　　　　　　　　*Past Participle:* **been torn**

INDICATIVE MOOD

Pres.	I, we, you, they **tear**	I **am torn**
		we, you, they **are torn**
	he, she, it **tears**	he, she, it **is torn**
Pres.	I **am tearing**	I **am being torn**
Prog.	we, you, they **are tearing**	we, you, they **are being torn**
	he, she, it **is tearing**	he, she, it **is being torn**
Pres.	I, we, you, they **do tear**	I, we, you, they **do get torn**
Int.	he, she, it **does tear**	he, she, it **does get torn**
Fut.	I, he, she, it,	I, he, she, it,
	we, you, they **will tear**	we, you, they **will be torn**
Past	I, he, she, it,	I, he, she, it **was torn**
	we, you, they **tore**	we, you, they **were torn**
Past	I, he, she, it **was tearing**	I, he, she, it **was being torn**
Prog.	we, you, they **were tearing**	we, you, they **were being torn**
Past	I, he, she, it,	I, he, she, it,
Int.	we, you, they **did tear**	we, you, they **did get torn**
Pres.	I, we, you, they **have torn**	I, we, you, they **have been torn**
Perf.	he, she, it **has torn**	he, she, it **has been torn**
Past	I, he, she, it,	I, he, she, it,
Perf.	we, you, they **had torn**	we, you, they **had been torn**
Fut.	I, he, she, it, we, you, they	I, he, she, it, we, you, they
Perf.	**will have torn**	**will have been torn**

IMPERATIVE MOOD

　　　　tear　　　　　　　　　　**be torn**

SUBJUNCTIVE MOOD

Pres.	if I, he, she, it,	if I, he, she, it,
	we, you, they **tear**	we, you, they **be torn**
Past	if I, he, she, it,	if I, he, she, it,
	we, you, they **tore**	we, you, they **were torn**
Fut.	if I, he, she, it,	if I, he, she, it,
	we, you, they **should tear**	we, you, they **should be torn**

Transitive and intransitive. The verb TEAR meaning to "fill with tears" is intransitive and has the past tense and past participle form TEARED.

tell
(active voice)

PRINCIPAL PARTS: **tells, telling, told, told**

be told
(passive voice)

Infinitive: **to tell**
Perfect Infinitive: **to have told**
Present Participle: **telling**
Past Participle: **told**

Infinitive: **to be told**
Perfect Infinitive: **to have been told**
Present Participle: **being told**
Past Participle: **been told**

INDICATIVE MOOD

Pres.	I, we, you, they **tell**	I **am told**
		we, you, they **are told**
	he, she, it **tells**	he, she, it **is told**
Pres. *Prog.*	I **am telling**	I **am being told**
	we, you, they **are telling**	we, you, they **are being told**
	he, she, it **is telling**	he, she, it **is being told**
Pres. *Int.*	I, we, you, they **do tell**	I, we, you, they **do get told**
	he, she, it **does tell**	he, she, it **does get told**
Fut.	I, he, she, it, we, you, they **will tell**	I, he, she, it, we, you, they **will be told**
Past	I, he, she, it, we, you, they **told**	I, he, she, it **was told** we, you, they **were told**
Past *Prog.*	I, he, she, it **was telling** we, you, they **were telling**	I, he, she, it **was being told** we, you, they **were being told**
Past *Int.*	I, he, she, it, we, you, they **did tell**	I, he, she, it, we, you, they **did get told**
Pres. *Perf.*	I, we, you, they **have told** he, she, it **has told**	I, we, you, they **have been told** he, she, it **has been told**
Past *Perf.*	I, he, she, it, we, you, they **had told**	I, he, she, it, we, you, they **had been told**
Fut. *Perf.*	I, he, she, it, we, you, they **will have told**	I, he, she, it, we, you, they **will have been told**

IMPERATIVE MOOD

tell   **be told**

SUBJUNCTIVE MOOD

Pres.	if I, he, she, it, we, you, they **tell**	if I, he, she, it, we, you, they **be told**
Past	if I, he, she, it, we, you, they **told**	if I, he, she, it, we, you, they **were told**
Fut.	if I, he, she, it, we, you, they **should tell**	if I, he, she, it, we, you, they **should be told**

Transitive and intransitive.

think
(active voice)

be thought
(passive voice)

Infinitive: **to think**
Perfect Infinitive: **to have thought**
Present Participle: **thinking**
Past Participle: **thought**

Infinitive: **to be thought**
Perfect Infinitive: **to have been thought**
Present Participle: **being thought**
Past Participle: **been thought**

INDICATIVE MOOD

Pres.	I, we, you, they **think**	I **am thought**
		we, you, they **are thought**
	he, she, it **thinks**	he, she, it **is thought**
Pres. *Prog.*	I **am thinking** we, you, they **are thinking** he, she, it **is thinking**	I **am being thought** we, you, they **are being thought** he, she, it **is being thought**
Pres. *Int.*	I, we, you, they **do think** he, she, it **does think**	I, we, you, they **do get thought** he, she, it **does get thought**
Fut.	I, he, she, it, we, you, they **will think**	I, he, she, it, we, you, they **will be thought**
Past	I, he, she, it, we, you, they **thought**	I, he, she, it **was thought** we, you, they **were thought**
Past *Prog.*	I, he, she, it **was thinking** we, you, they **were thinking**	I, he, she, it **was being thought** we, you, they **were being thought**
Past *Int.*	I, he, she, it, we, you, they **did think**	I, he, she, it, we, you, they **did get thought**
Pres. *Perf.*	I, we, you, they **have thought** he, she, it **has thought**	I, we, you, they **have been thought** he, she, it **has been thought**
Past *Perf.*	I, he, she, it, we, you, they **had thought**	I, he, she, it, we, you, they **had been thought**
Fut. *Perf.*	I, he, she, it, we, you, they **will have thought**	I, he, she, it, we, you, they **will have been thought**

IMPERATIVE MOOD

think

be thought

SUBJUNCTIVE MOOD

Pres.	if I, he, she, it, we, you, they **think**	if I, he, she, it, we, you, they **be thought**
Past	if I, he, she, it, we, you, they **thought**	if I, he, she, it, we, you, they **were thought**
Fut.	if I, he, she, it, we, you, they **should think**	if I, he, she, it, we, you, they **should be thought**

Transitive and intransitive.

thread
(active voice)

be threaded
(passive voice)

Infinitive: **to thread**
Perfect Infinitive: **to have threaded**
Present Participle: **threading**
Past Participle: **threaded**

Infinitive: **to be threaded**
Perfect Infinitive: **to have been threaded**
Present Participle: **being threaded**
Past Participle: **been threaded**

INDICATIVE MOOD

Pres.	I, we, you, they **thread**	I **am threaded**
		we, you, they **are threaded**
	he, she, it **threads**	he, she, it **is threaded**
Pres.	I **am threading**	I **am being threaded**
Prog.	we, you, they **are threading**	we, you, they **are being threaded**
	he, she, it **is threading**	he, she, it **is being threaded**
Pres.	I, we, you, they **do thread**	I, we, you, they **do get threaded**
Int.	he, she, it **does thread**	he, she, it **does get threaded**
Fut.	I, he, she, it,	I, he, she, it,
	we, you, they **will thread**	we, you, they **will be threaded**
Past	I, he, she, it,	I, he, she, it **was threaded**
	we, you, they **threaded**	we, you, they **were threaded**
Past	I, he, she, it **was threading**	I, he, she, it **was being threaded**
Prog.	we, you, they **were threading**	we, you, they **were being threaded**
Past	I, he, she, it,	I, he, she, it,
Int.	we, you, they **did thread**	we, you, they **did get threaded**
Pres.	I, we, you, they **have threaded**	I, we, you, they **have been threaded**
Perf.	he, she, it **has threaded**	he, she, it **has been threaded**
Past	I, he, she, it,	I, he, she, it,
Perf.	we, you, they **had threaded**	we, you, they **had been threaded**
Fut.	I, he, she, it, we, you, they	I, he, she, it, we, you, they
Perf.	**will have threaded**	**will have been threaded**

IMPERATIVE MOOD

thread   **be threaded**

SUBJUNCTIVE MOOD

Pres.	if I, he, she, it,	if I, he, she, it,
	we, you, they **thread**	we, you, they **be threaded**
Past	if I, he, she, it,	if I, he, she, it,
	we, you, they **threaded**	we, you, they **were threaded**
Fut.	if I, he, she, it,	if I, he, she, it,
	we, you, they **should thread**	we, you, they **should be threaded**

Transitive and intransitive.

Infinitive: **to thrive**
Perfect Infinitive: **to have thrived**
Present Participle: **thriving**
Past Participle: **thrived**

INDICATIVE MOOD

Pres. I, we, you, they **thrive**
he, she, it **thrives**

Pres. **I am thriving**
Prog. we, you, they **are thriving**
he, she, it **is thriving**

Pres. I, we, you, they **do thrive**
Int. he, she, it **does thrive**

Fut. I, he, she, it,
we, you, they **will thrive**

Past I, he, she, it,
we, you, they **thrived**

Past I, he, she, it **was thriving**
Prog. we, you, they **were thriving**

Past I, he, she, it,
Int. we, you, they **did thrive**

Pres. I, we, you, they **have thrived**
Perf. he, she, it **has thrived**

Past I, he, she, it,
Perf. we, you, they **had thrived**

Fut. I, he, she, it, we, you, they
Perf. **will have thrived**

IMPERATIVE MOOD

thrive

SUBJUNCTIVE MOOD

Pres. if I, he, she, it,
we, you, they **thrive**

Past if I, he, she, it,
we, you, they **thrived**

Fut. if I, he, she, it,
we, you, they **should thrive**

Intransitive verb. The *Oxford Dictionary* prefers THROVE for the past tense and THRIVEN for the past participle.

throw
(active voice)

be thrown
(passive voice)

Infinitive: **to throw**
Perfect Infinitive: **to have thrown**
Present Participle: **throwing**
Past Participle: **thrown**

Infinitive: **to be thrown**
Perfect Infinitive: **to have been thrown**
Present Participle: **being thrown**
Past Participle: **been thrown**

INDICATIVE MOOD

Pres.   I, we, you, they **throw**

he, she, it **throws**

I **am thrown**
we, you, they **are thrown**
he, she, it **is thrown**

Pres.
Prog.
I **am throwing**
we, you, they **are throwing**
he, she, it **is throwing**

I **am being thrown**
we, you, they **are being thrown**
he, she, it **is being thrown**

Pres.
Int.
I, we, you, they **do throw**
he, she, it **does throw**

I, we, you, they **do get thrown**
he, she, it **does get thrown**

Fut.   I, he, she, it,
we, you, they **will throw**

I, he, she, it,
we, you, they **will be thrown**

Past   I, he, she, it
we, you, they **threw**

I, he, she, it **was thrown**
we, you, they **were thrown**

Past
Prog.
I, he, she, it **was throwing**
we, you, they **were throwing**

I, he, she, it **was being thrown**
we, you, they **were being thrown**

Past
Int.
I, he, she, it,
we, you, they **did throw**

I, he, she, it,
we, you, they **did get thrown**

Pres.
Perf.
I, we, you, they **have thrown**
he, she, it **has thrown**

I, we, you, they **have been thrown**
he, she, it **has been thrown**

Past
Perf.
I, he, she, it,
we, you, they **had thrown**

I, he, she, it,
we, you, they **had been thrown**

Fut.
Perf.
I, he, she, it, we, you, they
will have thrown

I, he, she, it, we, you, they
will have been thrown

IMPERATIVE MOOD

throw   **be thrown**

SUBJUNCTIVE MOOD

Pres.   if I, he, she, it,
we, you, they **throw**

if I, he, she, it,
we, you, they **be thrown**

Past   if I, he, she, it,
we, you, they **threw**

if I, he, she, it,
we, you, they **were thrown**

Fut.   if I, he, she, it,
we, you, they **should throw**

if I, he, she, it,
we, you, they **should be thrown**

Transitive and intransitive.

thrust
(active voice)

PRINCIPAL PARTS: **thrusts, thrusting, thrust, thrust**

be thrust
(passive voice)

Infinitive: **to thrust**
Perfect Infinitive: **to have thrust**
Present Participle: **thrusting**
Past Participle: **thrust**

Infinitive: **to be thrust**
Perfect Infinitive: **to have been thrust**
Present Participle: **being thrust**
Past Participle: **been thrust**

INDICATIVE MOOD

Pres.	I, we, you, they **thrust**	I **am thrust**
		we, you, they **are thrust**
	he, she, it **thrusts**	he, she, it **is thrust**
Pres.	I **am thrusting**	I **am being thrust**
Prog.	we, you, they **are thrusting**	we, you, they **are being thrust**
	he, she, it **is thrusting**	he, she, it **is being thrust**
Pres.	I, we, you, they **do thrust**	I, we, you, they **do get thrust**
Int.	he, she, it **does thrust**	he, she, it **does get thrust**
Fut.	I, he, she, it,	I, he, she, it,
	we, you, they **will thrust**	we, you, they **will be thrust**
Past	I, he, she, it,	I, he, she, it **was thrust**
	we, you, they **thrust**	we, you, they **were thrust**
Past	I, he, she, it **was thrusting**	I, he, she, it **was being thrust**
Prog.	we, you, they **were thrusting**	we, you, they **were being thrust**
Past	I, he, she, it,	I, he, she, it,
Int.	we, you, they **did thrust**	we, you, they **did get thrust**
Pres.	I, we, you, they **have thrust**	I, we, you, they **have been thrust**
Perf.	he, she, it **has thrust**	he, she, it **has been thrust**
Past	I, he, she, it,	I, he, she, it,
Perf.	we, you, they **had thrust**	we, you, they **had been thrust**
Fut.	I, he, she, it, we, you, they	I, he, she, it, we, you, they
Perf.	**will have thrust**	**will have been thrust**

IMPERATIVE MOOD

thrust

be thrust

SUBJUNCTIVE MOOD

Pres.	if I, he, she, it,	if I, he, she, it,
	we, you, they **thrust**	we, you, they **be thrust**
Past	if I, he, she, it,	if I, he, she, it,
	we, you, they **thrust**	we, you, they **were thrust**
Fut.	if I, he, she, it,	if I, he, she, it,
	we, you, they **should thrust**	we, you, they **should be thrust**

Transitive and intransitive.

tie
(active voice)

PRINCIPAL PARTS: **ties, tying, tied, tied**

be tied
(passive voice)

Infinitive: **to tie**
Perfect Infinitive: **to have tied**
Present Participle: **tying**
Past Participle: **tied**

Infinitive: **to be tied**
Perfect Infinitive: **to have been tied**
Present Participle: **being tied**
Past Participle: **been tied**

INDICATIVE MOOD

Pres.	I, we, you, they **tie** he, she, it **ties**	I **am tied** we, you, they **are tied** he, she, it **is tied**
Pres. *Prog.*	I **am tying** we, you, they **are tying** he, she, it **is tying**	I **am being tied** we, you, they **are being tied** he, she, it **is being tied**
Pres. *Int.*	I, we, you, they **do tie** he, she, it **does tie**	I, we, you, they **do get tied** he, she, it **does get tied**
Fut.	I, he, she, it, we, you, they **will tie**	I, he, she, it, we, you, they **will be tied**
Past	I, he, she, it, we, you, they **tied**	I, he, she, it **was tied** we, you, they **were tied**
Past *Prog.*	I, he, she, it **was tying** we, you, they **were tying**	I, he, she, it **was being tied** we, you, they **were being tied**
Past *Int.*	I, he, she, it, we, you, they **did tie**	I, he, she, it, we, you, they **did get tied**
Pres. *Perf.*	I, we, you, they **have tied** he, she, it **has tied**	I, we, you, they **have been tied** he, she, it **has been tied**
Past *Perf.*	I, he, she, it, we, you, they **had tied**	I, he, she, it, we, you, they **had been tied**
Fut. *Perf.*	I, he, she, it, we, you, they **will have tied**	I, he, she, it, we, you, they **will have been tied**

IMPERATIVE MOOD

tie   **be tied**

SUBJUNCTIVE MOOD

Pres.	if I, he, she, it, we, you, they **tie**	if I, he, she, it, we, you, they **be tied**
Past	if I, he, she, it, we, you, they **tied**	if I, he, she, it, we, you, they **were tied**
Fut.	if I, he, she, it, we, you, they **should tie**	if I, he, she, it, we, you, they **should be tied**

Transitive and intransitive.

train
(active voice)

be trained
(passive voice)

Infinitive: **to train**
Perfect Infinitive: **to have trained**
Present Participle: **training**
Past Participle: **trained**

Infinitive: **to be trained**
Perfect Infinitive: **to have been trained**
Present Participle: **being trained**
Past Participle: **been trained**

INDICATIVE MOOD

Pres.	I, we, you, they **train**	I **am trained**
		we, you, they **are trained**
	he, she, it **trains**	he, she, it **is trained**
Pres.	I **am training**	I **am being trained**
Prog.	we, you, they **are training**	we, you, they **are being trained**
	he, she, it **is training**	he, she, it **is being trained**
Pres.	I, we, you, they **do train**	I, we, you, they **do get trained**
Int.	he, she, it **does train**	he, she, it **does get trained**
Fut.	I, he, she, it,	I, he, she, it,
	we, you, they **will train**	we, you, they **will be trained**
Past	I, he, she, it,	I, he, she, it **was trained**
	we, you, they **trained**	we, you, they **were trained**
Past	I, he, she, it **was training**	I, he, she, it **was being trained**
Prog.	we, you, they **were training**	we, you, they **were being trained**
Past	I, he, she, it,	I, he, she, it,
Int.	we, you, they **did train**	we, you, they **did get trained**
Pres.	I, we, you, they **have trained**	I, we, you, they **have been trained**
Perf.	he, she, it **has trained**	he, she, it **has been trained**
Past	I, he, she, it,	I, he, she, it,
Perf.	we, you, they **had trained**	we, you, they **had been trained**
Fut.	I, he, she, it, we, you, they	I, he, she, it, we, you, they
Perf.	**will have trained**	**will have been trained**

IMPERATIVE MOOD

train | **be trained**

SUBJUNCTIVE MOOD

Pres.	if I, he, she, it,	if I, he, she, it,
	we, you, they **train**	we, you, they **be trained**
Past	if I, he, she, it,	if I, he, she, it,
	we, you, they **trained**	we, you, they **were trained**
Fut.	if I, he, she, it,	if I, he, she, it,
	we, you, they **should train**	we, you, they **should be trained**

Transitive and intransitive.

tread
(active voice)

PRINCIPAL PARTS: **treads, treading, trod/treaded, trodden/trod**

be trodden/trod
(passive voice)

Infinitive: **to tread**
Perfect Infinitive: **to have trodden**
Present Participle: **treading**
Past Participle: **trodden**

Infinitive: **to be trodden**
Perfect Infinitive: **to have been trodden**
Present Participle: **being trodden**
Past Participle: **been trodden**

INDICATIVE MOOD

Pres.	I, we, you, they **tread** he, she, it **treads**	I **am trodden** we, you, they **are trodden** he, she, it **is trodden**
Pres. *Prog.*	I **am treading** we, you, they **are treading** he, she, it **is treading**	I **am being trodden** we, you, they **are being trodden** he, she, it **is being trodden**
Pres. *Int.*	I, we, you, they **do tread** he, she, it **does tread**	I, we, you, they **do get trodden** he, she, it **does get trodden**
Fut.	I, he, she, it, we, you, they **will tread**	I, he, she, it, we, you, they **will be trodden**
Past	I, he, she, it, we, you, they **trod**	I, he, she, it **was trodden** we, you, they **were trodden**
Past *Prog.*	I, he, she, it **was treading** we, you, they **were treading**	I, he, she, it **was being trodden** we, you, they **were being trodden**
Past *Int.*	I, he, she, it, we, you, they **did tread**	I, he, she, it, we, you, they **did get trodden**
Pres. *Perf.*	I, we, you, they **have trodden** he, she, it **has trodden**	I, we, you, they **have been trodden** he, she, it **has been trodden**
Past *Perf.*	I, he, she, it, we, you, they **had trodden**	I, he, she, it, we, you, they **had been trodden**
Fut. *Perf.*	I, he, she, it, we, you, they **will have trodden**	I, he, she, it, we, you, they **will have been trodden**

IMPERATIVE MOOD

tread   **be trodden**

SUBJUNCTIVE MOOD

Pres.	if I, he, she, it, we, you, they **tread**	if I, he, she, it, we, you, they **be trodden**
Past	if I, he, she, it, we, you, they **trod**	if I, he, she, it, we, you, they **were trodden**
Fut.	if I, he, she, it, we, you, they **should tread**	if I, he, she, it, we, you, they **should be trodden**

Transitive and intransitive.

treat
(active voice)

be treated
(passive voice)

Infinitive: **to treat**
Perfect Infinitive: **to have treated**
Present Participle: **treating**
Past Participle: **treated**

Infinitive: **to be treated**
Perfect Infinitive: **to have been treated**
Present Participle: **being treated**
Past Participle: **been treated**

INDICATIVE MOOD

Pres.	I, we, you, they **treat**	I **am treated**
		we, you, they **are treated**
	he, she, it **treats**	he, she, it **is treated**
Pres.	I **am treating**	I **am being treated**
Prog.	we, you, they **are treating**	we, you, they **are being treated**
	he, she, it **is treating**	he, she, it **is being treated**
Pres.	I, we, you, they **do treat**	I, we, you, they **do get treated**
Int.	he, she, it **does treat**	he, she, it **does get treated**
Fut.	I, he, she, it,	I, he, she, it,
	we, you, they **will treat**	we, you, they **will be treated**
Past	I, he, she, it,	I, he, she, it **was treated**
	we, you, they **treated**	we, you, they **were treated**
Past	I, he, she, it **was treating**	I, he, she, it **was being treated**
Prog.	we, you, they **were treating**	we, you, they **were being treated**
Past	I, he, she, it,	I, he, she, it,
Int.	we, you, they **did treat**	we, you, they **did get treated**
Pres.	I, we, you, they **have treated**	I, we, you, they **have been treated**
Perf.	he, she, it **has treated**	he, she, it **has been treated**
Past	I, he, she, it,	I, he, she, it,
Perf.	we, you, they **had treated**	we, you, they **had been treated**
Fut.	I, he, she, it, we, you, they	I, he, she, it, we, you, they
Perf.	**will have treated**	**will have been treated**

IMPERATIVE MOOD

treat	**be treated**

SUBJUNCTIVE MOOD

Pres.	if I, he, she, it,	if I, he, she, it,
	we, you, they **treat**	we, you, they **be treated**
Past	if I, he, she, it,	if I, he, she, it,
	we, you, they **treated**	we, you, they **were treated**
Fut.	if I, he, she, it,	if I, he, she, it,
	we, you, they **should treat**	we, you, they **should be treated**

Transitive and intransitive.

try
(active voice)

be tried
(passive voice)

Infinitive: **to try**
Perfect Infinitive: **to have tried**
Present Participle: **trying**
Past Participle: **tried**

Infinitive: **to be tried**
Perfect Infinitive: **to have been tried**
Present Participle: **being tried**
Past Participle: **been tried**

INDICATIVE MOOD

Pres.	I, we, you, they **try**	I **am tried**
		we, you, they **are tried**
	he, she, it **tries**	he, she, it **is tried**
Pres.	I **am trying**	I **am being tried**
Prog.	we, you, they **are trying**	we, you, they **are being tried**
	he, she, it **is trying**	he, she, it **is being tried**
Pres.	I, we, you, they **do try**	I, we, you, they **do get tried**
Int.	he, she, it **does try**	he, she, it **does get tried**
Fut.	I, he, she, it,	I, he, she, it,
	we, you, they **will try**	we, you, they **will be tried**
Past	I, he, she, it,	I, he, she, it **was tried**
	we, you, they **tried**	we, you, they **were tried**
Past	I, he, she, it **was trying**	I, he, she, it **was being tried**
Prog.	we, you, they **were trying**	we, you, they **were being tried**
Past	I, he, she, it,	I, he, she, it,
Int.	we, you, they **did try**	we, you, they **did get tried**
Pres.	I, we, you, they **have tried**	I, we, you, they **have been tried**
Perf.	he, she, it **has tried**	he, she, it **has been tried**
Past	I, he, she, it,	I, he, she, it,
Perf.	we, you, they **had tried**	we, you, they **had been tried**
Fut.	I, he, she, it, we, you, they	I, he, she, it, we, you, they
Perf.	**will have tried**	**will have been tried**

IMPERATIVE MOOD

try   **be tried**

SUBJUNCTIVE MOOD

Pres.	if I, he, she, it,	if I, he, she, it,
	we, you, they **try**	we, you, they **be tried**
Past	if I, he, she, it,	if I, he, she, it,
	we, you, they **tried**	we, you, they **were tried**
Fut.	if I, he, she, it,	if I, he, she, it,
	we, you, they **should try**	we, you, they **should be tried**

Transitive and intransitive.

turn
(active voice)

be turned
(passive voice)

Infinitive: **to turn**
Perfect Infinitive: **to have turned**
Present Participle: **turning**
Past Participle: **turned**

Infinitive: **to be turned**
Perfect Infinitive: **to have been turned**
Present Participle: **being turned**
Past Participle: **been turned**

INDICATIVE MOOD

Pres.	I, we, you, they **turn**	I **am turned**
		we, you, they **are turned**
	he, she, it **turns**	he, she, it **is turned**
Pres.	I **am turning**	I **am being turned**
Prog.	we, you, they **are turning**	we, you, they **are being turned**
	he, she, it **is turning**	he, she, it **is being turned**
Pres.	I, we, you, they **do turn**	I, we, you, they **do get turned**
Int.	he, she, it **does turn**	he, she, it **does get turned**
Fut.	I, he, she, it,	I, he, she, it,
	we, you, they **will turn**	we, you, they **will be turned**
Past	I, he, she, it,	I, he, she, it **was turned**
	we, you, they **turned**	we, you, they **were turned**
Past	I, he, she, it **was turning**	I, he, she, it **was being turned**
Prog.	we, you, they **were turning**	we, you, they **were being turned**
Past	I, he, she, it,	I, he, she, it,
Int.	we, you, they **did turn**	we, you, they **did get turned**
Pres.	I, we, you, they **have turned**	I, we, you, they **have been turned**
Perf.	he, she, it **has turned**	he, she, it **has been turned**
Past	I, he, she, it,	I, he, she, it,
Perf.	we, you, they **had turned**	we, you, they **had been turned**
Fut.	I, he, she, it, we, you, they	I, he, she, it, we, you, they
Perf.	**will have turned**	**will have been turned**

IMPERATIVE MOOD

turn

be turned

SUBJUNCTIVE MOOD

Pres.	if I, he, she, it,	if I, he, she, it,
	we, you, they **turn**	we, you, they **be turned**
Past	if I, he, she, it,	if I, he, she, it,
	we, you, they **turned**	we, you, they **were turned**
Fut.	if I, he, she, it,	if I, he, she, it,
	we, you, they **should turn**	we, you, they **should be turned**

Transitive and intransitive.

unbend
(active voice)

be unbent
(passive voice)

Infinitive: **to unbend**
Perfect Infinitive: **to have unbent**
Present Participle: **unbending**
Past Participle: **unbent**

Infinitive: **to be unbent**
Perfect Infinitive: **to have been unbent**
Present Participle: **being unbent**
Past Participle: **been unbent**

INDICATIVE MOOD

Pres.	I, we, you, they **unbend**	I **am unbent**
		we, you, they **are unbent**
	he, she, it **unbends**	he, she, it **is unbent**
Pres.	I **am unbending**	I **am being unbent**
Prog.	we, you, they **are unbending**	we, you, they **are being unbent**
	he, she, it **is unbending**	he, she, it **is being unbent**
Pres.	I, we, you, they **do unbend**	I, we, you, they **do get unbent**
Int.	he, she, it **does unbend**	he, she, it **does get unbent**
Fut.	I, he, she, it,	I, he, she, it,
	we, you, they **will unbend**	we, you, they **will be unbent**
Past	I, he, she, it,	I, he, she, it **was unbent**
	we, you, they **unbent**	we, you, they **were unbent**
Past	I, he, she, it **was unbending**	I, he, she, it **was being unbent**
Prog.	we, you, they **were unbending**	we, you, they **were being unbent**
Past	I, he, she, it,	I, he, she, it,
Int.	we, you, they **did unbend**	we, you, they **did get unbent**
Pres.	I, we, you, they **have unbent**	I, we, you, they **have been unbent**
Perf.	he, she, it **has unbent**	he, she, it **has been unbent**
Past	I, he, she, it,	I, he, she, it,
Perf.	we, you, they **had unbent**	we, you, they **had been unbent**
Fut.	I, he, she, it, we, you, they	I, he, she, it, we, you, they
Perf.	**will have unbent**	**will have been unbent**

IMPERATIVE MOOD

unbend   **be unbent**

SUBJUNCTIVE MOOD

Pres.	if I, he, she, it,	if I, he, she, it,
	we, you, they **unbend**	we, you, they **be unbent**
Past	if I, he, she, it,	if I, he, she, it,
	we, you, they **unbent**	we, you, they **were unbent**
Fut.	if I, he, she, it,	if I, he, she, it,
	we, you, they **should unbend**	we, you, they **should be unbent**

Transitive and intransitive.

unbind
(active voice)

be unbound
(passive voice)

Infinitive: **to unbind**
Perfect Infinitive: **to have unbound**
Present Participle: **unbinding**
Past Participle: **unbound**

Infinitive: **to be unbound**
Perfect Infinitive: **to have been unbound**
Present Participle: **being unbound**
Past Participle: **been unbound**

INDICATIVE MOOD

Pres.	I, we, you, they **unbind**	I **am unbound**
		we, you, they **are unbound**
	he, she, it **unbinds**	he, she, it **is unbound**
Pres.	I **am unbinding**	I **am being unbound**
Prog.	we, you, they **are unbinding**	we, you, they **are being unbound**
	he, she, it **is unbinding**	he, she, it **is being unbound**
Pres.	I, we, you, they **do unbind**	I, we, you, they **do get unbound**
Int.	he, she, it **does unbind**	he, she, it **does get unbound**
Fut.	I, he, she, it,	I, he, she, it,
	we, you, they **will unbind**	we, you, they **will be unbound**
Past	I, he, she, it,	I, he, she, it **was unbound**
	we, you, they **unbound**	we, you, they **were unbound**
Past	I, he, she, it **was unbinding**	I, he, she, it **was being unbound**
Prog.	we, you, they **were unbinding**	we, you, they **were being unbound**
Past	I, he, she, it,	I, he, she, it,
Int.	we, you, they **did unbind**	we, you, they **did get unbound**
Pres.	I, we, you, they **have unbound**	I, we, you, they **have been unbound**
Perf.	he, she, it **has unbound**	he, she, it **has been unbound**
Past	I, he, she, it,	I, he, she, it,
Perf.	we, you, they **had unbound**	we, you, they **had been unbound**
Fut.	I, he, she, it, we, you, they	I, he, she, it, we, you, they
Perf.	**will have unbound**	**will have been unbound**

IMPERATIVE MOOD

unbind

be unbound

SUBJUNCTIVE MOOD

Pres.	if I, he, she, it,	if I, he, she, it,
	we, you, they **unbind**	we, you, they **be unbound**
Past	if I, he, she, it,	if I, he, she, it,
	we, you, they **unbound**	we, you, they **were unbound**
Fut.	if I, he, she, it,	if I, he, she, it,
	we, you, they **should unbind**	we, you, they **should be unbound**

underbid
(active voice)

PRINCIPAL PARTS: **underbids,
underbidding, underbid, underbid**

be underbid
(passive voice)

Infinitive: **to underbid**
Perfect Infinitive: **to have underbid**
Present Participle: **underbidding**
Past Participle: **underbid**

Infinitive: **to be underbid**
Perfect Infinitive: **to have been underbid**
Present Participle: **being underbid**
Past Participle: **been underbid**

INDICATIVE MOOD

Pres.	I, we, you, they **underbid**	I **am underbid**
		we, you, they **are underbid**
	he, she, it **underbids**	he, she, it **is underbid**
Pres.	I **am underbidding**	I **am being underbid**
Prog.	we, you, they **are underbidding**	we, you, they **are being underbid**
	he, she, it **is underbidding**	he, she, it **is being underbid**
Pres.	I, we, you, they **do underbid**	I, we, you, they **do get underbid**
Int.	he, she, it **does underbid**	he, she, it **does get underbid**
Fut.	I, he, she, it,	I, he, she, it,
	we, you, they **will underbid**	we, you, they **will be underbid**
Past	I, he, she, it,	I, he, she, it **was underbid**
	we, you, they **underbid**	we, you, they **were underbid**
Past	I, he, she, it **was underbidding**	I, he, she, it **was being underbid**
Prog.	we, you, they **were underbidding**	we, you, they **were being underbid**
Past	I, he, she, it,	I, he, she, it,
Int.	we, you, they **did underbid**	we, you, they **did get underbid**
Pres.	I, we, you, they **have underbid**	I, we, you, they **have been underbid**
Perf.	he, she, it **has underbid**	he, she, it **has been underbid**
Past	I, he, she, it,	I, he, she, it,
Perf.	we, you, they **had underbid**	we, you, they **had been underbid**
Fut.	I, he, she, it, we, you, they	I, he, she, it, we, you, they
Perf.	**will have underbid**	**will have been underbid**

IMPERATIVE MOOD

underbid	**be underbid**

SUBJUNCTIVE MOOD

Pres.	if I, he, she, it,	if I, he, she, it,
	we, you, they **underbid**	we, you, they **be underbid**
Past	if I, he, she, it,	if I, he, she, it,
	we, you, they **underbid**	we, you, they **were underbid**
Fut.	if I, he, she, it,	if I, he, she, it,
	we, you, they **should underbid**	we, you, they **should be underbid**

Transitive and intransitive.

undergo
(active voice)

Infinitive: **to undergo**
Perfect Infinitive: **to have undergone**
Present Participle: **undergoing**
Past Participle: **undergone**

Infinitive: **to be undergone**
Perfect Infinitive: **to have been undergone**
Present Participle: **being undergone**
Past Participle: **been undergone**

INDICATIVE MOOD

Pres.	I, we, you, they **undergo**	I **am undergone**	
		we, you, they **are undergone**	
	he, she, it **undergoes**	he, she, it **is undergone**	
Pres.	I **am undergoing**	I **am being undergone**	
Prog.	we, you, they **are undergoing**	we, you, they **are being undergone**	
	he, she, it **is undergoing**	he, she, it **is being undergone**	
Pres.	I, we, you, they **do undergo**	I, we, you, they **do get undergone**	
Int.	he, she, it **does undergo**	he, she, it **does get undergone**	
Fut.	I, he, she, it,	I, he, she, it,	
	we, you, they **will undergo**	we, you, they **will be undergone**	
Past	I, he, she, it,	I, he, she, it **was undergone**	
	we, you, they **underwent**	we, you, they **were undergone**	
Past	I, he, she, it **was undergoing**	I, he, she, it **was being undergone**	
Prog.	we, you, they **were undergoing**	we, you, they **were being undergone**	
Past	I, he, she, it,	I, he, she, it,	
Int.	we, you, they **did undergo**	we, you, they **did get undergone**	
Pres.	I, we, you, they **have undergone**	I, we, you, they **have been undergone**	
Perf.	he, she, it **has undergone**	he, she, it **has been undergone**	
Past	I, he, she, it,	I, he, she, it,	
Perf.	we, you, they **had undergone**	we, you, they **had been undergone**	
Fut.	I, he, she, it, we, you, they	I, he, she, it, we, you, they	
Perf.	**will have undergone**	**will have been undergone**	

IMPERATIVE MOOD

undergo   **be undergone**

SUBJUNCTIVE MOOD

Pres.	if I, he, she, it,	if I, he, she, it,
	we, you, they **undergo**	we, you, they **be undergone**
Past	if I, he, she, it,	if I, he, she, it,
	we, you, they **underwent**	we, you, they **were undergone**
Fut.	if I, he, she, it,	if I, he, she, it,
	we, you, they **should undergo**	we, you, they **should be undergone**

456

PRINCIPAL PARTS: **understands, understanding, understood, understood**

Infinitive: **to understand**
Perfect Infinitive: **to have understood**
Present Participle: **understanding**
Past Participle: **understood**

Infinitive: **to be understood**
Perfect Infinitive: **to have been understood**
Present Participle: **being understood**
Past Participle: **been understood**

INDICATIVE MOOD

Pres.	I, we, you, they **understand**	I **am understood**
		we, you, they **are understood**
	he, she, it **understands**	he, she, it **is understood**
Pres. *Prog.*	I **am understanding**	I **am being understood**
	we, you, they **are understanding**	we, you, they **are being understood**
	he, she, it **is understanding**	he, she, it **is being understood**
Pres. *Int.*	I, we, you, they **do understand**	I, we, you, they **do get understood**
	he, she, it **does understand**	he, she, it **does get understood**
Fut.	I, he, she, it, we, you, they **will understand**	I, he, she, it, we, you, they **will be understood**
Past	I, he, she, it, we, you, they **understood**	I, he, she, it **was understood** we, you, they **were understood**
Past *Prog.*	I, he, she, it **was understanding** we, you, they **were understanding**	I, he, she, it **was being understood** we, you, they **were being understood**
Past *Int.*	I, he, she, it, we, you, they **did understand**	I, he, she, it, we, you, they **did get understood**
Pres. *Perf.*	I, we, you, they **have understood** he, she, it **has understood**	I, we, you, they **have been understood** he, she, it **has been understood**
Past *Perf.*	I, he, she, it, we, you, they **had understood**	I, he, she, it, we, you, they **had been understood**
Fut. *Perf.*	I, he, she, it, we, you, they **will have understood**	I, he, she, it, we, you, they **will have been understood**

IMPERATIVE MOOD

understand **be understood**

SUBJUNCTIVE MOOD

Pres.	if I, he, she, it, we, you, they **understand**	if I, he, she, it, we, you, they **be understood**
Past	if I, he, she, it, we, you, they **understood**	if I, he, she, it, we, you, they **were understood**
Fut.	if I, he, she, it, we, you, they **should understand**	if I, he, she, it, we, you, they **should be understood**

Transitive and intransitive.

undertake
(active voice)

be undertaken
(passive voice)

Infinitive: **to undertake**
Perfect Infinitive: **to have undertaken**
Present Participle: **undertaking**
Past Participle: **undertaken**

Infinitive: **to be undertaken**
Perfect Infinitive: **to have been undertaken**
Present Participle: **being undertaken**
Past Participle: **been undertaken**

INDICATIVE MOOD

Pres.	I, we, you, they **undertake**	I **am undertaken**
		we, you, they **are undertaken**
	he, she, it **undertakes**	he, she, it **is undertaken**
Pres.	I **am undertaking**	I **am being undertaken**
Prog.	we, you, they **are undertaking**	we, you, they **are being undertaken**
	he, she, it **is undertaking**	he, she, it **is being undertaken**
Pres.	I, we, you, they **do undertake**	I, we, you, they **do get undertaken**
Int.	he, she, it **does undertake**	he, she, it **does get undertaken**
Fut.	I, he, she, it,	I, he, she, it,
	we, you, they **will undertake**	we, you, they **will be undertaken**
Past	I, he, she, it,	I, he, she, it **was undertaken**
	we, you, they **undertook**	we, you, they **were undertaken**
Past	I, he, she, it **was undertaking**	I, he, she, it **was being undertaken**
Prog.	we, you, they **were undertaking**	we, you, they **were being undertaken**
Past	I, he, she, it,	I, he, she, it,
Int.	we, you, they **did undertake**	we, you, they **did get undertaken**
Pres.	I, we, you, they **have undertaken**	I, we, you, they **have been undertaken**
Perf.	he, she, it **has undertaken**	he, she, it **has been undertaken**
Past	I, he, she, it,	I, he, she, it,
Perf.	we, you, they **had undertaken**	we, you, they **had been undertaken**
Fut.	I, he, she, it, we, you, they	I, he, she, it, we, you, they
Perf.	**will have undertaken**	**will have been undertaken**

IMPERATIVE MOOD

undertake   **be undertaken**

SUBJUNCTIVE MOOD

Pres.	if I, he, she, it,	if I, he, she, it,
	we, you, they **undertake**	we, you, they **be undertaken**
Past	if I, he, she, it,	if I, he, she, it,
	we, you, they **undertook**	we, you, they **were undertaken**
Fut.	if I, he, she, it,	if I, he, she, it,
	we, you, they **should undertake**	we, you, they **should be undertaken**

undo
(active voice)

be undone
(passive voice)

Infinitive: **to undo**
Perfect Infinitive: **to have undone**
Present Participle: **undoing**
Past Participle: **undone**

Infinitive: **to be undone**
Perfect Infinitive: **to have been undone**
Present Participle: **being undone**
Past Participle: **been undone**

INDICATIVE MOOD

Pres.	I, we, you, they **undo**	I **am undone**
		we, you, they **are undone**
	he, she, it **undoes**	he, she, it **is undone**
Pres.	I **am undoing**	I **am being undone**
Prog.	we, you, they **are undoing**	we, you, they **are being undone**
	he, she, it **is undoing**	he, she, it **is being undone**
Pres.	I, we, you, they **do undo**	I, we, you, they **did get undone**
Int.	he, she, it **does undo**	he, she, it **does get undone**
Fut.	I, he, she, it,	I, he, she, it,
	we, you, they **will undo**	we, you, they **will be undone**
Past	I, he, she, it,	I, he, she, it **was undone**
	we, you, they **undid**	we, you, they **were undone**
Past	I, he, she, it **was undoing**	I, he, she, it **was being undone**
Prog.	we, you, they **were undoing**	we, you, they **were being undone**
Past	I, he, she, it,	I, he, she, it,
Int.	we, you, they **did undo**	we, you, they **did get undone**
Pres.	I, we, you, they **have undone**	I, we, you, they **have been undone**
Perf.	he, she, it **has undone**	he, she, it **has been undone**
Past	I, he, she, it,	I, he, she, it,
Perf.	we, you, they **had undone**	we, you, they **had been undone**
Fut.	I, he, she, it, we, you, they	I, he, she, it, we, you, they
Perf.	**will have undone**	**will have been undone**

IMPERATIVE MOOD

undo　　　　**be undone**

SUBJUNCTIVE MOOD

Pres.	if I, he, she, it,	if I, he, she, it,
	we, you, they **undo**	we, you, they **be undone**
Past	if I, he, she, it,	if I, he, she, it,
	we, you, they **undid**	we, you, they **were undone**
Fut.	if I, he, she, it,	if I, he, she, it,
	we, you, they **should undo**	we, you, they **should be undone**

Transitive and intransitive.

unfreeze
(active voice)

Principal Parts: **unfreezes,
unfreezing, unfroze, unfrozen**

be unfrozen
(passive voice)

Infinitive: **to unfreeze**
Perfect Infinitive: **to have unfrozen**
Present Participle: **unfreezing**
Past Participle: **unfrozen**

Infinitive: **to be unfrozen**
Perfect Infinitive: **to have been unfrozen**
Present Participle: **being unfrozen**
Past Participle: **been unfrozen**

INDICATIVE MOOD

Pres.	I, we, you, they **unfreeze**	I **am unfrozen**
		we, you, they **are unfrozen**
	he, she, it **unfreezes**	he, she, it **is unfrozen**
Pres.	I **am unfreezing**	I **am being unfrozen**
Prog.	we, you, they **are unfreezing**	we, you, they **are being unfrozen**
	he, she, it **is unfreezing**	he, she, it **is being unfrozen**
Pres.	I, we, you, they **do unfreeze**	I, we, you, they **do get unfrozen**
Int.	he, she, it **does unfreeze**	he, she, it **does get unfrozen**
Fut.	I, he, she, it,	I, he, she, it,
	we, you, they **will unfreeze**	we, you, they **will be unfrozen**
Past	I, he, she, it,	I, he, she, it **was unfrozen**
	we, you, they **unfroze**	we, you, they **were unfrozen**
Past	I, he, she, it **was unfreezing**	I, he, she, it **was being unfrozen**
Prog.	we, you, they **were unfreezing**	we, you, they **were being unfrozen**
Past	I, he, she, it,	I, he, she, it,
Int.	we, you, they **did unfreeze**	we, you, they **did get unfrozen**
Pres.	I, we, you, they **have unfrozen**	I, we, you, they **have been unfrozen**
Perf.	he, she, it **has unfrozen**	he, she, it **has been unfrozen**
Past	I, he, she, it,	I, he, she, it,
Perf.	we, you, they **had unfrozen**	we, you, they **had been unfrozen**
Fut.	I, he, she, it, we, you, they	I, he, she, it, we, you, they
Perf.	**will have unfrozen**	**will have been unfrozen**

IMPERATIVE MOOD

unfreeze   **be unfrozen**

SUBJUNCTIVE MOOD

Pres.	if I, he, she, it,	if I, he, she, it,
	we, you, they **unfreeze**	we, you, they **be unfrozen**
Past	if I, he, she, it,	if I, he, she, it,
	we, you, they **unfroze**	we, you, they **were unfrozen**
Fut.	if I, he, she, it,	if I, he, she, it,
	we, you, they **should unfreeze**	we, you, they **should be unfrozen**

unite
(active voice)

PRINCIPAL PARTS: **unites, uniting, united, united**

be united
(passive voice)

Infinitive: **to unite**
Perfect Infinitive: **to have united**
Present Participle: **uniting**
Past Participle: **united**

Infinitive: **to be united**
Perfect Infinitive: **to have been united**
Present Participle: **being united**
Past Participle: **been united**

INDICATIVE MOOD

Pres.	I, we, you, they **unite** he, she, it **unites**	I **am united** we, you, they **are united** he, she, it **is united**
Pres. *Prog.*	I **am uniting** we, you, they **are uniting** he, she, it **is uniting**	I **am being united** we, you, they **are being united** he, she, it **is being united**
Pres. *Int.*	I, we, you, they **do unite** he, she, it **does unite**	I, we, you, they **do get united** he, she, it **does get united**
Fut.	I, he, she, it, we, you, they **will unite**	I, he, she, it, we, you, they **will be united**
Past	I, he, she, it, we, you, they **united**	I, he, she, it **was united** we, you, they **were united**
Past *Prog.*	I, he, she, it **was uniting** we, you, they **were uniting**	I, he, she, it **was being united** we, you, they **were being united**
Past *Int.*	I, he, she, it, we, you, they **did unite**	I, he, she, it, we, you, they **did get united**
Pres. *Perf.*	I, we, you, they **have united** he, she, it **has united**	I, we, you, they **have been united** he, she, it **has been united**
Past *Perf.*	I, he, she, it, we, you, they **had united**	I, he, she, it, we, you, they **had been united**
Fut. *Perf.*	I, he, she, it, we, you, they **will have united**	I, he, she, it, we, you, they **will have been united**

IMPERATIVE MOOD

unite

be united

SUBJUNCTIVE MOOD

Pres.	if I, he, she, it, we, you, they **unite**	if I, he, she, it, we, you, they **be united**
Past	if I, he, she, it, we, you, they **united**	if I, he, she, it, we, you, they **were united**
Fut.	if I, he, she, it, we, you, they **should unite**	if I, he, she, it, we, you, they **should be united**

Transitive and intransitive.

461

Infinitive: **to unwind**
Perfect Infinitive: **to have unwound**
Present Participle: **unwinding**
Past Participle: **unwound**

Infinitive: **to be unwound**
Perfect Infinitive: **to have been unwound**
Present Participle: **being unwound**
Past Participle: **been unwound**

INDICATIVE MOOD

Pres.	I, we, you, they **unwind**		I **am unwound**
			we, you, they **are unwound**
	he, she, it **unwinds**		he, she, it **is unwound**
Pres. *Prog.*	I **am unwinding**		I **am being unwound**
	we, you, they **are unwinding**		we, you, they **are being unwound**
	he, she, it **is unwinding**		he, she, it **is being unwound**
Pres. *Int.*	I, we, you, they **do unwind**		I, we, you, they **do get unwound**
	he, she, it **does unwind**		he, she, it **does get unwound**
Fut.	I, he, she, it, we, you, they **will unwind**		I, he, she, it, we, you, they **will be unwound**
Past	I, he, she, it, we, you, they **unwound**		I, he, she, it **was unwound** we, you, they **were unwound**
Past *Prog.*	I, he, she, it **was unwinding** we, you, they **were unwinding**		I, he, she, it **was being unwound** we, you, they **were being unwound**
Past *Int.*	I, he, she, it, we, you, they **did unwind**		I, he, she, it, we, you, they **did get unwound**
Pres. *Perf.*	I, we, you, they **have unwound** he, she, it **has unwound**		I, we, you, they **have been unwound** he, she, it **has been unwound**
Past *Perf.*	I, he, she, it, we, you, they **had unwound**		I, he, she, it, we, you, they **had been unwound**
Fut. *Perf.*	I, he, she, it, we, you, they **will have unwound**		I, he, she, it, we, you, they **will have been unwound**

IMPERATIVE MOOD

unwind　　　　　**be unwound**

SUBJUNCTIVE MOOD

Pres.	if I, he, she, it, we, you, they **unwind**	if I, he, she, it, we, you, they **be unwound**
Past	if I, he, she, it, we, you, they **unwound**	if I, he, she, it, we, you, they **were unwound**
Fut.	if I, he, she, it, we, you, they **should unwind**	if I, he, she, it, we, you, they **should be unwound**

Transitive and intransitive.

uphold
(active voice)

be upheld
(passive voice)

Infinitive: **to uphold**
Perfect Infinitive: **to have upheld**
Present Participle: **upholding**
Past Participle: **upheld**

Infinitive: **to be upheld**
Perfect Infinitive: **to have been upheld**
Present Participle: **being upheld**
Past Participle: **been upheld**

INDICATIVE MOOD

Pres.	I, we, you, they **uphold**	I **am upheld**
		we, you, they **are upheld**
	he, she, it **upholds**	he, she, it **is upheld**
Pres.	I **am upholding**	I **am being upheld**
Prog.	we, you, they **are upholding**	we, you, they **are being upheld**
	he, she, it **is upholding**	he, she, it **is being upheld**
Pres.	I, we, you, they **do uphold**	I, we, you, they **do get upheld**
Int.	he, she, it **does uphold**	he, she, it **does get upheld**
Fut.	I, he, she, it,	I, he, she, it,
	we, you, they **will uphold**	we, you, they **will be upheld**
Past	I, he, she, it,	I, he, she, it **was upheld**
	we, you, they **upheld**	we, you, they **were upheld**
Past	I, he, she, it **was upholding**	I, he, she, it **was being upheld**
Prog.	we, you, they **were upholding**	we, you, they **were being upheld**
Past	I, he, she, it,	I, he, she, it,
Int.	we, you, they **did uphold**	we, you, they **did get upheld**
Pres.	I, we, you, they **have upheld**	I, we, you, they **have been upheld**
Perf.	he, she, it **has upheld**	he, she, it **has been upheld**
Past	I, he, she, it,	I, he, she, it,
Perf.	we, you, they **had upheld**	we, you, they **had been upheld**
Fut.	I, he, she, it, we, you, they	I, he, she, it, we, you, they
Perf.	**will have upheld**	**will have been upheld**

IMPERATIVE MOOD

uphold   **be upheld**

SUBJUNCTIVE MOOD

Pres.	if I, he, she, it,	if I, he, she, it,
	we, you, they **uphold**	we, you, they **be upheld**
Past	if I, he, she, it,	if I, he, she, it,
	we, you, they **upheld**	we, you, they **were upheld**
Fut.	if I, he, she, it,	if I, he, she, it,
	we, you, they **should uphold**	we, you, they **should be upheld**

upset
(active voice)

be upset
(passive voice)

Infinitive: **to upset**
Perfect Infinitive: **to have upset**
Present Participle: **upsetting**
Past Participle: **upset**

Infinitive: **to be upset**
Perfect Infinitive: **to have been upset**
Present Participle: **being upset**
Past Participle: **been upset**

INDICATIVE MOOD

Pres.	I, we, you, they **upset**	I **am upset**
		we, you, they **are upset**
	he, she, it **upsets**	he, she, it **is upset**
Pres.	I **am upsetting**	I **am being upset**
Prog.	we, you, they **are upsetting**	we, you, they **are being upset**
	he, she, it **is upsetting**	he, she, it **is being upset**
Pres.	I, we, you, they **do upset**	I, we, you, they **do get upset**
Int.	he, she, it **does upset**	he, she, it **does get upset**
Fut.	I, he, she, it,	I, he, she, it,
	we, you, they **will upset**	we, you, they **will be upset**
Past	I, he, she, it,	I, he, she, it **was upset**
	we, you, they **upset**	we, you, they **were upset**
Past	I, he, she, it **was upsetting**	I, he, she, it **was being upset**
Prog.	we, you, they **were upsetting**	we, you, they **were being upset**
Past	I, he, she, it,	I, he, she, it,
Int.	we, you, they **did upset**	we, you, they **did get upset**
Pres.	I, we, you, they **have upset**	I, we, you, they **have been upset**
Perf.	he, she, it **has upset**	he, she, it **has been upset**
Past	I, he, she, it,	I, he, she, it,
Perf.	we, you, they **had upset**	we, you, they **had been upset**
Fut.	I, he, she, it, we, you, they	I, he, she, it, we, you, they
Perf.	**will have upset**	**will have been upset**

IMPERATIVE MOOD

upset

be upset

SUBJUNCTIVE MOOD

Pres.	if I, he, she, it,	if I, he, she, it,
	we, you, they **upset**	we, you, they **be upset**
Past	if I, he, she, it,	if I, he, she, it,
	we, you, they **upset**	we, you, they **were upset**
Fut.	if I, he, she, it,	if I, he, she, it,
	we, you, they **should upset**	we, you, they **should be upset**

Transitive and intransitive.

464

use
(active voice)

Principal Parts: **uses, using,**
used, used

be used
(passive voice)

Infinitive: **to use**
Perfect Infinitive: **to have used**
Present Participle: **using**
Past Participle: **used**

Infinitive: **to be used**
Perfect Infinitive: **to have been used**
Present Participle: **being used**
Past Participle: **been used**

INDICATIVE MOOD

Pres.	I, we, you, they **use** he, she, it **uses**	I **am used** we, you, they **are used** he, she, it **is used**
Pres. *Prog.*	I **am using** we, you, they **are using** he, she, it **is using**	I **am being used** we, you, they **are being used** he, she, it **is being used**
Pres. *Int.*	I, we, you, they **do use** he, she, it **does use**	I, we, you, they **do get used** he, she, it **does get used**
Fut.	I, he, she, it, we, you, they **will use**	I, he, she, it, we, you, they **will be used**
Past	I, he, she, it, we, you, they **used**	I, he, she, it **was used** we, you, they **were used**
Past *Prog.*	I, he, she, it **was using** we, you, they **were using**	I, he, she, it **was being used** we, you, they **were being used**
Past *Int.*	I, he, she, it, we, you, they **did use**	I, he, she, it, we, you, they **did get used**
Pres. *Perf.*	I, we, you, they **have used** he, she, it **has used**	I, we, you, they **have been used** he, she, it **has been used**
Past *Perf.*	I, he, she, it, we, you, they **had used**	I, he, she, it, we, you, they **had been used**
Fut. *Perf.*	I, he, she, it, we, you, they **will have used**	I, he, she, it, we, you, they **will have been used**

IMPERATIVE MOOD

use   **be used**

SUBJUNCTIVE MOOD

Pres.	if I, he, she, it, we, you, they **use**	if I, he, she, it, we, you, they **be used**
Past	if I, he, she, it, we, you, they **used**	if I, he, she, it, we, you, they **were used**
Fut.	if I, he, she, it, we, you, they **should use**	if I, he, she, it, we, you, they **should be used**

USED TO can form the past tense meaning "a former custom, or activity."

vary
(active voice)

PRINCIPAL PARTS: **varies, varying,**
varied, varied

be varied
(passive voice)

Infinitive: **to vary**
Perfect Infinitive: **to have varied**
Present Participle: **varying**
Past Participle: **varied**

Infinitive: **to be varied**
Perfect Infinitive: **to have been varied**
Present Participle: **being varied**
Past Participle: **been varied**

INDICATIVE MOOD

Pres.	I, we, you, they **vary**	I **am varied**
		we, you, they **are varied**
	he, she, it **varies**	he, she, it **is varied**
Pres.	I **am varying**	I **am being varied**
Prog.	we, you, they **are varying**	we, you, they **are being varied**
	he, she, it **is varying**	he, she, it **is being varied**
Pres.	I, we, you, they **do vary**	I, we, you, they **do get varied**
Int.	he, she, it **does vary**	he, she, it **does get varied**
Fut.	I, he, she, it,	I, he, she, it,
	we, you, they **will vary**	we, you, they **will be varied**
Past	I, he, she, it,	I, he, she, it **was varied**
	we, you, they **varied**	we, you, they **were varied**
Past	I, he, she, it **was varying**	I, he, she, it **was being varied**
Prog.	we, you, they **were varying**	we, you, they **were being varied**
Past	I, he, she, it,	I, he, she, it,
Int.	we, you, they **did vary**	we, you, they **did get varied**
Pres.	I, we, you, they **have varied**	I, we, you, they **have been varied**
Perf.	he, she, it **has varied**	he, she, it **has been varied**
Past	I, he, she, it,	I, he, she, it,
Perf.	we, you, they **had varied**	we, you, they **had been varied**
Fut.	I, he, she, it, we, you, they	I, he, she, it, we, you, they
Perf.	**will have varied**	**will have been varied**

IMPERATIVE MOOD

vary　　　　　　　　　　**be varied**

SUBJUNCTIVE MOOD

Pres.	if I, he, she, it,	if I, he, she, it,
	we, you, they **vary**	we, you, they **be varied**
Past	if I, he, she, it,	if I, he, she, it,
	we, you, they **varied**	we, you, they **were varied**
Fut.	if I, he, she, it,	if I, he, she, it,
	we, you, they **should vary**	we, you, they **should be varied**

Transitive and intransitive.

visit
(active voice)

PRINCIPAL PARTS: **visits, visiting,**
visited, visited

be visited
(passive voice)

Infinitive: **to visit**
Perfect Infinitive: **to have visited**
Present Participle: **visiting**
Past Participle: **visited**

Infinitive: **to be visited**
Perfect Infinitive: **to have been visited**
Present Participle: **being visited**
Past Participle: **been visited**

INDICATIVE MOOD

Pres.	I, we, you, they **visit**	I **am visited**
		we, you, they **are visited**
	he, she, it **visits**	he, she, it **is visited**
Pres.	I **am visiting**	I **am being visited**
Prog.	we, you, they **are visiting**	we, you, they **are being visited**
	he, she, it **is visiting**	he, she, it **is being visited**
Pres.	I, we, you, they **do visit**	I, we, you, they **do get visited**
Int.	he, she, it **does visit**	he, she, it **does get visited**
Fut.	I, he, she, it,	I, he, she, it,
	we, you, they **will visit**	we, you, they **will be visited**
Past	I, he, she, it,	I, he, she, it **was visited**
	we, you, they **visited**	we, you, they **were visited**
Past	I, he, she, it **was visiting**	I, he, she, it **was being visited**
Prog.	we, you, they **were visiting**	we, you, they **were being visited**
Past	I, he, she, it,	I, he, she, it,
Int.	we, you, they **did visit**	we, you, they **did get visited**
Pres.	I, we, you, they **have visited**	I, we, you, they **have been visited**
Perf.	he, she, it **has visited**	he, she, it **has been visited**
Past	I, he, she, it,	I, he, she, it,
Perf.	we, you, they **had visited**	we, you, they **had been visited**
Fut.	I, he, she, it, we, you, they	I, he, she, it, we, you, they
Perf.	**will have visited**	**will have been visited**

IMPERATIVE MOOD

visit

be visited

SUBJUNCTIVE MOOD

Pres.	if I, he, she, it,	if I, he, she, it,
	we, you, they **visit**	we, you, they **be visited**
Past	if I, he, she, it,	if I, he, she, it,
	we, you, they **visited**	we, you, they **were visited**
Fut.	if I, he, she, it,	if I, he, she, it,
	we, you, they **should visit**	we, you, they **should be visited**

Transitive and intransitive.

wait
(active voice)

be waited
(passive voice)

Infinitive: **to wait**
Perfect Infinitive: **to have waited**
Present Participle: **waiting**
Past Participle: **waited**

Infinitive: **to be waited**
Perfect Infinitive: **to have been waited**
Present Participle: **being waited**
Past Participle: **been waited**

INDICATIVE MOOD

Pres.	I, we, you, they **wait**	I **am waited**
		we, you, they **are waited**
	he, she, it **waits**	he, she, it **is waited**
Pres.	I **am waiting**	I **am being waited**
Prog.	we, you, they **are waiting**	we, you, they **are being waited**
	he, she, it **is waiting**	he, she, it **is being waited**
Pres.	I, we, you, they **do wait**	I, we, you, they **do get waited**
Int.	he, she, it **does wait**	he, she, it **does get waited**
Fut.	I, he, she, it,	I, he, she, it,
	we, you, they **will wait**	we, you, they **will be waited**
Past	I, he, she, it,	I, he, she, it **was waited**
	we, you, they **waited**	we, you, they **were waited**
Past	I, he, she, it **was waiting**	I, he, she, it **was being waited**
Prog.	we, you, they **were waiting**	we, you, they **were being waited**
Past	I, he, she, it,	I, he, she, it,
Int.	we, you, they **did wait**	we, you, they **did get waited**
Pres.	I, we, you, they **have waited**	I, we, you, they **have been waited**
Perf.	he, she, it **has waited**	he, she, it **has been waited**
Past	I, he, she, it,	I, he, she, it,
Perf.	we, you, they **had waited**	we, you, they **had been waited**
Fut.	I, he, she, it, we, you, they	I, he, she, it, we, you, they
Perf.	**will have waited**	**will have been waited**

IMPERATIVE MOOD

wait **be waited**

SUBJUNCTIVE MOOD

Pres.	if I, he, she, it,	if I, he, she, it,
	we, you, they **wait**	we, you, they **be waited**
Past	if I, he, she, it,	if I, he, she, it,
	we, you, they **waited**	we, you, they **were waited**
Fut.	if I, he, she, it,	if I, he, she, it,
	we, you, they **should wait**	we, you, they **should be waited**

Intransitive and transitive.

wake
(active voice)

PRINCIPAL PARTS: **wakes, waking,
woke/waked, waked/woken**

be waked/woken
(passive voice)

Infinitive: **to wake**
Perfect Infinitive: **to have waked**
Present Participle: **waking**
Past Participle: **waked**

Infinitive: **to be waked**
Perfect Infinitive: **to have been waked**
Present Participle: **being waked**
Past Participle: **been waked**

INDICATIVE MOOD

Pres.	I, we, you, they **wake**	I **am waked**
		we, you, they **are waked**
	he, she, it **wakes**	he, she, it **is waked**
Pres.	I **am waking**	I **am being waked**
Prog.	we, you, they **are waking**	we, you, they **are being waked**
	he, she, it **is waking**	he, she, it **is being waked**
Pres.	I, we, you, they **do wake**	I, we, you, they **do get waked**
Int.	he, she, it **does wake**	he, she, it **does get waked**
Fut.	I, he, she, it,	I, he, she, it,
	we, you, they **will wake**	we, you, they **will be waked**
Past	I, he, she, it,	I, he, she, it **was waked**
	we, you, they **woke**	we, you, they **were waked**
Past	I, he, she, it **was waking**	I, he, she, it **was being waked**
Prog.	we, you, they **were waking**	we, you, they **were being waked**
Past	I, he, she, it,	I, he, she, it,
Int.	we, you, they **did wake**	we, you, they **did get waked**
Pres.	I, we, you, they **have waked**	I, we, you, they **have been waked**
Perf.	he, she, it **has waked**	he, she, it **has been waked**
Past	I, he, she, it,	I, he, she, it,
Perf.	we, you, they **had waked**	we, you, they **had been waked**
Fut.	I, he, she, it, we, you, they	I, he, she, it, we, you, they
Perf.	**will have waked**	**will have been waked**

IMPERATIVE MOOD

wake   **be waked**

SUBJUNCTIVE MOOD

Pres.	if I, he, she, it,	if I, he, she, it,
	we, you, they **wake**	we, you, they **be waked**
Past	if I, he, she, it,	if I, he, she, it,
	we, you, they **woke**	we, you, they **were waked**
Fut.	if I, he, she, it,	if I, he, she, it,
	we, you, they **should wake**	we, you, they **should be waked**

Intransitive and transitive. The *Oxford Dictionary* prefers the past participle WOKEN. *Webster's* also lists as a past participle WOKE.

waken
(active voice)

be wakened
(passive voice)

Infinitive: **to waken**
Perfect Infinitive: **to have wakened**
Present Participle: **wakening**
Past Participle: **wakened**

Infinitive: **to be wakened**
Perfect Infinitive: **to have been wakened**
Present Participle: **being wakened**
Past Participle: **been wakened**

INDICATIVE MOOD

Pres.	I, we, you, they **waken**	I **am wakened**
		we, you, they **are wakened**
	he, she, it **wakens**	he, she, it **is wakened**
Pres.	I **am wakening**	I **am being wakened**
Prog.	we, you, they **are wakening**	we, you, they **are being wakened**
	he, she, it **is wakening**	he, she, it **is being wakened**
Pres.	I, we, you, they **do waken**	I, we, you, they **do get wakened**
Int.	he, she, it **does waken**	he, she, it **does get wakened**
Fut.	I, he, she, it,	I, he, she, it,
	we, you, they **will waken**	we, you, they **will be wakened**
Past	I, he, she, it,	I, he, she, it **was wakened**
	we, you, they **wakened**	we, you, they **were wakened**
Past	I, he, she, it **was wakening**	I, he, she, it **was being wakened**
Prog.	we, you, they **were wakening**	we, you, they **were being wakened**
Past	I, he, she, it,	I, he, she, it,
Int.	we, you, they **did waken**	we, you, they **did get wakened**
Pres.	I, we, you, they **have wakened**	I, we, you, they **have been wakened**
Perf.	he, she, it **has wakened**	he, she, it **has been wakened**
Past	I, he, she, it,	I, he, she, it,
Perf.	we, you, they **had wakened**	we, you, they **had been wakened**
Fut.	I, he, she, it, we, you, they	I, he, she, it, we, you, they
Perf.	**will have wakened**	**will have been wakened**

IMPERATIVE MOOD

waken   **be wakened**

SUBJUNCTIVE MOOD

Pres.	if I, he, she, it,	if I, he, she, it,
	we, you, they **waken**	we, you, they **be wakened**
Past	if I, he, she, it,	if I, he, she, it,
	we, you, they **wakened**	we, you, they **were wakened**
Fut.	if I, he, she, it,	if I, he, she, it,
	we, you, they **should waken**	we, you, they **should be wakened**

Transitive and intransitive.

walk
(active voice)

PRINCIPAL PARTS: **walks, walking,
walked, walked**

be walked
(passive voice)

Infinitive: **to walk**
Perfect Infinitive: **to have walked**
Present Participle: **walking**
Past Participle: **walked**

Infinitive: **to be walked**
Perfect Infinitive: **to have been walked**
Present Participle: **being walked**
Past Participle: **been walked**

INDICATIVE MOOD

Pres.	I, we, you, they **walk**	I **am walked**
		we, you, they **are walked**
	he, she, it **walks**	he, she, it **is walked**
Pres.	I **am walking**	I **am being walked**
Prog.	we, you, they **are walking**	we, you, they **are being walked**
	he, she, it **is walking**	he, she, it **is being walked**
Pres.	I, we, you, they **do walk**	I, we, you, they **do get walked**
Int.	he, she, it **does walk**	he, she, it **does get walked**
Fut.	I, he, she, it,	I, he, she, it,
	we, you, they **will walk**	we, you, they **will be walked**
Past	I, he, she, it,	I, he, she, it **was walked**
	we, you, they **walked**	we, you, they **were walked**
Past	I, he, she, it **was walking**	I, he, she, it **was being walked**
Prog.	we, you, they **were walking**	we, you, they **were being walked**
Past	I, he, she, it,	I, he, she, it,
Int.	we, you, they **did walk**	we, you, they **did get walked**
Pres.	I, we, you, they **have walked**	I, we, you, they **have been walked**
Perf.	he, she, it **has walked**	he, she, it **has been walked**
Past	I, he, she, it,	I, he, she, it,
Perf.	we, you, they **had walked**	we, you, they **had been walked**
Fut.	I, he, she, it, we, you, they	I, he, she, it, we, you, they
Perf.	**will have walked**	**will have been walked**

IMPERATIVE MOOD

walk

be walked

SUBJUNCTIVE MOOD

Pres.	if I, he, she, it,	if I, he, she, it,
	we, you, they **walk**	we, you, they **be walked**
Past	if I, he, she, it,	if I, he, she, it,
	we, you, they **walked**	we, you, they **were walked**
Fut.	if I, he, she, it,	if I, he, she, it,
	we, you, they **should walk**	we, you, they **should be walked**

Intransitive and transitive.

want
(active voice)

be wanted
(passive voice)

Infinitive: **to want**
Perfect Infinitive: **to have wanted**
Present Participle: **wanting**
Past Participle: **wanted**

Infinitive: **to be wanted**
Perfect Infinitive: **to have been wanted**
Present Participle: **being wanted**
Past Participle: **been wanted**

INDICATIVE MOOD

Pres.	I, we, you, they **want**	I **am wanted**
		we, you, they **are wanted**
	he, she, it **wants**	he, she, it **is wanted**
Pres.	I **am wanting**	I **am being wanted**
Prog.	we, you, they **are wanting**	we, you, they **are being wanted**
	he, she, it **is wanting**	he, she, it **is being wanted**
Pres.	I, we, you, they **do want**	I, we, you, they **do get wanted**
Int.	he, she, it **does want**	he, she, it **does get wanted**
Fut.	I, he, she, it,	I, he, she, it,
	we, you, they **will want**	we, you, they **will be wanted**
Past	I, he, she, it,	I, he, she, it **was wanted**
	we, you, they **wanted**	we, you, they **were wanted**
Past	I, he, she, it **was wanting**	I, he, she, it **was being wanted**
Prog.	we, you, they **were wanting**	we, you, they **were being wanted**
Past	I, he, she, it,	I, he, she, it,
Int.	we, you, they **did want**	we, you, they **did get wanted**
Pres.	I, we, you, they **have wanted**	I, we, you, they **have been wanted**
Perf.	he, she, it **has wanted**	he, she, it **has been wanted**
Past	I, he, she, it,	I, he, she, it,
Perf.	we, you, they **had wanted**	we, you, they **had been wanted**
Fut.	I, he, she, it, we, you, they	I, he, she, it, we, you, they
Perf.	**will have wanted**	**will have been wanted**

IMPERATIVE MOOD

want   **be wanted**

SUBJUNCTIVE MOOD

Pres.	if I, he, she, it,	if I, he, she, it,
	we, you, they **want**	we, you, they **be wanted**
Past	if I, he, she, it,	if I, he, she, it,
	we, you, they **wanted**	we, you, they **were wanted**
Fut.	if I, he, she, it,	if I, he, she, it,
	we, you, they **should want**	we, you, they **should be wanted**

Transitive and intransitive.

watch
(active voice)

be watched
(passive voice)

Infinitive: **to watch**
Perfect Infinitive: **to have watched**
Present Participle: **watching**
Past Participle: **watched**

Infinitive: **to be watched**
Perfect Infinitive: **to have been watched**
Present Participle: **being watched**
Past Participle: **been watched**

INDICATIVE MOOD

Pres.	I, we, you, they **watch**	I **am watched**
		we, you, they **are watched**
	he, she, it **watches**	he, she, it **is watched**
Pres.	I **am watching**	I **am being watched**
Prog.	we, you, they **are watching**	we, you, they **are being watched**
	he, she, it **is watching**	he, she, it **is being watched**
Pres.	I, we, you, they **do watch**	I, we, you, they **do get watched**
Int.	he, she, it **does watch**	he, she, it **does get watched**
Fut.	I, he, she, it,	I, he, she, it,
	we, you, they **will watch**	we, you, they **will be watched**
Past	I, he, she, it,	I, he, she, it **was watched**
	we, you, they **watched**	we, you, they **were watched**
Past	I, he, she, it **was watching**	I, he, she, it **was being watched**
Prog.	we, you, they **were watching**	we, you, they **were being watched**
Past	I, he, she, it,	I, he, she, it,
Int.	we, you, they **did watch**	we, you, they **did get watched**
Pres.	I, we, you, they **have watched**	I, we, you, they **have been watched**
Perf.	he, she, it **has watched**	he, she, it **has been watched**
Past	I, he, she, it,	I, he, she, it,
Perf.	we, you, they **had watched**	we, you, they **had been watched**
Fut.	I, he, she, it, we, you, they	I, he, she, it, we, you, they
Perf.	**will have watched**	**will have been watched**

IMPERATIVE MOOD

watch   **be watched**

SUBJUNCTIVE MOOD

Pres.	if I, he, she, it,	if I, he, she, it,
	we, you, they **watch**	we, you, they **be watched**
Past	if I, he, she, it,	if I, he, she, it,
	we, you, **watched**	we, you, they **were watched**
Fut.	if I, he, she, it,	if I, he, she, it,
	we, you, they **should watch**	we, you, they **should be watched**

Intransitive and transitive.

waylay
(active voice)

be waylaid
(passive voice)

Infinitive: **to waylay**
Perfect Infinitive: **to have waylaid**
Present Participle: **waylaying**
Past Participle: **waylaid**

Infinitive: **to be waylaid**
Perfect Infinitive: **to have been waylaid**
Present Participle: **being waylaid**
Past Participle: **been waylaid**

INDICATIVE MOOD

Pres.	I, we, you, they **waylay**	I **am waylaid**
		we, you, they **are waylaid**
	he, she, it **waylays**	he, she, it **is waylaid**
Pres.	I **am waylaying**	I **am being waylaid**
Prog.	we, you, they **are waylaying**	we, you, they **are being waylaid**
	he, she, it **is waylaying**	he, she, it **is being waylaid**
Pres.	I, we, you, they **do waylay**	I, we, you, they **do get waylaid**
Int.	he, she, it **does waylay**	he, she, it **does get waylaid**
Fut.	I, he, she, it,	I, he, she, it,
	we, you, they **will waylay**	we, you, they **will be waylaid**
Past	I, he, she, it,	I, he, she, it **was waylaid**
	we, you, they **waylaid**	we, you, they **were waylaid**
Past	I, he, she, it **was waylaying**	I, he, she, it **was being waylaid**
Prog.	we, you, they **were waylaying**	we, you, they **were being waylaid**
Past	I, he, she, it,	I, he, she, it,
Int.	we, you, they **did waylay**	we, you, they **did get waylaid**
Pres.	I, we, you, they **have waylaid**	I, we, you, they **have been waylaid**
Perf.	he, she, it **has waylaid**	he, she, it **has been waylaid**
Past	I, he, she, it,	I, he, she, it,
Perf.	we, you, they **had waylaid**	we, you, they **had been waylaid**
Fut.	I, he, she, it, we, you, they	I, he, she, it, we, you, they
Perf.	**will have waylaid**	**will have been waylaid**

IMPERATIVE MOOD

waylay

be waylaid

SUBJUNCTIVE MOOD

Pres.	if I, he, she, it,	if I, he, she, it,
	we, you, they **waylay**	we, you, they **be waylaid**
Past	if I, he, she, it,	if I, he, she, it,
	we, you, they **waylaid**	we, you, they **were waylaid**
Fut.	if I, he, she, it,	if I, he, she, it,
	we, you, they **should waylay**	we, you, they **should be waylaid**

474

wear
(active voice)

PRINCIPAL PARTS: **wears, wearing, wore, worn**

be worn
(passive voice)

Infinitive: **to wear**
Perfect Infinitive: **to have worn**
Present Participle: **wearing**
Past Participle: **worn**

Infinitive: **to be worn**
Perfect Infinitive: **to have been worn**
Present Participle: **being worn**
Past Participle: **been worn**

INDICATIVE MOOD

Pres.	I, we, you, they **wear**	I **am worn**
		we, you, they **are worn**
	he, she, it **wears**	he, she, it **is worn**
Pres. Prog.	I **am wearing**	I **am being worn**
	we, you, they **are wearing**	we, you, they **are being worn**
	he, she, it **is wearing**	he, she, it **is being worn**
Pres. Int.	I, we, you, they **do wear**	I, we, you, they **do get worn**
	he, she, it **does wear**	he, she, it **does get worn**
Fut.	I, he, she, it,	I, he, she, it,
	we, you, they **will wear**	we, you, they **will be worn**
Past	I, he, she, it,	I, he, she, it **was worn**
	we, you, they **wore**	we, you, they **were worn**
Past Prog.	I, he, she, it **was wearing**	I, he, she, it **was being worn**
	we, you, they **were wearing**	we, you, they **were being worn**
Past Int.	I, he, she, it,	I, he, she, it,
	we, you, they **did wear**	we, you, they **did get worn**
Pres. Perf.	I, we, you, they **have worn**	I, we, you, they **have been worn**
	he, she, it **has worn**	he, she, it **has been worn**
Past Perf.	I, he, she, it,	I, he, she, it,
	we, you, they **had worn**	we, you, they **had been worn**
Fut. Perf.	I, he, she, it, we, you, they	I, he, she, it, we, you, they
	will have worn	**will have been worn**

IMPERATIVE MOOD

wear　　　　**be worn**

SUBJUNCTIVE MOOD

Pres.	if I, he, she, it,	if I, he, she, it,
	we, you, they **wear**	we, you, they **be worn**
Past	if I, he, she, it,	if I, he, she, it,
	we, you, they **wore**	we, you, they **were worn**
Fut.	if I, he, she, it,	if I, he, she, it,
	we, you, they **should wear**	we, you, they **should be worn**

Transitive and intransitive.

weave
(active voice)

PRINCIPAL PARTS: **weaves, weaving, wove/weaved, woven/weaved**

be woven/weaved
(passive voice)

Infinitive: **to weave**
Perfect Infinitive: **to have woven**
Present Participle: **weaving**
Past Participle: **woven**

Infinitive: **to be woven**
Perfect Infinitive: **to have been woven**
Present Participle: **being woven**
Past Participle: **been woven**

INDICATIVE MOOD

Pres.	I, we, you, they **weave**	I **am woven** we, you, they **are woven** he, she, it **is woven**
	he, she, it **weaves**	
Pres. *Prog.*	I **am weaving** we, you, they **are weaving** he, she, it **is weaving**	I **am being woven** we, you, they **are being woven** he, she, it **is being woven**
Pres. *Int.*	I, we, you, they **do weave** he, she, it **does weave**	I, we, you, they **do get woven** he, she, it **does get woven**
Fut.	I, he, she, it, we, you, they **will weave**	I, he, she, it, we, you, they **will be woven**
Past	I, he, she, it, we, you, they **wove**	I, he, she, it **was woven** we, you, they **were woven**
Past *Prog.*	I, he, she, it **was weaving** we, you, they **were weaving**	I, he, she, it **was being woven** we, you, they **were being woven**
Past *Int.*	I, he, she, it, we, you, they **did weave**	I, he, she, it, we, you, they **did get woven**
Pres. *Perf.*	I, we, you, they **have woven** he, she, it **has woven**	I, we, you, they **have been woven** he, she, it **has been woven**
Past *Perf.*	I, he, she, it, we, you, they **had woven**	I, he, she, it, we, you, they **had been woven**
Fut. *Perf.*	I, he, she, it, we, you, they **will have woven**	I, he, she, it, we, you, they **will have been woven**

IMPERATIVE MOOD

weave   **be woven**

SUBJUNCTIVE MOOD

Pres.	if I, he, she, it, we, you, they **weave**	if I, he, she, it, we, you, they **be woven**
Past	if I, he, she, it, we, you, they **wove**	if I, he, she, it, we, you, they **were woven**
Fut.	if I, he, she, it, we, you, they **should weave**	if I, he, she, it, we, you, they **should be woven**

The transitive verb with the forms WOVE and WOVEN has to do with making cloth. The transitive and intransitive verb with the past tense and past participle WEAVED means "moving from side to side as through traffic." The *Oxford Dictionary* lists WOVE as an alternate form of the past participle.

wed
(active voice)

be wed/wedded
(passive voice)

Infinitive: **to wed**
Perfect Infinitive: **to have wed**
Present Participle: **wedding**
Past Participle: **wed**

Infinitive: **to be wed**
Perfect Infinitive: **to have been wed**
Present Participle: **being wed**
Past Participle: **been wed**

INDICATIVE MOOD

Pres.	I, we, you, they **wed**	I **am wed**
		we, you, they **are wed**
	he, she, it **weds**	he, she, it **is wed**
Pres.	I **am wedding**	I **am being wed**
Prog.	we, you, they **are wedding**	we, you, they **are being wed**
	he, she, it **is wedding**	he, she, it **is being wed**
Pres.	I, we, you, they **do wed**	I, we, you, they **do get wed**
Int.	he, she, it **does wed**	he, she, it **does get wed**
Fut.	I, he, she, it,	I, he, she, it,
	we, you, they **will wed**	we, you, they **will be wed**
Past	I, he, she, it,	I, he, she, it **was wed**
	we, you, they **wedded**	we, you, they **were wed**
Past	I, he, she, it **was wedding**	I, he, she, it **was being wed**
Prog.	we, you, they **were wedding**	we, you, they **were being wed**
Past	I, he, she, it,	I, he, she, it,
Int.	we, you, they **did wed**	we, you, they **did get wed**
Pres.	I, we, you, they **have wed**	I, we, you, they **have been wed**
Perf.	he, she, it **has wed**	he, she, it **has been wed**
Past	I, he, she, it,	I, he, she, it,
Perf.	we, you, they **had wed**	we, you, they **had been wed**
Fut.	I, he, she, it, we, you, they	I, he, she, it, we, you, they
Perf.	**will have wed**	**will have been wed**

IMPERATIVE MOOD

wed   **be wed**

SUBJUNCTIVE MOOD

Pres.	if I, he, she, it,	if I, he, she, it,
	we, you, they **wed**	we, you, they **be wed**
Past	if I, he, she, it,	if I, he, she, it,
	we, you, they **wedded**	we, you, they **were wed**
Fut.	if I, he, she, it,	if I, he, she, it,
	we, you, they **should wed**	we, you, they **should be wed**

Transitive and intransitive.

weep
(active voice)

be wept
(passive voice)

Infinitive: **to weep**
Perfect Infinitive: **to have wept**
Present Participle: **weeping**
Past Participle: **wept**

Infinitive: **to be wept**
Perfect Infinitive: **to have been wept**
Present Participle: **being wept**
Past Participle: **been wept**

INDICATIVE MOOD

Pres.	I, we, you, they **weep**		I **am wept**
			we, you, they **are wept**
	he, she, it **weeps**		he, she, it **is wept**
Pres.	I **am weeping**		I **am being wept**
Prog.	we, you, they **are weeping**		we, you, they **are being wept**
	he, she, it **is weeping**		he, she, it **is being wept**
Pres.	I, we, you, they **do weep**		I, we, you, they **do get wept**
Int.	he, she, it **does weep**		he, she, it **does get wept**
Fut.	I, he, she, it,		I, he, she, it,
	we, you, they **will weep**		we, you, they **will be wept**
Past	I, he, she, it,		I, he, she, it **was wept**
	we, you, they **wept**		we, you, they **were wept**
Past	I, he, she, it **was weeping**		I, he, she, it **was being wept**
Prog.	we, you, they **were weeping**		we, you, they **were being wept**
Past	I, he, she, it,		I, he, she, it,
Int.	we, you, they **did weep**		we, you, they **did get wept**
Pres.	I, we, you, they **have wept**		I, we, you, they **have been wept**
Perf.	he, she, it **has wept**		he, she, it **has been wept**
Past	I, he, she, it,		I, he, she, it,
Perf.	we, you, they **had wept**		we, you, they **had been wept**
Fut.	I, he, she, it, we, you, they		I, he, she, it, we, you, they
Perf.	**will have wept**		**will have been wept**

IMPERATIVE MOOD

weep   **be wept**

SUBJUNCTIVE MOOD

Pres.	if I, he, she, it,		if I, he, she, it,
	we, you, they **weep**		we, you, they **be wept**
Past	if I, he, she, it,		if I, he, she, it,
	we, you, they **wept**		we, you, they **were wept**
Fut.	if I, he, she, it,		if I, he, she, it,
	we, you, they **should weep**		we, you, they **should be wept**

Transitive and intransitive.

wet
(active voice)

be wet/wetted
(passive voice)

Infinitive: **to wet**
Perfect Infinitive: **to have wet**
Present Participle: **wetting**
Past Participle: **wet**

Infinitive: **to be wet**
Perfect Infinitive: **to have been wet**
Present Participle: **being wet**
Past Participle: **been wet**

INDICATIVE MOOD

Pres.	I, we, you, they **wet**	I **am wet**
		we, you, they **are wet**
	he, she, it **wets**	he, she, it **is wet**
Pres. *Prog.*	I **am wetting**	I **am being wet**
	we, you, they **are wetting**	we, you, they **are being wet**
	he, she, it **is wetting**	he, she, it **is being wet**
Pres. *Int.*	I, we, you, they **do wet**	I, we, you, they **do get wet**
	he, she, it **does wet**	he, she, it **does get wet**
Fut.	I, he, she, it,	I, he, she, it,
	we, you, they **will wet**	we, you, they **will be wet**
Past	I, he, she, it,	I, he, she, it **was wet**
	we, you, they **wet**	we, you, they **were wet**
Past *Prog.*	I, he, she, it **was wetting**	I, he, she, it **was being wet**
	we, you, they **were wetting**	we, you, they **were being wet**
Past *Int.*	I, he, she, it,	I, he, she, it,
	we, you, they **did wet**	we, you, they **did get wet**
Pres. *Perf.*	I, we, you, they **have wet**	I, we, you, they **have been wet**
	he, she, it **has wet**	he, she, it **has been wet**
Past *Perf.*	I, he, she, it,	I, he, she, it,
	we, you, they **had wet**	we, you, they **had been wet**
Fut. *Perf.*	I, he, she, it, we, you, they **will have wet**	I, he, she, it, we, you, they **will have been wet**

IMPERATIVE MOOD

wet   **be wet**

SUBJUNCTIVE MOOD

Pres.	if I, he, she, it,	if I, he, she, it,
	we, you, they **wet**	we, you, they **be wet**
Past	if I, he, she, it,	if I, he, she, it,
	we, you, they **wet**	we, you, they **were wet**
Fut.	if I, he, she, it,	if I, he, she, it,
	we, you, they **should wet**	we, you, they **should be wet**

Transitive and intransitive.

whip
(active voice)

be whipped/whipt
(passive voice)

Infinitive: **to whip**
Perfect Infinitive: **to have whipped**
Present Participle: **whipping**
Past Participle: **whipped**

Infinitive: **to be whipped**
Perfect Infinitive: **to have been whipped**
Present Participle: **being whipped**
Past Participle: **been whipped**

INDICATIVE MOOD

Pres.	I, we, you, they **whip**	I **am whipped**
		we, you, they **are whipped**
	he, she, it **whips**	he, she, it **is whipped**
Pres.	I **am whipping**	I **am being whipped**
Prog.	we, you, they **are whipping**	we, you, they **are being whipped**
	he, she, it **is whipping**	he, she, it **is being whipped**
Pres.	I, we, you, they **do whip**	I, we, you, they **do get whipped**
Int.	he, she, it **does whip**	he, she, it **does get whipped**
Fut.	I, he, she, it,	I, he, she, it,
	we, you, they **will whip**	we, you, they **will be whipped**
Past	I, he, she, it,	I, he, she, it **was whipped**
	we, you, they **whipped**	we, you, they **were whipped**
Past	I, he, she, it **was whipping**	I, he, she, it **was being whipped**
Prog.	we, you, they **were whipping**	we, you, they **were being whipped**
Past	I, he, she, it,	I, he, she, it,
Int.	we, you, they **did whip**	we, you, they **did get whipped**
Pres.	I, we, you, they **have whipped**	I, we, you, they **have been whipped**
Perf.	he, she, it **has whipped**	he, she, it **has been whipped**
Past	I, he, she, it,	I, he, she, it,
Perf.	we, you, they **had whipped**	we, you, they **had been whipped**
Fut.	I, he, she, it, we, you, they	I, he, she, it, we, you, they
Perf.	**will have whipped**	**will have been whipped**

IMPERATIVE MOOD

whip   **be whipped**

SUBJUNCTIVE MOOD

Pres.	if I, he, she, it,	if I, he, she, it,
	we, you, they **whip**	we, you, they **be whipped**
Past	if I, he, she, it,	if I, he, she, it,
	we, you, they **whipped**	we, you, they **were whipped**
Fut.	if I, he, she, it,	if I, he, she, it,
	we, you, they **should whip**	we, you, they **should be whipped**

Transitive and intransitive. The *Oxford Dictionary* prefers the form WHIPT for the past tense and past participle.

will
(active voice)

PRINCIPAL PARTS: **wills, willing, willed, willed**

be willed
(passive voice)

Infinitive: **to will**
Perfect Infinitive: **to have willed**
Present Participle: **willing**
Past Participle: **willed**

Infinitive: **to be willed**
Perfect Infinitive: **to have been willed**
Present Participle: **being willed**
Past Participle: **been willed**

INDICATIVE MOOD

Pres.	I, we, you, they **will**	I **am willed**
		we, you, they **are willed**
	he, she, it **wills**	he, she, it **is willed**
Pres.	I **am willing**	I **am being willed**
Prog.	we, you, they **are willing**	we, you, they **are being willed**
	he, she, it **is willing**	he, she, it **is being willed**
Pres.	I, we, you, they **do will**	I, we, you, they **do get willed**
Int.	he, she, it **does will**	he, she, it **does get willed**
Fut.	I, he, she, it,	I, he, she, it,
	we, you, they **will will**	we, you, they **will be willed**
Past	I, he, she, it,	I, he, she, it **was willed**
	we, you, they **willed**	we, you, they **were willed**
Past	I, he, she, it **was willing**	I, he, she, it **was being willed**
Prog.	we, you, they **were willing**	we, you, they **were being willed**
Past	I, he, she, it,	I, he, she, it,
Int.	we, you, they **did will**	we, you, they **did get willed**
Pres.	I, we, you, they **have willed**	I, we, you, they **have been willed**
Perf.	he, she, it **has willed**	he, she, it **has been willed**
Past	I, he, she, it,	I, he, she, it,
Perf.	we, you, they **had willed**	we, you, they **had been willed**
Fut.	I, he, she, it, we, you, they	I, he, she, it, we, you, they
Perf.	**will have willed**	**will have been willed**

IMPERATIVE MOOD

will

be willed

SUBJUNCTIVE MOOD

Pres.	if I, he, she, it,	if I, he, she, it,
	we, you, they **will**	we, you, they **be willed**
Past	if I, he, she, it,	if I, he, she, it,
	we, you, they **willed**	we, you, they **were willed**
Fut.	if I, he, she, it,	if I, he, she, it,
	we, you, they **should will**	we, you, they **should be willed**

Transitive and intransitive. As an auxiliary verb WILL has only two forms: WILL for the present and WOULD for the past.

481

win
(active voice)

be won
(passive voice)

Infinitive: **to win**
Perfect Infinitive: **to have won**
Present Participle: **winning**
Past Participle: **won**

Infinitive: **to be won**
Perfect Infinitive: **to have been won**
Present Participle: **being won**
Past Participle: **been won**

INDICATIVE MOOD

Pres.	I, we, you, they **win**	I **am won**
		we, you, they **are won**
	he, she, it **wins**	he, she, it **is won**
Pres.	I **am winning**	I **am being won**
Prog.	we, you, they **are winning**	we, you, they **are being won**
	he, she, it **is winning**	he, she, it **is being won**
Pres.	I, we, you, they **do win**	I, we, you, they **do get won**
Int.	he, she, it **does win**	he, she, it **does get won**
Fut.	I, he, she, it,	I, he, she, it,
	we, you, they **will win**	we, you, they **will be won**
Past	I, he, she, it,	I, he, she, it **was won**
	we, you, they **won**	we, you, they **were won**
Past	I, he, she, it **was winning**	I, he, she, it **was being won**
Prog.	we, you, they **were winning**	we, you, they **were being won**
Past	I, he, she, it,	I, he, she, it,
Int.	we, you, they **did win**	we, you, they **did get won**
Pres.	I, we, you, they **have won**	I, we, you, they **have been won**
Perf.	he, she, it **has won**	he, she, it **has been won**
Past	I, he, she, it,	I, he, she, it,
Perf.	we, you, they **had won**	we, you, they **had been won**
Fut.	I, he, she, it, we, you, they	I, he, she, it, we, you, they
Perf.	**will have won**	**will have been won**

IMPERATIVE MOOD

win   **be won**

SUBJUNCTIVE MOOD

Pres.	if I, he, she, it,	if I, he, she, it,
	we, you, they **win**	we, you, they **be won**
Past	if I, he, she, it,	if I, he, she, it,
	we, you, they **won**	we, you, they **were won**
Fut.	if I, he, she, it,	if I, he, she, it,
	we, you, they **should win**	we, you, they **should be won**

Intransitive and transitive.

wind
(active voice)

PRINCIPAL PARTS: winds, winding, winded, winded

be winded
(passive voice)

Infinitive: **to wind**
Perfect Infinitive: **to have winded**
Present Participle: **winding**
Past Participle: **winded**

Infinitive: **to be winded**
Perfect Infinitive: **to have been winded**
Present Participle: **being winded**
Past Participle: **been winded**

INDICATIVE MOOD

Pres.	I, we, you, they **wind**	I **am winded**
		we, you, they **are winded**
	he, she, it **winds**	he, she, it **is winded**
Pres.	I **am winding**	I **am being winded**
Prog.	we, you, they **are winding**	we, you, they **are being winded**
	he, she, it **is winding**	he, she, it **is being winded**
Pres.	I, we, you, they **do wind**	I, we, you, they **do get winded**
Int.	he, she, it **does wind**	he, she, it **does get winded**
Fut.	I, he, she, it,	I, he, she, it,
	we, you, they **will wind**	we, you, they **will be winded**
Past	I, he, she, it,	I, he, she, it **was winded**
	we, you, they **winded**	we, you, they **were winded**
Past	I, he, she, it **was winding**	I, he, she, it **was being winded**
Prog.	we, you, they **were winding**	we, you, they **were being winded**
Past	I, he, she, it,	I, he, she, it,
Int.	we, you, they **did wind**	we, you, they **did get winded**
Pres.	I, we, you, they **have winded**	I, we, you, they **have been winded**
Perf.	he, she, it **has winded**	he, she, it **has been winded**
Past	I, he, she, it,	I, he, she, it,
Perf.	we, you, they **had winded**	we, you, they **had been winded**
Fut.	I, he, she, it, we, you, they	I, he, she, it, we, you, they
Perf.	**will have winded**	**will have been winded**

IMPERATIVE MOOD

wind　　　　　　　　　　**be winded**

SUBJUNCTIVE MOOD

Pres.	if I, he, she, it,	if I, he, she, it,
	we, you, they **wind**	we, you, they **be winded**
Past	if I, he, she, it,	if I, he, she, it,
	we, you, they **winded**	we, you, they **were winded**
Fut.	if I, he, she, it,	if I, he, she, it,
	we, you, they **should wind**	we, you, they **should be winded**

Transitive and intransitive. This verb means to "expose to the air, or be short of breath." The verb is pronounced like the "wind" that blows.

wind
(active voice)

be wound
(passive voice)

Infinitive: **to wind**
Perfect Infinitive: **to have wound**
Present Participle: **winding**
Past Participle: **wound**

Infinitive: **to be wound**
Perfect Infinitive: **to have been wound**
Present Participle: **being wound**
Past Participle: **been wound**

INDICATIVE MOOD

Pres.	I, we, you, they **wind**	I **am wound**
		we, you, they **are wound**
	he, she, it **winds**	he, she, it **is wound**
Pres. Prog.	I **am winding**	I **am being wound**
	we, you, they **are winding**	we, you, they **are being wound**
	he, she, it **is winding**	he, she, it **is being wound**
Pres. Int.	I, we, you, they **do wind**	I, we, you, they **do get wound**
	he, she, it **does wind**	he, she, it **does get wound**
Fut.	I, he, she, it, we, you, they **will wind**	I, he, she, it, we, you, they **will be wound**
Past	I, he, she, it, we, you, they **wound**	I, he, she, it **was wound**
		we, you, they **were wound**
Past Prog.	I, he, she, it **was winding**	I, he, she, it **was being wound**
	we, you, they **were winding**	we, you, they **were being wound**
Past Int.	I, he, she, it, we, you, they **did wind**	I, he, she, it, we, you, they **did get wound**
Pres. Perf.	I, we, you, they **have wound**	I, we, you, they **have been wound**
	he, she, it **has wound**	he, she, it **has been wound**
Past Perf.	I, he, she, it, we, you, they **had wound**	I, he, she, it, we, you, they **had been wound**
Fut. Perf.	I, he, she, it, we, you, they **will have wound**	I, he, she, it, we, you, they **will have been wound**

IMPERATIVE MOOD

wind

be wound

SUBJUNCTIVE MOOD

Pres.	if I, he, she, it, we, you, they **wind**	if I, he, she, it, we, you, they **be wound**
Past	if I, he, she, it, we, you, they **wound**	if I, he, she, it, we, you, they **were wound**
Fut.	if I, he, she, it, we, you, they **should wind**	if I, he, she, it, we, you, they **should be wound**

Transitive and intransitive. This verb means to "turn or twirl around, like a watch."

wish
(active voice)

be wished
(passive voice)

Infinitive: **to wish**
Perfect Infinitive: **to have wished**
Present Participle: **wishing**
Past Participle: **wished**

Infinitive: **to be wished**
Perfect Infinitive: **to have been wished**
Present Participle: **being wished**
Past Participle: **been wished**

INDICATIVE MOOD

Pres.	I, we, you, they **wish**	I **am wished**
		we, you, they **are wished**
	he, she, it **wishes**	he, she, it **is wished**
Pres.	I **am wishing**	I **am being wished**
Prog.	we, you, they **are wishing**	we, you, they **are being wished**
	he, she, it **is wishing**	he, she, it **is being wished**
Pres.	I, we, you, they **do wish**	I, we, you, they **do get wished**
Int.	he, she, it **does wish**	he, she, it **does get wished**
Fut.	I, he, she, it,	I, he, she, it,
	we, you, they **will wish**	we, you, they **will be wished**
Past	I, he, she, it,	I, he, she, it **was wished**
	we, you, they **wished**	we, you, they **were wished**
Past	I, he, she, it **was wishing**	I, he, she, it **was being wished**
Prog.	we, you, they **were wishing**	we, you, they **were being wished**
Past	I, he, she, it,	I, he, she, it,
Int.	we, you, they **did wish**	we, you, they **did get wished**
Pres.	I, we, you, they **have wished**	I, we, you, they **have been wished**
Perf.	he, she, it **has wished**	he, she, it **has been wished**
Past	I, he, she, it,	I, he, she, it,
Perf.	we, you, they **had wished**	we, you, they **had been wished**
Fut.	I, he, she, it, we, you, they	I, he, she, it, we, you, they
Perf.	**will have wished**	**will have been wished**

IMPERATIVE MOOD

wish   **be wished**

SUBJUNCTIVE MOOD

Pres.	if I, he, she, it,	if I, he, she, it,
	we, you, they **wish**	we, you, they **be wished**
Past	if I, he, she, it,	if I, he, she, it,
	we, you, they **wished**	we, you, they **were wished**
Fut.	if I, he, she, it,	if I, he, she, it,
	we, you, they **should wish**	we, you, they **should be wished**

Transitive and intransitive.

withhold
(active voice)

PRINCIPAL PARTS: **withholds, withholding, withheld, withheld**

be withheld
(passive voice)

Infinitive: **to withhold**
Perfect Infinitive: **to have withheld**
Present Participle: **withholding**
Past Participle: **withheld**

Infinitive: **to be withheld**
Perfect Infinitive: **to have been withheld**
Present Participle: **being withheld**
Past Participle: **been withheld**

INDICATIVE MOOD

Pres.	I, we, you, they **withhold**	I **am withheld**
		we, you, they **are withheld**
	he, she, it **withholds**	he, she, it **is withheld**
Pres. *Prog.*	I **am withholding**	I **am being withheld**
	we, you, they **are withholding**	we, you, they **are being withheld**
	he, she, it **is withholding**	he, she, it **is being withheld**
Pres. *Int.*	I, we, you, they **do withhold**	I, we, you, they **do get withheld**
	he, she, it **does withhold**	he, she, it **does get withheld**
Fut.	I, he, she, it, we, you, they **will withhold**	I, he, she, it, we, you, they **will be withheld**
Past	I, he, she, it, we, you, they **withheld**	I, he, she, it **was withheld** we, you, they **were withheld**
Past *Prog.*	I, he, she, it **was withholding** we, you, they **were withholding**	I, he, she, it **was being withheld** we, you, they **were being withheld**
Past *Int.*	I, he, she, it, we, you, they **did withhold**	I, he, she, it, we, you, they **did get withheld**
Pres. *Perf.*	I, we, you, they **have withheld** he, she, it **has withheld**	I, we, you, they **have been withheld** he, she, it **has been withheld**
Past *Perf.*	I, he, she, it, we, you, they **had withheld**	I, he, she, it, we, you, they **had been withheld**
Fut. *Perf.*	I, he, she, it, we, you, they **will have withheld**	I, he, she, it, we, you, they **will have been withheld**

IMPERATIVE MOOD

withhold　　　　　　**be withheld**

SUBJUNCTIVE MOOD

Pres.	if I, he, she, it, we, you, they **withhold**	if I, he, she, it, we, you, they **be withheld**
Past	if I, he, she, it, we, you, they **withheld**	if I, he, she, it, we, you, they **were withheld**
Fut.	if I, he, she, it, we, you, they **should withhold**	if I, he, she, it, we, you, they **should be withheld**

Transitive and intransitive.

withstand
(active voice)

be withstood
(passive voice)

Infinitive: **to withstand**
Perfect Infinitive: **to have withstood**
Present Participle: **withstanding**
Past Participle: **withstood**

Infinitive: **to be withstood**
Perfect Infinitive: **to have been withstood**
Present Participle: **being withstood**
Past Participle: **been withstood**

INDICATIVE MOOD

Pres.	I, we, you, they **withstand**	I **am withstood**
		we, you, they **are withstood**
	he, she, it **withstands**	he, she, it **is withstood**
Pres.	I **am withstanding**	I **am being withstood**
Prog.	we, you, they **are withstanding**	we, you, they **are being withstood**
	he, she, it **is withstanding**	he, she, it **is being withstood**
Pres.	I, we, you, they **do withstand**	I, we, you, they **do get withstood**
Int.	he, she, it **does withstand**	he, she, it **does get withstood**
Fut.	I, he, she, it,	I, he, she, it,
	we, you, they **will withstand**	we, you, they **will be withstood**
Past	I, he, she, it,	I, he, she, it **was withstood**
	we, you, they **withstood**	we, you, they **were withstood**
Past	I, he, she, it **was withstanding**	I, he, she, it **was being withstood**
Prog.	we, you, they **were withstanding**	we, you, they **were being withstood**
Past	I, he, she, it,	I, he, she, it,
Int.	we, you, they **did withstand**	we, you, they **did get withstood**
Pres.	I, we, you, they **have withstood**	I, we, you, they **have been withstood**
Perf.	he, she, it **has withstood**	he, she, it **has been withstood**
Past	I, he, she, it,	I, he, she, it,
Perf.	we, you, they **had withstood**	we, you, they **had been withstood**
Fut.	I, he, she, it, we, you, they	I, he, she, it, we, you, they
Perf.	**will have withstood**	**will have been withstood**

IMPERATIVE MOOD

withstand

be withstood

SUBJUNCTIVE MOOD

Pres.	if I, he, she, it,	if I, he, she, it,
	we, you, they **withstand**	we, you, they **be withstood**
Past	if I, he, she, it,	if I, he, she, it,
	we, you, they **withstood**	we, you, they **were withstood**
Fut.	if I, he, she, it,	if I, he, she, it,
	we, you, they **should withstand**	we, you, they **should be withstood**

Transitive and intransitive.

wonder
(active voice)

be wondered
(passive voice)

Infinitive: **to wonder**
Perfect Infinitive: **to have wondered**
Present Participle: **wondering**
Past Participle: **wondered**

Infinitive: **to be wondered**
Perfect Infinitive: **to have been wondered**
Present Participle: **being wondered**
Past Participle: **been wondered**

INDICATIVE MOOD

Pres.	I, we, you, they **wonder**	I **am wondered**
		we, you, they **are wondered**
	he, she, it **wonders**	he, she, it **is wondered**
Pres.	I **am wondering**	I **am being wondered**
Prog.	we, you, they **are wondering**	we, you, they **are being wondered**
	he, she, it **is wondering**	he, she, it **is being wondered**
Pres.	I, we, you, they **do wonder**	I, we, you, they **do get wondered**
Int.	he, she, it **does wonder**	he, she, it **does get wondered**
Fut.	I, he, she, it,	I, he, she, it,
	we, you, they **will wonder**	we, you, they **will be wondered**
Past	I, he, she, it,	I, he, she, it **was wondered**
	we, you, they **wondered**	we, you, they **were wondered**
Past	I, he, she, it **was wondering**	I, he, she, it **was being wondered**
Prog.	we, you, they **were wondering**	we, you, they **were being wondered**
Past	I, he, she, it,	I, he, she, it,
Int.	we, you, they **did wonder**	we, you, they **did get wondered**
Pres.	I, we, you, they **have wondered**	I, we, you, they **have been wondered**
Perf.	he, she, it **has wondered**	he, she, it **has been wondered**
Past	I, he, she, it,	I, he, she, it,
Perf.	we, you, they **had wondered**	we, you, they **had been wondered**
Fut.	I, he, she, it, we, you, they	I, he, she, it, we, you, they
Perf.	**will have wondered**	**will have been wondered**

IMPERATIVE MOOD

wonder   **be wondered**

SUBJUNCTIVE MOOD

Pres.	if I, he, she, it,	if I, he, she, it,
	we, you, they **wonder**	we, you, they **be wondered**
Past	if I, he, she, it,	if I, he, she, it,
	we, you, they **wondered**	we, you, they **were wondered**
Fut.	if I, he, she, it,	if I, he, she, it,
	we, you, they **should wonder**	we, you, they **should be wondered**

Intransitive and transitive.

work
(active voice)

PRINCIPAL PARTS: **works, working,
worked/wrought, worked/wrought**

be worked/wrought
(passive voice)

Infinitive: **to work**
Perfect Infinitive: **to have worked**
Present Participle: **working**
Past Participle: **worked**

Infinitive: **to be worked**
Perfect Infinitive: **to have been worked**
Present Participle: **being worked**
Past Participle: **been worked**

INDICATIVE MOOD

Pres.	I, we, you, they **work**		I **am worked** we, you, they **are worked**
	he, she, it **works**		he, she, it **is worked**
Pres. *Prog.*	I **am working** we, you, they **are working** he, she, it **is working**		I **am being worked** we, you, they **are being worked** he, she, it **is being worked**
Pres. *Int.*	I, we, you, they **do work** he, she, it **does work**		I, we, you, they **do get worked** he, she, it **does get worked**
Fut.	I, he, she, it, we, you, they **will work**		I, he, she, it, we, you, they **will be worked**
Past	I, he, she, it, we, you, they **worked**		I, he, she, it **was worked** we, you, they **were worked**
Past *Prog.*	I, he, she, it **was working** we, you, they **were working**		I, he, she, it **was being worked** we, you, they **were being worked**
Past *Int.*	I, he, she, it, we, you, they **did work**		I, he, she, it, we, you, they **did get worked**
Pres. *Perf.*	I, we, you, they **have worked** he, she, it **has worked**		I, we, you, they **have been worked** he, she, it **has been worked**
Past *Perf.*	I, he, she, it, we, you, they **had worked**		I, he, she, it, we, you, they **had been worked**
Fut. *Perf.*	I, he, she, it, we, you, they **will have worked**		I, he, she, it, we, you, they **will have been worked**

IMPERATIVE MOOD

work   **be worked**

SUBJUNCTIVE MOOD

Pres.	if I, he, she, it, we, you, they **work**	if I, he, she, it, we, you, they **be worked**
Past	if I, he, she, it, we, you, they **worked**	if I, he, she, it, we, you, they **were worked**
Fut.	if I, he, she, it, we, you, they **should work**	if I, he, she, it, we, you, they **should be worked**

Intransitive and transitive. The past tense and past participle can be WORKED or WROUGHT.

worry
(active voice)

PRINCIPAL PARTS: **worries, worrying, worried, worried**

be worried
(passive voice)

Infinitive: **to worry**
Perfect Infinitive: **to have worried**
Present Participle: **worrying**
Past Participle: **worried**

Infinitive: **to be worried**
Perfect Infinitive: **to have been worried**
Present Participle: **being worried**
Past Participle: **been worried**

INDICATIVE MOOD

Pres.	I, we, you, they **worry**	I **am worried** we, you, they **are worried**
	he, she, it **worries**	he, she, it **is worried**
Pres. *Prog.*	I **am worrying** we, you, they **are worrying** he, she, it **is worrying**	I **am being worried** we, you, they **are being worried** he, she, it **is being worried**
Pres. *Int.*	I, we, you, they **do worry** he, she, it **does worry**	I, we, you, they **do get worried** he, she, it **does get worried**
Fut.	I, he, she, it, we, you, they **will worry**	I, he, she, it, we, you, they **will be worried**
Past	I, he, she, it, we, you, they **worried**	I, he, she, it **was worried** we, you, they **were worried**
Past *Prog.*	I, he, she, it **was worrying** we, you, they **were worrying**	I, he, she, it **was being worried** we, you, they **were being worried**
Past *Int.*	I, he, she, it, we, you, they **did worry**	I, he, she, it, we, you, they **did get worried**
Pres. *Perf.*	I, we, you, they **have worried** he, she, it **has worried**	I, we, you, they **have been worried** he, she, it **has been worried**
Past *Perf.*	I, he, she, it, we, you, they **had worried**	I, he, she, it, we, you, they **had been worried**
Fut. *Perf.*	I, he, she, it, we, you, they **will have worried**	I, he, she, it, we, you, they **will have been worried**

IMPERATIVE MOOD

worry	**be worried**

SUBJUNCTIVE MOOD

Pres.	if I, he, she, it, we, you, they **worry**	if I, he, she, it, we, you, they **be worried**
Past	if I, he, she, it, we, you, they **worried**	if I, he, she, it, we, you, they **were worried**
Fut.	if I, he, she, it, we, you, they **should worry**	if I, he, she, it, we, you, they **should be worried**

Intransitive and transitive.

worship
(active voice)

be worshiped/ worshipped
(passive voice)

Infinitive: **to worship**
Perfect Infinitive: **to have worshiped**
Present Participle: **worshiping**
Past Participle: **worshiped**

Infinitive: **to be worshiped**
Perfect Infinitive: **to have been worshiped**
Present Participle: **being worshiped**
Past Participle: **been worshiped**

INDICATIVE MOOD

Pres.	I, we, you, they **worship**	I **am worshiped**
		we, you, they **are worshiped**
	he, she, it **worships**	he, she, it **is worshiped**
Pres.	I **am worshiping**	I **am being worshiped**
Prog.	we, you, they **are worshiping**	we, you, they **are being worshiped**
	he, she, it **is worshiping**	he, she, it **is being worshiped**
Pres.	I, we, you, they **do worship**	I, we, you, they **do get worshiped**
Int.	he, she, it **does worship**	he, she, it **does get worshiped**
Fut.	I, he, she, it,	I, he, she, it,
	we, you, they **will worship**	we, you, they **will be worshiped**
Past	I, he, she, it,	I, he, she, it **was worshiped**
	we, you, they **worshiped**	we, you, they **were worshiped**
Past	I, he, she, it **was worshiping**	I, he, she, it **was being worshiped**
Prog.	we, you, they **were worshiping**	we, you, they **were being worshiped**
Past	I, he, she, it,	I, he, she, it,
Int.	we, you, they **did worship**	we, you, they **did get worshiped**
Pres.	I, we, you, they **have worshiped**	I, we, you, they **have been worshiped**
Perf.	he, she, it **has worshiped**	he, she, it **has been worshiped**
Past	I, he, she, it,	I, he, she, it,
Perf.	we, you, they **had worshiped**	we, you, they **had been worshiped**
Fut.	I, he, she, it, we, you, they	I, he, she, it, we, you, they
Perf.	**will have worshiped**	**will have been worshiped**

IMPERATIVE MOOD

worship be worshiped

SUBJUNCTIVE MOOD

Pres.	if I, he, she, it,	if I, he, she, it,
	we, you, they **worship**	we, you, they **be worshiped**
Past	if I, he, she, it,	if I, he, she, it,
	we, you, they **worshiped**	we, you, they **were worshiped**
Fut.	if I, he, she, it,	if I, he, she, it,
	we, you, they **should worship**	we, you, they **should be worshiped**

Transitive and intransitive. The *Oxford Dictionary* prefers the spelling with the double "pp" for the past tense and participles: WORSHIPPING, WORSHIPPED.

wound
(active voice)

be wounded
(passive voice)

Infinitive: **to wound**
Perfect Infinitive: **to have wounded**
Present Participle: **wounding**
Past Participle: **wounded**

Infinitive: **to be wounded**
Perfect Infinitive: **to have been wounded**
Present Participle: **being wounded**
Past Participle: **been wounded**

INDICATIVE MOOD

Pres.	I, we, you, they **wound**	I **am wounded**
		we, you, they **are wounded**
	he, she, it **wounds**	he, she, it **is wounded**
Pres. *Prog.*	I **am wounding**	I **am being wounded**
	we, you, they **are wounding**	we, you, they **are being wounded**
	he, she, it **is wounding**	he, she, it **is being wounded**
Pres. *Int.*	I, we, you, they **do wound**	I, we, you, they **do get wounded**
	he, she, it **does wound**	he, she, it **does get wounded**
Fut.	I, he, she, it, we, you, they **will wound**	I, he, she, it, we, you, they **will be wounded**
Past	I, he, she, it, we, you, they **wounded**	I, he, she, it **was wounded** we, you, they **were wounded**
Past *Prog.*	I, he, she, it **was wounding** we, you, they **were wounding**	I, he, she, it **was being wounded** we, you, they **were being wounded**
Past *Int.*	I, he, she, it, we, you, they **did wound**	I, he, she, it, we, you, they **did get wounded**
Pres. *Perf.*	I, we, you, they **have wounded**	I, we, you, they **have been wounded**
	he, she, it **has wounded**	he, she, it **has been wounded**
Past *Perf.*	I, he, she, it, we, you, they **had wounded**	I, he, she, it, we, you, they **had been wounded**
Fut. *Perf.*	I, he, she, it, we, you, they **will have wounded**	I, he, she, it, we, you, they **will have been wounded**

IMPERATIVE MOOD

wound　　　　　　　**be wounded**

SUBJUNCTIVE MOOD

Pres.	if I, he, she, it, we, you, they **wound**	if I, he, she, it, we, you, they **be wounded**
Past	if I, he, she, it, we, you, they **wounded**	if I, he, she, it, we, you, they **were wounded**
Fut.	if I, he, she, it, we, you, they **should wound**	if I, he, she, it, we, you, they **should be wounded**

Transitive and intransitive.

492

wrap
(active voice)

be wrapped/wrapt
(passive voice)

Infinitive: **to wrap**
Perfect Infinitive: **to have wrapped**
Present Participle: **wrapping**
Past Participle: **wrapped**

Infinitive: **to be wrapped**
Perfect Infinitive: **to have been wrapped**
Present Participle: **being wrapped**
Past Participle: **been wrapped**

INDICATIVE MOOD

Pres.	I, we, you, they **wrap**	I am **wrapped**
		we, you, they **are wrapped**
	he, she, it **wraps**	he, she, it **is wrapped**
Pres.	I **am wrapping**	I **am being wrapped**
Prog.	we, you, they **are wrapping**	we, you, they **are being wrapped**
	he, she, it **is wrapping**	he, she, it **is being wrapped**
Pres.	I, we, you, they **do wrap**	I, we, you, they **do get wrapped**
Int.	he, she, it **does wrap**	he, she, it **does get wrapped**
Fut.	I, he, she, it,	I, he, she, it,
	we, you, they **will wrap**	we, you, they **will be wrapped**
Past	I, he, she, it,	I, he, she, it **was wrapped**
	we, you, they **wrapped**	we, you, they **were wrapped**
Past	I, he, she, it **was wrapping**	I, he, she, it **was being wrapped**
Prog.	we, you, they **were wrapping**	we, you, they **were being wrapped**
Past	I, he, she, it,	I, he, she, it,
Int.	we, you, they **did wrap**	we, you, they **did get wrapped**
Pres.	I, we, you, they **have wrapped**	I, we, you, they **have been wrapped**
Perf.	he, she, it **has wrapped**	he, she, it **has been wrapped**
Past	I, he, she, it,	I, he, she, it,
Perf.	we, you, they **had wrapped**	we, you, they **had been wrapped**
Fut.	I, he, she, it, we, you, they	I, he, she, it, we, you, they
Perf.	**will have wrapped**	**will have been wrapped**

IMPERATIVE MOOD

wrap

be wrapped

SUBJUNCTIVE MOOD

Pres.	if I, he, she, it,	if I, he, she, it,
	we, you, they **wrap**	we, you, they **be wrapped**
Past	if I, he, she, it,	if I, he, she, it,
	we, you, they **wrapped**	we, you, they **were wrapped**
Fut.	if I, he, she, it,	if I, he, she, it,
	we, you, they **should wrap**	we, you, they **should be wrapped**

Transitive and intransitive.

wreak
(active voice)

be wreaked
(passive voice)

Infinitive: **to wreak**
Perfect Infinitive: **to have wreaked**
Present Participle: **wreaking**
Past Participle: **wreaked**

Infinitive: **to be wreaked**
Perfect Infinitive: **to have been wreaked**
Present Participle: **being wreaked**
Past Participle: **been wreaked**

INDICATIVE MOOD

Pres.	I, we, you, they **wreak**	I **am wreaked** we, you, they **are wreaked**
	he, she, it **wreaks**	he, she, it **is wreaked**
Pres. *Prog.*	I **am wreaking** we, you, they **are wreaking** he, she, it **is wreaking**	I **am being wreaked** we, you, they **are being wreaked** he, she, it **is being wreaked**
Pres. *Int.*	I, we, you, they **do wreak** he, she, it **does wreak**	I, we, you, they **do get wreaked** he, she, it **does get wreaked**
Fut.	I, he, she, it, we, you, they **will wreak**	I, he, she, it, we, you, they **will be wreaked**
Past	I, he, she, it, we, you, they **wreaked**	I, he, she, it **was wreaked** we, you, they **were wreaked**
Past *Prog.*	I, he, she, it **was wreaking** we, you, they **were wreaking**	I, he, she, it **was being wreaked** we, you, they **were being wreaked**
Past *Int.*	I, he, she, it, we, you, they **did wreak**	I, he, she, it, we, you, they **did get wreaked**
Pres. *Perf.*	I, we, you, they **have wreaked** he, she, it **has wreaked**	I, we, you, they **have been wreaked** he, she, it **has been wreaked**
Past *Perf.*	I, he, she, it, we, you, they **had wreaked**	I, he, she, it, we, you, they **had been wreaked**
Fut. *Perf.*	I, he, she, it, we, you, they **will have wreaked**	I, he, she, it, we, you, they **will have been wreaked**

IMPERATIVE MOOD

wreak **be wreaked**

SUBJUNCTIVE MOOD

Pres.	if I, he, she, it, we, you, they **wreak**	if I, he, she, it, we, you, they **be wreaked**
Past	if I, he, she, it, we, you, they **wreaked**	if I, he, she, it, we, you, they **were wreaked**
Fut.	if I, he, she, it, we, you, they **should wreak**	if I, he, she, it, we, you, they **should be wreaked**

---

wreck
(active voice)

PRINCIPAL PARTS: **wrecks, wrecking,
wrecked, wrecked**

be wrecked
(passive voice)

Infinitive: **to wreck**
Perfect Infinitive: **to have wrecked**
Present Participle: **wrecking**
Past Participle: **wrecked**

Infinitive: **to be wrecked**
Perfect Infinitive: **to have been wrecked**
Present Participle: **being wrecked**
Past Participle: **been wrecked**

INDICATIVE MOOD

Pres.	I, we, you, they **wreck**	I **am wrecked**
		we, you, they **are wrecked**
	he, she, it **wrecks**	he, she, it **is wrecked**
Pres.	I **am wrecking**	I **am being wrecked**
Prog.	we, you, they **are wrecking**	we, you, they **are being wrecked**
	he, she, it **is wrecking**	he, she, it **is being wrecked**
Pres.	I, we, you, they **do wreck**	I, we, you, they **do get wrecked**
Int.	he, she, it **does wreck**	he, she, it **does get wrecked**
Fut.	I, he, she, it,	I, he, she, it,
	we, you, they **will wreck**	we, you, they **will be wrecked**
Past	I, he, she, it,	I, he, she, it **was wrecked**
	we, you, they **wrecked**	we, you, they **were wrecked**
Past	I, he, she, it **was wrecking**	I, he, she, it **was being wrecked**
Prog.	we, you, they **were wrecking**	we, you, they **were being wrecked**
Past	I, he, she, it,	I, he, she, it,
Int.	we, you, they **did wreck**	we, you, they **did get wrecked**
Pres.	I, we, you, they **have wrecked**	I, we, you, they **have been wrecked**
Perf.	he, she, it **has wrecked**	he, she, it **has been wrecked**
Past	I, he, she, it,	I, he, she, it,
Perf.	we, you, they **had wrecked**	we, you, they **had been wrecked**
Fut.	I, he, she, it, we, you, they	I, he, she, it, we, you, they
Perf.	**will have wrecked**	**will have been wrecked**

IMPERATIVE MOOD

wreck   **be wrecked**

SUBJUNCTIVE MOOD

Pres.	if I, he, she, it,	if I, he, she, it,
	we, you, they **wreck**	we, you, they **be wrecked**
Past	if I, he, she, it,	if I, he, she, it,
	we, you, they **wrecked**	we, you, they **were wrecked**
Fut.	if I, he, she, it,	if I, he, she, it,
	we, you, they **should wreck**	we, you, they **should be wrecked**

Transitive and intransitive.

wring
(active voice)

be wrung
(passive voice)

Infinitive: **to wring**
Perfect Infinitive: **to have wrung**
Present Participle: **wringing**
Past Participle: **wrung**

Infinitive: **to be wrung**
Perfect Infinitive: **to have been wrung**
Present Participle: **being wrung**
Past Participle: **been wrung**

INDICATIVE MOOD

Pres.	I, we, you, they **wring**	I **am wrung**
		we, you, they **are wrung**
	he, she, it **wrings**	he, she, it **is wrung**
Pres.	I **am wringing**	I **am being wrung**
Prog.	we, you, they **are wringing**	we, you, they **are being wrung**
	he, she, it **is wringing**	he, she, it **is being wrung**
Pres.	I, we, you, they **do wring**	I, we, you, they **do get wrung**
Int.	he, she, it **does wring**	he, she, it **does get wrung**
Fut.	I, he, she, it,	I, he, she, it,
	we, you, they **will wring**	we, you, they **will be wrung**
Past	I, he, she, it,	I, he, she, it **was wrung**
	we, you, they **wrung**	we, you, they **were wrung**
Past	I, he, she, it **was wringing**	I, he, she, it **was being wrung**
Prog.	we, you, they **were wringing**	we, you, they **were being wrung**
Past	I, he, she, it,	I, he, she, it,
Int.	we, you, they **did wring**	we, you, they **did get wrung**
Pres.	I, we, you, they **have wrung**	I, we, you, they **have been wrung**
Perf.	he, she, it **has wrung**	he, she, it **has been wrung**
Past	I, he, she, it,	I, he, she, it,
Perf.	we, you, they **had wrung**	we, you, they **had been wrung**
Fut.	I, he, she, it, we, you, they	I, he, she, it, we, you, they
Perf.	**will have wrung**	**will have been wrung**

IMPERATIVE MOOD

wring   **be wrung**

SUBJUNCTIVE MOOD

Pres.	if I, he, she, it,	if I, he, she, it,
	we, you, they **wring**	we, you, they **be wrung**
Past	if I, he, she, it,	if I, he, she, it,
	we, you, they **wrung**	we, you, they **were wrung**
Fut.	if I, he, she, it,	if I, he, she, it,
	we, you, they **should wring**	we, you, they **should be wrung**

Transitive and intransitive.

write
(active voice)

be written
(passive voice)

Infinitive: **to write**
Perfect Infinitive: **to have written**
Present Participle: **writing**
Past Participle: **written**

Infinitive: **to be written**
Perfect Infinitive: **to have been written**
Present Participle: **being written**
Past Participle: **been written**

INDICATIVE MOOD

Pres.	I, we, you, they **write**	I **am written**
		we, you, they **are written**
	he, she, it **writes**	he, she, it **is written**
Pres.	I **am writing**	I **am being written**
Prog.	we, you, they **are writing**	we, you, they **are being written**
	he, she, it **is writing**	he, she, it **is being written**
Pres.	I, we, you, they **do write**	I, we, you, they **do get written**
Int.	he, she, it **does write**	he, she, it **does get written**
Fut.	I, he, she, it,	I, he, she, it,
	we, you, they **will write**	we, you, they **will be written**
Past	I, he, she, it,	I, he, she, it **was written**
	we, you, they **wrote**	we, you, they **were written**
Past	I, he, she, it **was writing**	I, he, she, it **was being written**
Prog.	we, you, they **were writing**	we, you, they **were being written**
Past	I, he, she, it,	I, he, she, it,
Int.	we, you, they **did write**	we, you, they **did get written**
Pres.	I, we, you, they **have written**	I, we, you, they **have been written**
Perf.	he, she, it **has written**	he, she, it **has been written**
Past	I, he, she, it,	I, he, she, it,
Perf.	we, you, they **had written**	we, you, they **had been written**
Fut.	I, he, she, it, we, you, they	I, he, she, it, we, you, they
Perf.	**will have written**	**will have been written**

IMPERATIVE MOOD

write **be written**

SUBJUNCTIVE MOOD

Pres.	if I, he, she, it,	if I, he, she, it,
	we, you, they **write**	we, you, they **be written**
Past	if I, he, she, it,	if I, he, she, it,
	we, you, they **wrote**	we, you, they **were written**
Fut.	if I, he, she, it,	if I, he, she, it,
	we, you, they **should write**	we, you, they **should be written**

Transitive and intransitive.

x-ray
(active voice)

PRINCIPAL PARTS: **x-rays, x-raying,**
x-rayed, x-rayed

be x-rayed
(passive voice)

Infinitive: **to x-ray**
Perfect Infinitive: **to have x-rayed**
Present Participle: **x-raying**
Past Participle: **x-rayed**

Infinitive: **to be x-rayed**
Perfect Infinitive: **to have been x-rayed**
Present Participle: **being x-rayed**
Past Participle: **been x-rayed**

INDICATIVE MOOD

Pres.	I, we, you, they **x-ray**	I **am x-rayed**
		we, you, they **are x-rayed**
	he, she, it **x-rays**	he, she, it **is x-rayed**
Pres.	I **am x-raying**	I **am being x-rayed**
Prog.	we, you, they **are x-raying**	we, you, they **are being x-rayed**
	he, she, it **is x-raying**	he, she, it **is being x-rayed**
Pres.	I, we, you, they **do x-ray**	I, we, you, they **do get x-rayed**
Int.	he, she, it **does x-ray**	he, she, it **does get x-rayed**
Fut.	I, he, she, it,	I, he, she, it,
	we, you, they **will x-ray**	we, you, they **will be x-rayed**
Past	I, he, she, it,	I, he, she, it **was x-rayed**
	we, you, they **x-rayed**	we, you, they **were x-rayed**
Past	I, he, she, it **was x-raying**	I, he, she, it **was being x-rayed**
Prog.	we, you, they **were x-raying**	we, you, they **were being x-rayed**
Past	I, he, she, it,	I, he, she, it,
Int.	we, you, they **did x-ray**	we, you, they **did get x-rayed**
Pres.	I, we, you, they **have x-rayed**	I, we, you, they **have been x-rayed**
Perf.	he, she, it **has x-rayed**	he, she, it **has been x-rayed**
Past	I, he, she, it,	I, he, she, it,
Perf.	we, you, they **had x-rayed**	we, you, they **had been x-rayed**
Fut.	I, he, she, it, we, you, they	I, he, she, it, we, you, they
Perf.	**will have x-rayed**	**will have been x-rayed**

IMPERATIVE MOOD

x-ray   **be x-rayed**

SUBJUNCTIVE MOOD

Pres.	if I, he, she, it,	if I, he, she, it,
	we, you, they **x-ray**	we, you, they **be x-rayed**
Past	if I, he, she, it,	if I, he, she, it,
	we, you, they **x-rayed**	we, you, they **were x-rayed**
Fut.	if I, he, she, it,	if I, he, she, it,
	we, you, they **should x-ray**	we, you, they **should be x-rayed**

498

xerox
(active voice)

be xeroxed
(passive voice)

Infinitive: **to xerox**
Perfect Infinitive: **to have xeroxed**
Present Participle: **xeroxing**
Past Participle: **xeroxed**

Infinitive: **to be xeroxed**
Perfect Infinitive: **to have been xeroxed**
Present Participle: **being xeroxed**
Past Participle: **been xeroxed**

INDICATIVE MOOD

Pres.	I, we, you, they **xerox**	I **am xeroxed**
		we, you, they **are xeroxed**
	he, she, it **xeroxes**	he, she, it **is xeroxed**
Pres.	I **am xeroxing**	I **am being xeroxed**
Prog.	we, you, they **are xeroxing**	we, you, they **are being xeroxed**
	he, she, it **is xeroxing**	he, she, it **is being xeroxed**
Pres.	I, we, you, they **do xerox**	I, we, you, they **do get xeroxed**
Int.	he, she, it **does xerox**	he, she, it **does get xeroxed**
Fut.	I, he, she, it,	I, he, she, it,
	we, you, they **will xerox**	we, you, they **will be xeroxed**
Past	I, he, she, it,	I, he, she, it **was xeroxed**
	we, you, they **xeroxed**	we, you, they **were xeroxed**
Past	I, he, she, it **was xeroxing**	I, he, she, it **was being xeroxed**
Prog.	we, you, they **were xeroxing**	we, you, they **were being xeroxed**
Past	I, he, she, it,	I, he, she, it,
Int.	we, you, they **did xerox**	we, you, they **did get xeroxed**
Pres.	I, we, you, they **have xeroxed**	I, we, you, they **have been xeroxed**
Perf.	he, she, it **has xeroxed**	he, she, it **has been xeroxed**
Past	I, he, she, it,	I, he, she, it,
Perf.	we, you, they **had xeroxed**	we, you, they **had been xeroxed**
Fut.	I, he, she, it, we, you, they	I, he, she, it, we, you, they
Perf.	**will have xeroxed**	**will have been xeroxed**

IMPERATIVE MOOD

xerox　　　　　　**be xeroxed**

SUBJUNCTIVE MOOD

Pres.	if I, he, she, it,	if I, he, she, it,
	we, you, they **xerox**	we, you, they **be xeroxed**
Past	if I, he, she, it,	if I, he, she, it,
	we, you, they **xeroxed**	we, you, they **were xeroxed**
Fut.	if I, he, she, it,	if I, he, she, it,
	we, you, they **should xerox**	we, you, they **should be xeroxed**

Transitive and intransitive.

yes
(active voice)

PRINCIPAL PARTS: **yeses, yessing,
yessed, yessed**

be yessed
(passive voice)

Infinitive: **to yes**
Perfect Infinitive: **to have yessed**
Present Participle: **yessing**
Past Participle: **yessed**

Infinitive: **to be yessed**
Perfect Infinitive: **to have been yessed**
Present Participle: **being yessed**
Past Participle: **been yessed**

INDICATIVE MOOD

Pres.	I, we, you, they **yes**	I **am yessed**
		we, you, they **are yessed**
	he, she, it **yeses**	he, she, it **is yessed**
Pres.	I **am yessing**	I **am being yessed**
Prog.	we, you, they **are yessing**	we, you, they **are being yessed**
	he, she, it **is yessing**	he, she, it **is being yessed**
Pres.	I, we, you, they **do yes**	I, we, you, they **do get yessed**
Int.	he, she, it **does yes**	he, she, it **does get yessed**
Fut.	I, he, she, it,	I, he, she, it,
	we, you, they **will yes**	we, you, they **will be yessed**
Past	I, he, she, it,	I, he, she, it **was yessed**
	we, you, they **yessed**	we, you, they **were yessed**
Past	I, he, she, it **was yessing**	I, he, she, it **was being yessed**
Prog.	we, you, they **were yessing**	we, you, they **were being yessed**
Past	I, he, she, it,	I, he, she, it,
Int.	we, you, they **did yes**	we, you, they **did get yessed**
Pres.	I, we, you, they **have yessed**	I, we, you, they **have been yessed**
Perf.	he, she, it **has yessed**	he, she, it **has been yessed**
Past	I, he, she, it,	I, he, she, it,
Perf.	we, you, they **had yessed**	we, you, they **had been yessed**
Fut.	I, he, she, it, we, you, they	I, he, she, it, we, you, they
Perf.	**will have yessed**	**will have been yessed**

IMPERATIVE MOOD

yes   be yessed

SUBJUNCTIVE MOOD

Pres.	if I, he, she, it,	if I, he, she, it,
	we, you, they **yes**	we, you, they **be yessed**
Past	if I, he, she, it,	if I, he, she, it,
	we, you, they **yessed**	we, you, they **were yessed**
Fut.	if I, he, she, it,	if I, he, she, it,
	we, you, they **should yes**	we, you, they **should be yessed**

zero
(active voice)

be zeroed
(passive voice)

Infinitive: **to zero**
Perfect Infinitive: **to have zeroed**
Present Participle: **zeroing**
Past Participle: **zeroed**

Infinitive: **to be zeroed**
Perfect Infinitive: **to have been zeroed**
Present Participle: **being zeroed**
Past Participle: **been zeroed**

INDICATIVE MOOD

Pres.	I, we, you, they **zero**	I **am zeroed**
		we, you, they **are zeroed**
	he, she, it **zeroes**	he, she, it **is zeroed**
Pres.	I **am zeroing**	I **am being zeroed**
Prog.	we, you, they **are zeroing**	we, you, they **are being zeroed**
	he, she, it **is zeroing**	he, she, it **is being zeroed**
Pres.	I, we, you, they **do zero**	I, we, you, they **do get zeroed**
Int.	he, she, it **does zero**	he, she, it **does get zeroed**
Fut.	I, he, she, it,	I, he, she, it,
	we, you, they **will zero**	we, you, they **will be zeroed**
Past	I, he, she, it,	I, he, she, it **was zeroed**
	we, you, they **zeroed**	we, you, they **were zeroed**
Past	I, he, she, it **was zeroing**	I, he, she, it **was being zeroed**
Prog.	we, you, they **were zeroing**	we, you, they **were being zeroed**
Past	I, he, she, it,	I, he, she, it,
Int.	we, you, they **did zero**	we, you, they **did get zeroed**
Pres.	I, we, you, they **have zeroed**	I, we, you, they **have been zeroed**
Perf.	he, she, it **has zeroed**	he, she, it **has been zeroed**
Past	I, he, she, it,	I, he, she, it,
Perf.	we, you, they **had zeroed**	we, you, they **had been zeroed**
Fut.	I, he, she, it, we, you, they	I, he, she, it, we, you, they
Perf.	**will have zeroed**	**will have been zeroed**

IMPERATIVE MOOD

zero

be zeroed

SUBJUNCTIVE MOOD

Pres.	if I, he, she, it,	if I, he, she, it,
	we, you, they **zero**	we, you, they **be zeroed**
Past	if I, he, she, it,	if I, he, she, it,
	we, you, they **zeroed**	we, you, they **were zeroed**
Fut.	if I, he, she, it,	if I, he, she, it,
	we, you, they **should zero**	we, you, they **should be zeroed**

Phrasal Verbs

Many English verbs occur with one or more prepositions or adverbs where the meaning is not readily apparent from the different elements. Here is a list of many of these combinations for the verbs conjugated in *501 English Verbs*. I have omitted most of the forms considered slang. In assembling the list I have relied primarily on the *American Heritage Dictionary of the English Language*.

Abide by: comply with, conform to
> *You should abide by your parents' wishes.*

Act out: dramatize
> *John and Sara acted out the dialogue.*

Act up: misbehave
> *Joe continues to act up during class.*

Act up: begin to bother
> *My old war injury started to act up again.*

Add up: be logical, make sense
> *Their main points in the discussion simply did not add up.*

Add up to be: amount to
> *Their arguments all added up to be a reasonable conclusion.*

Allow for: make provision for
> *We allowed for a slight overage in our calculations.*

Ask after: inquire about someone
> *He asked after you last evening.*

Ask for it (trouble): continue an action in spite of likely punishment
> *The kids were finally punished by their mother, who simply said: "They asked for it."*

Ask out: invite (as on a date)
> *I'm so happy that George asked me out to the prom.*

Be about: occupy self with
> *You should be about your business.*

Bear down: apply maximum effort
> *It's time for us to bear down and get this job completed.*

Bear down on: harm
> *The financial pressures are already beginning to bear down on him.*

Bear out: confirm
> *The results of the experiment bore out our worst fears.*

Bear up: withstand the pressure
> *Given all of the commotion, it is a wonder how well he is bearing up.*

Bear with: endure, persevere
> *Bear with me for just a minute as I try to explain.*

Beat off: repel
> *They ultimately beat off their attackers.*

Beat it: leave quickly
> *He beat it when the police arrived.*

Beat out: arrive first

> *He beat out the other candidate by just two votes.*

Become of: happen to

> *What becomes of a broken heart?*

Beg off: ask to be excused

> *Given the constraints on his time, he begged off the assignment.*

Bid up: force a price higher

> *They bid up the price of the painting to over a million dollars.*

Bind over: to hold someone on bail or bond

> *The prisoner was bound over for trial.*

Blow away: overwhelm

> *His performance blew me away.*

Blow off: release

> *Let him blow off some steam.*

Blow out: extinguish

> *Please don't forget to blow out the candles.*

Blow over: pass by (like a storm)

> *We're hoping the controversy will blow over with time.*

Blow up: enlarge

> *Can you blow up these photos?*

Blow up: explode

> *If you're not careful, you'll blow up the whole neighborhood with that explosive charge.*

Break down: cause to collapse

> *The elevator is always breaking down.*

Break down: become distressed

> *When confronted with the evidence the suspect broke down and cried.*

Break even: gain back the original investment

> *After many years of hard work they finally broke even.*

Break in: train

> *They were trying to break in the new horse.*

Break in: adapt for a purpose

> *He used the oil to break in his new baseball glove.*

Break in: enter illegally

> *The burglars broke in last evening.*

Break in/into: interrupt

> *The secretary broke into our conversation with an important message.*

Break into: enter a profession

> *He broke into the major leagues in 1947.*

Break off: cease

> *They broke off negotiations after the last round of talks.*

Break out: skin eruption

> *He broke out in a rash after eating just a few peanuts.*

Break out: escape

> *Last evening two criminals broke out of a maximum security prison.*

Break out: begin
> *Fighting broke out in the streets of Jerusalem.*

Break up: separate
> *The couple broke up after the argument on their last date.*

Bring around: convince one to adopt an opinion
> *The shop foreman finally brought the workers around to management's point of view.*

Bring around: restore to consciousness
> *They used smelling salts to bring her around.*

Bring back: recall to mind
> *Those songs bring back such fond memories.*

Bring down: cause to fall
> *The Russian Revolution brought down the Romanov dynasty.*

Bring forth: propose
> *They brought forth a series of new proposals at our meeting this morning.*

Bring forth: give birth
> *And she brought forth a son.*

Bring in: render a verdict
> *The jury brought in a verdict of "not guilty."*

Bring off: accomplish
> *I don't see how we can bring that off without help.*

Bring on: cause to appear
> *You can bring on the dancers.*

Bring out: reveal or expose
> *The lecture brought out the best and worst in him.*

Bring to: restore to consciousness
> *The doctor brought him to.*

Bring up: raise
> *I didn't want to bring this up, but since you mentioned it, I feel I must.*

Build in: include as an integral part
> *The car stereo is built in.*

Build on: use as a basis
> *These proposals finally give us something to build on.*

Build up: increase gradually
> *The errors continued to build up until they harmed his performance.*

Burn out: wear out from exhaustion
> *Toward the end of the race he felt like he was burning out.*

Burn up: make very angry
> *Your attitude really burns me up.*

Burst out: begin suddenly
> *They burst out laughing at the speaker.*

Buy into: buy a stock of
> *I bought into IBM when it was just beginning.*

Buy into: give credence to
> *He never bought into the company's philosophy.*

Buy off: bribe
>*They bought off the politician with a large contribution to her campaign.*

Buy out: purchase all the shares
>*The larger company bought them out.*

Buy up: purchase all that is available
>*The speculator keeps buying up the plots in that old neighborhood.*

Call back: ask to return
>*The workers were called back to the job as the strike vote was being counted.*

Call for: arrive to meet
>*The young gentlemen called for his new found friend.*

Call for: requires
>*That calls for a celebration.*

Call forth: evoke
>*Their attack called forth an immediate response.*

Call in: summon
>*A heart specialist was called in to review the diagnosis.*

Call in: use the telephone to communicate
>*Has the salesman called in yet?*

Call off: cancel
>*The ball game was called off on account of rain.*

Call up: summon to military duty
>*The reserves were called up during the Gulf War.*

Call upon: require
>*I call upon you to take up your arms in the defense of liberty.*

Call upon: visit
>*When can I call upon you to discuss this matter?*

Care for: provide for
>*I cared for the children while their Mom was away.*

Carry away: excite
>*She was carried away by the sound of his voice.*

Carry off: cause the death of
>*The entire population of the village was carried off by a new strain of the virus.*

Carry on: continue
>*The officer was pleased with the inspection and told his men to carry on with their duties.*

Carry out: put into practice
>*They carried out his orders without hesitation.*

Carry through: persevere to a goal or conclusion
>*He rarely carries through on his promises.*

Cast about: search for
>*He kept casting about for the answers.*

Cast around: search about for something
>*She was casting around for a friend.*

Cast off: throw away
>*She loves to cast off last year's fashions.*

Cast off: launch a boat
>*They cast off for the next destination.*

Cast out: expel
> *An exorcist casts out devils.*

Catch on: become popular
> *It didn't take long for colored hair to catch on with the younger generation.*

Catch up: overtake from behind
> *How do you ever expect me to catch up if you walk so fast?*

Change off: alternate performing tasks
> *We can change off in an hour or so if you get tired.*

Close down: discontinue, go out of business
> *The clothing store closed down after the Christmas season.*

Close in: advance, surround
> *The enemy used the darkness of night to close in on our positions.*

Close up: block up or shut down
> *They closed up the entrance to the cave.*

Close out: dispose, terminate
> *We must close out this particular product at the end of the month.*

Come about: happen
> *It just came about.*

Come across: find, meet
> *I was lucky to come across just the perfect gift.*

Come along: go with someone else
> *You may come along if you wish.*

Come around (round): regain consciousness
> *The boxer finally came around in the dressing room.*

Come at: approach
> *You can come at that problem from a number of angles.*

Come back: regain past state
> *He came back quickly after the knee operation.*

Come by: acquire
> *How did you come by this money?*

Come down: lose position, money, standing
> *He has certainly come down in the opinion polls.*

Come in: arrive
> *The new spring fashions have just come in.*

Come into: acquire or inherit
> *My brother recently came into a small fortune.*

Come off: happen, occur
> *The concert came off without any problems.*

Come on: show an interest in
> *He came on to her all evening at the party.*

Come out: make known
> *They finally came out with the official statement.*

Come through: deliver on a promise
> *I am so happy he finally came through with his contribution.*

Come to: regain consciousness
> *He came to an hour after the operation.*

Come over: drop by for a visit
> *Why don't you come over this evening?*

Come to pass: happen
> *And so it came to pass that they parted as friends.*

Come up: appear
> *Everything is coming up on the screen as we expected.*

Come upon: discover
> *I came upon the evidence quite by accident.*

Cover up: conceal after the fact
> *They tried to cover up their wrongdoing.*

Cry down: belittle someone
> *The speaker was cried down by the unruly audience.*

Cry out: exclaim
> *The wounded soldier cried out in pain.*

Cut back: reduce
> *We are cutting back production as of next Monday.*

Cut down: kill
> *He was cut down by a stray bullet on the street last evening.*

Cut down: reduce
> *You should cut down on the amount of fat in your diet.*

Cut in: break into a line
> *It is rude to cut in, when we have been standing here over an hour.*

Cut off: stop
> *I am afraid that I must cut off this discussion right now.*

Cut off: separate
> *They were cut off from the exit by the progress of the fire.*

Cut out: form or shape by cutting
> *Little children love to cut out paper dolls.*

Cut out: exclude
> *Let's cut her out of the final decision.*

Cut out: suited for
> *He is not cut out to be a doctor.*

Cut short: interrupt
> *Our trip was cut short by my wife's accident.*

Cut up: clown about
> *The little boy loves to cut up when the teacher turns his back.*

Cut up: destroy completely
> *The division was cut up by the air attack.*

Dial in: access by telephone or modem
> *He often dials in from home to check his e-mail.*

Dial out: access a telephone line for a phone call
> *How can I dial out from this phone?*

Die down: subside
> *The controversy died down after a month.*

508

Die off: decline dramatically
>*The tribal members died off.*

Die out: become extinct
>*The tigers in India are dying out.*

Dig in: hold on stubbornly
>*Let's dig in and meet the challenge.*

Dig in: begin to eat
>*Let's dig in, guys. I'm so hungry I could eat a horse.*

Do in: ruin or kill
>*He was done in by his fellow inmates.*

Do up: dress elaborately
>*The little girl was all done up for her school play.*

Do without: manage in spite of a lack of something
>*The kids can't do without television.*

Drag on: go on for a long time
>*The hours seem to drag on endlessly.*

Drag out: extend
>*I can't understand why they are dragging this matter out so long.*

Draw away: pull ahead
>*We must continue drawing away from the other colleges.*

Draw back: retreat
>*Let's draw back and regroup.*

Draw down: deplete resources
>*We will have to draw down on our grain supplies.*

Draw out: prolong
>*Just how long can she draw out the committee meeting?*

Draw up: compose
>*Let's just draw up a contract.*

Dream up: invent
>*Who dreamed up that idea?*

Drink in: listen closely
>*He drank in her every word.*

Drink to: raise a toast
>*Let's drink to days gone by.*

Drive at: hint, lead in a direction
>*What are you driving at?*

Drop behind: fall behind
>*The little kids kept dropping behind their parents on the walk.*

Drop by: stop in for a visit
>*Don't forget to drop by when you are in town.*

Drop off: go to sleep
>*I finally dropped off at midnight.*

Drop out: withdraw from school
> *Continue your studies. Don't drop out of school.*

Dwell on/upon: write, speak, or think at length
> *We have been dwelling on this topic for over a week.*

Eat into: deplete
> *The number of returns began to eat into their profits.*

Eat out: dine in a restaurant
> *Do you eat out often?*

Eat up: enjoy enormously
> *She ate up the evening's entertainment.*

End up: reach a place
> *I don't know how, but I ended up in Cleveland.*

Enter into: take an active role in
> *He entered into politics late in life.*

Enter on/upon: set out, begin
> *Today we enter on the new phase of our project.*

Explain away: minimize
> *He kept trying to explain away the illegal contributions.*

Face down: confront and overcome
> *He faced down his opponent in the first match.*

Face off: start or resume play in hockey, lacrosse and other games
> *They faced off in their opponents' zone.*

Face off: take sides against one another
> *The two warring factions had faced off at the first meeting.*

Face up: deal with an issue
> *It's time for you to face up to your obligations.*

Fall apart: break down
> *After his wife's death he completely fell apart.*

Fall back: lag behind
> *The others fell back after the first mile of the hike.*

Fall back on: rely on
> *What can I fall back on if this doesn't work?*

Fall behind: fail to pay on time
> *When he lost his job, they fell behind in their mortgage payments.*

Fall down: fail to meet expectations
> *Unfortunately the new boss fell down on the job.*

Fall for: succumb to, fall in love
> *He fell for her at first glance.*

Fall for: be deceived
> *He fell for the con artist's scam.*

Fall in: take a place
> *All of the principal investors fell in after the initial presentation.*

Fall off: decrease

The interest in foreign languages has been gradually falling off.

Fall on: attack

Those waiting in ambush fell on the unsuspecting soldiers.

Fall out: leave military formation

The sergeant roared, "Company, fall out!"

Fall through: fail

The deal fell through at the last moment.

Fall to: approach energetically

The new maid fell to the cleaning.

Fall short: fail to obtain

His efforts to earn a million dollars fell short.

Feel like: wish or want to

I feel like taking a walk.

Feel out: try to find out something indirectly

Could you feel out the opposition before we meet next week?

Feel up to: be prepared for

I don't really feel up to a five mile run.

Fight back: suppress one's feeling

He fought back tears at the announcement.

Fight off: repel an attack

They fought off the attackers until their ammunition ran out.

Figure in: include

Be sure to figure in the extra expenses.

Figure on: depend upon someone

I never thought we could figure on their support.

Figure on: consider

Figure on at least a one-hour delay in your flight.

Figure out: resolve

Now how are we going to figure that out?

Fill in: provide with new information

Could you fill me in on the latest news?

Fill in: substitute for

He filled in for her when she was on vacation.

Fill out: complete a form or application

Be sure to fill out both sides of the form.

Find out: learn or discover

Let's see what we can find out about tigers.

Finish off: end or complete

Let's finish off for the evening.

Finish off: destroy or kill

He finished them off with a hunting knife.

Finish up: conclude, bring to an end

He finished up at midnight.

Fit in: be compatible
>*He doesn't fit in with that crowd.*

Fly at: attack someone
>*He flew at him in a rage.*

Follow along: move in unison with
>*The others just followed along with the song.*

Follow through: pursue something to completion
>*We simply have to follow through on our commitments.*

Follow through: complete the motion of a baseball, golf, or tennis swing
>*When you hit the ball, be sure to follow through.*

Follow out: comply with
>*They followed out his instructions precisely.*

Follow up: check the progress
>*Did you ever follow up on those sales leads?*

Freeze out: exclude
>*They froze him out of the negotiations.*

Get about: walk again
>*It was a week before he could get about.*

Get across: make something comprehensible
>*I keep trying to get the same point across to you.*

Get after: encourage, follow up
>*It's time to get after those kids again.*

Get along: co-exist
>*Can't you find a way to get along with one another?*

Get around: avoid
>*There is no way we can get around this situation.*

Get at: reach successfully
>*Put the cookies where the children can't get at them.*

Get at: suggest
>*What are you trying to get at with that question?*

Get back: receive
>*Did you ever get your money back?*

Get back at: exact revenge
>*He tried unsuccessfully to get back at his enemies.*

Get by: go past
>*Excuse me, can I get by here?*

Get by: barely succeed
>*He did just enough homework to get by.*

Get down: descend
>*Please get down from the table.*

Get down: devote your attention
>*Let's get down to work.*

Get down: discourage
>*Don't let her criticism get you down.*

Get in: enter
>*We were lucky to get in before they closed the doors.*

Get in: succeed in accomplishing
>*They got the game in before the rain.*

Get into: become involved
>*I really can get into this assignment.*

Get off: depart
>*Did he ever get off last evening?*

Get off: fire a shot
>*Try to get off a shot if he appears.*

Get off: send a message
>*He got off a quick note before he left the office.*

Get off: escape punishment
>*He got off with only two years.*

Get off: finish the work day
>*When do you get off?*

Get on: continue on good terms
>*They seem to be getting on well together.*

Get on: make progress
>*Let's get on with it. Time is money.*

Get out: escape
>*How did the bird get out of its cage?*

Get out: publish a newspaper
>*They got the paper out last evening.*

Get over: prevail
>*How will they ever get over the loss of their home?*

Get over: recover from difficult experience
>*He never got over the death of his son.*

Get through: make contact
>*I tried calling, but I couldn't get through.*

Get to: make contact with
>*How can we get to the head of the corporation?*

Get to: affect
>*The strain of the job finally got to him.*

Get together: gather
>*We should all get together on Friday morning.*

Get up: arise from bed
>*It's six o'clock and time to get up.*

Get up: initiate
>*He got up a petition against the property tax.*

Give away: present at a wedding
>*The father gave his daughter away with a tear in his eye.*

Give away: reveal accidentally
>*He gave away the secret in the press conference.*

Give back: return
>*Don't forget to give me the book back.*

Give in: surrender
>*Don't give in—regardless of the pressure.*

Give of: devote
>*He gave generously of himself in the cause of peace.*

Give off: emit
> *The lawn mower was giving off strange smells.*

Give out: distribute
> *The company representative was giving out free samples.*

Give out: stop functioning
> *His heart gave out last night.*

Give over: place in another's care
> *He gave over his assets to his attorney for safekeeping.*

Give over: devote oneself
> *He gave himself over to helping humanity.*

Give over: surrender oneself
> *He gave himself over to her with his heart and soul.*

Give up: surrender, desist, lose hope
> *Don't give up, try again.*

Go about: continue
> *He should go about his business.*

Go along: agree
> *They will go along with whatever we suggest.*

Go at: attack
> *He went at his opponent determined to prevail.*

Go at: approach
> *How many ways can we go at this problem?*

Go by: elapse
> *As time goes by we grow wiser.*

Go by: pay a short visit
> *They went by the new neighbors' house to say hello.*

Go down: set
> *The sun goes down very early in winter.*

Go down: fall to ground
> *The boxer went down after being hit on the chin.*

Go down: lose
> *They went down to defeat.*

Go down: be recorded
> *This will go down as a very important event of the decade.*

Go for: like, have an urge for
> *I could go for an ice cream.*

Go in for: participate
> *He goes in for tennis and swimming.*

Go off: explode
> *The bomb went off on a deserted street.*

Go off: depart
> *He went off to the navy after high school.*

Go on: happen
> *What's going on here?*

Go on: continue
> *Life goes on.*

Go on: keep on doing
> *He went on reading even after the sun went down.*

Go out: become extinguished
> *The fire went out.*

Go out: go outdoors
> *Mommy, can we go out?*

Go out: partake in social life
> *Since her husband died, she never goes out anymore.*

Go over: review
> *Can we go over these figures one more time?*

Go over: gain acceptance
> *The presentation went over very well.*

Go through: examine carefully
> *We have to go through the clothes and papers.*

Go through: experience
> *I hope I never have to go through that again.*

Go through: perform
> *He went through his lines like a professional actor.*

Go under: fail
> *The business went under after only six months of mismanagement.*

Go under: lose consciousness to anesthesia
> *The patient wanted to see her before he went under.*

Go with: date regularly
> *Sally has been going with John since eighth grade.*

Grind out: produce by hard work
> *He keeps grinding out those articles for the newspaper.*

Grow into: develop
> *He is growing into a handsome young man.*

Grow on: become acceptable
> *That music grows on you.*

Grow out of: become too mature for something
> *He grew out of those children's books.*

Grow out of: come into existence
> *This project grew out of preliminary discussions last year.*

Grow up: become an adult
> *When will you grow up?*

Hang around: loiter
> *Why does he hang around with those kids every afternoon?*

Hang back: hold back
> *Be sure to hang back at the start of the match.*

Hang in: persevere
> *You just have to hang in there with him.*

Hang on: persevere
> *We must hang on until the rescue helicopter arrives.*

Hang together: be united
> *Let's hang together in the salary negotiations.*

Hang up: end a telephone conversation
> *Don't you dare hang up on me.*

Hang up: hinder
What's hanging up the parade?

Have on: wear
What did he have on when you saw him?
Have to: must
I just have to see that movie.

Hear from: be notified
When will we hear from you about the application?
Hear from: be reprimanded
He certainly will hear from his superiors about that error.
Hear of: be aware of
Have you heard of the new family in town?
Hear out: listen fully
I would like you to hear me out on this matter before you proceed.

Heave to: turn into the wind or to the seas before a storm
With the storm approaching, the captain gave the order to heave to.

Hide out: conceal yourself
He hid out for two months in the hills.

Hold back: restrain oneself
All evening I held back my applause.
Hold down: restrict
Please hold down the noise.
Hold forth: talk at length
The president held forth on international relations all during dinner.
Hold off: withstand
Can anyone hold off the invaders?
Hold on: persist
We will just hold on until our wish is granted.
Hold out: last
The supplies held out for two months.
Hold over: delay
The sale has been held over one more week.
Hold to: remain loyal
He held to his promises.
Hold up: delay
What is holding up the construction?
Hold up: rob
He held up a bank in Chicago.
Hold with: agree
No one seriously holds with his opinions.

Join in: participate
They joined in at the end of the first verse.

Keep at: persevere
>*Just keep at it and you'll succeed.*

Keep down: restrain
>*They kept the cost of college education down as long as they could.*

Keep off: stay away from
>*Keep off the grass!*

Keep to: stay with
>*Let's keep to the main idea.*

Keep up: maintain properly
>*You must keep up your dues to remain a member in good standing.*

Kill off: eliminate
>*All the rats were killed off by the poison.*

Knock around: be rough with someone
>*You won't be able to knock her around any more.*

Knock around: travel
>*They knocked around California for a month.*

Knock back: gulp down
>*They both knocked back the vodka in true Russian style.*

Knock down: topple
>*The little girl knocked down the sand castle her father had just completed.*

Knock off: stop work
>*Let's knock off today at four.*

Knock off: kill
>*They knocked off the drug dealer in a back alley.*

Knock out: render unconscious
>*That last punch knocked him out for two minutes.*

Knock out: be confined by illness or injury
>*The flu really knocked him out for a week.*

Knock together: make something quickly
>*Let's see if we can knock this table together before evening.*

Knock up: wake or summon by knocking at the door (British English)
>*Don't forget to knock me up tomorrow.*

Knock up: make pregnant (American English—crude and vulgar)

Lay aside: give up
>*Lay aside your arms and come out.*

Lay away: reserve for the future
>*Be sure to lay away some extra funds for a vacation.*

Lay in: store for the future
>*It's time to lay in some seed for the spring.*

Lay into: reprimand
>*The boss is really laying into the new employee.*

Lay off: terminate one's employment
>*Ten thousand people are scheduled to be laid off tomorrow.*

Lay on: prepare
>*They laid on a reception for fifty people.*

Lay out: present
Can you lay out your intentions for us?
Lay out: clothe a corpse
She was laid out in her finest dress.
Lay over: make a stopover
We will have to lay over in Moscow enroute to Siberia.

Lead off: start
Johnny will lead off the discussion.
Lead on: entice, encourage, deceive
The young man led her on for almost two years.

Lean on: apply pressure
I want you to lean on him until his performance improves.

Leave alone: refrain from disturbing
Please leave me alone. I'm busy.
Leave go: relax one's grasp
She left go of the girl's hand.
Leave off: cease doing something
She left off in the middle of the sentence.
Leave out: omit
She left out two answers.

Lend itself to: be suitable for
That story lends itself well to a screen adaptation.

Let down: disappoint
In the end his friends let him down.
Let on: admit knowing
We finally had to let on to the fact that we had known all along.
Let out: end
School let out at 2:00 PM.
Let up: diminish
The rain did not let up for two hours.

Lie down: do little
He keeps lying down on the job.
Lie with: depend upon
The final word lies with you.

Light into: attack
Did you see how she lit into him?
Light out: depart hastily
He certainly lit out after work.
Light up: become animated
Whenever he started talking, her face lit up.
Light up: start smoking
They both lit up after the play.

Listen in: eavesdrop
> *The teacher tried to listen into the conversation at the next table.*

Listen in: tune in to a radio broadcast
> *They listened in to the show every Sunday morning.*

Live down: overcome the shame
> *Can he ever live down that disgraceful performance?*

Live it up: enjoy life in an extravagant fashion
> *After we won the lottery, we lived it up for a year.*

Live out: go through a period of time
> *They lived out their days in peace.*

Live with: resign oneself to
> *He learned to live with his limitations.*

Live up to: achieve
> *How can you live up to your parents' expectations?*

Look after: take care of
> *She will look after you while I'm gone.*

Look down on: despise
> *They always looked down on the new students.*

Look for: expect
> *What can we look for in the new year?*

Look for: search
> *Look for tea in the coffee aisle of the supermarket.*

Look forward to: await with great anticipation
> *I am looking forward to our meeting.*

Look like: appear as
> *It looks like rain.*

Look on/upon: regard
> *They looked upon him with skepticism.*

Look out: be careful
> *Look out. It's a dangerous crossing.*

Look to: expect from
> *We looked to you for guidance.*

Look up: search and find
> *What words do you have to look up in a dictionary?*

Look up to: admire
> *She really looks up to her daddy.*

Lose out: fail to achieve
> *Those who came late lost out on a golden opportunity.*

Make for: promote, lead to, results in
> *That approach makes for better productivity.*

Make off: depart hastily
> *The thieves made off with their jewelry.*

Make out: discern
> *Without my glasses I can't make out this note.*

Make out: understand
> *I can't make out what he means.*

Make out: compose
>Have you made out a will?

Make out: get along with
>How did you make out with the new eyeglasses?

Make over: redo
>She was completely made over for the new part.

Make up: construct
>Let's make up a new proposal.

Make up: alter appearance
>They made her up to be an old woman for the play.

Make up: apply cosmetics
>She always makes herself up before she goes out.

Make up: resolve a quarrel
>After an hour they decided to make up and start over again.

Make up: take an exam later
>The student who had been ill had a chance to make up the math exam.

Mark down: decrease the price
>They marked down the toys after the Christmas holidays.

Mark out: plan something
>He marked out a course of action.

Mark up: deface
>They marked up the subway car with spray paint.

Mark up: increase the price
>As soon as the New Year came they marked up the new car models.

Measure up: match requirements
>He just didn't measure up to our qualifications.

Meet with: be received
>The outline of the plan met with his approval.

Mete out: allot
>It is the responsibility of the judge to mete out punishment.

Move in/into: occupy a place
>We are moving into the new offices next week.

Move on: begin a passage
>It's time to move on and try something new.

Move out: leave a place
>When will they be moving out of their apartment?

Mow down: destroy (as in cutting grass)
>Every time the enemy soldiers attacked, they were mowed down by the machine gun.

Open up: unfold
>She opened up the letter with mixed emotions.

Open up: begin the business day
>We open up at 7:00 AM on Sundays.

Open up: speak candidly

> *Only after we became good friends did she begin to open up.*

Open up: start

> *They opened up the newsstand as soon as the dawn came.*

Pass away: die

> *He passed away last year.*

Pass off: offer an imitation as the original

> *He tried to pass it off as a Picasso painting.*

Pass out: lose consciousness

> *After drinking ten bottles of beer he passed out.*

Pass over: omit

> *They passed over the difficult items on the agenda.*

Pass over: skip

> *He was passed over for promotion.*

Pass up: miss an opportunity

> *He passed up a chance to sing with the Beatles.*

Pay off: pay the full amount

> *He paid off the mortgage last year.*

Pay off: return a profit

> *Their investment in real estate paid off handsomely.*

Pay out: spend

> *He paid out twenty dollars for the gift.*

Pay up: give the requested amount

> *He paid up his bar tab on Friday evening.*

Pick apart: refute by careful analysis

> *He picked apart the prosecution's argument in front of the jury.*

Pick at: pluck with fingers

> *He picked at the guitar strings before playing a song.*

Pick on: tease

> *You shouldn't pick on your baby sister.*

Pick out: select

> *Pick out a nice tie for me.*

Pick out: distinguish in a large group

> *He could always pick her out in a crowd.*

Pick up: retrieve by hand

> *He picked up a newspaper on the way to work.*

Pick up: organize, clean

> *Let's pick up this room right now.*

Play at: take half-heartedly

> *He only played at being the boss.*

Play back: replay

> *We played back the tape.*

Play down: minimize

> *We want to play down the weakest aspects of our proposal.*

Play on: take advantage of

> *He often played on her fears.*

Play out: exhaust
This type of approach played itself out long ago.
Play up: emphasize
They played up her good looks.

Pull away: withdraw
They pulled away from the attack.
Pull away: move ahead
He pulled away in the public opinion polls.
Pull back: withdraw
Let's pull back and regroup.
Pull in: arrive at destination
The train pulled in at 10:00 PM.
Pull out: depart
The train pulled out on time.
Pull over: bring a vehicle to a stop
The policeman asked him to pull over.
Pull through: endure and emerge successfully
He finally pulled through after much extra work.
Pull up: bring to a halt
The riders pulled up at the gate.

Put across: make comprehensible
He was able to put across his main points.
Put away: renounce
They put away their thoughts of revolution.
Put down: write down
He put down his thoughts on paper.
Put down: to end
We must put down the revolt.
Put down: criticize
Someone was always putting her down.
Put forth: exert
He put forth his best effort in the race.
Put forward: propose
He put forward his ideas in his presentation.
Put in: apply
He put in for the new position at his office.
Put in: spend time
He put in ten extra hours last week.
Put off: postpone
They put off the meeting until after the harvest.
Put on: clothe oneself
Put on a hat.
Put out: extinguish
He put out the fire.
Put out: publish
She put out a small literary journal.
Put over on: get across deceptively
He tried to put over his schemes on the people.

Put through: bring to a successful end
> *He put the bill through in the Senate.*

Put together: construct
> *She put together the model airplane with her dad.*

Put upon: imposed
> *He was often put upon by friends.*

Read out: read aloud
> *The teacher read out the names at the beginning of class.*

Read up: learn or study by reading
> *I'll have to read up on my history for the exam.*

Read out of: be expelled from
> *He was read out of the party organization.*

Ride out: survive
> *They rode out the latest dip in the stock market.*

Ring up: record a sale
> *I can ring those items up at this register.*

Ring up: extend out a series
> *They rang up ten victories without a loss.*

Rise above: be superior to
> *You must rise above these petty squabbles.*

Run across: find by chance
> *They simply ran across each other at the shopping mall.*

Run after: seek attention
> *Stop running after her and maybe she'll pay you more attention.*

Run against: encounter
> *He kept running against new obstacles.*

Run against: oppose
> *He ran against the incumbent senator.*

Run along: leave
> *Run along now, children.*

Run away: flee
> *The prisoners tried to run away.*

Run down: stop because of lack of power
> *The tractor simply ran down.*

Run down: tire
> *He was very run down after the basketball season.*

Run down: collide with
> *They ran down that poor little dog.*

Run down: chase and capture
> *They ran him down in Philadelphia.*

Run down: review
> *Let's run down the list of our options.*

Run in: take into legal custody
> *He was run in by the two officers.*

Run into: meet by chance
I ran into my wife at the post office.
Run into: amount to
This could run into millions of dollars.
Run off: print, duplicate
He ran off a hundred copies.
Run off: escape
He ran off with all their money.
Run off: flow or drain away
The water ran off the roof.
Run off: decide a contest
They are running off the tie vote today.
Run on: continue to talk
How he runs on when he gets to the podium.
Run out: deplete
I never want to run out of money.
Run over: knock down
Who ran over the dog?
Run over: review quickly
I ran over my notes before the speech.
Run over: overflow
My cup runneth over.
Run over: exceed the limit
I don't want any of you to run over budget this month.
Run through: pierce
He ran the knife through the butter.
Run through: use up quickly
We have run through all our copy paper.
Run through: rehearse
Let's run through the play one more time.
Run through: go over main points
Let's run through the first two points.
Run up: make larger
He ran up a huge bar bill.
Run with: adopt an idea
Let's run with this idea for the time being.

See after: take care of
She will see after you until I return.
See off: take leave of
They saw the children off at the airport.
See out: escort to the door
Judy will see you out. Please come again.
See through: understand the true nature
I can see through his plans.
See through: continue
I will see this deal through until they sign on the bottom line.
See through: support in difficult times
My dad saw us through financially the first few years.

See to: attend to
> *See to the new patient and I'll find his chart.*

Sell off: get rid of at discount prices
> *We will be selling off any leftover items at the end of the month.*

Sell out: dispose of all
> *The tickets were all sold out by mid-morning.*

Send for: summon
> *They sent for the police.*

Send in: cause to arrive
> *They sent in dozens of e-mail messages.*

Send out: order from
> *They sent out for two pizzas and some beer.*

Send up: confined to jail
> *He was sent up for five years on a drug charge.*

Set about: begin
> *They set about their business.*

Set apart: distinguish
> *Her qualifications clearly set her apart from the other candidates.*

Set aside: reserve
> *Can you set aside two tickets for us?*

Set aside: reject
> *Their claim was set aside by the service manager.*

Set at: attack
> *The dogs set at the two little boys throwing stones.*

Set back: slow down
> *The family was severely set back by the flood.*

Set back: cost a lot
> *That new part for the car set me back one hundred dollars.*

Set down: seat someone
> *They set the baby down at the table.*

Set down: put in writing
> *He wanted to set down his thoughts before the meeting.*

Set down: land a plane
> *The pilot set down in a grassy field.*

Set forth: express
> *He set forth his principles in his campaign speech.*

Set forth: propose
> *The attorneys set forth the necessary conditions of the tentative agreement.*

Set in: insert
> *His last words are set in stone.*

Set in: begin happening
> *The storm set in overnight.*

Set off: initiate
> *His words set off a rally on Wall Street.*

Set off: explode
> *He set off the bomb.*

Set out: undertake
>*He set out to conquer the world.*

Set out: lay out graphically
>*He set out the new plans for the museum.*

Set to: begin
>*Can we set to work?*

Set up: put forward, select
>*He was set up as the group's leader.*

Set up: assemble
>*He set up the train set in the living room.*

Set up: establish business
>*What do we still need to set up production?*

Set up: arrange
>*Please set up the glasses on the rear shelf of the cabinet.*

Set upon: attack violently
>*The dogs set upon the cat.*

Sew up: complete successfully
>*We finally sewed up the deal.*

Shake down: subject to search
>*I want you to shake down his apartment for evidence in the case.*

Shake hands: greet by clasping one another's hands
>*Americans often shake hands when they meet one another.*

Shake off: dismiss
>*He shook off the injury and continued to play.*

Shake off: get rid of
>*How can I shake off this cold?*

Shake up: upset
>*The death of his father really shook him up.*

Shake up: rearrange drastically.
>*He will really shake up the industry.*

Shape up: develop
>*This is shaping up to be a close contest.*

Shape up: improve to the standard.
>*He will have to shape up or he'll be fired.*

Shoot down: bring down
>*They shot down the enemy aircraft.*

Shoot for: aspire
>*You ought to shoot for the top job.*

Shoot up: increase dramatically
>*The stock prices shot up toward the end of the day.*

Shoot up: damage or terrorize a town
>*The guerrillas shot up the entire village.*

Shoot straight: be truthful
>*I love someone who shoots straight in negotiations.*

Shop around: look for bargains
>*The girls love to shop around at the discount stores.*

Shop around: look for something better, like a job.
    We decided to shop around for a while, before we make a career decision.

Show around: act as a guide
    My daughter can show you around the city if you have time.
Show off: display
    The goods were shown off to their best advantage.
Show off: behave ostentatiously
    He always likes to show off in front of his friends.
Show up: be visible
    The cancer showed up clearly on the x-ray.
Show up: arrive
    Will they ever show up?

Shut down: stop something from operating
    They shut the plant down.
Shut off: stop the flow
    Shut off the electricity before you work on the outlet.
Shut off: isolate
    He was shut off from all news for two months.
Shut out: prevent from scoring
    We were able to shut them out in the last inning of the game.
Shut up: silence, be silent
    You should shut up before you get in more trouble.

Sing out: cry out
    He sang out from the rear of the crowd.

Sit down: take a seat
    Please sit down until you are called.
Sit in: participate
    They sat in on the discussions.
Sit in: participate in a sit-in demonstration
    The demonstrators intend to sit in at the plant gates tomorrow.
Sit on: consider
    Can we sit on this for a day or two and then give you our response?
Sit on: suppress
    The defense attorneys sat on the new evidence.
Sit out: stay to the end
    We will sit this out until it is over.
Sit out: not participate
    I sat out the second match and let my brother play.
Sit up: rise from lying to sitting position
    After his nap he sat up in bed.
Sit up: sit with spine erect
    Mothers always want you to sit up straight.
Sit up: stay up late
    They sat up until past midnight waiting for their daughter to come home.
Sit up: become suddenly alert
    He sat up at the sound of shots.

Sleep in: sleep late
> *I like to sleep in on Sundays.*

Sleep out: sleep away from one's home
> *The parents are sleeping out this weekend.*

Sleep over: spend the night at another home
> *The girls slept over at their friend's house.*

Sleep with: have sexual relations
> *He slept with her for the first time on their vacation.*

Slip away: depart without taking one's leave
> *They just slipped away from the party.*

Slip out: depart unnoticed
> *He slipped out for a cigarette break.*

Smell out: discover through investigation
> *They smelled out the criminal after years of investigation.*

Sound off: express an opinion
> *He sounded off about taxes at the town meeting.*

Sound out: elicit an opinion
> *Sound out the board on this matter before Monday.*

Speak out: talk freely
> *He spoke out at our weekly meeting.*

Speak up: talk loud enough to be heard
> *We can't hear you. Would you please speak up?*

Speak up: talk without fear
> *You must learn to speak up for your rights.*

Spell out: read slowly
> *Try to spell it out if you can't understand the meaning.*

Spell out: make clear
> *Would you please spell out your specific objections?*

Spell out: decipher
> *Let's see if we can spell out the new proposal and write a response.*

Spin off: develop from an existing project
> *They spun off two shows from the original.*

Spin out: rotate out of control
> *The car spun out on the ice when he hit the brakes.*

Split up: part company
> *After ten years of marriage they decided to split up.*

Stand by: be ready
> *Stand by for the commercial.*

Stand by: remain uninvolved
> *He just stood by and watched.*

Stand by: remain loyal
She stood by me in my time of trouble.
Stand down: withdraw, cease work
The soldiers on duty stood down at midnight.
Stand for: represent
What do you stand for?
Stand for: put up with
I don't know why I stand for this nonsense.
Stand in: replace
She stood in for the sick actress.
Stand off: stay at a distance
They stood off and observed from afar.
Stand on: be based on
These findings stand on my previous calculations.
Stand on: insist on
There are times when you must stand on ceremony.
Stand out: be conspicuous
She really stood out in the green dress.
Stand out: refuse compliance
He is going to stand out against the tax people.
Stand over: supervise
She stood over him the entire test.
Stand to: prepare to act
The police were ordered to stand to.
Stand up: remain valid
His conclusions stood up to various attacks.
Stand up: miss an appointment
She stood him up again last evening.
Stand up for: defend
I stood up for you in my meeting with the school board.

Start out: begin a trip
They started out for Miami at dawn.

Stave off: prevent
They staved off the attackers countless times.

Stay put: remain in place
Now you kids stay put until I get the ice cream.
Stay up: remain awake
They stayed up all night talking about old times.

Stick around: remain
He stuck around for an hour after the press conference to sign autographs.
Stick out: be prominent
He really sticks out in a crowd.
Stick up: to rob at gunpoint
They were stuck up twice in six months.
Stick up for: defend
He always sticks up for his kid brother.

Stop by: visit
> *They stopped by for coffee after the theater.*

Stop off: interrupt a trip
> *They stopped off in Rome for two days.*

Strike down: fell with a blow
> *He was struck down by a lightning bolt.*

Strike out for: begin a course of action
> *He struck out for California on his own.*

Strike out: fail in one's attempts
> *He struck out in his attempts to get approval for the highway.*

Strike up: start
> *Strike up the band!*

String along: entice by giving false hope
> *They strung him along for a few weeks before telling him they had hired someone else.*

String out: prolong
> *How long can we string out these talks?*

String up: hang someone
> *They strung him up without a trial.*

Swear at: verbally abuse
> *She swore at them like a sailor.*

Swear by: rely on
> *I swear by these calculations.*

Swear by: take an oath
> *Do you swear by the Bible?*

Swear in: administer a legal oath
> *He was sworn in as Governor.*

Swear off: renounce
> *I have sworn off cigarettes.*

Swear out: process
> *The detectives swore out a warrant for his arrest.*

Sweat out: await anxiously
> *Some students sweated out the two weeks before grades were mailed home.*

Take after: follow the example of, resemble
> *She takes after her father.*

Take apart: separate
> *He took the motor apart in an afternoon.*

Take back: retract
> *I take back my original comments.*

Take down: lower
> *He was taken down a notch or two by the negative fitness report.*

Take down: record in writing
> *He took down the minutes of the meeting.*

Take for: regard
> *What do you take me for?*

Take in: grant admittance
>
> *She was taken in as a member of the law firm.*

Take in: reduce
>
> *She took in his new slacks at the waist.*

Take in: include
>
> *This article takes in all of the existing information.*

Take in: deceive
>
> *He was taken in by her flashy business card.*

Take in: observe thoroughly
>
> *He took in the entire scene with a single glance.*

Take off: remove
>
> *Take off your hat indoors.*

Take off: depart by aircraft
>
> *Our flight to Madrid took off on schedule.*

Take off: deduct
>
> *He took off ten percent from the marked price.*

Take on: hire
>
> *We took him on temporarily for the job.*

Take on: accept
>
> *We took on the new responsibilities cheerfully.*

Take on: oppose
>
> *He took on the taller man in a fistfight.*

Take out: secure a license
>
> *I took out a hunting license.*

Take out: escort
>
> *I took out our guests for a look at the city.*

Take out: vent
>
> *He took out his anger on the punching bag.*

Take out: kill
>
> *He took out the enemy sniper with his first shot.*

Take over: assume control
>
> *I am taking over here as of today.*

Take to: develop habit or ability
>
> *He took to swimming at an early age.*

Take to: escape
>
> *The escapees took to the hills.*

Take up: assume
>
> *He took up the burden of his family's debts.*

Take up: reduce
>
> *She took up the dress a full inch.*

Take up: use time
>
> *It took up all morning.*

Talk around: persuade
>
> *He tried to talk me around to his point of view.*

Talk around: avoid
>
> *He tried talking his way around the parking ticket.*

Talk at: address
>
> *He talked at the rotary club.*

Talk back: reply rudely
> *Don't talk back to your parents.*

Talk down: deprecate
> *He loves to talk down to his secretary.*

Talk down: silence
> *By the end of the meeting he had successfully talked down all the dissenting voices.*

Talk out: resolve
> *Can we not talk this out in a friendly fashion?*

Talk over: consider
> *We talked it over before deciding.*

Talk over: persuade
> *They talked her over by the end of the day.*

Talk up: promote, exaggerate
> *Let's talk up our accomplishments.*

Tear at: attack like an animal
> *They tore at the package like wild animals.*

Tear at: distress oneself
> *Stop tearing at yourself.*

Tear down: vilify
> *They love to tear other people down.*

Tear down: demolish
> *They love to tear down the walls that separate the people in our community.*

Tear into: attack vigorously
> *They tore into their opponents.*

Tear up: destroy
> *We tore up the lease.*

Tell off: reprimand
> *They certainly told him off.*

Throw away: get rid of
> *We throw the boxes away.*

Throw away: waste
> *She threw away her life's savings in Las Vegas.*

Throw away: fail to take advantage
> *They threw away their chance.*

Throw back: hinder the progress
> *They were completely thrown back by his critical comments.*

Throw back: revert
> *They were thrown back to the beginning by the new discovery.*

Throw in: insert
> *Throw in your opinions whenever ready.*

Throw off: rid oneself
> *They threw the dogs off their scent by crossing a stream.*

Throw off: emit
> *The new plant throws off a foul odor.*

Throw off: divert
> *They were thrown off course by a faulty computer.*

Throw open: make accessible
> *We must throw open our doors to every deserving student.*

Throw out: emit
> *It throws out a powerful signal to other countries.*

Throw out: reject
> *The new design was thrown out by the board of directors.*

Throw out: force to leave
> *Throw the bum out.*

Throw over: overturn
> *They threw over the leftist government in the sixties.*

Throw over: reject
> *The new tax laws were thrown over by the voters in a special vote.*

Throw up: vomit
> *I was so sick I threw up twice.*

Throw up: abandon
> *She threw up her attempts to gain the money.*

Throw up: refer to something repeatedly
> *He kept throwing up her name.*

Throw up: construct hastily
> *Those buildings were thrown up in a matter of months.*

Throw up: project
> *Please throw that image up on the screen.*

Tie in: connect
> *Can we tie in these findings with our previous data?*

Tie into: attack
> *He tied into her.*

Tie up: block
> *They tied up traffic for hours.*

Tie up: occupy
> *I was tied up in the office all last week.*

Try on: check out clothes for size
> *Try on the shoes before you buy them.*

Try out: undergo a competitive qualifying exam
> *He must try out for the soccer team.*

Try out: test or examine
> *Can I try out these new glasses before I purchase a pair?*

Turn away: dismiss
> *They were turned away at the hotel because it was full.*

Turn away: reject
> *They were turned away at the last moment by a violent counterattack.*

Turn back: reverse direction
> *Can you turn back time?*

Turn back: halt advance
> *The invaders were turned back by the courageous citizens of the village.*

Turn down: reject
> *She was turned down by the police department.*

Turn down: fold down
>The bed was turned down by the chambermaid before they returned last evening.

Turn in: give over
>Turn in your papers at the end of class.

Turn in: inform on
>They turned in their own brother to the authorities.

Turn off: stop operation
>Turn off the electricity.

Turn off: offend
>He was turned off by their use of profanity.

Turn off: cease paying attention
>He turned them off and played all by himself.

Turn on: begin operation
>Turn on the television.

Turn on: alter the mind with drugs
>In the sixties people were eager to turn on.

Turn on: interest
>That course turned him on.

Turn out: produce
>They turn out dozens of autos an hour.

Turn out: gather
>Hundreds turned out for his speech.

Turn out: develop
>The cake turned out wonderfully.

Turn over: shift position
>Turn over on your side if you snore.

Turn over: reflect upon
>He turned the request over and over in his mind for a long time.

Turn over: transfer to another
>The papers were turned over to the judge.

Turn over: sell
>How many of these cars can we turn over by the end of the month?

Turn to: seek assistance
>Whom can I turn to?

Turn to: begin
>He turned his attention to the new project.

Turn up: increase volume
>Turn up the radio. I want to hear the weather report.

Turn up: find
>Where did you turn up the missing wallet?

Turn up: appear, be found
>The ring turned up among her dirty socks.

Turn up: just happen
>In every translation, some new difficulty turns up.

Use up: exhaust the supply
>He used up all the sugar for the cake.

Wait on/upon: attend to
>She waited on him day and night.

Wait out: endure
> *We will have to wait out the storm in a hotel.*

Wait up: postpone sleep
> *Daddy still waits up for his daughters even though they are grown up.*

Walk out: go on strike
> *The workers walked out at midnight without a contract.*

Walk out: leave suddenly
> *He just got up and walked out.*

Walk over: gain easy victory
> *They walked all over their opponents.*

Walk over: treat poorly
> *They walk all over the staff.*

Walk through: perform
> *They walked through their lines for the last time.*

Watch out: be careful
> *Watch out, it's very slippery.*

Watch over: be in charge of
> *I was told to watch over him until the doctor came.*

Watch it: be careful
> *I'm telling you, you'd better watch it, or they'll be trouble.*

Wear down: exhaust by continuous pressure
> *They finally wore him down by constant interrogation.*

Wear off: diminish gradually
> *The paint has worn off the siding.*

Wear out: become unusable
> *These jeans will never wear out.*

Win out: prevail
> *He finally won out over his competitors.*

Win over: persuade
> *He won them over with his charm.*

Wind down: relax
> *After work they wound down for an hour in the hot tub.*

Wind up: end
> *They wound up the party at midnight.*

Work in: insert
> *They worked in an hour of relaxation.*

Work off: rid by effort
> *She worked off ten pounds at the gym.*

Work out: accomplish
> *That worked out well.*

Work out: develop
> *They worked out a satisfactory arrangement for them both.*

Work out: engage in strenuous activity
> *She works out every afternoon for two hours.*

Work over: repeat, revise
They are working over their papers for submission on Monday.
Work up: get excited
She got all worked up over her grade.
Work up: increase ability or capacity
She worked her way up to ten pages an hour.

Wrap up: complete
Let's wrap up the meeting and go home.
Wrap up: summarize
Can you wrap up the presentation with your main points?
Wrap up: intensely involved
She's all wrapped up in her schoolwork.

Write down: record
She wrote down the assignment.
Write in: insert
She wrote in a new opening scene for the main actress.
Write in: submit name of candidate not on the ballot
They wrote her in for the post of treasurer.
Write in: write to organization
They wrote in to the maker of the toy with their complaint.
Write off: dismiss
They wrote her off even before the tryouts.
Write out: write in full
She had to write out the complete sentence.
Write up: report
She wrote up the minutes of the meeting.

Zero in: concentrate on
They zeroed in on their long-term goals during the afternoon session.

Another 500 Problem Verbs

Listed below are an additional 500 English Verbs whose principal parts may cause confusion or difficulty in spelling. Their principal parts are listed here to correspond to the order of the full *501 English Verbs*.

Basic Form	3rd Person Singular	Present Participle	Past Tense	Past Participle
abet	abets	abetting	abetted	abetted
abhor	abhors	abhorring	abhorred	abhorred
accompany	accompanies	accompanying	accompanied	accompanied
accede	accedes	acceding	acceded	acceded
access	accesses	accessing	accessed	accessed
acquit	acquits	acquitting	acquitted	acquitted
ad-lib	ad-libs	ad-libbing	ad-libbed	ad-libbed
allay	allays	allaying	allayed	allayed
allot	allots	allotting	allotted	allotted
annul	annuls	annulling	annulled	annulled
answer	answers	answering	answered	answered
antique	antiques	antiquing	antiqued	antiqued
argue	argues	arguing	argued	argued
bat	bats	batting	batted	batted
bed	beds	bedding	bedded	bedded
befit	befits	befitting	befitted	befitted
belie	belies	belying	belied	belied
benefit	benefits	benefit/benefitting	benefited/ benefitted	benefited/ benefitted
betake	betakes	betaking	betook	betaken
binge	binges	binging/bingeing	binged	binged
blab	blabs	blabbing	blabbed	blabbed
blot	blots	blotting	blotted	blotted
blur	blurs	blurring	blurred	blurred
bob	bobs	bobbing	bobbed	bobbed
bobsled	bobsleds	bobsledding	bobsledded	bobsledded
boo	boos	booing	booed	booed
bop	bops	bopping	bopped	bopped
brim	brims	brimming	brimmed	brimmed
bug	bugs	bugging	bugged	bugged
bum	bums	bumming	bummed	bummed
bus	buses/busses	busing/bussing	bused/bussed	bused/bussed
can	can		could	
cancel	cancels	canceling/ cancelling	canceled/ cancelled	canceled/ cancelled
cane	canes	caning	caned	caned
cap	caps	capping	capped	capped

Basic Form	3rd Person Singular	Present Participle	Past Tense	Past Participle
channel	channels	channeling/ channelling	channeled/ channelled	channeled/ channelled
chap	chaps	chapping	chapped	chapped
chat	chats	chatting	chatted	chatted
chin	chins	chinning	chinned	chinned
chip	chips	chipping	chipped	chipped
chug	chugs	chugging	chugged	chugged
chum	chums	chumming	chummed	chummed
clad	clads	cladding	clad	clad
clap	claps	clapping	clapped	clapped
clip	clips	clipping	clipped	clipped
clog	clogs	clogging	clogged	clogged
clot	clots	clotting	clotted	clotted
club	clubs	clubbing	clubbed	clubbed
combat	combats	combating/ combatting	combated/ combatted	combated/ combatted
commit	commits	committing	committed	committed
confer	confers	conferring	conferred	conferred
control	controls	controlling	controlled	controlled
coo	coos	cooing	cooed	cooed
cop	cops	copping	copped	copped
cope	copes	coping	coped	coped
counsel	counsels	counseling/ counselling	counseled/ counselled	counseled/ counselled
crab	crab	crabbing	crabbed	crabbed
crop	crops	cropping	cropped	cropped
dab	dabs	dabbing	dabbed	dabbed
debug	debugs	debugging	debugged	debugged
debut	debuts	debuting	debuted	debuted
defat	defats	defatting	defatted	defatted
deter	deters	deterring	deterred	deterred
dip	dips	dipping	dipped	dipped
disagree	disagrees	disagreeing	disagreed	disagreed
disbar	disbars	disbarring	disbarred	disbarred
disbud	disbuds	disbudding	disbudded	disbudded
dog	dogs	dogging	dogged	dogged
don	dons	donning	donned	donned
dot	dots	dotting	dotted	dotted
drip	drips	dripping	dripped	dripped
drivel	drivels	driveling/drivelling	driveled/drivelled	driveled/drivelled
drug	drugs	drugging	drugged	drugged
drum	drums	drumming	drummed	drummed
dry	dries	drying	dried	dried
dub	dubs	dubbing	dubbed	dubbed
duel	duels	dueling/duelling	dueled/duelled	dueled/duelled
dun	duns	dunning	dunned	dunned

Basic Form	3rd Person Singular	Present Participle	Past Tense	Past Participle
emit	emits	emitting	emitted	emitted
empty	empties	emptying	emptied	emptied
entrap	entraps	entrapping	entrapped	entrapped
envy	envies	envying	envied	envied
enwrap	enwraps	enwrapping	enwrapped	enwrapped
equal	equals	equaling/equalling	equaled/equalled	equaled/equalled
equip	equips	equipping	equipped	equipped
exhibit	exhibits	exhibiting	exhibited	exhibited
expel	expels	expelling	expelled	expelled
eye	eyes	eyeing	eyed	eyed
fan	fans	fanning	fanned	fanned
fat	fats	fatting	fatted	fatted
fatten	fattens	fattening	fattened	fattened
fib	fibs	fibbing	fibbed	fibbed
fine	fines	fining	fined	fined
flag	flags	flagging	flagged	flagged
flap	flaps	flapping	flapped	flapped
flip	flips	flipping	flipped	flipped
flog	flogs	flogging	flogged	flogged
flop	flops	flopping	flopped	flopped
flub	flubs	flubbing	flubbed	flubbed
fog	fogs	fogging	fogged	fogged
frag	frags	fragging	fragged	fragged
fret	frets	fretting	fretted	fretted
frit	frits	fritting	fritted	fritted
fry	fries	frying	fried	fried
fuel	fuels	fueling/fuelling	fueled/fuelled	fueled/fuelled
fur	furs	furring	furred	furred
gainsay	gainsays	gainsaying	gainsaid	gainsaid
gap	gaps	gapping	gapped	gapped
gape	gapes	gaping	gaped	gaped
gas	gases/gasses	gassing	gassed	gassed
gel	gels	gelling	gelled	gelled
geld	gelds	gelding	gelded/gelt	gelded/gelt
gem	gems	gemming	gemmed	gemmed
gib	gibs	gibbing	gibbed	gibbed
gibe	gibes	gibing	gibed	gibed
gig	gigs	gigging	gigged	gigged
gin	gins	ginning	ginned	ginned
glut	gluts	glutting	glutted	glutted
grab	grabs	grabbing	grabbed	grabbed
gravel	gravels	graveling/gravelling	graveled/gravelled	graveled/gravelled
grin	grins	grinning	grinned	grinned
grip	grips	gripping	gripped	gripped
gripe	gripes	griping	griped	griped

Basic Form	3rd Person Singular	Present Participle	Past Tense	Past Participle
grit	grits	gritting	gritted	gritted
grub	grubs	grubbing	grubbed	grubbed
gum	gums	gumming	gummed	gummed
gun	guns	gunning	gunned	gunned
gut	guts	gutting	gutted	gutted
gyp	gyps	gypping	gypped	gypped
ham	hams	hamming	hammed	hammed
hat	hats	hatting	hatted	hatted
hoe	hoes	hoeing	hoed	hoed
hog	hogs	hogging	hogged	hogged
hug	hugs	hugging	hugged	hugged
impel	impels	impelling	impelled	impelled
imperil	imperils	imperiling/ imperilling	imperiled/ imperilled	imperiled/ imperilled
inbreed	inbreeds	inbreeding	inbred	inbred
incur	incurs	incurring	incurred	incurred
infer	infers	inferring	inferred	inferred
inherit	inherits	inheriting	inherited	inherited
input	inputs	inputting	inputted/input	inputted/input
inter	inters	interring	interred	interred
interbreed	interbreeds	interbreeding	interbred	interbred
intercrop	intercrops	intercropping	intercropped	intercropped
intercut	intercuts	intercutting	intercut	intercut
intermit	intermits	intermitting	intermitted	intermitted
intrigue	intrigues	intriguing	intrigued	intrigued
intromit	intromits	intromitting	intromitted	intromitted
intuit	intuits	intuiting	intuited	intuited
issue	issues	issuing	issued	issued
jab	jabs	jabbing	jabbed	jabbed
jag	jags	jagging	jagged	jagged
jam	jams	jamming	jammed	jammed
jar	jars	jarring	jarred	jarred
jet	jets	jetting	jetted	jetted
jib	jibs	jibbing	jibbed	jibbed
jig	jigs	jigging	jigged	jigged
job	jobs	jobbing	jobbed	jobbed
jog	jogs	jogging	jogged	jogged
jot	jots	jotting	jotted	jotted
jug	jugs	jugging	jugged	jugged
junket	junkets	junketing	junketed	junketed
jut	juts	jutting	jutted	jutted
ken	kens	kenning	kenned/kent	kenned/kent
kid	kids	kidding	kidded	kidded

Basic Form	3rd Person Singular	Present Participle	Past Tense	Past Participle
kidnap	kidnaps	kidnapping/ kidnaping	kidnapped/ kidnaped	kidnapped/ kidnaped
knap	knaps	knapping	knapped	knapped
knee	knees	kneeing	kneed	kneed
knot	knots	knotting	knotted	knotted
label	labels	labeling/labelling	labeled/labelled	labeled/labelled
lag	lags	lagging	lagged	lagged
lap	laps	lapping	lapped	lapped
lasso	lassos/lassoes	lassoing	lassoed	lassoed
laurel	laurels	laureling/laurelling	laureled/laurelled	laureled/laurelled
level	levels	leveling/levelling	leveled/levelled	leveled/levelled
libel	libels	libeling/libelling	libeled/libelled	libeled/libelled
lid	lids	lidding	lidded	lidded
lip	lips	lipping	lipped	lipped
lob	lobs	lobbing	lobbed	lobbed
log	logs	logging	logged	logged
loop	loops	looping	looped	looped
lop	lops	lopping	lopped	lopped
lope	lopes	loping	loped	loped
lug	lugs	lugging	lugged	lugged
mad	mads	madding	madded	madded
madden	maddens	maddening	maddened	maddened
magic	magics	magicking	magicked	magicked
man	mans	manning	manned	manned
manumit	manumits	manumitting	manumitted	manumitted
map	maps	mapping	mapped	mapped
mar	mars	marring	marred	marred
marvel	marvels	marveling/ marvelling	marveled/ marvelled	marveled/ marvelled
mat	mats	matting	matted	matted
mate	mates	mating	mated	mated
maul	mauls	mauling/maulling	mauled/maulled	mauled/maulled
may	may		might	
medal	medals	medaling/medalling	medaled/medalled	medaled/medalled
merchandise	merchandises	merchandising	merchandised	merchandised
metal	metals	metaling/metalling	metaled/metalled	metaled/metalled
midwife	midwifes/midwives	midwifing/ midwiving	midwifed/ midwived	midwifed/ midwived
misdeal	misdeals	misdealing	misdealt	misdealt
misdo	misdoes	misdoing	misdid	misdone
misfuel	misfuels	misfueling/ misfuelling	misfueled/ misfuelled	misfueled/ misfuelled
mislabel	mislabels	mislabeling/ mislabelling	mislabeled/ mislabelled	mislabeled/ mislabelled
misunderstand	misunderstands	misunderstanding	misunderstood	misunderstood

Basic Form	3rd Person Singular	Present Participle	Past Tense	Past Participle
miswrite	miswrites	miswriting	miswrote	miswritten
mob	mobs	mobbing	mobbed	mobbed
model	models	modeling/ modelling	modeled/ modelled	modeled/ modelled
monogram	monograms	monogramming/ monograming	monogrammed/ monogramed	monogrammed/ monogramed
monolog	monologs	monologging	monologed	monologed
monologue	monologues	monologuing	monologued	monologued
mop	mops	mopping	mopped	mopped
mope	mopes	moping	moped	moped
mortgage	mortgages	mortgaging	mortgaged	mortgaged
mosaic	mosaics	mosaicking	mosaicked	mosaicked
mud	muds	mudding	mudded	mudded
mug	mugs	mugging	mugged	mugged
mum	mums	mumming	mummed	mummed
must	must		had to	
nap	naps	napping	napped	napped
nag	nags	nagging	nagged	nagged
nap	naps	napping	napped	napped
net	nets	netting	netted	netted
nip	nips	nipping	nipped	nipped
nod	nods	nodding	nodded	nodded
omit	omits	omitting	omitted	omitted
one-step	one-steps	one-stepping	one-stepped	one-stepped
one-up	one-ups	one-upping	one-upped	one-upped
ought	ought		ought	
out	outs	outing	outed	outed
outbreed	outbreeds	outbreeding	outbred	outbred
outgo	outgoes	outgoing	outwent	outgone
outgrow	outgrows	outgrowing	outgrew	outgrown
outlay	outlays	outlaying	outlaid	outlaid
outshine	outshines	outshining	outshone	outshone
outstrip	outstrips	outstripping	outstripped	outstripped
outwear	outwears	outwearing	outwore	outworn
outwork	outworks	outworking	outworked/ outwrought	outworked/ outwrought
overbear	overbears	overbearing	overbore	overborne
overbid	overbids	overbidding	overbidded	overbidded
overblow	overblows	overblowing	overblew	overblown
overdo	overdoes	overdoing	overdid	overdone
overcommit	overcommits	overcommitting	overcommitted	overcommitted
override	overrides	overriding	overrode	overridden
pad	pads	padding	padded	padded
pal	pals	palling	palled	palled

Basic Form	3rd Person Singular	Present Participle	Past Tense	Past Participle
pale	pales	paling	paled	paled
pall	palls	palling	palled	palled
pan	pans	panning	panned	panned
panel	panels	paneling/panelling	paneled/panelled	paneled/panelled
par	pars	parring	parred	parred
parallel	parallels	paralleling/parallelling	paralleled/parallelled	paralleled/parallelled
parcel	parcels	parceling/parcelling	parceled/parcelled	parceled/parcelled
partake	partakes	partaking	partook	partaken
pat	pats	patting	patted	patted
patrol	patrols	patrolling	patrolled	patrolled
pedal	pedals	pedaling/pedalling	pedaled/pedalled	pedaled/pedalled
peg	pegs	pegging	pegged	pegged
pencil	pencils	penciling/pencilling	penciled/pencilled	penciled/pencilled
pep	peps	pepping	pepped	pepped
pet	pets	petting	petted	petted
photo	photos	photoing	photoed	photoed
picnic	picnics	picnicking	picnicked	picnicked
pig	pigs	pigging	pigged	pigged
pin	pins	pinning	pinned	pinned
pip	pips	pipping	pipped	pipped
pipe	pipes	piping	piped	piped
pique	piques	piquing	piqued	piqued
pit	pits	pitting	pitted	pitted
plague	plagues	plaguing	plagued	plagued
plod	plods	plodding	plodded	plodded
plop	plops	plopping	plopped	plopped
plot	plots	plotting	plotted	plotted
plug	plugs	plugging	plugged	plugged
ply	plies	plying	plied	plied
pod	pods	podding	podded	podded
pop	pops	popping	popped	popped
pot	pots	potting	potted	potted
pray	prays	praying	prayed	prayed
prep	preps	prepping	prepped	prepped
prig	prigs	prigging	prigged	prigged
prim	prims	primming	primmed	primmed
prime	primes	priming	primed	primed
prod	prods	prodding	prodded	prodded
prop	props	propping	propped	propped
pry	pries	prying	pried	pried
pug	pugs	pugging	pugged	pugged
pun	puns	punning	punned	punned
putt	putts	putting	putted	putted

Basic Form	3rd Person Singular	Present Participle	Past Tense	Past Participle
quip	quips	quipping	quipped	quipped
quiver	quivers	quivering	quivered	quivered
rag	rags	ragging	ragged	ragged
rage	rages	raging	raged	raged
rally	rallies	rallying	rallied	rallied
ram	rams	ramming	rammed	rammed
ramble	rambles	rambling	rambled	rambled
rattle	rattles	rattling	rattled	rattled
rebut	rebuts	rebutting	rebutted	rebutted
recap	recaps	recapping	recapped	recapped
recede	recedes	receding	receded	receded
recur	recurs	recurring	recurred	recurred
reflag	reflags	reflagging	reflagged	reflagged
rely	relies	relying	relied	relied
remit	remits	remitting	remitted	remitted
remodel	remodels	remodeling/ remodelling	remodeled/ remodelled	remodeled/ remodelled
repel	repels	repelling	repelled	repelled
rerun	reruns	rerunning	reran	rerun
rescue	rescues	rescuing	rescued	rescued
reset	resets	resetting	reset	reset
retread	retreads	retreading	retreaded/retrod	retreaded/ retrodden
rev	revs	revving	revved	revved
reveal	reveals	revealing	revealed	revealed
revel	revels	reveling/revelling	reveled/revelled	reveled/revelled
rewind	rewinds	rewinding	rewound	rewound
rib	ribs	ribbing	ribbed	ribbed
rim	rims	rimming	rimmed	rimmed
rip	rips	ripping	ripped	ripped
rival	rivals	rivaling/rivalling	rivaled/rivalled	rivaled/rivalled
rivet	rivets	riveting	riveted	riveted
rot	rots	rotting	rotted	rotted
rub	rubs	rubbing	rubbed	rubbed
rue	rues	ruing	rued	rued
sag	sags	sagging	sagged	sagged
sap	saps	sapping	sapped	sapped
scab	scabs	scabbing	scabbed	scabbed
scan	scans	scanning	scanned	scanned
scar	scar	scarring	scarred	scarred
scare	scares	scaring	scared	scared
scram	scrams	scramming	scrammed	scrammed
scrap	scraps	scrapping	scrapped	scrapped
scrape	scrapes	scraping	scraped	scraped
scrub	scrubs	scrubbing	scrubbed	scrubbed

Basic Form	3rd Person Singular	Present Participle	Past Tense	Past Participle
scrunch	scrunches	scrunching	scrunched	scrunched
scud	scuds	scudding	scudded	scudded
scum	scums	scumming	scummed	scummed
shag	shags	shagging	shagged	shagged
shall	shall		should	
sham	shams	shamming	shammed	shammed
shellac	shellacs	shellacking	shellacked	shellacked
shin	shins	shinning	shinned	shinned
ship	ships	shipping	shipped	shipped
shot	shots	shotting	shotted	shotted
shrivel	shrivels	shriveling/ shrivelling	shriveled/ shrivelled	shriveled/ shrivelled
shrug	shrugs	shrugging	shrugged	shrugged
shy	shies	shying	shied	shied
sin	sins	sinning	sinned	sinned
skid	skids	skidding	skidded	skidded
skim	skims	skimming	skimmed	skimmed
skin	skins	skinning	skinned	skinned
skip	skips	skipping	skipped	skipped
sky	skies	skying	skied	skied
slab	slabs	slabbing	slabbed	slabbed
slam	slams	slamming	slammed	slammed
slap	slaps	slapping	slapped	slapped
sled	sleds	sledding	sledded	sledded
slew	slews	slewing	slewed	slewed
slim	slims	slimming	slimmed	slimmed
slog	slogs	slogging	slogged	slogged
slop	slops	slopping	slopped	slopped
slope	slopes	sloping	sloped	sloped
slot	slots	slotting	slotted	slotted
slub	slubs	slubbing	slubbed	slubbed
slue	slues	sluing	slued	slued
slug	slugs	slugging	slugged	slugged
slum	slums	slumming	slummed	slummed
slur	slurs	slurring	slurred	slurred
smut	smuts	smutting	smutted	smutted
snag	snags	snagging	snagged	snagged
snap	snaps	snapping	snapped	snapped
snip	snips	snipping	snipped	snipped
snipe	snipes	sniping	sniped	sniped
snub	snubs	snubbing	snubbed	snubbed
snug	snugs	snugging	snugged	snugged
sob	sobs	sobbing	sobbed	sobbed
sod	sods	sodding	sodded	sodded
sop	sops	sopping	sopped	sopped
spat	spats	spatting	spatted	spatted
spec	specs	spec'ing/speccing	spec'd/specced	spec'd/specced

Basic Form	3rd Person Singular	Present Participle	Past Tense	Past Participle
spiral	spirals	spiraling/spiralling	spiraled/spiralled	spiraled/spiralled
spot	spots	spotting	spotted	spotted
sprig	sprigs	sprigging	sprigged	sprigged
spur	spurs	spurring	spurred	spurred
spy	spies	spying	spied	spied
squat	squats	squatting	squatted	squatted
squelch	squelches	squelching	squelched	squelched
squib	squibs	squibbing	squibbed	squibbed
squirrel	squirrels	squirreling/ squirrelling	squirreled/ squirrelled	squirreled/ squirrelled
stab	stabs	stabbing	stabbed	stabbed
stag	stags	stagging	stagged	stagged
stage	stages	staging	staged	staged
star	stars	starring	starred	starred
stare	stares	staring	stared	stared
steer	steers	steering	steered	steered
stem	stems	stemming	stemmed	stemmed
step	steps	stepping	stepped	stepped
stir	stirs	stirring	stirred	stirred
stitch	stitches	stitching	stitched	stitched
stoop	stoops	stooping	stooped	stooped
stope	stopes	stoping	stoped	stoped
strap	straps	strapping	strapped	strapped
strip	strips	stripping	stripped	stripped
stripe	stripes	striping	striped	striped
strop	strops	stropping	stropped	stropped
strum	strums	strumming	strummed	strummed
strut	struts	strutting	strutted	strutted
stub	stubs	stubbing	stubbed	stubbed
stud	studs	studding	studded	studded
stun	stuns	stunning	stunned	stunned
sub	subs	subbing	subbed	subbed
subdue	subdues	subduing	subdued	subdued
submit	submits	submitting	submitted	submitted
sum	sums	summing	summed	summed
summon	summons	summoning	summoned	summoned
summons	summonses	summonsing	summonsed	summonsed
sun	suns	sunning	sunned	sunned
sunburn	sunburns	sunburning	sunburned/ sunburnt	sunburned/ sunburnt
sup	sups	supping	supped	supped
swab	swabs	swabbing	swabbed	swabbed
swag	swags	swagging	swagged	swagged
swap	swaps	swapping	swapped	swapped
swivel	swivels	swiveling/ swivelling	swiveled/ swivelled	swiveled/ swivelled
sync	syncs	syncing	synced	synced
synch	synches	synching	synched	synched

Basic Form	3rd Person Singular	Present Participle	Past Tense	Past Participle
tab	tabs	tabbing	tabbed	tabbed
taboo	taboos	tabooing	tabooed	tabooed
tabu	tabus	tabuing	tabued	tabued
tag	tags	tagging	tagged	tagged
talc	talcs	talcking/talcing	talcked/talced	talcked/talced
tan	tans	tanning	tanned	tanned
tap	taps	tapping	tapped	tapped
tar	tars	tarring	tarred	tarred
tax	taxes	taxing	taxed	taxed
teasel	teasels	teaseling/teaselling	teaseled/teaselled	teaseled/teaselled
tech	techs	teching	teched	teched
tee	tees	teeing	teed	teed
telecast	telecast	telecasting	telecast/telecasted	telecast/telecasted
thin	thins	thinning	thinned	thinned
throb	throbs	throbbing	throbbed	throbbed
thrum	thrums	thrumming	thrummed	thrummed
thud	thuds	thudding	thudded	thudded
tic	tics	ticcing	ticced	ticced
tick	ticks	ticking	ticked	ticked
ticket	tickets	ticketing	ticketed	ticketed
tin	tins	tinning	tinned	tinned
tip	tips	tipping	tipped	tipped
toe	toes	toeing	toed	toed
tog	togs	togging	togged	togged
top	tops	topping	topped	topped
total	totals	totaling/totalling	totaled/totalled	totaled/totalled
trammel	trammels	trammeling/ trammelling	trammeled/ trammelled	trammeled/ trammelled
trap	traps	trapping	trapped	trapped
travel	travels	traveling/travelling	traveled/travelled	traveled/travelled
tree	trees	treeing	treed	treed
trek	treks	trekking	trekked	trekked
trifle	trifles	trifling	trifled	trifled
trim	trims	trimming	trimmed	trimmed
trip	trips	tripping	tripped	tripped
trolley	trolleys	trolleying	trolleyed	trolleyed
trot	trots	trotting	trotted	trotted
tub	tubs	tubbing	tubbed	tubbed
tug	tugs	tugging	tugged	tugged
tumble	tumbles	tumbling	tumbled	tumbled
unbuckle	unbuckles	unbuckling	unbuckled	unbuckled
underwrite	underwrites	underwriting	underwrote	underwritten
unify	unifies	unifying	unified	unified
unmake	unmakes	unmaking	unmade	unmade
unravel	unravels	unraveling/ unravelling	unraveled/ unravelled	unraveled/ unravelled
untie	unties	untying	untied	untied

Basic Form	3rd Person Singular	Present Participle	Past Tense	Past Participle
up	ups	upping	upped	upped
uphold	upholds	upholding	upheld	upheld
value	values	valuing	valued	valued
van	vans	vanning	vanned	vanned
vat	vats	vatting	vatted	vatted
vet	vets	vetting	vetted	vetted
veto	vetoes	vetoing	vetoed	vetoed
vial	vials	vialing/vialling	vialed/vialled	vialed/vialled
vie	vies	vying	vied	vied
volley	volleys	volleying	volleyed	volleyed
wad	wads	wadding	wadded	wadded
wade	wades	wading	waded	waded
wag	wags	wagging	wagged	wagged
wage	wages	waging	waged	waged
wainscot	wainscots	wainscoting/ wainscotting	wainscoted/ wainscotted	wainscoted/ wainscotted
waltz	waltzes	waltzing	waltzed	waltzed
wan	wans	wanning	wanned	wanned
wane	wanes	waning	waned	waned
war	wars	warring	warred	warred
weasel	weasels	weaseling/ weaselling	weaseled/ weaselled	weaseled/ weaselled
web	webs	webbing	webbed	webbed
whet	whets	whetting	whetted	whetted
whir	whirs	whirring	whirred	whirred
whiz	whizzes	whizzing	whizzed	whizzed
whop	whops	whopping	whopped	whopped
wig	wigs	wigging	wigged	wigged
wigwag	wigwags	wigwagging	wigwagged	wigwagged
will	will		would	
woo	woos	wooing	wooed	wooed
wow	wows	wowing	wowed	wowed
yak	yaks	yakking	yakked	yakked
yap	yaps	yapping	yapped	yapped
yip	yips	yipping	yipped	yipped
yodel	yodels	yodeling/yodelling	yodeled/yodelled	yodeled/yodelled
yo-yo	yo-yos	yo-yoing	yo-yoed	yo-yoed
zag	zags	zagging	zagged	zagged
zap	zaps	zapping	zapped	zapped
zig	zigs	zigging	zigged	zigged
zigzag	zigzags	zigzagging	zigzagged	zigzagged
zinc	zincs/zincks	zincing/zincking	zinced/zincked	zinced/zincked
zing	zings	zinging	zinged	zinged
zip	zips	zipping	zipped	zipped

Index of the 501 English Verbs

All of the verbs conjugated in *501 English Verbs* are listed below in alphabetical order. Irregular (or possibly confusing) principal parts are listed in *italics* underneath each verb to assist you in finding the basic form of the verb you need.

abide
 abode
accept
achieve
act
add
admit
agree
allow
announce
annoy
appear
apply
arise
 arose, arisen
ask
assume
attack
attend
avoid
awake
 awoke
awaken

bar
bare
base
be
 is, am, are,
 was, were,
 been
bear
 bore, borne
beat
become
beg
beget
 begot,
 begotten
begin
 began, begun
behold
 beheld
believe

bend
 bent
bereave
 bereft
beseech
 besought
beset
bestride
 bestrode,
 bestridden
bet
bid
bid
 bade, bidden
bide
 bode
bind
 bound
bite
 bit, bitten
bleed
 bled
blend
 blent
bless
 blest
blow
 blew, blown
bother
break
 broke, broken
breed
 bred
bring
 brought
broadcast
build
 built
burn
 burnt
burst
bust
buy
 bought

call
can
care
carry
cast
catch
 caught
cause
change
chide
 chid, chidden
choose
 chose,
 chosen
cleave
 cleft, clove,
 cloven
cling
 clung
close
clothe
 clad
come
 came
compare
concern
confuse
connect
consider
contain
continue
cost
cover
create
creep
 crept
cry
 cried
cut

dare
deal
 dealt
decide

deep-freeze
 deep-froze,
 deep-frozen
describe
design
determine
develop
dial
die
 dying
die
 dieing
dig
 dug
discover
discuss
dive
 dove
do
 did, done
drag
draw
 drew, drawn
dream
 dreamt
drink
 drank, drunk
drive
 drove, driven
drop
dwell
dye

earn
eat
 ate, eaten
echo
embarrassed
end
enjoy
enter
envelop
establish
excuse

exist
expect
explain
express
extend

face
fail
fall
 fell, fallen
feed
 fed
feel
 felt
fell
fight
 fought
figure
fill
find
 found
finish
fit
flee
 fled
fling
 flung
fly
 flew, flown,
 flied
focus
follow
forbear
 forbore,
 forborne
forbid
 forbad,
 forbade,
 forbidden
force
forecast
foresee
 foresaw,
 foreseen

foretell
foretold
forget
forgot,
forgotten
forgive
forgave,
forgiven
forgo
forewent,
foregone
form
forsake
forsook,
forsaken
forswear
forswore,
forsworn
found
founded
free
freed
freeze
froze, frozen
frighten

gamble
get
got, gotten
gild
gilt
gird
girt
give
gave, given
go
gone, went
grind
ground
grow
grew, grown
guess

hamstring
hamstrung
handle
hang
hung
hang
hanged
happen

hate
have
has, had
hear
heard
heave
hove
help
hem
hew
hewn
hide
hid, hidden
hide
hided
hit
hold
held
hop
hopping,
hopped
hope
hoping,
hoped
hurt

imagine
improve
include
increase
indicate
inset
involve

join

keep
kept
kill
kneel
knelt
knit
knock
know
knew,
known

lade
laden
lay
laid

lead
led
lean
leant
leap
leapt
learn
learnt
leave
left, leaved
lend
lent
let
lie
lying, lay, lain
lie
lied
light
lit
lighten
like
limit
listen
live
load
look
loose
loosen
lose
lost
love

maintain
make
made
manage
mark
marry
mean
meant
measure
meet
met
mention
mete
mimic
mimicking,
mimicked
mind
mislead
misled

misspeak
misspoke,
misspoken
misspell
misspelt
misspend
misspent
mistake
mistook,
mistaken
move
mow
mown

need
note
notice

observe
obtain
occur
offer
offset
open
operate
order
outbid
outbidden
outdo
outdid,
outdone
outfight
outfought
outfit
outgrow
outgrew,
outgrown
outrun
outran
overcast
overcome
overcame
overeat
overate,
overeaten
overfeed
overfed
override
overrode,
overridden

overrun
overran,
overrun
overshoot
overshot
oversleep
overslept
overtake
overtook,
overtaken
overthrow
overthrew,
overthrown

panic
panicking,
panicked
partake
partook,
partaken
pass
pay
paid
pen
permit
pick
place
plan
planning,
planned
plane
planing,
planed
play
plead
pled
please
point
precede
prefer
prepare
present
prevent
proceed
produce
program
prove
proven
provide
pull
put

quarrel	require	see	sit	stave
quit	reread	*saw, seen*	*sat*	*stove*
quiz	rescue	seek	ski	stay
	rest	*sought*	slay	steal
radio	result	seem	*slew, slain*	*stole, stolen*
radioing,	retell	sell	sleep	stick
radioed	*retold*	*sold*	*slept*	*stuck*
raise	rethink	send	slide	sting
rap	*rethought*	*sent*	*slid*	*stung*
rapped, rapt	return	serve	sling	stink
reach	rewrite	set	*slung*	*stank, stunk*
react	*rewrote,*	sew	slink	stop
read	*rewritten*	*sewn*	*slunk*	strew
realize	rid	shake	slip	*strewn*
rebind	*ridding,*	*shook, shaken*	slit	stride
rebinding,	*ridded*	shampoo	smell	*strode,*
rebound	ride	shape	*smelt*	*stridden*
rebound	*riding, rode,*	shave	smile	strike
rebounding,	*ridden*	*shaven*	smite	*struck,*
rebounded	rig	shear	*smote, smitten*	*stricken*
rebuild	ring	*shorn*	sneak	string
rebuilt	*rang, rung*	shed	*snuck*	*strung*
receive	ring	sheer	sound	strive
recognize	*ringed*	shine	sow	*strove, striven*
redo	rise	*shone*	*sown*	stroke
redid, redone	*rose, risen*	shoe	speak	study
reduce	rive	*shod, shod-*	*spoke, spoken*	suggest
refer	*riven*	*den, shoed*	speed	support
regret	rob	shoot	*sped*	suppose
relate	*robbing,*	*shot*	spell	surprise
re-lay	*robbed*	shop	*spelt*	swear
re-laid,	robe	short	spend	*swore, sworn*
re-laying	*robing,*	shorten	*spent*	sweat
relay	*robed*	shovel	spill	sweep
relayed,	rout	show	*spilt*	*swept*
relaying	*routing,*	*shown*	spin	swell
remain	*routed*	shred	*span, spun*	swim
remake	route	shrink	spit	*swam, swum*
remade	*routing,*	*shrank,*	*spat*	swing
remember	*routed*	*shrunk,*	split	*swung*
remove	ruin	*shrunken*	spoil	
rend	run	shrive	*spoilt*	take
rent	*ran*	*shrove,*	spread	*took, taken*
rent		*shriven*	spring	talk
rented	save	shut	*sprang,*	taxi
repay	saw	sing	*sprung*	*taxies, taxying*
repaid	*sawn*	*sang, sung*	stand	teach
reply	say	singe	*stood*	*taught*
report	*said*	sink	start	tear
represent	seat	*sank, sunk*	state	*tore, torn*

tell
told
think
thought
thread
thrive
throve,
thriven
throw
threw,
thrown
thrust
tie
tying
train
tread
trod,
trodden
treat
try
turn

unbend
unbent
unbind
unbound
underbid
undergo
underwent,
undergone
understand
understood
undertake
undertook,
undertaken
undo
undid, undone
unfreeze
unfroze,
unfrozen
unite
unwind
unwound

uphold
upheld
upset
use

vary
visit

wait
wake
woke,
woken
waken
walk
want
watch
waylay
waylaid
wear
wore,
worn

weave
wove, woven
wed
weep
wept
wet
whip
whipt
will
win
won
wind
wound
wind
winded
wish
withhold
withheld
withstand
withstood
wonder

work
wrought
worry
worship
wound
wrap
wrapt
wreak
wreck
wring
wrung
write
wrote,
written

x-ray
xerox

yes

zero